Integrating Ecology and Evolution in a Spatial Context

The 14th Special Symposium of the British Ecological Society held at Royal Holloway College, University of London, 29–31 August, 2000

EDITED BY

JONATHAN SILVERTOWN

Department of Biological Sciences
The Open University

AND

JANIS ANTONOVICS

Department of Biology
University of Virginia

b

**Blackwell
Science**

© 2001 the British Ecological Society
and published for them by
Blackwell Science Ltd
Editorial Offices:
Osney Mead, Oxford OX2 0EL
25 John Street, London WC1N 2BS
23 Ainslie Place, Edinburgh EH3 6AJ
350 Main Street, Malden
   MA 02148-5018, USA
54 University Street, Carlton
   Victoria 3053, Australia
10, rue Casimir Delavigne
   75006 Paris, France

Other Editorial Offices:
Blackwell Wissenschafts-Verlag GmbH
Kurfürstendamm 57
10707 Berlin, Germany

Blackwell Science KK
MG Kodenmacho Building
7–10 Kodenmacho Nihombashi
Chuo-ku, Tokyo 104, Japan

Iowa State University Press
A Blackwell Science Company
2121 S. State Avenue
Ames, Iowa 50014-8300, USA

First published 2001

Set by Best-set Typesetter Ltd.,
Hong Kong
Printed and bound in Great Britain by
MPG Books, Ltd., Bodmin, Cornwall.

The Blackwell Science logo is a
trade mark of Blackwell Science Ltd,
registered at the United Kingdom
Trade Marks Registry

A catalogue record for this title
is available from the British Library

ISBN 0-632-05824-2 Paperback
      0-632-05823-4 Hardback

Library of Congress
Cataloging-in-Publication Data
has been applied for

DISTRIBUTORS

Marston Book Services Ltd
PO Box 269
Abingdon, Oxon OX14 4YN
(*Orders*: Tel: 01235 465500
           Fax: 01235 465555)

The Americas
Blackwell Publishing
c/o AIDC
P.O. Box 20
50 Winter Sport Lane
Williston, VT 05495-0020
(*Orders*: Tel: 800 216-2522
           Fax: 802 864-7626)

Australia
Blackwell Science Pty Ltd
54 University Street
Carlton, Victoria 3053
(*Orders*: Tel: 3 9347 0300
           Fax: 3 9347 5001)

For further information on
Blackwell Science, visit our website:
www.blackwell-science.com

Contents

v

List of Contributors

J. Antonovics

Department of Biology, University of Virginia, Charlottesville, VA 22904-4328, USA

C. M. Barr

Department of Ecology and Evolutionary Biology, University of California, Irvine,
CA 92697-2525, USA

S. C. H. Barrett

Department of Botany, University of Toronto, 25 Willcocks Street, Toronto, Ontario M5S 3B2,
Canada

N. H. Barton

Institute of Cell, Animal and Population Biology, University of Edinburgh, Edinburgh
EH9 3JT, UK

G. Bell

Department of Biology, McGill University, 1205 Avenue Dr Penfield, Montreal, Quebec
H3A 1B1, Canada; and Redpath Museum, McGill University, 859 Sherbrooke Street West,
Montreal, Quebec H3K 1B6, Canada

B. J. Best

Department of Biology, Duke University, Durham, NC 27708, USA. Current address:
Department of Economics, University of Washington, Seattle, WA 98195-3330, USA

R. Bialozyt

Institute of Forest Genetics, Sieker Landstrasse 2, D-22927 Grosshansdorf, Germany

S. Brewer

IMEP, CNRS UPRES A6116, Faculté de Jérôme, case 451, 13397 Marseille cedex 20, France;
and European Pollen Database, Centre Univeritaire d'Arles, 13200 Arles, France

S. J. Brunsfeld

College of Natural Resources, University of Idaho, Moscow, ID 83844, USA

J. J. Burdon

Centre for Plant Biodiversity Research, CSIRO-Plant Industry, GPO Box 1600, Canberra,
ACT 2601, Australia

A. L. Case

Department of Botany, University of Toronto, 25 Willcocks Street, Toronto, Ontario M5S 3B2,
Canada

D. Charlesworth

Institute of Cell, Animal and Population Biology, University of Edinburgh, Edinburgh
EH9 3JT, UK

R. Cheddadi

IMEP, CNRS UPRES A6116, Faculté de Jérôme, case 451, 13397 Marseille cedex 20, France;
and European Pollen Database, Centre Univeritaire d'Arles, 13200 Arles, France

B. Comps
Laboratory of Ecological Genetics, University of Bordeaux I, F-33405 Talence, France

U. Dieckmann
Adaptive Dynamics Network, International Institute for Applied Systems Analysis, A-2361 Laxenburg, Austria

M. E. Dorken
Department of Botany, University of Toronto, 25 Willcocks Street, Toronto, Ontario M5S 3B2, Canada

J. Ehrlén
Department of Botany, Stockholm University, SE-106 91 Stockholm, Sweden

S. N. Emery
Department of Biological Sciences, Vanderbilt University, Nashville, TN 37235, USA

R. A. Ennos
Institute of Ecology and Resource Management, University of Edinburgh, Darwin Building, King's Buildings, Mayfield Road, Edinburgh EH9 3JU, UK

O. Eriksson
Department of Botany, Stockholm University, SE-106 91 Stockholm, Sweden

S. A. Frank
Department of Ecology and Evolutionary Biology, University of California, Irvine, CA 92697-2525, USA

I. Hanski
Metapopulation Research Group, Department of Ecology and Systematics, PO Box 17, FIN-00014 University of Helsinki, Finland

G. M. Hewitt
School of Biological Sciences, University of East Anglia, Norwich NR4 7TJ, UK

S. P. Hubbell
Department of Botany, University of Georgia, Athens, GA 30602; and Smithsonian Tropical Research Institute, Box 2072, Balboa, Panama

K. M. Ibrahim
School of Biological Sciences, University of East Anglia, Norwich NR4 7TJ, UK

R. Law
Department of Biology, University of York, York YO10 5YW, UK

M. J. Lechowicz
Department of Biology, McGill University, 1205 Avenue Dr Penfield, Montreal, Quebec H3A 1B1, Canada

D. E. McCauley
Department of Biological Sciences, Vanderbilt University, Nashville, TN 37235, USA

J. W. McGlothlin
Department of Biological Sciences, Vanderbilt University, Nashville, TN 37235, USA

D. J. Murrell
Department of Biology, University of York, York YO10 5YW, UK

T. J. Newman
Departments of Biology and Physics, University of Virginia, Charlottesville, VA 22904-4328, USA

I. Olivieri
Institut des Sciences de l'Evolution, UMR 5554, Université de Montpellier 2, Place Eugéne Bataillon, 34095 Montpellier cedex 05, France

J. R. Pannell
Department of Plant Sciences, University of Oxford, Oxford OX2 6UD, UK

R. J. Petit
Institut National de la Recherche Agronomique, Station de Recherches Forestières, BP 45, F-33611 Gazinet cedex, France

D. W. Purves
Department of Biology, University of York, York YO10 5YW, UK

C. M. Richards
Department of Biological Sciences, Vanderbilt University, Nashville, TN 37235, USA. Current address: USDA/ARS, National Seed Storage Laboratory, 1111 South Mason Street, Fort Collins, CO 80521, USA

J. Silvertown
Department of Biological Sciences, The Open University, Walton Hall, Milton Keynes MK7 6AA, UK

R. A. Smith
Department of Biological Sciences, Vanderbilt University, Nashville, TN 37235, USA. Current address: Department of Biology, Duke University, Durham, NC 27708, USA

D. E. Soltis
Department of Botany and the Genetics Institute, University of Florida, Gainesville, FL 32611, USA

P. S. Soltis
Florida Museum of Natural History and the Genetics Institute, University of Florida, Gainesville, FL 32611, USA

J. Sullivan
Department of Biological Sciences, University of Idaho, Moscow, ID 83844, USA

P. H. Thrall
Centre for Plant Biodiversity Research, CSIRO-Plant Industry, GPO Box 1600, Canberra, ACT 2601, Australia

M. J. Waterway
Department of Plant Sciences, Macdonald Campus, McGill University, Lakeshore Boulevard, Ste-Anne-de-Bellevue, Quebec H9X 3V9, Canada

History of the British Ecological Society

The British Ecological Society is a learned society, a registered charity and a company limited by guarantee. Established in 1913 by academics to promote and foster the study of ecology in its widest sense, the Society currently has around 5000 members spread around the world. Members include research scientists, environmental consultants, teachers, local authority ecologists, conservationists and many others with an active interest in natural history and the environment. The core activities are the publication of the results of research in ecology, the development of scientific meetings and the promotion of ecological awareness through education. The Society's mission is:

> To advance and support the science of ecology and publicize the outcome of research, in order to advance knowledge, education and its application.

The Society publishes four internationally renowned journals and organizes at least two major conferences each year plus a large number of smaller meetings. It also initiates a diverse range of activities to promote awareness of ecology at the public and policy maker level in addition to developing ecology in the education system, and it provides financial support for approved ecological projects. The Society is an independent organization that receives little outside funding.

British Ecological Society
26 Blades Court
Deodar Road, Putney
London SW15 2NU
United Kingdom
Tel.: +44 (0)20 8871 9797 Fax: +44 (0)20 8871 9779
E-mail: general@ecology.demon.co.uk
ULR: http://www.demon.co.uk/bes

The British Ecological Society is a limited company, registered in England No. 15228997 and a Registered Charity No. 281213.

Preface

This book contains written versions of papers presented at a special symposium of the British Ecological Society held in August 2000 at Royal Holloway College, London. The title of the meeting, *Plant stand still, but their genes don't*, captured (if somewhat obliquely) the essence of our theme and the imagination of delegates. This symposium title was also a testimony to the remarkable influence of John Harper on plant population biology, whose celebrated truism 'plants stand still to be counted' has been a rallying cry of plant biologists relieved at not having to cope with trapping and the statistical headache of mark—recapture techniques. On the last evening of the meeting, delegates signed a poster of the meeting which John Harper later received with much pleasure. The meeting was heavily oversubscribed and, to our regret, many people who wished to participate were unable to do so. This volume, now presented under a more formal title, is an opportunity for those who were unable to attend to share in the intellectual excitement of the meeting, and for all to own a permanent record of a ground-breaking event.

The purpose of the symposium was to advance understanding of ecological and evolutionary processes by integrating them within a common frame of reference. That frame of reference was space. The first chapter echoes the original title of the meeting, and explains just why ecological and evolutionary processes are most readily integrated in an explicitly spatial context. While the focus of the book is largely on basic science, the topics are also of direct relevance to conservation biology and resource management. Moreover, while focusing largely on plants, all of the questions addressed in this volume are just as applicable to animals. Indeed several authors write about both, but plants provide ideal model systems for the study of spatial processes because their locations in the adult phase are fixed.

Any work that addresses spatial processes must explicitly consider scale. The contents of the book are therefore divided into three sections that progressively ascend in scale from (1) populations, through (2) metapopulations to (3) geography. Certain themes recur at different scales. For example spatial population dynamics (Chapters 2, 7, 8, 9, 10, 13, 14, 15), population genetics at boundaries (Chapters 1, 5, 17), the imprint of spatial population dynamics upon genetic structure (Chapters 3, 9, 11, 13, 14, 15), adaptation (Chapters 6, 12, 17), evolution of mating systems (Chapters 4, 11, 16) and the consequences of population genetics for ecological dynamics (Chapters 1, 5, 9, 10, 17). Finally, Stephen Hubbell summarizes his unified neutral theory that emulates the neutral theory of population genetics for large-scale ecological processes (Chapter 18), while Graham Bell and co-authors point the way to empirical tests of neutral theory (Chapter 6).

We wish to thank the many people who made the meeting a success and who helped this book come to fruition. First and foremost we thank the contributors who created a stimulating atmosphere at the meeting and who eagerly captured its essence in print. We also wish to thank the many reviewers (who unfortunately have to remain nameless) for their comments; they not only improved the quality of individual chapters, but also contributed to the unification of the different contributions. We are grateful to Kenny Leung, Amanda Thomas and all at the BES office who handled the logistics of the meeting so efficiently; to Godfrey Hewitt, Tony Davy, Nigel Webb and Malcolm Press who advised us; to Members of the BES Meetings Committee who backed the idea; and to Ian Sherman and Delia Sandford at Blackwell Science who saw the book through the press.

Jonathan Silvertown
Janis Antonovics

Part 1

Populations

Chapter 1

Plants stand still, but their genes don't: non-trivial consequences of the obvious

*J. Silvertown**

Introduction

The observation that 'plants stand still, but their genes don't' may seem obvious, but it contains the germ of some fundamental concepts in plant population biology that have profound consequences. Because the location of adult plants is fixed, their ecological interactions are with neighbours and the geometry of these interactions is important to population and community structure (see Chapter 2). The area around a focal plant containing the neighbours that significantly influence its growth, often as few as six in number (e.g. Kenkel 1988), is its ecological neighbourhood. Because plants are sessile, selection pressures are often local and intense, leading to local genetic differentiation and adaptation being the norm rather than the exception in plant populations (Linhart & Grant 1996). By contrast, seeds and pollen transgress the boundaries of ecological neighbourhoods and as vehicles of gene flow determine the size of genetic neighbourhoods and the foundation and initial genetic composition of new populations. Gene flow has the potential to prevent genetic differentiation and local adaptation, with potential consequences for the evolution of geographical range limits (see Chapter 17).

During its comparatively brief history, plant population biology has tended to develop along two parallel tracks: one genetic and the other ecological. This was not because either discipline was unaware of the other; Ledyard Stebbins and John Harper, the founding fathers of the subject in, respectively, genetics (Stebbins 1950) and ecology (Harper 1977) were well known to each other, and there have been repeated attempts at synthesis (e.g. Haeck & Woldendorp 1985; Jacquard *et al.* 1985; Berry *et al.* 1992). Furthermore, although the field of ecological genetics formed a bridge between the disciplines, it never produced a synthesis between the two. Arguably, the reason no synthesis was forthcoming was because each discipline worked within a different frame of reference. Population genetics dealt explicitly with spatial structure, while population ecology generally did not (Silvertown 1991). The limitations of this for population ecology were appreciated. J. L. Harper (pers. comm.) was insistent that density, the variable favoured in population ecology, was an abstraction because plant–plant interactions are all between neighbours (e.g. Mack & Harper

* *Department of Biological Sciences, The Open University, Walton Hall, Milton Keynes, MK7 6AA, UK.*

1977). Antonovics and Levin (1980) pointed out that the ecological and genetical concepts of a 'population' were different, and they made an early attempt at synthesis by proposing an ecological analogue for the genetic neighbourhood. This term now has common currency.

Recent developments in spatial ecology mean that ecological as well as genetic procesess can now be understood within a spatial frame of reference (see Chapter 2; Tilman & Kareiva 1997; Dieckmann *et al.* 2000). This is the first, essential step towards the unification of plant population biology, but it immediately raises the question of the appropriateness of scale. Finding the relevant scale has always been an important question in ecology, but now a new dimension has been added to the question. Namely, at what spatial scales do demographic and ecological variables affect evolutionary processes and (especially) vice versa, and when can either be safely ignored when considering the other? As a prelude to the more detailed discussion in later chapters, I will discuss three examples relevant to these questions, which are central to the theme of this book. In ascending order of spatial scale they are:
1 the influence of population size structure and intraspecific competition on effective population size;
2 the influence of mating system and genetic diversity on metapopulation dynamics in the Park Grass Experiment;
3 integrating ecology and evolution at geographical range limits.

Population size structure, resource competition and effective population size

Effective population size
In an idealized, panmictic population of infinite size with no mutation or selection, all genotypes should make equal contributions to future generations, and hence gene and genotype frequencies should not change over time. Real populations, of course, have finite size and are not like this. Thus, even for selectively neutral alleles, frequencies will change due to the sampling variance of gametes (drift), non-random mating and inequalities of fecundity among parents. Wright (1931) introduced the concept of effective population size, N_e, which can be used to quantify the effect of such sources of bias on gene frequency change (Caballero 1994). There are several alternative definitions of the concept, but the relevant one for the example which follows is the *variance* effective population size. This is defined as the number of individuals that, if they behaved like an idealized population, would give rise to the same sampling variance of gene frequency as observed in an actual population (Falconer & Mackay 1996). The distribution of family size among parents in the idealized population is Poisson, each generation is censused at birth, and there is assumed to be no mortality between birth and adulthood (Caballero 1994).

N_e is a key parameter in population genetics, with consequences for drift, selection, genetic substructuring and the maintenance of heterozygosity. Small N_e increases the likelihood of genetic drift and the rate at which deleterious alleles are fixed. Biparental inbreeding resulting from small N_e can result in inbreeding depression with deleterious consequences for population viability. Newman and Pilson (1997) constructed small experimental populations of the outcrossing, annual herb *Clarkia pulchella* with different values of N_e. Populations with the low N_e treatment had a significantly increased extinction rate compared to populations of the same census size that had a higher N_e.

Estimates of N_e for natural populations tend to be made in the form of the quotient N_e/N which indicates how far the effective population size deviates from the behaviour of an ideal population of census size N. A problem here is that the census size of the idealized population is made at birth and there is no juvenile mortality, while real populations can experience extremely heavy juvenile mortality. The estimated size of a real population therefore depends upon when the census is taken. If it is taken at birth, N_e/N will be severely reduced by the inclusion in the estimate of N of juveniles that will never reproduce. In practice, N_e/N is almost always estimated using a census of the adult or the breeding population (not necessarily identical to one another) (Nunney & Elam 1994; Frankham 1995). An exception is a study of N_e in the palm *Astrocaryum mexicanum*, which included juveniles in the census population size (Eguiarte *et al.* 1993). However N is defined, N_e in natural populations is invariably smaller than the census number (N). In a review, Frankham (1995) found that the ratio N_e/N averaged about 0.1 when all relevant variables had been taken into account, although values varied widely between studies depending upon, among other things, how estimates were made.

The influence of neighbourhood competition upon N_e/N

Three spatial processes are of particular importance in reducing the ratio of N_e/N in plant populations:

1 the fact that mating occurs predominantly among neighbours;
2 the limited dispersal of the majority of seeds from the maternal parent;
3 neighbourhood competition for light, which creates hierarchies of plant size and fecundity.

The first two of these factors have been well studied and are discussed elsewhere in this volume (see Chapters 3 and 4). By contrast, the influence of size hierarchies on N_e in plant populations has received much less attention, although there is evidence from studies of annuals that it can be significant (Crawford 1984; Heywood 1986; Husband & Barrett 1992; Johnson 1998).

Light is a directional resource, so that only slight differences in height between competing neighbours results in very large differences in the amount of light captured by taller individuals compared to shorter ones (Figure 1.1). Larger plants suppress smaller neighbours out of all proportion to their difference in size, and small plants have little or no effect on neighbours that are larger than them. This size asymmetry in competition for light, combined with exponential growth by the largest plants, causes size frequency distributions that start off normal to rapidly skew to lognormal in crowded stands (Figure 1.2). Thus, competition for light produces a hierarchy of size that contains many small individuals and a few large dominants.

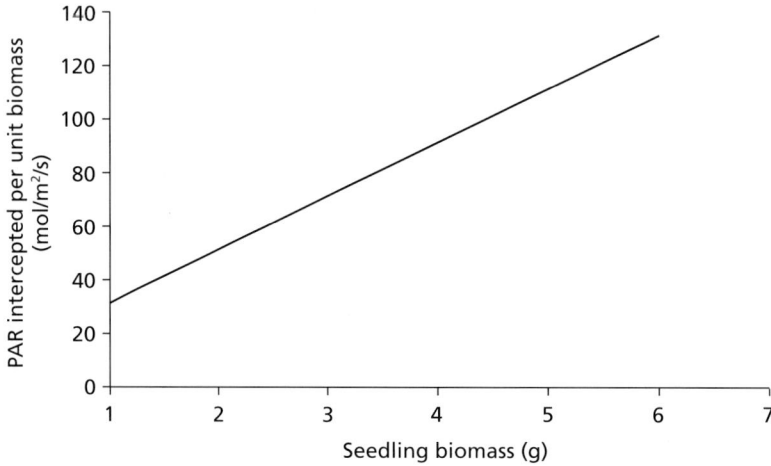

Figure 1.1 Light (PAR) captured per gram of biomass by seedlings of yellow birch growing at a density of 265 m^{-2} in relation to size after 6 weeks growth. (Data from Wayne & Bazzaz 1997.)

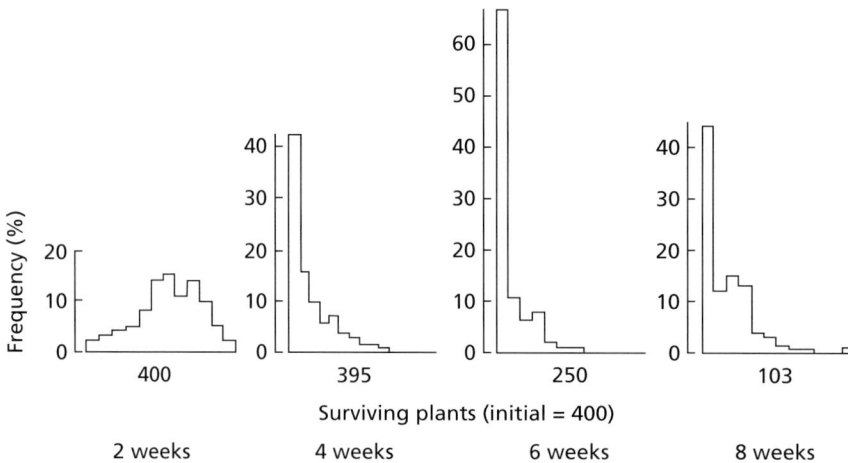

Figure 1.2 The development of a size hierarchy in a population of marigolds (*Tagetes patula*) during 8 weeks of growth. (From Ford 1975.)

Fecundity is correlated with size in most plant populations, and in annual species where there is typically no lower threshold size for reproduction, all surviving plants will flower, producing a highly unequal distribution of fecundity in the population. For example, in a study of poppy *Papaver dubium* by Mackay (cited by Crawford 1984), 2% of the 2316 plants in a population produced 50% of the seeds and the variance of seed output was 1 488 630 with a mean per plant of only 245. Ignoring other

6

causes of deviation from the idealized population structure, Crawford (1984) calculated a value of $N_e/N = 0.07$ for this population, indicating the enormous potential impact of asymmetric competition upon N_e. Heywood (1986) estimated the influence of fecundity hierarchies on N_e/N in 27 species of annual plants and found a ratio of <0.5 in most of them.

Levin and Wilson (1978; Wilson & Levin 1986) ran simulation models to explore the evolutionary consequences of L-shaped vs. Poisson-distributed fecundity variation in plant populations. They found that L-shaped fecundity hierarchies resulted in faster response to directional selection, faster extinction of rare alleles, and a greater propensity for genetic drift. Collectively, these studies demonstrate that neighbourhood competition for light can generate hierarchies of size and inequalities in fecundity that may reduce N_e anywhere between a half and one-10th of census size, with potentially important evolutionary consequences. An important link between ecological and evolutionary processes has therefore been demonstrated, but some important questions remain. In particular, it is important to ask how ecological factors that influence the formation of size hierarchies alter evolutionary processes.

Size-frequency distributions and the competitive processes that generate them have been extensively studied in plants, and because plant size and fecundity are generally closely correlated, this means that genetic predictions about N_e/N ought to be derivable from this ecological knowledge. The following are some examples of predictions derived in this way.

Predictions

Competitive symmetry: N_e/N *should vary positively with the symmetry of intraspecific competition*

Competitive asymmetry is responsible for the size hierarchies that lower N_e/N. It therefore follows that the quotient should be higher in populations occupying nutrient-poor and arid environments where limiting resources are below ground and competition is size symmetric, than in nutrient-rich and mesic environments where light is limiting and competition is consequently size asymmetric.

Arid environments are subject to large seasonal variation in rainfall, and population numbers of annuals fluctuate hugely in response to this (Venable & Pake 1999). Thus, temporal variance in population size may restrict N_e more than any inequality of fecundity within individual years. It is notable that the 27 N_e/N values calculated by Heywood were for annuals grown by Salisbury (1942) in the mesic environment of the British Isles.

Size-thresholds for reproduction: N_e/N *should be higher in species in which there is a size threshold for reproduction*

A size threshold for reproduction truncates the size frequency distribution of reproductive plants, making it less leptokurtic. It follows from this that N_e/N should be higher in perennials, including semelparous species, which tend to exhibit a size threshold, than in annual species, which generally do not. This prediction is sensitive to the definition of N, and assumes that it is based only upon adult plants.

Density-dependent mortality (self-thinning): N_e/N *should be higher in populations subject to intense density-dependent mortality (self-thinning)*
In perennials, particularly trees, size-frequency distributions for crowded stands during early life go through the same transformation from normal to lognormal that is seen in annuals (see Figure 1.1). However, in trees, density-dependent mortality (self-thinning) culls more and more of the smallest individuals as time proceeds and size distributions become less skewed again as a cohort nears maturity. Self-thinning will tend to cull small reproductives and so N_e/N should be higher in larger, longer-lived species with late ages at first reproduction such as forest trees. Once again, this prediction assumes that only adults are counted.

The effect of self-thinning on population size structure through time can be seen for populations of balsam fir *Abies balsamea* in Figure 1.3. These data, from Mohler *et al.* (1978), were collected in subalpine fir wave forests at Whiteface Mountain in the Adirondacks, New York State. A peculiarity of wave forests is that cohorts of successively greater age occur in ordered fashion along a chronosequence from seedlings at one end to senescent adults at the other. The spatial process that gives rise to this structure is described by Sato and Iwasa (1993), but for present purposes the important feature of these populations is that they have a stable age and size structure and therefore it is possible to use the size structure of reproductives present in the population to calculate N_e/N by the method of Heywood (1986).

Dodd and Silvertown (2000) used the size structure of natural populations of balsam fir in three waves at Whiteface Mountain to estimate N_e/N and found a value of 0.78 (± 0.027). This is far higher than the values found by Heywood (1986) for annual species and confirms the expectation that N_e should be less affected by fecundity inequalities in trees than in annuals. The effect of the existence of a size threshold for reproduction upon the size-frequency distribution of reproductives in *A. balsamea* may be seen in Figure 1.4.

Genetics and metapopulation dynamics in the Park Grass Experiment
Thanks to seed dispersal, plant populations can be quite mobile. We tend to think of this mobility in terms of species invading new territory, either in the form of sometimes troublesome invasions by alien species, or in terms of postglacial recolonization of the temperate zone (see Chapters 13–15). Only in the rare instances where a small area has been the subject of detailed botanical recording over a long period of time do we see movements at the local scale. Although it is unusual to find long-term observations made at this scale, there is no reason to suppose that local movements are themselves unusual. Undoubtedly one of the best, if not the best, records of this kind that we have is for the Park Grass Experiment at Rothamsted in England. This unique experiment is briefly described before discussing what it tells us about a potential link between the genetics and dynamics of plants at the local scale.

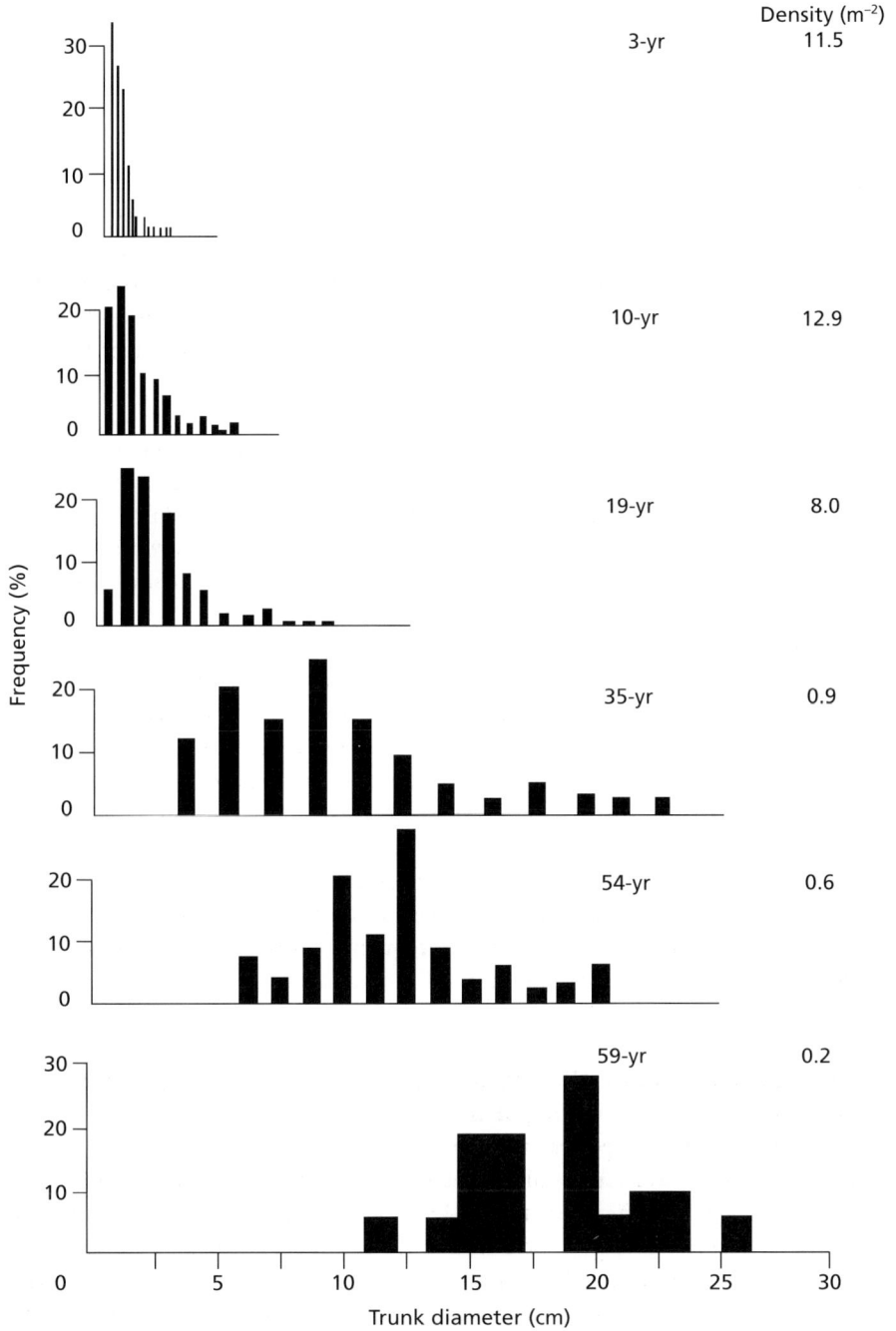

Figure 1.3 Size-frequency distributions for successively older cohorts of *Abies balsamea*. (From Mohler *et al.* 1978.)

(a) Wave forest

(b) Non-wave forest

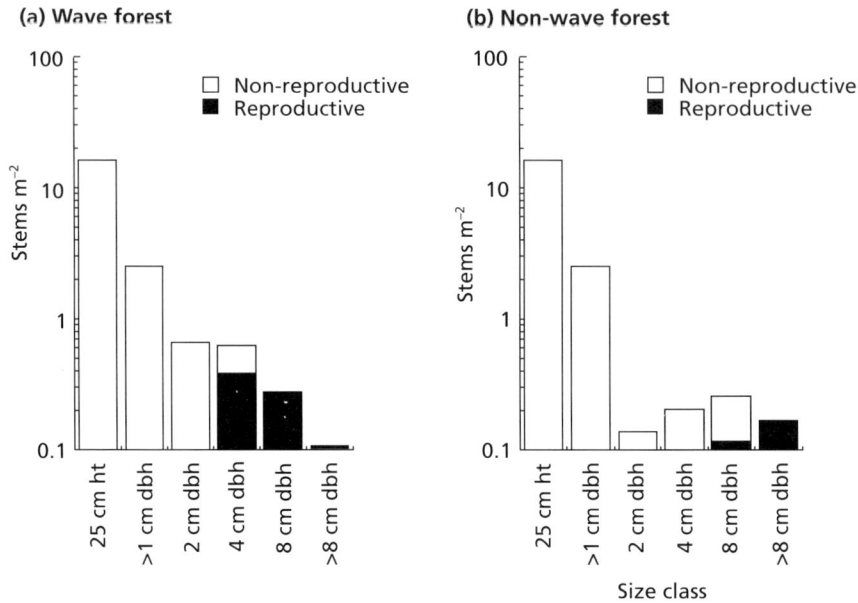

Figure 1.4 Size-frequency distribution of trees in wave and normal populations of *Abies balsamea* at Whiteface Mountain. Reproductives are shown in black. (From Dodd & Silvertown, 2000.)

The Park Grass Experiment

The Park Grass Experiment was begun in 1856 when Lawes and Gilbert (1863) divided a hay meadow at Rothamsted Experimental Station into plots of between 0.1 and 0.2 ha and applied different fertilizer treatments to them. Two plots (nos. 3 and 12) were maintained as unfertilized controls, but fertilizer (farmyard manure) was applied to another plot (no. 2) only between 1856 and 1863, so there are now effectively three unfertilized plots. The original plots have been subdivided, and some subdivisions have been limed, but fertilizer treatments and a regular regime of hay-cutting have been maintained from 1856 until the present day. Botanical records of the species present on all plots have been made with varying frequency and in varying degrees of detail from soon after the experiment began until the present (Williams 1978; M. J. Crawley, unpublished). Changes in botanical composition were at first rapid, as species that were once present throughout the Park Grass meadow were selectively favoured or eliminated on particular plots by the fertilizer treatments being applied. There have been no important invasions from outside Park Grass and virtually all species now found in the Park Grass Experiment were present in the flora of the original meadow. At the present time the control plots are the most species rich and certain plots with acidified soil (caused by ammonium sulphate fertilizer) possess only one or two grasses (*Anthoxanthum odoratum* and *Holcus lanatus*) (Dodd *et al.* 1994).

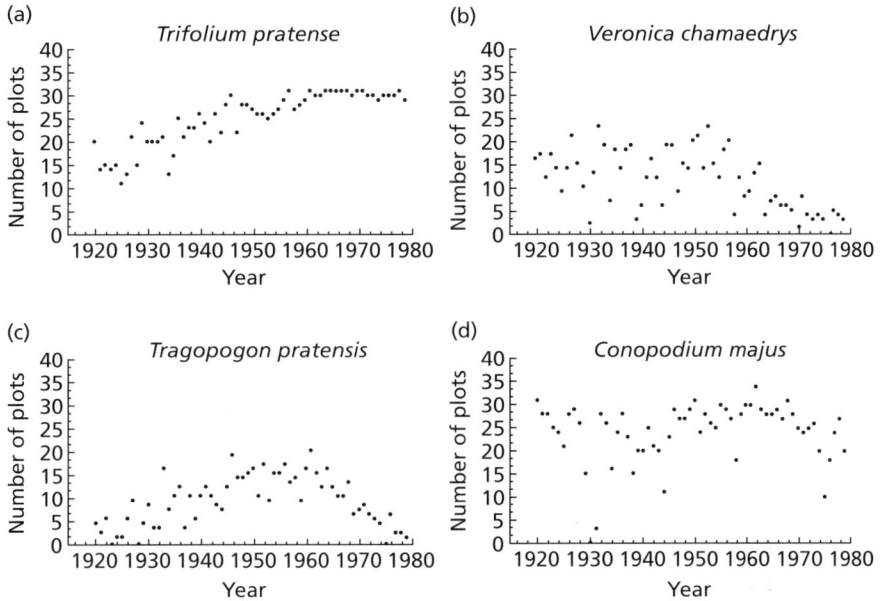

Figure 1.5 Four patterns of long-term dynamics observed in the Park Grass Experiment between 1920 and 1979. (a) Increase, exemplified by *Trifolium pratense*; (b) decrease, exemplified by *Veronica chamaedrys*; (c) outbreak, exemplified by *Tragopogon pratensis*; and (d) fluctuations without a trend, exemplified by *Conopodium majus*. (From Dodd *et al.* 1995.)

Metapopulation dynamics and genetics

Analysis of the gross composition of the plots, broken down into the components grasses, legumes and other species (G/L/O) has shown that, following a period of initial change in the 19th century, the ratio of these components during the 20th century has been at dynamic equilibrium on most plots. Each plot has a characteristic average G/L/O ratio determined by fertilizer and liming treatment, and returns towards this value when perturbed by annual variation in the weather (Silvertown 1980, 1987; Silvertown *et al.* 1994). However, the stability of the botanical composition of Park Grass plots at the gross level conceals a much more dynamic situation for the individual species that comprise each of the major components.

From annual, visual surveys of the presence/absence of species on plots over 60 years 1920–1979, Dodd *et al.* (1995) discovered that species varied greatly from one another in their long-term dynamics, as measured by changes in their frequency of occurrence across the experiment. Four patterns were detected: increase, decrease, outbreak and fluctuation with no trend (Figure 1.5). On non-acidified plots, nearly one-quarter of the 43 species analysed showed the outbreak pattern. Discriminant analysis was used to identify life-history traits that might be associated with the different patterns, and this revealed two important correlations: increase and outbreak species were both more ruderal (*sensu* Grime *et al.* 1988) than other species, and

increase species had mating systems that were more outcrossing than the outbreak species (Dodd *et al.* 1995).

The results of the discriminant analysis suggest the following two-part hypothesis
to explain why different species showed different long-term dynamics. We propose
that the initial increase in plot frequency seen in increase and outbreak species was
triggered by some climatic event such as drought, and that the species with a higher
intrinsic rate of natural increase (a ruderal characteristic) were the ones best able to
spread. The 10 increase species reached their zenith of abundance between about
1945 and 1952 and then declined over the ensuing 30 years, while the increase species
continued to occur across many plots. We propose that the difference in mating system between the two groups was responsible for this difference. We suggest that the
outcrossing species possessed the genetic diversity required to adapt and thrive in
the wide range of environments represented by the different plots, while the more
inbreeding species did not, and consequently declined after reaching their peak.
Both parts of this hypothesis are currently being tested, but only the genetical
hypothesis is relevant in the present context and is discussed further here.

The increase species include the outcrossing grass *Anthoxanthum odoratum*
which Snaydon and Davies (1972; Snaydon 1970; Davies & Snaydon 1976) showed
had adapted to local conditions on different plots. A reciprocal transplant experiment between three pairs of contrasting plots showed that after 18 months all alien
transplants had lower growth (tillering) and survival rates than natives. Selection
coefficients upon aliens ($s = 1 -$ alien/native performance) had values in the range
0.23–0.57 for tillering rate and 0.09–0.77 for survival (Davies & Snaydon 1976).
Plants sampled from different plots and grown in common garden conditions were
different in height, disease resistance to mildew and rust, and growth response to pH.

Snaydon and Davies' studies of *Anthoxanthum* support the idea that the occurrence of this species across a large number of Park Grass plots requires local adaptation. This could only be achieved in the short time scales over which it has been
observed to arise if the starting population contained sufficient genetic diversity
upon which selection could act. There is no reason to suppose that other increase
species have not also become locally adapted, although the experiments to test this
have not yet been done.

The spatial dynamics of *Tragopogon pratensis* at the plot level show how this outbreak species first began to appear on plots from which it had been absent, becoming
a constant feature of some of them in the period 1945–1960 until a retreat to its core
distribution on plots 18, 19 and 2 in 1975 (Figure 1.6). We do not know for certain
whether these increases represent actual extinction and dispersal between plots or
just large *in situ* changes of abundance. If the latter, then species that were not recorded in visual surveys may have been present at very low abundance on some plots
where they later appeared. Seeds of *T. pratensis* have a very large pappus that would
permit dispersal between plots, and the plant is short-lived, so local colonization and
extinction may well explain the observed dynamics.

We have scored allozyme loci (PGI, PGM) that are polymorphic in other species at
Park Grass and found them to be monomorphic in *T. pratensis* and in the grass *Bro-*

Tragopogon pratensis at the Park Grass Experiment

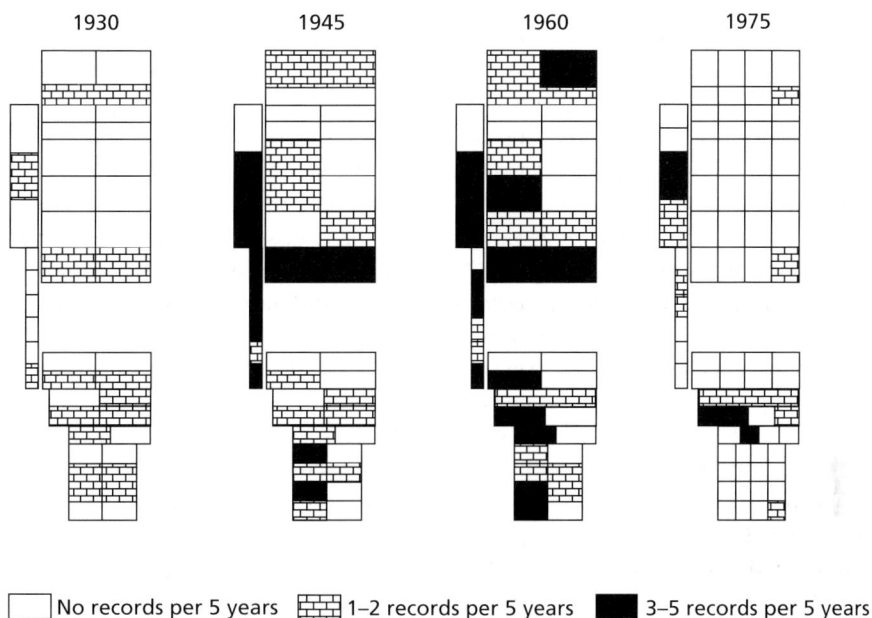

No records per 5 years   1–2 records per 5 years   3–5 records per 5 years

Figure 1.6 Maps of the Park Grass Experiment at four intervals between 1930 and 1975 showing the spatial dynamics of *Tragopogon pratensis* on non-acidified plots. (From Dodd *et al.* 1995.)

mus hordeaceus, another outbreak species, as one would expect in selfing species. DNA markers (ISSRs: intersimple-sequence repeats, Zietkiewicz *et al.* 1994) have also been used for mating-system estimation on both these species. In *T. pratensis*, 12 ISSR loci showed no variation at all, either within or between 10 families of 12 progeny each. Roose and Gottlieb (1976) and Soltis *et al.* (1995) also found American populations of *T. pratensis* to be monomorphic at allozyme and DNA loci. Lack of polymorphism in this outbreak species is consistent with our hypothesis but makes it impossible to estimate the mating system quantitatively. Polymorphism at ISSR loci was found in *B. hordeaceus*, but this variation occurred only between families, and progeny were nearly all identical with their mothers. We estimated the multilocus outcrossing rate of this species to be $t = 0.001$. ISSR markers are dominant, but genotypes were inferred by maximum likelihood using Ritland's (1990) MLDT program and all maternal genotypes tested were inferred to be homozygous at all the loci examined. The pattern of genetic variation in *B. hordeaceus* at Park Grass suggests that the mating system varies with time and that occasional outcrossing events occur in some years. Low levels of allozyme variation in *B. hordeaceus* have been found in Mediterranean populations (Ainouche *et al.* 1995, 1999) and in Swedish populations where allozyme markers are correlated with variation in soil moisture (Lönn 1993).

Integrating ecology and evolution at geographical range limits

The stable boundaries of a species' range are where its ecological and evolutionary limits coincide on the map. Range limits are therefore a good place to look if one is interested in a synthesis of ecological and evolutionary processes (see Chapter 5). Stable range limits are all the more interesting because it is not clear why they exist, and why natural selection not does drive species range boundaries ever outwards (Hoffman & Blows 1994). Of course, not all present-day range limits are stable, but the speed of postglacial recolonization of the temperate zone by trees and the often spectacular rates of spread by alien species invading new territory both attest to the fact that plants can rapidly approach their geographical range limits when climate ameliorates or physical barriers are overcome (see Chapters 13–15). This, and the often close correlation of range limits with current climatic parameters (e.g. Beerling 1993; Jeffree & Jeffree 1994; Beerling *et al.* 1995; Carey *et al.* 1995; Collatz *et al.* 1998), implies that many native species are at or near their stable range limits. To illustrate how ecological and evolutionary processes interact at range boundaries, I briefly discuss two related ways in which plants may escape those boundaries.

Escape from range boundaries, I: evolution of reproductive isolation

Holt and Gomulkiewicz (1997) and Kirkpatrick and Barton (1997) show that stable range boundaries can be expected if populations in these locations are demographic sinks that are dependent for their persistence upon propagule migration from the hinterland. These migrants will be adapted to the conditions of the hinterland rather than to the environment at the range boundary, and gene flow from source to sink can prevent local adaptation in the sink, without which the range boundary cannot expand. Barton (Chapter 17) reviews and extends this theory.

Escape from a range boundary sink requires local adaptation, permitting the net reproductive rate to be raised above the value of unity required to turn a sink into a source of migrants. If local adaptation is prevented by gene flow in pollen, then a mutant in the sink must achieve pre-mating reproductive isolation from the source population before local selection can be effective. This can be achieved in a variety of ways. For example, in the Park Grass Experiment, plants of *Anthoxanthum odoratum* occurring on the boundaries between plots flower significantly earlier than plants half a metre either side of the boundary (Snaydon & Davies 1976). Presumably this produces pre-mating isolation in the boundary plants that helps to preserve local adaptation in their progeny in the face of pollen flow from adjacent populations that we know are adapted to different conditions. Over the larger, geographical scale, gene flow may be limited not only by distance itself but also by climatic gradients that produce phenological differences in flowering. Therefore, it is not at all clear whether or not there is enough gene flow from the hinterland into marginal plant populations to select for reproductive isolating mechanisms of the kind seen at the local scale. It is most likely to apply when environmental gradients are steep (see Chapter 17).

Assuming that distances between populations in the hinterland and those at a range boundary are not so great as to prevent significant gene flow, two other possible routes by which reproductive isolation may arise are through the evolution of parthenogenesis (apomixis) or selfing. These traits do not evolve independently of one another and both may occur through polyploidization. Most apomicts are polyploid while, in plants with gametophytic self-incompatibility systems, polyploidization disrupts the self-recognition system and produces self-compatible genotypes (de Nettancourt 1977). The reverse sequence of events may also occur; once selfing has evolved, it appears that selfing plant taxa have higher rates of polyploidization than outcrossers (Ramsey & Schemske 1998). Selfing and apomixis can be favoured in marginal populations in two ways. First, as already discussed, apomicts or selfers may gain an advantage over outcrossers because they are reproductively isolated from the source of non-adapted genes. Secondly, selfers and apomicts have an advantage in colonizing situations because their fecundity is not limited by the availability of mates ('Baker's rule') (Pannell & Barrett 1998). To varying degrees, apomixis and selfing both show geographical distributions that are consistent with the gene-flow hypothesis, although the patterns are potentially confounded by correlations between these traits and polyploidy.

Escape from range boundaries, II: polyploidization

Apomixis in plants is associated with populations at high latitudes and high elevations where the terrain has been colonized since the last glaciation (Bierzychudek 1987). These apomicts are usually polyploid derivatives of diploid ancestors with a more southerly distribution. Peck *et al.* (1998) describe a model that shows that such distribution patterns, known as geographic parthenogenesis, can be explained if there is gene flow from regions with a longer growing season to regions with a shorter one, which prevents the evolution of local adaptation among sexual genotypes in the poorer environment.

Although theoretical models and the geography of apomixis would both appear to lend some support to the gene-flow hypothesis, it is possible that the relationship between apomixis and marginal habitats is the result of selection for other, ecological traits associated with polyploidy. Ecological differences between diploid and polyploid cytotypes of the same species are common, and indeed are expected to be the rule. This is because mixed populations of different ploidy levels are not stable; the minority cytotype in a mixed population suffers a frequency-dependent disadvantage because it lacks compatible mates (Levin 1975; Burton & Husband 1999). Of course this problem does not exist if a polyploid is apomictic, but the barrier to the establishment of new polyploids can also be overcome if there are ecological niche differences between cytotypes so that the polyploid can colonize areas where the diploid is absent (Fowler & Levin 1984; Felber 1991; Rodriguez 1996). This is probably much more common than apomixis.

The ecological and/or geographical range distributions of polyploids have been compared with those of diploid species in several regional surveys and in numerous more detailed studies of closely related or individual species with different cytotypes. For example, in the floras of the Pyrenees (Petit & Thompson 1999) and in Europe more broadly, niche and/or distributional differences between cytotypes appear to be the rule. Studies of the grasses *Anthoxanthum alpinum, Dactylis glomerata, Deschampsia caespitosa, Festuca apennina* and *Spartina anglica* in Europe and in North America of *Antennaria rosea, Solidago nemoralis* and other species all report niche, habitat and/or range differences between cytotypes. Not all polyploids are apomictic of course, but because the reverse is virtually true it is not clear whether it is selection for apomixis or some other polyploid trait that accounts for the pattern of geographic parthenogenesis in plants.

Approximately 70% of angiosperms are thought to be polyploid in origin (Masterson 1994), including some major angiosperm clades (Soltis & Soltis 2000), raising the possibility that events at range boundaries have been of more than peripheral significance in the evolutionary origins of plant diversity.

Conclusions

Three questions were raised in the Introduction, which we can now re-visit with respect to the three particular examples I have discussed. The first question was, 'At what scales do ecological variables affect evolutionary processes?' We have seen that local, neighbourhood competition among plants for light produces size structures that influence effective population size (N_e), with potentially important evolutionary consequences.

The second question was the reverse of the first and asked at what spatial scales evolutionary processes have ecological consequences. In this case I argued that mating system has ecological consequences at the scale of the metapopulation and that this can explain some aspects of the long-term dynamics of plant species in the Park Grass Experiment. A feature of this experiment is that local adaptation has evolved in the wind-pollinated, outcrossing grass *Anthoxanthum odoratum* despite the close proximity of adjacent populations adapted to quite different local environments. At this local scale gene flow has apparently not prevented local adaptation.

The third question was, 'At what spatial scales can evolutionary or ecological proceses be considered in isolation from each other?' The evolutionary theory of geographical range limits is a clear case where demography and population genetics are interdependent. In contradistinction to the situation at Park Grass, where gene flow has not prevented local adaptation, the evolutionary hypothesis holds that at the geographical scale gene flow *should* be capable of preventing local adaptation. It seems counterintuitive that gene flow should be a more powerful inhibitor of adaptation at a geographical scale than at a local one, but this matter has scarcely been addressed in the field, so there is little hard evidence to go on. The subject is further discussed for the local scale by Antonovics *et al.* (Chapter 5) and at the geographical scale by Barton (Chapter 17).

Summary

The interaction of ecological and evolutionary processes is illustrated by examples at three spatial scales. At the population scale I describe how neighbourhood competition for light generates size hierarchies which, when translated into skewed distributions of reproductive success, reduces the ratio of effective to census population size (N_e/N). This has implications for genetic drift and the response to directional selection. In general, ecological factors that affect the symmetry of intraspecific competition or the shape of the size distribution of reproductive individuals can be expected to influence N_e/N.

There is evidence from the Park Grass Experiment, begun in 1856 and still running, that mating system differences between plant species affect their dynamics at the scale of the metapopulation. Outcrossing species such as the grass *Anthoxanthum odoratum* sustain populations on a large number of experimental plots with quite different soils. Selfing species such as *Tragopogon pratensis* have colonized similar numbers of plots for periods of a decade or two, but appear unable to sustain populations across the full range of environments for longer than this. We suggest that local adaptation is required for the long-term maintenance of populations on different plots and that selfing species have insufficient genetic diversity to achieve this.

At the geographical scale, the stable boundaries of a species' range are where its ecological and evolutionary limits coincide on the map. Understanding why species have ecological and geographic boundaries requires an answer to the evolutionary question as to why natural selection not does drive species' range boundaries ever outwards. An hypothesis with a long pedigree (e.g. Huxley 1942, page 267) is that gene flow from the centre of the range to the periphery could prevent local adaptation and thus limit populations at the range boundary from spreading. The evolution of pre-mating reproductive isolation or apomixis in boundary populations would cut off pollen flow from the hinterland, making the evolution of local adaptation and range extension possible. While apomicts often are found at range boundaries as the hypothesis would predict, these plants are polyploids. Thus, ecological traits associated with polyploidy and not apomixis *per se* may explain this geographical distribution.

Acknowledgements
I thank Mike Dodd for his crucial contribution to our joint research described here. I am grateful to Nick Barton, John Pannell and Janis Antonovics for comments on the manuscript at various stages of its preparation and to the Natural Environment Research Council for financial support.

References
Ainouche, M., Misset, M.T. & Huon, A. (1995). Genetic diversity in Mediterranean diploid and tetraploid *Bromus* L (Section *Bromus* Sm) populations. *Genome*, **38**, 879–888.

Ainouche, M.L., Bayer, R.J., Gourret, J.P., De-

fontaine, A. & Misset, M. T. (1999). The allotetraploid invasive weed *Bromus hordeaceus* L. (Poaceae): Genetic diversity, origin and molecular evolution. *Folia Geobotanica*, **34**, 405–419.

Antonovics, J. & Levin, D.A. (1980). The ecological

and genetic consequences of density-dependent regulation in plants. *Annual Review of Ecology and Systematics*, **11**, 411–452.

Beerling, D.J. (1993). The impact of temperature on the northern distribution-limits of the introduced species *Fallopia japonica* and *impatiens-glandulifera* in north-west europe. *Journal of Biogeography*, **20**, 45–53.

Beerling, D.J., Huntley, B. & Bailey, J.P. (1995). Climate and the distribution of *Fallopia japonica* — use of an introduced species to test the predictive capacity of response surfaces. *Journal of Vegetation Science*, **6**, 269–282.

Berry, R.J., Crawford, T.J. & Hewitt, G.M., ed. (1992). *Genes in Ecology*. Blackwell Scientific Publications, Oxford.

Bierzychudek, P. (1987). Patterns in plant parthenogenesis. In: *The Evolution of Sex and its Consequences* (ed. S.C. Stearns), pp. 197–217. Birkhaüser, Basel.

Burton, T.L. & Husband, B.C. (1999). Population cytotype structure in the polyploid Galax urceolata (Diapensiaceae). *Heredity*, **82**, 381–390.

Caballero, A. (1994). Developments in the prediction of effective population size. *Heredity*, **73**, 657–679.

Carey, P.D., Watkinson, A.R. & Gerard, F.F.O. (1995). The determinants of the distribution and abundance of the winter annual grass *Vulpia ciliata* ssp *ambigua*. *Journal of Ecology*, **83**, 177–187.

Collatz, G.J., Berry, J.A. & Clark, J.S. (1998). Effects of climate and atmospheric CO_2 partial pressure on the global distribution of C-4 grasses: present, past, and future. *Oecologia*, **114**, 441–454.

Crawford, T.J. (1984). What is a population? In: *Evolutionary Ecology* (ed. B. Shorrocks), pp. 135–173. Blackwell Scientific Publications, Oxford.

Davies, M.S. & Snaydon, R.W. (1976). Rapid population differentiation in a mosaic environment. III. Measures of selection pressures. *Heredity*, **36**, 59–66.

de Nettancourt, D. (1977). *Incompatibility in Angiosperms*. Springer-Verlag, Berlin.

Dieckmann, U., Law, R. & Metz, J.A.J., ed. (2000). *The Geometry of Ecological Interactions: Simplifying Spatial Complexity*. Cambridge University Press, Cambridge.

Dodd, M.E. & Silvertown, J. (2000). Size-specific fecundity and the influence of lifetime size variation upon effective population size in *Abies balsamea*. *Heredity*, **85**, 604–609.

Dodd, M.E., Silvertown, J., Mcconway, K., Potts, J. & Crawley, M. (1994). Application of the British National Vegetation Classification to the communities of the Park Grass Experiment through time. *Folia Geobotanica et Phytotaxonomica*, **29**, 321–334.

Dodd, M., Silvertown, J., Mcconway, K., Potts, J. & Crawley, M. (1995). Community stability: A 60-year record of trends and outbreaks in the occurrence of species in the Park Grass Experiment. *Journal of Ecology*, **83**, 277–285.

Eguiarte, L.E., Burquez, A., Rodriguez, J., Martinez Ramos, M., Sarukhan, J. & Pinero, D. (1993). Direct and indirect estimates of neighborhood and effective population size in a tropical palm, *Astrocaryum mexicanum*. *Evolution*, **47**, 75–87.

Falconer, D.S. & Mackay, T.F.C. (1996). *Introduction to Quantitative Genetics*. Longman, Harlow.

Felber, F. (1991). Establishment of a tetraploid cytotype in a diploid population — effect of relative fitness of the cytotypes. *Journal of Evolutionary Biology*, **4**, 195–207.

Ford, E.D. (1975). Competition and stand structure in some even-aged plant monocultures. *Journal of Ecology*, **63**, 311–333.

Fowler, N.L. & Levin, D.A. (1984). Ecological constraints on the establishment of a novel polyploid in competition with its diploid progenitor. *American Naturalist*, **124**, 703–711.

Frankham, R. (1995). Effective population-size adult-population size ratios in wildlife — a review. *Genetical Research*, **66**, 95–107.

Grime, J.P., Hodgson, J.G. & Hunt, R. (1988). *Comparative Plant Ecology*. Allen & Unwin, London.

Haeck, J. & Woldendorp, J.W., ed. (1985). *Structure and Functioning of Plant Populations 2*. North Holland, Amsterdam.

Harper, J.L. (1977). *Population Biology of Plants*. Academic Press, London.

Heywood, J.S. (1986). The effect of plant size variation on genetic drift in populations of annuals. *American Naturalist*, **127**, 851–861.

Hoffmann, A.A. & Blows, M.W. (1994). Species borders — ecological and evolutionary perspectives. *Trends in Ecology and Evolution*, **9**, 223–227.

Holt, R.D. & Gomulkiewicz, R. (1997). How does immigration influence local adaptation? A reexamination of a familiar paradigm. *American Naturalist*, **149**, 563–572.

Husband, B.C. & Barrett, S.C.H. (1992). Genetic drift and the maintenance of the style length polymorphism in tristylous populations of *Eichhornia paniculata* (Pontederiaceae). *Heredity*, **69**, 440–449.

Huxley, J.S. (1942). *Evolution: the Modern Synthesis*. Allen & Unwin, London.

Jacquard, P., Heim, G. & Antonovics, J., ed. (1985). *Genetic Differentiation and Dispersal in Plants*. Springer-Verlag, Heidelberg.

Jeffree, E.P. & Jeffree, C.E. (1994). Temperature and the biogeographical distributions of species. *Functional Ecology*, **8**, 640–650.

Johnson, R.C. (1998). Genetic structure of regeneration populations of annual ryegrass. *Crop Science*, **38**, 851–857.

Kenkel, N.C. (1988). Pattern of self-thinning in Jack pine: testing the random mortality hypothesis. *Ecology*, **69**, 1017–1024.

Kirkpatrick, M. & Barton, N.H. (1997). Evolution of a species' range. *American Naturalist*, **150**, 1–23.

Lawes, J.B. & Gilbert, J.H. (1863). The effect of different manures on the mixed herbage of grassland. *Journal of the Royal Agricultural Society of England*, **24**, 131–164.

Levin, D.A. (1975). Minority cytotype exclusion in local plant populations. *Taxon*, **24**, 35–43.

Levin, D.A. & Wilson, J.B. (1978). The genetic implications of ecological adaptations in plants. *Structure and Functioning of Plant Communities* (eds A.H.J. Freysen & J.W. Woldendorp), pp. 75–100. PUDOC, Wageningen.

Linhart, Y.B. & Grant, M.C. (1996). Evolutionary significance of local genetic differentiation in plants. *Annual Review of Ecology and Systematics*, **27**, 237–277.

Lönn, M. (1993). Genetic structure and allozyme-microhabitat associations in *Bromus hordeaceus*. *Oikos*, **68**, 99–106.

Mack, R. & Harper, J.L. (1977). Interference in dune annuals: Spatial pattern and neighbourhood effects. *Journal of Ecology*, **65**, 345–363.

Masterson, J. (1994). Stomatal size in fossil plants — evidence for polyploidy in majority of angiosperms. *Science*, **264**, 421–424.

Mohler, C.L., Marks, P.L. & Sprugel, D.G. (1978). Stand structure and allometry of trees during self-thinning of pure stands. *Journal of Ecology*, **66**, 599–614.

Newman, D. & Pilson, D. (1997). Increased probability of extinction due to decreased genetic effective population size: experimental populations of *Clarkia pulchella*. *Evolution*, **51**, 354–362.

Nunney, L. & Elam, D.R. (1994). Estimating the effective population-size of conserved populations. *Conservation Biology*, **8**, 175–184.

Pannell, J.R. & Barrett, S.C.H. (1998). Baker's law revisited: Reproductive assurance in a metapopulation. *Evolution*, **52**, 657–668.

Peck, J.R., Yearsley, J.M. & Waxman, D. (1998). Explaining the geographic distributions of sexual and asexual populations. *Nature*, **391**, 889–892.

Petit, C. & Thompson, J.D. (1999). Species diversity and ecological range in relation to ploidy level in the flora of the Pyrenees. *Evolutionary Ecology*, **13**, 45–66.

Ramsey, J. & Schemske, D.W. (1998). Pathways, mechanisms, and rates of polyploid formation in flowering plants. *Annual Review of Ecology and Systematics*, **29**, 467–501.

Ritland, K. (1990). A series of fortran computer-programs for estimating plant mating systems. *Journal of Heredity*, **81**, 235–237.

Rodriguez, D.J. (1996). A model for the establishment of polyploidy in plants. *American Naturalist*, **147**, 33–46.

Roose, M.L. & Gottlieb, L.D. (1976). Genetic and biochemical consequences of polyploidy in *Tragopogon*. *Evolution*, **30**, 818–830.

Salisbury, E.J. (1942). *The Reproductive Capacity of Plants*. Bell & Sons, London.

Sato, K. & Iwasa, Y. (1993). Modelling of wave regeneration in sub-alpine *Abies* forests — population dynamics with spatial structure. *Ecology*, **74** 1538–1550.

Silvertown, J.W. (1980). The dynamics of a grassland ecosystem: botanical equilibrium in the Park Grass Experiment. *Journal of Applied Ecology*, **17**, 491–504.

Silvertown, J.W. (1987). Ecological stability: a test case. *American Naturalist*, **130**, 807–810.

Silvertown, J. (1991). Dorothy's dilemma and the unification of plant population biology. *Trends in Ecology and Evolution*, **6**, 346–348.

Silvertown, J., Dodd, M.E., Mcconway, K., Potts, J. & Crawley, M. (1994). Rainfall, biomass variation, and community composition in the Park Grass Experiment. *Ecology*, **75**, 2430–2437.

Snaydon, R.W. (1970). Rapid population differentiation in a mosaic environment. I. Response of *Anthoxanthum odoratum* to soils. *Evolution*, **24**, 257–269.

Snaydon, R.W. & Davies, M.S. (1972). Rapid population differentiation in a mosaic environment. II. Morphological variation in *Anthoxanthum odoratum* L. *Evolution*, **26**, 390–405.

Snaydon, R.W. & Davies, M.S. (1976). Rapid population differentiation in a mosaic environment. IV. Populations of *Anthoxanthum odoratum* L. at sharp boundaries. *Heredity*, **36**, 9–25.

Soltis, P.S. & Soltis, D.E. (2000). The role of genetic and genomic attributes in the success of polyploids. *Proceedings of the National Academy of Sciences of the United States of America*, **97**, 7051–7057.

Soltis, P.S., Plunkett, G.M., Novak, S.J. & Soltis, D.E. (1995). Genetic variation in *Tragopogon* species — additional origins of the allotetraploids *T. mirus* and *T. miscellus* (Compositae). *American Journal of Botany*, **82**, 1329–1341.

Stebbins, G.L. (1950). *Variation and Evolution in Plants*. Columbia University Press, New York.

Tilman, D. & Kareiva, P. (1997). *Spatial Ecology*. Princeton University Press, Princeton, New Jersey.

Venable, D.L. & Pake, C.E. (1999). Population ecology of Sonoran Desert annual plants. *Ecology of Sonoran Desert Plants and Plant Communities* (ed. R.H. Robichaux), pp. 115–141. University of Arizona Press, Tucson, AZ.

Wayne, P.M. & Bazzaz, F.A. (1997). Light acquisition and growth by competing individuals in CO_2-enriched atmospheres: Consequences for size structure in regenerating birch stands. *Journal of Ecology*, **85**, 29–42.

Williams, E.D. (1978). *Botanical Composition of the Park Grass Plots at Rothamsted 1856–1976*. Rothamsted Experimental Station, Harpenden, UK.

Wilson, J.B. & Levin, D.A. (1986). Some genetic consequences of skewed fecundity distributions in plants. *Theoretical and Applied Genetics*, **73**, 113–121.

Wright, S. (1931). Evolution in Mendelian populations. *Genetics*, **16**, 97–159.

Zietkiewicz, E., Rafalski, A. & Labuda, D. (1994). Genome fingerprinting by simple sequence repeat (ssr)-anchored polymerase chain-reaction amplification. *Genomics*, **20**, 176–183.

Chapter 2

Causes and effects of small-scale spatial structure in plant populations

R. Law,* D. W. Purves,* D. J. Murrell* and U. Dieckmann†

Introduction

If plants in a community were located in space independently of one another, and if each small part of the space had the same probability of being occupied, the community would have no spatial structure. Such randomness is unusual. Plants in mesic environments are commonly clustered together in groups of conspecifics, and the spatial pattern of plants in arid environments can sometimes have the opposite property—a striking overdispersion of individuals (Cody 1986). *Spatial structure* (a departure from a homogeneous Poisson process) is the norm.

The existence of spatial structure has profound implications for plant ecology because plants interact primarily with their close neighbours. The effects of neighbours of a plant are most evident above ground through shading, and are also felt below ground through the uptake of nutrients and water. Individuals outside the neighbourhood have relatively little effect on these processes—in particular, there is no reason to suppose that density averaged over some large spatial region, the so-called 'mean-field' assumption (Law *et al.* 2000), is of any significance (Mack & Harper 1977).

These points might seem too trivially obvious to mention were it not for the great difficulty plant ecologists have had in constructing a theory of population dynamics that holds them properly in place. Historically, plant population dynamics has taken its framework from animal ecology, together with the mean-field approximation widely used there. Yet this is not enough: somehow the information on local spatial structure, on which the growth of plants and ultimately their vital rates crucially depend, has to be accounted for. Without this, models at the theoretical core of plant ecology are dynamically insufficient (Lewontin 1974, page 8), and predictions about future states are liable to be seriously in error.

This chapter is concerned with small-scale spatial structure in plant communities, the readiness with which such structure is generated, how it can be built into plant–community dynamics, and the implications of such structure for plant population genetics. The thread that runs through all this is the need to replace the mean-

*Biology Department, University of York, PO Box 373, York YO10 5YW, UK and † Adaptive Dynamics Network, International Institute for Applied Systems Analysis, A-2361 Laxenburg, Austria.

field assumption with what might be termed the 'plant's eye view' (Turkington & Harper 1979; Mahdi & Law 1987) of the community. General interest in the spatial structure of plant communities goes back to the early days of plant ecology (Blackman 1935), but building the plant's eye view into dynamical systems is a recent development.

Measuring the plant's eye view of the community

How can the plant's eye view of the community be defined and measured? An appropriate measure must make use of the locations of individuals relative to one another, and a sensible starting point is a map showing the positions of individuals, or at least their presence and absence, at an appropriate spatial scale.

We suggest here a measure for a discrete spatial lattice, based on spatial covariance functions (see Condit *et al.* (2000) and Law and Dieckmann (2000a) for an equivalent measure in continuous space). To show how this is done, we use some maps of the presence and absence of species living in a flat alluvial meadow in the lower Derwent Valley National Nature Reserve near York, England (Purves & Law 2001). The site is cut for hay in the early summer, then grazed regularly by sheep until flooding in the winter, and is species-poor, dominated by the grasses *Agrostis stolonifera*, *Holcus lanatus* and *Lolium perenne*. Maps of two of the species in a single quadrat are shown in Figure 2.1(a,b); the species are quite abundant, and it is not immediately obvious whether there is any spatial structure. Nevertheless, if the cells containing the plants are randomized (Figure 2.1c,d), the resulting layouts appear less patchy, suggesting some spatial structure is present.

The plant's eye looks out at a neighbourhood surrounding the plant, rather than taking a global view of the mean density or cover ('global' here means the region covered by the whole map). One can think of concentric rings of increasing radius around a plant (Figure 2.1b), a 'myopic' plant sensing only its very nearest neighbours, a less myopic one sensing the density further away. Near the plant, any local spatial structure causes departures from the global mean, giving a higher density of neighbours if there is aggregation, and a lower density if there is overdispersion. The neighbours may be conspecifics, but they can equally well be other species and ultimately every species can contribute to the neighbourhood.

Each plant has its own unique neighbourhood, and it is more helpful to have a summary statistic of the plant's eye view averaged over the neighbourhoods of all individuals of a species in a given area. Stationarity of the spatial process needs to be assumed, as it does not make sense to think of an average of the neighbourhoods if the statistical properties of the map change from one location to another. Consider a grid of K cells, writing $p_i^{(x)}$ as the density of species i in cell with coordinates $x = (x_1, x_2)$ (density taking values 1 or 0 in Fig. 2.1). The mean density is given by

$$n_i = \frac{1}{K} \cdot \sum_x p_i^{(x)} \qquad (1)$$

(a)

(b)

(c)

(d)

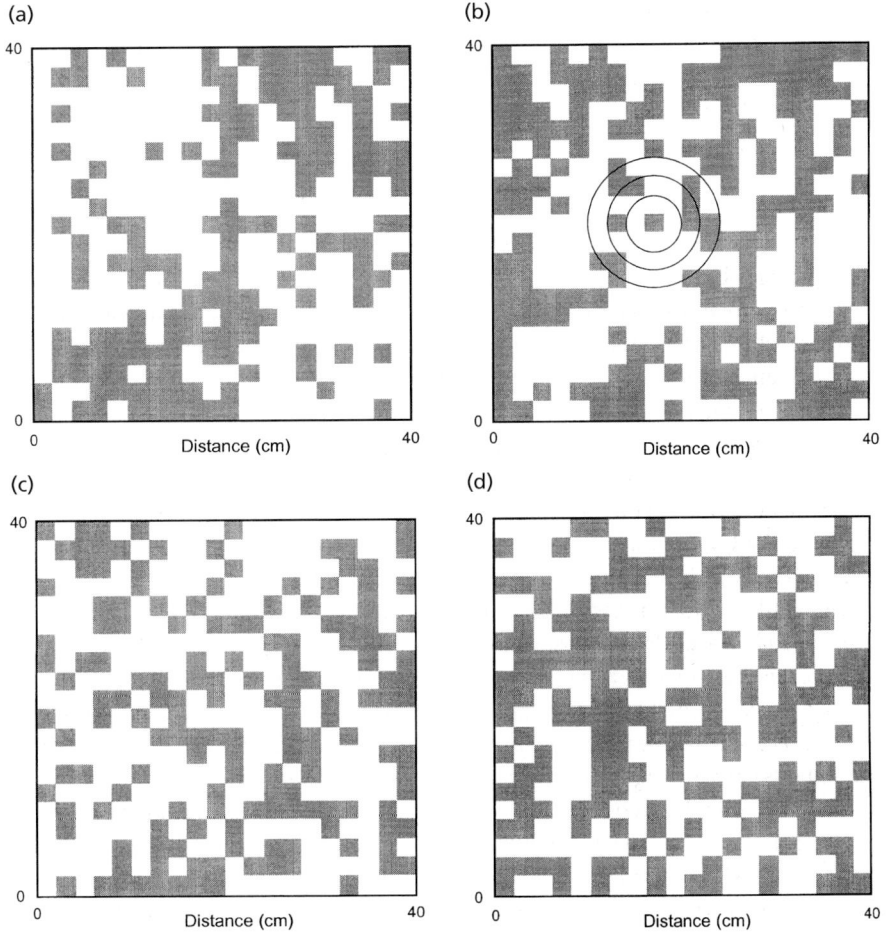

Figure 2.1 Maps showing presence (grey) and absence (white) of (a) *Agrostis stolonifera* and (b) *Lolium perenne* rooting in a grid of 2 × 2 cm cells measured in an alluvial meadow. Maps after randomization of locations of (c) *A. stolonifera* and (d) *L. perenne*. The concentric rings around a plant in (b) are used to construct the plant's eye view of the community.

and a statistic for the mean density of neighbours of species j displaced by a distance $\xi = (\xi_1, \xi_2)$ from individuals of i is

$$c_{ij\xi} = \frac{1}{|S_\xi|} \cdot \sum_{x \in S_\xi} p_i^{(x)} \cdot p_j^{(x+\xi)}, \qquad (2)$$

where $S_\xi = \{(x, x + \xi)\}$ is the set of pairs of cells with a displacement ξ, and $|S_\xi|$ is the number of such pairs and also allows for the finite size of the grid. The statistic can alternatively be measured in polar coordinates of radius r and angle ϕ (if there is no directionality, i.e. if the spatial process is isotropic, the radial dependence suffices). In

(a)

(b)

(c)

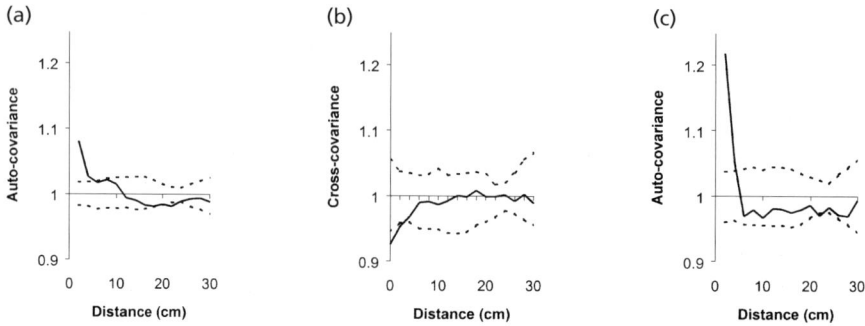

Figure 2.2 Radial covariance functions computed for eight randomly positioned quadrats, including the one in Figure 2.1. (a) Autocovariance function of *Agrostis stolonifera*, (b) cross-covariance function of *A. stolonifera* and *Lolium perenne*, (c) autocovariance function of *L. perenne*. Continuous lines are values obtained from the data, and dashed lines are envelopes, showing the range within which 99% of the lines would lie under the assumption of randomness.

statistical terms $c_{ij\xi}$ measures the spatial covariance with lag ξ, an autocovariance for conspecific neighbours and a cross-covariance for neighbours of other species. Notice that $c_{ij\xi}$ is not a central moment because the cover is not expressed as a deviation from the means (n_i and n_j); the moment is chosen to be as simple as possible because we use it later as a state variable of a dynamical system. Various alternative statistics are to be found in the literature (Ripley 1981; Lotwick & Silverman 1982; Renshaw & Ford 1984; Burrough 1987).

Figure 2.2 shows three covariance functions, each averaged over eight quadrats (like the one in Figure 2.1), randomly located within a visually uniform region of the meadow. To display the functions, they are expressed in radial form (*L. perenne* is isotropic, but there is some anisotropy in *A. stolonifera*). The functions are normalized by dividing by the value they would take in the absence of spatial structure, so that the functions are unity if spatial structure is absent; the normalizing value is close to $n_i \cdot n_j$, but also allows for the finite size and boundaries of the quadrat (details in Purves & Law 2001). In both species, the autocovariance functions are peaked at short distances, indicating some clumping of conspecifics, the clumps tending to be larger in *A. stolonifera* than in *L. perenne*, perhaps reflecting the stolon-forming habit of the former (regeneration from seed is relatively rare in mesic grasslands). The decline to around unity means that, as the neighbourhood becomes large, the auto-covariance function comes close to the mean-field value; thus, over the spatial scale investigated, structure is confined to a small neighbourhood. In contrast to the autocovariance functions, the cross-covariance function between species is at a minimum at short distances, suggesting some spatial separation of the species.

Some variation in covariance functions would be expected simply as a matter of chance, and this needs to be distinguished from genuine spatial structure. This could be done in various ways (e.g. Lotwick & Silverman 1982; Coomes *et al.* 1999); we use the following Monte Carlo methods. For autocovariances, the locations of cells containing the species are completely randomized, as illustrated in Figure 2.1(c,d), and the autocovariance recomputed. For cross-covariances, the spatial structure within species is held in place and the patterns of one species displaced by a random amount, wrapping the edges around on a torus (the displacement is constrained to be greater than the larger spatial structure within species, a distance of 10 cm here). The randomization is repeated a large number of times (we used 1000 replicates) to compute envelopes within which 99% of the functions would lie under the assumption of randomness, as shown in Figure 2.2. The envelopes confirm the aggregation within species, the observed autocovariance functions being outside or on the margin of the envelopes up to about 10 cm in the case of *A. stolonifera* and 4 cm in the case of *L. perenne*. There is also some separation of the species at very short distances.

We suggest that spatial covariance functions of the kind described above provide a useful measure of the plant's eye view of the neighbourhood. How far from the origin the plants sense their neighbourhoods depends on the context, as the distance is obviously affected by plant size. But it is clear in the meadow example that the composition of the immediate neighbourhood is far from the spatial average: individuals find themselves in an environment in which conspecifics are overrepresented and heterospecifics underrepresented when compared with the mean-field.

Causes of spatial structure

There are many processes that contribute to small-scale spatial structure and result in a plant's eye view that differs from the mean field.

Plant growth in even-aged monocultures

You need do no more than grow some plants together from uniform seed under uniform environmental conditions to break their initial symmetry and generate spatial structure. Those plants that emerge first are larger than later-emerging neighbours; those that have more space are larger before they come into contact with neighbours; larger plants have an advantage over their smaller neighbours in competition for limited resources. A well-documented size hierarchy develops (e.g. Obeid *et al.* 1967; Ford 1975; Weiner 1985), often accompanied by an increased risk of death of small individuals (e.g. Mithen *et al.* 1984).

Spatial structure in this kind of experiment becomes evident when the locations of large and small plants are measured. This was first demonstrated by Hozumi *et al.* (1955) and Yoda *et al.* (1957), growing corn in rows with 2-cm and 3-cm spacing between plants. After 16 days, they observed a negative autocorrelation of the fresh weight of a plant with its first, third and fifth neighbours, and a positive autocorrelation with the second, fourth and sixth; as one might expect, the autocorrelations changed with increasing age (and size) of the plants. Later, using a more elaborate design, Franco and Harper (1988) grew the annual *Kochia scoparia* in concentric arcs and found that plants in several odd-numbered arcs were shorter in height than those in even arcs; along a single arc, there was also a negative autocorrelation in weight of successive plants. It is though that an arc of relatively large plants leads to suppression of the plants in the next arc, which releases the next arc from competition, and so on.

The close proximity of two plants may lead to the death of one or both, bringing about further change in spatial structure: aggregations break up, causing a shift towards overdispersion (Antonovics & Levin 1980). An experiment by Mithen *et al.* (1984) on an even-aged stand of the annual plant *Lapsana communis* illustrates this; Figure 2.3 shows the spatial arrangement of seedlings immediately after germination, distinguishing the plants destined to die from those still alive 15 weeks later. The radial covariance functions (Figure 2.3b–d) show strong aggregation among those that died (the function is peaked close to distance zero), although there are rather too few surviving individuals to draw conclusions about their spatial structure. The cross-covariance drops below unity at short distances suggesting some separation of the survivors from those that died, but this is not statistically significant. A similar analysis was carried out by Kenkel (1988) on locations of dead and living individuals in a natural stand of jack pine *Pinus banksiana* following synchronous regeneration after a fire in the 1920s. This analysis also showed spatial aggregation of dead individuals and independence of the survivors from those that died, although in this case the survivors were themselves overdispersed.

Interaction kernels

At the heart of the structure that emerges in even-aged monocultures must lie some dependence of growth of an individual on its own state and the state of its neighbourhood. The function presumably depends on the size s and location x of the plant, and size s' and location x' of each neighbour, written here as the interaction kernel $w(s,s',x'-x)$. The overall effect of neighbours is the convolution product obtained from weighting the kernel by the density $p(x',s')$ of plants of size s' at x', and integrating over s' and x':

$$W(s, x, p) = \int\int w(s, s', x'-x) \cdot [p(s', x') - \delta_s(s') \cdot \delta_x(x')] dx' ds' \tag{3}$$

The δs are Dirac delta functions introduced so that each plant is not counted as a neighbour of itself. Ultimately these neighbour-dependent effects on growth impact on reproductive output and risk of mortality: our understanding of plant population dynamics would be much improved if interaction kernels could be specified.

Attempts to characterize w have come primarily from theoretical reasoning (Benjamin & Hardwick 1986). The zone-of-influence model is particularly promising biologically (Wyszomirski 1983; Firbank & Watkinson 1985; Bonan 1988; Miller & Weiner 1989), although not altogether tractable mathematically. This model equates the size of a plant to a zone of influence around it: as plants grow, the zones of different plants meet, leading to competition in areas of overlap; competition can be symmetric, or asymmetric if the largest plant gets a disproportionate share of the resources (Weiner 1990).

Little is known about w from experimental studies. Silander and Pacala (1985) used an even-aged stand of *Arabidopsis thaliana* to search for a function of the neighbourhood of a plant that would minimize residual variation in its reproductive

(a)

(b)

(c)

(d)

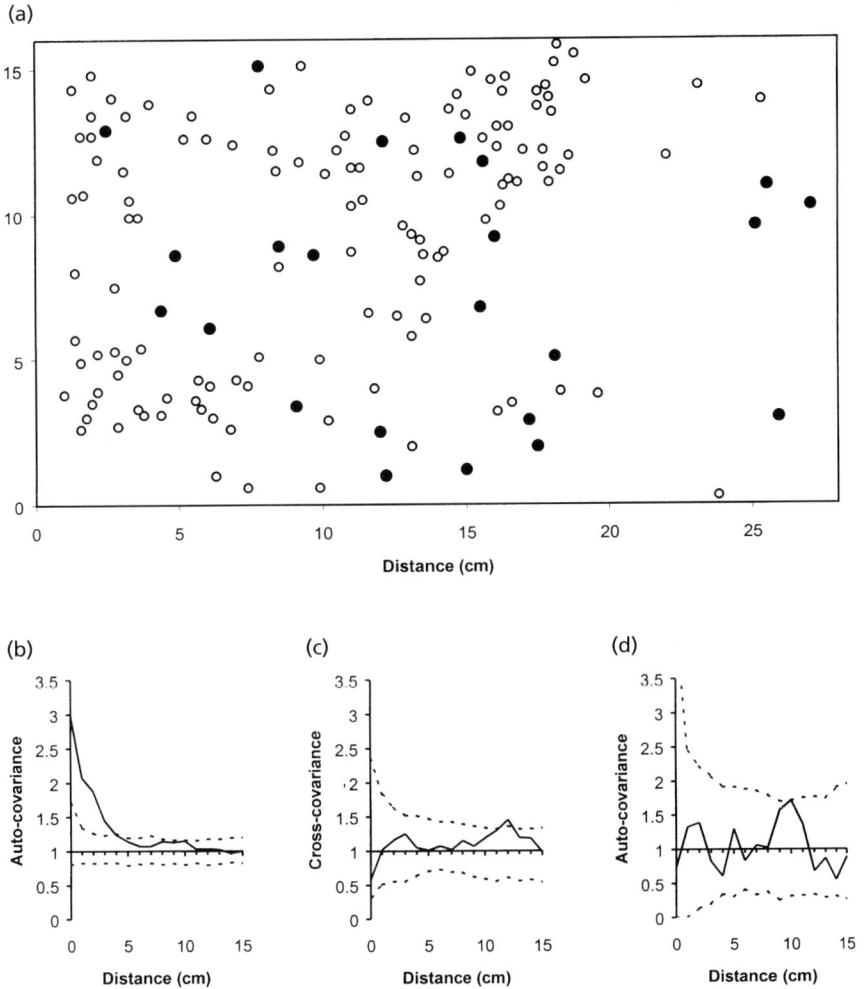

Figure 2.3 (a) Map of seedlings of *Lapsana communis* at emergence, redrawn from Mithen *et al.* (1984); those still alive 15 weeks later are filled circles, those that died are open circles. (b) Radial autocovariance function for plants that died; (c) cross-covariance function for surviving and dead plants; (d) autocovariance function for plants that survived. Continuous lines are values obtained from the data, and dashed lines are envelopes showing the range within which 99% of the lines would lie under the assumption of randomness, calculated as in Figure 2.2.

output. Simply counting the number of neighbours in a circle of 5-cm radius turned out to be as successful as a function incorporating distance to each neighbour. Nevertheless, a closer examination of the effect of distance, growing plants of *A. thaliana* with a single neighbour matched in size but increasingly distant, does show the expected quantitative dependence on distance (Figure 2.4).

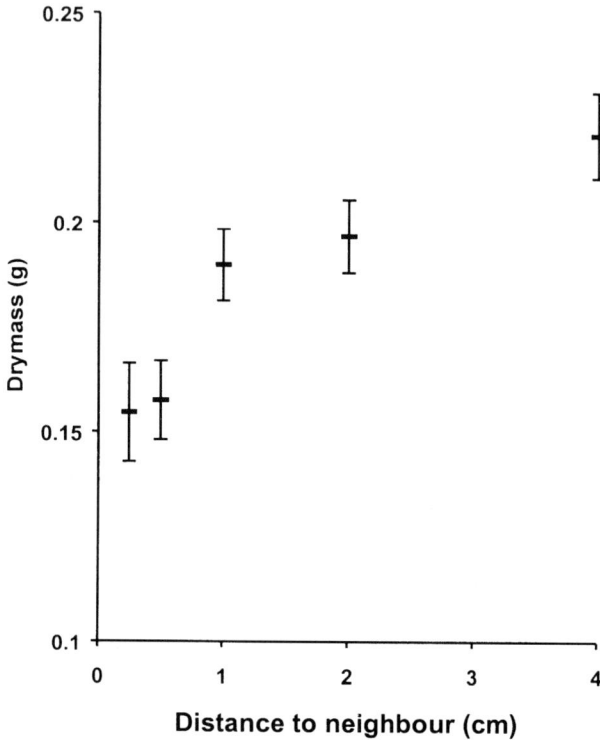

Figure 2.4 Mean (± standard error) plant dry mass after 37 days of *Arabidopsis thaliana*, grown from seed with a single neighbour placed at various distances. (From Purves unpublished data.)

Dispersal kernels

The neighbourhood interactions above apply once plants are rooted to the spot. Beyond the context of plant growth and mortality in even-aged monocultures, spatial structure is obviously affected by the new locations that individuals come to occupy through reproduction and dispersal of propagules. Passive dispersal typically counteracts the breakdown of aggregations because most seeds fall close to the parent plant even if there are specific adaptations for dispersal (e.g. Harper 1977, page 33 *et seq.*); events such as occasional wind gusts that cause seeds to travel much farther (van Dorp *et al.* 1996) would not normally change this. Seed dispersal by animals can, however, lead to movement over much longer distances (see Chapter 3; Isagi *et al.* 2000).

Dispersal kernels have been studied more than interaction kernels because of the insight they give into two important phenomena. First is the size of the area over which individuals can be thought of coming from a panmictic unit, which depends both on pollen and seed dispersal (Crawford 1984; Meagher & Thompson 1987). Second are the paradoxically high rates of migration observed, for instance, in the

1 interactions among conspecifics that typically tend to break up aggregations of conspecifics;

2 dispersal that tends to generate aggregations;

3 spatial structure of the abiotic environment; and

4 interactions with other species that generate or break up aggregations, depending on the kind of interaction.

The examples above show repeatedly that the plant's eye view can be far from the mean field. Neither is the plant's eye view fixed. As plants grow, give birth and die, there is continual flux in local spatial structure: the vital processes determine local spatial structure, and local spatial structure determines the vital processes. The challenge is to construct a theory of plant community dynamics that couples them together.

Here we describe some work towards this coupling. We develop the ideas in a continuous space because this is a good representation of the space that plants in reality occupy, and assume that edge effects are negligible by using periodic boundaries. (See Wissel (2000) for simulations in discrete spatial lattices and Rand (1999) for pair approximation methods to describe their dynamics.)

Individual-based models

The approach favoured by ecologists when faced with complex spatial ecological processes is to simulate them as individual-based models (IBMs), in effect to compute realizations of the stochastic process (e.g. Cain *et al.* 1995; Pacala *et al.* 1996; Wissel 2000); this is the so-called Lagrangian approach (Turchin 1998, page 36). There is much to recommend this approach to the ecologist: it has appeal because it is algorithmic rather than mathematical; it allows much biological detail to be included, and gets closer than other approaches to the complexity of real ecological systems. We illustrate stochastic IBMs with two examples below.

The first example describes the growth of an even-aged monoculture of plants, in the absence of births and deaths. The IBM is specified by the state $p(s,x)$ at some point in time, comprising the size (mass) s and location x of each plant, together with the rate at which plants lose g^- and gain g^+ an 'atom' of mass δ

$$g^-(s) = \alpha \cdot s \tag{4a}$$

$$g^+(x, s, p) = \beta \cdot s^{2/3} \cdot [1 + W(s, x, p)]^{-1} \tag{4b}$$

The terms $\alpha \cdot s$ and $\beta \cdot s^{2/3}$ describe size changes of an isolated plant: losses are assumed to be proportional to mass, and increments proportional to area; parameters α and β scale to rate of change of mass. The remaining term in Eq. 4b reduces the rate of gain of area in the presence of neighbours, and thus depends on the spatial pattern; this uses the convolution product Eq. 3, with an interaction kernel

$$w(s, s', x' - x) = \frac{\gamma \cdot s'^{2/3}}{(x' - x)^2} \cdot \begin{cases} 1 & \text{if } s' \geq s \\ 1 - \varepsilon & \text{if } s' < s \end{cases} \tag{4c}$$

(Thomas & Weiner 1989). The parameter γ denotes the overall strength of competition and ε determines competitive asymmetry (Weiner 1990), from symmetric

(a)

(b)

(c)

(d)

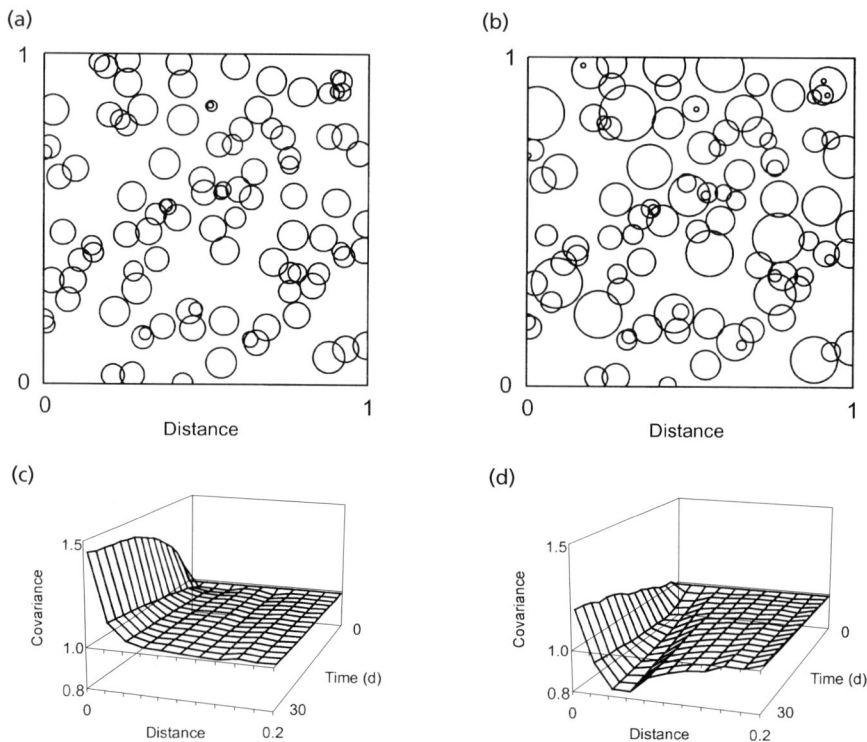

Figure 2.6 An individual-based model (IBM) of growth of plants in an even-aged monoculture. At time 0, 100 individuals of mass 0.1 units are placed at random locations in the unit area; individuals grow as shown in Eq. 4 depending on their current size and the size of neighbouring individuals with which they compete. (a) Size of individuals (area of circle proportional to mass$^{2/3}$) after 32 days with symmetric competition ($\varepsilon = 0$); (b) size of individuals with asymmetric competition ($\varepsilon = 0.9$); locations of individuals are the same in the two realizations. Time series of the radial covariance of plant mass averaged over 50 realizations (c) with symmetric competition, and (d) with asymmetric competition. The radial moment is centralized by taking the deviation of plant mass from the mean plant mass at the current time. Other parameter values are $\alpha = 2.8, \beta = 14, \gamma = 4.1 \times 10^{-4}, \delta = 0.05$.

($\varepsilon = 0$) to completely asymmetric ($\varepsilon = 1$); the strength of competition attenuates with the square of the distance between the plants, and is proportional to the area of the neighbour.

Figure 2.6(a,b) shows the outcome of two realizations of the IBM, contrasting in the asymmetry of competition, the plants being positioned at the same locations at the start. Asymmetry has large effects on local spatial structure: neighbouring plants show mutual inhibition under symmetric competition, whereas one plant gets an advantage over another under asymmetric competition. As a result, the spatial covariances of plant size develop differently over time (Figure 2.6c,d). Under symmetric competition, adjacent individuals become similar in size, and deviations in the covariance from the mean field decrease nearly monotonically with increasing distance between plants. Under asymmetric competition, small plants tend to have large plants as neighbours at intermediate distances, in keeping with the results of experiments (Hozumi *et al.* 1955; Yoda *et al.* 1957; Franco & Harper 1988), and the covariance function develops a minimum.

The second example is a simple birth–death process of a single species in a spatial setting, taken from Law and Dieckmann (2000b) (similar to IBMs used by Bolker and Pacala (1997) and Dieckmann *et al.* (1997)). The IBM is specified by the locations of plants $p(x)$, together with the death and birth rate for an individual at location x:

$$D(x, p) = d + d' \cdot \int w(x' - x) \cdot [p(x') - \delta_x(x')] dx' \qquad (5a)$$

$$B(x' - x) = b \cdot m(x' - x) \qquad (5b)$$

The death rate $D(x,p)$ contains an intrinsic death term d, and a neighbour-dependent term; the latter makes use of the interaction kernel $w(x' - x)$ (for simplicity now independent of size) to give each neighbour a weight according to its distance, and sums over all neighbours (the Dirac delta function δ excludes the target individual itself), finally scaling the overall effect of neighbours by d'. $B(x' - x)$ is the rate at which an individual at x gives rise to a new individual at x', assumed here to depend only on an intrinsic birth rate b and the dispersal kernel $m(x' - x)$.

Figure 2.7 shows the outcome of some realizations of the IBM. In Figure 2.7(a), the kernel parameters are set such that the neighbourhoods of interaction and dispersal are large, giving little spatial structure (Figure 2.7d); the population then settles slightly below the mean-field density of 200 in the unit area. Reducing the neighbourhoods of interaction and dispersal by the same amount emphasizes the role of the dispersal kernel in generating aggregations (Figure 2.7b,e). The plant's eye then perceives a crowded neighbourhood, and the population declines to a lower density (≈ 140). A sufficiently big reduction in the interaction neighbourhood on its own has the consequence that two plants living close together are unlikely both to survive; the population thus becomes overdispersed at very short distances (Figure 2.7c,f). To the plant's eye, the area is sparsely inhabited, and the population increases to a greater density (≈ 270). Throughout these simulations b, d and d' are held constant; the changes in population density are caused entirely by the effects the kernels have on spatial structure. Evidently, even in this particularly simple ecological stochastic process (essentially a spatial, stochastic version of the logistic equation), the kernel parameters can lead to anything from a decline to low densities (some parameters can even cause rapid extinction), to densities much greater than the mean-field value. The spatial extension has fundamental effects on the dynamics.

Dynamics of spatial moments

Insightful though IBMs are, there are limits to what they can tell us about, for instance, the equilibrium states, attractors, and parameter dependencies of the dynamics. If you doubt this, consider how hard it would be to establish the main features of competition in the Lotka–Volterra model from simulations of IBMs.

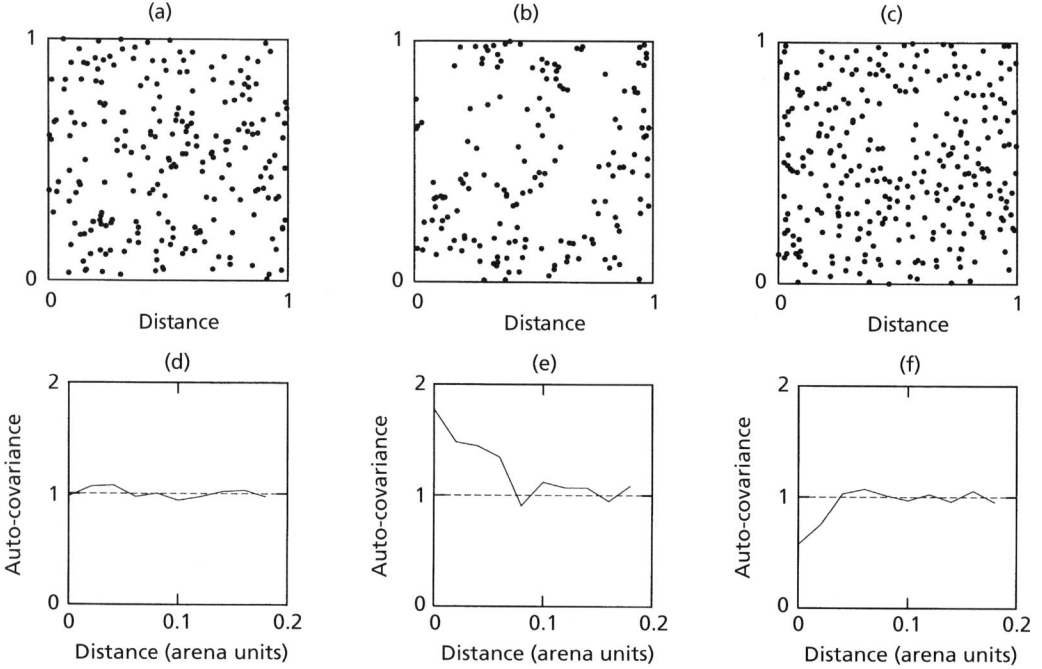

Figure 2.7 An individual-based model (IBM) of growth of a single-species population. At time 0, 200 individuals are randomly located in an arena of unit area; individuals die and give birth according to the rates shown in Eq. 5. Spatial patterns (a), (b), (c) depict the locations of individuals after 50 time units have elapsed; (d), (e), (f) give the corresponding autocovariance functions. Gaussian kernels are used, truncated at a 3× standard deviation (sd). The realizations differ in their kernel parameter values: (a) $sd_w = sd_m = 0.12$; (b) $sd_w = sd_m = 0.04$; (c) $sd_w = 0.02$, $sd_m = 0.12$; parameter values common to all realizations are: $b = 0.4$, $d = 0.2$, $d' = 0.001$.

To gain deeper insights it helps to have dynamical systems that give good approximations to the IBMs. Recent research shows that dynamical systems of spatial moments can be derived from the stochastic processes, and in a sense these form a natural extension of the non-spatial dynamics used in ecology in the past. (The derivations are somewhat technical and are given elsewhere (Bolker & Pacala 1997, 1999; Pacala & Levin 1997, 2000; Dieckmann & Law 2000; Murrell & Law 2000).) Here we concentrate on the general form of the equations and give an example to illustrate the ideas.

First some notation: We consider a multispecies community comprising a set of species $L = \{1, 2, \ldots l\}$, living in a continuous, two-dimensional space of area A, large enough for edge effects to be negligible. The spatial moments are defined as:

$$N_i(p) = \frac{1}{A} \cdot \int p_i(x) dx \qquad \bullet \qquad (6a)$$

$$C_{ij}(\xi, p) = \frac{1}{A} \cdot \int p_i(x) \cdot \left[p_j(x+\xi) - \delta_{ij} \cdot \delta(\xi) \right] dx \qquad (6b)$$

$$T_{ijk}(\xi, \xi', p) = \frac{1}{A} \cdot \int p_i(x) \cdot [p_j(x+\xi) - \delta_{ij} \cdot \delta(\xi)]$$
$$\cdot [p_k(x+\xi') - \delta_{ik} \cdot \delta(\xi')] dx \qquad (6c)$$

where $p_i(x)$ is the density of plants of species i at x, and the δs are Dirac delta functions that remove self pairs. The diagram beside each equation tries to make clear the object being averaged across space; each circle represents a plant. Thus, Eq. 6a is the average density of single plants, the first spatial moment, and is a continuous version of Eq. 1. Eq. 6b is the average density of pairs of plants displaced by ξ, the second spatial moment, a continuous version of Eq. 2; we take the second moment as measuring the plant's eye view and normalize by dividing by $N_i(p) \cdot N_j(p)$ for graph plotting (which gives the second moment a value of unity if the plants are randomly dispersed). The hierarchy of moments can be continued: Eq. 6c is the average density of triples of plants displaced by ξ and ξ', the third spatial moment, and so on.

Moment dynamics deal with the average change of the moments over time, the average being over the ensemble of stochastic realizations; we therefore remove the p argument, and introduce t to emphasize the dependence on time. For notational simplicity, we use the sets $N = \{N_i(t)|i \in L\}$, $C = \{C_{ij}(\xi,t)|i,j \in L\}$, $T = \{T_{ijk}(\xi,\xi',t)|i,j,k \in L\}$. In principle, a system of differential equations describing the rate of change of the spatial moments with respect to time can be constructed of the form:

$$\dot{N}_i(t) = F_i(N, C) \quad \text{for all } i \in L \qquad (7a)$$

$$\dot{C}_{ij}(\xi, t) = F_{ij}(N, C, T) \quad \text{for all } i, j \in L \qquad (7b)$$

$$\dot{T}_{ijk}(\xi, \xi', t) = F_{ijk}(N, C, T, \ldots) \quad \text{for all } i, j, k \in L \qquad (7c)$$

Eq. 7a deals with the flux in average density of individuals, a familiar-enough concept in ecology. Less familiar is Eq. 7b: this describes the flux in density of pairs of individuals displaced by ξ, in effect accounting for changes in the second-order spatial structure caused by growth, birth and death of individuals. In other words, Eq. 7b tracks the changing plant's eye view (see pp. 22–27). Eqs 7a and 7b are just the start of a hierarchy of equations: 7c describes the dynamics of density of triples, and so on.

Consider, for instance, the spatial version of the logistic equation (Law & Dieckmann 2000b); variations on this theme were given by Bolker and Pacala (1997), and Dieckmann *et al.* (1997), with a detailed analysis of the model in the case of Bolker and Pacala (1997). The stochastic process in Eq. 5 gives dynamics of the first moment:

$$\dot{N}(t) = b \cdot N(t) \qquad (a)$$

$$-d \cdot N(t) \qquad (b)$$

$$-d' \cdot \int w(\xi') \cdot C(\xi', t) d\xi' \qquad (c) \qquad (8)$$

In case it is not intuitive what these contributions to flux of the first moment are, the diagrams on the right summarize the events, with the convention here and below that a grey circle represents birth of a new individual, an open circle a death, and a double circle a neighbour. Term (a) on the right-hand side is thus the contribution to the flux due to birth, (b) is the contribution due to the intrinsic tendency to die, and (c) modifies the death rate due to interactions with other individuals in the vicinity. It is instructive to compare Eq. 8 with the familiar non-spatial (mean-field) logistic equation

$$\dot{N}(t) = b \cdot N(t) - d \cdot N(t) - d' \cdot N^2(t) \tag{9}$$

the only difference is that the density-dependent term N^2 is replaced by an integral weighting the plant's eye view by the interaction kernel. In other words, the density-dependent effects in Eq. 8 are mediated by other plants in the neighbourhood, rather than by the average density; the dynamics of the first moment are now coupled to the second moment as in Eq. 7a.

Dynamics of the second moment are inevitably a good deal more complicated than those of the first moment, because they deal with the flux in density of *pairs* of individuals displaced by ξ. From Eq. 5

$$\dot{C}(\xi, t) = b \cdot \int m(\xi') \cdot C(-\xi + \xi', t) d\xi' \qquad \text{(a)}$$

$$+ b \cdot \int m(\xi') \cdot C(\xi + \xi', t) d\xi' \qquad \text{(b)}$$

$$+ 2 \cdot d \cdot m(\xi) \cdot N(t) \qquad \text{(c) (d)}$$

$$- 2 \cdot b \cdot C(\xi, t) \qquad \text{(e) (f)}$$

$$- d' \cdot \int w(\xi') \cdot T(\xi, \xi + \xi', t) d\xi' \qquad \text{(g)}$$

$$- d' \cdot \int w(\xi') \cdot T(\xi, \xi', t) d\xi' \qquad \text{(h)}$$

$$- 2 \cdot d' \cdot w(\xi) \cdot C(\xi, t) \qquad \text{(i) (j)} \tag{10}$$

This is less daunting than it might seem at first sight: each term still has a precise geometric interpretation, which we try to make intuitive in the corresponding diagram.

Terms (a) and (b) describe the rate at which new pairs are formed due to births at a distance ξ' from the parent; the integration accounts for all locations of the parent, and makes use of the dispersal kernel of seeds $m(\xi')$. Terms (c) and (d) arise because one of the pair can itself be the parent. Terms (e) and (f) describe the intrinsic rate at which individuals die. Terms (g) and (h) modify the death rate due to neighbours located at a distance ξ', using the interaction kernel $w(\xi')$, the integration allowing for all individuals in the neighbourhood. Terms (i) and (j) allow for modifications to the death rate due to the other individual in the pair. Notice that all these terms come in groups of two because each kind of change applies to both individuals in the pair. Notice also that this equation has the general form of Eq. 7b, depending on the first, second and third moments.

The extension from a single species to a two-species (or multispecies) community is straightforward. For two species, the dynamics of first and second moments, $N_1(t)$, $N_2(t)$, $C_{11}(\xi,t)$, $C_{12}(\xi,t)$, $C_{22}(\xi,t)$ keep track of local spatial structure both within and between species (Bolker & Pacala 1999; Law & Dieckmann 2000a). The extension to a spatially heterogeneous physical environment, such as that caused by the variation in soil depth in Figure 2.5, also raises no further difficulties. Environmental heterogeneity can be treated as fixed on the time scale of population dynamics, but as having effects on local birth and death rates. Thus, for a single species (indexed 1) living in a heterogeneous environment (indexed 2), dynamics of $N_1(t)$, $C_{11}(\xi,t)$, $C_{12}(\xi,t)$ are used, the information about the environment entering through the cross-covariance. A version of this was given by Murrell and Law (2000) to describe the dynamics of movements of beetles in a complex ecological landscape, further simplified by the absence of births and deaths, with the result that the average density (first moment) could not change, leaving only the second moments $C_{11}(\xi,t)$, $C_{12}(\xi,t)$ as state variables.

Moment closures

It should be understood that Eqs 7 do not themselves form a closed dynamical system. The dynamics of the first moments depend on the second moments, the dynamics of the second moments depend on the third, and so on; the hierarchy of equations is coupled such that each depends on the next. To obtain a dynamical system, somehow the moment hierarchy has to be closed. Moment closures are unfamiliar in ecology, although the mean-field approximation, which has served ecology since the early part of the 20th century, can be thought of as a first-order closure with $C_{ij}(\xi,t)$ replaced by $N_i(t) \cdot N_j(t)$, leaving a dynamical system

$$\dot{N}_i(t) = F_i(N) \quad \text{for all } i \in L \tag{11}$$

This can be seen, for instance, by comparing dynamics of the first moments in the spatial and non-spatial versions of the logistic equation, Eqs 8 and 9. The step plant ecology needs to make to hold the plant's eye view in place is to replace the first-order closure with a second-order closure. This means replacing the third moment by some function of the first and second moments, to get a closed dynamical system of the form

$$\dot{N}_i(t) = F_i(N, C) \quad \text{for all } i \in L \tag{12a}$$

$$\dot{C}_{ij}(\xi, t) = F_{ij}(N, C) \quad \text{for all } i, j \in L. \tag{12b}$$

The choice of closure is an important research question that has yet to be fully re-solved; Dieckmann and Law (2000) describe some closures and investigate their properties. To illustrate the use of a dynamical system to approximate the stochastic process, we use here a new power-2 closure (D. J. Murrell, unpublished). Figure 2.8 shows the fit between the first and second moments of the stochastic process and the moments obtained by integrating Eqs 8 and 10. The dynamical system captures some important features of the first and second moments, the density moving above or below the mean-field value of 200 given by the non-spatial logistic equation (Figure 2.8a, b). This comes about because the dynamical system keeps track of changes in the second moment, i.e. changes in the plant's eye view. Corresponding to the aggregations that build up in the IBM in Figure 2.7b, the second moment of the dynamical system increases at short distances (Figure 2.8c), and this feeds back to the dynamics of the first moment (Eq. 8, term c). Where overdispersion develops in the IBM (Figure 2.7c), the second moment of the dynamical system decreases at short distances (Figure 2.8d), which again feeds back to the dynamics of the first moment.

We suggest that important effects of local spatial structure on populations can be dealt with by dynamical systems with second-order moment closures. These systems in effect introduce the dynamics of the plant's eye view of the community, and elim-inate the mean-field assumption that penetrates so deeply into ecological theory. But two notes of caution. First the success of the second-order closure depends on the absence of important higher-order spatial structure, and there are conditions under which it must fail as a satisfactory approximation. Second, there is still much to learn about appropriate moment closures, and it may be premature to go too deeply into analysis of the dynamical systems until issues about closures are resolved.

Local spatial structure in population genetics

The dynamical consequences of local spatial structure are potentially profound. This should not come as a surprise. Compare, for instance, the intricate feedbacks in the spatial version of the logistic equation Eqs 8 and 10 with the much simpler non-spatial version Eq. 9: it would be unrealistic to expect properties of a mean-field model in general to carry over to a spatially structured one. New phenomena are al-ready emerging from spatial dynamics theory, such as the dependence of the equi-librium densities on the interaction and dispersal kernels shown above (see also Bolker & Pacala 1999; Rand 1999; Bolker *et al.* 2000; Law & Dieckmann 2000a). It would be surprising if plant community dynamics in the field were not also contin-gent on local spatial structure. For example, in dune annual plants, aggregation of conspecifics and segregation of heterospecific individuals have major effects on competitive interactions (Rees *et al.* 1996); in weeds, aggregation of conspecifics can promote persistence of species that are weaker competitors (Stoll & Prati 2001).

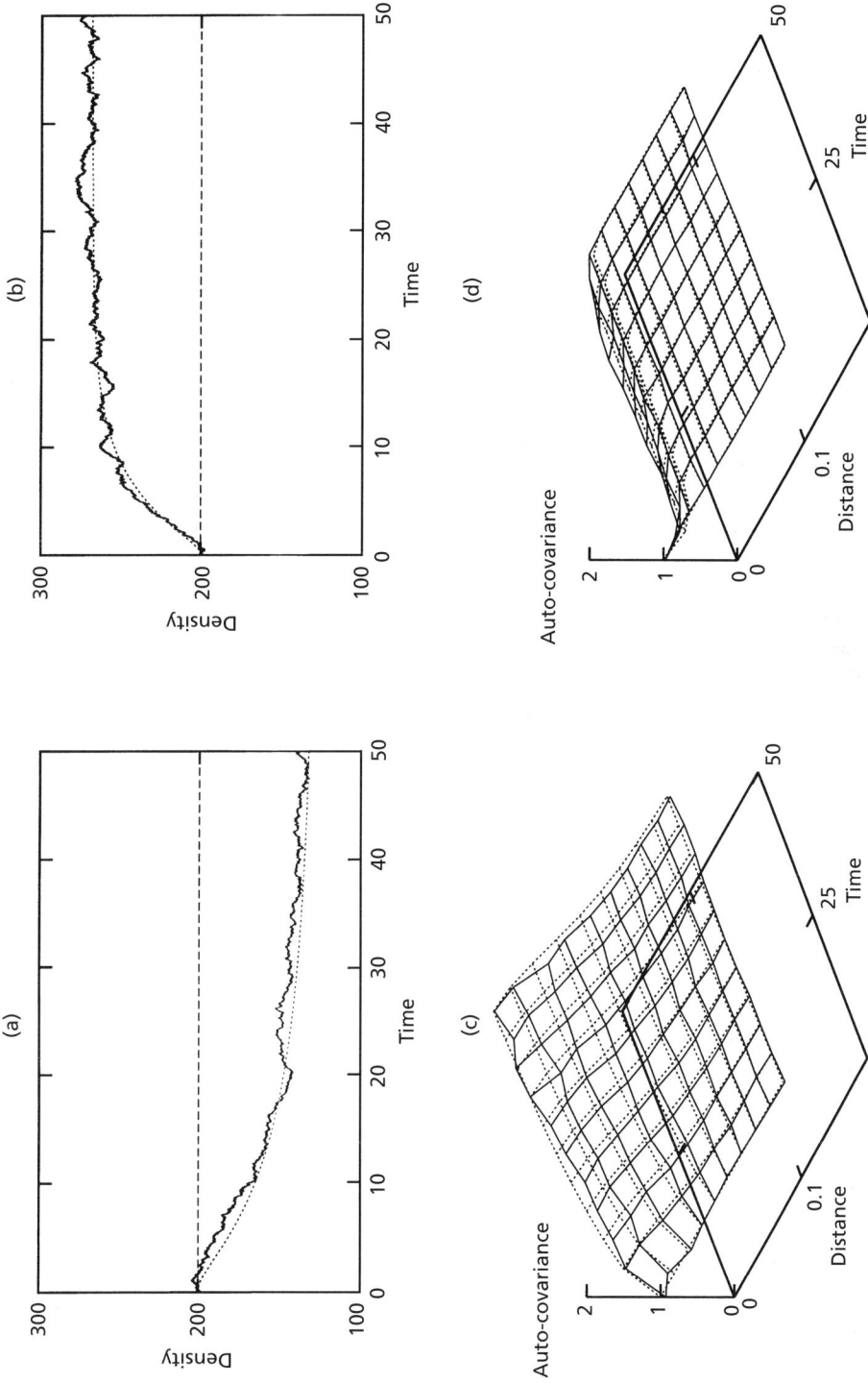

Figure 2.8 Comparison of first and second spatial moments of a single-species population over time, modelled as an individual-based model (IBM) (continuous lines) and as a dynamical system (dotted lines). Simulations of the IBM start with 200 individuals randomly distributed over space, and periodic boundary conditions are used. Parameters are as in Figure 2.7, with 'low density' values $sd_w = sd_m = 0.04$ in (a) and (c), and 'high density' values $sd_w = 0.02$, $sd_m = 0.12$ in (b) and (d). Moments of the IBM are computed from the spatial patterns and averaged over 20 realizations. Moments of the dynamical system are found from numerical integration of Eqs 8 and 10; distance units of the autocovariances are as in Figure 2.7. The dashed line in (a) and (b) gives the mean-field dynamics obtained from solving the logistic equation Eq. 9.

39

Having said this, there are clearly circumstances under which mean-field models would be good approximations; for instance, if there is little spatial structure, or if individuals compete over large distances. Pacala and Silander (1990), for example, describe an experiment on two annual weed species with relatively weak spatial structure, where the mean-field approximation worked well.

What implications does local spatial structure have for plant population genetics? Broadly, this depends on the extent to which results from population genetics depend on the mean-field assumption.

Invasion of new mutants

Consider, for instance, the fate of a rare mutant gene. When calculating the mutant's initial rate of increase in a well-mixed, mean-field system, one would assume a mutant frequency close to zero and a resident gene frequency close to one. However, in a spatially structured system with limited seed dispersal, a local cluster of individuals carrying the mutant gene builds up, giving a frequency of mutant individuals in the neighbourhood far in excess of the mutant's mean frequency in the population. The initial growth of the mutant is then not settled by the dynamics of the first spatial moment alone: it also depends on the local spatial structure of the resident and mutant, given above by the dynamics of both their first and second moments. Invasion criteria allowing for spatial structure have been suggested both for lattices (van Baalen & Rand 1998; Ferrière & Le Galliard 2000) and for continuous space (Bolker & Pacala 1999). It is evident from these studies that results from population genetics that depend on the rate of increase of mutants, such as protected polymorphisms and evolutionarily stable strategies (ESSs) can be altered by small-scale spatial structure.

Maintenance of polymorphism

It is well known that spatial structure in the abiotic environment combined with limited movement can permit genetic polymorphism (Levene 1953). This was nicely demonstrated in cultures of *Pseudomonas fluorescens*, initially comprising a single genotype. Cultures without stirring (little movement) became polymorphic within 3 days and showed some spatial separation of the predominant phenotypes, whereas those with stirring (much movement) remained monomorphic (Rainey & Travasino 1998). Small-scale spatial structure generated by biotic processes increases the potential for genetic polymorphism still further. In a population with spatial aggregation, competition in small neighbourhoods can cause stronger inhibition of genes of common maternal ancestry at least (Kalisz *et al.* 1999), promoting the coexistence of genes of different ancestries.

Evolution of dispersal

Particularly interesting are mutants that affect local spatial structure itself (see Chapter 12). Many phenotypic traits have effects on dispersal kernels, including plant growth form, inflorescence size, and mechanisms for pollen and seed dispersal, and genetic variation in such traits has been documented for many years (e.g. Clausen *et al.* 1948; Aston & Bradshaw 1966). The capacity of such genes to increase when rare is very likely to be influenced by the small-scale spatial structures they generate (van Baalen & Rand 1998; Ferrière & Le Galliard 2000). Individuals carrying genes with low dispersal cluster more closely together than those with genes for greater dispersal, and are more adversely affected by their neighbours (also tending to carry the gene for low dispersal); Hamilton and May (1977) gave a schematic model to show the advantage of dispersal in these circumstances. On the other hand, in a spatially heterogeneous environment with small patches suitable for growth, poor dispersal could be a positive asset (Bolker & Pacala 1999). Models for evolution of dispersal that fail to keep track of local spatial structure could be misleading.

You have only to scratch the surface of plant population genetics to see the importance of local spatial structure of plants on the fate of genes; some of the most interesting predictions have in fact come from abandoning the mean-field assumption, for instance in the spread of populations (see Chapter 5). There already exists a large body of theory in population genetics for the dynamics in metapopulations on lattices with constant population size and no selection, stemming from the work of Wright and of Malécot (see review by Nagylaki 1989). A synthesis that brings together population-genetic and ecological theory, allowing for small-scale spatial structure, would be of much interest.

Summary

Small-scale spatial structure is important in plant ecology. Plants interact primarily with their immediate neighbours, and the view of the community as seen by an individual plant can be quite different from the large-scale spatial average. We describe a spatial statistic that captures the plant's eye view and use it to illustrate the strong spatial structure present in a grassland community. Many processes affect small-scale spatial structure, including intraspecific competition, dispersal of propagules, interactions with other species, and the spatial structure of the environment. Spatial structure in turn affects the the vital processes of growth, birth and death; the dynamics of plant communities thus involve a coupling of spatial structure and the vital processes. We describe recent work towards making this coupling explicit by means of individual-based models and the dynamics of spatial moments.

Acknowledgements

We thank David Grey, Tomás Herben, Vivian Hutson, Hans Metz and Peter Lee for advice during the work towards this chapter, and English Nature and the Derbyshire Wildlife Trust for permission to use their nature reserves. The research was supported by an NERC studentship (DWP), a NERC/CASE studentship with the Central Science Laboratory MAFF (DJM), the International Institute for Applied Systems Analysis (Laxenburg Austria), and the Wissenschaftskolleg zu Berlin.

References

Antonovics, J. & Levin, D.A. (1980). The ecological and genetic consequences of density-dependent regulation in plants *Annual Review of Ecology and Systematics*, 11, 411–452.

Aston, J.L. & Bradshaw, A.D. (1966). Evolution in closely adjacent plant populations II. *Agrostis stolonifera* in maritime habitats. *Heredity*, 21, 649–664.

Augspurger, C.K. (1984). Seedling survival of tropical tree species: interactions of dispersal distance, light gaps, and pathogens. *Ecology*, 65, 1705–1712.

Benjamin, L.R. & Hardwick, R.C. (1986). Sources of variation and measures of variability in even-aged stands of plants. *Annals of Botany*, 58, 757–778.

Blackman, G.E. (1935). A study by statistical methods of the distribution of species in grassland association. *Annals of Botany*, 49, 749–777.

Bolker, B. & Pacala, S.W. (1997). Using moment equations to understand stochasticaly driven spatial pattern formation in ecological systems. *Theoretical Population Biology*, 52, 179–197.

Bolker, B. & Pacala, S.W. (1999). Spatial moment equations for plant competition: understanding spatial strategies and the advantages of short dispersal. *American Naturalist*, 153, 575–602.

Bolker, B.M., Pacala, S.W. & Levin, S.A. (2000). Moment methods for ecological processes in continuous space. In: *The Geometry of Ecological Interactions: Simplifying Spatial Complexity* (eds U. Dieckmann, R. Law & J.A.J. Metz), pp. 388–411. Cambridge University Press, Cambridge, UK.

Bonan, G.B. (1988). The size structure of theoretical plant populations: spatial patterns and neighborhood effects. *Ecology*, 69, 1721–1730.

Brooker, R.W. & Callaghan, T.V. (1998). The balance between positive and negative plant interactions and its relationship to environmental gradients: a model. *Oikos*, 81, 196–207.

Burrough, P.A. (1987). Spatial aspects of ecological data. In: *Data Analysis in Community and Landscape Ecology* (eds R.H.G. Jongman, C.J.F. ter Braak & O.F.R. van Tongeren), pp. 213–251. Pudoc, Wageningen, the Netherlands.

Cain, M.L., Pacala, S.W., Silander, J.A. Jr & Fortin, M.J. (1995). Neighbourhood models of clonal growth in the white clover *Trifolium repens: American Naturalist*, 145, 888–917.

Carlsson, B.Å. & Callaghan, T.V. (1991). Positive plant interactions in tundra vegetation and the importance of shelter. *Journal of Ecology*, 79, 973–983.

Clark, J.S., Fastie, C., Hurtt, G., Jackson, S.T., Johnson, C., King, G.A., Lewis, M., Lynch, J., Pacala, S., Prentice, C., Schupp, E.W., Webb, T. & Wyckoff, P. (1998). Reid's paradox of rapid plant migration: dispersal theory and interpretation of paleoecological records. *BioScience*, 48, 13–24.

Clausen, J., Keck, D.D. & Hiesey, W.M. (1948). *Experimental Studies on the Nature of Species III. Environmental Responses of Climatic Races of* Achillea. Carnegie Institution of Washington Publication, 581.

Cody, M.L. (1986). Spacing patterns in Mojave Desert plant communities: near-neighbor analyses. *Journal of Arid Environments*, 11, 199–217.

Condit, R., Ashton, P.S., Baker, P., Bunyavejchewin, S., Gunatilleke, S., Gunatilleke, N., Hubbell, S.P., Foster, R.B., Itoh, A., LaFrankie, J.V., Lee, H.S., Losos, E., Manokaran, N., Sukumar, R. & Yamakura, T.Y. (2000). Spatial patterns in the distribution of tropical tree species. *Science*, 288, 1414–1418.

Coomes, D.A., Rees, M. & Turnbull, L. (1999). Identifying aggregation and association in fully mapped spatial data. *Ecology*, 80, 554–565.

Connell, J.H. (1971). On the role of natural enemies in preventing competitive exclusion in some marine animals and in rain forests. In: *Dynamics of Populations* (eds P.J. den Boer & G.R. Gradwell), pp. 298–310. Center for Agricultural Publishing and Documentation, Wageningen, The Netherlands.

Crawford, T.J. (1984). What is a population? In: *Evolutionary Ecology* (ed. B. Shorrocks), pp. 135–173. Blackwell Scientific Publications, Oxford.

Dieckmann, U., Herben, T. & Law, R. (1997). Spatio-temporal processes in plant communities. In: *Yearbook 1995/1996* (ed. W. Lepenies), pp. 296–326. Nicolaische Verlagsbuchhandlung, Berlin, Germany.

Dieckmann, U., Herben, T. & Law, R. (1999). Spatio-temporal processes in ecologial communities. *CWI Quarterly*, 12, 213–238.

Dieckmann, U. & Law, R. (2000). Relaxation projections and the method of moments. In: *The Geometry of Ecological Interactions: Simplifying Spatial*

Complexity (eds U. Dieckmann, R. Law & J.A.J. Metz), pp. 412–455. Cambridge University Press, Cambridge, UK.

Ferrière, R. & Le Galliard, J.-F. (2000). Invasion fitness and adaptive dynamics in spatial population models. In: *Causes, Consequences and Mechanisms of Dispersal at the Individual, Population and Community Level* (eds J. Clobert, J.D. Nichols, E. Danchin & A. Dhondt). Oxford University Press, Oxford, UK.

Firbank, L.G. & Watkinson, A.R. (1985). A model of interference within plant monocultures. *Journal of Theoretical Biology*, **116**, 291–311.

Ford, E.D. (1975). Competition and stand structure in some even-aged monocultures. *Journal of Ecology*, **63**, 311–333.

Franco, M. & Harper, J.L. (1988). Competition and the formation of spatial pattern in spacing gradients: an example using *Kochia scoparia*. *Journal of Ecology*, **76**, 959–974.

Greene, D.F. & Johnson, E.A. (1996). Wind dispersal of seeds from a forest into a clearing. *Ecology*, **77**, 595–609.

Hamilton, W.D. & May, R.M. (1977). Dispersal in stable habitats. *Nature*, **269**, 578–581.

Harper, J.L. (1977). *Population Biology of Plants*. Academic Press, London.

Holzapfel, C. & Mahall, B.E. (1999). Bidirectional facilitation and interference between shrubs and annuals in the Mojave Desert. *Ecology*, **80**, 1747–1761.

Hozumi, K., Koyama, H. & Kira, T. (1955). Intraspecific competition among higher plants. IV. A preliminary account on the interaction between adjacent individuals. *Journal of the Institute Polytechnic Osaka City University*, **6**(D), 121–130.

Isagi, Y., Kanazashi, T., Suzuki, W., Tanaka, H. & Abe, T. (2000). Microsatellite analysis of the regeneration process of *Magnolia obovata* Thunb. *Heredity*, **84**, 143–151.

Janzen, D.H. (1970). Herbivores and the number of tree species in tropical forests. *American Naturalist*, **104**, 501–528.

Kalisz, S., Hanzawa, F.M., Tonsor, S.J., Thiede, D.A. & Voigt, S. (1999). Ant-mediated seed dispersal alters pattern of relatedness in a population of *Trillium grandiflorum*. *Ecology*, **80**, 2620–2634.

Kenkel, N.C. (1988). Pattern of self-thinning in jack pine: testing the random mortality hypothesis. *Ecology*, **69**, 1017–1024.

Law, R. & Dieckmann, U. (2000a). A dynamical system for neighborhoods in plant communities. *Ecology*, **81**, 2137–2148.

Law, R. & Dieckmann, U. (2000b). Moment approximations of individual-based models. In: *The Geometry of Ecological Interactions: Simplifying Spatial Complexity* (eds U. Dieckmann, R. Law & J.A.J. Metz), pp. 252–270. Cambridge University Press, Cambridge, UK.

Law R., Dieckmann, U. & Metz, J.A.J. (2000). Introduction. In: *The Geometry of Ecological Interactions: Simplifying Spatial Complexity* (eds U. Dieckmann, R. Law & J.A.J. Metz), pp. 1–6. Cambridge University Press, Cambridge, UK.

Levene, H. (1953). Genetic equilibrium when more than one ecological niche is available. *American Naturalist*, **87**, 311–313.

Lewontin, R.C. (1974). *The Genetic Basis of Evolutionary Change*. Columbia University Press, New York.

Lotwick, H.W. & Silverman, B.W. (1982). Methods for analysing spatial processes of several types of points. *Journal of the Royal Statistical Society B*, **44**, 406–413.

Mack, R.N. & Harper, J.L. (1977). Interference in dune annuals: spatial pattern and neighbourhood effects. *Journal of Ecology*, **65**, 345–363.

Mahdi, A. & Law, R. (1987). On the spatial organization of plant species in a limestone grassland community. *Journal of Ecology*, **75**, 459–476.

Mahdi, A., Law, R. & Willis, A.J. (1989). Large niche overlaps among coexisting plant species in a limestone grassland community. *Journal of Ecology*, **77**, 386–400.

Meagher, T.R. & Thompson, E. (1987). Analysis of parentage for naturally established seedlings of *Chamaelirium luteum*. *Ecology*, **68**, 803–812.

Miller, T.E. & Weiner, J. (1989). Local density variation may mimic effects of asymmetric competition on plant size variability. *Ecology*, **70**, 1188–1191.

Mithen, R., Harper, J.L. & Weiner, J. (1984). Growth and mortality of individual plants as a function of 'available area'. *Oecologia (Berlin)*, **62**, 57–60.

Murrell, D.J. & Law, R. (2000). Beetles in fragmented woodlands: a formal framework for dynamics of movement in ecological landscapes. *Journal of Animal Ecology*, **69**, 471–483.

Nagylaki, T. (1989). Gustave Malécot and the transition from classical to modern population genetics. *Genetics*, **122**, 253–268.

Nathan, R. & Muller-Landau, H.C. (2000). Spatial patterns of seed dispersal, their determinants and consequences for recruitment. *Trends in Ecology and Evolution*, 15, 278–285.

Obeid, M., Machin, D. & Harper, J.L. (1967). Influence of density on plant to plant variation in fiber flax, *Linum usitatissimum* L. *Crop Science*, 7, 471–473.

Pacala, S.W. & Levin, S.A. (1997). Biologically generated spatial pattern and the coexistence of competing species. In: *Spatial Ecology: the Role of Space in Population Dynamics and Interspecific Interactions* (eds D. Tilman & P. Karieva), pp. 204–232. Princeton University Press, Princeton, NJ.

Pacala, S.W. & Silander, J.A. Jr. (1990). Field tests of neighborhood population dynamic models of two annual weed species. *Ecological Monographs*, 60, 113–134.

Pacala, S.W., Canham, C.D., Saponara, J., Silander, J.A. Jr., Kobe, R.K. & Ribbens, E. (1996). Forest models defined by field measurements: estimation, error analysis and dynamics. *Ecological Monographs*, 66, 1–43.

Packer, A. & Clay, K. (2000). Soil pathogens and spatial paterns of seedling mortality in a temperate tree. *Nature*, 404, 278–281.

Purves, D.W. & Law, R. (2001). Fine scale spatial structure in a grassland community: quantifying the plant's eye view. *Journal of Ecology*, in press.

Rainey, P.B. & Travasino, M. (1998). Adaptive radiation in a heterogeneous environment. *Nature*, 394, 69–72.

Rand, D.A. (1999). Correlation equations and pair approximations for spatial ecologies. In: *Advanced Ecological Theory: Principles and Applications* (ed. J. McGlade), pp. 100–142. Blackwell Science, Oxford.

Rees, M., Grubb, P.J. & Kelly, D. (1996). Quantifying the impact of competition and spatial heterogeneity on the structure and dynamics of a four-species guild of winter annuals. *American Naturalist*, 147, 1–32.

Renshaw, E. & Ford, E.D. (1984). The description of spatial pattern using two-dimensional spectral analysis. *Vegetatio*, 56, 75–85.

Ripley, B.D. (1981). *Spatial Statistics*. Wiley, New York.

Silander, J.A. Jr. & Pacala, S.W. (1985). Neighborhood predictors of plant performance. *Oecologia (Berlin)*, 66, 256–263.

Stoll, P. & Weiner, J. (2000). A neighborhood view of interactions among individual plants. In: *The Geometry of Ecological Interactions: Simplifying Spatial Complexity* (eds U. Dieckmann, R. Law & J.A.J. Metz), pp. 11–27. Cambridge University Press, Cambridge, UK.

Stoll, P. & Prati, D. (2001). Intraspecific aggregation alters competitive interactions in experimental plant communities. *Ecology*, 82, 319–327.

Thomas, S.C. & Weiner, J. (1989). Including competitive asymmetry in measures of local interference in plant populations. *Oecologia*, 80, 349–355.

Turchin, P. (1998). *Quantitative Analysis of Movement*. Sinauer, Sunderland, MA.

Turkington, R. & Harper, J.L. (1979). The growth, distribution and neighbour relationships of *Trifolium repens* in a permanent pasture. I. Ordination, pattern and contact. *Journal of Ecology*, 67, 201–208.

van Baalen, M. & Rand, D.A. (1998). The unit of selection in viscous populations and the evolution of altruism. *Journal of Theoretical Biology*, 193, 631–648.

van Dorp, D., van den Hoek, W.P.M. & Daleboudt, C. (1996). Seed dispersal capacity of six perennial grassland species measured in a wind tunnel at varying wind speed and height. *Canadian Jounal of Botany*, 74, 1956–1963.

Weiner, J. (1985). Size hierarchies in experimental populations of annual plants. *Ecology*, 66, 743–752.

Weiner, J. (1990). Asymmetric competition in plant populations. *Trends in Ecology and Evolution*, 5, 360–364.

Wissel, C. (2000). Grid-based models as tools for ecological research. In: *The Geometry of Ecological Interactions: Simplifying Spatial Complexity* (eds U. Dieckmann, R. Law & J.A.J. Metz), pp. 94–115. Cambridge University Press, Cambridge, UK.

Wyszomirski, T. (1983). A simulation model of the growth of competing individuals of a plant population. *Ekologia Polska*, 31, 73–92.

Yoda, K., Kira, T. & Hozumi, K. (1957). Intraspecific competition among higher plants. IX. Further analysis of the competitive interaction between adjacent individuals. *Journal of the Institute Polytechnic Osaka City University*, 8(D), 161–178.

Chapter 3

Inferences about spatial processes in plant populations from the analysis of molecular markers

*R. A. Ennos**

Introduction

Plants and their genes move within populations by vegetative growth, and by dispersal of asexual propagules, pollen and seed. These processes determine the physical placement of individuals and the spatial location of genotypes within populations. Understanding the spatial dynamics brought about by vegetative growth, pollen and seed dispersal within populations is central to an understanding of plant demography. It is also important to appreciate how these processes influence the spatial genetic structure of populations. In particular we need to know the extent to which they lead to non-random distribution of genotypes throughout the population, and influence spatial patterns of genetic relatedness. The objective of this chapter is to illustrate how molecular markers can be used as tools for describing the structuring of genetic variation within plant populations, and for measuring the dynamic processes of vegetative growth, pollen and seed dispersal that generate this genetic structure.

Molecular markers

Molecular markers represent differences in the genetic information possessed by individuals within a species. They are detected either by analysing the DNA directly, or indirectly, by distinguishing variation in the products of enzyme coding genes (isozyme variation). In plants, molecular markers can be situated in any of the three genomes: nuclear, chloroplast or mitochondrial. Nuclear markers are inherited biparentally in a Mendelian fashion. Chloroplast and mitochondrial DNA markers are inherited uniparentally. In angiosperms, chloroplast and mitochondrial genomes are normally maternally inherited, while in gymnosperms, chloroplast markers are generally paternally inherited.

These different modes of inheritance mean that, over the course of one generation, nuclear genes (and paternally inherited chloroplast genes in conifers) are dispersed by both pollen and seed. In contrast, the maternally inherited chloroplast

* *Institute of Ecology and Resource Management, University of Edinburgh, Darwin Building, King's Buildings, Mayfield Road, Edinburgh EH9 3JU, Scotland.*

genes in angiosperms, and mitochondrial genes in angiosperms and gymnosperms are only dispersed in seed. This difference in marker behaviour can be exploited to separate gene flow within populations into its pollen and seed components (see later).

Another important difference associated with chromosomal location relates to the extent of recombination among marker loci. In the nuclear genome of outcrossing species, recombination takes place among molecular markers unless they are extremely tightly linked. The molecular markers at different genetic loci will become randomly associated with one another (a situation termed gametic or linkage equilibrium). As a consequence, information derived from one nuclear marker is likely to be relatively independent of that from another nuclear marker.

However, in inbreeding species the opportunities for recombination between nuclear loci are severely reduced and gametic disequilibrium is commonly present, even between unlinked loci (see Chapter 4). Data from different loci do not provide independent measures of spatial structure. Likewise in the organelle genomes there is a complete lack of recombination. As a consequence each of these genomes behaves as if it were a single gene. The multilocus genotypes (haplotypes) of these genomes are best regarded as alleles of a single gene.

An important property of nuclear molecular markers is their dominance relationship. For the vast majority of isozyme variants inheritance is codominant. Among DNA markers traditional restriction fragment length polymorphisms (RFLP), polymerase chain reaction (PCR) RFLP variants and microsatellite variants also show codominant inheritance. However, for certain PCR-based markers (randomly amplified polymorphic DNA (RAPD) and amplified fragment length polymorphisms (AFLP)) the variation among individuals is due to amplification or non-amplification of a sequence. This leads to a dominant mode of inheritance with a maximum of two alleles. Markers of this type are far less powerful than multiallelic codominant markers for many applications, particularly paternity exclusion and parentage analysis (Milligan & McMurray 1993). However, they can be used effectively for the study of haploids or where haploid tissue is available (e.g. conifer megagametophytes).

Another property of molecular markers affecting their diversity and population behaviour is mutation rate. Nuclear markers other than microsatellites have a low mutation rate (10^{-5} per generation typically). At polymorphic loci only two or three alleles are generally present within populations. This limits their power for paternity and parentage analysis. However, mutation takes place at too low a rate to affect significantly the spatial distribution of genetic marker variation. Codominant markers of this kind, such as isozymes, are therefore ideal for measuring genetic structure and making inferences about pollen and gene flow.

In contrast, the mutation rate of nuclear microsatellite markers may be orders of magnitude higher than for isozymes, reaching 10^{-2} per generation in some cases. As a consequence microsatellite markers show enormous variation, with over 20 alleles commonly being maintained per locus within a single population. This makes them the markers of choice for paternity and parentage analysis (Chase *et al.* 1996a).

When mutation rates are this high, however, mutation cannot be ignored as a factor influencing the spatial distribution of marker variation (Hedrick 1999).

In organelle markers, rates of mutation per gene are orders of magnitude lower than for nuclear markers (Wolfe *et al.* 1987). However, in the chloroplast genome many different sequences can be assayed for PCR-RFLP variation using universal primers for coding, non-coding or microsatellite sequences (Taberlet *et al.* 1991; Powell *et al.* 1995). By combining information from different sequences in the cpDNA genome, a high diversity of chloroplast haplotypes can often be found within single populations (Caron *et al.* 2000). This cytoplasmic DNA (cpDNA) variation is extremely useful for studies both of genetic structure and parentage (Ziegenhagen *et al.* 1998). In mitochondrial genomes the PCR-RFLP approach for detecting variation has not been so widely applied due to the difficulty in obtaining reliable universal primers. However, traditional RFLP analysis that detects large rearrangements in the mitochondrial genome can detect useful levels of marker variation within populations (Samitou-Laprade *et al.* 1993).

When using molecular markers as tools for studying spatial processes, a fundamental assumption is that the molecular marker variation is not under selection. As a working hypothesis this is reasonable. However, in a small proportion of cases, marker variation may not be selectively neutral. Moreover, in genomes that do not recombine (nuclear genomes in apomictic and highly inbreeding species, and possibly in chloroplast and mitochondrial genomes (Ennos *et al.* 1999)), selection at other loci that are in gametic disequilibrium will affect the behaviour of genetic marker variation (see Chapter 4). This means that it is dangerous to make inferences about spatial processes in apomictic and inbreeding species from data on molecular markers distribution, because the effects of pollen and seed flow will be confounded with the effects of selection.

Inferences from analysis of spatial genetic structure

Causes of genetic structuring for molecular markers in plant populations
Vegetative reproduction
Many adult plants do not stand still, but are highly mobile within populations as a consequence of vegetative spread. Vegetative spread may lead to spatial clustering of multilocus genotypes. The extent to which this occurs will be dependent on the characteristics of vegetative spread, being most marked where ramets establish very close to parent genets, and a phalanx strategy of spread with little intermingling of clones is found. In species that reproduce through apomictic seed, clustering of multilocus marker genotypes can occur as a consequence of restricted seed dispersal.

Restricted pollen and seed flow in continuous populations
If gene dispersal by pollen and seed is restricted within a continuous plant population, Wright (1943) showed analytically that genetic structure will develop by genetic drift in the absence of selection. The relatedness of individuals increases with their

spatial proximity. This process of genetic isolation-by-distance can readily be simulated in spatially explicit models relevant to plant populations (Turner *et al.* 1982; Ohsawa *et al.* 1993; Hardy & Vekemans 1999).

If loss of genetic variation from the finite population is balanced by mutation or long-distance gene flow, a quasi-equilibrium becomes established within 20 to 30 generations. At this quasi-equilibrium the population is genetically structured and comprises patches or neighbourhoods of related genotypes (Figure 3.1). The scale of these neighbourhoods depends critically on the dispersal distributions of pollen and seed. The more restricted the gene flow, the more genetically differentiated are the neighbourhoods and the more closely related are nearest neighbours.

Patches of similar genotype that develop in this fashion are not expected to be coincident across marker loci. On the other hand the spatial scales of genetic structuring should be similar across all loci with a common mode of inheritance because the genetic structure for any marker is determined by shared processes of gene flow. An exception to this rule is found in models where a high mutation rate, rather than long-distance gene flow, is used to balance loss of genetic variation

Figure 3.1 Spatial genetic structuring generated by simulating highly restricted pollen and seed flow in a continuous population of 10 000 individuals after 200 generations. Genetic marker genotypes A_1A_1, A_1A_2 and A_2A_2 are represented by white, grey and black, respectively. (From Epperson 1995b.)

from the population. Here, variation in the value of the mutation rate may significantly affect the genetic structure shown by a marker (Slatkin & Arter 1991). Genetic structure within the population is always expected to be greater for maternally inherited organelle markers, that are only dispersed in seed, than for paternally inherited or nuclear markers that are dispersed in both pollen and seed (Hu & Ennos 1997, 1999).

Sampling events during population foundation and regeneration
Spatial genetic structure may be generated in plant populations as a consequence of sampling events that occur when the population is founded or regenerated (see Chapter 9). The genotypes establishing in different areas of the population may be derived from a limited and distinct subset of the parents contributing to the total population, and may therefore be more closely related to one another than to individuals drawn randomly from the population.

Spatial genetic structure generated in this fashion will be greatest where regeneration sites are colonized from a limited number of maternal and paternal seed parents and should be most marked for maternally inherited markers that travel only in the seed.

Important features of spatial structure generated in this manner are that a patch of individuals may be distinguishable using more than one independent marker. Individuals within a patch should show a high coefficient of relatedness detectable initially on the basis of linkage disequilibrium over a number of loci (Queller & Goodnight 1989). A key difference between this form of genetic structure, and that generated purely by restricted gene flow (described above), is that it represents a non-equilibrium situation. To establish that genetic structure has been generated in this manner, ecological data on the historical processes of population foundation or of regeneration in existing populations is required (see Chapter 9).

Selection
There is ample evidence that where selection regimes differ spatially within a single plant population, genetic differentiation will evolve leading to genetic structuring for the loci that are affected by this selection (Bradshaw 1972). The working hypothesis for genetic markers is that they are selectively neutral and therefore, in outcrossing species, selection will not influence their spatial distribution. However, in inbreeding and apomictic taxa where there is gametic disequilibrium, significant genetic marker structuring is anticipated, caused by natural selection on associated loci under selection (Hamrick & Holden 1979).

Detecting spatial genetic structure
Spatial autocorrelation analysis
The utility of spatial autocorrelation analysis (SAA) for detecting genetic structure has been thoroughly demonstrated since its introduction by Sokal and Oden (1978a,b). SAA statistics measure the correlation in allelic or genotypic state between individuals separated by defined distances within the whole population.

Positive autocorrelation implies that individuals within a particular distance class are more genetically similar than would be expected under random spatial distribution of genotypes within the population.

The data required for conducting SAA are the spatial coordinates and genotype of all, or a sample of plants from within a population. Using this information two types of analysis can be conducted. In the first the number of joins between individuals of like (or unlike) genotype separated by a certain range of distances (within a distance class) are determined. This joint count value is compared with that expected under random distribution of genotypes. When the difference between them is divided by their standard deviation this yields a standard normal deviate (SND) statistic. Positive SND values for like joins within short-distance classes indicate spatial clumping of individual genotypes, whereas negative values indicate hyperdispersion of like genotypes. The changes in SND value with increasing distance class can be plotted in a correlogram. Such correlograms can be used to illustrate features of spatial pattern such as the size of patches of like genotype (Figure 3.2a).

An alternative SAA technique for detecting spatial structure involves the calculation of Moran's autocorrelation statistic I (Moran 1950) for a relevant range of distance classes. I measures the correlation in gene frequencies between samples of genotypes within the distance class. Positive values of I indicate clumping of like genotypes and greater genetic relatedness within a distance class. Moran's I can be calculated using allele frequencies estimated from samples that comprise many genotypes. Alternatively, each sample may comprise a single individual (Epperson 1995a). In this case the frequency of alleles within the individuals (0.0, 0.5 or 1.0 for individuals lacking, heterozygous and homozygous for an allele, respectively) are used in the correlation. When applied in the latter manner I is an estimator of Wright's coefficient of relationship $\rho_{(x)}$ (Heywood 1991; Hardy & Vekemans 1999), and there is a direct link between spatial autocorrelation and population genetic analysis. A correlogram showing the change in I with distance class can be drawn to visualize the spatial genetic structure (Figure 3.2b). Individual loci may be analysed separately, or data can be combined over loci to produce a single correlogram (Smouse & Peakall 1999).

Exhaustive simulations of equilibrium genetic structure generated by isolation-by-distance have demonstrated the power and efficiency of both SND and Moran's I statistic for detecting genetic structure within populations (Epperson 1995b; Epperson & Li 1996, 1997; Epperson et al. 1999). If spatial structure has been generated purely through isolation-by-distance and populations are at equilibrium, the SAA correlograms can be interpreted so as to provide quantitative information about gene flow within the population (Hardy & Vekemans 1999).

Spatial autocorrelation analysis has limitations because it is a statistical description of the *average* spatial genetic structure of the whole population. There may be good biological reasons why genetic structure and the correlation of genotypes within a distance class may be high in some areas of a population, but low in other areas of the same population (because of different origins, for instance). Spatial autocorrelation analysis will not pick up such distinctions, and may indicate no overall

(a)

(b)

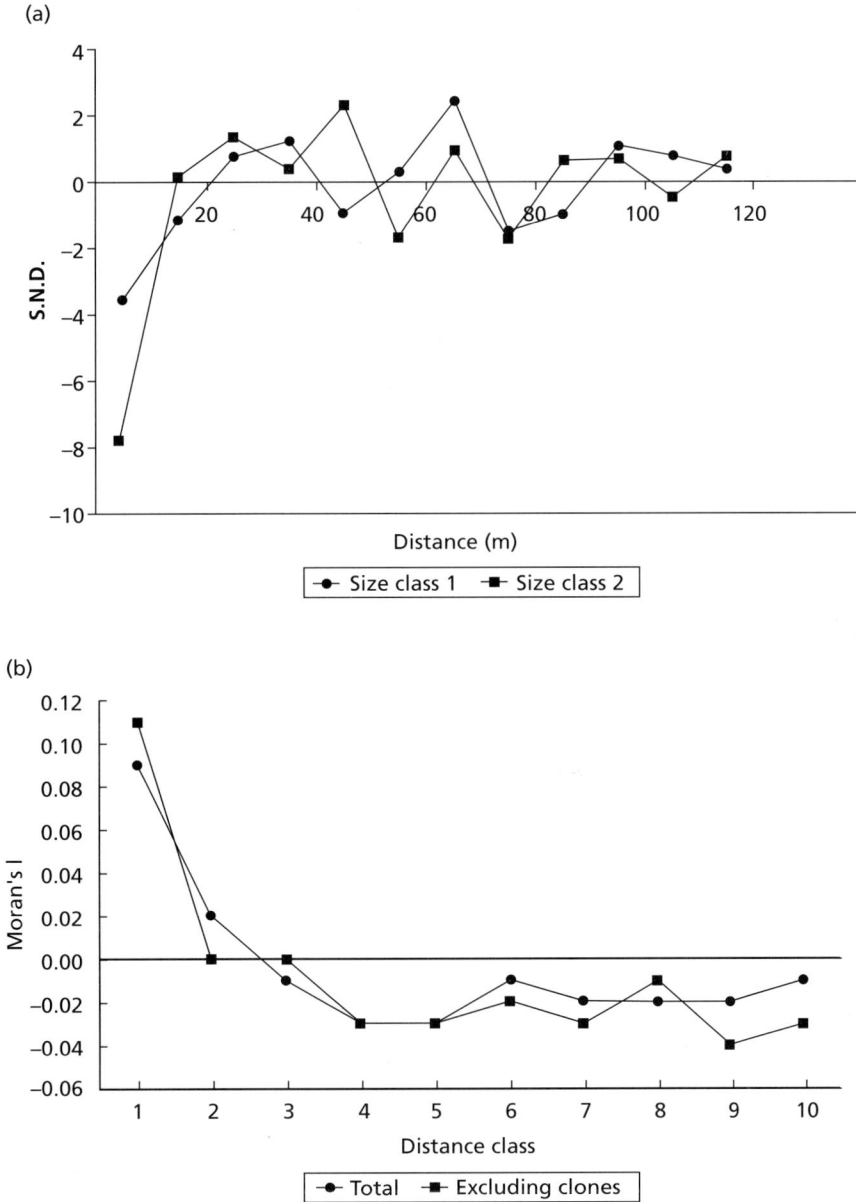

Figure 3.2 Spatial autocorrelation analysis of *Eurya emarginata*. (a) SND analysis of unlike joins among multilocus genotypes for two size classes of tree. Significant spatial structuring occurs with a patch width of 20 m. (b) Analysis of spatial autocorrelation among nuclear markers in the same population using Moran's *I* statistics. Results of two analyses are shown, with or without vegetative spread being accounted for. Spatial genetic structure is significant for the smallest distance class in both cases. (From Chung & Epperson 2000.)

R. A. ENNOS

genetic structure in the population, even though genetic structure may be very well developed locally.

Analysis of F *statistics*
An alternative approach for detecting and quantifying genetic structure within plant populations is to measure structure in terms of inbreeding due to population subdivision using Wright's F statistics (Wright 1951; Weir & Cockerham 1984). Analysis of F_{st} is most straightforward to apply where subpopulations with potentially different origins can be readily identified. For example it may be possible to delineate regeneration gaps suspected of containing offspring derived from a restricted number of maternal genotypes. F_{st} analysis can be used to test the hypothesis of genetic structuring due to recruitment of related individuals within these regeneration gaps. However, there will be many situations in which there are no ecological criteria for delineating subpopulations, e.g. neighbourhoods generated by isolation by distance. It will then be necessary to estimating F_{st} using arbitrary subdivisions of increasing size to determine at what scale genetic structure, if it is present, is found (Wright 1978). The problem with such an analysis is that as subpopulation size decreases, sample size decreases and statistical power to detect population genetic structure also decreases. In these situations it is claimed that SAA has the advantages over F_{st} analysis of using all the available genetic information and of providing greater statistical power to detect small-scale population genetic structure (Epperson *et al.* 1999).

Spatial genetic structure in natural populations
Table 3.1 summarizes results from 43 studies in which the spatial genetic structure of plant populations has been investigated using the techniques outlined above. The studies cover species with a range of breeding systems: inbreeding (two), mixed vegetative reproduction and outcrossing (nine), and outcrossing (29). Among the purely outcrossing species, 10 are herbs, and 19 are woody perennials.

Both of the inbreeding species displayed significant genetic structuring within populations as anticipated from theory. However, it is not possible to make inferences about spatial processes from these data because the spatial structure of genetic markers is potentially affected by selection (see above). Indeed the study of *Avena barbata* provides strong evidence for genetic differentiation as a consequence of selection in contrasting xeric and mesic environments (Hamrick & Holden 1979).

Of the 10 studies involving species with vegetative reproduction, non-random spatial distribution of genotypes was found in eight cases. However, this was not always attributable to clonal growth. Long-distance dispersal by vegetative growth may be sufficient to prevent the non-random distribution of ramets within a population (Chung & Epperson 2000; Chung *et al.* 2000). Also ramets from different genotypes may be sufficiently intermingled at small scales that spatial genetic structure cannot be detected (Kudoh *et al.* 1999). Molecular marker analysis can highlight differences in patterns of clonal diversity between environments and may allow inferences to be made about the conditions under which recruitment of sexual offspring takes place (Kudoh *et al.* 1999).

52

Among outcrossing herbs, six of the 11 studies showed no evidence of genetic structuring for nuclear markers within populations. In four of the five studies where structuring was detected, it was attributed to founder effects rather than to an isolation-by-distance mechanism. Finally, for outcrossing woody perennials, 14 of the 19 studies showed some evidence of genetic structuring. In five of these cases, factors relating to the founding of the population were implicated in the generation of the genetic structure. Only in nine cases was pure isolation-by-distance implicated, and in all instances genetic structure was weak and confined to positive spatial autocorrelation in the shortest-distance class.

The results above refer to nuclear markers. In five studies of outcrossing species, genetic structure was compared between nuclear or paternally inherited markers, and maternally inherited markers. No genetic structuring was found for nuclear and paternally inherited markers. However, significant genetic structure was detected for maternally inherited markers in every case (McCauley *et al.* 1996; Tarayre *et al.* 1997; Latta *et al.* 1998; Levy & Neal 1999; Caron *et al.* 2000). This contrast between the results obtained for different markers is as anticipated from theory (Hu & Ennos 1997, 1999). It implies that seed flow is limited, encouraging the development or maintenance of genetic structure for maternal markers. On the other hand, pollen flow is extensive in these outcrossing species, preventing the build-up and retention of significant genetic structure for nuclear markers.

Taken together, these data strongly suggest that extensive non-random spatial genetic structure for nuclear markers generated by isolation-by-distance is neither a universal nor a significant feature of outcrossing plant populations. However, very small scale spatial associations of related individuals caused by restricted gene flow are not unusual. On the other hand, non-equilibrium sampling processes that occur during population foundation and regeneration appear to be very important causes of genetic structure.

These processes may include colonization by related individuals dispersed in family groups either passively, as in *Silene dioica* (Ingvarsson & Giles 1999), or by animal vectors, as is the case for *Pinus albicaulis* whose families of seed are cached by nutcrackers (Furnier *et al.* 1987). Related individuals may be found associated when populations are regenerated from a limited number of scattered parents (Schnabel *et al.* 1991). This can occur in harvested forests where seed trees are left to regenerate a new stand (Knowles *et al.* 1992; Takahashi *et al.* 2000). If it is suspected that the individuals within an area comprise related individuals, further confirmation of this may be sought by calculating their relatedness using nuclear or organelle markers (Queller & Goodnight 1989; Giles *et al.* 1998; Latta *et al.* 1998).

Another situation where related individuals can establish in small defined areas is where gap regeneration occurs, and only a limited number of parents contribute genetically to the seedlings within a gap. Xie and Knowles (1991) suggest that this process may have contributed to the spatial structure observed in *Acer saccharum* stands. Strong evidence for structuring, generated by gap regeneration, was obtained by Epperson and Alvarez-Bayella (1997). They demonstrated high spatial autocorrelation within gaps for seedlings of the tropical tree *Cecropia obtusifolia*,

Table 3.1 Summary of studies of genetic structure within plant populations that have used genetic markers.

Species	Breeding system	Marker	Method*	Evidence†	Cause‡	Reference
Avena barbata	Selfing	Isozymes	Environment/ genotype correlation	Strong correlation present	S	Hamrick & Holden (1979)
Sclerolaena dicantha	Inbreeding	Isozymes	M	+ve in 1/3 populations	R	Peakall & Beattie (1995)
Adenophora grandiflora	Vegetative and outcrossing	Isozymes	SND M	+ve	V and R	Chung & Epperson (1999)
Androcymbium gramineum	Vegetative and mixed mating	Isozymes	M	+ve	V and R	Caujape-Castells & Pedrola-Monfort (1997)
Antherosperma moschata	Vegetative and mixed mating	Isozymes	SND	+ve	V	Shapcott (1995)
Calluna vulgaris	Vegetative and outcrossing	Isozymes	M F_{st}	+ve n.s.	V and R	Mahy & Neve (1997)
Calluna vulgaris	Vegetative and outcrossing	Isozymes	M	n.s.		Mahy *et al.* (1999)
Eurya emarginata	Vegetative and outcrossing	Isozymes	SND M	+ve +ve	R	Chung & Epperson (2000)
Rhus javanica	Vegetative and dioecious	Isozymes	SND M	+ve in 1/2 populations	R	Chung *et al.* (2000)

Species	Breeding system	Marker	Result	Method	Category	Reference
Uvularia perfoliata	Vegetative and outcrossing	Isozymes	+ve > 1 m; n.s. < 1 m.	M	V	Kudoh et al. (1999)
Zostera marina	Vegetative and outcrossing	Isozymes	n.s.	SND		Ruckelshaus (1998)
Zostera marina	Vegetative and outcrossing	Microsatellites	+ve; +ve	SND; M	V	Reusch et al. (1999)
Delphinium nelsonii	Outcrossing	Isozymes	n.s.	M		Waser (1987)
Delphinium nuttallianum	Outcrossing	Isozymes	n.s.	M		Williams & Waser (1999)
Ipomopsis aggregata	Outcrossing	Isozymes	+ve	M	R	Campbell & Dooley (1992)
Lathyrus sylvestris	Outcrossing	Isozymes	+ve	M	F	Hossaert McKey et al. (1996)
Phacelia dubia	Mixed mating	Isozymes and cpDNA (maternal)	n.s. Isozymes +cpDNA	F_{st}	RS	Levy & Neal (1999)
Silene acaulis	Gynodioecious	Isozymes	+ve; +	M; F_{st}	F	Gehring & Delph (1999)
Silene alba	Dioecious	Isozymes and cpDNA (maternal)	n.s. Isozymes +ve cpDNA	SND; M; F_{st}	RS	McCauley et al. (1996)
Silene dioica	Dioecious	Isozymes	+	F_{st}	F	Giles et al. (1998)
Silene dioica	Dioecious	Isozymes	+	F_{st}	F	Ingvarsson & Giles (1999)

Continued p. 56

Table 3.1 *Continued*

Species	Breeding system	Marker	Method*	Evidence[†]	Cause[‡]	Reference
Stylidium coroniforme	Mixed mating	Isozymes	M	n.s.		Coates (1992)
Thymus vulgaris	Gynodioecious	Isozymes and cpDNA (maternal)	F_{st} F_{st}	n.s. Isozymes +cpDNA	RS	Tarayre *et al.* (1997)
Acer saccharum	Outcrossing	Isozymes	M	+ve	F	Perry & Knowles (1991)
Carapa procera	Outcrossing	Isozymes	M	n.s. in seedlings +ve in adults	R	Doligez & Joly (1997)
Camellia japonica	Outcrossing	Microsatellites	M	+ve	R	Ueno *et al.* (2000)
Cecropia obtusifolia	Outcrossing	Isozymes	SND F_{st}	+ve +	F	Epperson & Alvarez-Baylla (1997)
Dicorynia guianensis	Outcrossing	Isozymes and cpDNA (maternal)	F_{st} M	n.s. Isozymes +ve cpDNA	RS	Caron *et al.* (2000)
Fagus crenata	Outcrossing	Isozymes	M	n.s. in primary forest +ve in cut forest	F	Takahashi *et al.* (2000)
Gledista tricanthos	Dioecious	Isozymes	M	+ve	RS	Schnabel *et al.* (1991)
Helicteres brevispira	Outcrossing	Isozymes	M F_{st}	+ve +	R	Franceschinelli & Kesseli (1999)

Species	Breeding system	Marker	Statistic	Result	Reference
Larix laricina	Outcrossing	Isozymes	M	n.s. in field population +ve in cutover population	Knowles *et al.* (1992)
Maclara pomifera	Dioecious	Isozymes	M	+ve	Schnabel *et al.* (1991)
Pinus albicaulis	Outcrossing	Isozymes	M	+ve	Furnier *et al.* (1987)
Pinus banksiana	Outcrossing	Isozymes	M	+ve in 2/3 populations	Xie & Knowles (1991)
Pinus contorta	Outcrossing	Isozymes	SND	n.s.	Epperson & Allard (1989)
Pinus ponderosa	Outcrossing	cpDNA (paternal) and mtDNA (maternal)	SND	n.s. cpDNA +ve mtDNA	Latta *et al.* (1998)
Psychotria nervosa	Outcrossing	Isozymes	M	n.s.	Dewey & Heywood (1988)
Psychotria officinalis	Outcrossing	Isozymes	M F_{st}	n.s. n.s.	Loirelle *et al.* (1995)
Quercus laevis	Outcrossing	Isozymes	M	+ve	Berg & Hamrick (1995)
Quercus robur and *Q. petraea*	Outcrossing	Isozymes and microsatellites	M F_{st}	+ve +	Streiff *et al.* (1998)

* SND = spatial autocorrelation join count statistic; M = Moran's *I* statistic; F_{st} = Wright's F_{st} statistic.
† +ve = significant positive spatial autocorrelation; + = significant F_{st} value; n.s. = non significant.
‡ S = selection; V = vegetative reproduction; R = restricted pollen and seed flow; RS = restricted seed flow; F = founder event. cpDNA, chloroplast DNA; mtDNA, mitochondrial DNA.

significant genetic differentiation among seedlings from different gaps, and a reduction in spatial autocorrelation in juvenile and adult trees as self-thinning took place.

Direct analysis of pollen and seed movement within populations

Analysis of snapshot data on spatial genotypic distributions can provide useful insights into spatial processes within plant populations. However, the approach suffers from the weakness of any spatial pattern analysis, namely that many different processes could be responsible for the observed results. Without information on the dynamics of the situation, inferences about process are weak. Direct methods have therefore been developed that use genetic markers to measure, over a single generation, the movement of genes within populations.

Pollen flow

The methods described in this section exploit the fact that seeds are retained on, and can be collected from, maternal parents. This allows the genotype of the ovule involved in seed formation to be inferred, and provides information on the distribution of successful fertilization events measured at seed formation. This may differ from realized pollen flow distributions measured over the entire generation if there are systematic differences in the fitness of ovules produced by pollen dispersed over different distances (Fenster 1991).

Unique alleles

In this approach, an adult plant carrying a putative unique genetic marker is taken as the focal male parent (Figure 3.3a). Female parents and their offspring are sampled around this individual, and scored for the presence of the unique allele. The presence of the marker in their progeny represents a pollen fertilization event by the focal male parent. Although straightforward in principle, there are many problems with using this method. There is the difficulty of detecting and confirming the status of unique alleles, and the need for exponential increases in female plus offspring sample sizes as distance from the focal male increases to provide the same power of detection of pollen flow events. The maximum pollen flow distances observed will be limited by the maximum distance between sampled females and the focal male. The data obtained will be unique to the focal male chosen, and it may be difficult to extrapolate this pollination behaviour to that of the whole population.

Paternity exclusion analysis

In paternity exclusion analysis the multilocus genotype of a focal maternal plant and a sample of her seeds are determined, together with the multilocus genotypes of all potential fathers (Figure 3.3b). For each seed, adults that could not have acted as pollen parents are excluded on the basis of their genotype. If the exclusion probability generated by the genetic marker variation is sufficiently high, a single adult will be left that can be uniquely assigned as the male parent (Chakraborty et al. 1988). The more variable the suite of genetic markers used in terms of allele diversity and

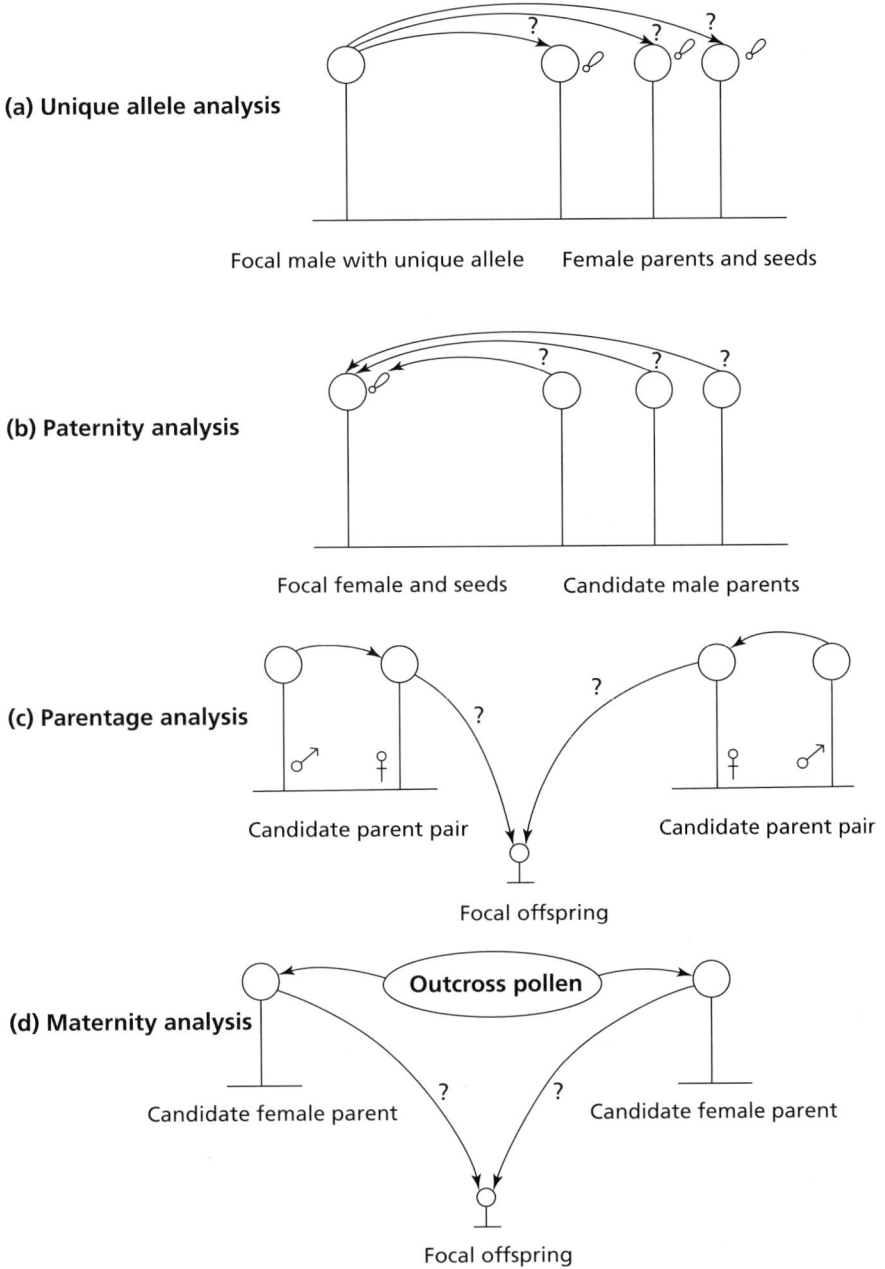

Figure 3.3 Sampling procedures for direct analyses of spatial processes in plant populations. (a) Measuring pollen flow using unique alleles. (b) Measuring pollen flow using paternity analysis. (c) Measuring pollen and seed flow using parentage analysis. (d) Measuring seed flow using maternity analysis.

evenness of allele frequency, the greater the exclusion probability. With a relatively small number (four to six) of highly variable microsatellite markers possessing 20 or more alleles per locus, exclusion probabilities close to one can be achieved, and male parents can be uniquely identified even in populations of 100 individuals (Dow & Ashley 1996). In conifer populations, where the multilocus genotype of the female gamete can be determined from the megagametophyte tissue of the seed, the probability of identifying male parents is much enhanced, and complete exclusion of non-parental individuals can be achieved when marker variation is lower (Schuster & Mitton 2000).

It is often the case with less variable isozyme and microsatellite loci in angio-sperms that a number of potential male parents, rather than an unique male parent, are identified after paternity exclusion analysis. In such circumstances a number of options are open for deciding upon paternity. Complete paternity can be assigned on the basis of the most likely father given the genotypes of the mother, maternal offspring and potential fathers (Meagher 1986). Alternatively, fractional paternity can be assigned to a number of fathers according to their genetic likelihood of being the true father (Devlin *et al.* 1988).

Both of these methods may be criticized on the grounds that they do not take into account variation in the 'prior probability' of paternity, namely the influence of non-genetic factors (isolation, flowering phenology) in determining the likelihood of a male parent being the true father (Adams *et al.* 1992). If additional data on factors that may affect prior probability have been collected (interplant distances, flowering phenology), these may be incorporated in the paternity assignment procedure to produce what may be a less biased distribution of pollen-flow distributions. This prevents any tendency to overestimate pollen flow. This would otherwise arise because a male genotype with very high genetic probability of paternity is more likely by chance to be found among the many individuals a long distance away in the population, than among the few individuals at shorter distances.

Although feasible in small populations with a restricted number of potential fathers, paternity exclusion analysis becomes impractical in large continuous populations where the number of potential fathers is enormous. In these situations it may more appropriate to apply the approach of Burczyk *et al.* (1996). Here a neighbourhood is delineated around focal maternal parents. Pollen flow is then divided into a within-neighbourhood component, and a component representing migration from outside the neighbourhood. A model of male fertility within the neighbourhood can then be fitted to account for the offspring genotype arrays of the focal maternal parents. This model can include pollination distance and direction of pollen flow as factors influencing male success, and these parameters can be estimated.

Seed flow

Parentage analysis

The ultimate objective of parentage analysis is to use genetic marker data from adults and established seedlings within a population to infer the male and female parents of a focal offspring individual (Figure 3.3c). Such an analysis is far more difficult than is paternity analysis, since neither of the parents of the offspring in question are known.

As in the case of paternity analysis, the problem is most tractable if highly variable marker loci are available and the potential number of maternal and paternal parents contributing to the offspring are small. Under these conditions it is possible to write down the range of complementary pairs of multilocus gametes that could have fused to produce the offspring genotype observed. Potential male and female parental genotype pairs can be scanned to see whether they could have contributed one or both of the complementary gametes. Provided the exclusion probability is sufficiently high three outcomes are possible (Dow & Ashley 1996). The first is that only one pair of potential parents is found that could have contributed a pair of complementary gametes to produce the offspring. In this case both parents are identified uniquely. The distance between the parents measures effective pollen flow in one generation. If the species is dioecious the distance from female parent to offspring measures effective seed dispersal. If the species is hermaphrodite, realized seed flow could be estimated by making the *ad hoc* assumption that offspring lie closest to their female parent (Dow & Ashley 1996). Another option would be to score maternally inherited markers to unambiguously identify the female parent, although so far this does not seem to have been attempted.

Alternative outcomes of parentage analysis when exclusion probabilities are very close to one are that all potential parents are excluded, or all except one. In this case the inference is that the missing parent or parents have not been sampled either because they are no longer alive, or because they lie outside the sampled population.

The desirable situation where parentage exclusion probabilities are so high that parents can be uniquely identified may not apply either because sufficiently variable markers are not available, or because the effort required to achieve such high exclusion probabilities severely limits the number of offspring that can be analysed. In these situations, other strategies must be used for parentage assignment. If the potential number of fathers is relatively small and pollen flow is likely to be restricted to the adults within the population, maximum likelihood methods for assignment of parentage can be applied (Meagher & Thompson 1987). If long-distance pollen flow is substantial (i.e. from outside the immediate population) and it is not possible to score all potential fathers, yet information is required on seed flow, a form of 'maternity analysis' may be applied.

Maternity analysis
Maternity analysis is appropriate where it is reasonable to assume that established offspring are derived by random mating of existing maternal parents with a homogeneous outcross pollen poll (Schnabel *et al.* 1998). To apply maternity analysis, data are required on marker genotypes of focal offspring, marker allele frequencies in the outcross pollen pool, and the marker genotypes of potential female parents (Figure 3.3d). A mating model, in which fertility of potential female parents is allowed to vary, is fitted to account for the observed distribution of offspring genotypes. Seed-dispersal patterns can then be derived by measuring the distances between

established offspring and inferred maternal parent. If the population involved is large, and seed flow is substantial, it may be desirable to modify the model by delineating a neighbourhood around the focal offspring and jointly analyse maternity within the neighbourhood and seed flow from outside the neighbourhood (Adams 1992).

Direct estimates of pollen and seed dispersal

Pollen dispersal

Despite its limitations, the unique marker approach has yielded very useful information on pollen flow. Data from seed orchards suggests that while pollination is more likely to occur between nearest neighbours than would be expected under random mating, this effect is not large. Only 11% and 2% of all pollinations were nearest neighbour pollinations in two studies of *Pinus sylvestris* (Muller 1977; Yasdani *et al.* 1989). Although pollen flow drops off sharply away from the male parent, the tail of the distribution may be very long (Figure 3.4). Thus, in the neotropical tree *Cordia alliodora* pollen flow events are still detectable at 275 metres from a focal male parent (Boshier *et al.* 1995).

Studies of pollen flow using paternity exclusion methods are summarized in Table 3.2. A number of points stand out. The first is that far from being restricted to movement between nearest neighbours, pollination distances in both animal- and wind-pollinated species are extensive. For some wind-pollinated species, e.g. *Pinus flexilis* (Schuster & Mitton 2000) the distribution of pollination distances does not differ from that expected under random mating between individuals (Figure 3.5a). In

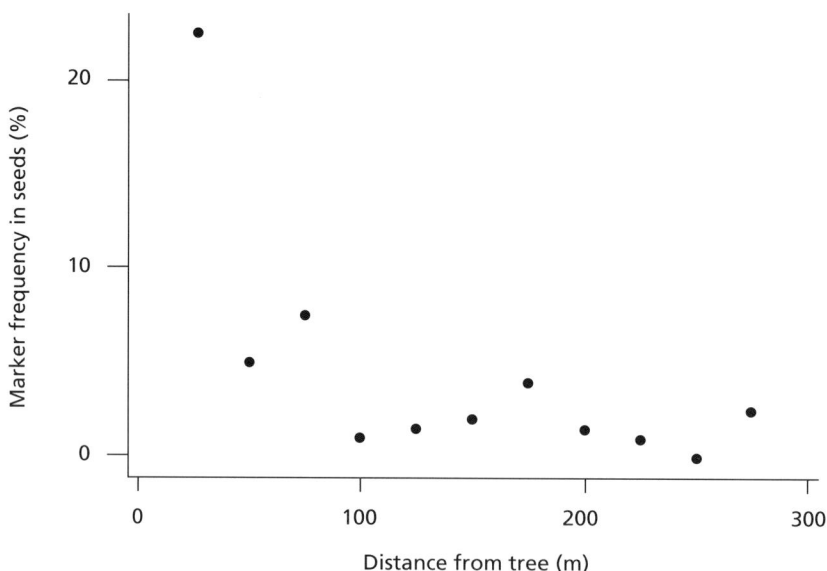

Figure 3.4 Estimated pollen-dispersal distribution in the neotropical tree *Cordia alliodora* using unique marker analysis. (From Boshier *et al.* 1995.)

other wind-pollinated species and in insect-pollinated species of both trees (Isagi *et al.* 2000) and herbs (Meagher 1986) a tendency towards an excess of nearest neighbour compared with random pollination is seen (Figure 5.5b).

Realized pollination distances in animal-pollinated species are significantly larger than inferred from pollen tracking or pollinator movement (Campbell 1991; Meagher 1986; Massey & Hamrick 1999). This suggests possible selection against pollen involved in very-short-distance dispersal events. The explanation may be that very-short-distance pollination involves mating between closely related individuals because there is genetic structuring of the population at this small scale (see earlier). These inbred seeds may not survive to be assayed.

A further important result is that a high proportion of pollinations involve male parents that are from outside the study population. The frequency of these interpopulation pollination events may be 30–50% depending upon the study (Godt & Hamrick 1993; Dow & Ashley 1998; Isagi *et al.* 2000). The effect of high levels of migrant pollen flow will be to decrease the probability of the development of genetic

Table 3.2 Mean and range of pollen flow distance estimated within natural populations using paternity analysis techniques, together with estimates of percentage successful pollen that has migrated into the population.

Species	Mean pollen flow (m)	Range (SE) (m)	Migrant pollen %	Reference
Chamaelerium luteum	10.4	(0.4)	—	Meagher & Thompson (1987)
Gleditsia triacanthos	150	85–240	17–30	Schnabel & Hamrick (1995)
Lathyrus latifolius	11.6–14.8	(1.5–4.1)	16–46	Godt & Hamrick (1993)
Magnolia obovata	131	3–540	30	Isagi *et al.* (2000)
Pinus flexilis	140	68–300	6.5	Schuster & Mitton (2000)
Pithecellobium elegans	142	27–350	29	Chase *et al.* (1996a)
Quercus macrocarpa	77	63–88	71	Dow & Ashley (1998)
Quercus petraea/robur	43	38–65	67	Streiff *et al.* (1999)
Yucca filamentosa	118	6–293	10	Massey & Hamrick (1999)

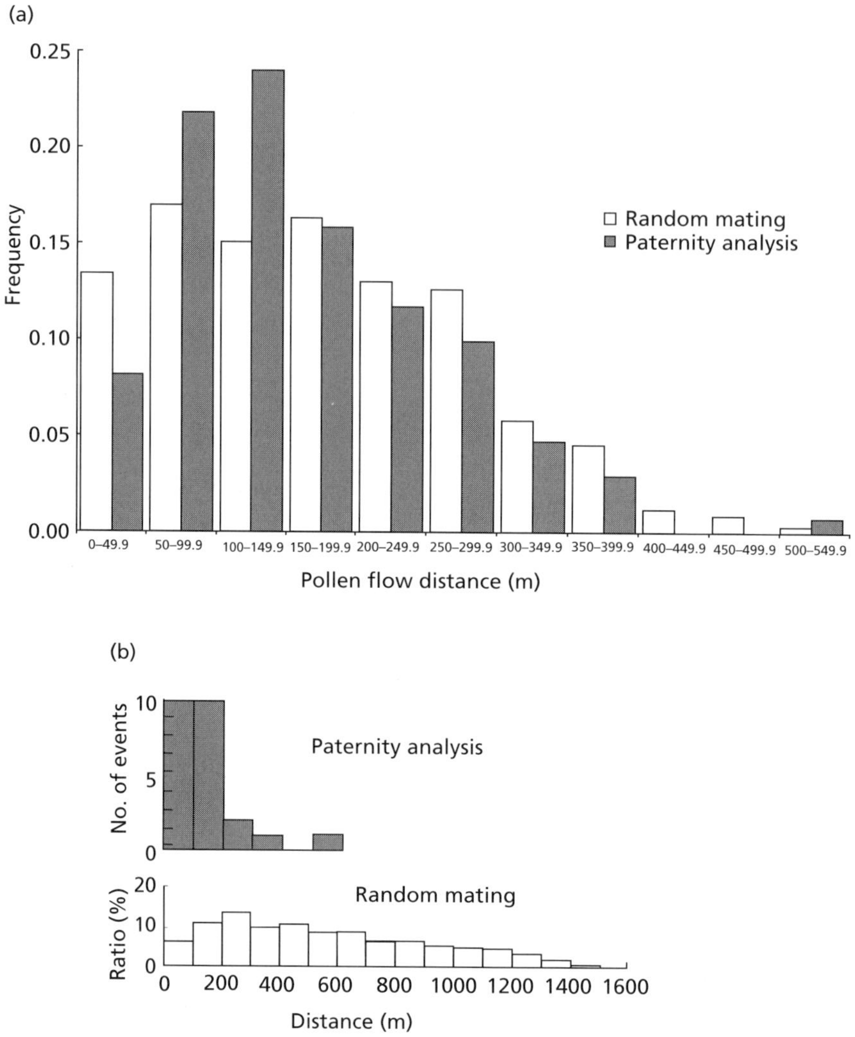

R. A. ENNOS

Figure 3.5 Comparison of pollen-flow distributions inferred from paternity analysis with those expected under random mating of individuals. Data are for (a) wind-pollinated *Pinus flexilis* (Schuster & Mitton 2000) and (b) insect-pollinated *Magnolia obovata* (Isagi *et al.* 2000).

structure within the population by isolation-by-distance processes (Hu & Ennos 1999).

Seed dispersal

Few direct measurements of realized seed dispersal within populations have been made using parentage and maternity analysis, although the number is likely to increase as microsatellite markers become more widely employed. Table 3.3 summa-

64

Table 3.3 Mean and range of seed-flow distance estimated within natural populations using parentage analysis techniques, together with estimates of percentage successful seed that has migrated into the population.

Species	Mean seed flow (m)	Range (SE) (m)	Migrant seed %	Reference
Chamaelerium luteum	10.1	(0.4)	—	Meagher & Thompson (1987)
Gleditsia triacanthos	(a) 60* (b) 80*	(a) 0–180* (b) 10–160*	2.1	Schnabel *et al.* (1998)
Magnolia obovata	265†	32–563†	40	Isagi *et al.* (2000)
Quercus macrocarpa	26	0–165	14	Dow & Ashley (1996)

* Estimates for two populations (a) and (b).
† Estimates of parent–offspring dispersal that include pollen flow as well as seed flow.

rizes the data that comprise one study of a perennial herb with gravity-dispersed seeds and three studies of trees with animal-dispersed fruits. Although generalizations are difficult with so few studies, a number of features are apparent. Animal dispersal of fruit may be very substantial both within and between populations. In *Quercus macrocarpa* and *Magnolia obovata* 14% and 40%, respectively, of the seedlings establishing were from seed formed outside the stand being studied. Seed dispersal within populations can occur over hundreds of metres from one side of the population to the other (Dow & Ashley 1996; Isagi *et al.* 2000) (Figure 3.6).

An equally important conclusion is that the patterns of realized seed flow are likely to be a function not merely of seed dispersal potential, but also of the spatial pattern of regeneration sites in relation to parent plants. For instance in *Q. macrocarpa* regeneration occurs in canopy gaps. If canopy gaps are available near the parent tree, realized seed-dispersal distances may be short, whereas in the same population realized seed dispersal may be much greater if the canopy gap is further from the parent tree (Figure 3.6) (Dow & Ashley 1996).

Conclusions

Before the introduction of molecular markers, spatial dynamic processes in plant populations were inferred from pollen- and seed-dispersal profiles. Levin and Kerster (1974) used such methods to support the contention that gene flow within plant populations is very restricted. This view has coloured our perception of spatial dynamics within plant populations for many years. The advent of molecular markers has provided us with the opportunity to test the validity of Levin and Kerster's contention, and its predicted genetic consequences. Sensitive analysis of spatial genetic structure in large numbers of outcrossing species has now indicated that the

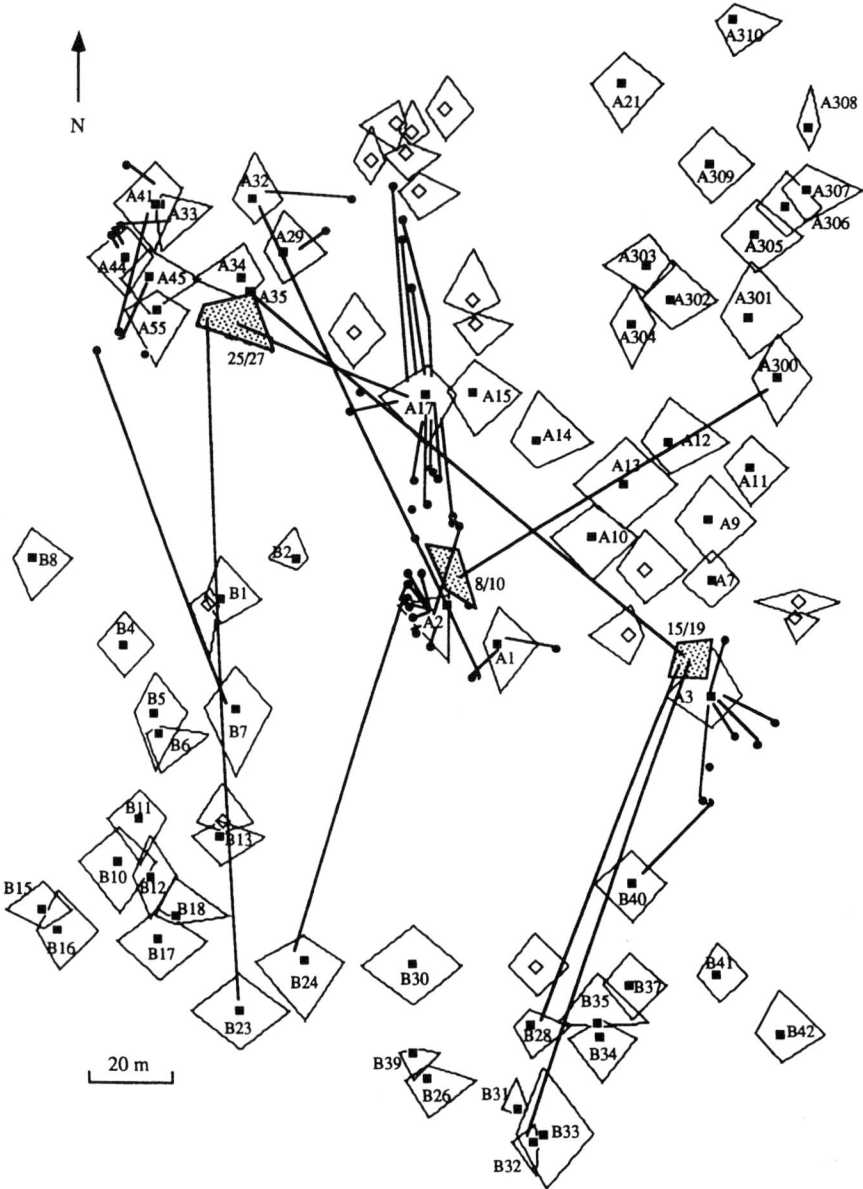

Figure 3.6 Spatial pattern of seed dispersal in *Quercus macrocarpa* inferred from parentage analysis. Diagram indicates position of tree canopies. Lines indicate dispersal of seeds from maternal parents. Shaded areas indicate sapling clusters. Fractions indicate number of offspring derived from nearest maternal parent over total number of saplings in the cluster. (From Dow & Ashley 1996.)

anticipated high levels of subpopulation differentiation generated by isolation-by-distance processes with restricted gene flow are not found. Where genetic structure attributable to isolation-by-distance is present, it appears to be weak, limited to very small spatial scales, or detectable only for maternally inherited markers that do not disperse in pollen. On the other hand, genetic structure resulting from founder effects during population establishment and regeneration can be detected, and may be an important cause of subpopulation differentiation even for nuclear markers.

These results suggest that gene flow, and in particular pollen flow, is far more extensive within outcrossing plant populations than was envisaged by Levin and Kerster. Direct measurements in a limited range of species using paternity and parentage analysis support the contention that there are high levels of pollen dispersal within outcrossing plant populations. Direct measures of seed flow suggest that it too may have been underestimated, particularly in plants with animal dispersed seed. Data from a wider range of species, particularly short-lived herbs, are now required to see whether these conclusions are generally true.

The realization that non-equilibrium processes may be widely responsible for generating genetic structure suggests a need to realign studies of spatial processes in plant populations. Greater emphasis is needed on the spatial genetic consequences of stochastic events within plant populations and non-equilibrium dynamics. This can be achieved most efficiently by introducing genetic marker analysis into established long-term ecological research programmes concerned with understanding population dynamic behaviour. The potential of genetic markers for investigating spatial processes can then be exploited to the full, and the results interpreted within the appropriate ecological context.

Summary

A wide variety of molecular markers are now available as tools for studying the spatial dynamics of vegetative growth, pollen and seed dispersal within plant populations. Choosing the correct marker is crucial to the success of any such investigation. Key properties of the markers that affect their suitability are their mode of inheritance, rate of mutation, level of variability and linkage relationships.

Indirect approaches for measuring spatial processes use molecular markers to reveal the spatial distribution of genotypes within populations. Genetic structuring is detected and measured using spatial autocorrelation analysis or analysis of F_{st}. The spatial processes giving rise to this genetic structure are then inferred. Inferences about spatial processes from genetic structure may be problematic because they rely either on assumptions of drift/migration equilibrium or on knowledge of the ecological history of the population.

A review of the literature suggests that in many plant populations, genetic structure detected with molecular markers is weak, and confined to association of like genotypes over very short distance classes. Where more substantial genetic structure has been observed this is often attributable to sampling events during foundation and regeneration of populations.

Direct approaches to the study of spatial processes use highly variable codominant molecular markers to conduct paternity, maternity and parentage analyses within plant populations. These provide data on contemporary patterns of pollen and seed movement. Early results from these studies suggest that effective pollen and seed flow within populations are more extensive than anticipated from ecological measurements of pollen and seed dispersal profiles.

The results of molecular marker-based studies indicate that the traditional view of restricted pollen and seed flow within plant populations needs to be revised. Integration of molecular marker based approaches into ecological and demographic studies has enormous potential to further our understanding of spatial processes in plant populations.

References

Adams, W.T. (1992). Gene dispersal within forest tree populations. *New Forests*, **6**, 217–240.

Adams, W.T., Griffin, A.R. & Moran, G.F. (1992). Using paternity analysis to measure effective pollen dispersal in plant populations. *American Naturalist*, **140**, 762–780.

Berg, E.E. & Hamrick, J.L. (1995). Fine scale genetic structuring of a turkey oak forest. *Evolution*, **49**, 110–120.

Boshier, D.H., Chase, M.R. & Bawa, K.S. (1995). Population genetics of *Cordia alliodora* (Boraginaceae), a neotropical tree. 3. Gene flow, neighbourhood and population substructure. *American Journal of Botany*, **82**, 484–490.

Bradshaw, A.D. (1972). Some of the evolutionary consequences of being a plant. *Evolutionary Biology*, **5**, 25–47.

Burczyk, J., Adams, W.T. & Shimizu, J.Y. (1996). Mating patterns and pollen dispersal in a natural knobcone pine (*Pinus attenuata* Lemmon.) stand. *Heredity*, **77**, 251–260.

Campbell, D.R. (1991). Comparing pollen dispersal and gene flow in a natural population. *Evolution*, **45**, 1965–1968.

Campbell, D.R. & Dooley, J.L. (1992). The spatial scale of genetic differentiation in a hummingbird-pollinated plant: comparison with models of isolation by distance. *American Naturalist*, **139**, 735–748.

Caron, H., Dumas, S., Marque, G., Messier, C., Bandou, E., Petit, R.J. & Kremer, A. (2000). Spatial and temporal distribution of chloroplast DNA polymorphism in a tropical tree species. *Molecular Ecology*, **9**, 1089–1098.

Caujape-Castells, J. & Pedrola-Monfort, J. (1997). Space–time patterns of genetic structure within a stand of *Androcymbium gramineum* (Cav.) McBride (Colchicaceae). *Heredity*, **79**, 341–349.

Chakraborty, R., Meagher, T.R. & Smouse, P.E. (1988). Parentage analysis with genetic markers in natural populations. I. The expected proportion of offspring with unambiguous paternity. *Genetics*, **118**, 527–536.

Chase, M.R., Kesseli, R. & Bawa, K. (1996a). Microsatellite markers for population and conservation genetics of tropical trees. *American Journal of Botany*, **83**, 51–57.

Chase, M.R., Moller, C., Kesseli, R. & Bawa, K.S. (1996b). Distant gene flow in tropical trees. *Nature*, **383**, 398–399.

Chung, M.G. & Epperson, B.K. (1999). Spatial genetic structure of clonal and sexual reproduction in populations of *Adenophora grandiflora* (Campanulaceae). *Evolution*, **53**, 1068–1078.

Chung, M.G. & Epperson, B.K. (2000). Clonal and spatial genetic structure in *Eurya emarginata* (Theaceae). *Heredity*, **84**, 170–177.

Chung, M.G., Chung, J.M., Chung, M.Y. & Epperson, B.K. (2000). Spatial distribution of allozyme polymorphisms following clonal and sexual reproduction in populations of *Rhus javanica* (Anacardiaceae). *Heredity*, **84**, 178–185.

Coates, D.J. (1992). Genetic consequences of a bottleneck and spatial genetic structure in the triggerplant *Stylidium coroniforme* (Stylidiaceae). *Heredity*, **69**, 512–520.

Devlin, B., Roeder, K. & Ellstrand, N.C. (1988). Fractional paternity assignment: theoretical development and comparison to other methods. *Theoretical and Applied Genetics*, **76**, 369–380.

Dewey, S.E. & Heywood, J.S. (1988). Spatial genetic structure in a population of *Psychotria nervosa* I. Distribution of genotypes. *Evolution*, **42**, 834–838.

Doligez, A. & Joly, H.I. (1997). Genetic diversity and spatial structure within a natural stand of a tropical forest tree species, *Carapa procera* (Meliaceae). *Heredity*, **79**, 72–82.

Dow, B.D. & Ashley, M.V. (1996). Microsatellite analysis of seed dispersal and parentage of saplings on bur oak, *Quercus macrocarpa*. *Molecular Ecology*, **5**, 615–627.

Dow, B.D. & Ashley, M.V. (1998). High levels of gene flow in bur oak revealed by paternity analysis using microsatellites. *Journal of Heredity*, **89**, 62–70.

Ennos, R.A., Sinclair, W.T., Hu, X.-S. & Langdon, A. (1999). Using organelle markers to elucidate the history, ecology and evolution of plant populations. In: *Molecular Systematics and Plant Evolution* (ed. P.M. Hollingsworth, R.M. Bateman & R.J. Gornall), pp. 1–19. Taylor & Francis, London.

Epperson, B.K. (1995a). Fine-scale spatial structure: correlations for individual genotypes differ from those for local gene frequencies. *Evolution*, **49**, 1022–1026.

Epperson, B.K. (1995b). Spatial distributions of genotypes under isolation by distance. *Genetics*, **140**, 1431–1440.

Epperson, B.K. & Allard, R.W. (1989). Spatial autocorrelation analysis of the distribution of genotypes within populations of lodgepole pine. *Genetics*, **121**, 369–377.

Epperson, B.K. & Alvarez-Baylla, E.R. (1997). Limited seed dispersal and genetic structure in lifestages of *Cecropia obtusifolia*. *Evolution*, **51**, 275–282.

Epperson, B.K. & Li, T. (1996). Measurement of genetic structure within populations using Moran's spatial autocorrelation statistics. *Proceedings of the National Academy of Sciences of the USA*, **93**, 10528–10532.

Epperson, B.K. & Li, T.-Q. (1997). Gene dispersal and genetic structure. *Evolution*, **51**, 672–681.

Epperson, B.K., Huang, Z. & Li, T.Q. (1999). Measures of spatial structure in samples of genotypes for multiallelic loci. *Genetical Research Cambridge*, **73**, 251–261.

Fenster, C.B. (1991). Gene flow in *Chamaecrista fasciculata* (Leguminosae) II. Gene establishment. *Evolution*, **45**, 410–422.

Franceschinelli, E.V. & Kesseli, R. (1999). Population structure and gene flow of the Brasilian shrub *Helicteres brevispira*. *Heredity*, **82**, 355–367.

Furnier, G.R., Knowles, P., Clyde, M.A. & Dancik, B.P. (1987). Effects of avian seed dispersal on the genetic structure of whitebark pine populations. *Evolution*, **41**, 607–612.

Gehring, J.L. & Delph, L.F. (1999). Fine scale genetic structure and clinal variation in *Silene acaulis* despite high gene flow. *Heredity*, **82**, 628–637.

Giles, B.E., Lundqvist, E. & Goudet, J. (1998). Restricted gene flow and subpopulation differentiation in *Silene dioica*. *Heredity*, **80**, 715–723.

Godt, M.J.W. & Hamrick, J.L. (1993). Patterns and levels of pollen-mediated gene flow in *Lathyrus latifolius*. *Evolution*, **47**, 98–110.

Hamrick, J.L. & Holden, L.R. (1979). Influence of microhabitat heterogeneity on gene frequency distribution and gametic phase disequilibrium in *Avena barbata*. *Evolution*, **33**, 521–533.

Hardy, O.J. & Vekemans, X. (1999). Isolation by distance in a continuous population: reconciliation between spatial autocorrelation analysis and population genetic models. *Heredity*, **83**, 145–154.

Hedrick, P.W. (1999). Perspective: Highly variable loci and their interpretation in evolution and conservation. *Evolution*, **53**, 313–318.

Heywood, J.S. (1991). Spatial analysis of genetic variation in plant populations. *Annual Review of Ecology and Systematics*, **22**, 335–355.

Hossaert-McKey, M., Valdero, M., Magda, O., Jary, M., Cuguen, J. & Vernet, P. (1996). The evolving genetic history of a population of *Lathyrus sylvestris*: evidence for temporal and spatial genetic structure. *Evolution*, **50**, 1808–1821.

Hu, X.-S. & Ennos, R.A. (1997). On estimation of the ratio of pollen to seed flow among plant populations. *Heredity*, **79**, 541–552.

Hu, X.-S. & Ennos, R.A. (1999). Impacts of seed and pollen flow on population genetic structure for plant genomes with three contrasting modes of inheritance. *Genetics*, **152**, 441–450.

Ingvarsson, P.K. & Giles, B.E. (1999). Kin-structured colonisation and small-scale genetic differentiation in *Silene dioica*. *Evolution*, **53**, 606–611.

Isagi, Y., Kanazashi, T., Suzuki, W., Tanaka, H. & Abe,

T. (2000). Microsatellite analysis of the regeneration process of *Magnolia obovata* Thunb. *Heredity*, **84**, 143–151.

Knowles, P., Perry, D.J. & Foster, H.A. (1992). Spatial genetic structure in two tamarak (*Larix laricina* Du Roi K. Koch) populations with different establishment histories. *Evolution*, **46**, 572–576.

Kudoh, H., Shibaike, H., Takasu, H., Whigham, D.F. & Kawano, S. (1999). Genet structure and determinants of clonal structure in a temperate deciduous woodland herb, *Uvularia perfoliata*. *Journal of Ecology*, **87**, 244–257.

Latta, R.G., Linhart, Y.B., Fleck, D. & Elliot, M. (1998). Direct and indirect estimates of seed versus pollen movement within a population of ponderosa pine. *Evolution*, **52**, 61–67.

Levin, D.A. & Kerster, H.W. (1974). Gene flow in seed plants. *Evolutionary Biology*, **7**, 139–220.

Levy, F. & Neal, C.L. (1999). Spatial and temporal genetic structure in chloroplast and isozyme markers in *Phacelia dubia* implicate genetic drift. *Heredity*, **82**, 422–431.

Loirelle, B.A., Sork, V.L., Nason, J. & Graham, C. (1995). Spatial genetic structure of a tropical understory shrub, *Psychotria officinalis* (Rubiaceae). *American Journal of Botany*, **82**, 1420–1425.

Mahy, G. & Neve, G. (1997). The application of spatial autocorrelation methods to the study of *Calluna vulgaris* population genetics. *Belgian Journal of Botany*, **129**, 131–139.

Mahy, G., Vekemans, X. & Jacquemart, A.-L. (1999). Patterns of allozymic variation within *Calluna vulgaris* populations at seed bank and adult stages. *Heredity*, **82**, 432–440.

Massey, L.K. & Hamrick, J.L. (1999). Breeding structure of a *Yucca filamentosa* (Agavaceae) population. *Evolution*, **53**, 1293–1298.

McCauley, D.E., Stevens, J.E., Peroni, P.A. & Raveill, J.A. (1996). The spatial distribution of chloroplast DNA and allozyme polymorphisms within a population of *Silene alba* (Caryophyllaceae). *American Journal of Botany*, **83**, 727–731.

Meagher, T.R. (1986). Analysis of paternity within a natural population of *Chamaelerium luteum*. I. Identification of most likely parents. *American Naturalist*, **128**, 199–215.

Meagher, T.R. & Thompson, E. (1987). Analysis of parentage for naturally established seedlings of *Chamaelerium luteum* (Liliaceae). *Ecology*, **68**, 803–812.

Milligan, B.G. & McMurray, C.K. (1993). Dominant vs. codominant genetic-markers in the estimation of male mating success. *Molecular Ecology*, **2**, 275–283.

Moran, P.A.P. (1950). Notes on continuous stochastic phenomena. *Biometrika*, **37**, 17–23.

Muller, G. (1977). Short note: cross-fertilisation in a conifer stand inferred from enzyme gene-markers in seeds. *Silvae Genetica*, **26**, 223–226.

Ohsawa, R., Furuya, N. & Ukai, Y. (1993). Effect of spatially restricted pollen flow on spatial genetic structure of an animal-pollinated allogamous plant population. *Heredity*, **71**, 64–73.

Peakall, R. & Beattie, A.J. (1995). Does ant dispersal of seeds in *Sclerolaena diacantha* (Chenopodiaceae) generate local spatial structure? *Heredity*, **75**, 351–361.

Perry, D.J. & Knowles, P. (1991). Spatial genetic structure within three sugar maple (*Acer saccharum* Marsh.) stands. *Heredity*, **66**, 137–142.

Powell, W.M., Morgante, M., McDevitt, R., Vendramin, G.G. & Rafalski, J.A. (1995). Polymorphic simple sequence repeat regions in chloroplast genomes: application to the population genetics of pines. *Proceedings of the National Academy of Sciences of the USA*, **92**, 7759–7763.

Queller, D.C. & Goodnight, K.F. (1989). Estimating relatedness using genetic markers. *Evolution*, **43**, 258–275.

Reusch, T.B.H., Hukriede, W., Stam, W.T. & Olsen, J.L. (1999). Differentiating between clonal growth and limited gene flow using spatial autocorrelation of microsatellites. *Heredity*, **83**, 120–126.

Ruckelshaus, M.H. (1998). Spatial scale of genetic structure and an indirect estimate of gene flow in eelgrass, *Zostera marina*. *Evolution*, **52**, 330–343.

Samitou-Laprade, P., Rouwendale, G.J.A., Cuguen, J., Krens, F.A. & Michaelis, G. (1993). Different CMS sources found in *Beta vulgaris* ssp. *maritima*: mitochondrial variability in wild populations revealed by a rapid screening procedure. *Theoretical and Applied Genetics*, **85**, 529–535.

Schnabel, A. & Hamrick, J.L. (1995). Understanding the population genetic structure of *Gleditsia triacanthos* L.: The scale and pattern of pollen gene flow. *Evolution*, **49**, 921–931.

Schnabel, A., Laushman, R.H. & Hamrick, J.L. (1991). Comparative genetic structure of two co-occurring tree species *Maclura pomifera*

(Moraceae) and *Gleditsis tricanthos*. *Heredity*, **67**, 357–364.

Schnabel, A., Nason, J.D. & Hamrick, J.L. (1998). Understanding the population genetic structure of *Gleditsia triacanthos* L.: seed dispersal and variation in female reproductive success. *Molecular Ecology*, **7**, 819–832.

Schuster, W.S.F. & Mitton, J.B. (2000). Paternity and gene dispersal in limber pine (*Pinus flexilis* James). *Heredity*, **84**, 348–361.

Shapcott, A. (1995). The spatial genetic structure in natural populations of the Australian temperate rainforest tree *Antherosperma moschatus* (Labill.). *Heredity*, **74**, 28–38.

Slatkin, M. & Arter, H.E. (1991). Spatial autocorrelation methods in population genetics. *American Naturalist*, **138**, 499–517.

Smouse, P.E. & Peakall, R. (1999). Spatial autocorrelation analysis of individual multiallelic and multilocus genetic structure. *Heredity*, **82**, 561–573.

Sokal, R.R. & Oden, N.L. (1978a). Spatial autocorrelation in biology 1. Methodology. *Biological Journal of the Linnean Society*, **10**, 199–228.

Sokal, R.R. & Oden, N.L. (1978b). Spatial autocorrelation in biology 2. Some biological implications and four applications of evolutionary and ecological interest. *Biological Journal of the Linnean Society*, **10**, 229–249.

Streiff, R., Ducousso, A., Lexer, C., Steinkellner, H., Gloessl, J. & Kremer, A. (1999). Pollen dispersal inferred from paternity analysis in a mixed stand of *Quercus robur* L. and *Q. petraea* (Matt.) Liebl. *Molecular Ecology*, **8**, 831–841.

Streiff, R., Labbe, T., Bacilien, R., Steinkellness, H., Glossl, J. & Kremer, A. (1998). Within-population genetic structure in *Quercus robur* L. and *Q. petraea* (Matt.) Liebl. assessed with isozymes and microsatellites. *Molecular Ecology*, **7**, 317–328.

Taberlet, P., Gielly, L., Patou, G. & Bouvet, J. (1991). Universal primers for amplification of three non-coding regions of chloroplast DNA. *Plant Molecular Biology*, **17**, 1105–1109.

Takahashi, M., Mukuoda, M. & Koono, K. (2000). Differences in genetic structure between two Japanese beech (*Fagus crenata* Blume) stands. *Heredity*, **84**, 103–115.

Tarayre, M., Saumitou-Laprade, P., Cuguen, J.,

Couvet, D. & Thompson, J.D. (1997). The spatial genetic structure of cytoplasmic (cpDNA) and nuclear (allozyme) markers within and among populations of the gynodioecious *Thymus vulgaris* (Labiateae) in southern France. *American Journal of Botany*, **84**, 1675–1684.

Turner, M.E., Stephens, J.C. & Anderson, W.W. (1982). Homozygosity and patch structure in plant populations as a result of nearest-neighbor pollination. *Proceedings of the National Academy of Sciences of the USA*, **79**, 203–207.

Ueno, S., Tomaru, N., Yoshima, H., Manabe, T. & Yamamoto, S. (2000). Genetic structure of *Camellia japonica* L. in an old growth evergreen forest. *Molecular Ecology*, **9**, 647–656.

Waser, N.M. (1987). Spatial genetic heterogeneity in a population of the montane perennial plant *Delphinium nelsonii*. *Heredity*, **58**, 249–256.

Weir, B.S. & Cockerham, C.C. (1984). Estimating F-statistics for the analysis of population structure. *Evolution*, **38**, 1358–1370.

Williams, C.F. & Waser, N.M. (1999). Spatial genetic structure of *Delphinium nuttallianum* populations: inferences about gene flow. *Heredity*, **83**, 541–550.

Wolfe, K.H., Li, W. & Sharp, P.M. (1987). Rates of nucleotide substitution vary greatly among plant mitochondrial, chloroplast and nuclear DNAs. *Proceedings of the National Academy of Sciences of the USA*, **84**, 9054–9058.

Wright, S. (1943). Isolation by distance. *Genetics*, **28**, 114–138.

Wright, S. (1951). The genetical structure of populations. *Annals of Eugenics*, **15**, 323–354.

Wright, S. (1978). *Evolution and the Genetics of Populations*, Vol. 4: *Variability Within and Among Natural Populations*. University of Chicago Press, Chicago.

Xie, C.Y. & Knowles, P. (1991). Spatial genetic substructure within natural populations of jack pine (*Pinus banksiana*). *Canadian Journal of Botany*, **69**, 547–551.

Yasdani, R., Lindgren, D. & Stewart, S. (1989). Gene dispersion within a population of *Pinus sylvestris*. *Scandinavian Journal of Forest Research*, **4**, 295–306.

Ziegenhagen, B., Scholtz, F., Madaghiele, A. & Vendramin, G.G. (1998). Chloroplast microsatellites as markers for paternity analysis. *Canadian Journal of Forest Research*, **28**, 317–321.

Chapter 4

Mating systems and population genetic structure in the light of coalescent theory

D. Charlesworth* and J. R. Pannell†

Introduction

It is well known that plants vary greatly in their mating systems, with species ranging from highly outcrossed to moderately or even highly self-fertilizing (Darwin 1876, 1877; Baker 1953, 1959; Stebbins 1957). Early evidence on mating systems was based on floral morphology supplemented by estimates of self-fertility. Recently, the use of genetic markers has allowed quantitative estimates of self-fertilization rates in natural populations of cosexual (hermaphroditic or monoecious) plants, and in angiosperms several clear trends have become evident. Outcrossing is commoner in long-lived plants than in annuals (Baker 1959; Barrett *et al.* 1996), whereas few trees or shrubs are highly inbreeding. Overall, although the distribution of self-fertilization rates is somewhat bimodal (Barrett *et al.* 1996), intermediate selfing is common (e.g. Baker 1959; Lloyd 1979).

It is also well established that mating systems affect genetic variability both within and between populations. Ideally, closely related taxa with similar life histories and ecological situations should be compared. Although this has rarely been done, all types of variability (morphological, quantitative, or diversity estimated with genetic markers) seem to be lower in inbreeding than outbreeding populations. Considering morphological variability, Baker (1953, page 114) noted that, 'In no case does a self-compatible culture show greater variety than the outbreeders'. Few studies have been done on quantitative variability, but the conclusions are the same (Carr & Fenster 1993; Charlesworth & Charlesworth 1995). Finally, the large body of enzyme electrophoresis data consistently shows higher levels of within-population diversity in outcrossing than in selfing or apomictic populations (Hamrick & Godt 1990; Schoen & Brown 1991). At the level of species as a whole, however, inbreeding and outcrossing species appear to differ less, although species-wide diversity again tends to be slightly lower in inbreeders than in outbreeders (Hamrick & Godt 1990; Charlesworth *et al.* 1997; Table 4.1).

More work is still needed to compare diversity levels between populations whose outcrossing rates have been quantified, so that populations are not merely characterized as in- or outbreeding, as has mostly been done in the past (Hamrick & Godt

* *Institute of Cell, Animal and Population Biology (ICAPB), University of Edinburgh, Edinburgh EH9 3JT, Scotland and* † *Department of Plant Sciences, University of Oxford, Oxford, OX2 6UD, UK.*

Table 4.1 Isozyme and microsatellite diversity (either means reported in the papers listed or unweighted means over all populations reported) in congeneric species with different selfing rates (S). When S values for the populations were not given in the cited references, the selfing rates are categorized as low or high. D_{st} represents $H_t - H_s$.

Genus	Species or population	S	H_s	H_t	D_{st}	G_{st}	Reference
Isozymes							
Arabidopsis	lyrata	0	0.29	0.27	—	0.41	van Treuren et al. (1997)
	thaliana	0.99	0.023	0.061	0.038	0.62	Abbott & Gomes (1988)
Phlox	drummondii	0	0.18	0.25	0.07	0.28	Levin (1978)
	roemeriana	0	0.28	0.36	0.08	0.22	
	cuspidata	high	0.05	0.07	0.03	0.37	
Oenothera	grandis	0	0.19	0.22	0.03	0.14	Ellstrand & Levin
	laciniata	high	0.14	0.18	0.04	0.22	(1980)
Plectritis	congesta	0.30	0.23	0.27	0.04	0.15	Layton &
	brachystemon	0.98	0.06	0.17	0.11	0.64	Ganders (1984)
Gilia	achillefolia 4 pops	0.21	0.21	0.27	0.06	0.23	Schoen (1982)
	achillefolia 3 pops	0.71	0.14	0.30	0.16	0.54	
Lolium	3 species	0.08	0.34	0.38	0.04	0.10	Loos (1993)
	remotum	high	0.004	0.44	0.44	0.75	
Plantago	lanceolata	0	0.13	0.13	0.006	0.05	Wolff (1991)
	major	high	0.05	0.06	0.02	0.32	
Mimulu	guttatus	low	0.24	0.36	0.09	0.26	Fenster &
	micranthus	high	0.04	0.06	0.02	0.34	Ritland (1992)
Lilium	parryi CA	low	0.25	0.29	0.03	0.11	Linhart & Premoli
	parryi AZ	high	0.06	0.06	0.003	0.06	(1994)
Arenaria	uniflora 2 pops	low	0.134	—	—	—	Wyatt et al.
	uniflora 5 pops	high	0.017	—	—	—	(1992)
Scutellaria	angustifolia	low	0.080	0.131	0.051	0.389	Olmstead (1990)
	a. micrantha	high	0.026	0.107	0.081	0.755	
Microsatellites							
Mimulus	guttatus	0.49	0.51	0.66	0.15	0.23	Awadalla &
	laciniatus	0.88	0.31	0.64	0.32	0.52	Ritland (1997)
Arabidopsis	lyrata	0	0.15	0.24	—	0.59	van Treuren et al. (1997)
	thaliana	0.99	0	0.67	—	1	Todokoro et al. (1995)

1996). Plants provide ideal material for such studies, because there are multiple evolutionarily independent cases of the evolution of inbreeding by self-fertilization from outcrossing (Stebbins 1957). In some cases, ecologically similar inbreeding and outcrossing species are found within genera (e.g. Holtsford & Ellstrand 1989; Macnair et al. 1989; Husband & Barrett 1993; Schoen et al. 1997; Bena et al. 1998).

Both inbreeding and outcrossing populations can even occur within single species, and in two well-studied cases, inbreeding populations have lower isozyme diversity (Lloyd 1965; Rick *et al.* 1977; Barrett & Husband 1990).

These facts are well known. However, since Brown's valuable paper dealing with allozyme diversity (Brown 1979), there has been surprisingly little clear discussion in the empirical literature about why breeding system differences lead to differences in diversity, and empirical studies of genetic diversity frequently ignore the mating systems of the populations studied. The situation today remains little different from that in 1953, when Baker (1953, page 114) wrote:

> When one consults the literature appropriate to this subject, one cannot
> fail to be impressed by the mass of calculations and deductions as to the
> probable course of evolution in species with different kinds of breeding
> systems which have been made by those I will call 'theoretical
> evolutionists'. On the other hand, several of the more practical
> 'biosystematists' (or 'genecologists' or 'experimental taxonomists')
> appear to have paid very little attention to these conclusions and, in some
> cases, have published extensive works containing little or no reference to
> the reproductive methods of the plants involved.

In this review, we show that many of the patterns outlined above can be understood in the context of a growing and rigorous theoretical framework. We first briefly review the salient population genetic properties of different types of markers, emphasizing their advantages and disadvantages for the interpretation of population structure and mating-system variation, together with the relevant theory needed to interpret diversity data. Finally, we discuss in detail the patterns that are emerging from empirical studies of natural populations, relating them to the population genetic theory. Throughout, we emphasize the similarity between geographic subdivision of a species and the genetic subdivision caused by inbreeding. Because of this similarity, a discussion of the effects of both spatial structure and mating systems on patterns of genetic diversity can be approached within the same framework, by rescaling times to coalescence of lineages (Nordborg 2000; Wakeley 2000).

Neutral markers and diversity measures

Studies based on genetic markers are particularly important for several reasons. First, they can provide quantitative diversity estimates of variability that can be compared between different loci, populations and species. Secondly, diversity patterns can be understood based on well-defined theoretical models. Finally, marker variants can often be assumed to be selectively neutral. Such variants are often found in repetitive or other non-coding parts of the DNA (including restriction fragment length polymorphism (RFLP) markers in DNA sequences that lie outside the coding region of the genes, or in introns), or as silent changes (which do not change the amino acid sequence) in coding sequences (see Miller & Tanksley 1990; Ouborg *et al.* 1999).

Different types of markers are useful for different purposes (see Ouborg *et al.* 1999). Among the different diversity measures available, gene diversity, calculated from allele frequencies in a population or species, and nucleotide diversity, estimated from DNA sequence data, are particularly important, because theoretical predictions of their behaviour are available. For gene diversity estimates, codominant markers, such as isozymes and microsatellites are needed, while dominant markers require either the assumption of Hardy–Weinberg genotype frequencies (e.g. Innan *et al.* 1999), which is inappropriate for inbreeders, or special experimental designs (Szmidt *et al.* 1996, Lynch & Milligan 1994; Zhivotovsky 1999). Dominant markers are nevertheless useful for comparisons between populations, such as estimates of F_{st} (or its equivalent for multiple alleles, G_{st}).

The gene diversity, H_e, at a locus is the chance that two randomly chosen alleles will be different (Nei 1987). It is calculated from:

$$H_e = 1 - \sum_i p_i^2 \qquad (1)$$

where p_i is the frequency of the *i*th allele type. Confusion has been caused because H_e is sometimes referred to as 'heterozygosity' (since it is the same as the expected frequency of heterozygotes in a random-mating population); this term should be reserved for the observed frequency of heterozygotes in a population, H_o. For microsatellites, diversity is often estimated using measures, such as the variance in the number of repeats, that take into account the special features of the way these variants may arise (Estoup & Cornuet 1999). Many microsatellite loci have numerous alleles, and diversity can approach unity (e.g. Todokoro *et al.* 1995).

With recent advances in polymerase chain reaction (PCR) and DNA sequencing methods, data can be obtained on variation at individual nucleotide sites. Here we concentrate on silent diversity, which is more likely to be neutral than nonsynonymous amino acid replacements (see Nei 1987). For DNA sequence data, the diversity measure 'nucleotide diversity' (π) is the fraction of nucleotides at which differences are found between pairs of allelic sequences, similar to the concept used to estimate the gene diversity measure, H_e (Nei 1987; Tajima 1993). Nucleotide diversity can also be estimated from RFLP data (Stephan & Langley 1998).

For species distributed into discrete populations, H_s is often used to refer to within-population allelic diversity, and H_t for total species-wide diversity (Nei 1987); π_s and π_t are used for nucleotide diversity. Population structure is often expressed in terms of F_{st}, the ratio of between-population to total species-wide diversity (Nei 1987); for DNA sequences, $F_{st} = (\pi_t - \pi_s)/\pi_t$ (Charlesworth 1998).

There is a growing body of data on nucleotide diversity in plant genes, from both crops and natural populations (see Table 4.3, page 86). Values tend to be less than 1–2% (except for a few special cases such as self-incompatibility alleles). Outcrossing species, such as maize, may have high nucleotide diversity (e.g. Wang *et al.* 1999; Stephan & Langley 1998) relative to those found in the only other well-studied species, *Drosophila* and humans. Inbreeding species tend to have lower diversity, both for allozymes, as already mentioned, and for nucleotide variants (Miller & Tanksley 1990; Stephan & Langley 1998; Dvorak *et al.* 1998). Before showing how these differences may be understood, we briefly review the theory of molecular diversity in panmictic populations, and then extend this framework successively to inbreeding and subdivided populations, and finally to the effects of the combination of both these factors.

Theoretical background

Coalescent trees in panmictic populations

Genetic diversity can be understood within the framework of the neutral theory of molecular evolution (Kimura 1983). Diversity for neutral variants depends on their arising by mutation, and their random loss through genetic drift. Variability, as defined above, depends on the amount of time during which the sequences to be compared have been accumulating differences by mutation (Figure 4.1), and on the mutation rate in the sequence (e.g. Nei 1987). This is similar to the familiar concept of distance based on divergence between homologous sequences of different species used in phylogenetic inference.

To model isozyme variants, the 'infinite-alleles model' assumes that each mutation generates a new allele (Figure 4.1) at rate u (see Nei 1987). The expected gene

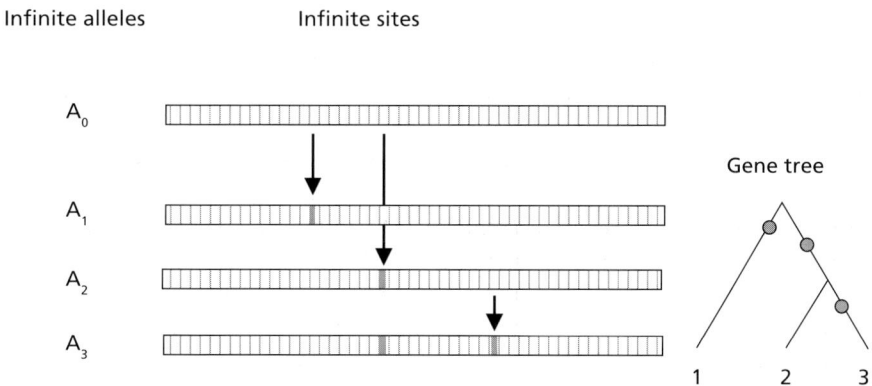

Figure 4.1 The infinite alleles and infinite sites mutation models. A gene sequence is schematically shown, with three different sites where mutations (denoted by arrows from ancestral to descendant sequences) have occurred. In the infinite sites model, each mutation changes a unique site (and these sites could be distinguished by sequencing). The sequences contain information on descent: since the bottom sequence (3) carries two mutations, one of which is the also in the sequence above (number 2), sequences 2 and 3 must be more closely related than either of them is to sequence 1, and a gene tree can be drawn (with grey circles representing the mutations). Under the infinite alleles model, each new sequence created by mutation is a different allele. There are enough sites in a gene sequence that this is a reasonable assumption. There is no information on descent under this model, and a gene tree cannot be constructed from the information on alleles at a locus.

diversity at equilibrium in a panmictic population is then:

$$H \simeq 4N_e u \qquad\qquad\qquad (2)$$

Here, N_e is the 'effective size' of the population (see, for example, Nei 1987). N_e relates the diversity in an actual population, with a particular population size, structure and breeding system, to that expected in a panmictic population under the Wright–Fisher model (a homogeneous, constant-sized cosexual population with Poisson-distributed individual reproductive success). Effects of population structure and the mating system on genetic diversity can often be accurately summarized by relating N_e to N.

We shall mainly focus on results from the infinite-sites model (see Kimura 1983), because nucleotide sequence data are most relevant to thinking about gene trees. These are particularly helpful in understanding what happens when populations deviate from the Wright–Fisher model, for instance when there is population structure and/or inbreeding. In the infinite-sites model, each mutation occurs at a different site in the sequence (Figure 4.1). This is a reasonable assumption, as mutation rates at individual sites, and thus nucleotide site diversity, are usually low (occasionally polymorphic nucleotide site have multiple variants, so this simple model is not perfect for real sequences). Under this mutation model, the expected equilibrium nucleotide diversity in a population with effective size N_e and a mutation rate μ per nucleotide per generation, is $\pi = 4N_e\mu$, the 'scaled mutation rate'.

Coalescent analysis uses a phylogenetic perspective, in which we think about the ancestry of a samples of alleles at a single locus, going backwards in time (Hudson 1990; Figure 4.2). This approach straightforwardly yields predictions of expected diversity and other population properties, and the clarity it gives permits extension to give an intuitive understanding of the effects of population structure and the mating system. To illustrate coalescence reasoning, it explains the expression above for differences between pairs of sequences (π), as follows (ignoring, for the moment, the occurrence of recombination). In an outcrossing 'Wright–Fisher' population of N diploid individuals, the probability that two alleles in a population will coalesce (have the same common ancestor) in the previous generation is $1/(2N)$, regardless of whether the alleles are in the same or in different individuals. The expected number of generations back to the most recent common ancestor of two DNA sequences in a sample is thus $2N$. Independent mutations accumulate in each sequence over those $2N$ generations at rate μ per base pair per generation, so the expected number of differences between the sequences is $2 \times 2N\mu$.

Another important aspect of the coalescent perspective is that it is easy to simulate the ancestry of samples of sequences. This permits statistical testing of deviations in patterns of variation from those expected under a null model (often selective neutrality and panmixis; e.g. Tajima 1989). π varies greatly between samples, partly due to 'mutational' variance (stochastic differences in numbers of mutations in a given time), but mainly due to the great randomness of gene genealogies, the 'evolutionary' variance. The outcome of a given evolutionary model is stochastic, and a sample of sequences from a single non-recombining locus is a single unreplicated geneal-

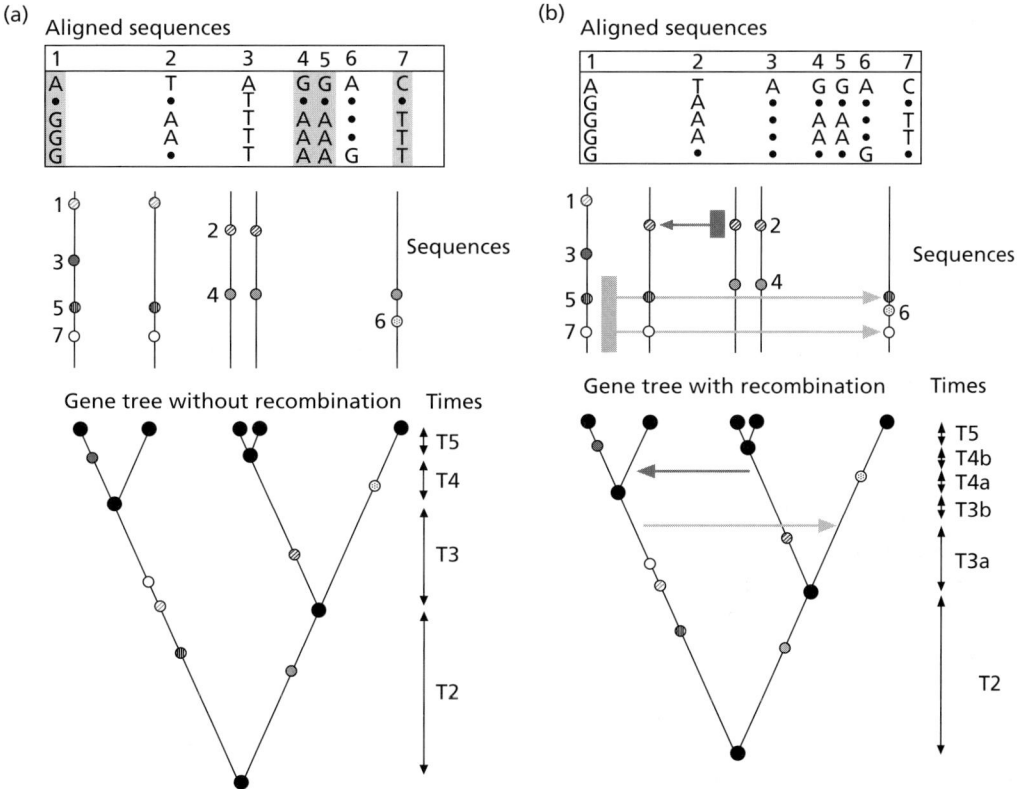

Figure 4.2 Coalescents without (a) and with (b) recombination. In each part of the figure, the bottom section shows the gene tree, with the sample sequences at the top and sequences ancestral to the sample shown as large black circles. Mutations during the ancestry of the sample are shown as smaller circles, with different patterns, indicating different mutations. Above the tree are shown schematic diagrams of the sequences that might be generated by the tree, for particular locations of the mutations. At the top, the same sequence information is transformed into aligned sequences with particular variants at the sites within the sequence that have undergone mutation. Sites in grey boxes indicate sites in linkage disequilibrium. In the absence of recombination, many sites are correlated (they indicate the same tree). With recombination (indicated by arrows in the gene tree and the sequences, to show which portions of the gene are inserted into the recipient sequences), this structure is not seen.

ogy (see Nordborg 2000). One cannot therefore estimate a population's diversity accurately from a single locus. Loci that segregate independently will have different genealogies, so having data from several loci increases accuracy. Because diversity is measured per nucleotide site, and individual sites accumulate variants independently in the infinite sites model, recombination does not affect the expected diversity (Hudson 1990), but it breaks up the sample's ancestry into somewhat independent genealogical trees. Recombination within a gene thus reduces the evolutionary variance of the sampled gene tree (similar to sampling several different loci) and diversity estimates become more accurate.

A further important effect of recombination is to alter the ancestry of samples (Hudson 1990; Figure 4.2). Without recombination, half of the expected total coalescence time of a sample of sequences is the time for the last two sequences in the gene tree to go back to the common ancestor, so the sequences tend to fall into two subsets, or haplotypes, corresponding to the two branches of the gene tree. Recombination obliterates this dichotomy in the sequences.

The effect of the mating system on diversity

The first important effect of non-random mating is a short-term redistribution of diversity in the population. Each generation of complete self-fertilization, for instance, increases the population's homozygosity by 50%. Under the 'mixed-mating' model, with all individuals assumed to reproduce with the same selfing rate S (Brown 1979), the expected equilibrium inbreeding coefficient is:

$$F = S/(2 - S) \tag{3}$$

This, by itself, does not affect genetic diversity. In the long term, however, inbreeding has another, more profound, effect, reducing the effective population size, such that

$$N_e = N/(1 + F) \tag{4}$$

(Pollak 1987). A completely self-fertilizing population at mutation-drift equilibrium should therefore have half the neutral genetic diversity of a completely outcrossing species with the same population size. In the coalescent perspective, the probability of coalescence of two alleles in partially or completely self-fertilizing population depends on whether they are in the same or in different individuals, unlike the situation under outcrossing just outlined. The coalescence of two randomly sampled lineages requires two steps. First, the two lineages must trace back into a single diploid individual. With N diploid individuals in the population, this will take, on average, N generations. Once in the same individual, the two lineages must then descend from the same common ancestral allele (coalesce). Under complete selfing, this has a probability of 1/2, and an average waiting time of two generations. If N is large, this second time is negligible, relative to the first one, so the expected coalescence time is approximately N generations, half that for an equivalent outcrossing population (see Nordborg 2000).

Effects of the mating system on recombination

Another important consequence of inbreeding is to break up a species into different genetic 'islands' (or lineages), between which gene flow is limited. In panmictic sexual populations, chromosome pairs are assigned randomly to diploid individuals each generation, and so recombination occurs between sequences that are no more closely related than pairs randomly sampled from the population. Under self-fertilization, in contrast, closely related genomes recombine. This reduces the effective recombination rate (Nordborg 2000), since crossing-over between identical sequences has no genetic effect (i.e. does not generate recombinant progeny). In fully selfing (completely homozygous) populations, recombination will have no effect at all: individuals will behave genetically as if they were clonally reproducing. If the probability of crossing-over between two base pairs in a given generation is r, the quantity $R = 4N_e r$ (the 'scaled effective recombination rate') in an outcrossing population is reduced (Nordborg 2000) in a partially selfing population with the same N_e to:

$$R_s = R(1 - F) \tag{5}$$

This reduced effective recombination rate due to selfing has two main implications for genetic diversity. First, samples of sequences from inbreeding populations will behave like those from non-recombining populations, which, as just explained, often fall into two divergent lineages, with linkage disequilibrium between different polymorphic sites within the sample (Figure 4.3). Comparing the estimated ratio of the scaled mutation and recombination rates from a population with those from a related outcrossing population can provide an estimate of the 'long-term' selfing rate in a population, which determines patterns of diversity and linkage disequilibrium, as opposed to recent inbreeding which determines the population's current genotype frequencies (Nordborg 2000).

Secondly, selection at linked sites is more important in inbreeding than outcross-

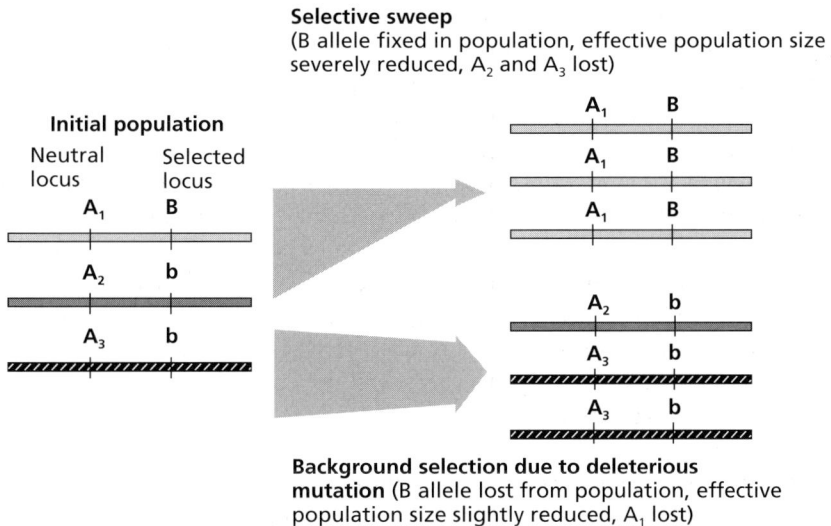

Figure 4.3 The effects of a selective sweep and of an ongoing process of background selection on a population with three variants at a neutral site or locus (A). The selected site or locus is assumed to be completely linked to the neutral site. (B) is either fixed (for the B variant in the case of a selective sweep), or (in the case of background selection) the B alleles are deleterious and are eliminated from the population. Either process reduces variation at the neutral site.

ing populations. Three categories of effects are important (see Table 4.2, page 84). Two forms of genetic hitch-hiking decrease variability (see Figure 4.3). In self-fertilizing populations, the selection and rapid fixation of any advantageous mutation will cause a 'selective sweep' at linked sites, reducing neutral diversity (Maynard Smith & Haigh 1974; Barton 1998). Similarly, the continuous occurrence of deleterious mutations reduces the effective population size of linked loci (background selection), because individuals carrying them have a lower than average chance of leaving progeny (Charlesworth *et al.* 1993). Both processes reduce the time to a sample's most recent common ancestor, and thus reduce genetic diversity in non-recombining regions of the genome (Begun & Aquadro 1992; Charlesworth *et al.* 1993; Stephan & Langley 1998).

In contrast, coalescence times may be increased at loci where a balanced polymorphism is maintained, and at closely linked sites (Strobeck 1983). This third process, balancing selection, maintains two or more classes of alleles at roughly constant frequencies over time (e.g. *S*-alleles in self-incompatible plants). Coalescence of sequences in different allelic classes is retarded because they must first enter the same allelic class by recombination (see Charlesworth *et al.* 1997). Consequently, variants linked to different alleles at a site with a balanced polymorphism have magnified coalescence times and increased expected diversity, similar to the divergence of geographically isolated alleles in different populations. This probably explains the high silent and replacement diversity at self-incompatibility loci (e.g. Richman *et al.* 1996). Peaks of sequence diversity may disclose loci with balanced polymorphisms. The expected width of the peak of increased polymorphism is proportional to $1/(Nr)$, so that in large outcrossing populations it may be very narrow and the effect difficult to observe (Charlesworth *et al.* 1997), but it could be detectable in selfing species. Selfing populations are unlikely to have balanced polymorphisms maintained by overdominance, because heterozygotes are rare (Kimura & Ohta 1971), but other forms of selection, such as frequency dependence, may be important.

Effects of population subdivision on diversity

Before discussing how inbreeding affects population structure, we must understand the effects of subdivision on patterns of genetic diversity. These are strongly affected by ecological processes. Geographic subdivision affects neutral diversity similarly to the 'genetic subdivision' due to balancing selection. If deme sizes remain constant, coalescence times of sequences sampled from different demes will be increased, because they must trace their ancestry back to the same deme, by migration, and then coalesce within it. Subdivision may thus increase a species' total diversity. Under simple models of population structure and migration, such as the island or stepping-stone models, the expected nucleotide diversity π_s is equal to the π value for a panmictic population with the same total number of breeding individuals (Strobeck 1987; Slatkin 1987). This is no longer true if some demes contribute more migrants than others (Nagylaki 2000). While simple population subdivision with non-directional migration does not lead to changes in the average value of π_s, restricted migration can lead to greatly increased differences between sequences from different demes, and to high π_t, while π_t approaches π_s with increases in migration.

'Source-sink' situations, for instance due to temporal size fluctuations, reduce species' effective size and genetic diversity, and both π_t and π_s approach the diversity of the 'source' (Nagylaki 2000; Whitlock & Barton 1997). Relative to subdivided populations with stable deme sizes, demographic fluctuations greatly reduce diversity, both within demes (Pannell & Charlesworth 1999) and species-wide (Slatkin 1977; Whitlock & Barton 1997). In addition, local extinctions and recolonizations may occur (metapopulation dynamics).

Again, these effects can be understood intuitively by considering coalescent times. Population turnover increases the rate at which sequences from different demes trace back to the same deme, and rapid deme growth after colonization greatly reduces coalescence times within demes. Both π_s and π_t are thus reduced (Pannell & Charlesworth 2000). The effect on F_{st} depends on the colonization model (Whitlock & McCauley 1990; Pannell & Charlesworth 2000). Under biologically reasonable assumptions, F_{st} is expected to increase if new demes are colonized by less than roughly twice the number of immigrants per generation into established populations. Most current results are based on the island model, but stepping-stone and other models have been studied with respect to total species-wide diversity (Maruyama & Kimura 1980), and F_{st} (Whitlock & Barton 1997). Recurrent population bottlenecks resulting from metapopulation dynamics should also reduce the frequencies of rare alleles within local populations (Luikart & Cornuet 1998).

Loci under balancing selection will tend to be less differentiated than neutral variants in spatially subdivided populations, because variants that immigrate into a population experience selection pressure to increase to the equilibrium frequency (Schierup *et al.* 2000a). Neutral polymorphic variants linked to such loci are affected similarly and have lower F_{st} than unlinked ones (Schierup *et al.* 2000b).

Interactions between the mating system and population structure

We have seen that, all else being equal, fully selfing populations are expected to maintain half the genetic diversity of outcrossing populations of the same census size, and that within-population diversity may be further reduced by selection in the genome, owing to selfers' low effective recombination rate. Low within-deme diversity, when species-wide diversity is high, implies high F_{st} values (Charlesworth *et al.* 1997; Nagylaki 1998). The evolution of self-fertilization from outcrossing also often coincides with the evolution of other reproductive and life-history traits that further affect genetic diversity. Simple contrasts between selfing and outcrossing species will thus typically confound several possible causes of differences (Table 4.2, Figure 4.4).

First, selfers tend to have reduced allocation to male function (Darwin 1876), both in terms of pollen production as well as investment in floral display and pollinator rewards (Lloyd 1965; Charlesworth & Charlesworth 1987). Interpopulation dispersal of pollen is thus likely to be lower in selfers than in outcrossers, with consequently reduced overall actual migration rates (increasing F_{st}). Secondly, population turnover in metapopulations probably reduces diversity even more in

Table 4.2 Factors that can affect neutral variability.

Factor	Effect on diversity
Inbreeding	Reduced N_e; maximum effect is to halve N_e under complete selfing
Selection at linked loci	
Selective sweeps	Hitch-hiking due to directional selection for new, advantageous mutations (decreased diversity in neighbourhood of selected locus; inbreeding expands the region)
Background selection	Hitch-hiking due to directional selection against new, deleterious mutations (inbreeding enhances the effect)
Linkage to balanced polymorphism	Increased diversity in neighbourhood of selected locus; inbreeding expands the region
Local selection	Affects neutral variants similarly to balanced polymorphism, if migration is free, but in subdivided populations increases differentiation between subpopulations

Effects of inbreeding

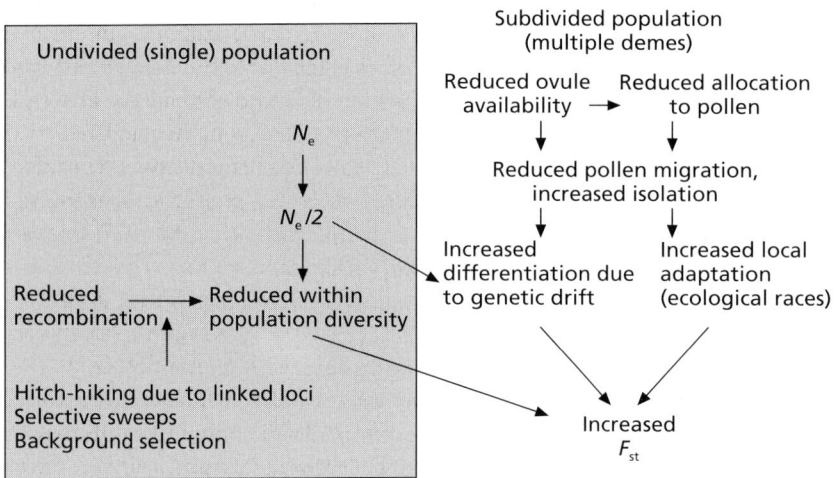

Figure 4.4 The effects of inbreeding on diversity in undivided and subdivided populations.

inbreeding than outcrossing species, because both factors reduce species' effective population sizes and increase identities by descent (Kaj & Lascoux 1999). Furthermore, selfers can colonize new habitat as single individuals (Baker 1955; Lloyd 1980). Thus, when self-fertilization has evolved from outcrossing through selection for reproductive assurance during recurrent local extinction and recolonization (e.g. Pannell & Barrett 1998), within-population diversity should be low, because demes will often be founded by single highly homozygous individuals. N_e for the entire species can thus be reduced to a value similar to just the number of demes, with greatly decreased species-wide diversity (Schoen *et al.* 1996). F_{st} may be high or low, depending on the relative rates of colonization and immigration (as just explained for outcrossing populations), although further theoretical work is still required to understand more fully how selfing and population turnover interact.

Finally, due to isolation, different selection pressures between localities may lead to locally adapted genotypes, especially in inbreeders (so that outbreeding depression may occur in selfers). Such adaptive differences cause greater differentiation at linked loci in selfers relative to outcrossers, because of selfers' reduced effective recombination rate (Charlesworth *et al.* 1997). Inbreeding populations may differ in allele frequencies at loci at considerable distances from locally selected genes, particularly when background selection reduces within-deme diversity. Such divergence will cause elevated F_{st} values, and linkage disequilibrium between loci due to the population differences (Charlesworth *et al.* 1997).

Patterns of genetic diversity in plants

Diversity within populations

A major prediction of the theory outlined above is that selfers should have reduced within-population diversity, due to reduced coalescent times caused by the direct effect of inbreeding on the effective population size, but also to the effects of hitchhiking, local adaptation and background selection. This can explain the low H_s for isozyme loci in selfers, mentioned above. Taking the data from the published literature as a whole, inbreeders have about half the diversity of outcrossers (Hamrick & Godt 1990), although a much larger effect is seen when populations of the same species with different outcrossing rates are compared (Rick *et al.* 1977; Barrett & Husband 1990), and in paired comparisons within genera, inbreeders' diversity is about a quarter that of outcrossers (see Table 4.1). Within British *Arabidopsis thaliana* populations (Abbott & Gomes 1988), isozyme H_s was considerably lower than the mean value of 0.11 for other annual plant species (Hamrick & Godt 1990). It is also lower than the mean value for other 'selfers' (0.07), which probably include a range of inbreeding coefficients. In the related self-incompatible outcrosser *A. lyrata*, H_s in four populations was much higher (between 0.23 and 0.40; van Treuren *et al.* 1997). Similarly, no microsatellite variation was found within *A. thaliana* populations (Todokoro *et al.* 1995), but *A. lyrata* populations are quite variable (van Treuren *et al.* 1997).

There are as yet few within-population DNA sequence data from plants, and most studies involve samples taken from widely different populations of the species and thus represent species-level diversity (π_t), which, as explained above, is expected to be less sensitive than π_s to breeding system differences. It is nevertheless already becoming clear that considerable sequence diversity may exist within populations. It is frequently easier to find genetic variants at the DNA level than isozyme variants (Table 4.3), probably reflecting high variability of silent sites and non-coding DNA.

Comparison of six orthologous genes in two pairs of closely related *Leavenworthia* species (Brassicaceae), found inbreeding to be associated with greatly lowered π_s

Table 4.3 Effect of selfing rates on *Adh* DNA sequence diversity within natural and cultivated plant populations (or, where noted, in the species as a whole). Diversity values shown are the published estimates of π (or the alternative estimate of $4N\mu$, θ; see Nei 1987 for cases where π values were not given and could not be calculated from data given). Silent variability is shown where this is available, but in some cases total diversity, regardless of site type, are the only data available.

| Loci studied | Species | Diversity per base (π or $\theta \times 10^3$) | | Source of data |
		Intron sites	Coding sequence silent or all sites	
Cross-fertilizing populations				
Adh1	*Zea mays**	20.9	49.3	Cummings & Clegg (1998)
	*Pennisetum glaucum**	2.43	6.66	Cummings & Clegg (1998)
	Leavenworthia stylosa	43.7	23.0	Liu *et al.* (1998)
	Arabidopsis lyrata	—	0.97 (all)	Savolainen *et al.* (2000)
Other loci				
teosinte-branched1	*Zea mays* ssp. *mays**	—	1.74	Wang *et al.* (1999)
teosinte-branched1	*Zea mays* ssp. *parviglumis**	—	4.62	Wang *et al.* (1999)
chalcone synthase-A	*Ipomoea purpurea**	—	2.10 (all)	Huttley *et al.* (1997)
	Leavenworthia stylosa	23.0 (2 loci)	30.2 (5 loci)	Liu (1998)
various	*Leavenworthia crassa* (outbreeding)	23.1 (5 loci)	16.2 (5 loci)	Liu (1998) (inbreeding)
CAULIFLOWER	*Brassica oleracea*	—	5.3 (all)	Purugganan *et al.* (2000)
Self-fertilizing populations				
Adh1	*Arabidopsis thaliana*	—	0.52 (all, incl. non-coding)	Bergelson *et al.* (1998)
	*Arabidopsis thaliana**	8.2	2.2	Miyashita *et al.* (1998)
	Leavenworthia uniflora	0	0	Liu *et al.* (1998)
	Leavenworthia torulosa	0	0	Liu *et al.* (1998)
	*Hordeum vulgare**	2.29	4.73	Cummings & Clegg (1998)
Other loci	*Arabidopsis thaliana**	—	0.29, 0.38 (all, 2 loci)	Bergelson *et al.* (1998)
	*Arabidopsis thaliana**	—	0.53–1.04 (all, 5 loci)	Purugganan & Suddith (1999)
	Leavenworthia crassa (inbreeding)	22.0 (3 loci)	5.90 (6 loci)	Liu (1998)

* Total species-wide diversity.

86

(Liu 1998; Liu *et al.* 1998, 1999). Because π_s is at most halved as a consequence of selfing alone, larger differences than this suggest the operation of some of the other factors discussed above. It is unclear whether such differences are general, as few comparisons yet exist between pairs of similar species, but data are starting to become available from *A. thaliana* and the related outcrosser *A. lyrata*. An RFLP study of three loci within 13 *A. thaliana* populations yielded polymorphism at <0.05% of sites ($\pi_s = 0.00029$–0.00052; Bergelson *et al.* 1998). These data include both coding sequences and flanking non-coding regions of the loci surveyed. One locus, *Adh*, has also been studied in *A. lyrata* (for a more constrained region of the *Adh* gene, which would be expected to have lower diversity): π_s values in three populations averaged about 0.00097, roughly twice the *A. thaliana* value (Savolainen *et al.* 2000). Unfortunately, sample sizes were small and the comparison is based on only one locus.

Given the high variances expected for pairwise diversity measures (see above), we must interpret these data with caution. Certainly, more data on within-population diversity are needed, ideally comparing orthologous loci in related species with contrasting breeding systems. It will also be valuable to report diversity patterns for silent sites separately from those that might be under selection, since the theories we have outlined apply to measures of neutral diversity. Table 4.3 summarizes the available comparisons between inbreeding and outcrossing populations, for silent variability where this is available. The overall picture is not yet clear, especially as much information is either from cultivars or from single species that offer no comparisons between different breeding systems.

Species-wide diversity

In outcrossers, within-population diversity and species-wide diversity are generally similar, both for isozymes (Hamrick & Godt 1990) and for nucleotide diversity (Liu *et al.* 1998, 1999), and genetic differentiation between populations is low (measured by $H_t - H_s$, $\pi_t - \pi_s$, or by F_{st}). This is expected, since such species will behave genetically as a panmictic unit unless gene flow among populations is extremely reduced (see above). In inbreeders, in contrast to the low (or entirely absent) within-population allozyme diversity, total species-wide diversity often differs little from that of outcrossers (H_t for selfers is 75% of that for outcrossers according to Hamrick and Godt (1990), or almost 60% in paired comparisons, see Table 4.1). These results are generally consistent with the theory for undivided populations, predicting species-wide diversity in selfers to be at least half that of outcrossers with the same population sizes, due to reduced N_e.

Table 4.1 includes several instances of higher diversity in inbreeders than outcrossers. A high degree of isolation between demes in a selfer could outweigh the reduction in N_e, and a selfing species could thus have higher neutral diversity than an outcrosser (Charlesworth *et al.* 1997). For *A. thaliana*, most current DNA sequence diversity data are from single plants from different 'ecotypes' (inbred strains each originating from a different natural population). These results thus estimate $\pi_t - \pi_s$, or π_t as there is almost no diversity within these highly selfing populations. Based on the few available data, this measure of diversity is similar to that in the outcrosser, *A. lyrata* (Bergelson *et al.* 1998; Savolainen *et al.* 2000), and for *Adh* the *A. thaliana* π_t (0.69%; Innan *et al.* 1996) is higher than that for *A. lyrata* (0.38%).

The theory used to interpret these comparisons assumes equivalent population sizes, which may often be untrue. Population sizes are notoriously difficult to estimate, especially for species with subdivided populations. Taking geographic range as a crude indicator of the total population size, the total allozyme diversity (H_t) in narrow endemics is, as expected, lower than that of more widespread species (Karron 1987; Hamrick & Godt 1996; Gitzendanner & Soltis 2000). The effect is found over a range of mating systems, but narrow endemic selfers had the lowest H_t values (Hamrick & Godt 1996), perhaps because H_t depends strongly on the number of populations in the species rather than on the numbers of individuals within populations (see above).

Other factors may also reduce diversity in selfing species. The evolution of selfing from outcrossing involves a selective sweep of a new genotype, eliminating genotypic diversity throughout the population, particularly if selfing evolves due to selection for reproductive assurance, and if selfing is complete (Schoen *et al.* 1996). The same is true for asexuality.

Structuring of genetic diversity between populations

The higher F_{st} or G_{st} of selfing than outcrossing species is a striking and repeatable obervation (Hamrick & Godt 1990; see Table 4.1). In the *A. thaliana* RFLP study, G_{st} was 0.83 (Bergelson *et al.* 1998), while in the related outcrosser *A. lyrata* the estimate from *Adh* sequences was zero (Savolainen *et al.* 2000). In *Leavenworthia crassa*, a species with both self-incompatible and highly selfing populations (Lloyd 1965), similar differences are clearly apparent (Liu 1998; Liu *et al.* 1999). This may largely be due to low within-population diversity in selfers (see above). Because $F_{st} = (\pi_t - \pi_s)/\pi_t$, decreased π_s necessarily increases apparent differentiation (Charlesworth *et al.* 1997; Charlesworth 1998; Nagylaki 1998).

However, the data also suggest a true increase in isolation in the inbreeders. In more than half of the comparisons of allozyme diversity in Table 4.1, $H_t - H_s$ (D_{st}) is higher in the inbreeders than their outcrossing relatives, and this increase is often a major reason for the inbreeders' high F_{st} values (Table 4.1). This is not expected if the inbreeders' low H_s were caused by extinction and recolonization, as this would also reduce H_t. It would be valuable to get more direct evidence on extinction and recolonization in the field for some of these species.

Linkage disequilibrium in inbreeders and outcrossing species

Linkage disequilibrium of closely linked polymorphic sites is clearly extensive in *A. thaliana*. Many loci show two distinct haplotypes, or divergent sequence types (Miyashita *et al.* 1998). This is expected in a highly selfing population, because recombination is infrequent so that the sequences evolve essentially by a coalescent process without recombination (see above). The isolation of populations of inbreeders should also lead to greater linkage disequilibrium than in outcrossers, even for loosely linked loci. Most *A. thaliana* sequence diversity data give evidence for within-locus recombination (Innan *et al.* 1996), even though the sequences were sampled from different populations, so isolation is clearly not extreme. Different loci should therefore show no strong associations unless they are tightly linked. This is empirically verified (Miyashita *et al.* 1999; Sharbel *et al.* 2000), although the scale at which linkage disequilibrium decays in *A. thaliana* is unknown. Again, comparisons with outcrossing species are not yet available, but data from outcrossing plant populations suggest much higher recombination rates per nucleotide than in *A. thaliana*, and extensive linkage disequilibrium is only occasionally found within loci, except when there is evidence for balancing selection (Liu 1998; Liu *et al.* 1998, 1999).

Asexual populations

Like inbreeding, apomictic reproduction has important population genetic consequences. Apomixis merely propagates the single genotype in which the mutation causing asexuality arose. However, in contrast to the effects of inbreeding, which leads to fully homozygous genotypes within a few generations, apomictic genotypes may be heterozygous at some or even many loci, particularly if they evolved from hybrids (see Gornall 1999). Strictly speaking, then, apomictic populations often contain genetic diversity. However, there are usually just a few multilocus genotypes, with diversity between genomes within individuals. Clonal diversity in apomicts (e.g. Ellstrand & Roose 1987) may be due to multiple independent origins of apomixis followed by seed migration, or to facultative asexuality with the possibility of gene flow through pollen, or apomixis may have evolved long ago and mutation has subsequently generated new diversity. It may become possible to estimate the age of apomicts, using DNA sequence differences, to distinguish between these alternatives, and test whether apomicts (and selfers) have shorter evolutionary lifespans than sexual species (Barrett *et al.* 1996; Schoen *et al.* 1997; Bena *et al.* 1998).

Conclusions

The theory outlined here can explain many of the patterns noted by H. G. Baker: the reduced genetic diversity in selfing species, both species-wide, and, particularly, within populations, and the high F_{st} values of selfers. Race differences have long been recognized in selfers, in studies of both morphology and isozymes. Baker (1953) suggested that, 'ecological races will tend to be more easily distinguished and will be more likely to correspond with the taxa of the systematist (who is particularly concerned with discrete morphological variation in making his classification) if the species tend towards inbreeding rather than outbreeding'.

As we have indicated, there are many possible reasons for the reduced diversity of inbreeders, ranging from the effects of selection on a more tightly linked genome in selfers than in outcrossers (Charlesworth *et al.* 1997), to the effects of differences in population demography and population structure between species with different breeding systems (Kaj & Lascoux 1999). There is clearly a need to investigate the causes of these patterns further. Most analyses of diversity patterns have sought broad-scale comparisons between patterns of diversity and empirically observed characteristics of populations, including breeding systems but also many other variables (e.g. Hamrick & Godt 1996). To broaden our understanding of empirical patterns in genetic diversity we now need to test aspects of the theory in suitable paired (or similar) comparisons.

More ecological studies are particularly needed to test whether extinction and recolonization alone are sufficient to explain low diversity in selfers. Severely reduced within-population diversity caused by extinction and recolonization will often be accompanied by low species-wide diversity, which affects all loci. If low diversity is caused by genetic hitch-hiking, on the other hand, only regions linked to the selected locus will be affected. Such differences can help to test whether highly differentiated population structure in selfers is caused by population demographic processes or requires selection at linked sites (Table 4.2). More data from reciprocal transplant experiments would also be useful to test for local selective differences (Bell 1996; Argyres & Schmitt 1991; Linhart & Grant 1996), including comparisons between selfers and outcrossers.

Clearly, breeding system differences are not the only factors affecting genetic diversity. For example, life-history differences, such as more or less extensive overlap of the generations, may sometimes explain differences in genetic differentiation between populations (Austerlitz et al. 2000), and actual population size differences will also affect genetic diversity. Different factors will thus often be confounded. This is, of course, a frequent difficulty with comparisons involving data from observational rather than experimental studies. It further emphasizes the need to increase the number of comparisons available, preferably focusing on comparisons that control each of the factors under inspection.

In trying to understand genetic diversity, we have focused on the effects of breeding systems because they are frequently neglected in the interpretation of variation. Given the agreed importance of genetic diversity in plant population biology, conservation biology, and systematics, this major cause of a number of clear patterns ought to be widely understood. The theoretical framework now available explains several of the major differences in diversity patterns between selfers and outcrossers, and we are now beginning to understand more quantitatively what our predecessors observed (e.g. Baker 1959):

> Whereas the outbreeding form presents a continuously variable complex of characters, the inbreeding one is liable to display a circumscribed set, not only by fewer alleles but with fewer combinations of those alleles which are present. The reaction of an unsuspecting taxonomist may well be a tendency to seize gratefully upon the sharply defined form as a species, separate from the polymorphic 'unsatisfactory' residue.

Summary

Plant mating systems are very varied, and, since H. G. Baker's pioneering work, it has been recognized that inbreeders commonly have lower genetic variability than outcrossing species, and this variability tends to be chiefly found between populations in inbreeding species rather than within them. Molecular markers, including allozymes and DNA-sequence differences, allow Baker's observations, and his ideas for explaining them, to be put in a precise quantitative form. Genetic markers are invaluable for quantifying populations' selfing rates, probably the most important breeding system parameter affecting genetic variability. Markers also allow us to quantify variability and partition it into within- and between-population diversity. Along with the increasingly quantitative nature of diversity data, advances in population genetics have provided a clear understanding of the causes of the differences observed between inbreeding and outcrossing species. Important departures from predictions for 'ideal' outcrossing populations can be due to self-fertilization and to population structure. Most current theory for structured populations deals with deme structure, based on non-spatially explicit island models (with or without extinction and recolonization), although in realistic situations gene flow is likely to decrease with distance between populations. Nevertheless, such models show that population structure can have important effects, which depend on the species' breeding system. Inbreeding accentuates isolation, so the effects of inbreeding on variability should be magnified in subdivided populations, relative to panmictic ones. Inbreeding also reduces effective recombination rates, so that diversity within inbreeding populations will be affected by genetic processes acting on other loci in the genome. We relate these theoretical ideas to empirical data from plant populations, and show that many observed differences in the structure of variability between inbreeding and outcrossing populations are now well understood.

Acknowledgements

D. Charlesworth is supported by a NERC Senior Research fellowship. J. R. Pannell gratefully acknowledges support from a British Ecological Society Early Careers Grant.

This paper is dedicated to the memory of the plant population biologist Herbert G. Baker, who died on July 2, 2001.

References

Abbott, R.J. & Gomes, M.F. (1988). Population genetic structure and outcrossing rate of *Arabidopsis thaliana* (L.) Heynh. *Heredity*, **62**, 411–418.

Argyres, A.Z. & Schmitt, J. (1991). Microgeographic genetic structure of morphological and life history traits in a natural population of *Impatiens capensis. Evolution*, **45**, 178–189.

Austerlitz, F., Mariette, S., Machon, N., Gouyon, P.-H. & Godelle, B. (2000). Effects of colonization processes on genetic diversity: differences between annual plants and tree species. *Genetics*, **154**, 1309–1321.

Awadalla, P. & Ritland, K. (1997). Microsatellite variation in Mimulus species of contrasting mating systems. *Molecular Biology and Evolution*, **14**, 1023–1034.

Baker, H.G. (1953). Race formation and reproductive method in flowering plants. *SEB Symposia*, **7**, 114–145.

Baker, H.G. (1955). Self-compatibility and establishment after 'long-distance' dispersal. *Evolution*, **9**, 347–348.

Baker, H.G. (1959). Reproductive methods as a factor in speciation in flowering plants. *Science*, **24**, 9–24.

Barrett, S.C.H. & Husband, B.C. (1990). Variation in outcrossing rates in *Eichhornia paniculata*: the role of demographic and reproductive factors. *Plant Species Biology*, **5**, 41–55.

Barrett, S.C.H., Harder, L.D. & Worley, A.C. (1996). Comparative biology of plant reproductive traits. *Philosophical Transactions of the Royal Society of London B*, **351**, 1272–1280.

Barton, N.H. (1998). The effect of hitch-hiking on neutral genealogies. *Genetical Research*, **72**, 123–133.

Begun, D.J. & Aquadro, C.F. (1992). Levels of naturally occurring DNA polymorphism correlate with recombination rates in *D. melanogaster*. *Nature*, **356**, 519–520.

Bell, G. (1996). *Selection. The Mechanism of Evolution*. Chapman & Hall, New York.

Bena, G., Prosperi, J.M., Lejeune, B. & Olivieri, I. (1998). Evolution of annual species of the genus *Medicago*: A molecular phylogenetic approach. *Molecular Phylogenetics and Evolution*, **9**, 552–559.

Bergelson, J., Stahl, E.A., Dudek, S. & Kreitman, M. (1998). Genetic variation within and among populations of *Arabidopsis thaliana*. *Genetics*, **148**, 1311–1323.

Brown, A.H.D. (1979). Enzyme polymorphism in plant populations. *Theoretical Population Biology*, **15**, 1–42.

Carr, D.E. & Fenster, C.B. (1993). Levels of genetic variation and covariation for *Mimulus* (Scrophulariaceae) floral traits. *Heredity*, **72**, 606–618.

Charlesworth, B. (1998). Measures of divergence between populations and the effect of forces that reduce variability. *Molecular Biology and Evolution*, **15**, 538–543.

Charlesworth, B., Morgan, M.T. & Charlesworth, D. (1993). The effect of deleterious mutations on neutral molecular variation. *Genetics*, **134**, 1289–1303.

Charlesworth, B., Nordborg, M. & Charlesworth, D. (1997). The effects of local selection, balanced polymorphism and background selection on equilibrium patterns of genetic diversity in subdivided populations. *Genetical Research*, **70**, 155–174.

Charlesworth, D. & Charlesworth, B. (1987). The effect of investment in attractive structures on allocation to male and female functions in plants. *Evolution*, **41**, 948–968.

Charlesworth, D. & Charlesworth, B. (1995). Quantitative genetics in plants: the effect of breeding system on genetic variability. *Evolution*, **49**, 911–920.

Cummings, M.P. & Clegg, M.T. (1998). Nucleotide sequence diversity at the alcohol dehydrogenase 1 locus in wild barley (*Hordeum vulgare* ssp. *spontaneum*): An evaluation of the background selection hypothesis. *Proceedings of the National Academy of Sciences of the USA*, **95**, 5637–5642.

Darwin, C.R. (1876). *The Effects of Cross and Self Fertilization in the Vegetable Kingdom*. John Murray, London.

Darwin, C.R. (1877). *The Different Forms of Flowers on Plants of the Same Species*. John Murray, London.

Dvorak, J., Luo, M.C. & Yang, Z.L. (1998). Restriction fragment length polymorphism and divergence in the genomic regions of high and low recombination in self-fertilizing and cross-fertilizing *Aegilops* species. *Genetics*, **148**, 423–434.

Ellstrand, N.C. & Levin, D.A. (1980). Recombination system and population structure in *Oenothera*. *Evolution*, **34**, 923–933.

Ellstrand, N.C. & Roose, M.L. (1987). Patterns of genotypic diversity in clonal plant-species. *American Journal of Botany*, **74**, 123–131.

Estoup, A. & Cornuet, J.M. (1999). Microsatellite evolution: inferences from population data. In: *Microsatellites. Evolution and Applications* (eds D.B. Goldstein & C. Schlötterer), pp. 50–65. Oxford University Press, Oxford.

Fenster, C.B. & Ritland, K. (1992). Chloroplast DNA and isozyme diversity in two *Mimulus* species (Scrophulariaceae) with contrasting mating systems. *American Journal of Botany*, **79**, 1440–1447.

Gitzendanner, M.A. & Soltis, P.S. (2000). Patterns of variation in rare and widespread plant congeners. *American Journal of Botany*, **87**, 783–792.

Gornall, R.J. (1999). Population genetic structure in agamospermous plants. In: *Molecular Systematics and Plant Evolution* (eds P.M. Hollingsworth,

R.M. Bateman & R.J. Gornall), pp. 118–138. Taylor & Francis, London.

Hamrick, J.L. & Godt, M.J. (1990). Allozyme diversity in plant species. In: *Plant Population Genetics, Breeding, and Genetic Resources* (eds A.H.D. Brown, M.T. Clegg, A.L. Kahler & B.S. Weir), pp. 43–63. Sinauer, Sunderland, MA.

Hamrick, J.L. & Godt, M.J.W. (1996). Effects of life history traits on genetic diversity in plant species. *Philosophical Transactions of the Royal Society of London B*, **351**, 1291–1298.

Holtsford, T.P. & Ellstrand, N.C. (1989). Variation in outcrossing rate and population genetic structure of *Clarkia tembloriensis* (Onagraceae). *Theoretical Applied Genetics*, **78**, 480–488.

Hudson, R.R. (1990). Gene genealogies and the coalescent process. *Oxford Surveys of Evolutionary Biology*, **7**, 1–45.

Husband, B.C. & Barrett, S.C.H. (1993). Multiple origins of self-fertilization in tristylous *Eichhornia paniculata* (Pontederiaceae): inferences from style morph and isozyme variation. *Journal of Evolutionary Biology*, **6**, 591–608.

Huttley, G.A., Durbin, M.L., Glover, D.E. & Clegg, M.T. (1997). Nucleotide polymorphism in the chalcone synthase-A locus and evolution of the chalcone synthase multigene family of common morning glory *Ipomoea purpurea*. *Molecular Ecology*, **6**, 549–558.

Innan, H., Tajima, F., Terauchi, R. & Miyashita, N.T. (1996). Intragenic recombination in the *Adh* locus region of the wild plant *Arabidopsis thaliana*. *Genetics*, **143**, 1761–1770.

Innan, H., Terauchi, R., Kahl, G. & Tajima, F. (1999). A method for estimating nucleotide diversity from AFLP data. *Genetics*, **151**, 1157–1164.

Kaj, I. & Lascoux, M. (1999). Probability of identity by descent in metapopulations. *Genetics*, **152**, 1217–1228.

Karron, J.D. (1987). A comparison of levels of genetic polymorphism and self-compatibility in geographically restricted and widespread plant congeners. *Evolutionary Ecology*, **1**, 47–58.

Kimura, M. (1983). *The Neutral Theory of Molecular Evolution*. Cambridge University Press, Cambridge, UK.

Kimura, M. & Ohta, T. (1971). *Theoretical Topics in Population Genetics*. Princeton University Press, Princeton, NJ.

Layton, C.R. & Ganders, F.R. (1984). The genetic consequences of contrasting breeding systems in *Plectritis* (Valerianaceae). *Evolution*, **38**, 1308–1325.

Levin, D.A. (1978). Genetic variation in annual *Phlox*: self-compatible vs. self-incompatible species. *Evolution*, **32**, 245–263.

Linhart, Y.B. & Grant, M.C. (1996). Evolutionary significance of local genetic differentiation in plants. *Annual Review of Ecology and Systematics*, **27**, 237–277.

Linhart, J. & Premoli, A.C. (1994). Genetic variation in central and disjunct populations of *Lilium parryi*. *Canadian Journal of Botany*, **72**, 79–85.

Liu, F. (1998). *Genetic diversity in Leavenworthia populations with different inbreeding levels. The Effect of Breeding System on the Level and Pattern of Molecular Variation in Plant populations*. PhD, University of Chicago.

Liu, F., Zhang, L. & Charlesworth, D. (1998). Genetic diversity in *Leavenworthia* populations with different inbreeding levels. *Proceedings of the Royal Society of London B*, **265**, 293–301.

Liu, F., Charlesworth, D. & Kreitman, M. (1999). The effect of mating system differences on nucleotide diversity at the phosphoglucose isomerase locus in the plant genus *Leavenworthia*. *Genetics*, **151**, 343–357.

Lloyd, D.G. (1965). Evolution of self-compatibility and racial differentiation in *Leavenworthia* (Cruciferae). *Contributions to the Gray Herbarium Harvard University*, **195**, 3–134.

Lloyd, D.G. (1979). Some reproductive factors affecting the selection of self-fertilization in plants. *American Naturalist*, **113**, 67–79.

Lloyd, D.G. (1980). Demographic factors and mating patterns in angiosperms. In: *Demography and Evolution in Plant Populations* (ed. O.T. Solbrig), pp. 209–224. Blackwell Scientific Publications, Oxford.

Loos, B.P. (1993). Allozyme variation within and between populations in *Lolium* (Poaceae). *Plant Systematics and Evolution*, **188**, 101–113.

Luikart, G. & Cornuet, J.M. (1998). Empirical evaluation of a test for identifying recently bottlenecked populations from allele frequency data. *Conservation Biology*, **12**, 228–237.

Lynch, M. & Milligan, B.G. (1994). Analysis of population genetic structure with RAPD markers. *Molecular Ecology*, **3**, 91–99.

Macnair, M.R., Macnair, V.E. & Martin, B.E. (1989). Adaptive speciation in *Mimulus*: an ecological comparison of *M. cupriphilus* with its presumed progenitor *M. guttatus*. *New Phytologist*, **112**, 269–279.

Maruyama, T. & Kimura, M. (1980). Genetic variability and effective population size when local extinction and recolonization of subpopulations are frequent. *Proceedings of the National Academy of Sciences of the USA*, **77**, 6710–6714.

Maynard Smith, J. & Haigh, J. (1974). The hitch-hiking effect of a favorable gene. *Genetical Research (Cambridge)*, **219**, 1114–1116.

Miller, J.C. & Tanksley, S.D. (1990). RFLP analysis of phylogenetic relationships and genetic variation in the genus *Lycopersicon*. *Theoretical Applied Genetics*, **80**, 437–448.

Miyashita, N.T., Kawabe, A. & Innan, H. (1999). DNA variation in the wild plant *Arabidopsis thaliana* revealed by amplified fragment length polymorphism analysis. *Genetics*, **152**, 1723–1731.

Miyashita, N.T., Kawabe, A., Innan, H. & Terauchi, R. (1998). Intra- and interspecific DNA variation and codon bias of the alcohol dehydrogenase (*Adh*) locus in *Arabis* and *Arabidopsis* species. *Molecular Biology and Evolution*, **15**, 1420–1429.

Nagylaki, T. (1998). Fixation indices in subdivided populations. *Genetics*, **148**, 1325–1332.

Nagylaki, T. (2000). Geographical invariance and the strong migration limit in subdivided populations. *Journal of Mathematical Biology*, **41**, 123–142.

Nei, M. (1987). *Molecular Evolutionary Genetics*. Columbia University Press, New York.

Nordborg, M. (1997). Structured coalescent processes on different time scales. *Genetics*, **146**, 1501–1514.

Nordborg, M. (2000). Linkage disequilibrium, gene trees and selfing: an ancestral recombination graph with partial self-fertilization. *Genetics*, **154**, 923–929.

Olmstead, R.G. (1990). Biological and historical factors influencing genetic diversity in the *Scutellaria angustifolia* complex (Labiatae): inference from morphology and molecular data. *Evolution*, **44**, 54–70.

Ouborg, N.J., Piquot, Y. & Groenendael, J.M.V. (1999). Population genetics, molecular markers and the study of dispersal in plants. *Journal of Ecology*, **87**, 551–568.

Pannell, J.R. & Barrett, S.C.H. (1998). Baker's law revisited: Reproductive assurance in a metapopulation. *Evolution*, **52**, 657–668.

Pannell, J.R. & Charlesworth, B. (1999). Neutral genetic diversity in a metapopulation with recurrent local extinction and recolonization. *Evolution*, **53**, 664–676.

Pannell, J.R. & Charlesworth, B. (2000). Effects of metapopulation processes on measures of genetic diversity. *Philosophical Transactions of the Royal Society, Series B*, **355**, 1851–1864.

Pollak, E. (1987). On the theory of partially inbreeding finite populations. I. Partial selfing. *Genetics*, **117**, 353–360.

Purugganan, M.D. & Suddith, J.I. (1998). Molecular population genetics of the *Arabidopsis* CAULIFLOWER regulatory gene: nonneutral evolution and naturally occurring variation in floral homeotic function. *Proceedings of the National Academy of Sciences of the USA*, **95**, 8130–8134.

Purugganan, M.D. & Suddith, J.I. (1999). Molecular population genetics of floral homeotic loci: departures from the equilibrium-neutral model at the APETALA3 and PISTILLATA genes of *Arabidopsis thaliana*. *Genetics*, **151**, 839–848.

Purugganan, M.D., Boyles, A.L. & Suddith, J.I. (2000). Variation and selection at the CAULIFLOWER floral homeotic gene accompanying the evolution of domesticated *Brassica oleracea*. *Genetics*, **155**, 855–862.

Richman, A.D., Uyenoyama, M.K. & Kohn, J.R. (1996). Allelic diversity and gene genealogy at the self-incompatibility locus in the Solanaceae. *Science*, **273**, 1212–1216.

Rick, C.M., Fobes, J.F. & Holle, M. (1977). Genetic variation in *Lycopersicon pimpinellifolium*: evidence of evolutionary change in mating systems. *Plant Systems and Evolution*, **127**, 139–170.

Savolainen, O., Langley, C.H., Lazzaro, B.P. & Freville, H. (2000). Contrasting patterns of nucleotide polymorphism at the alcohol dehydrogenase locus in the outcrossing *Arabidopsis lyrata* and the selfing *Arabidopsis thaliana*. *Molecular Biology and Evolution*, **17**, 645–655.

Schierup, M.H., Vekemans, X. & Charlesworth, D. (2000a). The effect of hitch-hiking on genes linked to a balanced polymorphism in a subdivided population. *Genetic Research (Cambridge),* **76**, 63–73.

Schierup, M.H., Vekemans, X. & Charlesworth, D. (2000b). The effect of subdivision on variation at multi-allelic loci under balancing selection. *Genetic Research (Cambridge),* **76**, 51–62.

Schoen, D.J. (1982). Genetic variation and the breeding system of *Gilia achilleifolia. Evolution,* **36**, 361–370.

Schoen, D.J. & Brown, A.H.D. (1991). Intraspecific variation in population gene diversity and effective population size correlates with the mating system in plants. *Proceeding of the National Academy of Sciences of the USA,* **88**, 4494–4497.

Schoen, D.J., Morgan, M.T. & Bataillon, T. (1996). How does self-pollination evolve? Inferences from floral ecology and molecular genetic variation. *Philosophical Transactions of the Royal Society of London B,* **351**, 1281–1290.

Schoen, D.J., L'Heureux, A.-M., Marsolais, J. & Johnston, M.O. (1997). Evolutionary history of the mating system in *Amsinckia* (Boraginaceae). *Evolution,* **51**, 1090–1099.

Sharbel, T.F., Haubold, B. & Mitchell-Olds, T. (2000). Genetic isolation by distance in *Arabidopsis thaliana:* biogeography and postglacial colonisation of Europe. *Molecular Ecology,* **9**, 2109–2118.

Slatkin, M. (1977). Gene flow and genetic drift in a species subject to local extinctions. *Theoretical Population Biology,* **12**, 253–262.

Slatkin, M. (1987). The average number of sites separating (DNA) sequences drawn from a subdivided population. *Theoretical Population Biology,* **32**, 42–49.

Stebbins, G.L. (1957). Self fertilization and population variation in the higher plants. *American Naturalist,* **91**, 337–354.

Stephan, W. & Langley, C.H. (1998). DNA polymorphism in *Lycopersicon* and crossing-over per physical length. *Genetics,* **150**, 1585–1593.

Strobeck, C. (1983). Expected linkage disequilibrium for a neutral locus linked to a chromosomal arrangement. *Genetics,* **103**, 545–555.

Strobeck, C. (1987). Average number of nucleotide differences in a sample from a single population: a test for population subdivision. *Genetics,* **117**, 149–153.

Szmidt, A.E., Wang, X.R. & Lu, M.Z. (1996). Empirical assessment of allozyme and RAPD variation in *Pinus sylvestris* (L) using haploid tissue analysis. *Heredity,* **76**, 412–420.

Tajima, F. (1993). Measurement of DNA polymorphism. In: *Mechanisms of Molecular Evolution* (eds N. Takahata & A.G. Clark), pp. 37–59. Sinauer, Sunderland, MA.

Tajima, F. (1989). Statistical method for testing the neutral mutation hypothesis. *Genetics,* **123**, 585–595.

Todokoro, S., Terauchi, R. & Kawano, S. (1995). Microsatellite polymorphisms in natural populations of *Arabidopsis thaliana* in Japan. *Japanese Journal of Genetics,* **70**, 543–554.

van Treuren, R., Kuittinen, H., Karkkainen, K., Baena-Gonzalez, E. & Savolainen, O. (1997). Evolution of microsatellites in *Arabis petraea* and *Arabis lyrata,* outcrossing relatives of *Arabidopsis thaliana. Molecular Biology and Evolution,* **14**, 220–229.

Wakeley, J. (2000). The effects of subdivision on the genetic divergence of populations and species. *Evolution,* **54**, 1092–1101.

Wang, R.-L., Stec, A., Hey, J., Doebley, J.F. & Lukens, L. (1999). The limits of selection during maize domestication. *Nature,* **398**, 236–239.

Whitlock, M.C. & Barton, N.H. (1997). The effective size of a subdivided population. *Genetics,* **146**, 427–441.

Whitlock, M.C. & McCauley, D.E. (1990). Some population genetic consequences of colony formation and extinction: genetic correlations within founding groups. *Evolution,* **44**, 1717–1724.

Wolff, K. (1991). Analysis of allozyme variability in three Plantago species and a comparison to morphological variability. *Theoretical and Applied Genetics,* **81**, 119–126.

Wyatt, R., Evans, E.A. & Sorenson, J.C. (1992). The evolution of self-pollination in granite outcrop species of *Arenaria* (Caryophyllaceae). VI. Electrophoretically detectable genetic variation. *Systematic Botany,* **17**, 201–209.

Zhivotovsky, L.A. (1999). Estimating population structure in diploids with multilocus dominant DNA markers. *Molecular Ecology,* **8**, 907–913.

Chapter 5

Spatially explicit studies on the ecology and genetics of population margins

J. Antonovics,* T. J. Newman† and B. J. Best‡

Introduction

There has been a growing realization that the numerical and genetic dynamics of populations can be profoundly different when individuals do not have equal probabilities of interacting with every other individual, but instead interact in a distance-dependent way with a local subset of the population (Kareiva 1994; Rhodes *et al.* 1996; Tilman & Kareiva 1997). Much of this realization has come from comparing the outcome of spatially explicit simulations with standard unstructured population models (so called 'mean-field' models; Levin & Pacala 1997). For example, the inclusion of spatial structure in host–parasitoid models not only increases the likelihood of long-term host–parasitoid coexistence, but it also leads to complex spatio-temporal patterns, even in homogeneous external environments (Comins *et al.* 1992). Such complexity occurs quite generally when these models are applied to other host–pathogen systems (J. Antonovics and M. P. Hassell, unpublished).

Most of such studies have focused on the emergence of patterns within large patches, and edges have been seen as 'nuisances' to be taken care of by algorithms that wrap, reflect or absorb at boundary regions. However, in nature, populations are characterized by real borders and edges. The processes and dynamics occurring at such margins have been shown to be critical for understanding limits to range extension (Antonovics 1976; Carter & Prince 1981; Watkinson 1985; Best 1990), responses to environmental change (Camill & Clark 1998), genetic divergence (Slatkin 1973; Endler 1977; Mallet & Barton 1989) and speciation (Caisse & Antonovics 1978).

Nevertheless, processes at margins and zones of contact have generally been described in terms of the behaviour of 'one-dimensional', transect-like, mean-field models. These studies have used either 'connected lattice' models in one dimension (e.g. 'stepping-stone' models in population genetics), or partial differential equations describing spatial change in abundance or gene frequency over one or two dimensions (Fisher 1937; Turchin 1998). While there have been a number of spatially explicit studies of dispersal from point sources (Turchin 1998) and the spread of in-

* *Department of Biology, University of Virginia, Charlottesville, VA 22904-4328, USA.*

† *Departments of Biology and Physics, University of Virginia, Charlottesville, VA 22904-4328, USA.*

‡ *Department of Botany, Duke University, Durham, NC 27708, USA. Current address: Department of Economics, University of Washington, Seattle, WA 98195-3330, USA.*

vading populations into 'empty' habitat (Hengeveld 1989; Lewis 1997), there have
been almost no studies of spatially explicit processes in marginal populations. In this
chapter we will use spatially explicit, individual-based models to study the patterns
and dynamics that develop in population margins as they expand into regions that
become more and more unsuitable (or perhaps as they retreat in response to environmental change). We begin by considering purely ecological models where there is
no genetic variation in the population and only environmentally imposed variation
in demographic parameters. Then, we examine colonization of a novel habitat,
where genetic change accompanies the range expansion of a population.

Demographic limits to population spread

The basic model
To investigate the dynamics of populations at the edges of their range, we use a spatially explicit model of a distributional limit caused by an environmental gradient
which imposes an increasing death rate in one dimension. We use a two-dimensional
square lattice, where each cell represents a site that can be potentially occupied by an
individual plant. Each individual (with some probability) can then die or reproduce,
and the ensuing offspring are dispersed according to a normal distribution around
the centre point of the parent (which itself is immobile). Dispersal involves placing
an individual into an unoccupied cell using a smooth bivariate Gaussian weighting
function so as to minimize the anisotropic influence of the underlying lattice. We
impose exclusion dynamics, meaning that each cell of the lattice can at most be occupied by a single individual. This represents density dependence at the smallest
scale. We model an environmental gradient as a sigmoid increase in individual mortality rate in one direction, perpendicular to a boundary. We use the hyperbolic tan-
gent function to describe this mortality rate $\mu(x)$, where x measures the distance
along the gradient from the mid-point of the gradient. If reproduction exceeds mortality, and the gradient is sufficiently steep, a margin to the population is established
at some position on the gradient. We use serial updating (representing perennials),
and use a $n \times n$ lattice with wrap-around edges perpendicular to the margin. All runs
are started by allowing invasion of a few individuals in the region of the gradient
where population growth is positive (i.e. in the figures, the gradient of increasing
mortality runs from bottom to top). Simulations are run until there is visually an
overall steady state with only random fluctuations (i.e. the population has reached
an ergodic state).

The influence of space on species margins determined by
an environmental gradient
The distribution pattern of the individuals at the population edges is extremely different from that obtained by simple diffusion theory with only dispersal (Figure
5.1). In the former, biologically more realistic case, the edges are much 'rougher' because clusters of individuals arising by chance at the margins produce invading

(a)

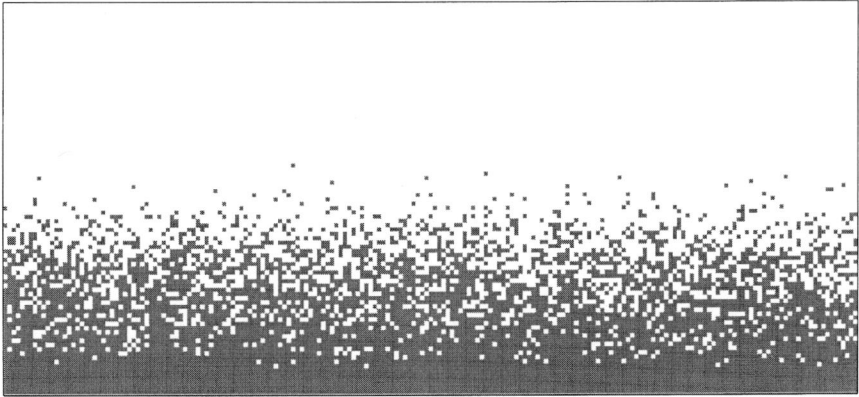

(b)

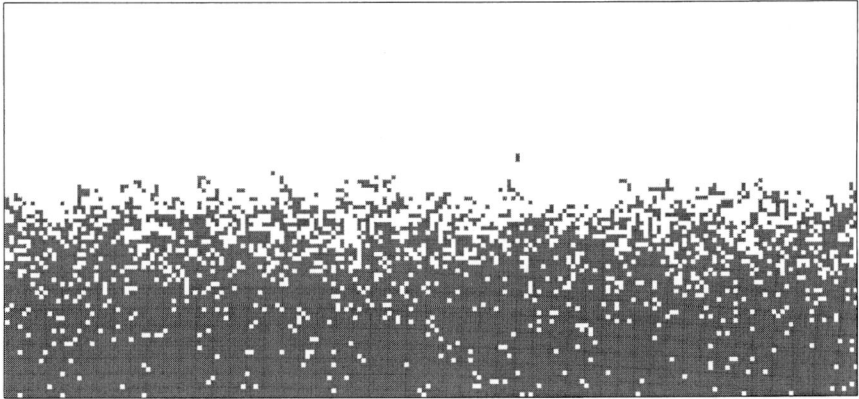

Figure 5.1 Typical spatial structure of a population margin where there is either, (a) movement of adults (= diffusion) but no births, or (b) no movement of adults, but dispersal of newly born individuals. In both cases mortality rate increases smoothly towards the top of the figure, but is uniform in the horizontal direction. Note the rough edge and flame-like extensions of the population margin boundary in (b)

flame-like phalanxes maintained by high local recruitment rates. We have also found from our simulation that the mean-field estimate of the steady-state density profile may substantially overestimate the ability of the population margin to advance along the gradient, depending on the steepness of the gradient relative to the dispersal distance (Figure 5.2). Note that the agreement is worse for one dimension than for two dimensions. To estimate the expected population profile we invoke a spatially implicit mean-field model which includes density-dependent reproduction and mortality. Denoting the density of the population as $\rho(x,t)$, the birth term is $r\rho(1 - \rho)$ and the death term is $-\mu(x)\rho$ (where we have scaled the density to its carrying capacity). Equating these two in the steady-state yields $\rho(x) = 1 - \mu(x)/r$.

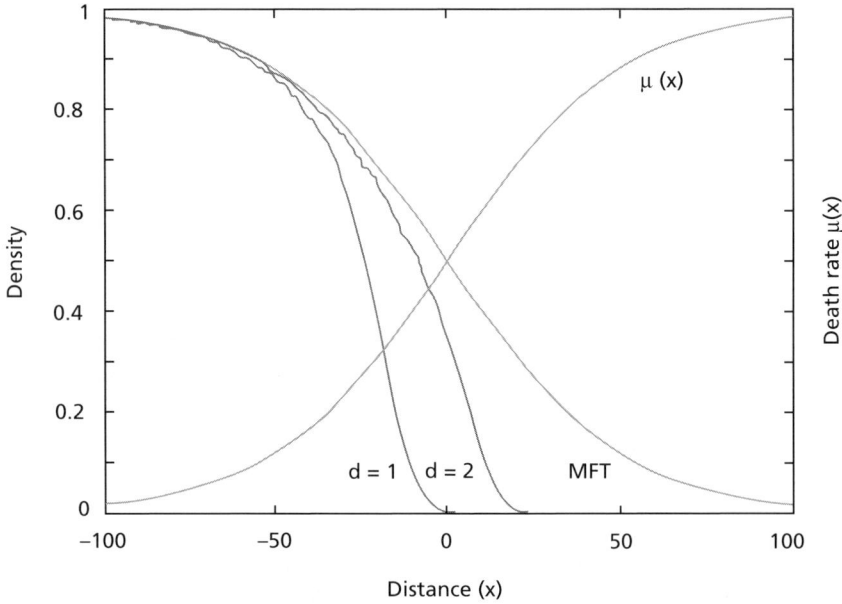

Figure 5.2 Density profiles as a function of distance along the environmental gradient (represented by increasing mortality rate, μ) for a marginal population with dispersal of newborns, but no adult movement (case b, Figure 5.1). Density profiles are plotted for the cases of one dimension ($d = 1$, a linear habitat) and two dimensions ($d = 2$), compared to expectations from mean-field theory (MFT)

This discrepancy may be understood heuristically as follows. As a cluster of individuals climbs the environmental gradient, its size fluctuates through birth and death processes. In a mean-field description, the individuals are described by a density which, however small, never vanishes. However, in our simulations, as in the real world of discrete organisms, the population is composed of clusters of a finite number of individuals. As a cluster extends into the margin it often becomes reduced to a single organism. This is where discrete effects are crucial. If this single organism dies, the entire cluster dies as there can be no subsequent recovery. It is the finite time extinction of clusters due to large fluctuations that is lost in mean-field theories.

We have also contrasted instantaneous and cumulative population distributions. The former is a snapshot of the population at a given time, while the latter is a time-integrated distribution such as would be obtained by sampling specimens over a period of time (as occurs when collections are accrued by museums and herbaria). We find that the cumulative distributions are (as expected) broader than the instantaneous distributions. But the edges of such cumulative distributions are not smoother. Instead, they are much rougher and have a great deal of spatial and temporal structure that seems to bear no consistent relationship to the instantaneous distributions (Figure 5.3). This is because the cumulative distribution incorporates

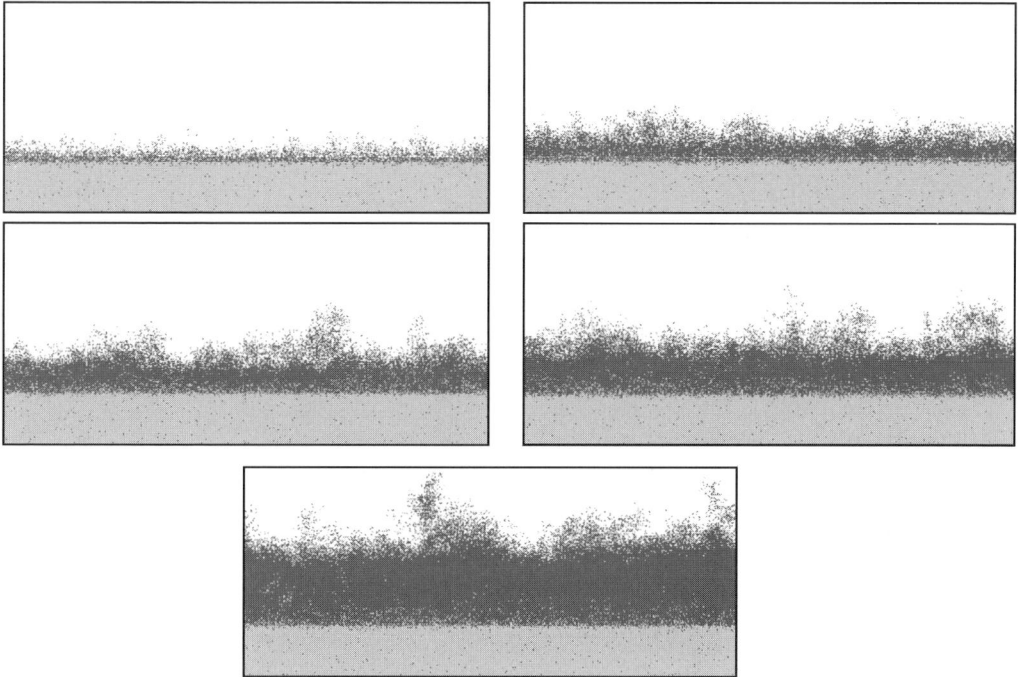

Figure 5.3 Time sequence (left to right, top to bottom) of typical distribution patterns at a population boundary as seen from a single generation census (grey) and as seen from a cumulative census (dark) obtained when all occupied sites are noted over successive periods of several hundred time steps.

rare events which include individuals at extreme points along the gradient. As time proceeds, the cumulative distribution changes increasingly slowly because increasingly extreme events are required to effect any change. However, no matter how long one observes the system, the cumulative distribution remains spatially inhomogeneous.

On viewing the cumulative distribution one would be tempted to infer much about the underlying environmental gradient, especially regarding its position and shape. However, one's inferences would be false, as the real demographic gradient lies hidden far behind the edge of the cumulative distribution and is much smoother. In our own studies, we have recorded similar differences between distributions obtained by a one-time intensive sampling vs. that obtained from cumulative sampling as occurs, for example, with collections of herbarium specimens (Figure 5.4).

Populations which are colonizing a new area across a demographic barrier
The study of a demographic barrier is a natural extension to our study of an environmental gradient. It is also of prime ecological significance in questions of species colonization. We represent this barrier by a bell-shaped (normally distributed)

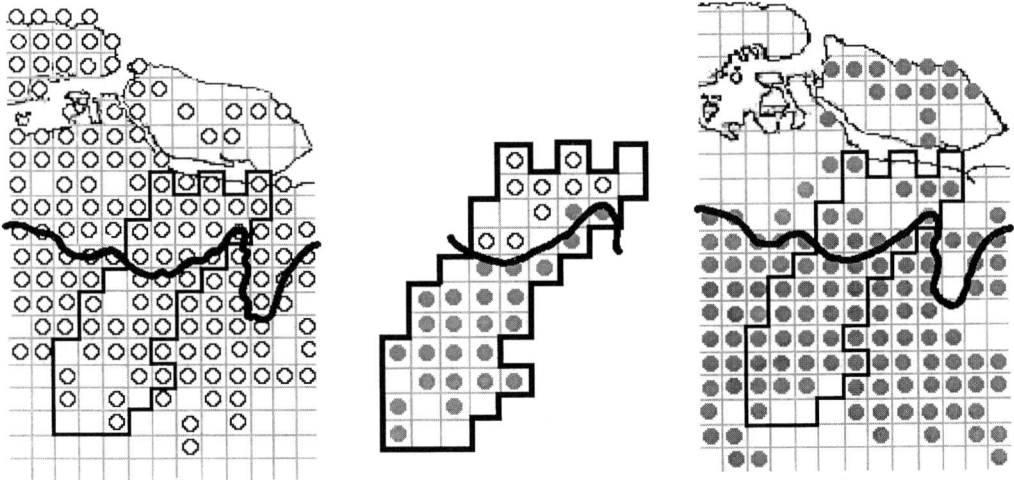

Figure 5.4 Distribution of *Silene alba* (left, open circles) and *Silene dioica* (right, solid circles) in north-central Kent, England, as given by the cumulative county distribution maps (Philp 1982), and distributions recorded in a 1992 census of part of the same region (centre figure). Data are from J. Antonovics and W. E. Kunin, unpublished results. Each square is 2 × 2 km. The dark line shows the approximate position of the fall line between the North Downs and the lowland, arable region of the Thames Valley. Note the relatively sharp boundary seen in the 'instantaneous' census, and the broad overlap seen in the cumulative census.

region of increased mortality centred across the lattice in one direction. So long as the demographic barrier is not too small (in which case it is easily surmounted by an advancing population), we can expect that colonization will occur via individuals in the advancing front of the population distribution. However, as we saw in the previous section, the position of this leading edge is strongly suppressed in the spatially explicit model as compared to the predictions of mean-field theory. Thus, we expect colonization to be more difficult when spatial stochastic effects are correctly accounted for! As pointed out already, the overall effect of fluctuations at a margin appear to be antidiffusional due to the finite time extinction of small outlying clusters. It is very interesting to see that even when outlying clusters diffuse over the peak of the barrier, colonization does not necessarily occur. Although over the barrier, the cluster is still in a very unfavourable region and its most likely fate is to shrink to zero before making it far enough into the favourable habitat to begin prospering.

The colonization time scale depends on the model parameters. For example, increasing the reproduction rate enables clusters to live longer and thus have a higher probability of descending far enough down the far side of the barrier to firmly seed the colonization event. One can view this process as that of condensation, in which a bubble of sufficient size is required to initiate the condensation process. Such a critical nucleation size is a well-known concept in the field of phase transitions in

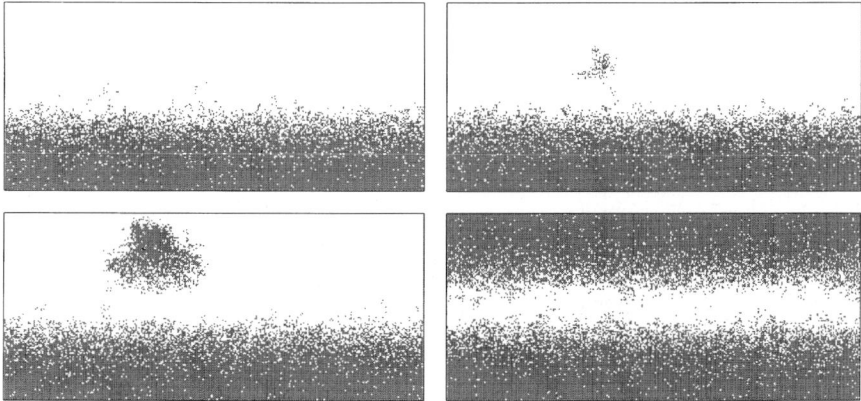

Figure 5.5 Time sequence (left to right, top to bottom) of colonization over a demographic barrier. The demographic barrier is a Gaussian-shaped region of increased mortality (not shown) across the centre of the region being colonized. Top left, outlying clusters at barrier; top right, successful cluster seeding new habitat; bottom left, growth of new population; and bottom right, complete population on both sides of barrier.

liquid–gas systems (Gunton *et al.* 1983). When colonization does occur it is often due to a single cluster, with the spread of the new population starting at a single longitudinal point in the virgin habitat (Figure 5.5).

One can then ask about the ensuing patterning of population spread along and further down the far side of the demographic barrier. Our initial results show that spread into the favourable habitat is not necessarily as an ever-widening wedge/ triangle as might be expected intuitively, but that it is more often relatively amorphous. After colonization has occurred, the instantaneous distribution reflects two thriving populations separated by a very sparsely populated region (the barrier). As might be expected, the cumulative distribution comes to show no features whatsoever, because traversal events back and forth across the barrier eradicate any signal of the barrier.

Populations whose margins are determined by the changes in abundance of another species: host–pathogen interactions at a species boundary

We have seen that populations at margins have complicated spatial patterning and are dominated by spatiotemporal fluctuations. It is therefore extremely interesting to examine the process of infection of such a population by an invading species, for example a pathogen. It is intuitively appealing to imagine that marginal populations, although fragile, may actually be refugia from pathogen spread. An example of this is the persistence of healthy stands of American chestnut in marginal areas of the species distribution, following the spread of chestnut blight.

In our model, we establish the host species on an environmental gradient, and after a steady state has been reached we introduce a pathogen into the bulk of the host

(a)

(b)

(c)

(d)

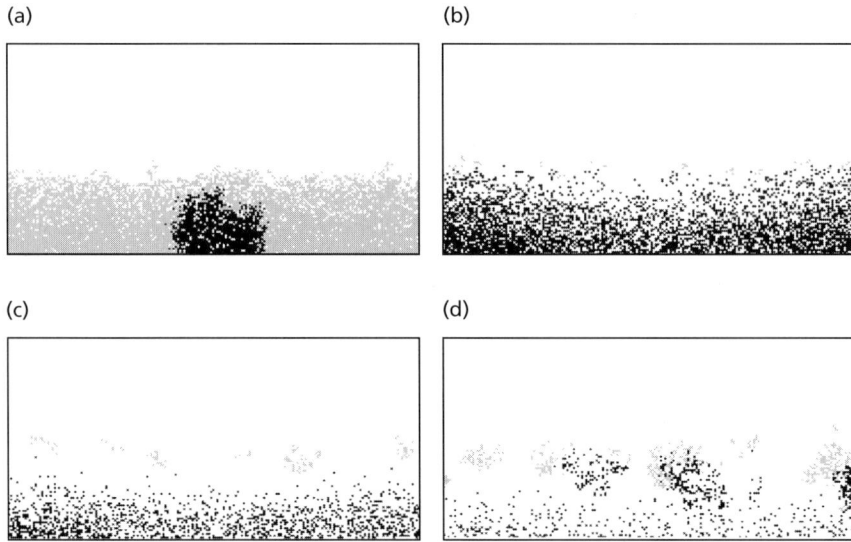

Figure 5.6 Time sequence (left to right, top to bottom) of pathogen spread into a marginal population. The healthy host individuals are represented by grey squares and the diseased hosts by black squares. Panels are: (a) early stages of pathogen spread; (b) a few individuals in the margin escape infection; (c) retreat of infected individuals and regrowth of healthy population; and (d) subsequent reinfection of advancing healthy population. Disease transmission is a Gaussian function around infected individuals, there is no recovery, and the disease increases host mortality rate.

population. The pathogen spreads, sterilizes the host, and slightly increases its mortality (cf. *Silene alba* and *Microbotryum violaceum*; Alexander & Antonovics (1988), Alexander *et al.* (1996)).

In many cases the population furthest up the gradient does act as a refuge, at least in the early stages of the pathogen spread (Figure 5.6). We then have a strip of healthy individuals high up on the gradient and a sea of infected individuals lower down which gradually die off. Because of the increased mortality further up the gradient, the infected individuals higher up die off faster leaving an empty band between the healthy marginal population and the infected central population. The healthy individuals then exploit this empty habitat and begin reclaiming the gradient lower down. However, they inevitably make contact with long-lived infected individuals in the bulk which reinfect them sending a wave of infection back up the gradient, and so the process repeats itself (Figure 5.6).

It is important to stress that this process of infection, recovery and reinfection (which is accompanied by advancement and recession of the healthy population) is dominated by rare events at the population margin. Thus, the cycles are not periodic, but seemingly random, in both size and duration. Such cycles are not seen in the 'body' of the population. In this sense, the mass infection events resemble earthquakes and avalanches, which are events on a wide range of spatiotemporal scales.

Such systems have attracted a lot of interest over the past 10 years under the heading 'self-organized criticality' (Bak 1994).

Genetic limits to population spread

Most natural plant populations have distinct boundaries, but it is often unclear why the boundaries occur precisely where they do. In the previous section we tacitly assumed that population limits were due to some physiological tolerance, perhaps modulated by the effects of competition, disease and predation (Harper 1977). These explanations are mechanistic, making the assumption that the observed tolerances or competitive abilities are fixed. However, physiological limits are under selection, and should continue to evolve. Viewed in this light, our explanations for the species distributions we observe must include factors which limit the rate and extent of evolutionary change (Chapter 17; Antonovics 1968, 1976).

On a large geographic scale, ecotypic variation allows individuals of a species to occupy a wide range of environmental conditions (Turesson 1922; Clausen *et al.* 1948). Similarly, the adaptation of individuals within a population to local conditions should lead to the exploitation of novel resources (Wilson & Turelli 1986) or the colonization of adjacent habitats and microsites (Ludwig 1950; Levene 1953; Antonovics *et al.* 1971; Antonovics 1990).

Genetic differentiation and expansion of a population into a different marginal habitat can be reduced to a three part process.

1 Production of 'preadapted' genotypes. This may occur by mutation and/or recombination. This may be limited by finite population size since rare mutations and gene combinations may be effectively unachievable.

2 Dispersal. High seed dispersal will increase the frequency with which a neighbouring habitat is sampled by offspring from the original habitat.

3 Gene flow through seed and pollen dispersal. This will determine the degree which the offspring of any new colonists resemble their parents.

4 Population growth within the newly exploited habitat. This will affect the availability of colonists and the level of effective gene flow. Gene flow will depend on the number of individuals in the new habitat relative to the number of individuals in the source population. Because this ratio will change as colonization proceeds, population size should be included explicitly in any model of the invasion of new habitats.

Population growth itself will depend on several conflicting factors.

1 Continued immigration from the source population by seed may augment population size. Immigration by pollen dispersal may also result in additional fertilizations if, for example, the colonizing population is sparse.

2 Gene flow either by seed or pollen may serve to limit adaptation to the new habitat. Alternatively, it may reduce the effects of inbreeding that might be occurring in the individuals at the margins.

3 Stochastic spatial processes may allow immigration where in deterministic models such immigration may be impossible. The effects may be genetical (e.g. chance increase and fixation of chromosome variants that are disadvantageous in the heterozygous condition) or they may be ecological (e.g. spatial clumping of individuals in one region may minimize gene flow into that clump).

Numerous empirical and theoretical studies have now demonstrated localized differentiation for adaptive characters and determined the conditions that are likely to promote or retard such adaptation. Several studies (see Chapter 17) have recently modelled gene flow and selection where the number of surviving individuals is a direct function of localized genetic differentiation along an environmental gradient. However, these studies have not considered finite populations from an individually based context, where chance processes may be particularly important at boundaries. We therefore simulated conditions at the margin of a finite, two-dimensional plant population to test the general hypothesis that population boundaries may be determined by ecological factors which limit local adaptation to novel conditions, rather than by an absolute lack of genetic variation for the character(s) determining distribution.

The model

A source population was placed in one habitat, next to an unexploited habitat. The source population held rare alleles at three loci, and these alleles had low fitness in the source habitat but very high fitness in the novel environment. The actual ability of the source population to colonize the adjacent, novel habitat was monitored for varying seed and pollen dispersal distances under different spatial patterns of natural selection. Several specific questions were addressed in the context of whether the source population colonizes the unexploited habitat. In particular we asked: How long does the colonization process take? What are the specific effects of the patterns of natural selection and seed and pollen dispersal distances on population expansion? How are genetic differentiation and population growth in the new habitat related?

A two-dimensional area was defined with a grid of cells arranged on 50 rows and 100 columns. A maximum of seven different habitat types, numbered 0 to 6, were also defined to represent different selection regimes. Each point on the grid could be assigned a different habitat type, and any seed landing at that point would be subject to the corresponding selection regime. Thus, any spatial pattern of natural selection could be imposed by assigning groups of points the same number in the desired pattern.

Selection acted on phenotypes determined by three unlinked loci in the simplest possible model for a quantitative trait. Each locus had two alleles (0 or 1) with completely additive effects, so phenotypic values ranged from 0 (homozygous for 0) to 6 (homozygous for 1). Each phenotype had its maximum fitness in the habitat defined by the same number, and its fitness decreased in habitats defined by smaller or larger numbers according to a normal density function with a standard deviation of one habitat (Figure 5.7). Thus, the 0 allele was favoured in habitats with low numbers, the 1 allele was advantageous in habitats defined by high numbers. Relative fitnesses were translated into absolute fitnesses by multiplying by the maximum possible seed production for an individual. If the absolute fitness (seed number per individual)

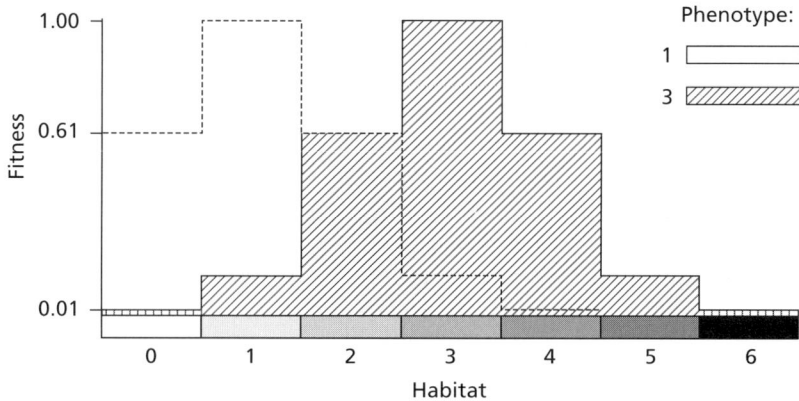

Figure 5.7 Relative fitnesses of two representative phenotypes, 1 and 3, in six habitats of differing quality. Note that each phenotype has the highest fitness in its correspondingly numbered habitat.

was less than 1, a fitness of 0 was assigned to the individual. We assumed no pollen limitation to seed set.

Population dynamics were determined by the occupancy of individual cells or sites on the grid, but only 10% of the points on the grid were designated at random as safe sites (i.e. occupiable). The maximum possible population size was 500, but actual sizes were less if safe sites were not colonized.

Each generation, the following series of events occurred. Maternal parents were mated to pollen parents, randomly one seed at a time. Gametes were sampled randomly from the maternal and paternal genotypes in each mating event, and no selfing was allowed. Seeds were dispersed individually onto the grid. At sites in which more than one seed landed, the surviving occupant was chosen at random. Seeds became the new adults, and their fitnesses (seed production) were calculated as above.

Dispersal of pollen and seed followed a normal distribution. For seeds, the site to which a seed was dispersed was selected randomly from among all sites the chosen distance away from the maternal parent. For pollen dispersal, a pollen parent was selected randomly for each mating event from among all plants the chosen distance away from the maternal parent. The average dispersal distances used (measured in rows and columns) were low (s.d. = 2), and high (s.d. = 10). Seeds that were dispersed to unsafe sites on the grid, or to sites off the grid, were lost (absorbing boundaries).

Three spatial patterns of natural selection were imposed. Each used habitat 0 as the native habitat and habitat 5 as the new habitat to be colonized, but the patterns differed at the transition zone between the two habitats (Figure 5.8). The 'sharp' pattern of selection had no intermediate habitat between habitats 0 and 5, the 'stepped' pattern of selection had a region of habitat 2 between habitats 0 and 5, and the

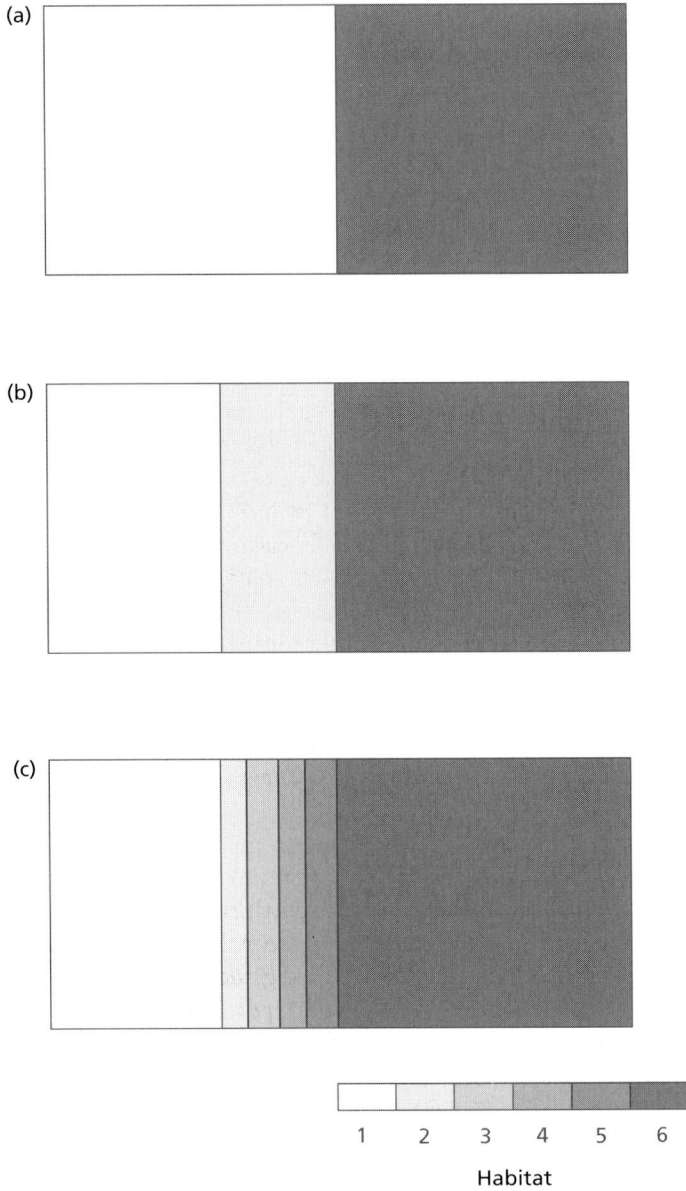

Figure 5.8 Three types of habitat distribution at boundary regions: (a) sharp; (b) stepped; (c) gradual.

'graded' pattern of selection had sequentially arranged sections of habitats 1 to 4 between habitats 0 and 5.

Each run started with a source population of 125 individuals in habitat 0. Most of these individuals were phenotype 0, but randomly chosen individuals were assigned

Table 5.1 Colonization success and average time to start of colonization for a population adapting to an adjacent marginal habitat characterized by three spatial patterns of selection at the boundary, and with different levels of seed and pollen dispersal (see text). Based on 50 simulation runs.

	Spatial pattern of selection	Seed dispersal low		Seed dispersal high	
		Pollen low	Pollen high	Pollen low	Pollen high
Percentage colonization	Sharp	0 (–)	0 (–)	32 (45)	8 (52)
success and time to	Stepped	16 (29)	0 (–)	100 (4)	100 (4)
colonization	Graded	82 (45)	0 (–)	100 (14)	100 (15)
(generations)					

a single 1 allele (and therefore were phenotype 1) such that the initial frequency of the 1 allele was 0.05 at each locus. The frequency of the 1 allele at any locus was not allowed to fall below 0.05 because preliminary simulations had shown that without resetting gene frequency, rare alleles were frequently lost at one locus.

The following information was obtained for each run:

1 colonization success—the new habitat was considered colonized when it held more than 50 individuals;

2 time to start of colonization defined as the generation at which the novel environment was continuously occupied by at least one individual;

3 distributions of gene frequency and plant density across the habitat boundary. At five-generation intervals, average gene frequency and population size were calculated for regions of each habitat defined by adjacent five-column sections of the grid.

Results

Colonization success

Invasion of a new habitat was much more likely when seed dispersal was high, and when intermediate habitats were included between the source population and the novel environment (Table 5.1). The stepped and graded spatial patterns of selection had similar effects on colonization success, except when seed and pollen dispersal distances were both low. In this case, individuals were more likely to colonize the new area when the change in selection was graded than when it was stepped. The average distance travelled by pollen had little effect on colonization success when seed dispersal was high, but when seed dispersal was low, long-distance pollen dispersal prevented population expansion under all three patterns of natural selection (Table 5.1). A supplemental run of 1000 generations with graded selection, and with low seed and high pollen dispersal distances showed successful colonization at generation 975, indicating that colonization under such conditions is not impossible, but rather highly improbable.

Time to start of colonization

In runs with no selection, it always took 10 generations for seeds to colonize the new habitat when seed dispersal was low, and one generation when seed dispersal was

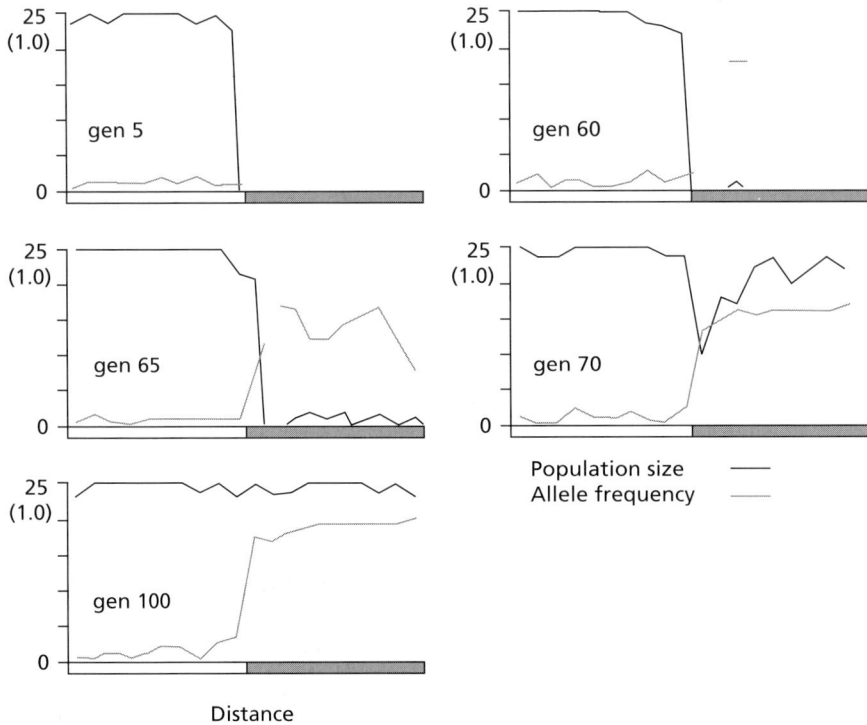

Figure 5.9 Plant density (solid line) and gene frequency (grey line) of a population colonizing and simultaneously adapting to a new habitat across an abrupt gradient, and where there is low pollen dispersal but high seed dispersal.

high. When selection was applied and colonization was successful, the generation in which colonization occurred was highly variable among replicates. Despite this variability, a trend towards earlier colonization can be seen under stepped selection as compared to graded selection (Table 5.1).

In many runs, the novel habitat was continuously inhabited from an early generation (often as early as generation 15 or 20), but was not colonized by the criteria used here, because the population of colonists never grew beyond about 10 individuals. This situation was seen frequently in the stepped pattern of selection, when seed- and pollen-dispersal distances were both low.

Spatial distribution
When seed dispersal was high, the temporal changes in the distribution of individuals during a successful colonization event were similar for all spatial patterns of selection and all pollen dispersal distances (Figures 5.9 and 5.10). Within approximately 10 generations, the density rose so that more than 90% of all safe sites were occupied. A cline in gene frequency was quickly established.

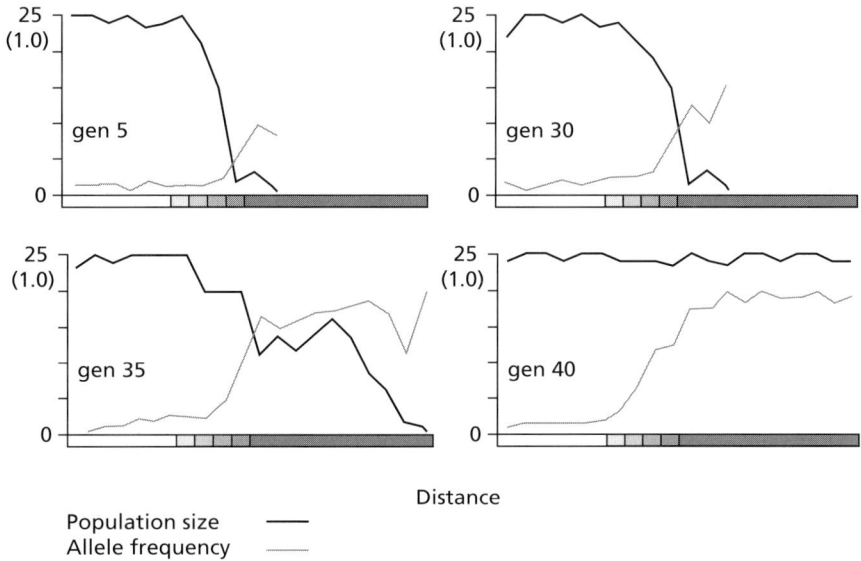

Figure 5.10 Plant density (solid line) and gene frequency (grey line) of a population colonizing and simultaneously adapting to a new habitat across a gradual habitat gradient, and where there is low pollen dispersal but high seed dispersal.

With a low seed-dispersal distance, the changes in population distribution depended on the spatial pattern of selection and on the pollen-dispersal distance. Under the sharp pattern of selection, no local adaptation occurred regardless of the pollen-dispersal distance, and the population ended abruptly at the edge of the novel habitat. An occasional colonist, weakly genetically adapted, extended the population boundary beyond the source habitat, but complete colonization never followed. When the selection pattern included intermediate habitats, the low and high pollen-dispersal distances gave different results. The low pollen-dispersal distance led to considerable local differentiation in the intermediate habitat, even when colonization was unsuccessful. When colonization occurred, the population advanced slowly at its margin into the new habitat (Figure 5.10), so that much of the time the margin of the population was characterized by a gradual decrease in population density. When the pollen-dispersal distance was high, colonization never occurred (within 100 generations) but genetic differentiation nevertheless developed in the intermediate habitats. (Figure 5.11).

Discussion
These simulations indicate it may be erroneous to make the simple inference that the absence of a species from a particular habitat means that neighbouring populations hold no genetic variation for the relevant characters. Instead, there are ecological and genetic factors which could inhibit the evolution of locally adapted subpopulations, thereby decreasing the likelihood that a new habitat can be exploited.

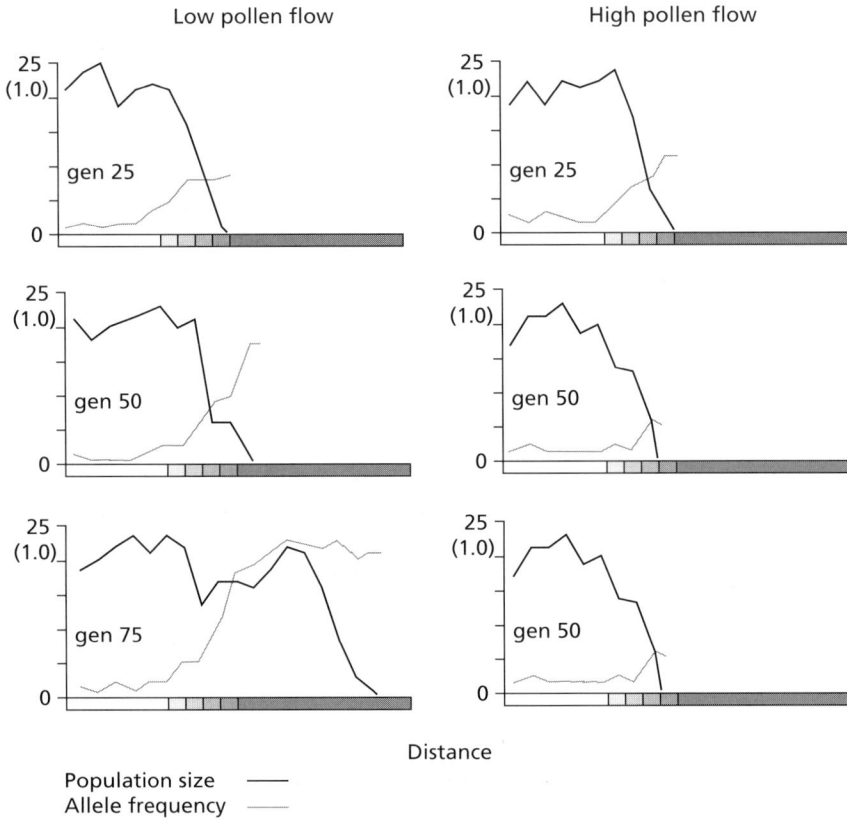

Low pollen flow

High pollen flow

gen 25

gen 25

gen 50

gen 50

gen 75

gen 50

Distance

Population size ——
Allele frequency ——

Figure 5.11 Plant density (solid line) and gene frequency (grey line) of a population colonizing and simultaneously adapting to a new habitat across a gradual habitat gradient, under conditions of low seed dispersal and either low or high pollen dispersal.

Long-distance seed dispersal had quite different effects from long-distance pollen dispersal. In fact, colonization was more likely when seed dispersal was greater, and the latter could completely mask the inhibitory effects of high pollen dispersal on colonization. There are several reasons why long-distance seed dispersal would have different consequences from long-distance pollen dispersal. First, selection acted on diploids, so ill-adapted seeds were screened from the migrants. Genes carried by migrant pollen, however, were not selected before mating, and so colonists often produced offspring ill-adapted to the new habitat. Secondly, if seeds are dispersed far into the new habitat, they may receive smaller amounts of ill-adapted pollen from the source population, making local differentiation easier to maintain. Thirdly, by increasing the number of offspring landing in the novel environment, a high seed-dispersal distance provided a greater number of opportunities for selection to pick out a locally adapted type. And finally, rapid population growth in the new habitat resulting from wide seed dispersal could have quickly increased the population size above some critical level, so that enough pollen was available from colonists to proportionally reduce the amount of ill-adapted pollen received from elsewhere. If long-distance seed dispersal had any negative effect on the maintenance of local differences in gene frequency, the effect was confounded with, and counteracted by, other effects which promoted colonization.

The presence of intermediate habitats greatly facilitated the colonization of the extreme habitat because incremental selection promoted a local increase in the frequency of genes favoured in the new habitat, ultimately resulting in a genetic change that could not be achieved in a single step. This is not unlike methods employed in artificial selection programmes, where breeders can achieve drastic results, but only through gradual, incremental changes. It has never been demonstrated in the field to what extent the power of natural selection to achieve certain results is determined by spatial patterns of selection.

Replicate runs often gave qualitatively different outcomes, such that predictions could only be made in probabilistic terms about whether or not a colonization would occur in a particular ecological situation. The most striking illustration of the stochastic nature of colonization was the supplemental run of 1000 generations, using a high pollen-dispersal distance, a low seed-dispersal distance, and graded selection. For the first 974 generations, the population boundary remained static (as in the 100-generation replicate runs), with little or no evidence of local differentiation. Colonization suddenly occurred at generation 975. If this was a real population under observation for a substantial period of time (5, 10, or even 100 years), one might conclude erroneously that the population had reached the extent of its distribution, and would not invade adjacent habitats without the input of new genetic variation. This indicates that there is (as above in the purely ecological model) some critical event necessary for colonization that may or may not occur by chance. The critical event could be the chance production of a well preadapted genotype, genetic drift towards the favourable state in the new habitat, or the attainment of a local threshold population size which decreases effective pollen flow from the original habitat. To determine this, future studies will need to include 'pedigree tracing' (to show whether new establishments were migrants from the source population or offspring of the colonists), and explicit study of the two-dimensional spatial distribution of genotypes in successful vs. unsuccessful colonization events.

Conclusions

While there has been general recognition that processes at population margins are critical in determining the distribution and abundance of species, there has been remarkably little study of such margins at a population level. The goal of the studies presented here has been to develop a rigorous theory of such margins. Such a theory is timely because of the recent advances in computational techniques associated with mapping and remote sensing technology. Until now, the time and effort needed to do fine-scale mapping has been prohibitive, with the consequence that ecological margins have largely been studied at a coarse scale in terms of the correlation of individual abundance with topographic, climatic or other readily measured variables.

Processes occurring at marginal populations may not only determine range extension and distribution, but these marginal populations may in turn have an influence on the dynamics of the more 'central' or source population. This is particularly likely where populations are small (or localized to small habitat patches), because in these cases boundary conditions will contribute relatively more to global dynamics than where populations are large. For example, we have shown (using mean-field models) that the presence of a 'passive refuge' can greatly influence the conditions for chaotic behaviour to emerge in the parent population (Newman *et al.* 2001). It is also well known that seed banks and resting stages (which can be considered as passive refuges) can have large consequences for above ground dynamics (Cohen & Levin 1991; Ellner & Hairston 1994), as can source–sink structuring of populations (Pulliam 1996).

Our studies have shown that processes occurring at margins can have counterintuitive outcomes, and reaffirm that a simple correlational approach to causes of species distributions may be very misleading. In addition, we can expect that detailed analysis of marginal patterns (which we have not attempted) may give substantial insight into factors limiting populations at their ranges, as well as whether such ranges are expanding or retreating. Clearly this is important in understanding the effect of climatic or other environmental changes on distribution patterns, as well as in understanding the processes impinging on rare species and small populations where edge effects may predominate.

Summary

The distribution of species is often limited by environmental gradients, such that the abundance of a species declines in concert with some spatial change in biotic or abiotic factors. We use spatially explicit individually based models to investigate the patterns that occur at these boundaries, and to investigate range extension beyond the boundary as a result of genetic change. Our results show that patterns at population margins that result form birth, death and dispersal are quite different from those observed as a result of simple diffusion against a gradient. Distance moved along such a gradient is less than would be predicted by a mean field model. At the margins, local, short-lived 'flame-like' patterns develop, and such heterogeneity is accentuated rather than minimized in cumulative plots of individual distributions. Classical distribution maps based on cumulative records are therefore likely to exaggerate the heterogeneity of species boundaries and show poorer correlation with environmental gradients, relative to distributions obtained by intensive one time sampling. Interaction of abiotic gradients with biotic gradients was investigated by introducing a pathogen and allowing it to spread into the margin of the host population. While the low density of individuals at population margins initially prevents the invasion of disease into those margins, in the long term marginal populations and disease are sustained by a complex colonization–extinction dynamic where there is no clear gradient in pathogen abundance at the margin. When genetic variants are introduced that can colonize an extreme habitat at the edge of a population, the success of these variants depends not only on the patterns of seed and pollen movement, but also on the steepness of the environmental gradient connecting the habitats. Colonization accompanied by genetic change is facilitated by a gradual environmental change. Even when colonization is unsuccessful, local clinal patterns can develop at the population margins. In simulation runs, the time to colonization was often highly variable, suggesting that spatially driven stochastic events (e.g. local aggregation) may be extremely important for successful invasion of a new habitat in the face of gene flow.

Acknowledgements

We wish to thank W. E. Kunin for help with collecting the distribution data for *Silene* in Kent. J.A. wishes to acknowledge a Guggenheim Fellowship which made such collections possible. B.J.B. is grateful to the National Research Council of Canada for a fellowship. This work was partly supported by grants NSF-DEB9119626 and NIH-GM60776.

References

Alexander, H.M. & Antonovics, J. (1988). Disease spread and population dynamics of anther-smut infection of *Silene alba* caused by the fungus *Ustilago violacea*. *Journal of Ecology*, **75**, 91–104.

Alexander, H.M., Thrall, P.H., Antonovics, J., Jarosz, A.M. & Oudemans, P.V. (1996). Population dynamics and genetics of plant disease: a case study of anther-smut disease of *Silene alba* caused by the fungus *Ustilago violacea*. *Ecology*, **77**, 990–996.

Antonovics, J. (1968). Evolution in closely adjacent plant populations. VI. Manifold effects of gene flow. *Heredity*, **23**, 507–524.

Antonovics, J. (1976). The nature of limits to natural selection. *Annals of the Missouri Botanical Garden*, **63**, 224–247.

Antonovics, J. (1990). Wilhelm Ludwig and his contributions to population genetics. *Trends in Ecology and Evolution*, **5**, 87–90.

Antonovics, J., Bradshaw, A.D. & Turner, R.G. (1971). Heavy metal tolerance in plants. *Advances in Ecological Research*, **7**, 1–85.

Bak, P. (1994). Self-organized criticality: a holistic view of nature. In: *Complexity: Metaphors, Models, and Reality* (eds A.C. Cowan, D. Pines & D. Meltzer), pp. 477–496. Addison-Wesley, Reading.

Best, B. (1990). *A Stochastic Model of Genetic Differentiation at the Margin of a Finite Plant Population*. MS Thesis, Duke University, Durham, North Carolina.

Caisse, M. & Antonovics, J. (1978). Evolution in closely adjacent plant populations. IX. Evolution of reproductive isolation in clinal populations. *Heredity*, **40**, 371–384.

Camill, P. & Clark, J.S. (1998). Climate change disequilibrium of boreal permafrost peatlands caused by local processes. *American Naturalist*, **151**, 207–222.

Carter, R.N. & Prince, S.D. (1981). Epidemic models used to explain biogeographical distribution limits. *Nature*, **293**, 644–645.

Clausen, J., Keck, D.D. & Hiesey, W.M. (1948). *Experimental Studies on the Nature of Species: 3. Environmental Responses of Climatic Races of Achillea*. Carnegie Institute of Washington Publication No. 581.

Cohen, D. & Levin, S.A. (1991). Dispersal in patchy environments: the effects of temporal and spatial structure. *Theoretical Population Biology*, **39**, 63–99.

Comins, H.N., Hassell, M.P. & May, R.M. (1992). The spatial dynamics of host–parasitoid systems. *Journal of Animal Ecology*, **61**, 735–748.

Ellner, S. & Hairston, N.G. (1994). Role of overlapping generations in maintaining genetic variation in a fluctuating environment. *American Naturalist*, **143**, 403–414.

Endler, J. (1977). *Geographic Variation, Speciation, and Clines.* Princeton University Press, Princeton, NJ.

Fisher, R.A. (1937). The wave of advance of advantageous genes. *Annals of Eugenics*, **7**, 355–369.

Gunton, J.D., San Miguel, M. & Sahni, P.S. (1983). The dynamics of first order phase transitions. In: *Phase transitions and critical phenomena*, Vol. 8 (eds C. Domb & J.L. Lebowitz), pp. 267–466. Academic Press, New York.

Harper, J.L. (1977). *Population Biology of Plants.* Academic Press, New York.

Hengeveld, R. (1989). *Dynamics of Biological Invasions.* Chapman & Hall, London.

Kareiva, P. (1994). Space: the final frontier for ecological theory. *Ecology*, **75**, 1–47 (special feature).

Levene, H. (1953). Genetic equilibrium when more than one ecological niche is available. *American Naturalist*, **87**, 331–333.

Levin, S.A. & Pacala, S.W. (1997). Theories of simplification and scaling of spatially distributed processes. In: *Spatial Ecology: The Role of Space in Population Dynamics and Interspecific Interactions* (eds D. Tilman & P. Kareiva), pp. 271–295. Princeton University Press, Princeton, NJ.

Lewis, M.A. (1997). Variability, patchiness, and jump dispersal in the spread of an invading population. In: *Spatial Ecology: The Role of Space in Population Dynamics and Interspecific Interactions* (eds D. Tilman & P. Kareiva), pp. 46–69. Princeton University Press, Princeton, NJ.

Ludwig, W. (1950). Zur Theorie der Konkurrenz. Die Annidation (Einnischung) als funfter Evolutionsfaktor. In: *Neue Ergebnisse und Probleme der Zoologie (Klatt-Festschrift)* (ed. W. Herre), pp. 516–537. Akademische Verlagsgesellschaft Geest and Portig, K-G., Leipzig.

Mallet, J. & Barton, N. (1989). Inference from clines stabilized by frequency-dependent selection. *Genetics*, **122**, 967–976.

Newman, T.J., Antonovics, J. & Wilbur, H.M. (2001). Population dynamics with a refuge: fractal basins and the suppression of chaos. *Theoretical Population Biology*, submitted.

Philp, E.G. (1982). *Atlas of the Kent Flora.* Kent Field Club, Maidstone.

Pulliam, H.R. (1996). Sources and sinks: empirical evidence and population consequences. In: *Population Dynamics in Ecological Space and Time* (eds O.E. Rhodes, R.K. Chesser & M.H. Smith), pp. 45–69. University of Chicago Press, Chicago, IL.

Rhodes, O.E., Chesser, R.K. & Smith, M.H. (1996). *Population Dynamics in Ecological Space and Time.* University of Chicago Press, Chicago, IL.

Slatkin, M. (1973). Gene flow and selection in a cline. *Genetics*, **75**, 733–756.

Tilman, D. & Kareiva, P. (1997). *Spatial Ecology: The Role of Space in Population Dynamics and Interspecific Interactions.* Princeton University Press, Princeton, NJ.

Turchin, P. (1998). *Quantitative Analysis of Movement.* Sinauer Press, Sunderland, MA.

Turesson, G. (1922). The genotypical response of the plant species to the habitat. *Hereditas*, **3**, 211–350.

Watkinson, A.R. (1985). On the abundance of plants along an environmental gradient. *Journal of Ecology*, **23**, 569–578.

Wilson, D.S. & Turelli, M. (1986). Stable underdominance and the evolutionary invasion of empty niches. *American Naturalist*, **127**, 835–850.

Chapter 6
The scale of local adaptation in forest plants

G. Bell,*† M. J. Lechowicz* and M. J. Waterway‡

Introduction: theories of distribution and abundance

Distribution and abundance are the central themes of community ecology. They emerge from biological surveys in which the organisms collected or recorded from a number of sites are assigned to taxa, typically species. The output of a biological survey is thus a species × sites occurrence matrix. The sum of each row is the abundance of that species, if the number of individuals (or a measure of cover or biomass) found at each site has been recorded; otherwise, if only the presence or absence of the species has been recorded, it is the range of the species within the area sampled. Surveys thus lead to two related questions about the ecological characteristics of species. The first is to explain the variation in abundance or range among species. The second is to explain why the range of a species includes some sites and not others. Five kinds of hypothesis, of different levels of complexity, have been put forward to answer these questions.

1 *The random model.* The simplest hypothesis is that distribution and abundance are determined by chance alone: each individual, anywhere within the area sampled, belongs to a given species with a fixed probability. Species are thus distributed at random among sites, and range or abundance follow a Poisson distribution.

2 *The neutral model.* In practice, however, it has been found that most species are not randomly distributed, but are instead patchy or aggregated. The simplest hypothesis to explain aggregation is that it arises through local dispersal alone, without any systematic differentiation among species or sites. The observed pattern is then the outcome of chance plus history. This situation is represented by a neutral community model, or NCM (Bell 2000).

3 *The ecological model.* A patchy distribution may arise from a spatial NCM, but need not necessarily do so. It might instead arise from a patchy distribution of resource input, so that sites differ in productivity. Some sites may then support many more individuals, and thereby many more species, than others. The observed patterns are then caused by chance plus history plus environmental variance.

4 *The evolutionary model.* When the environment is heterogeneous, lineages will tend to become adapted to local conditions of growth. Observed patterns will then

* Biology Department, McGill University, 1205 Ave Dr Penfield, Montreal, Quebec, Canada H3A 1B1,
† Redpath Museum, McGill University, 859 Sherbrooke St West, Montreal, Quebec, Canada H3K 1B6
and ‡ Department of Plant Sciences, Macdonald Campus, McGill University, Lakeshore Boulevard, Ste-Anne-de-Bellevue, Quebec, Canada H9X 3V9.

be caused by chance plus history plus environmental variance plus selection. The distribution of a species will then depend in part on the distribution of the particular factor or combination of factors to which it is adapted.

5 *The coevolutionary model.* The growth of a species at a site may itself change the characteristics of that site. This will be true for any depletable resource, and there may be complex interactions, involving continual mutual adaptation and counter-adaptation, among antagonists such as predators and prey. In any case, the distribution of a species is constrained by the distributions of others.

In this chapter we are primarily concerned to evaluate the evolutionary model: to what extent do distributions reflect local adaptation in heterogeneous environments? Local adaptation is caused by selection within local populations that favours individuals with high fitness over some relatively narrow range of conditions of growth. Divergent selection causes species to be locally adapted to different conditions of growth. When a landscape is occupied by a species, through dispersal, it will tend to flourish at sites which provide the conditions of growth to which it has in the past become locally adapted, whereas it will often fail to become established at sites to which it is not well adapted. Because species have become adapted to different kinds of site, the continued dispersal of a group of species into a region will lead to distributions that are to some extent segregated from one another. This can be called selection, or sorting, or competition, or community assembly; these terms all refer to the process whereby observed patterns of distribution are generated by differential success over sites, itself the consequence of previous natural selection acting within populations. The restriction of a species to certain kinds of site is thus a consequence of local adaptation. Moreover, the degree of specialization displayed by a species, that is, the narrowness of the range of sites in which it is found, will reflect the degree of local adaptation. These are the main propositions that we shall examine in this paper.

Evidence from experiments and surveys

Identification of local adaptation by transplant experiments

The evolutionary model is tested directly by experiments in which families whose provenance is known are grown in different sites where their performance is measured. 'Performance' is ideally the same as 'fitness'; in practice, a complete seed-to-seed measure of increase is difficult to obtain, and in most cases some component of fitness, such as ramet survival or seed set, which we refer to generically as performance, is used instead. When plants are transferred between sites that have experienced different kinds of artificial disturbance, there is often unmistakeable evidence of divergent specialization (e.g. explant studies by Jain and Bradshaw (1966), or reciprocal transplant studies by Davies and Snaydon (1976)). Transplant experiments involving natural communities also tend to demonstrate local adaptation quite readily, provided that they are conducted on sufficiently large geographical scales. This was the object of the extensive common garden trials set up early in the 20th century (see Hiesey 1940). Reciprocal transplants involving seminatural sites several hundred kilometres apart often show that residents are consistently superior to incomers for at least some components of fitness (Antonovics & Primack 1982; Schmidt & Levin 1988; Jordan 1992). The same effect has sometimes been found at much smaller scales of 100 m or less, for example between grassland and woodland sites (Antonovics 1976; Lovett Doust 1981). A related observation is that the fitness of a family may decrease with distance from the parental site (Schmitt & Gamble 1990). Other experiments conducted over small distances, however, have failed to demonstrate any consistent superiority of residents (Cheplick 1988; van Tienderen & van der Toorn 1991). In brief, there is considerable experimental evidence for local adaptation, especially at rather large spatial scales.

Biological surveys

Surveys are much easier to do than experiments, so we often know the occurrence of species among sites but not their performance. It may be possible, nevertheless, to demonstrate local adaptation. The reason is that the response of species to sites is presumed to be caused by the ecological characteristics of those sites, so that if we can demonstrate a correlation between the abundance of a species and the level of some environmental factor, then this is evidence for local adaptation, subject to the condition of repeatability described below. Unfortunately, it is not possible to use biological surveys to *falsify* a general hypothesis of local adaptation, for the simple reason that imagination cannot be relied on to identify the factor to which species are adapted. The best that can be done with survey data alone is to guess which factor may be responsible for shaping a given species distribution, and then test the specific hypothesis of local adaptation with respect to this factor. The first problem raised by this approach, then, is how to make this guess.

The approach that we have followed is to take overall productivity as the first-order environmental factor (or, more precisely, as reflecting the underlying environmental factor or factors that most strongly influence plant growth); then to consider the known components of overall productivity; and only then to speculate about the idiosyncratic responses of particular species. Productivity is determined primarily by nutrient concentrations, and secondarily by factors which influence the rate of nutrient utilization, such as radiant flux, water availability and pH. These can be measured on the ground, or, failing that, inferred from maps of topography, climate or geology.

Measurement of local adaptation from survey data

The consequence of local adaptation apparent from survey data is that a species will occupy a restricted range of sites, relative to those available, with respect to a given environmental factor. The extent of local adaptation to a given factor is therefore appropriately measured by the variance of occupied sites as a fraction of the variance of all sites. To avoid the statistical shortcomings of proportions, and to obtain a measure that increases as adaptation becomes more precise, we define precision as

$$\text{Precision} = -\log(s^2_{occ}/s^2_{all}) \qquad (1)$$

where s^2_{occ} and s^2_{all} are the variances of occupied sites alone and of all sites, respectively.

The consequences of local adaptation for diversity and abundance depend not only on adaptation, but on divergent adaptation. The extent of divergence is measured by the variance of the mean values of occupied sites among a set of species. We shall use the standardized difference from the environmental mean as a measure that can be used to compare the response to different environmental factors:

$$\text{Eccentricity} = (m_{occ} - m_{all})/s_{all} \qquad (2)$$

Where m_{occ} and m_{all} are the mean values of occupied sites alone and of all sites, respectively. Divergence is then defined as the variance of eccentricity.

We can then formulate the question that we began with: To what extent do distributions reflect local adaptation in heterogeneous environments? In a more quantitative way as: What are the average values of precision and divergence, and how do they vary among taxa and among environmental factors?

General theory of adaptation in relation to ecological scale

The general answer to this question is, that it depends on the scale of the investigation. Any survey will involve a particular environmental scale, the size of the region surveyed and of the sites within it, and a particular phylogenetic scale, the relatedness of the organisms recorded. The interpretation of the survey is sensitive to both.

Consider first the environment, where the issue is whether sites within a region are occupied by different species as the consequence of local adaptation. The precision of adaptation will depend principally on the balance between selection and immigration. In a small region, the number of immigrants will be large relative to the number of births within the site, whereas in large regions the converse is likely to be the case. At a scale of 1 m, the pattern of vegetation is caused largely by the accidents of colonization, although adaptation to factors such as microtopographical relief may sometimes occur. At a scale of 1 km, the much greater variance of physical factors such as soil moisture and light leads to distributions that are restricted to (say) bogs or dry forest, although most species may be capable of growing at most sites. At a scale of a 1000 km, major differences in climate and geology are likely to occur, and almost all species will be restricted to a small fraction of sites.

Organisms do not measure their environment in units of metres, of course: they measure it in units of themselves. More precisely, their response to environmental heterogeneity will depend on two natural scales: the individual scale of the growth of single organisms, and the dispersal scale of the propagules they release. These will both be enormously different for, say, an alga and an aspen, so that any conclusions about scale and adaptation must take the organisms concerned into account. As a crude rule of thumb, we might expect local adaptation to be much more conspicuous within regions exceeding the dispersal scale than in smaller regions.

A second general rule applies to the organisms included in a survey: lineages are more likely to become distinctively specialized if they are only distantly related. The minimal genetic change, a single-base substitution, is likely to be neutral or nearly so; in all events, it is unlikely to give rise to two lines adapted to different conditions of growth. At the other extreme, lineages that have diverged very widely, such as a fern and a sedge, are almost certain to have accumulated a variety of substantial ecological differences. There are exceptions to both of these statements: single mutations do occasionally produce ecological differentiation, whereas organisms belonging to different phyla may share some specializations, at least, and occur together at the same sites. In general, however, the likelihood that two lineages will have evolved distinctive local adaptations increases with the genetic distance between them.

Putting these two rules together, we are led to the generalization that distinctive local adaptation is more likely to evolve as the environmental variation within the survey region increases, and as genetic variation among the organisms surveyed increases (see Kassen & Bell 2000). It synthesizes a number of ideas that have long been current in community ecology and population genetics, in particular community turnover (Whittaker 1970) and limiting similarity (see Hubbell & Foster 1986). In doing so, it makes it clear that the most pervasive generalizations that can be made about local adaptation, and thus about the diversity of sites and the abundance of species, hinge on concepts of scale.

The biological survey of Mont St-Hilaire

The survey
Biological surveys are the basis for all of our knowledge about the distribution and abundance of organisms, and therefore about the extent of local adaptation. Most published surveys are of little use because they were not conducted systematically; survey data can be interpreted only when all sites have been searched for all species with the same effort and using the same procedures. A few surveys, although unsystematic, are nearly exhaustive, after the records of generations of naturalists have accumulated, and these are perhaps the best available sources of information. All of them, however, exemplify the 'survey paradox'. We wish to use survey data to evaluate hypotheses about the natural processes that shape distribution and abundance, and must therefore conduct the survey in regions that have not been severely disturbed by recent human activity. Unfortunately, all the most rigorous and comprehensive surveys have been conducted in countries such as Britain, Germany and the Netherlands, where the landscape is almost completely humanized. The survey paradox is that where we have adequate data it cannot be used, and where we require data it is not available.

We are conducting a systematic biological survey of a large surviving fragment of old-growth forest in the St Lawrence valley in defiance of this paradox. The site is Mont St-Hilaire, an isolated hill some 1000 ha in extent, where the forest has never been cleared (see Maycock 1961). Most of the area is beech–maple forest characteristic of the region, with scattered oak and pine. Teams of trained recorders search each hectare for a given group of plants, following a fixed pattern. The groups for which we have complete information to date are ferns, sedges and trees, giving us consistent estimates of the distribution of a total of 125 species. Sedges form a group of closely related species within a single genus, *Carex*; ferns and trees are more diverse taxa. The survey thus encompasses groups of different phylogenetic extent within a region consisting chiefly of a single 'habitat'.

Data on landscape structure comes in part from topography and in part from extensive explant trials. The digital elevation model for the area yields estimates of elevation, slope, water flow and insolation for each 5 m × 5 m cell, which for the purposes of this analysis are used to obtain averages for each hectare. Soil samples were collected for each hectare. We measured pH and the production of three organisms: the chlorophyte *Chlamydomonas* and the sedges *Carex arctata* and *Carex prasina*. These procedures and the spatial structure of the eight components of productivity are described by G. Bell, M. Lechowicz and M. J. Waterway (unpublished). Briefly, the spatial structure of a given environmental factor can be characterized by the slope of the regression of log variance on log distance for all pairwise combinations of samples (Bell *et al.* 1993). A steep slope indicates a coarse-grained environment (with respect to the particular factor analysed), and a shallow slope a fine-grained environment. Our soil measures all have shallow slopes of about 0.1, indicating that there is a great deal of environmental variance within each hectare, below the grain of our plant survey. We are, of course, unable to identify any correlation between occurrence and environmental state at scales below the grain of the survey; these are the subject of further research (e.g. Richard *et al.* 2000).

Precision

The distribution of precision for two representative factors, insolation and *Chlamydomonas* production, are shown in Figure 6.1. They resemble left-skewed lognormal with a mode at small positive values. The overall mean for all eight factors was +0.0845, corresponding to 82% of the overall environmental variance. Thus, most species occupy a large fraction of the available range of growth conditions. Errors of estimation give rise to modest negative values, whereas the long tail to the right consists of progressively more specialized species.

Analysis of covariance shows that overall range has a strong effect on precision (Table 6.1). The relationship is triangular (Figure 6.2). Very widespread species that occupy a large fraction of sites are constrained to have precision of close to zero. In progressively less abundant species the range of precision extends to more positive values, reaching about +1 (10% of environmental variance) for species occupying 10 sites (1% of total area). Thus, although rare species may have any degree of specialization, the most specialized species are always rare.

Precision also varies among groups of organisms and among environmental

(a) Distribution of precision for insolation

(b) Distribution of precision for Chlamy BioAssay

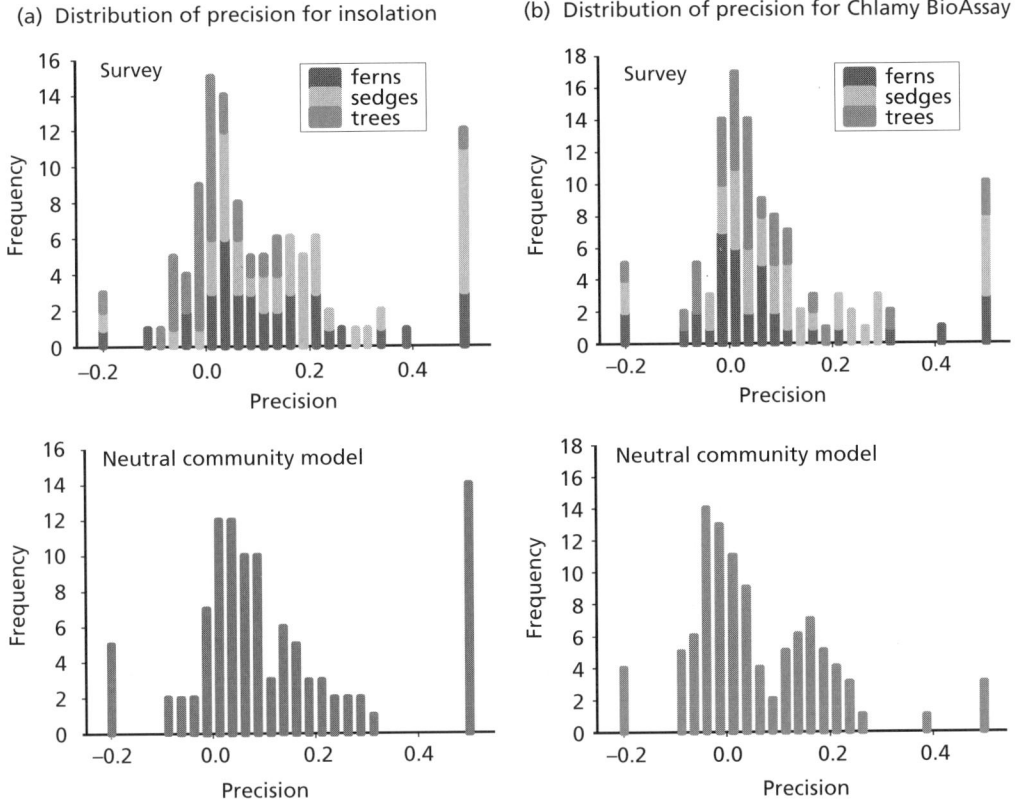

Figure 6.1 Frequency distribution of precision of local adaptation, in the Mont St-Hilaire survey and in the neutral community model (NCM). (a) Insolation; (b) *Chlamydomonas* bioassay.

factors (Figure 6.3). In almost all cases, the herbaceous plants, ferns and sedges have greater precision than trees. Some environmental factors (such as elevation and insolation) are associated with greater precision that others (such as water flow), but no more general pattern is apparent.

Precision is expected to vary with scale. If sites are agglomerated into progressively larger blocks, precision should increase with block size as selection becomes more effective. We found, however, that precision fluctuated with block size without any evident trend (Figure 6.4).

Eccentricity

Over all species, eccentricity is approximately normally distributed around zero (Figure 6.5). This is the outcome, however, of summing groups whose distributions may be skewed. Ferns are skewed towards negative values for insolation, for instance, whereas sedges are skewed towards positive values.

Table 6.1 Analysis of covariance of precision of adaptation. The continuous variate is range (number of hectares occupied by species). Factor is a categorical variable, representing the eight environmental factors whose spatial structure was measured. For the survey data, species were placed into one of four monophyletic groups: ferns, sedges, conifers and woody dicots. Variation among species within groups supplies the common error term.

Source	d.f.	MS	F	P
Biological survey of Mont St-Hilaire				
Range	1	2.3655	23.5	<0.0001
Group	3	0.2750	2.73	0.043
Factor	7	0.2960	2.94	0.005
Group × factor	21	0.0777	<1	
Species (group)	911	0.1006		
Spatial neutral community model				
Range	1	2.1534	51.4	<0.0001
Factor	7	0.3781	9.03	<0.0001
Species	815	0.0419		

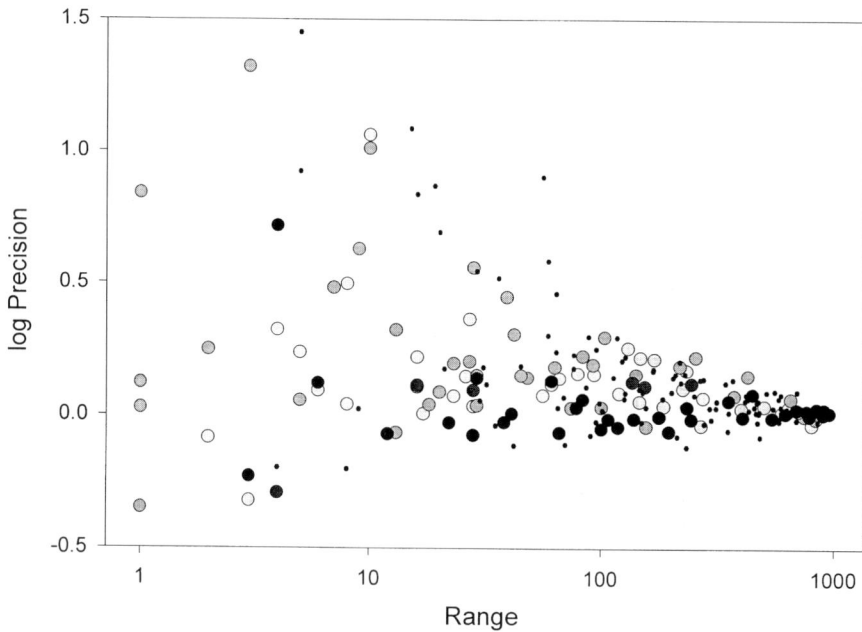

Figure 6.2 Relationship between precision and range for insolation. Symbols are: open circles, ferns; lightly shaded circles, coniferous trees; medium shaded circles, sedges; solid circles, broad-leaved trees; dots, neutral community model.

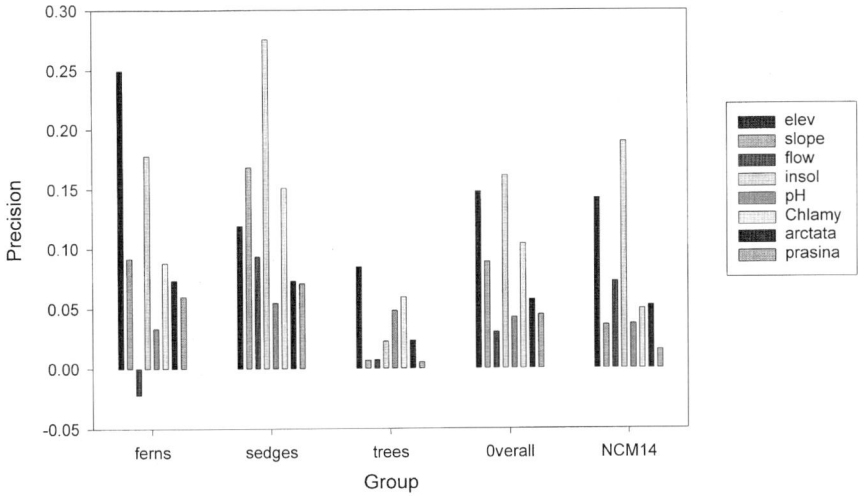

Figure 6.3 The precision of adaptation for different groups and environmental factors, in survey data and the neutral community model (NCM)

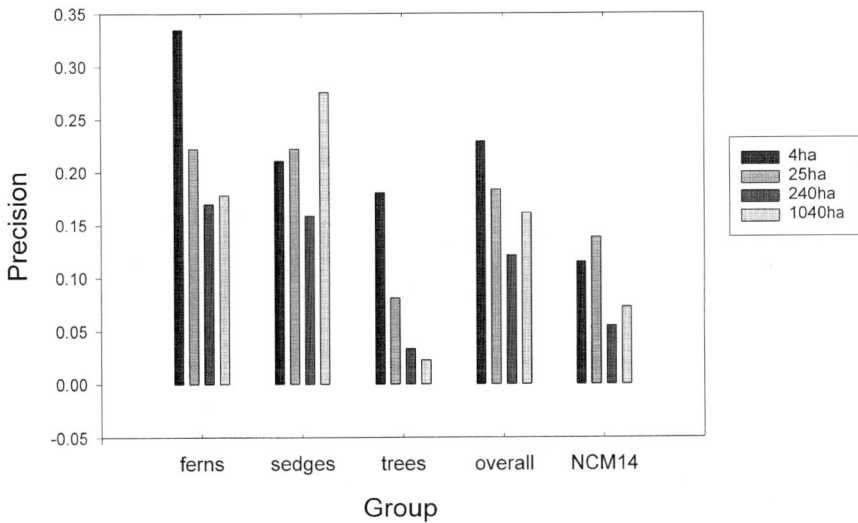

Figure 6.4 The precision of adaptation to insolation in relation to spatial scale, in the survey and the neutral community model (NCM)

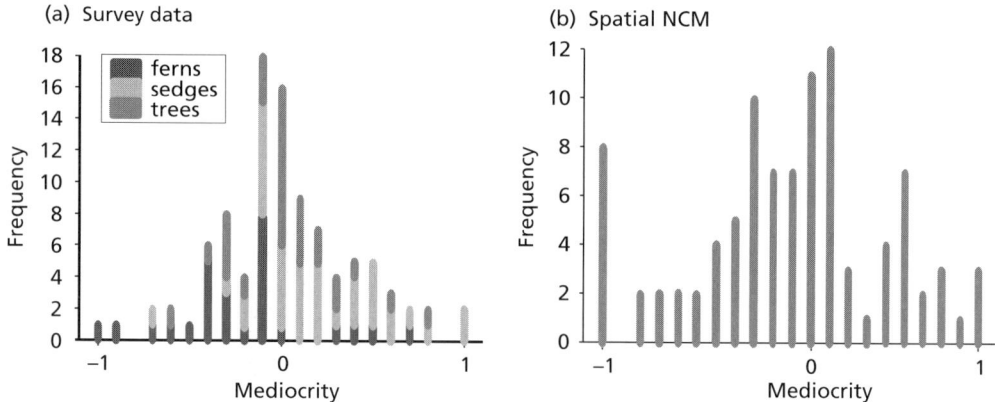

Figure 6.5 The distribution of eccentricity for insolation, in the survey and the neutral community model (NCM)

The average value of divergence was 0.41, so that somewhat more than 95% of species occupied sites with average values within 1 s.d. of the overall environmental mean (Figure 6.5). The extent of divergence varied among groups and among environmental factors (Figure 6.6). For most (14/16) comparisons, ferns and sedges have diverged more than trees. There is also a tendency, although not a very strong one, for divergence to be more marked for the factors related to topography than for those related to soil conditions.

In short, the survey shows that most species are specialized to some extent, with respect to any component of productivity; that high degrees of specialization are found predominantly among rare species; and that precision and divergence vary among groups and among environmental factors. We could now proceed to interpret these patterns in terms of the natural history of each species, investigating the extent to which each is restricted to a narrow range of conditions, and attempting to identify the physiological basis of each case of local adaptation. We shall instead ask first whether the patterns require any biological interpretation at all in terms of local adaptation, or whether they might arise instead through some simpler process.

Neutral community models

The spatially located NCM

The patterns emerging from the survey are clearly non-random, and the random model can be dismissed at once. It is not so easy to dismiss the neutral model, in which pattern arises solely through limited local dispersal without any ecological differences among individuals whatsoever. In order to investigate this possibility, we need to construct a neutral simulacrum of the survey, using the same number of

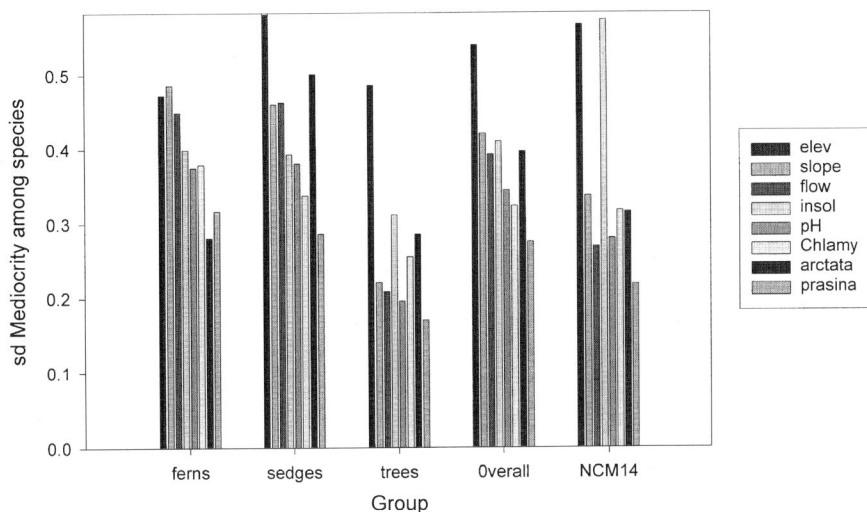

Figure 6.6 The magnitude of divergence (variance of eccentricity) in the survey and the neutral community model (NCM).

species in the same area, so that we can compare the output of the model directly with the analysis of the survey itself.

At a single site, an NCM can be constructed for a community comprising a fixed number of species by assuming that the rates of birth, death and immigration are identical for all species. This leads to a distribution of abundance among species that resembles a log-normal curve, skewed to the left by immigration; at the limit where immigration greatly exceeds birth, this approaches a log-series distribution (Bell 2000). This has been shown to represent a new distribution, the 'zero-sum multinomial' by Hubbell (Chapter 18 and Hubbell 2001). To represent processes within the region where a survey has been conducted, a spatial neutral model can be constructed by placing an NCM at each site on a lattice. Founding individuals are assigned to sites at random, so that the community is initially described by the random model. When an individual reproduces, however, its offspring may disperse away from the natal site. This can be simulated by a random walk: with fixed probability the newborn individual moves to one of the four adjacent sites that can be reached by a rook's move. Once there, it again moves, with the same probability, and so forth, until the condition for movement is not met, when it settles in the site it last occupied. Individuals that are born close to the edge of the region may stray over the edge and are then lost to the community; this loss is balanced by new immigration from an external source into the marginal sites. If the probability of movement is very low, most newborns will settle in their natal site, whereas if it is high they will become more or less widely dispersed away from it. In this way, a correlation between nearby sites is created, and the initially random distribution becomes more or less aggregated.

To create a simulated survey, founding individuals belonging to 125 species were settled at random on a 50 × 50 lattice and allowed to propagate for 2000 cycles. A piece shaped exactly like the hectare survey grid at Mont St-Hilaire was cut out of the centre of the lattice, avoiding any edge effects caused by immigration. The distributions of the species generated by the model within this region are then used to compute precision and divergence, using the observed spatial structure of the environmental factors. Comparing this output with the survey results is not a statistical test, however. To run the NCM requires specifying five parameters—birth rate, death rate, dispersal probability, immigration rate and carrying capacity per site—all of which are unknown. They will be unknown for almost any conceivable survey. We are necessarily restricted to asking whether the patterns that emerge from the NCM are qualitatively similar to survey data.

The NCM readily generates species distributions that look uncannily like the results of real surveys, with great variation in range or overall abundance among species. Within a site, the distribution of abundance among species resembles a skewed log-normal, as found previously for isolated communities (Bell 2000). We have extended this result by finding that the distribution of both overall abundance and range among species within a region comprising many sites that exchange migrants resembles a geometric or log-series distribution, as predicted by Hubbell (2001). The model output depends in detail on parameter values. We chose parameter values that led to a distribution of range similar to that found in the survey, with a broad band of species at intermediate abundance. Specifically, we assigned a birth rate very slightly higher than the death rate ($b = 0.505$, $d = 0.500$ per individual per cycle), to counter the leakage of dispersing offspring across the edge of the lattice; a low immigration rate ($m = 0.00025$ per species per marginal cell) to forestall species extinctions; a moderate dispersal rate for offspring ($s = 0.1$); and a carrying capacity of 500 individuals per site, which eventually results in a total population of about half a million individuals on the Mont St-Hilaire cut-out. We have restricted our comparison to a single realization of this parameter set. Different realizations produce similar results. Changing the parameters can cause substantial changes in the distribution of range, but our results seem broadly applicable to moderate dispersal probabilities of 0.05–0.5 or so.

Patterns in neutral communities

The basic properties of the model were as follows. The distribution of precision is left-skewed log-normal, with a mode at small negative values (see Figure 6.1). The overall mean precision was +0.0742, corresponding to 84% of the environmental variance. Abundance has a highly significant effect on precision (see Table 6.1). The relationship is again triangular, with high degrees of specialization being restricted to rare species (see Figure 6.2). Species cannot be assigned to groups in this model, but precision varies among environmental factors (see Table 6.1). Elevation and insolation are associated with the greatest negative values of average precision (see

Figure 6.3). There is no consistent relationship between precision and block size (see Figure 6.4). Eccentricity was more or less normally distributed about zero (see Figure 6.5), with an average value of divergence over all factors of 0.3855. The degree of divergence varied among factors, the greatest values being associated with topographically derived variables (see Figure 6.6).

In short, the NCM-generated patterns that are strikingly similar to the survey. No attempt was made to study the whole parameter space of the model, so it would be surprising if this conclusion applies only to a very narrow and unrealistic range of parameters. (It may well apply only to parameter sets that generate abundance and range distributions that approximate real data, however.) Much of our preceding analysis therefore not only fails to provide a measure of the extent of local adaptation, it fails even to demonstrate that any local adaptation has occurred.

Accuracy

In the light of the NCM results, it is easy to appreciate that the weakness of the concept of precision is that no value of this statistic, however large, can be interpreted as evidence for local adaptation. Suppose that a species were to arrive at some site by chance, grow there and in time disperse to a group of nearby sites. These sites are likely to be similar, because of their proximity, and will therefore represent only a small part of the regional variance. The species would thus be judged to be locally adapted, whereas it is in fact merely locally dispersed. The hallmark of local adaptation is not that it causes a restricted pattern of distribution, but that it repeatedly causes the same pattern. It can be demonstrated from survey data, therefore, only by aggregating neighbouring sites into blocks, and showing not only that occupied sites have low variance but also that they have a similar mean throughout the region surveyed. More formally, suppose that having partitioned the region into blocks of neighbouring sites, we estimate the variances among sites within blocks, $s^2_{within,all}$, and among blocks, $s^2_{among,all}$. Furthermore, we estimate the corresponding variances for the sites occupied by a given species, $s^2_{within,occ}$ and $s^2_{among,occ}$. These estimates can then be used to derive two measures of local adaptation.

1 The precision of adaptation is the within-block variance of occupied sites, normalized by the overall within-block variance: it is expressed as precision = $-\log(s^2_{within,occ} / s^2_{within,all})$, so that greater values indicate more precise adaptation.

2 The accuracy of adaptation is the among-block variance of occupied sites, normalized by the overall among-block variance: accuracy = $-\log(s^2_{among,occ} / s^2_{among,all})$.

This provides a method of distinguishing between local adaptation and neutral processes. In practice, it should be applied only to blocks of moderate size that provide adequate degrees of freedom for estimating both within-block and among-block variance components. Figure 6.7 shows the results of a plot of precision on accuracy for 25-ha blocks. Many apparently high-precision species turn out to have low accuracy, making it difficult to interpret their restricted range of occurrence as being caused by selection. It is true that the NCM results show somewhat lower accuracy than the survey, but the cloud of points produced by the NCM overlaps so

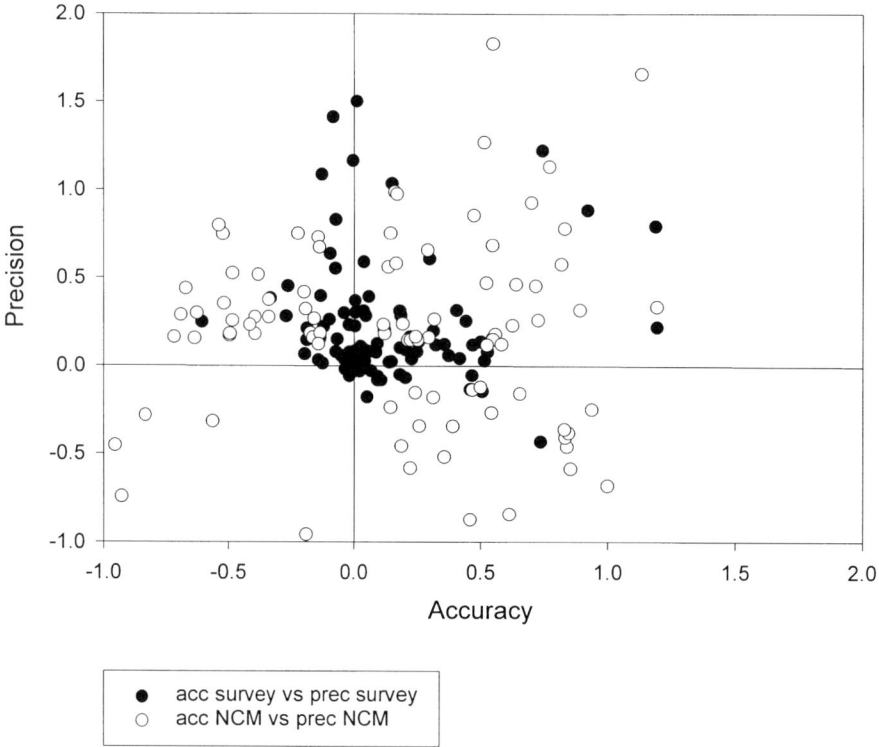

Figure 6.7 Precision and accuracy of local adaptation in the survey and the neutral community model (NCM)

broadly with the survey that it is difficult to argue that the analysis strengthens the case for local adaptation. This conclusion applies to all block sizes between 4 ha and 240 ha.

The experimental evidence

Extensive implant experiments carried out at Mont St Hilaire have been reported in a previous paper (Bell *et al.* 2000). They involved setting out several thousand ramets of 15 species of *Carex* along 3 km of transects within the forest. The overall survival of ramets in the first year showed that most sites in the forest would support growth. The habitat requirements of these species are therefore quite broad, and as most forest sedges usually grow as spaced plants, which are unlikely to compete directly with one another, they are unlikely to express precise or divergent adaptation. The rate of survival, moreover, was not correlated with range or abundance; indeed, the most successful species in these implant trials was *Carex bromoides*, which ranked only 31st in range of the 45 species found in the survey. It may be that establishment is more sensitive to germination than to the survival of large ramets. We now know, however, that the species with the most rapid and consistent germination of fresh seed is *Carex prasina* (unpublished data), again a rather uncommon species which ranked 21st in the survey. Furthermore, we have conducted targetted implant experiments which failed to show any tendency for ramets to survive better when planted close to a resident plant of the same species (Bell *et al.* 2001).

The explant experiments allow us to compare the growth of *Carex arctata* and *Carex prasina* in soil samples from sites where they were present with growth in samples from sites where they did not occur. The two species have contrasting ranges: *Carex prasina* was found in only 4% of sites, whereas *Carex arctata* is the third most abundant sedge in the forest, and was found at 74% of sites. The mean dry weight of *Carex arctata* grown in soil from sites from which the species was recorded was 73.5 mg (s.e. 0.9 mg) and in unoccupied sites was 74.9 mg (s.e. 1.8 mg). The dry weight of *Carex prasina* for occupied sites was 72.5 mg (s.e. 5.6 mg) and for unoccupied sites was 81.4 mg (s.e. 1.1 mg). There is no evidence that either species is specialized to the soil of its neighbourhood.

Both implant and explant experiments are consistent with a neutralist interpretation of distribution for sedges within the forest.

The comparative evidence

It might be argued that our failure to detect the local adaptation that is well known to be characteristic of many plants is simply because our data are unreliable. This is not the case. The biological survey and the environmental mapping that we have conducted are among the most systematic and comprehensive on record. When particular species are isolated, they usually have the expected properties. Bracken fern (*Pteridium aquilinum*), for example, is well known to grow chiefly in open sunny areas. When its distribution is analysed against insolation, it has an eccentricity of +0.57 and a precision of +0.21, while at a block size of 25 ha its accuracy is +0.37. It therefore appears on Figure 6.7 as one of the minority of species with a combination of precision and accuracy. This is an exceptional case; most species are not as clearly specialized. Our analysis does not refute the existence of conventional patterns of local adaptation, however. Indeed, the difference in eccentricity among groups is the clearest signal of local adaptation to emerge from our data. Rather, it refutes the possibility that the average or ensemble properties of species distributions can be used directly to demonstrate the existence of local adaptation or to estimate its precision.

Model structure

It is easy to specify parameter values such that the NCM would not generate patterns resembling survey data. If the probability of local dispersal is set to zero, for example, the distributions set up by initial colonization are retained indefinitely; at the other extreme, if offspring are nearly certain to disperse they settle almost at random, after a very long sequence of moves from site to site. Moderate levels of dispersal, however, always generate survey-like patterns. Nevertheless, many correspondents and reviewers have argued that a five-parameter model can be tuned to produce almost any result, and that the qualitative correspondence between the survey results and the NCM output cannot be taken as support for a neutral interpretation of species distributions and the associated phenomena of diversity and abundance. We answer as follows. In the first place, *all community models have the same number of parameters*. They differ only in the number that may be varied. A model of simple exponential growth may appear to have only a single parameter, but this is because all other parameters (the rate of immigration, for example) have been set to some fixed value (zero, in this case), so that they do not appear in the presentation of the model. This approach was necessary before the advent of high-speed computing made it possible to study individual-based, equation-free community models, and it remains a useful heuristic device, but its simplicity is apparent rather than real. Secondly, if the number of variable parameters is the criterion, neutral models are necessarily simpler than any theory of local adaptation, which will require many additional, explicitly defined values for site-specific fitness. Finally, we do not claim that the patterns we have found provide decisive evidence for a neutral interpretation of communities, although we do claim that these patterns cannot henceforth be used as evidence for any non-neutral interpretation. More precisely: when the grain and extent of a surveyed area are such that there are moderate rates of local dispersal between adjacent sites, the spatial structure of species composition will not reflect local adaptation.

Grain and extent

The actual level of dispersal achieved by plants will depend in part on the nature of the propagules they produce, but it will also depend on the design of the survey or the blocking of the data: dispersal will be low when grain is large, regardless of extent, but high when both grain and extent are small. The prominence of local adaptation in the structure of communities is likely to depend on the grain and extent at which the region concerned is surveyed or analysed. Our conclusions, therefore, apply only to the scale of the survey that we have used, with a grain of 1 ha and an extent of about 1000 ha. We expect that a more extensive survey should display more pronounced local adaptation, because larger areas will contain more environmental variance. In practice, however, this may not necessarily be the case. The most authoritative published surveys, such as the grid-based surveys of European regions and the county-based surveys of the USA, all comprise similar numbers of sites, from several hundreds to a few thousands. This is because there is a correlation between grain and extent: more extensive surveys have coarser grain. A survey of, say, 10^6 ha with a grain of 1 ha might well provide much more evidence of local adaptation than we have been able to document within 10^3 ha. No such survey exists, however, and none well ever be carried out. The *Atlas Florae Europaeae* (Jalas & Suominen 1972) deals with an area of about 10^9 ha, at a grain size of 2.5×10^5 ha; the *Atlas of the British Flora* (Perring & Walters 1962), an area of about 2.5×10^7 ha at a grain size of 10^4 ha; the best available British county atlases, such as that for the Leicestershire flora (Primavesi & Evans 1988), an area of about 1.5×10^5 ha at a grain size of 4×10^2 ha. These surveys therefore offer increased among-site variance, but at the expense of increased within-site variance. Just as adaptation cannot be detected at scales greater than the extent of a survey, neither can it be detected at scales less than the grain of a survey. The best available data may therefore be too coarse to reveal local adaptation, quite apart from referring to developed landscapes. The only satisfactory solution to this quandary is an extensive, fine-grained survey of a remote wilderness, and no such survey has yet been attempted.

Neutral macroecology

It might also be urged that real communities possess distinctive properties that are unlikely to be exhibited by neutral models. Species tend to be consistently abundant or rare, for example, when quite independent localities within the same region are sampled; thus, if we were to sample another Monteregian forest we would probably find that *Carex arctata* was much more abundant that *Carex prasina*, as it is at Mont St-Hilaire. This constitutes indirect evidence for local adaptation, in so far as it is consistent with the conclusion that some species are systematically more specialized than others. It is equally consistent with a neutral model, however. When the abundance of species at occupied sites is analysed for the NCM, the variance within sites is 56.7 and the variance among sites 301.6, yielding an intraclass correlation of 0.84. There is a pronounced tendency for some species to be locally abundant everywhere whereas others are locally scarce everywhere. The distribution of abundance among species at a site often resembles a left-skewed log-normal, whereas the distribution of range for the whole region is often more or less geometrical; both are properties of the NCM. It is also often found that local abundance is correlated with range, and this relationship has been held to demonstrate patterns of specialization (see Gaston 1996). This is likewise a feature of the NCM, however, where the regression of mean local abundance on range (both log-transformed) for the 125 species of the model was +0.37, with $r^2 = 0.74$.

The fact that a simple neutral model can generate spatial patterns resembling survey data has broad implications for community ecology (see also Chapter 18 and Hubbell 2001). Species diversity is thought to depend on the extent of local adaptation, and if neutral models mirror patterns of local adaptation then they will also mirror patterns of diversity. They will readily generate a species–area curve, for instance, or the relationship between diversity and environmental heterogeneity. Most theories of range and abundance also invoke the degree of specialization as the key attribute of species. Our results show that the use of survey data to evaluate theories of any kind about the diversity of sites or the abundance of organisms is likely to be completely misleading in the absence of an appropriate NCM.

Summary

The distribution of species is often explained in terms of divergent specialization: having become adapted in the past to particular conditions of growth, species are now found predominantly in sites that provide these conditions, so that there is a close fit between the composition of the community and the state of the environment. The major patterns of diversity and abundance that follow from species distributions can then be interpreted in terms of local adaptation. An alternative view is that all species have identical demographic properties, and that patterns of distribution, diversity and abundance arise solely as the consequence of local dispersal. We present the results of a detailed physical and biological survey of plants in an old-growth forest, and use them to calculate the degree of local adaptation in terms of the environmental variance of sites occupied by a species as a fraction of the overall variance among sites. We compare the outcome with a parallel analysis of the spatial patterns generated by a neutral community model (NCM). The patterns observed in the forest are qualitatively similar to those generated by the NCM. It is concluded that there is no evidence for community structure generated by local adaptation at the grain (1 ha) and extent (1000 ha) of our survey. Furthermore, we argue that fundamental ecological patterns such as the species–area and range–abundance relationships cannot be interpreted reliably except in the context of an appropriate NCM.

Acknowledgements

This research was supported by a grant from Fonds pour les Chercheurs et à l'Aide de la Recherche, Québec.

References

Antonovics, J. (1976). The nature of limits to selection. *Annals of the Missouri Botanical Garden*, **63**, 224–247.

Antonovics, J. & Primack, R.B. (1982). Experimental population genetics in *Plantago*. VI. The demography of seedling transplants of *P. lanceolata*. *Journal of Ecology*, **70**, 55–75.

Bell, G. (2000). The distribution of abundance in neutral communities. *American Naturalist*, **155**, 606–617.

Bell, G., Lechowicz, M.J., Appenzeller, A., Chandler, M., Deblois, E., Jackson, L., Mackenzie, B., Preziosi, R., Schallenberg, M. & Tinker, N. (1993). The spatial structure of the physical environment. *Oecologia*, **96**, 114–121.

Bell, G., Lechowicz, M.J. & Waterway, M.J. (2000). Environmental heterogeneity and species diversity of forest sedges. *Journal of Ecology*, **88**, 67–87.

Cheplick, G.P. (1988). Influence of environment and population origin on survivorship and reproduction in reciprocal transplants of amphicarpic peanutgrass (*Amphicarpum purshii*). *American Journal of Botany*, **75**, 1048–1056.

Davies, M.S. & Snaydon, R.W. (1976). Rapid population differentiation in a mosaic environment. III. Measures of selection pressures. *Heredity*, **36**, 59–66.

Gaston, K.J. (1996). The multiple forms of the interspecific abundance–distribution relationship. *Oikos*, **76**, 211–220.

Hiesey, W.M. (1940). Environmental influences and transplant experiments. *Botanical Review*, **6**, 181–203.

Hubbell, S.P. (2001). *A unified Theory of Biodiversity and Biogeography*. Princeton University Press, Princeton, NJ.

Hubbell, S.P. & Foster, R.B. (1986). Biology, chance and history and the structure of tropical rain forest tree communities. In: *Community Ecology* (eds J. Diamond & T.J. Case), pp. 314–329. Harper & Row, New York.

Jain, S.K. & Bradshaw, A.D. (1966). Evolution in closely adjacent plant communities. I. The evidence and its theoretical analysis. *Heredity*, **21**, 407–441.

Jalas, J. & Suominen, J., eds (1972). *Atlas Florae*

Europaeae, Vols 1–12. Cambridge University Press, Cambridge, UK.

Jordan, N. (1992). Path analysis of local adaptation in two ecotypes of the annual plant *Diodia teres* Walt (Rubiaceae). *American Naturalist*, **140**, 149–165.

Kassen, R.K. & Bell, G. (2000). The ecology and genetics of fitness in Chlamydomonas. XII. The phylogenetic and ecological structure of fitness. *Evolution*, **54**, 425–432.

Lovett Doust, L. (1981). Population dynamics and local specialization in a clonal perennial (*Ranunculus repens*). II. The dynamics of leaves, and a reciprocal transplant–replant experiment. *Journal of Ecology*, **69**, 757–768.

Maycock, P.F. (1961). Botanical studies on Mont St. Hilaire, Rouville County, Quebec. I. General description of the area and a floristic survey. *Canadian Journal of Botany*, **39**, 1293–1325.

Perring, F.H. & Walters, S.M. (1962). *Atlas of the British Flora*. Nelson, London.

Primavesi, A.L. & Evans, P.A. (1988). *Flora of Leicestershire*. Leicestershire Museums, Art Galleries and Records Service, Leicester.

Richard, M., Bell, G. & Berhadt, T. (2000). Environmental heterogeneity and the spatial structure of fern species diversity in one hectare of old-growth forest. *Ecography*, **23**, 231–245.

Schmidt, K.P. & Levin, D.A. (1988). The comparative demography of reciprocally sown populations of *Phlox drummondi* Hood. I. Survivorships, fecundities, and finite rates of increase. *Evolution*, **39**, 396–404.

Schmitt, J. & Gamble, S.E. (1990). The effect of distance from the parental site on offspring performance and inbreeding depression in *Impatiens capensis*: a test of the local adaptation hypothesis. *Evolution*, **44**, 2022–2030.

van Tienderen, P.H. & van der Toorn, J. (1991). Genetic differentiation between populations of *Plantago lanceolata*. II. Phenotypic selection in a transplant experiment in three contrasting habitats. *Journal of Ecology*, **70**, 43–59.

Whittaker, R.H. (1970). *Communities and Ecosystems*. Macmillan, London.

Part 2

Metapopulations

Chapter 7

Spatially realistic models of metapopulation dynamics and their implications for ecological, genetic and evolutionary processes

I. Hanski*

Introduction

A chapter that seemingly does not fit an otherwise coherent volume can be justified in one of two ways, either by boasting that it brings a helpful perspective from a near-by field of research, or by promising that it helps convey the book's message to a broader audience. The focal organisms in this chapter are butterflies rather than plants. Butterflies don't stand still like plants do, but to my astonishment the very spatial population structures that my research group has documented in a large-scale butterfly study are strikingly similar to well-documented spatial population structures in a plant metapopulation. Not only that, but the hypothesized or proven processes that maintain these spatial structures might also be largely the same. Having thus convinced myself of the value of comparing plants and butterflies I venture to offer this chapter to others.

In the research that we have conducted an important challenge has been to find ways of incorporating the key effects of landscape structure on spatial population processes. We have focused on what I call highly fragmented landscapes, that is land-scapes in which the suitable habitat for the focal species occurs as relatively small and discrete fragments that altogether cover only a relatively small fraction of the total landscape area. The spatial dynamics are dominated by the turnover of local populations inhabiting individual habitat patches. In such situations, for which there are many well-studied examples (Hanski 1999), an ecologist is tempted to focus on local populations and to ignore within-population dynamics, although this has the draw-back that extending the analysis to evolutionary issues, primarily concerned with individuals, is not straightforward. The advantages are, however, many. The conceptual and mathematical models remain relatively simple, and it is possible to relate in a sensible manner the key metapopulation processes, local extinction and colonization, to the key structural features of highly fragmented landscapes. The models can be parameterized for real metapopulations (Hanski 1994a, 1999; Moilanen 1999), and a rigorous mathematical analysis is also possible (Ovaskainen & Hanski

* *Metapopulation Research Group, Department of Ecology and Systematics, PO Box 17, FIN-00014 University of Helsinki, Finland.*

2001a,b). I call such models spatially realistic models, which is more than spatially explicit models (typically based on regular lattice), as the spatially realistic models allow one to consider the features of real fragmented landscapes.

Integrating ecology and evolution in a spatial context, the title of this volume, is a mighty task. Ecologists have struggled for a long time to incorporate the spatial structure of populations into their research and theories (Hanski & Gilpin 1997; McCullough 1997; Tilman & Kareiva 1997; Bascompte & Solé 1998; Dieckmann et al. 2000), while time after time evolutionary ecologists have reminded us of the necessity of integrating ecological and evolutionary processes (Berry et al. 1992). Difficult as the synthesis of all three components will be — ecological dynamics, evolutionary dynamics, realistic description of space — there are reasons to believe that the effort is very much worthwhile. First, the time scale of metapopulation dynamics is necessarily relatively slow, so slow that there is ample time for evolutionary processes to operate. In a spatially realistic setting, when we take into account spatial variation in the structure of the landscape, selection may lead to spatial variation in the genotypic composition of local populations with possible consequences for ecological dynamics. Secondly, in metapopulations with a high rate of population turnover, which is often the case in highly fragmented landscapes (Hanski 1999), selection may operate not only at the level of individuals but also at the level of local populations as envisioned in the classical models of group selection (Wynne-Edwards 1962; Levins 1970; Gilpin 1975). With conflicting selection pressures operating at the individual and population levels, the evolutionary response cannot be properly understood without taking into account the spatial structure of the landscape. Thirdly, in highly fragmented landscapes many local populations are either permanently small (in small habitat patches) or temporally small (e.g. following population establishment; see Chapter 9). Genetic drift and inbreeding then amplify differences in the genetic composition of populations, and the genetic dynamics may have an impact on the ecological dynamics (e.g. inbreeding depression increasing extinction risk). Finally, it is worth stressing that while including the actual spatial structure of landscapes into our analyses may represent considerable complication, and therefore forces us to carefully consider exactly what to include in our models and designs for field studies, focus on the actual spatial structure of landscapes will facilitate quantitative tests of model predictions. In this chapter, I hope to illustrate all these considerations.

Butterflies and plants: two metapopulation studies

Over the past 9 years, I have conducted with a large number of students and post docs a large-scale study of metapopulation biology of a species of butterfly, the Glanville fritillary (*Melitaea cinxia*; Hanski 1999). Although metapopulation dynamics of many other species of butterfly (Thomas & Hanski 1997) and of other taxa (reviews in Hanski & Gilpin 1997; Hanski 1999; for plants see Chapter 8) have been studied over the past decade, these studies do not typically combine the large spatial scale and intensive work on the processes influencing the extinction and colonization rates that we have aimed at combining in the *M. cinxia* project. However, there is one other metapopulation study that is astonishingly similar in scope and in many of its aims to our butterfly project — the metapopulation study of the white campion plant (*Silene alba*), conducted in Virginia, USA, by Janis Antonovics and his colleagues. It is instructive to compare these two studies in some detail (Table 7.1).

The spatial scale of the two studies is almost identical, both metapopulations consisting of some 300–500 local populations in any one year, distributed across a network of several thousand suitable habitat patches. In the *Silene* metapopulation, the patches are arbitrarily delimited 40-m segments of roadside, embracing one or two genetic neighbourhoods as estimated from pollen and seed dispersal distances (Antonovics *et al.* 1997). In the study area, the plant is conveniently confined to the roadside habitat, making extensive census work of several thousand 'patches' feasible. In the *Melitaea* metapopulation, habitat patches are naturally delimited, small, dry meadows that contain one or both of the two larval host plants, *Plantago lanceolata* and *Veronica spicata*. Females lay eggs in large batches, and the larvae tend to remain in sib-groups throughout their development. The larvae spin a conspicuous web around the host plant, which makes it possible to census rather accurately

Table 7.1 Comparison between two metapopulation studies on the Glanville fritillary butterfly (*Melitaea cinxia*) and the white campion plant (*Silene alba*).

Attribute	Melitaea cinxia	Silene alba
Size of the study area	30×30 km^2	25×25 km^2
Number of habitat patches	4200	7500
Type of habitat patch	Small (typically <1 ha) discrete dry meadows	40-m segments of roadside
Number of person-months needed to survey the system	20	2
Number of local populations in any one year	300–500	400–500
Life history	Annual	Short-lived perennial
Annual extinction rate	42–50%	14–22%
Extinction risk increases with decreasing population size	Yes	Yes
Colonization probability increases with connectivity	Yes	Yes
Strong interaction with	Cotesia melitaearum (parasitoid wasp)	Ustilago violacea (fungal pathogen)
Fraction of host populations occupied by the natural enemy	9–20%	16–19%
Full sib mating decreases	Egg-hatching rate by 27%	Germination rate by 60%

References: *Melitaea cinxia*, Hanski (1999), Hanski *et al.* (1995), Saccheri *et al.* (1998), Haikola *et al.* (in preparation); *Silene alba*, Antonovics *et al.* (1997), Thrall *et al.* (1998), Richards (2000).

local populations in terms of the number of family groups. Still, the effort needed to census the entire butterfly metapopulation is by an order of magnitude greater (20 person-months) than the effort expended by Antonovics's crew (2 person-months). In both studies, local populations are censused twice a year, providing additional information on the processes influencing mortality and thereby population extinction.

One difference in the life histories of the two species is that while *Silene alba* is a short-lived perennial, *Melitaea cinxia* is an annual in our study area. The annual rate of population turnover is very high in both species (Table 7.1), because local populations are mostly very small. The annual extinction rate is even higher in the butterfly, but this difference would entirely or largely disappear if extinction rate would be calculated on a per-generation basis. In both species, the risk of local extinction increases with decreasing population size, and in both species colonization rate declines with increasing isolation of the focal patch from the existing local populations. One big advantage of working with butterflies rather than plants is that one may use straightforward mark–release–recapture techniques to study individual movement behaviour (Hanski *et al.* 1994, 2000; Kuussaari *et al.* 1996). Both females and males may disperse, although most butterflies actually stay in their natal patch throughout their life. Females typically mate soon after emergence in the natal patch, but if butterfly density is very low, females may remain unmated at least for some time (Kuussaari *et al.* 1998) and they may disperse unmated to another population. Mated females may deposit eggs in several habitat patches, but by and large male and female dispersal in *M. cinxia* are closely analogous to pollen and seed dispersal in *S. alba*.

Much of the research on the *S. alba* metapopulation has been focused on the interaction between the plant and its specific fungal pathogen, the anther smut *Ustilago violacea*. Infected flowers produce fungal spores instead of pollen, and the diseased plants are sterilized (Thrall *et al.* 1998). The butterfly has two specialist larval parasitoids, *Cotesia melitaearum* (Braconidae) and *Hyposoter horticola* (Ichneumonidae; Lei *et al.* 1997). The parasitoids have substantial differences in their biologies, which are reflected in their spatial dynamics (Lei & Hanski 1998). *Hyposoter horticola* disperses well and it tends to be present in most host populations regardless of their isolation. This parasitoid causes a rather constant level of larval mortality, around 30% (Lei *et al.* 1997; Lei & Hanski 1998). In contrast, *Cotesia melitaearum* has a much more dynamic interaction with the host butterfly, and is in this respect comparable with *Ustilago* in the *Silene* metapopulation. In 1995–99, *C. melitaearum* occupied 9–20% of the host populations, comparable to 16–19% of the *Silene* populations occupied by *Ustilago* in 1989–1993 (Antonovics *et al.* 1994; Thrall & Antonovics 1995). Both the parasitoid and the fungus increase the extinction risk of their host, and in both cases the mechanisms is exactly the same: infected populations become smaller and thereby more likely to go extinct. The *Melitaea–Cotesia* interaction is somewhat complicated by the presence of the second primary parasitoid (*H. horticola*) and an important hyperparasitoid (*Gelis agilis*; Lei *et al.* 1997; van Nouhuys & Hanski 2000).

In summary, there are striking similarities between the butterfly and the plant metapopulations, both of which consist of a large number of small local populations with a fast turnover, and both of which have a strong dynamic interaction with a specialist natural enemy. There are other similarities as well, to which I shall return below.

Adding realistic spatial structure into metapopulation models

Much of the theoretical work in metapopulation ecology continues to be based on the classic model introduced by Levins 30 years ago (Levins 1969, 1970). Similarly, much of the metapopulation genetic theory is based on the analogous 'island' model first employed by Wright (1931). The Levins model describes the rate of change in the scalar variable p, the fraction of habitat patches that are occupied at time t,

$$\frac{dp}{dt} = cp(1-p) - ep \tag{1}$$

where c and e are two parameters setting the rates of colonization and extinction of local populations. The model assumes 'mass action' in colonization, with the colonization rate being proportional to the product of the occupied (sources of migrants) and empty patches (targets of migrants). The model assumes a large number (strictly speaking infinite) of identical and equally connected habitat patches. Such assumptions, and the very simplicity of the model, have led some ecologists to distrust much of the metapopulation ecological theory (Harrison 1994). Evidently, real metapopulations live in finite patch networks with marked spatial variation in patch attributes. To what extent, then, does the Levins model remain a helpful theoretical tool for ecologists?

Perhaps the greatest problem with the Levins model and other 'island' models is the assumption of equal connectivity, which means that the models are not seriously spatial at all, as space is treated only indirectly through the implicit assumption that local dynamics are spatially uncorrelated. The cavalier treatment of space in Eq. 1 is well illustrated by the extension of the model to the question about the population dynamic consequences of habitat loss. Lande (1987) introduced the idea that fraction $1 - h$ of the patches are unsuitable for establishment of local populations, although migrating individuals still arrive randomly at all patches, including those that are not suitable (the immigrants are effectively killed in these patches). With this modification, the colonization rate is reduced to $chp(1 - p)$, where p is now the fraction of suitable patches ($=$ fraction h of all patches) that are occupied. The value of p at equilibrium is given by

$$p^\star = 1 - \frac{\delta}{h} \tag{2}$$

where $\delta = e/c$. It is apparent from this equation that the *spatial configuration* of habitat loss cannot be analysed at all with the Levins model or other comparable models.

Yet ecologists (McCarthy *et al.* 1997) have the strong intuition, backed up by simulation results (Hill & Caswell 1999; With & King 1999), that it makes a big difference where in-space habitat is lost.

Recent work by Ovaskainen and myself (Hanski & Ovaskainen 2000; Ovaskainen & Hanski 2001a,b) provides a simple way of expanding the Levins model into a spatially realistic model, appropriate for modelling metapopulation dynamics in highly fragmented landscapes. Space does not allow me to derive the following results in any detail, but this may actually make it easier to follow the main argument. Our models are based on the reasonable ecological assumptions that the risk of local extinction increases with decreasing patch size (a surrogate of expected local population size), and that the probability of colonization increases with increasing connectivity to neighbouring populations. Empirical findings for *Melitaea* and *Silene* metapopulations (Table 7.1), among many other studies (reviewed in Hanski 1994b, 1999), are consistent with these assumptions. We next construct a 'landscape' matrix **M**, which summarizes the effects of patch size and connectivity on the rates of local extinction and colonization. It turns out that in the spatially realistic version of the Levins model the size of the metapopulation at equilibrium is well approximated by

$$p_\lambda^\star = 1 - \frac{\delta}{\lambda_M} \tag{3}$$

where λ_M is the dominant eigenvalue of matrix **M**, called the metapopulation capacity of the fragmented landscape (Hanski & Ovaskainen 2000), and p_λ is the weighted average of the long-term probabilities of occupancy of individual patches, the weights being related to the contributions of individal patches to metapopulation capacity (Ovaskainen & Hanski 2001a; unpublished). Notice that Eq. 3 is structurally identical with Eq. 2. Therefore, λ_M plays exactly the same role in the spatially realistic model as h plays in the Levins model. The great advantage of λ_M, however, is that it measures not only the amount of habitat in the landscape but also, from the viewpoint of the metapopulation dynamic consequences, how that amount of habitat is distributed among a finite set of patches with particular spatial locations. Furthermore, it may be shown that the transient dynamics of the spatially realistic model are well approximated by the transient dynamics of the simple Levins model, when the parameters of the latter model are appropriately interpreted (Ovaskainen & Hanski 2001b). It now becomes straightforward to, for instance, analyse the metapopulation dynamic consequences of habitat loss and fragmentation, including the effects of the spatial configuration of the lost habitat (Figure 7.1).

I wish to underscore the conceptual and theoretical significance of these results. The simple one-dimensional Levins model can be used as a very good approximation of the *n*-dimensional spatially realistic model, with as many equations as there are habitat patches, each giving the rate of change in the probability of that patch being occupied. This means that we can very effectively summarize the effects of landscape configuration on metapopulation dynamics, and in a manner that can

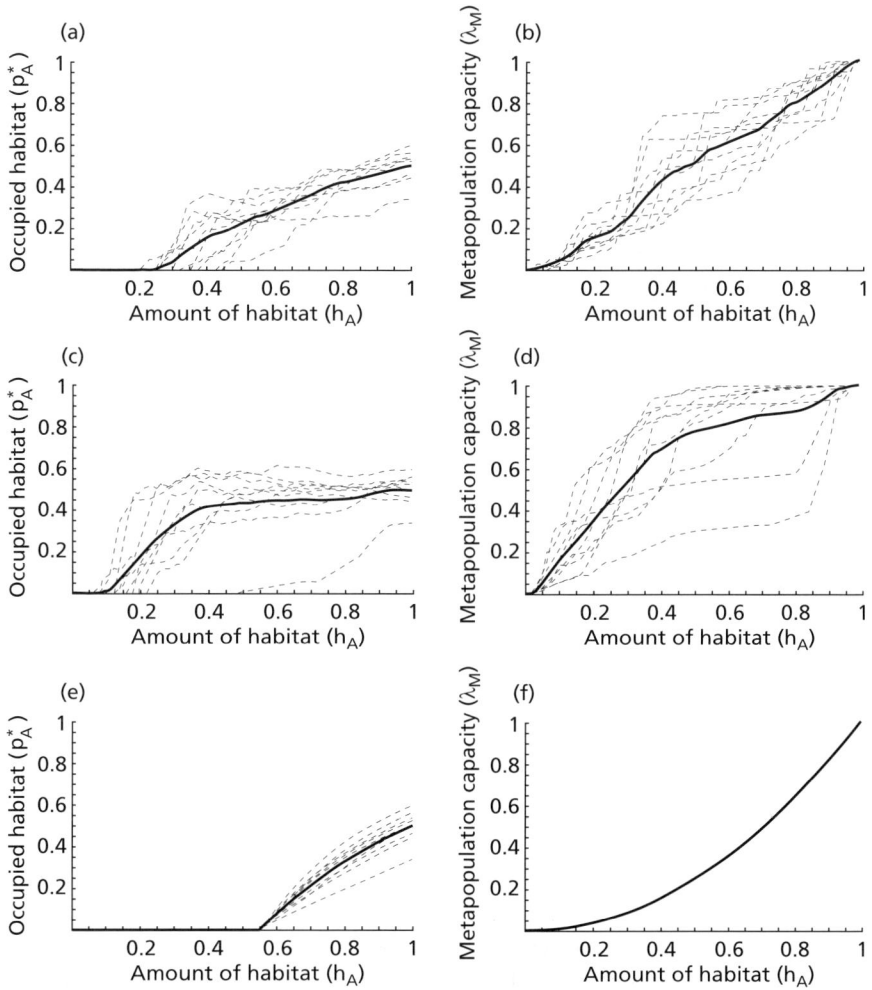

Figure 7.1 Consequences of habitat loss on patch occupancy and the threshold value for metapopulation persistence under three scenarios (the three rows of panels): (a) and (b), random loss of habitat patches; (c) and (d), systematic loss of patches from the margins of a square area; and (e) and (f), loss of area from each existing patch. The left-hand panels show the fraction of occupied habitat at equilibrium against the fraction of suitable habitat (h_A), the right-hand panels give the relationship between the metapopulation capacity (λ_M) and h_A. The results were calculated for hypothetical landscapes with 100 randomly located habitat patches. Patch areas are log-normally distributed. Model parameters have the values $\alpha = 1$ and $\delta = 0.3$. Results are shown for 10 replicates in each case, with the thick line showing the average. Patch areas in the replicates were scaled to give $\lambda_M = 1$. (From Hanski and Ovaskainen 2000. Reprinted by permission from *Nature*, Macmillan Magazines Ltd)

readily be applied to real metapopulations in real landscapes (λ_M can be calculated for patch networks for which patch areas and spatial locations are known). This is a major improvement upon the simple 'island' model, and should help us narrow down the gap between models and empirical research. One restriction of the new model is that it operates at the level of local populations inhabiting discrete habitat patches. As nothing is said about individuals and local dynamics, one cannot use this model to, for instance, construct evolutionary models at the individual level. Nevertheless, the challenge now is to incorporate, in one way or another, the same level of spatial realism into genetic and evolutionary models. The following sections attempt to make the point that including the description of landscape structure into our analyses of genetic and evolutionary processes is likely to lead to novel insights and conclusions.

Evolution of migration rate

Evolution of migration rate is one of the classic topics in evolutionary ecology (van Valen 1971; Gadgil 1971). The major forces thought to influence the evolution of migration rate include spatiotemporal variation in fitness, cost of migration in terms of elevated mortality, resource and kin competition, and inbreeding avoidance (Johnson & Gaines 1990; Hansson 1991; Olivieri & Gouyon 1997). All these processes depend more or less directly on the spatial structure of the landscape. Thus, kin competition and inbreeding are not likely to be important unless many local populations are often small, which is likely to be the case if many habitat patches are small. Spatiotemporal variation in fitness is likely to depend on the pattern of connectivity among the populations and hence on the spatial locations of the habitat patches.

Considering again the process of habitat loss, we may inquire about the consequences of habitat loss on the evolution of migration rate. Just as in the case of the ecological consequences discussed in the previous section, it is to be expected that the evolutionary consequences depend on exactly where inspace habitat is lost. We cannot analyse this question unless the modelling framework allows us to incorporate a realistic description of the landscape structure.

Heino and Hanski (2001) have constructed an individual-based simulation model to examine the evolution of migration rate (or some other traits) in spatially realistic landscapes. In our application of the model to metapopulations of *M. cinxia* and related butterflies, we used the ecological incidence function model to constrain the individual-based model to yield realistic long-term metapopulation dynamics (the incidence function model is a stochastic model in many ways comparable to the deterministic model described in the previous section and which can be parameterized for real metapopulations; Hanski 1994a, 1999; Moilanen 1999). We used a statistical model of mark–release–recapture data (Hanski *et al.* 2000) to model the movement patterns and rates of individuals in patch networks. We can rigorously estimate most of the model parameters, and those parameters that could not be estimated directly were used to tune the long-term dynamics. In the model, the emigration rate from patch i is given as

$$\varepsilon_i = \eta A_i^\zeta \tag{4}$$

where A_i is the area of patch i and ζ gives the scaling of emigration rate with patch area, an important landscape effect on movement patterns in highly fragmented landscapes (Thomas & Hanski 1997). In our study, parameter η, called the migration propensity, was allowed to evolve.

Applying the model to the real landscape of the false heath fritillary butterfly (*Melitaea diamina*), a close relative of *M. cinxia*, and allowing the migration propensity to evolve, produced the value of $\eta = 0.106$. The empirically estimated value was 0.130 (Hanski *et al.* 2000), which is not significantly different from the model-predicted value. There is nothing in the model to constrain the value of η, hence this is an enouraging result suggesting that with a spatially realistic model we may indeed be able to predict the migration propensity of species in real landscapes.

Real landscapes show spatial variation in landscape characteristics, and such variation may lead to local or regional adaptation in migration rate. We examined to what extent spatial variation in migration rate could be expected to evolve in the real habitat patch networks occupied by the butterfly metapopulations. The range of predicted η values for the landscapes investigated was rather limited, from 0.09 to 0.13, but none the less there were consistent differences between parts of the landscape with dissimilar network properties. The average extinction rate within a cluster of patches was positively correlated with the predicted η value (Figure 7.2), consistent with predictions of previous general models of the evolution of migration rate (van Valen 1971; Comins *et al.* 1980; Levin *et al.* 1984; but see Ronce *et al.* 2000; Parvinen *et al.* 2000; and Heino & Hanski 2001 for further analysis and discussion).

In a recent field experiment, we attempted to compare the migration propensity of *M. cinxia* females originating from a sparse and a dense patch network by releasing butterflies reared in a common environment into a small system of habitat patches and following their movement behaviour under the same environmental conditions. In qualitative terms, the model predicts that migration propensity first declines with increasing average isolation of habitat patches, due to increasing cost of migration (mortality), but with even greater average isolation, when an increasing fraction of habitat patches remains empty, migration propensity again increases (Heino & Hanski 2001). In the latter case, the opportunities for population establishment select for more migration. In both the sparse and the dense network, larvae were collected for the experiment from many newly-established and many older local populations. The results demonstrate a significant difference in the migration propensity of female butterflies originating from the two types of habitat patches, with butterflies from the newly-established populations being more mobile than butterflies from the older populations (Table 7.2). This result is consistent with the expectation that new populations are established by particularly mobile individuals. There is also a difference between the sparse and the dense networks in the expected

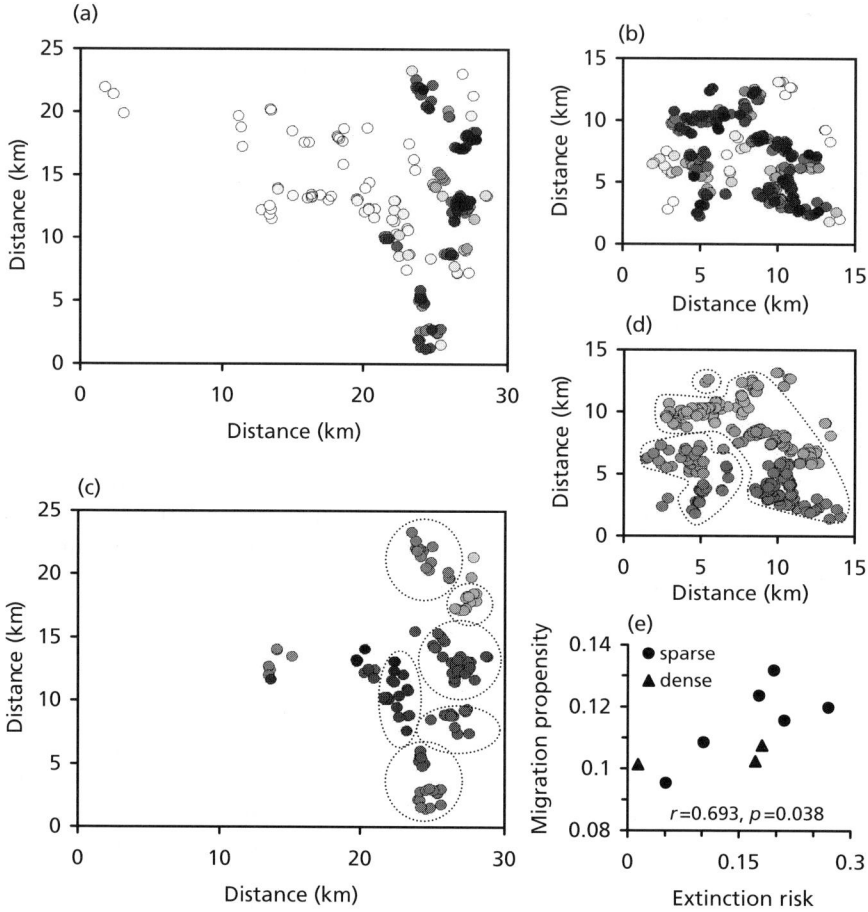

Figure 7.2 Relationship between extinction rate and migration propensity in the model of Heino and Hanski (2001). (a) and (b) show predicted patch occupancy, and (c) and (d) show the predicted migration propensity in two contrasting large habitat patch networks inhabited by *Melitaea cinxia* in the Åland Islands in south-west Finland. The network in (a) is sparse, and only the eastern part of the network supports a viable metapopulation using the field-estimated parameter values. Clustering of the patches allows some regional differences in migration propensity to evolve (c). The other network (b) is dense and less clustered. Migration propensity is fairly homogeneous over the network (d). Within-cluster average migration propensity is correlated with extinction risk (e). In calculating within-cluster averages, patches were weighted with their carrying capacity. Delineation of clusters is based on among-patch connectivities, with isolated single patches and clusters with very low incidence of occupancy ignored. The results are mean values for 10 replicates. (From Heino and Hanski 2001. Reprinted by permission from the University of Chicago Press)

Table 7.2 Experiment on emigration rate in *Melitaea cinxia*. Butterflies were collected as larvae from two different regions, with a dense and a sparse habitat patch network, and from some tens of individual local populations in each region, including newly-established and old populations. The larvae were reared in common environment, marked and released simultaneously in the same environment. The figures give the fraction of released butterflies that were observed outside the release patch (number of female individuals in brackets). The effect of the age of the population is significant ($P < 0.003$) but the effect of the region is not ($P = 0.31$; I. Hanski *et al.* unpublished).

Region	Newly-established	Old populations
Dense network	0.33 (33)	0.15 (119)
Sparse network	0.45 (22)	0.19 (26)

direction (taking into account that a large fraction of the patches is empty), but this difference is not statistically significant (Table 7.2). These empirical results suggest that the structure of the landscape may impose a substantial selection pressure on migration propensity. For reviews of related studies, including studies on plants, see Olivieri and Gouyon (1997) and Hanski (1999).

Inbreeding depression and metapopulation dynamics

Melitaea cinxia suffers from substantial inbreeding depression. One generation of mating between full sibs ($F = 0.25$) led to a 27% reduction on average in egg-hatching rate in three independent laboratory experiments (Haikola *et al.* 2002). In addition, the same level of inbreeding reduced the ability of larvae to construct the winter 'nest' within which they diapause (Nieminen *et al.* 2001), reduced larval weight after diapause but increased the length of pupal period (thereby possibly increasing pupal parasitism), reduced the rate of successful mating (Haikola *et al.* 2002) and adult longevity in the field (Saccheri *et al.* 1998). The fitness consequences of reduced egg-hatching rate are likely to be amplified by diapause in the field, as the probability of successful diapause is reduced by small larval group size (Kuussaari 1998). In the *S. alba* metapopulation, sibling-mated individuals showed a nearly 60% reduction in germination rate in comparison with outbred individuals (Richards 2000). Gene flow into local populations consisting of full sibs was observed to be higher than gene flow to comparable populations consisting of unrelated individuals (Richards 2000; see also Chapter 9). Dispersal may thus lead to 'genetic rescue' in addition to the familiar demographic rescue. The genetic rescue effect is apparently due to low fitness of inbred individuals, and hence high fitness of immigrants.

Inbreeding depression has substantial metapopulation dynamic consequences in *M. cinxia* in increasing the rate of local extinction. In an observational study involving 42 local populations with variation in population size and isolation, Saccheri *et al.* (1998) demonstrated that the extinction risk over 1 year was significantly increased by reduced average heterozygosity of individuals in the populations.

Given the population structure and dynamics of the butterfly, average heterozygosity is a reasonable measure of inbreeding in local populations. In this study, we controlled for the ecological causes of population extinction (the populations that went extinct were characterized by small size, they were isolated, and the habitat patch had a low density of nectar flowers, which increases emigration and decreases immigration). In a subsequent field experiment, small local populations were established with inbred (within-family crosses) and outbred individuals. As in the observational study (Saccheri *et al.* 1998), the rate of extinction over 1 year was higher among the populations consisting of inbred than outbred individuals (Nieminen *et al.* 2001). Our results are consistent with the vision (see Chapter 9) that many newly-established and still small populations quickly fail because of genetic as well as ecological reasons. Thrall *et al.* (1998) have investigated the metapopulation dynamic consequences of inbreeding in *S. alba* with a spatially realistic simulation model. They demonstrated that plausible scenarios exist in which the genetic rescue effect is essential for metapopulation persistence.

The common feature in the butterfly and the plant metapopulations is substantial genetic load and therefore strong inbreeding depression in spite of the local populations repeatedly going through population bottlenecks. One might expect that deleterious recessives are purged by such population structure. To some extent purging may be happening, as demonstrated by a comparison in inbreeding depression in *M. cinxia* from the naturally highly fragmented metapopulation in Åland, Finland, and a much more continuous population in South France—inbreeding depression was more severe in the latter (Haikola *et al.* in 2002). Nevertheless, substantial genetic load remains in the Åland metapopulation, most likely because of high probability of fixation of slightly deleterious recessives in small local populations and because of gene flow among neighbouring local populations. Evidently, the pattern of inbreeding and the maintenance of genetic load cannot be understood without considering the actual spatial structure and dynamics of the metapopulation. Richards (2000) suggests that the same sort of situation prevails in the *S. alba* metapopulation.

The general message from this section is that inbreeding might have especially marked population dynamic consequences in highly fragmented metapopulations. In large, continuous populations, inbreeding does not generally occur at all, whereas in smaller, but persistent and relatively isolated local populations purging may eliminate the harmful consequences of inbreeding. In contrast, in highly fragmented metapopulations mating among close relatives is likely to be a common phenomenon in small local populations and the population structure makes purging inefficient. However, exactly how the effects of mutation, selection, inbreeding and migration blend in metapopulations remains an exciting challenge for theoretical and empirical research (see also Chapter 9).

Evolution of oviposition preference

The spatial structure of metapopulations may influence the evolution of many other traits apart from migration rate. In our studies on the *M. cinxia* metapopulation, we have recently focused on the oviposition host plant preference of female butterflies, a trait that has been intensively studied from the behavioural (Parmesan *et al.* 1995), ecological (Singer 1983; Thomas & Singer 1987) and evolutionary (Singer *et al.* 1988; Singer *et al.* 1993) viewpoints in the related North American checkerspot butterflies. Like many other herbivorous insects, *M. cinxia* tends to exhibit local specialization, female butterflies in particular populations using only a subset of the host plants that are used within the entire geographic range of the species.

Local specialization is clearly a spatial phenomenon, but we may ask whether the actual process of local specialization is influenced by the spatial population structure and dynamics. Consider the landscape and metapopulation structure of *M. cinxia*. The landscape is naturally highly fragmented, consisting of small meadows that are typically less than 1 ha in size. In the entire study area, the butterfly has two host plants, *Plantago lanceolata* and *Veronica spicata*. Within a network of meadows, the species composition of host plants varies haphazardly, with one species typically dominating in any one region, but often the network also has 'atypical' patches dominated by the alternative host plant. The question we have asked is whether it makes a difference for the process of local specialization in exactly which manner the two host plants are distributed among the habitat patches.

Empirically, we have found strong evidence for a 'colonization effect' (Hanski & Singer 2001): the probability of an empty patch being colonized is influenced by the 'match' between the relative host plant composition in that patch and the genetically determined oviposition preference of migrating females. Here is a clear example of a particular life-history trait influencing extinction–colonization dynamics. Using a combination of modelling and empirical data, we have also demonstrated the reverse effect: the extinction–colonization dynamics appear to influence the evolution of oviposition preference (Hanski & Heino, in preparation). In brief, we have incorporated the colonization effect into a spatially realistic model to study the evolution of oviposition preference. The model-predicted optimal oviposition preference explained a significant fraction of the variation among replicate metapopulations in the use of the two host plants, on top of the variation explained by the overall abundances of the two host plants (Hanski & Heino, in preparation). In other words, the same amount of *Veronica* (or *Plantago*) has a dissimilar impact on both ecological and evolutionary dynamics depending on whether that amount of host plant is located in a patch that plays a minor vs. a major role in the dynamics of the metapopulation as a whole.

Conclusion

In this chapter, I have dwelled on models and analyses that incorporate the actual spatial structure of real fragmented landscapes in terms of the sizes and the spatial positions of individual habitat fragments. It may be asked whether this level of realism is really needed—the exact spatial structure of the landscape evidently has a quantitative influence on model results, but it is less clear that the qualitative conclusions would also be affected.

In the case of ecological metapopulation dynamics, one of the major questions is in fact a quantitative one: How does the actual spatial structure of the landscape influence the capacity of the landscape to support a viable metapopulation? The recent progress that has been made to answer this question with mathematical models (pp. 143–146) has substantial promise for practical applications. The hope is that we can develop predictive models that would find applications in management and conservation. With respect to theory, it is worth reiterating that the influence of the spatial structure of the landscape on metapopulation persistence can be absorbed into the simple Levins model via an appropriate reinterpretation of the model parameters (Ovaskainen & Hanski 2001b). This is a very pleasing result as it allows us to retain the clarity of the basic model and to effectively summarize the impact of landscape structure with a few parameters. However, it should be remembered that the models apply to 'highly fragmented' landscapes. It remains a big challenge to develop anything comparable for arbitrarily fragmented landscapes.

In the case of the evolution of migration rate, many of the qualitative results are not influenced by the inclusion of the exact spatial structure of the landscape (Heino & Hanski 2001). However, there are phenomena such as regional differentiation of migration rate in response to landscape structure that cannot be meaningfully analysed without considering the spatial configuration of the landscape. The same applies to the evolution of other life-history traits, such as oviposition preference discussed on pp. 150–151, and to the question about the maintenance of genetic load in metapopulations living in fragmented landscapes (pp. 149–150). I thus conclude that including the exact spatial structure of landscapes in our models is necessary both for the development of testable quantitative theory as well as for the qualitative analysis of many interesting population biological phenomena.

In the case of classical metapopulations with extinction-prone local populations, long-term persistence is possible only at the metapopulation level. Metapopulation-level persistence is not guaranteed, of course, and with increasing habitat loss and fragmentation of many landscapes, countless metapopulations approach the extinction threshold for persistence ($\lambda_M > \delta$ in Eq. 3). Genetic and evolutionary processes may interact with the ecological processes that influence metapopulation persistence. Recent studies of genetic 'meltdown' of isolated populations due to fixation of deleterious alleles (Lande 1995; Lynch et al. 1995) could be extended to metapopulations, in which recurrent extinctions and colonizations add another twist with still largely unexplored consequences. Thrall et al. (1998) have examined another kind of metapopulation meltdown in their study of S. alba, due to accumulated consequences of inbreeding depression.

The other side of the coin is the possibility that the ecological, genetic and evolutionary processes discussed in this chapter might lead to metapopulation rescue. The 'rescue effect' is most often discussed in term of demographic rescue of local populations, as originally envisioned by Brown and Kodric-Brown (1977) and discussed in Hanski (1999). In metapopulations with inbreeding depression, gene flow into small populations may lead to a genetic rescue, as demonstrated for the S. alba metapopulation by Richards (2000). Finally, Heino and Hanski (2001) analyse the possibility of evolutionary rescue in a deteriorating landscape due to the evolution of migration rate. They conclude that evolutionary rescue is a definite possibility, although in practice the rate of environmental change is so rapid, and the domain in the parameter space allowing for such rescue is so limited, that evolutionary rescue of endangered species is likely to remain an academic curiosity. One can also conceive interactions between the above-described ecological, genetic and evolutionary processes. Thus, the genetic rescue from harmful consequences of inbreeding may be strengthened by an evolutionary increase in migration propensity. In the *M. cinxia* metapopulation inbreeding depression is likely to be countered by elevated migration rate in low-density populations, which has been demonstrated experimentally by Kuussaari *et al.* (1996). The challenge is to find out which of such interactions make a truly significant difference in real metapopulations, and which interactions remain exciting theoretical possibilities.

Summary

Highly fragmented landscapes consist of networks of discrete habitat patches that collectively cover only a relatively small fraction of the total landscape area. Individual habitat patches are characterized by their size, spatial position and possibly by other attributes. Spatially realistic models take into account the effects of habitat patch area and connectivity (to existing local populations) on the rates of local extinction and establishment of new populations. With specific assumptions about the patch area and connectivity effects, we may write a set of equations for the rates of change in p_i, the probability of patch i being occupied. In the spatially realistic version of the familiar Levins model, an equilibrium solution with $p_i^* > 0$ for all i exists if and only if $\lambda_M > e/c$, where λ_M, called the metapopulation capacity of the fragmented landscape, is the leading eigenvalue of a matrix summarizing the patch area and connectivity effects on extinction and colonization. The metapopulation capacity can be calculated for real patch networks to assess their capacity to support a viable metapopulation.

These models may be used as templates into which various ecological, genetic and evolutionary processes may be attached to investigate how they may influence extinction–colonization dynamics in real landscapes and how, in turn, extinction–colonization dynamics might influence these processes. Several such processes are discussed drawing examples from a well-studied large metapopulation of the Glanville fritillary butterfly (*Melitaea cinxia*). Attention is also drawn to striking similarities in metapopulation structure and dynamics of *M. cinxia* and a well-studied plant species, the white campion (*Silene alba*).

First, in classical metapopulations migration among habitat patches and consequent colonization of currently empty patches are key processes. Spatial variation in landscape structure is expected to influence the evolution of migration rate and to lead to spatial (regional) variation in the rate of migration in real landscapes. At the same time, metapopulation persistence in increasingly fragmented landscapes may be influenced by the evolution of migration rate. Secondly, local populations in highly fragmented landscapes are often so small that mating occurs commonly among close relatives. In *M. cinxia*, inbreeding depression is sufficiently severe to increase the rate of local extinction, while the spatial population structure makes it unlikely that purging of mildly deleterious recessives is efficient. Thirdly, other habitat patch attributes apart from area and connectivity may influence extinction and colonization rates. One example is the host plant composition for oligophagous insects. In *M. cinxia*, the genetically based host plant preference of migrating females leads to biased colonization of habitat patches depending on their host plant species composition, and such biased colonizations in heterogeneous patch networks in turn influence the evolution of host plant preference. An important challenge for metapopulation biology is to integrate the various ecological, genetic and evolutionary processes into spatially realistic models.

References

Antonovics, J., Thrall, P., Jarosz, A. & Stratton, D. (1994). Ecological genetics of metapopulations: The Silene-Ustilago plant-pathogen system. In: *Ecological Genetics* (ed. L.A. Real), pp. 146–170. Princeton University Press, Princeton, NJ.

Antonovics, J., Thrall, P.H. & Jarosz, A.M. (1997). Genetics and the spatial ecology of species interaction. In: *Spatial Ecology* (eds D. Tilman & P. Kareiva), pp. 158–183. Princeton University Press, Princeton, NJ.

Bascompte, J. & Solé, R.V. (1998). *Modeling Spatiotemporal Dynamics in Ecology*. Springer-Verlag, New York.

Berry, R.J., Crawford, T.J. & Hewitt, G.M. (1992). *Genes in Ecology*. Blackwell Scientific Publications, Oxford.

Brown, J.H. & Kodric-Brown, A. (1977). Turnover rates in insular biogeography: effect of immigration on extinction. *Ecology*, **58**, 445–449.

Comins, H.N., Hamilton, W.D. & May, R.M. (1980). Evolutionary stable dispersal strategies. *Journal of Theoretical Biology*, **82**, 205–230.

Dieckmann, U., Law, R. & Metz, J.A.J. (2000). *The Geometry of Ecological Interaction: Simplifying Spatial Complexity*. Cambridge University Press, Cambridge, UK.

Gadgil, M. (1971). Dispersal: population consequences and evolution. *Ecology*, **52**, 253–261.

Gilpin, M.E. (1975). *Group Selection in Predator–Prey Communities*. Princeton University Press, Princeton, NJ.

Haikola, S., Fortelius, W., O'Hara, R.B., Kuussaari, M., Wahlberg, N., Saccheri, I.J., Singer, M.C. &

Hanski, I. (2002). Inbreeding depression and the maintenance of genetic load in *Melitaea cinxia* metapopulations. *Conservation Genetics*, in press.

Hanski, I. (1994a). A practical model of metapopulation dynamics. *Journal of Animal Ecology*, **63**, 151–162.

Hanski, I. (1994b). Patch-occupancy dynamics in fragmented landscapes. *Trends in Ecology and Evolution*, **9**, 131–135.

Hanski, I. (1999). *Metapopulation Ecology*. Oxford University Press, New York.

Hanski, I. & Gilpin, M.E. (1997). *Metapopulation Biology: Ecology, Genetics, and Evolution*. Academic Press, San Diego.

Hanski, I. & Ovaskainen, O. (2000). The metapopulation capacity of a fragmented landscape. *Nature*, **404**, 755–758.

Hanski, I. & Singer, M.C. (2001). Extinction–colonization dynamics and host plant choice in butterfly metapopulations. *American Naturalist*, in press.

Hanski, I., Kuussaari, M. & Nieminen, M. (1994). Metapopulation structure and migration in the butterfly *Melitaea cinxia*. *Ecology*, **75**, 747–762.

Hanski, I., Pakkala, T., Kuussaari, M. & Lei, G. (1995). Metapopulation persistence of an endangered butterfly in a fragmented landscape. *Oikos*, **72**, 21–28.

Hanski, I., Alho, J. & Moilanen, A. (2000). Estimating the parameters of survival and migration of individuals in metapopulations. *Ecology*, **81**, 239–251.

Hansson, L. (1991). Dispersal and connectivity in

metapopulations. *Biological Journal of the Linnean Society*, **42**, 89–103.

Harrison, S. (1994). Metapopulations and conservation. In: *Large-Scale Ecology and Conservation Biology* (eds P.J. Edwards, R.M. May & N.R. Webb), pp. 111–128. Blackwell Science, Oxford.

Heino, M. & Hanski, I. (2001). Evolution of migration rate in a spatially realistic metapopulation model. *American Naturalist*, **157**, 495–511.

Hill, M.F. & Caswell, H. (1999). Habitat fragmentation and extinction thresholds on fractal landscapes. *Ecology Letters*, **2**, 21–127.

Johnson, M.L. & Gaines, M.S. (1990). Evolution of dispersal: theoretical models and empirical tests using birds and mammals. *Annual Review of Ecology and Systematics*, **21**, 449–480.

Kuussaari, M. (1998). *Biology of the Glanville fritillary butterfly (Melitaea cinxia)*. PhD thesis, University of Helsinki.

Kuussaari, M., Nieminen, M. & Hanski, I. (1996). An experimental study of migration in the butterfly *Melitaea cinxia*. *Journal of Animal Ecology*, **65**, 791–801.

Kuussaari, M., Saccheri, I., Camara, M. & Hanski, I. (1998). Allee effect and population dynamics in the Glanville fritillary butterfly. *Oikos*, **82**, 384–392.

Lande, R. (1987). Extinction thresholds in demographic models of territorial populations. *American Naturalist*, **130**, 624–635.

Lande, R. (1995). Risk of population extinction from fixation of new deleterious mutations. *Evolution*, **48**, 1460–1469.

Lei, G. & Hanski, I.A. (1998). Spatial dynamics of two competing specialist parasitoids in a host metapopulation. *Journal of Animal Ecology*, **67**, 422–433.

Lei, G.C., Vikberg, V., Nieminen, M. & Kuussaari, M. (1997). The parasitoid complex attacking Finnish populations of the Glanville fritillary *Melitaea cinxia* (Lep: Nymphalidae), an endangered butterfly. *Journal of Natural History*, **31**, 635–648.

Levin, S.A., Cohen, D. & Hastings, A. (1984). Dispersal strategies in patchy environments. *Theoretical Population Biology*, **26**, 165–191.

Levins, R. (1969). Some demographic and genetic consequences of environmental heterogeneity for biological control. *Bulletin of the Entomological Society of America*, **15**, 237–240.

Levins, R. (1970). Extinction. *Lecture Notes in Mathematics*, **2**, 75–107.

Lynch, M., Conery, J. & Buerger, R. (1995). Mutation accumulation and the extinction of small populations. *American Naturalist*, **146**, 489–514.

McCarthy, M.A., Lindenmayer, D.B. & Dreschler, M. (1997). Extinction debts and risks faced by abundant species. *Conservation Biology*, **11**, 221–226.

McCullough, D.L. (1997). *Metapopulations and Wildlife Conservation*. Island Press, Washington DC.

Moilanen, A. (1999). Patch occupancy models of metapopulation dynamics: efficient parameter estimation using implicit statistical inference. *Ecology*, **80**, 1031–1043.

Nieminen, M., Singer, M.C., Fortelius, W., Schöps, K. & Hanski, I. (2001). Experimental confirmation that inbreeding depression increases extinction risk in butterfly populations. *American Naturalist*, **157**, 237–244.

Olivieri, I. & Gouyon, P.-H. (1997). Evolution of migration rate and other traits: The metapopulation effect. In: *Metapopulation Biology* (eds I.A. Hanski & M.E. Gilpin), pp. 293–324. Academic Press, San Diego.

Ovaskainen, O. & Hanski, I. (2001a). Spatially structured metapopulation models: global and local assessment of metapopulation capacity. *Theoretical Population Biology*, in press.

Ovaskainen, O. & Hanski, I. (2001b). Time delay in metapopulation response to perturbation. In preparation.

Parvinen, K., Dieckmann, U., Gyllenberg, M. & Metz, J.A.J. (2000). *Evolution of dispersal in metapopulations with local density dependence and demographic stochasticity*. Interim Report IR-00-035, IIASA, Laxenburg, Austria.

Parmesan, C., Singer, M. & Harris, I. (1995). Absence of adaptive learning from the oviposition foraging behaviour of a checkerspot butterfly. *Animal Behaviour*, **50**, 161–175.

Richards, C.M. (2000). Inbreeding depression and genetic rescue in a plant metapopulation. *American Naturalist*, **155**, 383–394.

Ronce, O., Perret, F. & Olivieri, I. (2000). Evolutionarily stable dispersal rates do not always increase with local extinction rates. *American Naturalist*, **155**, 485–496.

Saccheri, I.J., Kuussaari, M., Kankare, M., Vikman,

P., Fortelius, W. & Hanski, I. (1998). Inbreeding and extinction in a butterfly metapopulation. *Nature*, **392**, 491–494.

Singer, M.C. (1983). Determinants of multiple host use by a phytophagous insect population. *Evolution*, **37**, 389–403.

Singer, M.C., Ng, D. & Thomas, C.D. (1988). Heritability of oviposition preference and its relationship to offspring performance within a single insect population. *Evolution*, **42**, 977–985.

Singer, M.C., Thomas, C.D. & Parmesan, C. (1993). Rapid human-induced evolution of insect diet. *Nature*, **366**, 681–683.

Thomas, C.D. & Hanski, I.A. (1997). Butterfly metapopulations. In: *Metapopulation Biology* (eds I.A. Hanski & M.E. Gilpin), pp. 359–386. Academic Press, San Diego.

Thomas, C.D. & Singer, M.C. (1987). Variation in host preference affects movement patterns within a butterfly population. *Ecology*, **68**, 1262–1267.

Thrall, P.H. & Antonovics, J. (1995). Theoretical and empirical studies of metapopulations: population and genetic dynamics of the *Silene–Ustilago* system. *Canadian Journal of Botany*, **73**, 1249–1258.

Thrall, P.H., Richards, C.M., McCauley, D.E. & Antonovics, J. (1998). Metapopulation collapse: the consequences of limited gene-flow in spatially structured populations. In: *Modeling Spatiotemporal Dynamics in Ecology* (eds J. Bascompte & R.V. Solé), pp. 83–104. Springer-Verlag, New York.

Tilman, D. & Kareiva, P. (1997). *Spatial Ecology*. Princeton University Press, Princeton, NJ.

van Nouhuys, S. & Hanski, I. (2000). Apparent competition between parasitoids mediated by a shared hyperparasitoid. *Ecology Letters*, **3**, 82–84.

van Valen, L. (1971). Group selection and the evolution of dispersal. *Evolution*, **25**, 591–598.

With, K.A. & King, A.W. (1999). Extinction thresholds for species in fractal landscapes. *Conservation Biology*, **13**, 314–326.

Wright, S. (1931). Evolution in Mendelian populations. *Genetics*, **16**, 97–159.

Wynne-Edwards, V.C. (1962). *Animal Dispersion in Relation to Social Behaviour*. Oliver and Boyd, Edinburgh.

Chapter 8

Landscape fragmentation and the viability of plant populations

O. Eriksson* and J. Ehrlén*

Introduction

Plants live in patchy environments. This patchiness occurs at several different spatial scales, from the local neighbourhood of individual plants within populations to the whole distribution range of the species. At all spatial scales, suitable environments are located in a matrix of more or less inhospitable space. This means that for most plant species, a fragmented habitat is the arena for population dynamics, selection processes, adaptation and evolution (Wade & Goodnight 1998; Thompson 1999). In a long-term perspective, persistence of plant species necessitates mechanisms to cope with temporally and spatially unpredictable resources. Many plant life-history features, such as dispersal structures, seed dormancy, seed size and clonal propagation can be interpreted in this context (Venable & Brown 1988; Rees 1996). However, drastic human-induced changes of present-day landscapes implies an almost worldwide increase in the fragmentation of natural and seminatural habitats. Fragmentation is usually defined as an altered configuration of habitats with decreasing size and increasing average distance between habitats as distinguishing features. Although an altered population structure due to fragmentation may influence short-term adaptive response, for example concerning evolution of pathogen resistance (Ouborg *et al.* 2000) and dispersal (Olivieri *et al.* 1995), fragmentation occurs at a rate which makes adaptive tracking unlikely. As a result, fragmentation is viewed as one of the main causes of population and species loss, and it has become a key issue in conservation biology, stimulating development of both theory and empirical studies.

Predictions of fragmentation effects derive mainly from theories of island biogeography (MacArthur & Wilson 1967) and metapopulation dynamics (summarized by Hanski 1999). The main predictions are that fragmentation leads to: (i) an area-related reduction in populations sizes, in turn causing an increased local extinction rate of populations, for example due to demographic and environmental stochasticity (Menges 1992), inbreeding (Young *et al.* 1996) and Allee-effects (Stephens & Sutherland 1999); (ii) a decreased colonization rate due to the isolation of remaining habitats; and, as a result of these processes, (iii) a general decline in

* *Department of Botany, Stockholm University, SE-106 91 Stockholm, Sweden.*

local species richness. At some critical level of habitat fragmentation, dispersal among habitats is so unlikely that it does not counterbalance extinctions of local populations. As a result, the metapopulation will decline and ultimately go extinct at some threshold value (the extinction threshold) (Lawton *et al.* 1994; Hanski 1999). Because metapopulation theory usually focuses on single species (but see Holt 1997), it has become one of the dominating concepts for studies of fragmentation effects on viability of populations in a landscape perspective. Basically, metapopulation theory views landscapes as composed of discrete patches suitable for the target species and surrounded by an unsuitable matrix. Assuming that the metapopulations inhabiting the landscape are in equilibrium with the existing pattern of habitat configuration, incidence function models (Hanski 1999) can be fitted to the pattern of occupancy and used to derive estimates of colonization and extinction rates, and their dependence on habitat area and isolation.

Despite the rapidly increasing number of empirical studies, there is still a significant gap between the theory of fragmentation and the evidence from field studies (Harrison & Bruna 1999). There are several reasons for this. First of all, plant individuals sample the environment very locally and one would expect that this makes plants inherently resistant to fragmentation. Thus, from a 'plant point of view' a certain degree of fragmentation, as perceived by an investigator, may not be directly relevant for the response of a population. Furthermore, many plants occupy gradients in habitat quality. Although this can be handled theoretically (Moilanen & Hanski 1998) it complicates the estimation of occupancy patterns based on field surveys. Assessment of 'empty' but suitable patches is notoriously difficult in plants, and there are still only few studies that have used experiments to estimate occupancy in plants (Ehrlén & Eriksson 2000). On the other hand, experiments where the pattern of fragmentation is directly manipulated have been performed both on a large scale (e.g. Laurance *et al.* 1998a) and on a small scale (e.g. Robinson *et al.* 1992), but despite their potential power, such experiments are restricted to short-term responses. Yet another problem for empirical studies is that fragmentation is associated with a simultaneous reduction in overall habitat area, edge effects and, in many cases, habitat deterioration (Harrison & Bruna 1999). This holds also when fragmentation has been manipulated experimentally (e.g. Laurance *et al.* 1998a). The major cause of fragmentation is changes in land use, particularly exploitation of land for agriculture, forestry or urban development. Thus, changing distributions of habitats will unavoidably be accompanied by a multitude of other phenomena such as eutrophication, altered water availability, invasion by alien species and an increasing disturbance caused by demand for human recreation. While theory usually has focused on the effects of changing habitat configuration or reduced area *per se*, field data hardly allows us to distinguish between the different factors associated with fragmentation.

A major problem in fragmentation theory is the assumption of equilibrium of metapopulations. Many plant species may be very persistent even after a severe fragmentation of their habitat, provided that the local neighbourhood of plant individuals permits survival of local populations. Such species may remain 'quasi-persistent' for extended periods of time (Eriksson 1996a). Eriksson and Kiviniemi (1999) used data on species occupancy and sowing experiments to derive extinction thresholds for grassland plants, and compared the results with *a priori* assessments of the status of the species examined. A conclusion was that the method yielded realistic results only when the assumption of equilibrium was relaxed. If regional plant populations are not close to equilibrium, the use of incidence models based on occupancy data to derive estimates of colonization and extinction dynamics (e.g. Quintana-Ascencio & Menges 1996) may not be generally applicable. A naive use of occupancy data may yield an unwarranted 'positive' picture of the status of plant species, in effect similar to the 'extinction debt' in fragmented landscapes, suggested by Tilman *et al.* (1994). However, from a conservation point of view, there is also a possibility of population recovery in case of habitat improvement, even for species which theoretically have been doomed to extinction. A critical issue for evaluating the degree of equilibrium in plant metapopulations is therefore to assess the time scale of local population persistence, the rate of regional population decline, and how these processes depend on the plant life cycles.

In this chapter, we briefly review results from field studies with the objective to illustrate the diversity of responses of plant populations and communities to fragmentation. We will stress the importance of initiating studies on how factors other than direct area and isolation effects, for example disturbance regimes and habitat quality, interact with fragmentation. Based on our own studies from Scandinavian seminatural grasslands and deciduous forests, we discuss fragmentation effects on plant populations, at local and regional scales. In particular, we will focus on the relationship between plant life cycles and the time scale of local extinction processes. A major conclusion is that regional populations of many plant species are far from equilibrium in relation to the present landscape configuration of habitats.

Effects of fragmentation

Community-level effects

The effects of fragmentation at the level of plant communities, as judged from field evidence, are not straightforward (Table 8.1). One example is that fragmentation has variable effects on overall species richness in plant communities. Some studies document the expected decline in species richness, whereas other find no effect, or even positive effects. Harrison (1999) distinguished between habitat specialists and generalists on serpentine soil, and noted that while the overall species richness increased, the fraction of specialists decreased. A similar pattern (but with no overall change in species richness) has been documented in calcareous grasslands in Switzerland (Fischer & Stöcklin 1997). Thus, fragmentation seems to make communities more susceptible to invasion by generalists. Wiser *et al.* (1998) analysed the invasion of *Nothofagus* forests by a perennial herb, and found that early stages of invasion was promoted by edge effects. Other studies have found dramatic effects of fragmentation on community structure, for example a 'biomass collapse' and an

Table 8.1 Effects of fragmentation on plant communities and populations. The table illustrates the diversity of effects and does not provide a complete review.

Fragmentation effects	Direction of effects	References
Community level		
Total species richness	+	Harrison (1999)
	0	Eriksson *et al.* (1995); Fischer & Stöcklin (1997); Honnay *et al.* (1999)
	–	Holt *et al.* (1995); Köchy & Rydin (1997); Grashof-Bokdam (1997)
Fraction of habitat specialists	–	Fischer & Stöcklin (1997); Harrison (1999)
Invasibility	+	Wiser *et al.* (1998); Harrison (1999); Levine (2000)
Soil mineralization	0	Robinson *et al.* (1992)
Successional trends	0	Holt *et al.* (1995)
Biomass	–	Laurance *et al.* (1997)
Overall dynamics (turnover of individuals)	+	Laurance *et al.* (1998a)
Resilience	–	Leach & Givnish (1996)
Plant—animal interactions		
Pollination	– (0?)	Groom (1998); Renner (1999)
Seed dispersal by animals		
Direct effects	–	Grashof-Bokdam (1997); Grashof-Bokdam & Geertsema (1998)
Mediated by edge-effects	+	Restrepo *et al.* (1999)
Population level		
Local extinctions	+	Ouborg (1993); Quintana-Ascencio & Menges (1996)
Colonization	–	Ouborg (1993); Quintana-Ascencio & Menges (1996); Grashof-Bokdam (1997)
	0	Wolf *et al.* (1999)
Seed production	–	Morgan (1999); Kéry *et al.* (2000)
Seedling recruitment	–	Benitez-Malvido (1998); Jules (1998)
	+	Laurance *et al.* (1998b)
Local genetic variation	–	Oostermeijer *et al.* (1994, 1995)
related to individual fitness	0	Ouborg & van Treuren (1995)

altered population turnover in Amazonian rain forest (Laurance *et al.* 1997, 1998a). In contrast, Robinson *et al.* (1992) and Holt *et al.* (1995) did not document any effects on processes such as soil mineralization and succession. As most studies of fragmentation record short-term (a few years) responses, there is perhaps an overlooked phenomenon which is that landscape-scale disturbances (or human-induced prevention of disturbances) may cover areas that incorporate small habitat fragments. If recolonization following local habitat changes is hindered by lack of source populations, local assemblages of species may thereby lose their ability to persist or recover. In a longer-term perspective (decades, centuries) this reduces the resilience of the system and may cause the demise of whole communities (e.g. Leach & Givnish 1996).

Another aspect of community effects is how fragmentation influences interactions between plants and animals. Pollinators may not be able to maintain persistent populations in all fragments where animal pollinated plants occur. Bond (1994) suggested that plants lacking mechanisms that ameliorate effects of reduced visitation by pollinators, for example clonal propagation or selfing, will be particularly affected by fragmentation (e.g. Jennersten 1988). However, in a recent review, Renner (1999) concluded that the evidence for such effects is still rather limited. A handful of species have been found to suffer from reduced fruit set, and there are a few cases which indicate shifts in pollinators. Due to the higher frequency of bird and bat pollination (which seem particularly sensitive to fragmentation) and the higher frequency of specialist pollinators in the tropics, Renner argued that we may expect a latitudinal gradient in the general effects of fragmentation on pollination. Also, seed dispersal by animals may change in fragmented habitats, although these effects may go in either direction. Isolation of forest fragments has been found to reduce the incidence of plant species dispersed by animals (Grashof-Bokdam & Geertsema 1998). In contrast, a complex interplay with edge effects (Restrepo *et al.* 1999), which may increase efficiency of frugivory by birds, can also counteract isolation in small fragments having a higher ratio of edge to interior. A positive edge effect on bird-dispersed plants has been documented along hedgerows connecting forest fragments (Sarlöv-Herlin & Fry 2000). Thus, in comparison with plants having other dispersal systems, it is unclear whether the net effect of fragmentation is expected to be positive or negative in bird-dispersed plants. For interactions with herbivores and pathogens, fragmentation may influence plant performance in a positive way. Herbivores and pathogens may not be able to maintain populations in all fragments, particularly if they are specialized in their use of plants as a resource.

Effects on population dynamics

There is evidence that plants exhibit different forms of regional dynamics, including metapopulation, source–sink and remnant populations dynamics (Eriksson 1996a; Husband & Barrett 1996), but only few studies have analysed general differences in population dynamics in habitat fragments varying in size and isolation (e.g. Husband & Barrett 1998). Many population studies instead focus on population size. Assuming that population size generally correlates with fragment size (which is reasonable but largely untested, and may not hold true for all species, e.g. Figure 8.1), these studies are relevant for understanding fragmentation effects. Theoretically, a reduced population size elevates extinction rates, for example due to demographic end environmental stochasticity (Menges 1992) and Allee-effects (Groom 1998;

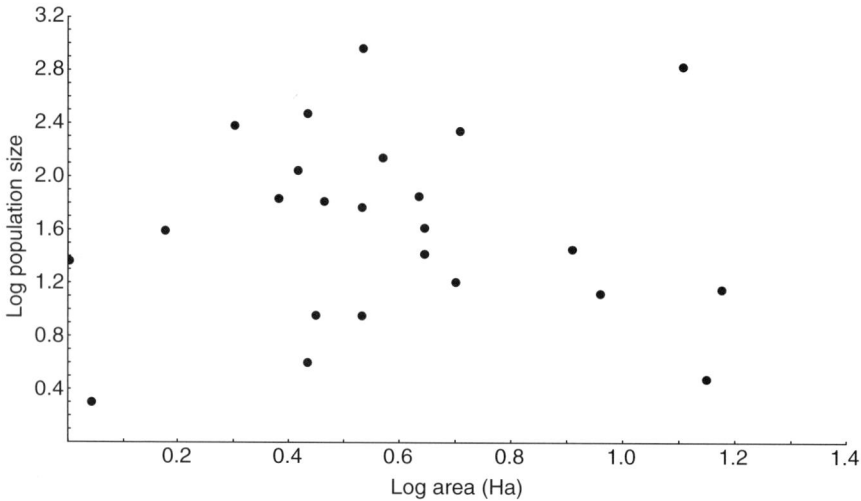

Figure 8.1 The relationship between local population size of *Gentianella campestris* and habitat fragment size (measured as area of isolated seminatural grasslands) in south-east Sweden ($r = 0.02$; $P = 0.94$). Local population size was measured as an average over 4–7 years for each population.

Stephens & Sutherland 1999). However, other factors may be more important for extinction rates (Schemske *et al.* 1994), particularly factors influencing habitat quality, for example disturbance regimes, edge effects and competition from invading species. Examination of demographic or genetic effects of small (or isolated) populations (e.g. Oostermeijer *et al.* 1994) with use of demographic modelling (Caswell 1989) and analyses of genetic markers (Ouborg *et al.* 1999) are tools that are particularly useful in addressing the direct effects of fragmentation on plant populations. Theory predicts that fragmentation will lead to an erosion of genetic variation, presumably resulting in a reduced population viability (Young *et al.* 1996). However, there is still limited evidence that reduced genetic variation also reduces local population viability (Schemske *et al.* 1994; Booy *et al.* 2000). Moreover, Young *et al.* (1996) remarked that fragmentation may in fact increase the likelihood of preserving genetic diversity, if the local genetic effects on viability are small and the between-population variation is maintained. However, rather few studies have examined these predictions, and, as with other fragmentation studies, the results are not conclusive. Some studies show a reduced variation and fitness in fragmented populations (Oostermeijer *et al.* 1994, 1995), but there are also examples where no such effects have been found (e.g. Ouborg & van Treuren 1995), as well as studies indicating that fragmentation may even increase local population viability (Ouborg *et al.* 2000).

Seed production and recruitment may be affected by fragmentation, but again the conclusions are not straightforward. Some studies have documented a reduced seed production (Morgan 1999) and a reduced recruitment (Benitez-Malvido 1998; Jules

1998), whereas others have found increased recruitment, probably due to interactions related to edge effects (Laurance *et al.* 1998b). It seems likely that the recruitment response is species specific, and that predictions on fragmentation effects have to account for the regenerative properties of each species. In forest habitats particularly, the local climate and the effects related to edges (e.g. abundance of animal dispersers) may either increase or decrease recruitment, depending on the niche requirements of the target species. If the causes of reduced population viability primarily are related to changing habitat conditions, rather than to area or isolation *per se*, species in the habitat (e.g. forest) interior will generally be negatively affected by fragmentation, whereas species using edge or transitional habitats may be favoured by fragmentation.

In a review of fragmentation effects on birds and mammals, Andrén (1994) concluded that overall area reduction has a dominating effect on regional populations until relatively little suitable habitat is left in a landscape, when local patch size and isolation become more influential. If this holds also for plants, we expect that habitat configuration in the present-day highly fragmented landscapes is important for the distribution of species. Some studies have documented that local extinction or colonization are related to habitat size or isolation (e.g. Ouborg 1993; Quintana-Ascencio & Menges 1996) and there is growing evidence for regional dispersal limitation in plants, both for grasslands (e.g. Primack & Miao 1992; Å. Eriksson 1998) and forests (e.g. Ehrlén & Eriksson 2000). These results suggest that fragmentation should influence the regional population dynamics, although such effects are probably not ubiquitous. For example, Wolf *et al.* (1999) found that a rare serpentine species managed to persist despite a high degree of fragmentation. However (as will be discussed below), if the time scale of population response considerably exceeds the monitoring period, such results may provide an erroneous view of regional population persistence. 'Corridors' in the landscape, i.e. habitat elements that would enhance dispersal between fragments, have become an important aspect of conservation planning, although Harrison and Bruna (1999) suggested that there is little evidence that corridors are important to counteract habitat isolation. However, corridors have an obvious effect on dispersal in riparian vegetation (Jansson *et al.* 2000). Moreover, in some forest plants, hedgerows have been found to aid dispersal (Corbit *et al.* 1999; Sarlöv-Herlin & Fry 2000), and for some grassland plants, road verges are likely to have a similar function (Eriksson & Kiviniemi 1999; S. A. O. Cousins & O. Eriksson, unpublished).

A new focus in fragmentation studies

Table 8.1 summarizes effects of fragmentation on plant populations and communities. Although there are several well-documented effects, the most obvious ones are related to disturbance regimes (Leach & Givnish 1996; Menges & Dolan 1998), influence from edges (Laurance *et al.* 1998a; Laurance 2000), and an altered species composition due to invasion of aliens or habitat generalists (Fischer & Stöcklin 1997; Harrison 1999). These effects are all resulting from the changing landscape structure but they are due to factors both at the scale of the focal habitat fragments and the habitat matrix surrounding the fragments. Thus, mechanistically they incorporate also other factors than area (population size) effects on extinction and isolation effects on colonization. The traditional opinion that community species richness is positively related to resistance against invasive species is not generally valid (Levine & D'Antonio 1999), and invasion of biodiversity 'hot spots' has been much discussed recently (e.g. Stohlgren *et al.* 1999; Stadler *et al.* 2000). Invading species may outcompete resident species, irrespective of the size and degree of isolation of the resident populations. Other factors than local species richness are probably critical for community invasibility, particularly availability of resources and source populations for invading species (Levine & D'Antonio 1999; Levine 2000). There are several factors that may lead to a positive relationship between fragmentation and risk of invasion: (i) an increased edge to area ratio of fragments supporting establishment of edge species (Robinson *et al.* 1995; Planty-Tabacchi *et al.* 1996); (ii) species loss in fragments opening niche space for invading species (Wiser *et al.* 1998; Levine 2000); and (iii) increasing size of source populations of invading species living in the surrounding landscape matrix. As pointed out by Harrison and Bruna (1999) a new focus in fragmentation research necessitates inclusive landscape level studies. Thus, an important challenge for future studies will be to incorporate landscape matrix effects in theory of fragmentation (see Chapter 7), and to examine how community invasibility depends on size of habitat patches.

Fragmented populations in seminatural grasslands and deciduous forests

Description of the study area

During the last decade we have conducted a series of studies on local and regional population dynamics of plants in Swedish seminatural grasslands and deciduous forests. The main study area is located within 100 km south of Stockholm, but some studies have also been performed further south in the Provinces of Östergötland, Småland and Öland. The focal habitats were chosen as representatives of vegetation types that are becoming increasingly rare in the modern landscape, due to abandonment of mowing and grazing, fertilization of grasslands, and a general transformation of forests to become dominated by conifers. Seminatural grasslands usually have a long history of traditional management, in some cases probably for more than a millenium (e.g. Å. Eriksson 1998). However, they may have been subjected to shorter periods of abandonment, or temporarily been used as arable fields. These grasslands have a high density of species, frequently between 30 and 40 vascular plant species per square metre, and they contain several species that are presently declining (e.g. Lennartsson & Svensson 1996). Typically, the remaining seminatural grasslands are of size about a couple of hectares (Å. Eriksson *et al.* 1995).

The deciduous forests are usually remnants of former wooded meadows or pastures which after abandonment of management, mainly during the first half of the 20th century, have developed to more dense forests. In many places invading spruce has been removed as a part of conservation plans. The dominating tree species are oak (*Quercus robur*), hazel (*Corylus avellana*), ash (*Fraxinus excelsior*), maple (*Acer platanoides*), birch (*Betula pendula*), elm (*Ulmus glabra*) and, in the southern parts, lime (*Tilia cordata*). The field layer flora is commonly species-rich, although the density of species is lower than in the seminatural grasslands.

In the modern landscape, both seminatural grasslands and deciduous forests are located in a matrix of environments, urban areas, arable fields or managed coniferous forests, which are inhospitable for many of grassland and deciduous forest species. However, road sides, infield islets and remnant habitats of former tradionally managed vegetation occurs in the landscape and host local populations, and, for some species, perhaps function as dispersal routes (Eriksson & Kiviniemi 1999).

Seed dispersal

We know very little about long-distance dispersal of seeds, but sowing experiments suggest that both local and regional distributions of plants in seminatural grasslands and deciduous forests are dispersal-limited. Given that these habitats are relatively isolated, and that traditional management, for example movement of hay and cattle, has ceased, this is hardly surprising. A good example of dispersal limitation is *Thymus serpyllum* (Å. Eriksson 1998), a species that inhabits dry grasslands in the study area. This species was found at 76% of 42 sites in which a long management was suggested by localization of Iron Age grave fields, but only at 12% of 42 sites presumably lacking a long management but otherwise regarded as suitable for the species. Establishment after sowing was equally good at both occupied and unoccupied sites, irrespective of management history. In fact, most grassland species we have examined in this respect establish after experimental sowing at unoccupied but presumably suitable sites (e.g. Eriksson 1996b; Kiviniemi & Eriksson 1999), results that are in agreement with studies performed in other grassland systems (e.g. Primack & Miao 1992; Turnbull *et al.* 1999).

Deciduous forest herbs are also dispersal-limited in the study area. We examined seven species with sowing and transplantation experiments and recorded establishment during a 4-year period (Ehrlén & Eriksson 2000). For six of the species, establishment was successful even at unoccupied sites. Interestingly, no evidence was found that abiotic soil factors were related to either occupancy or establishment success. As in the study of *T. serpyllum*, there were no indication that occupied and unoccupied sites differered in overall quality. An important limitation of sowing experiments is that they are not often followed until the established plants reach maturity (Turnbull *et al.* 1999). However, at present, when 8 years have passed since the experiment was initiated, four of the seven species we examined have reached adult stages, and the other species have reached a size corresponding to adult plants (C. Gustafsson, J. Ehrlén & O. Eriksson, unpublished). Thus, we consider this as convincing evidence that dispersal limitation really affects the regional distribution of these species.

If dispersal limits the distribution of species in seminatural grasslands and deciduous forests, we should expect that dispersal and colonization ability are positively related to the regional abundance of the species. Comparative studies of dispersal ability and abundance support this expectation for both these habitats (Eriksson & Jakobsson 1998, and unpublished). However, such relationships may as well reflect previous dispersal that occurred in a less fragmented landscape that existed several decades ago. A crucial question is therefore whether plants inhabiting present-day seminatural grasslands and deciduous forests are at all able to disperse among fragments, or if these habitats have become isolated. Estimates of local dispersal ability (such as the typical 'dispersal curve' estimates) are poor predictors of how plants disperse over larger distances (Cain *et al.* 1998; Clark 1998), and more direct estimates of dispersal are badly needed in order to assess the ability of plants to disperse beyond the local neighbourhood in fragmented landscapes. Extremely rare successful dispersal events may, in the long term, have a dominating role in plant migration. The time scale that we can follow the ongoing fragmentation of modern landscapes is in the magnitude of a few decades. In such a period of time, it seems highly unlikely that dispersal is common among habitat fragments separated by several kilometres, except perhaps for those species which are strongly favoured by dispersal agents such as wind or flying animals. This is not the case for the majority of species inhabiting the seminatural grasslands and deciduous forests in our study area. Based on evidence of dispersal limitation and fragmentation, we therefore suggest that local populations of species confined to these habitats are practically isolated in the modern landscape.

The time scale of local population decline

If local populations are isolated, or nearly so, then the effect of fragmentation will depend on the response of the local populations to the ongoing changes in the landscapes. Some grassland species show a fast response to habitat fragmentation. For example, the biennial species *Gentianella campestris* has declined drastically along with the overall fragmentation of seminatural grasslands in south-eastern Sweden (Lennartsson & Svensson 1996). This decline is probably associated with changing habitat conditions also within remaining habitats, for example eutrophication and reduced grazing intensity. In contrast to other grassland species (e.g. Eriksson & Kiviniemi 1999; Kiviniemi & Eriksson 1999), it is difficult to establish *G. campestris* by sowing at sites where it does not occur, suggesting that site quality may be poor. A sowing experiment that was initiated in 1993 at 12 sites resulted in an initial recruitment success at three sites. However, in 1999 these artificially established populations had disappeared. In *G. campestris*, there is no relationship between habitat area and local population size (Figure 8.1). Taken together, the results suggest that the quality of the sites has a dominating effect on the dynamics of local populations.

The rate of population decline (on an absolute time scale) in grassland plants after abandonment of grazing is directly related to their life cycles (Figure 8.2). Annual plants are strongly over-represented among species known to decline rapidly after cessation of grazing. However, the majority of species in these grasslands are perennial forbs and grasses, many of which possess clonal propagation. For these species

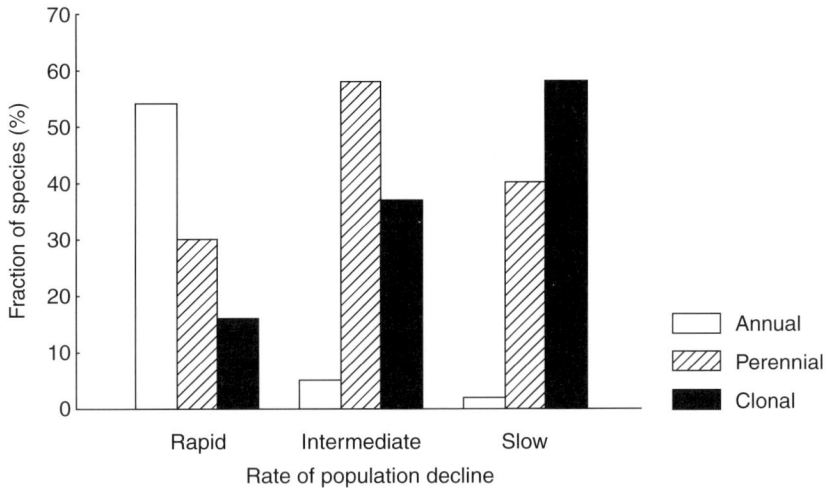

Figure 8.2 The distribution of annual, perennial (non-clonal) and clonal plant species among species categorized on the basis of their observed response to habitat deterioration in seminatural grasslands, rapid ($n = 92$), intermediate ($n = 116$) and slow ($n = 83$). (Based on Eriksson 1996b.)

the response is much slower. Figure 8.3 describes results of a study where seminatural grassland sites were categorized in relation to time since abandonment, and occupancy of 30 perennial species characteristic of grasslands was estimated within each site category. Within a time period of approximately 50 years, there was no reduction in the fraction of sites with remaining populations. Of course, the density of the local populations may have declined, but the results give an indication of the time lag in the response of perennial plants.

Long-term surveys of species occupancy, covering time periods of several decades, are very rare. An alternative and more common approach to estimate extinction rates of local populations is to use stochastic population modelling based on short-term demographic data (e.g. Menges 1990). Table 8.2 summarizes results for nine species from our study area. This kind of analyses must be viewed with much caution, because short-term variability in demographic parameters does not necessarily represent the variation that is relevant for longer time periods. Moreover, uncertainties in the underlying data set may also result in extinction estimates that have very wide confidence intervals (Ludwig 1999). For comparison with the results in Figure 8.3, we chose to present 'probability of local population extinction during 50 years' for the species. The two biennials experience a high extinction risk over this time period, suggesting that regional persistence depends on successful recruitment elsewhere in the grassland system. For the perennial species, both clonal and non-clonal, the simulation results indicate very low extinction risk, in accordance with the survey data in Figure 8.3. An exception was *Primula farinosa*, a generally declining species characteristic of moist seminatural grasslands. The analysis of this

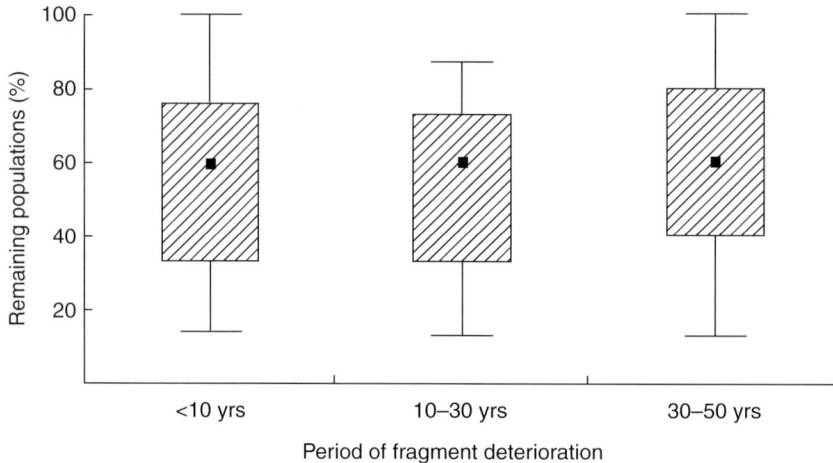

Figure 8.3 The response of populations of 30 perennial plant species (both clonal and non-clonal) in relation to the time period of habitat deterioration in dry seminatural grasslands in southern Sweden. Species presence was surveyed at sites which differ in time since abandonment of grazing: <10 years ($n = 21$), 10–30 years ($n = 15$) and 30–50 years ($n = 50$). The figure shows the median fraction of remaining populations (dot), the 25–75% range (hatched) and full range (bars). Comparisons among categories: $P = 0.90$ (ANOVA).

species was based on 17 population matrices, sampled from a variety of sites. At closer inspection, these sites differed much in dynamics of their populations (R. Lindborg, unpublished). Some local populations declined sharply some time after abandonment, whereas other populations increased steadily over the observation period. Thus, the analysis probably incorporates what may be different trajectories of population development. Populations of *P. farinosa* subjected to habitat deterioration thus seem to behave more like the short-lived biennials than other perennial species. Only two of the analysed species occur in deciduous forests, *Lathyrus vernus* and *Rubus saxatilis*. For both these species the risk of local population extinction was zero or close to zero. Survey data for other herbs and grasses in deciduous forests indicate an extremely slow local population dynamics. For example, populations of *Polygonatum multiflorum*, *Campanula latifolia* and *Bromus benekeni* in our study area have been more or less unchanged over a period of forty years (O. Eriksson & J. Ehrlén, unpublished).

Population synchronization

An unsynchronized group of populations has a smaller probability of collective chance extinction than a synchronized group of populations. If the dynamics of local populations are synchronized it indicates that landscape-scale factors, such as weather conditions or a general change in habitat conditions, have a dominating influence. As mentioned above, the studies of *G. campestris* suggest that local habitat

Table 8.2 'Extinction risk during 50 years' (E_{50}) of plant populations estimated from simulation of stochastic matrix models. E_{50} was defined as the proportion of populations declining to $N = 0$ during 50 simulated years. The investigated species inhabit fragmented seminatural grasslands or deciduous forests in Sweden. For all species the demographic information includes variation sampled during several years and/or at several sites (each matrix represents a year or a site). The life form, the number of matrices in the models and the size (in some cases an interval) of the initial simulated population (N_0) are also presented for each species. Sources of information: (1) Lennartsson (1997); (2) Löfgren *et al.* (2000); (3) R. Lindborg (unpublished); (4) Eriksson and Eriksson (2000); (5) Kiviniemi (1999); (6) Ehrlén (1995); (7) Eriksson (1994).

	Number of matrices	N_0	E_{50}
Biennials			
Gentianella campestris (1)	4	200–500	0.40–0.60
Carlina vulgaris (2)	8	64–400	0.42–0.72
Non-clonal perennials			
Primula farinosa (3)	17	50–500	0–0.99
Plantago media (4)	4	50–400	0
Agrimonia eupatoria (5)	5	50–400	0
Lathyrus vernus (6)	17	300	0
Clonal plants			
Geum rivale (5)	3	50–400	0
Potentilla anserina (7)	3	65–250	0
Rubus saxatilis (7)	3	65–250	0–0.07

quality strongly influences the dynamics (although we are still unaware of which local factors that are most important). In agreement with these results, there was no relationship between synchronization of 11 populations recorded between 1993 and 1999, and distance among sites (Figure 8.4). Thus, the emerging picture is that each local population basically follows its own trajectory. In the long run (i.e. within approximately 50 years, Table 8.2), most of the populations, which have less than 100 individuals flowering each year, are likely to go extinct. If there exists dispersal among populations (which we presently doubt), lack of population synchrony, in combination with a few large local populations (the largest in the study had a yearly average of more than 3000 flowering individuals) may, however, secure regional persistence even in a longer-term perspective.

Table 8.3 shows population synchronization obtained for the long-lived perennial *L. vernus* at six different sites, and, within one of these sites, at six different patches. The degree of synchronization were of a similar magnitude within and among sites. Although the variation in population growth rate was larger among sites than within sites, this suggests that in *L. vernus*, the dynamics to a large extent is determined at a scale smaller than the local population, and that landscape level factors have a minor influence on the local extinction risk experienced by the populations.

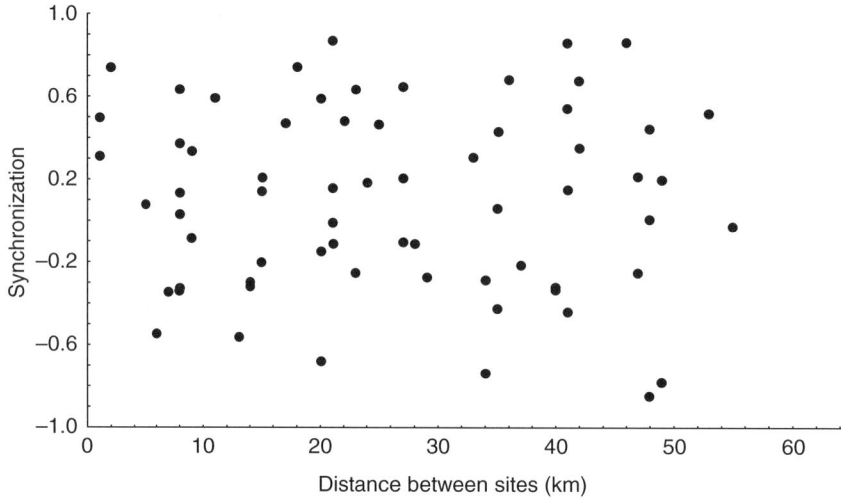

Figure 8.4 The relationship between population synchronization and distance between sites in *Gentianella campestris* in south-eastern Sweden. Synchronization was measured according to a method outlined in Hanski and Woiwod (1993): correlations were calculated for each pair of populations, based on the residuals of regressions between time series of populations sizes.

Table 8.3 Variation and synchronization of population growth rates (λ) in the perennial forest herb *Lathyrus vernus* among six sites (populations) and among six patches within one site. Data (from Ehrlén 1995) include three transition intervals (years) except for one of the populations which was studied over two transition intervals. Calculations of means and standard deviations were based on the averages of all transition intervals within populations or patches. Synchronization was measured as the average correlation coefficient for λ among all pairs of sites and all pairs of patches within one site. Statistical analyses were made with *F*-tests.

	Among sites	Within sites	*P*
Population growth rate			
Mean	1.014	0.989	0.57
Standard deviation	0.097	0.038	0.03
Population synchronization	0.056	0.080	>0.5

Conclusions

Habitat fragmentation has several effects on both plant populations and communities, including changes in the species richness and community structure of remaining habitat fragments, as well as changes in demographic properties of local populations. However, these effects are likely to be community and species specific, and it is essential to focus on the mechanisms behind each effect in order to achieve a solid generalization of the consequences of fragmentation. We suggest that analyses of occupancy patterns should include experimental sowing or transplantation in order to assess the fraction of unoccupied sites, and to examine how gradients in habitat quality influence these patterns. A mixture of approaches are useful to study fragmentation effects. The most crucial problem is to assess the actual dispersal of plants among fragments. Indirect evidence suggest that local populations of many plant species are practically isolated, but this may reflect that rare chance dispersal events are underestimated. Techniques using genetic markers will prove especially valuable for studies addressing dispersal among habitat fragments.

The effects of associated changes in habitat quality, the influence of the surrounding vegetation matrix, large-scale changes in disturbance regimes (i.e. covering areas larger than the fragments), and species invasions deserve particular attention in studies of fragmentation. Moreover, we suggest that many plants exhibit such a slow response to fragmentation that they are not likely to be in equilibrium with the current habitat configuration. As a result, patterns of occupancy may give a misleading picture of extinction and colonization rates, and the status of regional populations. A strong focus only on area effects on local extinctions and isolation effects on colonization is not likely to identify the major consequences of fragmentation for plant populations and communities.

Summary

This chapter reviews effects of habitat fragmentation on plant populations and communities, and summarizes results obtained from studies of plants in fragmented seminatural grasslands and deciduous forests in Sweden. Fragmentation is expected to lead to decreasing local population sizes, causing an elevated extinction risk of populations, and decreased colonization rates due to isolation of habitats. There is abundant evidence that fragmentation influences both plant populations and communities. However, the effects are not consistent, indicating that species- and site-specific factors interact with fragmentation. There are examples, for instance, of both increased and decreased local species richness, and some species are favoured by fragmentation. Fragmented habitats are subjected to an increased risk of invasion, probably due to an increasing edge–area ratio and increasing variance in community structure opening 'windows' for colonization by invaders. One of the reasons why observations do not consistently support predictions is the gap between theory of fragmentation, focusing on area and isolation effects *per se*, and empirical studies, which incorporate effects associated with changing habitat conditions, for example quality and edgy effects, and effects of the surrounding vegetation. In Swedish seminatural grasslands and deciduous forests many species are dispersal limited, and indirect evidence indicate that populations in habitat fragments are practically isolated. Thus, long-term effects of fragmentation will mainly reflect the rate of local extinctions. Whereas short-lived plants often show a fast response to fragmentation, leading to regional decline, many long-lived plants have a slow response. Time lags in the magnitude of at least 50–100 years are common among plants in Swedish seminatural grasslands and deciduous forests. Thus, occupancy patterns of many species in present-day landscapes are far from equilibrium. Interpretations of present distribution patterns, where colonization and extinction dynamics are inferred from occupancy, must therefore be used with much caution.

Acknowledgements

We are grateful to K. Lehtilä, J. Ouborg and two anonymous reviewers for comments on the manuscript, and to R. Lindborg for use of unpublished results. This study was supported financially by the Swedish Natural Science Research Council, (to O.E. and J.E.), the Swedish Council for Forestry and Agricultural Research (to O.E.) and MISTRA (to O.E. and J.E.).

References

Andrén, H. (1994). Effects of habitat fragmentation on birds and mammals in landscapes with different proportions of suitable habitat: a review. *Oikos*, **71**, 355–366.

Benitez-Malvido, J. (1998). Impact of forest fragmentation on seedling abundance in a tropical rain forest. *Conservation Biology*, **12**, 380–389.

Booy, G., Hendriks, R.J.J., Smulders, M.J.M., van Groenendael, J.M. & Vosman, B. (2000). Genetic diversity and the survival of populations. *Plant Biology*, **2**, 379–395.

Bond, W.J. (1994). Do mutualism matter? Assessing the impact of pollinator and disperser disruption on plant extinction. *Philosophical Transactions of the Royal Society of London* **B**, **344**, 83–90.

Cain, M., Damman, H. & Muir, L. (1998). Seed dispersal and the holocene migration of woodland herbs. *Ecological Monographs*, **68**, 325–347.

Caswell, H. (1989). *Matrix Population Models*. Sinauer, Sunderland, MA.

Clark, J.S. (1998). Why trees migrate so fast: confronting theory with dispersal biology and the paleorecord. *American Naturalist*, **152**, 204–224.

Corbit, M., Marks, P.L. & Gardescu, S. (1999). Hedgerows as habitat corridors for forest herbs in central New York, USA. *Journal of Ecology*, **87**, 220–232.

Ehrlén, J. (1995). Demography of the perennial herb *Lathyrus vernus*: II Herbivory and population dynamics. *Journal of Ecology*, **83**, 297–308.

Ehrlén, J. & Eriksson, O. (2000). Dispersal limitation and patch occupancy in forest herbs. *Ecology*, **81**, 1667–1674.

Eriksson, Å. (1998). Regional distribution of *Thymus serpyllum*: management history and dispersal limitation. *Ecography*, **21**, 35–43.

Eriksson, Å. & Eriksson, O. (2000). Population dynamics of the perennial *Plantago media* in seminatural grasslands. *Journal of Vegetation Science*, **11**, 245–252.

Eriksson, Å., Eriksson, O. & Berglund, H. (1995). Species abundance patterns of plants in Swedish semi-natural pastures. *Ecography*, **18**, 310–317.

Eriksson, O. (1994). Stochastic population dynamics of clonal plants: numerical experiments with ramet and genet models. *Ecological Research*, **9**, 257–268.

Eriksson, O. (1996a). Regional dynamics of plants: a review of evidence for remnant, source–sink and metapopulations. *Oikos*, **77**, 248–258.

Eriksson, O. (1996b). Population ecology and conservation — some theoretical considerations with examples from the Nordic flora. *Symbolae Botanicae Upsaliensis*, **31**, 159–167.

Eriksson, O. & Jakobsson, A. (1998). Abundance, distribution and life histories of grassland plants: a comparative study of 81 species. *Journal of Ecology*, **86**, 922–933.

Eriksson, O. & Kiviniemi, K. (1999). Site occupancy, recruitment and extinction thresholds in grassland plants; an experimental study. *Biological Conservation*, **87**, 319–325.

Fischer, M. & Stöcklin, J. (1997). Local extinctions of plants in remnants of extensively used calcareous grasslands 1950–1985. *Conservation Biology*, **11**, 727–737.

Grashof-Bokdam, C. (1997). Forest species in an agricultural landscape in the Netherlands: effects of habitat fragmentation. *Journal of Vegetation Science*, **8**, 21–28.

Grashof-Bokdam, C.J. & Geertsema, W. (1998). The effect of isolation and history on colonization patterns of plant species in secondary woodland. *Journal of Biogeography*, **25**, 837–846.

Groom, M.J. (1998). Allee effects limit population viability of an annual plant. *American Naturalist*, **151**, 487–496.

Hanski, I. (1999). *Metapopulation Ecology*. Oxford University Press, Oxford.

Hanski, I. & Woiwod, I.P. (1993). Spatial synchrony in the dynamics of moth and aphid populations. *Journal of Animal Ecology*, **62**, 656–668.

Harrison, S. (1999). Local and regional diversity in a patchy landscape: native, alien, and endemic herbs on serpentine. *Ecology*, **80**, 70–80.

Harrison, S. & Bruna, E. (1999). Habitat fragmentation and large-scale conservation: what do we know for sure? *Ecography*, **22**, 225–232.

Holt, R.D. (1997). From metapopulation dynamics to community structure: some consequences of spatial heterogeneity. In: *Metapopulation Biology — Ecology, Genetics and Evolution* (eds I. Hanski & M.E. Gilpin), pp. 149–164. Academic Press, San Diego.

Holt, R.D., Robinson, G.R. & Gaines, M.S. (1995). Vegetation dynamics in an experimentally fragmented landscape. *Ecology*, **76**, 1610–1624.

Honnay, O., Hermy, M. & Coppin, P. (1999). Nested plant communities in deciduous forest fragments: species relaxation or nested habitats? *Oikos*, **84**, 119–129.

Husband, B.C. & Barrett, S.C.H. (1996). A metapopulation perspective in plant population biology. *Journal of Ecology*, **84**, 461–469.

Husband, B.C. & Barrett, S.C.H. (1998). Spatial and temporal variation in population size of *Eichornia paniculata* in ephemeral habitats: implications for metapopulation dynamics. *Journal of Ecology*, **86**, 1021–1031.

Jansson, R., Nilsson, C. & Renöfält, B. (2000). Fragmentation of riparian floras in rivers with multiple dams. *Ecology*, **81**, 899–903.

Jennersten, O. (1988). Pollination in *Dianthus deltoides* (Caryophyllaceae): effects of habitat fragmentation on visitation and seed set. *Conservation Biology*, **2**, 359–366.

Jules, E.S. (1998). Habitat fragmentation and demographic change for a common plant: *Trillium* in old-growth forest. *Ecology*, **79**, 1645–1656.

Kéry, M., Matthies, D. & Spillman, H.-H. (2000). Reduced fecundity and offspring performance in small populations of the declining grassland plants *Primula veris* and *Gentiana lutea*. *Journal of Ecology*, **88**, 17–30.

Kiviniemi, K. (1999). *Evolution of seed attributes, dispersal and population dynamics of plants, with special emphasis on fragmented habitats*. PhD thesis, Department of Botany, Stockholm University.

Kiviniemi, K. & Eriksson, O. (1999). Dispersal, recruitment and site occupancy of grassland plants in fragmented habitats. *Oikos*, **86**, 241–253.

Köchy, M. & Rydin, H. (1997). Biogeography of vascular plants on habitat islands, peninsulas and mainlands in an east-central Swedish agricultural landscape. *Nordic Journal of Botany*, **17**, 215–223.

Laurance, W.F. (2000). Do edge effects occur over large spatial scales? *Trends in Ecology and Evolution*, **15**, 134–135.

Laurance, W.F., Laurance, S.G., Ferreira, L.V., Rankin-de Merona, J.M., Gascon, C. & Lovejoy, T.E. (1997). Biomass collapse in Amazonian forest fragments. *Science*, **278**, 1117–1118.

Laurance, W.F., Ferreira, L.V., Rankin-de Merona, J.M. & Laurance, S.G. (1998a). Rain forest fragmentation and the dynamics of Amazonian tree communities. *Ecology*, **79**, 2032–2040.

Laurance, W.F., Ferreira, L.V., Rankin-de Merona, J.M., Laurance, S.G., Hutchings, R.W. & Lovejoy, T.E. (1998b). Effects of forest fragmentation on recruitment patterns in Amazonian tree communities. *Conservation Biology*, **12**, 460–464.

Lawton, J.H., Nee, S., Letcher, A.J. & Harvey, P.H. (1994). Animal distributions: patterns and processes. In: *Large-Scale Ecology and Conservation Biology* (eds P.J. Edwards, R.M. May & N.R. Webb), pp. 41–58. Blackwell Science, Oxford.

Leach, M.K. & Givnish, T.J. (1996). Ecological determinants of species loss in remnant prairies. *Science*, **273**, 1555–1558.

Lennartsson, T. (1997). *Demography, reproductive biology and adaptive traits in* Gentianella campestris *and* G. amarella: *evaluation grassland management for conservation by using indicator plant species*. PhD thesis. Agraria 46. Swedish University of Agricultural Sciences.

Lennartsson, T. & Svensson, R. (1996). Patterns in

the decline of three species of *Gentianella* (Gentianacea) in Sweden, illustrating the deterioration of semi-natural grasslands. *Symbolae Botanicae Upsaliensis*, **31**, 169–184.

Levine, J.M. (2000). Species diversity and biological invasions: relating local process to community pattern. *Science*, **288**, 852–854.

Levine, J.M. & D'Antonio, C. (1999). Elton revisited: a review of evidence linking diversity and invasibility. *Oikos*, **87**, 15–26.

Löfgren, P., Lehtilä, K. & Eriksson, O. (2000). Population dynamics and the effect of disturbance in the monocarpic herb *Carlina vulgaris* (Asteraceae). *Annales Botanici Fennici*, **37**, 183–192.

Ludwig, D. (1999). Is it meaningful to estimate a probability of extinction? *Ecology*, **80**, 298–310.

MacArthur, R.H. & Wilson, E.O. (1967). *The Theory of Island Biogeography*. Princeton University Press, Princeton, NJ.

Menges, E.S. (1990). Population viability analysis for an endangered plant. *Conservation Biology*, **4**, 52–62.

Menges, E.S. (1992). Stochastic modeling of extinction in plant populations. In: *Conservation Biology—The theory and practice of nature conservation, preservation and management* (eds P.L. Fiedler & S.K. Jain), pp. 253–275. Chapman & Hall, New York.

Menges, E.S. & Dolan, R.W. (1998). Demographic viability of populations of *Silene regia* in midwestern prairies: relationships with fire management, genetic isolation, geographic location, population size and isolation. *Journal of Ecology*, **86**, 63–78.

Moilanen, A. & Hanski, I. (1998). Metapopulation dynamics: effects of habitat quality and landscape structure. *Ecology*, **79**, 2503–2515.

Morgan, J.W. (1999). Effects of population size on seed production and germinability in an endangered, fragmented grassland plant. *Conservation Biology*, **13**, 266–273.

Olivieri, I., Michalakis, Y. & Gouyon, P.-H. (1995). Metapopulation genetics and the evolution of dispersal. *American Naturalist*, **146**, 202–228.

Oostermeijer, J.G.B., van Eijck, M.W. & den Nijs, J.C.M. (1994). Offspring fitness in relation to population size and genetic variation in the rare perennial plant species *Gentiana pneumonanthe* (Gentianaceae). *Oecologia*, **97**, 289–296.

Oostermeijer, J.G.B., van Eijck, M.W., van Leeuwen, N.C. & den Nijs, J.C.M. (1995). Analysis of the relationship between allozyme heterozygosity and fitness in the rare *Gentiana pneumonanthe* L. *Journal of Evolutionary Biology*, **8**, 739–759.

Ouborg, N.J. (1993). Isolation, population size and extinction: the classical and metapopulation approaches applied to vascular plants along the Dutch Rhine-system. *Oikos*, **66**, 298–308.

Ouborg, N.J. & van Treuren, R. (1995). Variation in fitness-related characters among small and large populations of *Salvia pratensis*. *Journal of Ecology*, **83**, 369–380.

Ouborg, N.J., Piquot, Y. & van Groenendael, J.M. (1999). Population genetics, molecular markers and the study of dispersal in plants. *Journal of Ecology*, **87**, 551–568.

Ouborg, N.J., Biere, A. & Mudde, C.L. (2000). Inbreeding effects on resistance and transmission-related traits in the *Silene-Microbotryum* pathosystem. *Ecology*, **81**, 520–531.

Planty-Tabacchi, A., Tabacchi, E., Naiman, R.J., DeFerrari, C. & Décamps, H. (1996). Invasibility of species rich communities in riparian zones. *Conservation Biology*, **10**, 598–607.

Primack, R.B. & Miao, S.L. (1992). Dispersal can limit local plant distributions. *Conservation Biology*, **6**, 513–519.

Quintana-Ascencio, P.F. & Menges, E.S. (1996). Inferring metapopulation dynamics from patch-level incidence of Florida scrub plants. *Conservation Biology*, **10**, 1210–1219.

Rees, M. (1996). Evolutionary ecology of seed dormancy and seed size. *Philosophical Transactions of the Royal Society of London* **B**, **351**, 1299–1308.

Renner, S.S. (1999). Effects of habitat fragmentation on plant pollinator interactions in the tropics. In: *Dynamics of Tropical Communities* (eds D.M. Newberry, H.H.T. Prins & N.D. Brown), pp. 339–360. Blackwell Science, Oxford.

Restrepo, C., Gomez, N. & Heredia, S. (1999). Anthropogenic edges, treefall gaps, and fruit–frugivore interactions in a neotropical montane forest. *Ecology*, **80**, 668–685.

Robinson, G.R., Holt, R.D., Gaines, M.S., Hamburg, S.P., Johnson, M.L., Fitch, H.S. & Martinko, E.A. (1992). Diverse and contrasting effects of habitat fragmentation. *Science*, **257**, 524–526.

Robinson, G.R., Quinn, J.F. & Stanton, M.L. (1995). Invasibility of experimental habitat islands in a

California winter annual grassland. *Ecology*, **76**, 786–794.

Sarlöv-Herlin, I.L. & Fry, G.L.A. (2000). Dispersal of woody plants in forest edges and hedgerows in a Southern Swedish agricultural area: the role of site and landscape structure. *Landscape Ecology*, **15**, 229–242.

Schemske, D.W., Husband, B.C., Ruckelshaus, M.H., Goodwillie, C., Parker, I.M. & Bishop, J.G. (1994). Evaluating approaches to the conservation of rare and endangered plants. *Ecology*, **75**, 584–606.

Stadler, J., Trefflich, A., Klotz, S. & Brandl, R. (2000). Exotic plant species invade diversity hot spots: the alien flora of northwestern Kenya. *Ecography*, **23**, 169–176.

Stephens, P.A. & Sutherland, W.J. (1999). Consequences of the Allee effect for behaviour, ecology and conservation. *Trends in Ecology and Evolution*, **14**, 401–405.

Stohlgren, T.J., Binkley, D., Chong, G.W., Kalkhan, M.A., Schell, L.D., Bull, K.A., Otsuki, Y., Newman, G., Bashkin, M. & Son, Y. (1999). Exotic plant species invade hot spots of native plant diversity. *Ecological Monographs*, **69**, 25–46.

Thompson, J.N. (1999). Specific hypotheses on the geographic mosaic of coevolution. *American Naturalist*, **153** (Suppl.), 1–14.

Tilman, D., May, R.M., Lehman, C.L. & Nowak, M.A. (1994). Habitat destruction and the extinction debt. *Nature*, **371**, 65–66.

Turnbull, L.A., Crawley, M.J. & Rees, M. (1999). Are plant populations seed-limited? A review of seed sowing experiments. *Oikos*, **88**, 225–238.

Venable, D.L. & Brown, J.S. (1988). The selective interactions of dispersal, dormancy, and seed size as adaptations for reducing risk in variable environments. *American Naturalist*, **131**, 360–384.

Wade, M.J. & Goodnight, C.J. (1998). The theories of Fisher and Wright in the context of metapopulations: when nature does many small experiments. *Evolution*, **52**, 1537–1553.

Wiser, S.K., Allen, R.B., Clinton, P.W. & Platt, K.H. (1998). Community structure and forest invasion by an exotic herb over 23 years. *Ecology*, **79**, 2071–2081.

Wolf, A., Brodmann, P.A. & Harrison, S. (1999). Distribution of the rare serpentine sunflower, *Helianthus exilis* (Asteraceae): the roles of habitat availability, dispersal limitation and species interactions. *Oikos*, **84**, 69–76.

Young, A., Boyle, T. & Brown, T. (1996). The population genetic consequences of habitat fragmentation for plants. *Trends in Ecology and Evolution*, **11**, 413–418.

Chapter 9

The interaction of genetic and demographic processes in plant metapopulations: a case study of *Silene alba*

D. E. McCauley,* C. M. Richards,*† S. N. Emery,* R. A. Smith,*‡ and J. W. McGlothlin*

Introduction

Genes can move in two ways; between established populations and from an established population into a patch of empty habitat. In this chapter the movement of genes between populations will be referred to as gene flow, whereas the initial establishment of genes in previously empty habitat will be referred to as colonization or founding. In seed plants, genes generally move between established populations in seeds and/or pollen, but can only colonize empty habitat when carried by seed.

The distinction between gene movement leading to gene flow and gene movement leading to colonization is particularly useful when considering the genetic consequences of metapopulation dynamics. A metapopulation can be defined as a system of populations with frequent extinction of local populations offset by frequent colonization of empty habitat (Levins 1969, 1970; Hanski & Gilpin 1991; Hanski & Simberloff 1997). The ecology and evolution of metapopulations has received considerable attention over the past 15 years, both because of the recognition that natural systems are often less stable than thought previously, and because the consequences of metapopulation dynamics induced by human disturbance have become an issue in conservation biology. Theoretical attempts to understand the genetic consequences of metapopulation dynamics have focused on how the frequent turnover of populations influences both the absolute amount of selectively neutral genetic diversity maintained within metapopulations, and on how that diversity is partitioned within and among component populations (e.g. Slatkin 1977; Maruyama & Kimura 1980; Wade & McCauley 1988; Whitlock & McCauley 1990; Hedrick & Gilpin 1997; Whitlock & Barton 1997; Pannell & Charlesworth 1999). In these models, gene movement leading to gene flow and gene movement leading to colonization contribute separately to overall genetic structure. The influence of colonization on genetic structure increases with the rate of population turnover,

* Department of Biological Sciences, Vanderbilt University, Nashville, TN 37235, USA, † current address: USDA/ARS, National Seed Storage Laboratory, 1111 South Mason Street, Fort Collins, CO 80521, USA and ‡ current address: Department of Biology, Duke University, Durham, NC 27708, USA.

because with high rates of turnover most populations are just a few generations re-moved from founding. In plants this means that seed movement should be a partic-ularly important component of genetic structure when there is frequent extinction and recolonization of local populations.

While models of selectively neutral genetic variation have a long history in the field of theoretical population genetics, they are often motivated by an interest in how a given genetic structure influences fitness or the response to selection (Barton & Whitlock 1997). One reason that the genetic consequences of metapopulation dynamics could be of more than theoretical interest to plant biologists is the possibi-lity of an interaction between genetic structure and population viability. Generally, small numbers of founders are thought to lead to reduced genetic diversity within populations. This, in turn, could lead to inbreeding depression in the generations immediately after founding, a phenomenon whose expression at the population level could be reduced population growth rate or even increased threat of local ex-tinction. If this ultimately leads to a smaller pool of dispersing individuals and even smaller groups of colonists, then the feedback between genetics and demography could eventually lead to 'metapopulation collapse' (Thrall *et al.* 1998). The dynam-ics of this process cannot be evaluated in most formal metapopulation genetic models since the genetic composition of individual populations is not considered, nor is population viability considered to be a function of genetic composition.

While models provide a useful conceptual framework, understanding the dynamics of biological metapopulations requires additional empirical data. We are only beginning to understand the relationship between genetic and metapopulation dynamics in natural plant populations. Two important issues emerge. First, what is the genetic structure of real plant metapopulations, and how is this different from what might have been expected with less frequent population turnover? In plants this question might be rephrased as to what degree is genetic structure determined by the dispersal of seeds into patches of empty habitat, rather than the exchange of seeds or pollen between established populations? Secondly, is there any evidence that reduced genetic diversity in the generations immediately after population founding has negative demographic consequences and, if so, does this feedback to the genetic properties of the local population and the metapopulation? It would seem that answering this question would require a detailed understanding of the genetic properties of founding groups, and also of the genetic and demographic properties of populations over the first few generations following colonization.

Over the last 10 years, studies of natural populations of the ruderal plant *Silene alba* (= *latifolia*) have attempted to address some of these questions by combining demographic information with population and quantitative genetic studies. Studies conducted in the early to mid-1990s suggested that the genetic structure of this species in Virginia, USA, is indeed influenced by founding events (McCauley 1994; McCauley *et al.* 1995), and that the reduced genetic diversity associated with colo-nization by small numbers of individuals results in considerable inbreeding depres-sion (Richards 2000). Subsequent monitoring of the original study populations now allows us to understand how demographic and genetic processes might interact in the first few generations after a population is founded; events not usually considered in theoretical models.

In this chapter we address three main topics. First, we review theoretical models of metapopulation genetics and ask how they might be applied generally to the study of plant populations. Next, we discuss the population structure of *S. alba* as a specific example of how the genetics of one system might be influenced by metapopulation dynamics, including processes that occur in the first few generations following colonization. Finally, we discuss studies of inbreeding depression in *S. alba* that illustrate some of the ecological consequences of genetic erosion. Taken together, these three topics will lead to the conclusion that understanding the ecological consequences of genetic structure might be crucial to understanding plant metapopulation dynamics.

Theoretical studies of metapopulation genetics: moving plant genes when populations are ephemeral

Mathematical or computer models of metapopulations can be grouped into three admittedly arbitrary categories. The first consists of purely ecological models that are motivated by a desire to understand the conditions that permit the persistence of a species or group of interacting species when local populations are ephemeral. Since Levin's original work (Levins 1969, 1970), these models have tended to focus on increasingly realistic ecological scenarios such as spatially explicit patterns of migration or the interaction of local and regional demographic processes (Hanski & Simberloff 1997). The second category focuses on adaptive evolution in metapopulations. Here, the main focus has been the evolution of life histories, such as dispersal strategies, within the context of metapopulation dynamics (e.g. Olivieri *et al.* 1995; Gandon & Michalakis 1999; Ronce *et al.* 2000). Finally, population genetic models have focused on how metapopulation dynamics influence the amount and apportionment of genetic diversity within metapopulations. Models focus on either the absolute amount of genetic diversity maintained within a metapopulation and its components, or on how that diversity is apportioned. It is this last category of models that will be considered most closely here. While these models mostly consider selectively neutral genetic variation, one long-term goal is, of course, to understand how metapopulation structure influences fitness.

Interest in the effects of metapopulation dynamics on genetic structure can be traced back to Wright (1940), who considered a population structure with frequent local extinction and recolonization favourable for his 'shifting balance' mode of evolution. Among the first formal metapopulation genetic models are those developed by Slatkin (1977). Slatkin's models have two important attributes. First, they consider movement between established populations (gene flow) and movement into empty habitat (colonization) as distinct processes. Secondly, they consider two ways a group of colonists can be drawn from a pool of dispersing individuals. In the 'migrant pool' mode the individuals (actually the genes) that comprise a given colonizing group are drawn at random from the pool of individuals dispersing from all source populations. In the 'propagule pool' mode the individuals that comprise a given group of colonists are drawn from just one source (although other colonizing groups can be drawn from other sources). A colonization event then has two somewhat contradictory demographic and genetic consequences. It represents a population bottleneck and therefore an apparent opportunity for genetic drift (assuming that the number of colonists is much smaller than the carrying capacity of the patch), but also a condition under which genes move. Slatkin emphasized that frequent extinction with migrant pool recolonization can influence genetic structure much like gene flow in that colonization events mix individuals from different sources, which can diminish existing structure.

Papers by Wade and McCauley (1988) and Whitlock and McCauley (1990) provided follow-up to the Slatkin model. Wade and McCauley (1988) recast Slatkin's model in terms of Wright's F_{st} and asked what conditions enhance and what diminish F_{st}, relative to a case without extinction and recolonization (i.e. with an extinction rate $e = 0$). They found that extinction and recolonization could *either* enhance or diminish F_{st}. With propagule pool colonization extinction/recolonization dynamics always increases F_{st}, provided the size of the colonizing group (k) is smaller than the local carrying capacity (N). This is because there is no mixing of populations with propagule pool colonization. With migrant pool colonization the situation is more complicated because both population bottleneck and mixing effects come into play. The net effect of migrant pool colonization depends on the size of the colonizing group (k) relative to the number of individuals migrating between established populations (Nm, where m is the migration rate). Specifically, extinction/recolonization will increase F_{st}, relative to a case with $e = 0$ provided

$$4Nm + 1 > 2k \tag{1}$$

Notice that $4Nm + 1$ is the denominator in Wright's classic approximation for the equilibrium F_{st} under Island Model migration and $2k$ is the denominator for the F_{st} calculated from a binomial distribution of allele frequencies created by repeated sampling of k diploid individuals. Viewed this way, metapopulation-wide F_{st} approaches $1/(4Nm + 1)$ as $e \to 0$ and approaches $1/2k$ as $e \to 1$. When extinction is random and independent of time since founding, the age distribution at the level of populations is known, and the metapopulation-wide F_{st} can be calculated as the weighted average of the age-specific F_{st} values. Some properties of this model are illustrated in Figure 9.1.

Whitlock and McCauley (1990) extended the model to include modes of colonization intermediate to the migrant and propagule pool modes. Specifically, they include a parameter $\emptyset$ in the model which is the probability that two genes drawn at random from a colonizing group come from the same source population ($\emptyset = 0$ and $\emptyset = 1$ represent the migrant and propagule pool cases, respectively). They also describe the effect of kin structured colonization (colonists consist of related individuals drawn from the same source) on F_{st}. Their conclusion was that $\emptyset > 0$ and kin structured colonization both broaden the range of colonizing group size and migration rates under which extinction and recolonization can increase F_{st}.

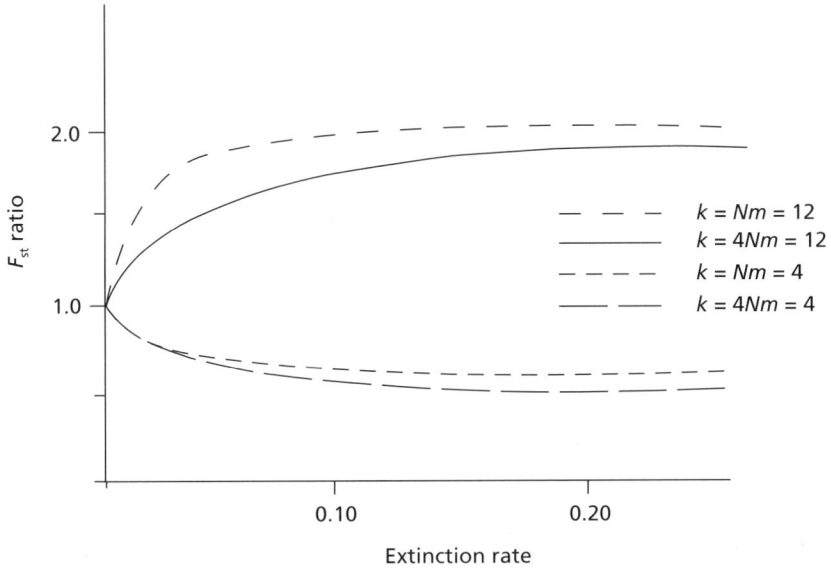

Figure 9.1 The ratio of the equilibrium F_{st} derived from the migrant pool metapopulation genetic model of Slatkin (1977) and Wade and McCauley (1988) to the equilibrium F_{st} derived from Wright's Island Model with no extinction. The ratio is given as a function of the extinction rate for colonizing groups (k) of size 4 or 12 in combination with Nm of 4 or 12. Note that an increase in population turnover can either increase or decrease F_{st}, depending on the combination of parameter values. (From Wade & McCauley 1988.)

Pannell and Charlesworth (1999) have shown how absolute measures of within- and among-population genetic diversity, such as might be obtained from DNA sequence data, respond to metapopulation dynamics, and can sometimes be more informative than F_{st}, since that is a measure of the *relative* amounts of within- and among-population genetic variance. In particular, the approach of Pannell and Charlesworth (1999) is useful for considering the effects of extinction and re-colonization on the total amount of diversity that can be maintained across the metapopulation.

These models have several specific applications to plants. First, in plants the number of genes moving between established populations can be much greater than the number of genes moving into patches of empty habitat because gene flow can be by seed or pollen, whereas colonization can only be by seed. Thus, when gene flow by pollen is extensive and $4Nm + 1$ (or its equivalent when considering movement by pollen) $\gg 2k$, extinction/recolonization would reduce F_{st} considerably compared to what might be expected from studies of gene flow alone. Secondly, when the fruit, rather than the individual seed, is the unit of dispersal, individuals founding a given population would tend to come from the same source population and be related, both factors that would increase F_{st} in a cohort of recently founded populations.

Most of the models cited above assume for mathematical convenience that populations increase in number from the starting size k to some maximum number N in just one generation. In natural populations there must often be a lag time between the initial colonization event and the maximum numbers that can be reached. This could be called the establishment phase. Thus, there must often be a number of generations early in the history of a population when its number falls somewhere between k and N. Ingvarsson (1997) showed that this can either increase or decrease F_{st}, relative to the case in which $k \rightarrow N$ in one generation. That is because, although the effective population size is below N during this establishment phase, opportunities for gene flow either increase or decrease depending on whether gene flow is considered as a constant proportion of the population (so that the *number* of immigrants is smaller when numbers are low) or a constant number (so that the *proportion* of immigrants is higher when numbers are low). In animal-pollinated plants this distinction might depend on how pollinators respond to such variables as patch size or flower number.

In these models, demography influences genetics but genetics does not influence demography. If, however, a reduction of within-population genetic diversity results in inbreeding depression, then there could well be population-level consequences in terms of numerical growth or persistence. It could be that the persistence of recently founded populations depends on the genetic consequences of colonization and on events that occur immediately postcolonization. Specifically, it has been suggested that postcolonization population growth and persistence depends on an infusion of genetic diversity via gene flow, especially by pollen (Thrall *et al.* 1998; Richards 2000) which can offset the loss of genetic diversity associated with colonization. In that view, those populations that maintain genetic diversity, either because they are founded by a genetically diverse group of founders, or because they receive subsequent gene flow, are more likely to increase numerically, persist for longer periods, and be a source of the seeds that are involved in future episodes of colonization. Populations that lose genetic diversity during colonization or the establishment phase are more likely to go extinct quickly without achieving much population growth or contributing substantially to the pool of dispersing seeds. These two trajectories are illustrated in Figure 9.2.

This view is not accommodated in standard metapopulation models because extinction rates are not considered to be a function of population age, size or genetic composition. Furthermore, the consequences of such a scenario cannot be extended to the level of the metapopulation because the genetic models assume that the number of occupied sites remains constant, as does k. Thrall *et al.* (1998) have used a computer simulation, however, to show that when population growth and persistence depend on levels of within-population genetic diversity there can be a feedback between levels of gene flow and metapopulation occupancy rates. In the simulation, reducing levels of gene flow by pollen reduced the persistence time of populations, which in turn reduced the size of the pool of seeds available for colonization and occupancy rates. This feedback can eventually result in 'metapopulation collapse', because reduced occupancy rates result in a greater spatial separation of established or recently founded population, and less opportunity for gene flow by pollen.

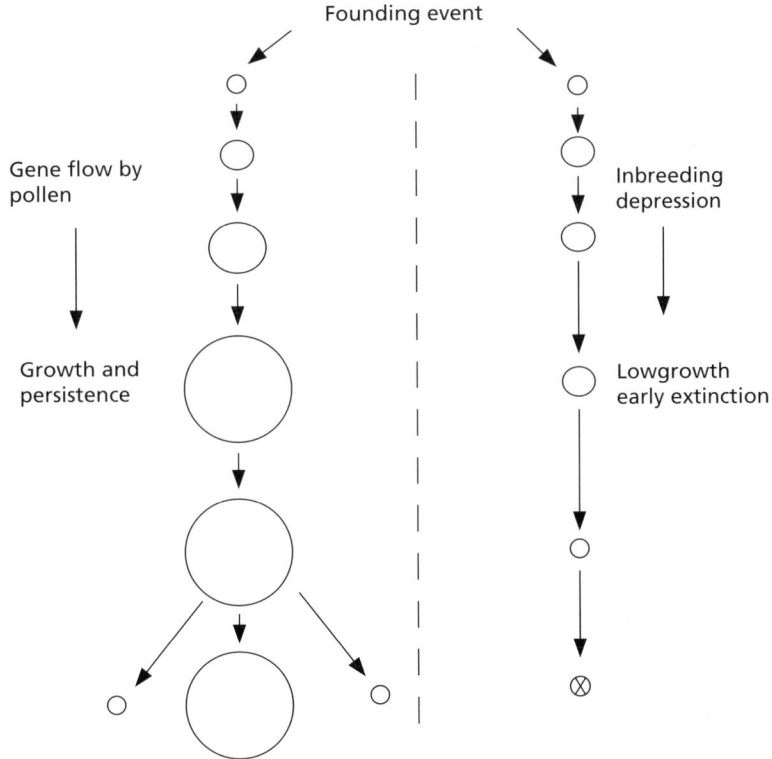

Figure 9.2 Schematic of two possible fates of newly founded plant populations. On the left side, genetic diversity is augmented by gene flow by pollen and the population grows, persists and produces dispersing propagules. On the right side, genetic diversity is lost, resulting in population decline and extinction without emigration.

The genetic structure of a plant metapopulation: *Silene alba* in Virginia

Young vs. old populations

In eastern North America, *Silene alba* (Caryophylaceae) is a short-lived perennial plant that can be found in fairly discrete patches along roadsides and in pastures (McNeill 1977). The species is dioecious and is primarily pollinated by hawk moths and bumble bees. Flowering begins in mid-May and can continue at least until mid-summer. Females can produce multiple seed capsules, each containing 100+ seeds. Seeds fall haphazardly from these capsules upon ripening in late summer, with no obvious adaptation for long-distance dispersal.

A long-term demographic study of *S. alba* has been conducted by Antonovics and colleagues near the Mountain Lake Biological Station in south-west Virginia, USA (see Antonovics *et al.* 1994, 1997 for results from earlier years). A yearly roadside census along a network of 150 km of country roads has shown that in the Mt. Lake area, *S. alba* is distributed into hundreds of local patches, ranging in size from fewer than five flowering individuals to greater than 100. Records taken since 1988 show a high rate of patch turnover rate, with most extinction and colonization events involving groups of fewer than 10 individuals. Given the high rate of patch turnover, the *S. alba* individuals found along the census route have been described as existing in a metapopulation (Antonovics *et al.* 1994; McCauley *et al.* 1995; Thrall *et al.* 1998).

In 1994 the genetic structure of *S. alba* in the study area was characterized in relation to the metapopulation dynamics (McCauley 1994; McCauley *et al.* 1995). Twenty-three patches were selected for study, 11 'old' patches that had been in existence since the onset of the census in 1988 and 12 'young' patches that had appeared in the records within the previous 3 years. Recall from the models that if extinction and recolonization enhances genetic structure (as measured by F_{st}) then the set of young patches would have a greater F_{st} value than the set of old patches. If extinction and recolonization reduces genetic structure, the reverse would be true.

Patches were characterized for allele frequency at seven polymorphic allozyme loci and with regard to chloroplast DNA (cpDNA) haplotype frequency. Several general points emerged. First, both young and old patches displayed significant among patch variation in allozyme allele frequencies, indicating that patches can be considered local breeding populations. Secondly, individual patches conformed to Hardy–Weinberg expectations, indicating approximate random mating within patches. Finally, among population differentiation as measured by cpDNA haplotype frequency was approximately fivefold greater than the measurement based on allozyme allele frequencies. This was considered notable in terms of the study of gene flow since the maternally inherited cpDNA cannot disperse in pollen.

Most important was a comparison between the young and old populations. The F_{st} value calculated for the allozyme data taken from the young populations was 50% greater than the same statistic calculated for the old populations, a statistically significant difference (Figure 9.3). A reasonable interpretation of these results is that the genetic structure seen in the young populations arises when populations are founded by a small number of individuals, presumably a result of seed dispersal. Based on their first appearance in the long-term census, the average size of the young populations at founding was 8.7 (harmonic mean 4.2), a sufficiently small number to generate a considerable amount of allele and haplotype frequency sampling variance, especially if members of a given founding group tend to be drawn from the same source ($\varnothing > 0$). Given the lower F_{st} value in the old populations, the genetic structure that is set up by founding events must then erode as a cohort of populations ages owing to subsequent gene flow, especially by pollen.

The generations immediately after colonization: small populations circling the drain?

How do the genetic and demographic properties of *S. alba* populations change as they age? The results of the 'young vs. old' study described above suggest that populations accumulate genetic diversity as they age, perhaps as a result of gene flow by pollen. Certainly, there is some increase numerically, as many populations on the

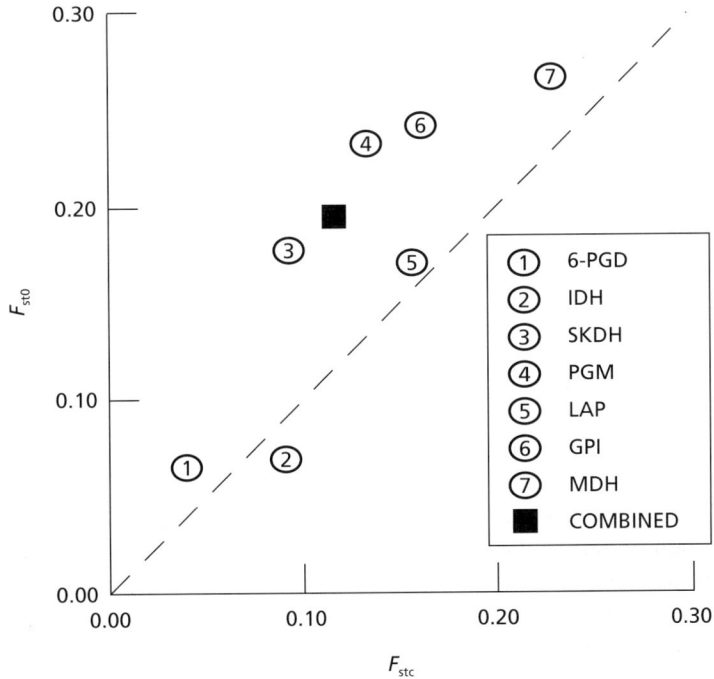

Figure 9.3 Paired values of F_{st} calculated for seven polymorphic allozymes based on information taken from newly formed populations of *Silene alba* (F_{st0}) and populations that had been in continued existence for 5+ years (F_{stc}). The filled rectangle represents F_{st} values based on information combined across loci. Note that the F_{st} value for the cohort of newly formed populations is nearly twice that of the established populations. (From McCauley *et al.* 1995.)

census route contain many more individuals than were found in even the largest 'young' population. Perhaps many other newly founded populations fail to prosper, and go extinct within a few generations after colonization. Thus, populations persisting long enough to be available for inclusion in our 'old' category might represent non-random samples of their respective founding cohorts.

In order to document events in the first few generations after colonization 12 of the 'young' populations were resampled for allozyme diversity in 1999 (C. M. Richards, D. E. McCauley & S. N. Emery, unpublished). Based on studies of survivorship in natural populations (C. M. Richards, unpublished), this is equivalent to an approximately 2.5-generation interval between allozyme samples, and an interval of perhaps five generations between the founding of the oldest 'young' population and the 1999 sample. Since sampling of these small populations includes information from all flowering individuals and most non-flowering individuals beyond the seedling stage, the sampling can also be used to evaluate demographic, as well as genetic, changes between years.

Table 9.1 Summary statistics for 12 small populations of *Silene alba* sampled in 1994 and then again in 1999. There are no statistically significant differences between years. Population size is based on direct count. Genetic parameters are based on six polymorphic allozyme loci.

	1994	1999
Mean population size	11.8	12.7
Mean heterozygosity	0.50	0.50
F_{st}	0.17	0.19
Mean number of alleles	17.2	16.7

The 1994 and 1999 samples are first summarized and compared in terms of population averages, such as mean population size, number of alleles and heterozygosity, as well as Wright's F_{st}. These calculations are presented in Table 9.1. It can be seen that there was very little change in these summary statistics between 1994 and 1999. However, minimal change in the summary statistics does not mean that individually the populations were static. For example, some populations tripled in size between 1994 and 1999, while others declined precipitously. In nearly every population, allozyme alleles seen in 1994 were missing in 1999, whereas some alleles not seen in those populations in 1994 appeared in the 1999 sample. This resulted in a net gain of alleles in some populations and a net loss in others.

Given that many populations appear to be numerically and genetically dynamic, it might prove useful to ask whether there are any correlations between the numeric and genetic properties of individual populations. To that end, graphs of the relationship between population growth and changes in allele number and heterozygosity are presented in Figure 9.4. It can be seen that in both cases there is a significant positive correlation. Populations that grew in size tended to exhibit an increase in genetic diversity as measured at the population level by allele number or at the individual level as measured by heterozygosity. Populations that declined in number tended to lose diversity.

Additional insight into the dynamics of these populations can be obtained from a sample taken in 1997. In that year cpDNA haplotypes were determined for individuals in eight of the 12 populations. A comparison of the cpDNA haplotype composition of these eight populations in 1994 and 1997 (an interval of a little more than one generation) yields a different picture from that gained from the allozymes (McGlothlin and McCauley, unpublished). As can be seen from Table 9.2, there was a clear decline in haplotype diversity. In 1997 no population had added a haplotype not seen in 1994, but several lost haplotypes. In fact, save for one individual in one population, no within-population haplotype diversity remained. The difference between the allozyme and cpDNA comparisons can be ascribed to the different modes of inheritance of the nuclear and chloroplast genomes. The chloroplast genome is inherited maternally (McCauley 1994). This has two effects, relative to biparental inheritance. First, it reduces the effective population size of cpDNA because *S. alba* is dioecious. Secondly, cpDNA can only be dispersed in seeds.

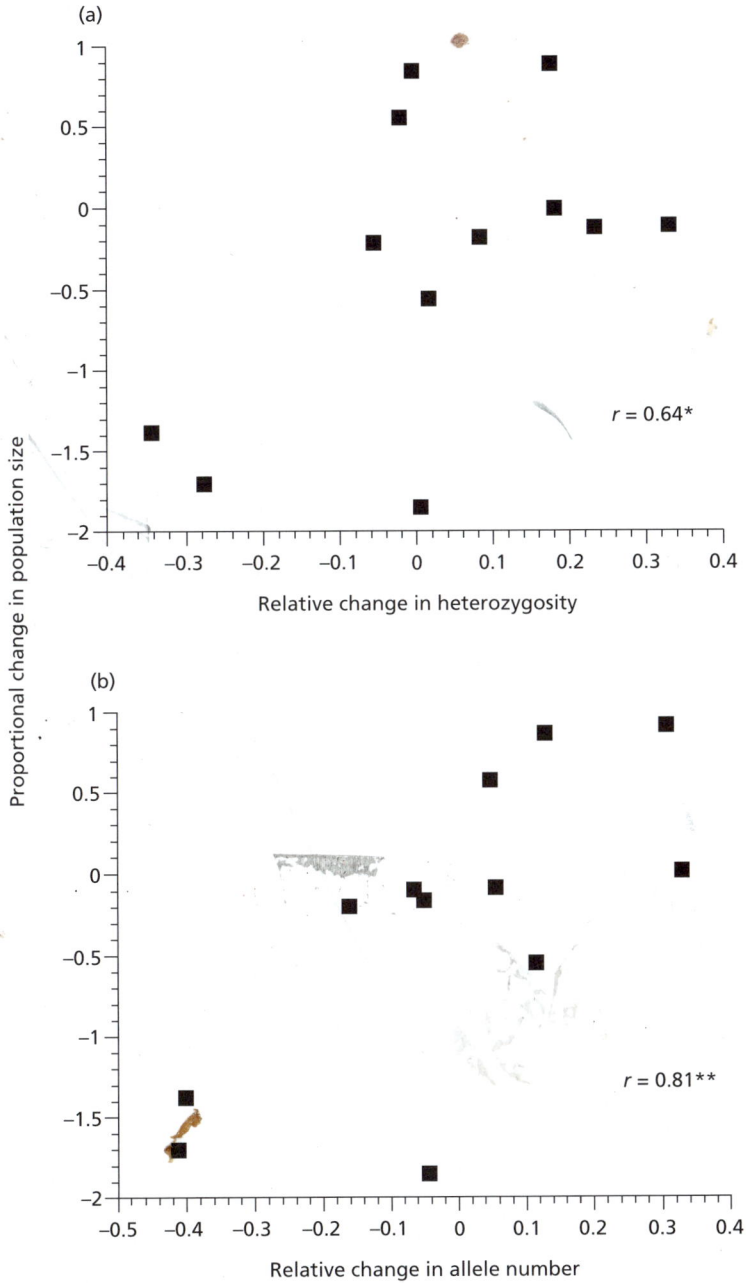

Figure 9.4 The relationship between changes in genetic diversity measured by either (a) heterozygosity or (b) allele number vs. the change in population size for 12 populations of *Silene alba* censused in 1994 and 1999. Genetic changes are measured as ((value 1999 – value 1994)/value 1994). Population size changes are measured as ln(size 1999/size 1994). In both (a) and (b) the product-moment correlation coefficient (*r*) is significantly greater than zero.

Table 9.2 Chloroplast DNA diversity in eight small populations of *Silene alba* sampled in 1994 and 1997. F_{st} values differ significantly ($P < 0.01$) by a jack-knifing method of comparison (Sokal & Rohlf 1995).

	1994	1997
Mean number of haplotypes	1.60	1.11
F_{st}	0.62	0.98

Several tentative conclusions can be drawn from these results. First, many of the 12 populations were small enough to be subject to rather severe genetic drift. This is illustrated by the moderate rate of loss of allozyme alleles and the more precipitous decline in within-population cpDNA haplotype diversity. Secondly, the addition of new allozyme alleles to many populations suggests at least a moderate rate of gene flow by pollen. New alleles could also appear owing to gene flow by seed, or the growth of seeds or seedlings present but not sampled in 1994. However, it is hard to imagine how seeds could be a source of new allozyme alleles without also contributing to the maintenance or enhancement of cpDNA diversity. Finally, the positive correlation between population growth and change in genetic diversity shows an interaction between genetics and demography. Perhaps most interesting would be a path of causation leading from genetics to demography, such as might be expected if gene flow offset any loss of vigour owing to genetic drift. Equally plausible might be causation leading from demography to genetics, such as might be expected if larger populations are more attractive to long-distance pollinators. Of course correlation need not imply any direct causation and both the genetic and demographic properties of these populations could be responding in a like way to some other, unknown variable.

In any event it is clear that recently founded populations lead a tenuous existence and are threatened by severe declines in both numbers and genetic diversity. Some of the 12 populations studied here are unlikely to persist for much longer. Perhaps the reduction in F_{st} seen in the 'old' populations in the earlier 'young vs. old' comparison was due to a hierarchical process in which the genetic diversity within newly founded populations is reduced relative to the metapopulation average owing to colonization of patches by a relatively small number of seeds, and then replenished with time via gene flow in some, but not all, populations. If it is these replenished populations that tend to persist, then *average* within-population diversity would increase with time (and F_{st} would decrease) in part due to differential extinction.

Does genetic erosion influence population persistence?

While theoretical studies have predicted that genetic variation is critical to continued population viability (Lacy 1987; Barret & Kohn 1991; Ellstrand & Elam 1993; Young *et al.* 1996), the specific ways in which drift, inbreeding and life-history characteristics affect plant population persistence is known only through a limited number of empirical studies. Experimental studies show that reductions in effective population size can lower fitness and can result in population extinction (Pollans & Allard 1989; Newman & Pilson 1997). In the field, documenting the process of genetic erosion and demographic decline has been typically examined by comparing populations of different sizes or ages. While the focal populations differed in their sizes or ages at the time of sampling, they represent the endpoints of different, unknown, population histories. It may be for this reason, that the apparent relationship between measures of genetic diversity (heterozygosity) and population fitness have been complex. While some studies of natural populations have shown strong correlation between measures of genetic diversity and population size (Raijman *et al.* 1994; Travis *et al.* 1996; Ouborg & van Treuren 1996; Fischer & Matthies 1998; Widen 1993) other species show little correlation (Meagher *et al.* 1978; Prober & Brown 1994; Schmidt & Jensen 2000). For example, in a series of studies of the genetics and population fitness of the threatened perennial *Scabiosa columbaria* in the Netherlands, results have shown a decrease in allozyme diversity with smaller populations, yet fitness estimates based on seed set, seed size and seedling size were mostly influenced by non-genetic maternal effects rather than by population origin (van Treuren *et al.* 1991). Similarly, in populations in the long-lived perennial *Gentiana pneumonanthe* there were positive correlations between population size and measures of early fitness, but correlations between population size and late fitness traits were not significant (Oostermeijer *et al.* 1994). In contrast, studies of the short-lived species *Gentianella germaninca* and *Ipomopsis aggregata*, showed a strong reduction in seed production and seedling fitness in smaller populations, which the authors attributed to genetic factors (Heschel & Paige, 1995; Fisher & Matthies 1998).

Given the emerging consensus that genetic erosion can influence the viability of small plant populations, two questions one might ask of the *S. alba* system are: (i) does *S. alba* display inbreeding depression in crosses of known pedigree, and (ii) is there evidence for inbreeding depression in recently founded populations in the field? Several recent studies have addressed one or both of these questions, answers to which might help identify the significance of the allozyme and cpDNA data.

Richards (2000) used a combination of within family and within and among population crosses to address these issues. In that study the germination probability of seeds was strongly influenced by the nature of the cross that produced them. The germination success of seeds produced by half-sib crosses was only about 70% that of outcross controls; whereas the products of full-sib crosses had only 40% the success of the controls (Richards 2000). Note that the increased homozygosity of the young natural populations ($F_{st} = 0.197$) is intermediate to the half-sib ($F = 0.125$) and full-sib ($F = 0.25$) experimental crosses.

A follow-up study (R. A. Smith & C. M. Richards, unpublished) examined some components of fitness beyond the seed-germination stage. In particular, seedling growth rate and pollen viability were compared for offspring produced by either outcrossing or full sib mating. Again there was a marked reduction in the germination success of seeds produced by full sib mating. Successfully germinating seeds were then grown under either low-fertilizer or high-fertilizer treatments. Products of full sib matings took longer to develop their first true leaves (relative to outcross controls) under the low-fertilizer treatment but not the high-fertilizer treatment. There was no effect of cross type on time to first flowering under the high-fertilizer treatment. The experiment was terminated before any plant flowered under the low-fertilizer treatment. Pollen viability (measured by a vital stain technique) was 13% higher in the outcross treatment. Interestingly, there was also a cross type by maternal line interaction (Figure 9.5).

Ouborg *et al.* (2000) studied the effects of inbreeding in *S. alba* on resistance to *Microbotryum violaceum*, a smut fungus. One might predict that a manifestation of inbreeding depression would be increased susceptibility to disease. Several generations of sib mating were conducted for several lines taken from each of several different natural populations found in the Netherlands. Infection rates were measured following artificial inoculations. Surprisingly, the overall average effect of inbreeding was to decrease infection rates. However, strong inbreeding × line and inbreeding × population interactions suggest that the population-specific resistance response to inbreeding could be very dependent on the population structure. Ouborg *et al.* (2000) also studied the effects of inbreeding on traits likely to influence the transmission of *M. violaceum* via pollinator transport of spores. Plant size and

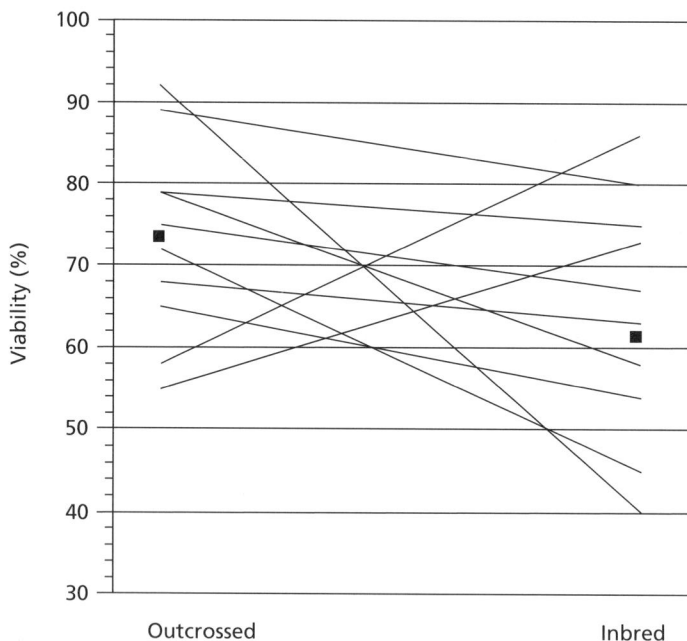

Figure 9.5 Viability of pollen produced by *Silene alba* males that were the product of either outcrossing or sib–sib inbreeding. Data are shown for 10 maternal lineages, as well as the cross treatment means (filled rectangle). Note that cross type and maternal lineage main effects, and the cross type × maternal line interaction were significant by ANOVA.

nectar volume were generally reduced by inbreeding, although again strong in-breeding × line effects were found.

Taken together, these results show that *S. alba* is highly susceptible to inbreeding depression, that the expression of inbreeding depression can be environment dependent, and that different lineages can respond to inbreeding differentially. They do not tell us if the population structure in nature results in a sufficient amount of inbreeding to manifest similar effects.

In order to answer this, Richards (2000) also conducted crosses within and among recently founded populations, which were subdivided into 'isolated' and 'central' categories according to their respective distances from nearest-neighbour populations. In the isolated group, within-population crosses displayed a marked reduction in seed germination relative to among population controls (Figure 9.6). This was not the case for the central populations. Again, there was a significant maternal line by cross-treatment interaction. It was suggested that the 'isolated vs. central' difference in seed germination was due to higher rates of gene flow by pollen into the less isolated central populations. Thus, if seed viability is a predictor of population viability it does seem that genetic erosion accompanying the early stages of population establishment could threaten persistence.

One demographic aspect of this system that is not yet well studied is the seed bank. While it is well known that seed banks can have a strong influence on the demography (Venable 1989) and genetics (Tonsor *et al.* 1993; Cabin 1996) of plant popula-

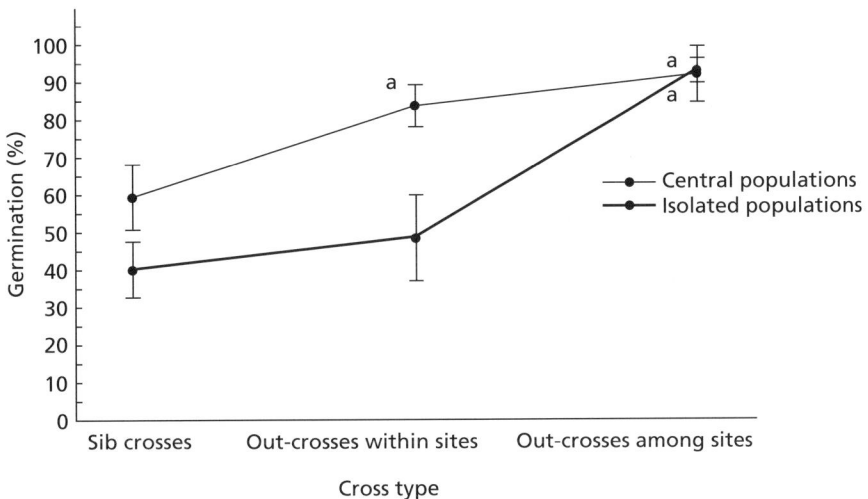

Figure 9.6 Mean germination (±s.e.) of *Silene alba* seeds produced by sib–sib crosses, and outcrosses within or among sites. Note that outcrossing within those sites near other established populations (central populations) resulted in germination equivalent to outcrossing among sites (these three statistically equivalent treatment means are denoted by 'a'). Outcrossing within isolated sites did not increase germination relative to sib–sib crosses. (From Richards 2000.)

tions, the study of seeds banks is not yet well integrated into either theoretical or empirical studies of the genetics of plant metapopulations. It is known that some *S. alba* seeds remain dormant in the soil in our study area (P. Peroni, pers. comm.), but their impact on the dynamics of established populations is not known. It is also not clear how the genetic consequences of colonization from below might differ from colonization from afar.

Conclusions

Clearly, when plant populations are ephemeral a key to understanding their dynamics would be understanding the conditions that permit population establishment. This chapter suggests that evaluation of the amount and consequences of gene movement during this process could be crucial. If one were to divide population establishment into two arbitrary steps, first a discrete colonization event and then subsequent population growth, the initial genetic composition of a population depends on patterns of seed dispersal. Genetic composition can then be modified during the second phase of establishment by the subsequent influx of genes in either seeds or pollen. Current mathematical models of metapopulation genetics provide some understanding of how colonization events influence genetic structure, but do not allow for the differential success of populations during the establishment phase. Empirical studies of *S. alba* demonstrate the influence of local extinction and recolonization on genetic structure, and suggest that the genetic composition of populations early in their history could influence their long-term persistence. However, neither the theoretical nor empirical study of metapopulation genetics has matured to the point where the interaction between genetics and demography of population establishment is well understood. The goal of these concluding paragraphs is to suggest some avenues for future study.

From a theoretical perspective, it would be useful to include non-random extinction in the models, either as a function of population size or genetic composition. This might require an individual–population-based approach (if not a true individual-based model) that keeps track of the properties of individual populations, rather than relying on metapopulation averages such as N, e, k or F_{st}. Further, it would be useful to connect the properties of individual populations to their respective contributions to the pool of seeds and pollen available for colonization and/or gene flow. In this way the influence of genetic structure on metapopulation-wide properties such as occupancy could be evaluated. Such an approach might require computer, rather than analytic, modelling. Efforts by Thrall *et al.* (1998) and Hedrick and Gilpin (1997) represent a first step in this regard.

A general goal for the empirical study of plant metapopulations would be, of course, to identify the ecological settings that cause plant populations to resemble the metapopulation metaphor. While the dynamics of ruderal species such as *S. alba* occupying habitat chronically disturbed by humans is an obvious case, the study of patch dynamics in naturally disturbed habitat has also come under close scrutiny by plant ecologists. Addition of a genetic component to the study of plant patch dynamics is rarer, however, with a series of genetic studies of Swedish island populations of *Silene dioica* being a nice exception (Giles & Goudet 1997a,b).

Perhaps most important would be more empirical studies of the conditions that permit population establishment. Studies of small plant populations are on the increase, both those considering purely ecological Allee effects such as pollinator limitation (Groom 1998), and more genetically orientated studies considering the effects of inbreeding on population viability (see references cited above). It is rarer, however, that the early stages of population establishment have been addressed explicitly, especially in a genetic context. For example, if the breeding system places a lower limit on the number of colonists needed for population establishment (i.e. all other things equal, it should require more colonists to establish populations of dioecious or self-incompatible species) then it is clear that there should be a biological lower limit on k, the size of colonizing groups in any effort to model that system. Similarly, understanding patterns of seed dispersal would help to parameterize Ø, the measure of the common origin of colonists. Finally, it is not clear at all how gene flow events alter the demography of small populations. There is no doubt that gene flow events can slow or reverse the effects of genetic drift, increase heterozygosity, and should, therefore, ameliorate the effects of inbreeding depression. What is not well know, however, is the empirical relationship between gene flow events in one generation and the numerical response by the population in future generations. Quantification of this numerical response would be critical to understanding the influence of postcolonization gene flow on population establishment.

Summary

Plants often occur in numerous discrete patches connected to one another by limited movements of seeds and/or pollen. When these patches are ephemeral, with patch extinctions more or less offset by colonization, the patch dynamics can approximate the metapopulation dynamics considered in many theoretical models. Most models of the genetic consequences of extinction/recolonization have considered the effects of demography on genetics, but not the effect of genetics on demography. For example, they rarely address how the genetic properties of recently established populations might influence their persistence, despite the fact that founding events often reduce genetic diversity.

This chapter considers the possibility that small numbers in the generations immediately after population founding can lead to inbreeding depression, which can limit further population growth and perhaps threaten that population with extinction. The potential for inbreeding depression might be ameliorated if gene flow by pollen were to occur during this period.

Evidence is presented that this scenario might be played out in *Silene alba*, a short-lived perennial plant often found in discrete patches along roadsides. Local patches (populations) show considerable genetic structure as a result of an ongoing process of extinction and recolonization. Smaller and more isolated patches display inbreeding depression as evidenced by reduced seed viability when compared to less isolated populations or among-population crosses. Finally, a comparison of the numerical and genetic properties of 12 small populations over 5 years shows a correlation between population growth and changes in genetic diversity. Generally, populations that increased in size increased in genetic diversity whereas those that decreased in population size during the study lost genetic diversity. This is the pattern expected if gene flow can offset inbreeding depression.

Acknowledgements

We would like to acknowledge the many people who contributed to this work, with special thanks to Janis Antonovics and Peter Thrall for introducing us to the science of psilonology. The research reported here was supported by several grants from the National Science Foundation; most recently award DEB-9610496.

References

Antonovics, J., Thrall, P., Jarosz, A. & Stratton, D. (1994). Ecological genetics of metapopulations: the *Silene–Ustilago* plant pathogen system. In: *Ecological Genetics* (ed. L. Real), pp. 146–170. Princeton University Press, Princeton, NJ.

Antonovics, J., Thrall, P.H. & Jarosz, A.M. (1997). Genetics and the spatial ecology of species interactions: the *Silene–Ustilago* system. In: *Spatial Ecology: The Role of Space in Population Dynamics and Interspecific Interactions.* (eds D. Tilman & P. Kareiva), pp. 158–180. Princeton University Press, Princeton, NJ.

Barrett, S.C.H. & Kohn, J. (1991). Genetic and evolutionary consequences of small population size in plants; implications for conservation. In: *Genetics and Conservation in Rare Plants* (eds D. Falk & K. Holsinger), pp. 3–30. Oxford University Press, New York.

Barton, N.H. & Whitlock, M.C. (1997). The evolution of metapopulations. In: *Metapopulation Biology, Ecology, Genetics, and Evolution* (eds I. Hanski & M.E. Gilpin,), pp. 183–210. Academic Press, New York.

Cabin, R.J. (1996). Genetic comparisons of seed bank and seedling populations of a perennial desert mustard *Lesquerella fendleri*. *Evolution*, **50**, 1830–1841.

Ellstrand, N. & Elam, D. (1993). Population genetic consequences of small population size: implications for plant conservation. *Annual Review of Ecology and Systematics*, **24**, 217–242.

Fischer, M. & Matthies, D. (1998). RAPD variation in relation to population size and plant fitness in the rare *Gentianella germanica* (Gentiaceae). *American Journal of Botany*, **85**, 811–819.

Gandon, S. & Michalakis, Y. (1999). Evolutionarily stable dispersal rate in a metapopulation with extinctions and kin competition. *Journal of Theoretical Biology*, **199**, 275–290.

Giles, B.E. & Goudet, J. (1997a). Genetic differentiation in *Silene dioica* metapopulations: estimation of spatio-temporal effects in a successional plant species. *American Naturalist*, **149**, 507–526.

Giles, B.E. & Goudet, J. (1997b). A case study of genetic structure in a plant metapopulation. In: *Metapopulation Biology, Ecology, Genetics, and Evolution* (eds I. Hanski & M.E. Gilpin), pp. 429–454. Academic Press, New York.

Groom, M. (1998). Allee effects limit population viability of an annual plant. *American Naturalist*, **151**, 487–496.

Hanski, I. & Gilpin, M. (1991). Metapopulation dynamics: brief history and conceptual domain. *Biological Journal of the Linnaean Society*, **42**, 73–88.

Hanski, I. & Simberloff, D. (1997). The metapopulation approach, its history, conceptual domain, and application to conservation. In: *Metapopulation Biology, Ecology, Genetics, and Evolution* (eds I. Hanski & M.E. Gilpin), pp. 5–26. Academic Press, New York.

Hedrick, P.W. & Gilpin, M.E. (1997). Genetic effective size of a metapopulation. In: *Metapopulation Biology, Ecology, Genetics, and Evolution* (eds I. Hanski & M.E. Gilpin), pp. 166–181. Academic Press, New York.

Heschel, M. & Paige, K. (1995). Inbreeding depression, environmental stress, and population size variation in Scarlet gillia (*Ipomopsis aggregata*). *Conservation Biology*, **9**, 126–133.

Ingvarsson, P.K. (1997). The effect of delayed population growth on the genetic differentiation of local populations subject to frequent extinctions and recolonizations. *Evolution*, **51**, 29–35.

Lacy, R.C. (1987). Loss of genetic diversity from managed populations: interacting effects of drift mutation, immigration, selection and population subdivision. *Conservation Biology*, **1**, 143–158.

Levins, R. (1969). Some demographic and genetic consequences of environmental heterogeneity for biological control. *Bulletin of the Entomological Society of America*, **15**, 237–240.

Levins, R. (1970). Extinction. In: *Some Mathematical Problems in Biology* (ed. M. Gerstenhaber), pp. 77–107. American Mathematical Society, Providence, RI.

Maruyama, T. & Kimura, M. (1980). Genetic variability and the effective size when local extinction and recolonization are frequent. *Proceedings of the National Academy of Sciences of the USA*, **77**, 6710–6714.

McCauley, D.E. (1994). Contrasting the distribution of chloroplast DNA and allozyme polymorphism among local populations of *Silene alba*: implications for studies of gene flow in plants. *Proceedings of the National Academy of Sciences of the USA*, **91**, 8127–8131.

McCauley, D.E., Raveill, J. & Antonovics, J. (1995). Local founding events as determinants of genetic structure in a plant metapopulation. *Heredity*, **75**, 630–636.

McNeill, J. (1977). The biology of Canadian weeds. 25. *Silene alba* (Miller) E.H.L. Krause. *Canadian Journal of Plant Science*, **57**, 1103–1114.

Meagher, T.R., Antonovics, J. & Primack, R. (1978). Experimental ecological genetics in *Plantago* III: Genetic variation and demography in relation to survival of *Plantago cordata*, a rare species. *Biological Conservation*, **14**, 243–258.

Newman, D. & Pilson, D. (1997). Increased probability of extinction due to decreased genetic

population size: Experimental populations of *Clarkia puchella*. *Evolution*, **51**, 354–362.

Olivieri, I., Michalakis, Y. & Gouyon, P.-H. (1995). Metapopulation genetics and the evolution of dispersal. *American Naturalist*, **146**, 202–228.

Oostermeijer, J.G.B., Van Eijck, M.W. & Den Nijs, H.C.M. (1994). Offspring fitness in relation to population size and genetic variation in the rare perennial plant species *Gentiana pneumonanthe* (Gentianaceae). *Oecologia*, **97**, 289–296.

Ouborg, N.J., Biere, A. & Mudde, C.L. (2000). Inbreeding effects on resistance and transmission-related traits in the *Silene–Microbotryum* pathosystem. *Ecology*, **81**, 520–531.

Ouborg, N.J. & van Treuren, R. (1995). Variation in fitness-related characters among small and large populations of *Salvia pratensis*. *Journal of Ecology*, **83**, 369–380.

Pannell, J.R. & Charlesworth, B. (1999). Neutral genetic diversity in a metapopulation with recurrent local extinction and recolonization. *Evolution*, **53**, 664–676.

Pollans, N. & Allard, R. (1989). An experimental evaluation of the recovery potential of rye grass. *Evolution*, **43**, 1320–1324.

Prober, S.M. & Brown, A.H.D. (1994). Conservation of the grassy whit box woodlands: Population genetics and fragmentation of *Eucalyptus albens*. *Conservation Biology*, **8**, 1003–1013.

Raijman, L.E.L., van Leewen, N.C., Kersten, R., Oostermeijer, J.G.B., den Nijs, H.C.M. & Menken, S.B. (1994). Genetic variation and outcrossing rate in relation to population size in *Gentiana pneumonanthe* L. *Conservation Biology*, **8**, 1014–1026.

Richards, C.M. (2000). Inbreeding depression and genetic rescue in a plant metapopulation. *American Naturalist*, **155**, 383–394.

Ronce, O., Perret, F. & Olivieri, I. (2000). Evolutionarily stable dispersal rates do not always increase with local extinction rates. *American Naturalist*, **155**, 485–496.

Schmidt, K. & Jensen, K. (2000). Genetic structure and AFLP variation of remnant populations in the rare plant *Pedicularis palustris* (Scrophulariaceae) and its relation to population size and reproductive components. *American Journal of Botany*, **87**, 678–689.

Slatkin, M. (1977). Gene flow and genetic drift in a

species subject to frequent local extinctions. *Theoretical Population Biology*, **12**, 253–262.

Sokal, R.R. & Rohlf, F.J. (1995). *Biometry*, 3rd edn. Freeman, New York.

Thrall, P.H., Richards, C.M., McCauley, D.E. & Antonovics, J. (1998). Metapopulation collapse: The consequences of limited gene flow in spatially structured populations. In: *Modeling Spatiotemporal Dynamics in Ecology* (eds J. Bascompte & R.V. Sole), pp. 83–104. Springer-Verlag, Berlin.

Tonsor, S.J., Kalisz, S. & Fisher, J. (1993). A life-history based study of population genetic structure: seed bank to adults in *Plantago lanceolata*. *Evolution*, **47**, 833–843.

Travis, S.E., Maschinski, J. & Keim, P. (1996). An analysis of genetic variation in *Astragulus cremnophylax* var. *cremnophlax*, a critically endangered plant, using AFLP markers. *Molecular Ecology*, **5**, 735–745.

Van Treuren, R., Bijlsma R., Van Delden, W. & Ouborg, N.J. (1991). The significance of genetic erosion in the process of extinction. 1. Genetic differentiation in *Salvia pratensis* and *Scabies columbaria* in relation to population size. *Heredity*, **66**, 181–189.

Venable, D.L. (1989). Modelling the evolutionary ecology of seed banks. In: *Ecology of Soil Seed Banks* (eds M.A. Leck, V.T. Parker & R.L. Simpson), pp. 67–90. Academic Press, New York.

Wade, M.J. & McCauley, D.E. (1988). Extinction and recolonization: their effects on the genetic differentiation of local populations. *Evolution*, **42**, 995–1005.

Whitlock, M.C. & Barton, N.H. (1997). The effective size of a subdivided population. *Genetics*, **146**, 427–441.

Whitlock, M.C. & McCauley, D.E. (1990). Some population genetic consequences of colony formation and extinction: genetic correlations within founding groups. *Evolution*, **44**, 1717–1724.

Widen, B. (1993). Demographic and genetic effects on reproduction as related to population size in a rare, perennial herb, *Senecio integrifolius. Biological Journal of the Linnean Society*, **50**, 179–195.

Wright, S. (1940). Breeding structure of populations in relation to speciation. *American Naturalist*, **74**, 232–248.

Young, A., Boyle, T. & Brown, A.H.D. (1996). The population genetic consequences of habitat fragmentation for plants. *Trends in Ecology and Evolution*, **11**, 413–418.

Chapter 10

The demography and genetics of host–pathogen interactions

J. J. Burdon and P. H. Thrall**

Introduction

The interplay of demographic and genetic processes in spatially structured groups of populations (metapopulations) is among the most fertile ground of study for evolutionary biologists. It is there that the consequences of interpopulation asynchrony, drift, local extinction and chance colonization events combine to produce the long-term dynamics characteristic of the ecological and evolutionary behaviour of whole systems. Nevertheless, while both empirical and theoretical biologists have embraced the central role of space in shaping biotic interactions, to date relatively few studies have integrated ecological and genetic processes in a spatial context. In the past, ecologists have tended to ignore the possibilities of changes in the genetic structure of populations to focus on factors influencing fluctuations in numerical dynamics, as well as species diversity at the community level. Population genetics, on the other hand, has developed a rich body of theory that emphasizes the evolution and maintenance of genetic variation but which largely ignores the importance of demographic change. Moreover, in a more empirical mode, it too has failed to embrace its partner discipline, focusing more commonly on surveys of genetic variation for neutral markers both within and among populations.

Without doubt a significant factor in this divide between the demographic and genetic components of populations has been the relative lack of experimentally tractable characters that may have consequences for demographic patterns, are easily assessed, have a clear genetic basis, and that are likely to be under significant selective pressure. In this regard, studies of the coevolutionary biology of plants and their fungal pathogens are particularly attractive because of the obvious and potentially tight interaction between resistance in the host and virulence (=ability to cause a susceptible response) in the pathogen, as well as the clear ecological effects of disease on numerical abundance of the host. Such interactions are, however, an order of magnitude more complex than studies of single species requiring, as they do, monitoring of a four-way interplay of both host and pathogen numbers and assessment of changes in an explicit set of genes (resistance and virulence) for which there may be

* Centre for Plant Biodiversity Research, CSIRO-Plant Industry, GPO Box 1600, Canberra, ACT 2601, Australia.

no simple biochemical markers or surrogates. A consequence of this complexity has been the relatively slow development of empirical research on natural plant–pathogen interactions. Despite this, a long history of disease epidemics in agricultural systems clearly shows that the severity of epidemics is frequently greater in genetically uniform than more diverse stands (Browning 1974; Wolfe 1985). Moreover, it has been shown that deliberate changes in crop resistance can have major consequences for the genetic structure of associated pathogen populations (Watson 1981), as well as for subsequent disease dynamics. Do these patterns apply to natural systems where species diversity and an extensive range of other factors vary unpredictably? In essence, how does the genetic composition of host and pathogen populations reciprocally affect their numerical size and survival through time at both local and regional spatial scales? Just what is the ecological importance of genetic diversity in nature? Ultimately, what factors determine the direction and magnitude of coevolutionary change?

Host–pathogen interactions are diverse, ranging from situations where demographic effects predominate, through to full coevolutionary associations where the size and genetic structure of both host and pathogen populations vary through time and space. The extent and impact of these interactions are influenced by a myriad of abiotic and biotic factors. Broad spatial scale differences in climate have been repeatedly shown to influence disease dynamics (Miller 1966) while much more subtle changes associated with nutrient status, moisture and humidity can produce similar effects on a micro-scale (Lukens & Mullany 1972; Palti 1981). Similarly, a range of biotic factors, not the least being the temporal match of the respective life histories of host and pathogen, can greatly influence both ecological and evolutionary dynamics. In this chapter, we begin by focusing on single population studies, but use these to make the central point that such studies must be embedded within a broader metapopulation context in order to understand long-term ecological and genetic patterns.

What have we learned from single population studies?

In some host–pathogen associations, neither demographic nor genetic effects are discernible (e.g. pathogens that are naturally rare across their entire range or where pathogens are close to the edge of their climatic range). In these circumstances, pathogens exhibit endemic-type dynamics, being found as occasional oddities on their hosts but never at sufficient levels to substantially affect demographic or genetic parameters. In a provocative paper, Harper (1990) considered the role of pests and pathogens in shaping plant populations, and pointed out that pathogen damage that results in lower fecundity or even the death of individuals does not in itself necessarily result in a significant effect on the host population. Such damage may simply be 'harvesting' individuals that were doomed to die as a consequence of later-acting, density-dependent factors or preventing the production of more propagules than would ever become established. Thus, host species whose establishment is severely limited by the availability of 'safe sites' rather than by seed numbers may be able to incur individual reductions in fecundity without any detectable effect on the size of the next generation (but see below for potential genetic effects). For example, studies of the impact of a seedling damping-off disease on a range of tropical forest tree species showed that there could be a total loss of individual fitness (seedling death) (Augspurger 1983; Augspurger & Kelly 1984) but there was no evidence this would have a discernible impact on adult plant population size. However, in that study there certainly was some potential for the disease to have an ecological effect. Because the severity of disease was influenced by distance to conspecific adults and local seedling density, the disease might promote community diversity by contributing to overdispersion of its host (cf. Janzen 1970).

Demographic effects of pathogens on their hosts

As a counterbalance to situations where diseases may have substantial fitness effects at the individual level and no impact on host abundance, it is equally the case that diseases may have significant impacts on host dynamics without themselves regulating host density (e.g. sexually transmitted and vector-borne diseases, Thrall *et al.* 1993; Thrall & Jarosz 1994). Numerous examples dot the literature where pathogen attack leads to reductions in the size of host populations. Without doubt the most dramatic of these occur when a naive host population or species is exposed to a new pathogen. Massive declines in American chestnut as a result of susceptibility to *Cryphonectria parasitica*, of a suite of highly susceptible Myrtaceous and Proteaceous species to *Phytophthora cinnamomi* (Wills & Keighery 1994), of live oak populations in Texas to *Ceratocystis fagacearum* (McDonald *et al.* 1998) and of elms to *Ophistoma novo-ulmi* have all occurred with little, if any, evidence of a shift in the resistance structure of remnant populations. Such large-scale effects may also occur in long-established associations as illustrated by the consequences of the spread of the root-rot fungus *Phellinus weirii* through stands of *Tsuga mertensiana* in the Pacific north-west of the USA. There the pathogen spreads outwards as a wave from infection foci, killing adult trees and, in many situations, changing the diversity and species balance of the community (Cook *et al.* 1989; Holah *et al.* 1993, 1997).

For annual or short-lived perennials where the aftermath of infection is usually far less apparent, the general lack of longitudinal studies has hampered proper documentation of the extent of the demographic effects of pathogens on their hosts. However, in the case of *Silene* species attacked by the systemic sterilizing anther smut *Microbotyrum violaceum*, it has been shown that heavily infected populations expand at a significantly slower rate than healthy ones (Carlsson & Elmqvist 1992; Antonovics *et al.* 1994, 1997). The *Silene–Microbotryum* system is characterized by endemic dynamics with relatively stable levels of disease, but it is worth stressing that diseases can have important consequences for host dynamics even though their prevalence in individual populations may be highly unpredictable through time. Thus, in a long-term study of *Linum marginale*, significant declines in population size have been very tightly associated with major disease epidemics of its rust pathogen *Melampsora lini* (Jarosz & Burdon 1992; J. J. Burdon unpublished). In intervening years when the disease was absent or only present at a low ebb, the death rate of individual host cohorts was low and, as a consequence, the overall population size slowly increased.

Demographic effects of hosts on their pathogens

There is very little firm descriptive or experimental data available concerning the effect of hosts on the numerical dynamics of their pathogens in natural systems. Host density, but not population size, has often (but not exclusively) been positively associated with disease levels (Burdon & Chilvers 1982; Thrall *et al.* 2001a). In fact, simple theoretical models of disease have shown that transmission mode is likely to play a major role in determining the interaction between host abundance and pathogen dynamics and persistence (Getz & Pickering 1983; Thrall *et al.* 1993). In systems characterized by density-dependent transmission (most representative of many aerially and indirectly transmitted diseases), there will be a minimum threshold host density below which pathogens will not be able to successfully invade and persist (especially through periods unsuitable for pathogen development). The size of such minima will clearly be strongly influenced by aspects of the life histories of both host and pathogen (Anderson & May 1981). Thus, in the interaction between the local lesion rust pathogen *Triphragmium ulmariae* and its host *Filipendula ulmaria*, which is characterized by severe winter population bottlenecks, the minimum size of host populations needed to ensure a 50% probability of local survival of the rust is in the range of 150–1000 individuals (Burdon *et al.* 1995).

On the other hand, systemic diseases that perennate within their hosts will require lower host population sizes for local survival than will pathogens without this advantage. Indeed, when transmission is frequency dependent, as in the case of sexually transmitted diseases (STDs), then (at least theoretically) there is no host density below which pathogen invasion cannot occur (Getz & Pickering 1983; Thrall *et al.* 1993, 1995). Indeed, the effective host population size needed for the local survival of vector-transmitted, systemic anther smuts may approach unity for *Microbotryum violaceum* infections of *Silene alba*. Studies of this interaction within a large roadside metapopulation have further shown that while disease incidence (presence/absence) is positively related to population size, prevalence is generally higher in smaller populations (Antonovics *et al.* 1994). This pattern is also predicted by population dynamical models incorporating frequency-dependent transmission. Such models also demonstrate that STD persistence requires independent regulation of host density, otherwise either the pathogen will be lost from the population or will completely infect its host population, leading to total extinction (Getz & Pickering 1983; Alexander & Antonovics 1988; Thrall *et al.* 1995).

Genetic effects of pathogens on their hosts

Regardless of whether there are obvious demographic effects, there may still be significant genetic consequences of the interaction between host and pathogen. Indeed, if pathogen transmission rates are positively correlated with host density (as is often the case; Burdon & Chilvers 1982) or are frequency dependent (cf. vector-transmitted diseases), and infection reduces individual host fitness, then the opportunity exists for subtle genetic changes to occur in host populations independent of fluctuations in size. Without the benefit of long-term studies in which disease levels are manipulated, it is obviously not possible to completely disentangle demographic and genetic effects and hence assert with total confidence that genetic changes have occurred in the total absence of demographic ones. However, the relative ease with which resistance to pathogens can be detected in host populations of all sizes (e.g. Snaydon & Davies 1972; Burdon 1980, 1987; Parker 1985; de Nooij & van Damme 1988; Bevan *et al.* 1993; Schmidt 1994; Morrison 1996) provides at least some support for this possibility. Despite this, situations in which genetic changes occur without any apparent demographic consequences may be difficult to identify. Indeed, it was only by chance in an experiment designed to assess variation in a range of morphological characters in *Anthoxanthum odoratum* that Snaydon and Davies (1972) identified subtle changes in the resistance structure of demes of *A. odoratum* growing in adjacent treatments of the Park Grass experiment.

That genetic changes in the resistance architecture of plant populations can occur in a consistent direction that reflects the selective impact of a pathogen has been documented in a biological control programme aimed at controlling the introduced, agamospermous species *Chondrilla juncea* in southern Australia. In its home range in Europe, populations of *C. juncea* are composed of a complex mixture of lines that show resistance to different pathotypes of the rust pathogen *Puccinia chondrillina* (Table 10.1). In Australia where only three resistance phenotypes occur, a single pathotype virulent against the most widespread host resistance type was introduced in 1970 (Cullen *et al.* 1973). The immediate effect of this introduction was a marked reduction in the fitness of the targeted host phenotype and a long-term decline in density. However, within a few years this change was followed by a marked surge in the distributional range and density of one of the previously more restricted but still resistant forms (Figure 10.1), leading to the development of populations comprised of mixtures of the two agamospermous lines (Burdon *et al.* 1981). A particularly attractive feature of this example has been the subsequent introduction of additional pathotypes of *P. chondrillina* exhibiting virulence against this newly

Table 10.1 Frequencies of *Chondrilla juncea* clones and the occurrence of rust caused by *Puccinia chondrillina* in 16 apomictic populations in eastern Turkey. For each population, the most common clone is designated as C1, and the second most common clone as C2. (Data from Chaboudez & Burdon 1995.)

Number of populations	Population size	Number of genotypes	% Plants infected	Common clone frequency		Number of populations with:			
				1st clone	2nd clone	C1	C2	C1+C2	C1+Other
One infected genotype									
13	42	4.46	11	0.64	0.17	10	3	—	—
Two infected genotypes									
3	50	6.33	14	0.67	0.16	—	—	1	2

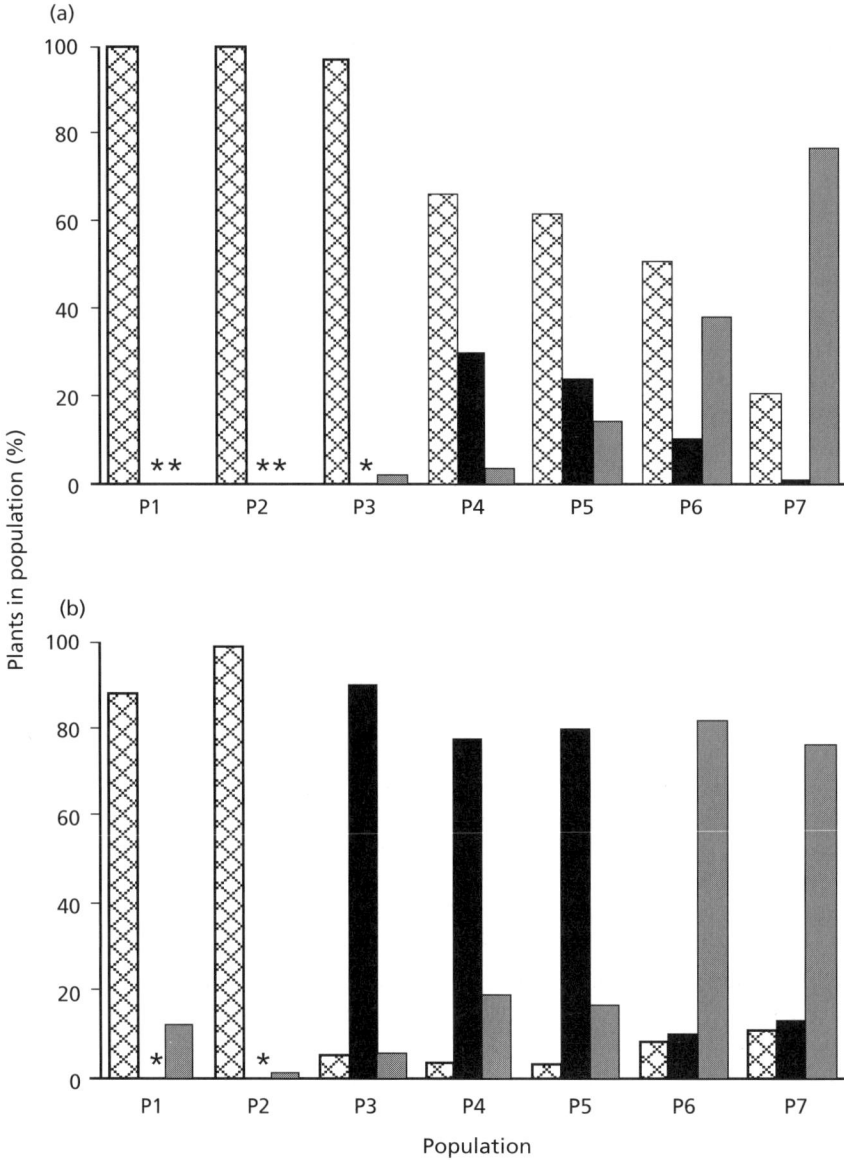

Figure 10.1 Patterns of genetic change in the resistance of Australian populations of the invasive weed *Chondrilla juncea* to attack by pathotypes of the rust fungus *Puccinia chondrillina* introduced as a biological control agent. (a) Census data from 1969, prior to release of the pathogen; (b) census data from 1980, 11 years after release. The three resistance phenotypes (narrow-leaved, intermediate-leaved, broad-leaved) are represented by cross-hatched, solid black and solid grey bars, respectively. * = total absence of a given resistance phenotype. (From Burdon *et al.* 1981.)

aggressive form of *C. juncea*. In turn, these pathotypes have reduced the fitness of this form creating a partly vacant niche into which the last resistant form of *C. juncea* is currently spreading (R. H. Groves, pers, comm.).

Normally, field-based 'experiments' do not have the luxury of tight control over both host and pathogen structure. Despite this, however, the challenge provided by a naturally occurring and usually variable pathogen population has the distinct advantage of providing an overall assessment of the likely response of a host population to its pathogen population. Indeed, in a controlled field experiment involving mixtures of a range of different clones of *Solidago altissima* and natural infection by the mildew fungus *Erysiphe cichoracearum*, Schmidt (1994) not only showed the existence of variation for resistance within the host but also that pathogen severity became greater in genetically less diverse stands, and susceptible lines suffered significant reductions in above-ground biomass.

Much of the available data on host resistance structure is based on surveys performed with bulk pathogen populations, which can obscure the genetic basis of any observed resistance and makes studies of the precise nature of interactions more difficult. Infection responses induced by bulk population inoculation onto multiple host lines are likely to show continuous variation. For the unwary, such results may suggest a system of disease resistance based on the interactive effect of multiple genes, each with small phenotypic effect. However, this interpretation is based on the implicit presumption that variation in the pathogen is based on uniform virulence and continuous variation in aggressiveness. Without supporting evidence, such assumptions are unwarranted (particularly in the case of biotrophic pathogens like rusts and mildews, populations of which are typically composed of multiple pathotypes; Pinon & Frey 1997; Burdon & Jarosz 1991). Indeed, as Kinloch and Walkinshaw (1991) have shown, a similar pattern of continuous variation may be generated in situations where: (i) disease resistance is controlled by genes with major phenotypic effects (cf. gene-for-gene; Flor 1955); (ii) many such genes are present; (iii) virulence/avirulence in the pathogen is controlled by single genes; and finally (iv) the pathogen population is composed of multiple genetically different individuals. All these features are commonly encountered in the real world.

In contrast to the use of bulk pathogen populations, the use of individual genetically uniform isolates results in a more restricted view of the resistance response of a host population, but allows a reasonable estimate to be made about the genetic control of resistance and pathogenicity. Thus, the near continuous variation in disease response seen in a population of *Plantago lanceolata* to infection by single isolates of *Phomopsis subordinaria* (de Nooij & van Damme 1988) provides solid circumstantial evidence for an interaction in which the genetic control of both aggressiveness in the pathogen and resistance in the host is based on multiple genes of minor phenotypic effect. On the other hand, patterns of discontinuous variation in disease resistance as were found in *Amphicarpaea bracteata* (Parker 1985), *Glycine canescens* (Burdon 1987), *Senecio vulgaris* (Bevan *et al.* 1993) and *Linum marginale* (Burdon 1994) to *Synchytrium, Phakopsora, Erysiphe* and *Melampsora*, respectively, are consistent with the expression of single genes with major phenotypic effects (cf. gene-for-gene). In all these examples subsequent genetic analysis confirmed this mode of control.

Genetic effects of hosts on their pathogens

With the exception of a few notable studies involving natural populations of *Cryphonectria parasitica* (Anagnostakis & Kranz 1987), *Melampsora lini* (Burdon & Jarosz 1991), *M. epitea* (Pei *et al.* 1996) and *M. larici-populina* (Pinon & Frey 1997), studies of the phenotypic or genetic structure of pathogen populations have been dominated by a series of on-going yearly surveys of a range of agricultural crop pathogens. A common feature of these surveys is the occurrence of variation such that even though individual populations (generally encompassing whole agricultural regions) may be dominated by a single pathotype, many other pathotypes often possessing quite different virulence spectra are usually present at low frequency. Such studies also provided the first conclusive evidence of evolutionary change in the structure and pathogenicity profile of pathogen populations in response to changes in the resistance structure of crop cultivars. This 'human-guided' evolution was particularly apparent in wheat stem rust (*Puccinia graminis* f.sp. *tritici*) during the 1950s as individually deployed resistance genes were sequentially rendered ineffective as a result of mutational changes (Watson 1981; Burdon & Silk 1997).

Evidence of similar temporal changes in the structure of pathogen populations parasitizing wild plant populations is very limited but recent work on the occurrence of the rust *Melampsoridium betulinum* in a coppice stand of *Betula pubescens* provides circumstantial evidence for temporal fluctuations in the structure and hence the direction of the selective pressure exerted by the pathogen (J. J. Burdon & L. Ericson, unpublished). Over the 3-year period 1998–2000, severe epidemics of *M. betulinum* occurred in 1998 and 2000 with a virtual absence of the pathogen in the drier intervening year. Comparison of the severity of disease suffered by 100 marked individuals at the epidemic peak in each of the 2 years shows strong evidence that some host individuals carry resistance that is effective over multiple years; others that were heavily diseased in both years appear to carry no effective resistance; while yet others sustained intermediate levels of disease in both years (Figure 10.2). In addition to these obvious differences some other host individuals showed marked differences in disease severity between the two years (high in 1998, low in 2000 and vice versa). These patterns are strongly suggestive of the impact of a variable pathogen population (showing variation both within and among years) attacking a host population in which resistance based on the presence of both major and minor gene resistance plays a role.

The interface between demography and genetics

Taken together, the above studies provide circumstantial evidence of a range of links between numbers and genetics. Individually, however, they provide no clear picture of the consequences of an integrated effect. Indeed, at the population level, the genetic outcome of the interaction of host and pathogen populations may often be counterintuitive, particularly in systems where colonization and extinction process-

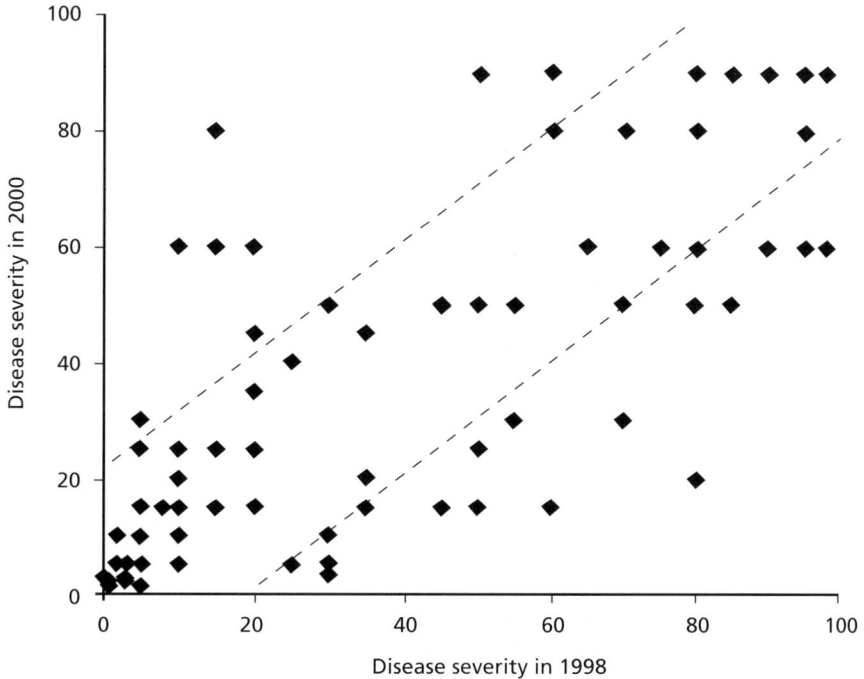

Figure 10.2 Comparison of severity of disease caused by *Melampsoridium betulinum* on 100 individuals of *Betula pubescens* in a single stand in northern Sweden in the epidemic years 1998 and 2000. Data points within the two dotted lines potentially represent host individuals responding in a qualitatively similar manner to the pathogen populations present in the 2 years; those outside the lines are more indicative of individuals responding differently to the two pathogen populations (J. J. Burdon & L. Ericson, unpublished).

es play major roles in determining patterns of disease incidence. This is particularly well shown in the interaction occurring between a single population of *Linum marginale* and its co-occurring rust pathogen *Melampsora lini* (Burdon & Thompson 1995). Over the period 1986–1992 the size of the *L. marginale* population showed an inverse correlation with that of the pathogen, with the former being relatively high and stable in the years leading up to and including 1989 (Figure 10.3a,b). This was followed by a massive decline in population size in 1990 after which a slow recovery in numbers began (J. J. Burdon, unpublished). Over the same period the pathogen was present at very low levels until 1989 when a major epidemic occurred.

While these patterns show the fitness consequences of high disease levels (see also Jarosz & Burdon 1992), the full significance of the 1989 epidemic is only apparent when the resistance structure of the host population in the epidemic and postepidemic years is compared (Figure 10.3c,d). Prior to the epidemic, the host population was dominated by two resistance phenotypes (I and II; determined by the response of individual plants to nine pathotypes of *M. lini*; Burdon & Thompson 1995) with a further 13 being present at low frequency. In the year following the epidemic the

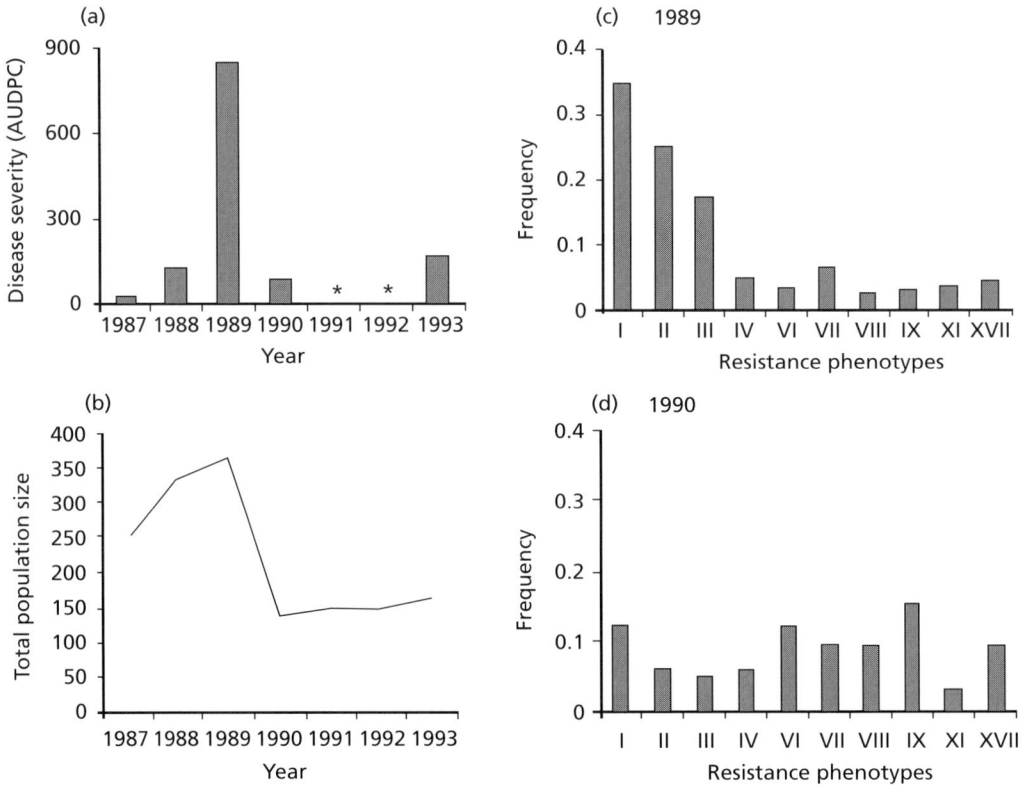

Figure 10.3 Demographic patterns and their genetic consequences in a single population of *Linum marginale* attacked by the rust pathogen *Melampsora lini.* (a) Epidemiological patterns in the mean severity of disease over a 7-year period (AUDPC = area under the disease progress curve; * = disease present at trace amounts); (b) *L. marginale* population size over the same 7-year period; (c) the resistance structure of the host population in the epidemic year 1989 (resistance phenotypes were identified by their response to six pathogen isolates (see Burdon & Thompson 1995)); (d) the resistance structure of the host population in the immediate post-epidemic year 1990.

resistance structure of the population changed markedly resulting in a more even distribution of frequencies of different resistances. In particular, resistance pheno-types I and II fell in frequency from 35% and 25% to 12% and 6%, respectively, while previously uncommon phenotypes such as VI and IX increased dramatically.

Superficially these changes appear to provide strong evidence for frequency-dependent selection. However, when considered in light of the pathotypic composi-tion of the pathogen population occurring during the epidemic, they are far more difficult to explain. Indeed, those resistance phenotypes that were susceptible to the majority of the pathogen population present at the time of the epidemic were the ones that increased most in frequency (e.g. resistance type IX rose in frequency from 2.9% to 15.6%, Figure 10.3c,d). The reasons for these apparently maladaptive changes are unclear but may result from genetic hitch-hiking or aspects of the interaction between plant size, disease increase and mortality rates (Burdon & Thompson 1995).

Studies that integrate the ecology and genetics of species ultimately involve determining how the genetic composition of populations affects their numerical size and survival through time at both local and regional spatial scales. In a broad sense, results from single population studies underline the problems of trying to understand the dynamics of host–pathogen systems beyond immediate, very short-term interactions. For an assessment of longer-term ecological and coevolutionary dynamics, we must turn to studies encompassing multiple populations over multiple years. Indeed, at the spatial scale at which evolutionary change leads to on-going interactions between hosts and their pathogens, most phenomena of importance (e.g. local adaptation) are ones for which occurrence in any given population is not assured. Rather, these phenomena are average expectations, the importance of which can only be seen in studies of multiple populations (i.e. metapopulations).

Host–pathogen dynamics in a metapopulation context

Effects of colonization and extinction on disease incidence and prevalence

A major driving force behind much of the work on host–pathogen metapopulations is the general difficulty of explaining long-term pathogen persistence within local populations. For example, both theoretical and empirical studies of the within-population dynamics of the *Silene–Microbotryum* system have emphasized that local pathogen extinction is much more likely than coexistence (Thrall & Jarosz 1994), while long-term persistence is readily obtainable in spatially structured situations (Thrall & Antonovics 1995). In fact, perhaps the most noticeable feature of the metapopulation dynamics of many host–pathogen associations is the unpredictable and stochastic nature of the strength of individual population level interactions. When viewed across the multiple populations of a metapopulation, the incidence, prevalence and intensity (severity) of interactions varies markedly from deme to deme and from time to time. Host populations that are heavily infected in one year may occur in close juxtaposition with others that are free of disease, while through time these patterns may be reversed or change in unpredictable ways (Antonovics *et al.* 1994; Thrall & Antonovics 1995; Ericson *et al.* 1999; Thrall *et al.* 2001b). However, even where rates of local colonization and extinction are relatively high, regional levels of disease appear to be relatively stable for many plant–pathogen associations (Burdon & Thrall 1999; Ericson *et al.* 1999), thus underscoring the central role of metapopulation structure in maintaining host–pathogen interactions.

The relative ease with which these patterns can be measured belies the importance of the processes that go hand in hand with such changes. Indeed, such deceptively simple patterns are often the numerically visual tip of an iceberg of genetic change that provides the selective pressures that drive coevolutionary interactions. The

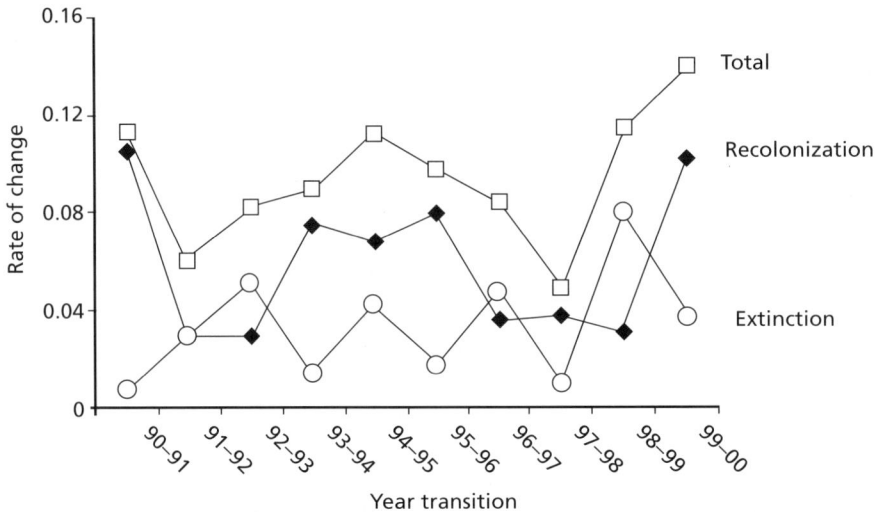

Figure 10.4 Year-to-year rates of colonization and extinction of *Triphragmium ulmariae* in the *Filipendula ulmaria* metapopulation occurring in the Skeppsvik archipelago (J. J. Burdon & L. Ericson, unpublished data).

dramatic fluctuations in the size of pathogen populations provides considerable scope for the processes of migration, drift, extinction and recolonization to influence both individual population and local among-population scale interactions. Compounding these interactions are almost inevitable differences between individual populations in the length of time coevolutionary pressures are continuously applied before local extinction leads to at least a temporary relaxation of those pressures (Burdon *et al.* 1995; Ericson *et al.* 1999). Extinction and recolonization events are potentially the easiest to detect and further underline the ephemeral nature of individual interactions between host and pathogen populations. Thus, over an 11-year period, rates of extinction and recolonization of the rust pathogen *Triphragmium ulmariae* occurring on stands of *Filipendula ulmaria* have fluctuated from year to year (Figure 10.4) but with an average of 9% of populations showing a change in status every year. In a very different system involving floral smuts and insect-vectored spore dispersal, Antonovics *et al.* (1994) showed even higher colonization and extinction rates, although these were also roughly in balance.

Resistance and virulence structure of plant–pathogen metapopulations

Extinction and subsequent recolonization is not just a numerical issue. Rather, in the majority of natural systems this is a stage at which the direction of selection on individuals within host populations is particularly vulnerable to dramatic shifts. In an explicit test of the hypothesis that the resistance structure of host populations might be related to local history, Thrall and Antonovics (1995) established experimental populations of *Silene latifolia* using seed collections from natural populations that were either: (i) healthy; (ii) diseased; or (iii) newly established (these were identified on the basis of data from an on-going and long-term demographic study of the metapopulation dynamics of the *Silene–Microbotryum* system (Antonovics *et al.* 1994; Thrall & Antonovics 1995; Alexander *et al.* 1996)). Their results showed that plants that became infected did so earlier when they came from diseased populations than when they came from healthy or newly established populations.

More subtle changes also occur in demes where population crashes have not been the prelude to extinction. In the interaction between *Linum marginale* and its rust pathogen *Melampsora lini*, such large-scale declines are often accompanied by a changing spectrum of pathotype identities as individual pathotypes blink in and out over a period of years (Burdon 1997). Conversely, even within established local interactions, the arrival of novel pathotypes (through immigration) may lead to significant shifts in the virulence profile of a pathogen population. Thus, in the *Linum–Melampsora* system a novel pathotype that first appeared in the summer of 1988 rose rapidly to a frequency of >35% 2 years later before disappearing in a subsequent population crash (J. J. Burdon, unpublished). In this instance, the pathotype in question did not appear to have any selective advantage over the pre-existing dominant one. However, it is not difficult to imagine situations where this sort of change will have direct implications for the fitness of the host population.

To date there is only one natural host–pathogen association (*Linum marginale* and *Melampsora lini*) for which extensive information is available concerning the genetic structure of both host and pathogen populations and the way in which these interact across a metapopulation landscape. By concentrating our attention on this interaction we hope to show conclusively the necessity to consider the dynamics of such interactions within and among multiple populations in order to develop an overall picture of the coevolutionary trajectory of the association as a whole. We also note, however, that the picture we paint is for one metapopulation of the wider association of these two species. Throughout the range in which they occur together, this interaction remains that of a host and its parasite. However, there is no doubt that differences in evolutionary history, environmental factors, chance events, and life-history attributes from one geographic region to the next have resulted in a series of separate coevolutionary interactions that follow distinctly different trajectories involving different suites of resistance genes (J. J. Burdon, P. H. Thrall & G. J. Lawrence, unpublished) and different breeding systems (Burdon *et al.* 1999).

Migration, drift, extinction, recolonization and local selection provide a complex mix of demographic and genetic parameters within the *Linum–Melampsora* system that give rise to a series of patterns of responses clearly indicative of an on-going interplay of numerical and genetic dynamics. In this host–pathogen system where pathogen generation times are measured in days during the growing season and host generation times are measured in years, the adaptation of pathogen populations to sympatric host demes is at least partly countered by the relatively high frequency of local pathogen extinctions. As a consequence, the length of time over which a pathogen population is associated with that of its host is unpredictable, and the degree of evolutionary adjustment of individual pathogen populations to those of their host will vary.

The influence of genetic variation on disease dynamics

A wide range of analytical and simulation models have demonstrated that genetic variation in host populations can have major consequences for the numerical dynamics and persistence of pathogens (e.g. May & Anderson 1983; Frank 1993; Antonovics 1994; Thrall *et al.* 1995). Simple models incorporating frequency-dependent disease transmission predict that shifts in average transmission rates can lead to qualitatively different dynamical outcomes (e.g. coexistence vs. loss of the pathogen). This prediction was explicitly tested in a multi-year study involving a large number of experimental populations of *Silene latifolia* and *Microbotryum violaceum*, where host populations were initiated with different levels of resistance (Thrall & Jarosz 1994). Results from this experiment were consistent with model predictions that resistant populations would lose the disease, while susceptible hosts and pathogens would coexist.

The overall resistance of host populations is influenced not only by the relative frequency of individual resistances within the population but also by their diversity (Figure 10.5). But just what effect does the structure of host populations really have on the epidemiology of their pathogens? Certainly in agricultural situations the use of resistance genes either in monoculture or mixture has a long and successful

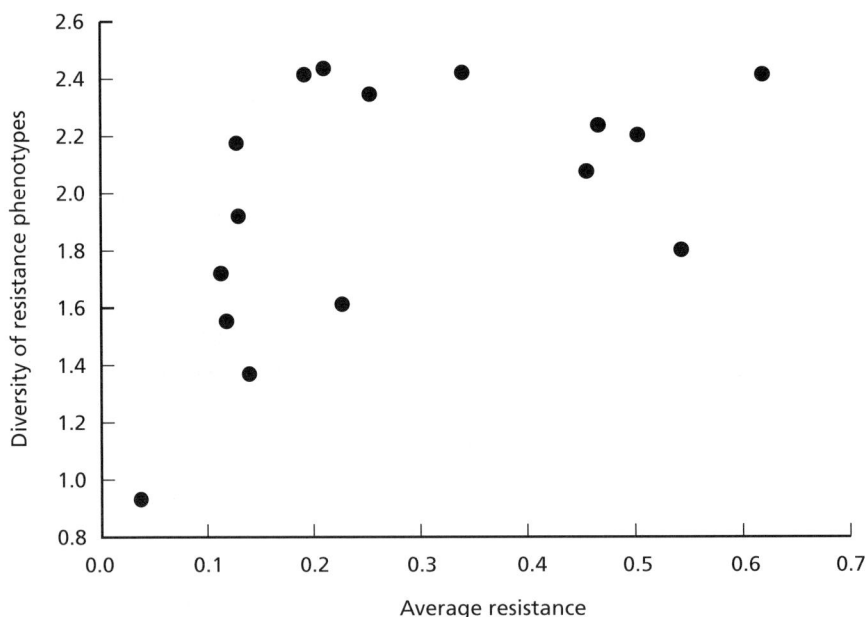

Figure 10.5 Average resistance of populations of *Linum marginale* from the Kiandra metapopulation to the rust pathogen *Melampsora lini* vs. the diversity (corrected Shannon–Weaver index) of resistance phenotypes in these populations. Mean resistance was scored on the basis of susceptibility to a standard set of pathogen isolates. The pattern of resistant and susceptible responses shown by individual host lines to the range of rust isolates was used to determine a 'multipathotype resistance phenotype'.

record in controlling disease. To date, direct evidence of this kind has been lacking in natural systems. However, Thrall and Burdon (2000) have recently found strong evidence for an inverse relationship between the resistance structure of a range of natural populations of *L. marginale* and the prevalence of disease caused by *M. lini*. Although the disease was present in all populations, in environmentally unfavourable years when disease was at a low ebb, no relationship existed. However, in epidemic years an inverse relationship existed between the mean resistance of individual populations or their resistance diversity and the prevalence of disease (Figure 10.6).

Local adaptation in a metapopulation context

Empirically, local adaptation can be tested in two contrasting ways: (i) pathogen performance on sympatric vs. allopatric hosts; (ii) sympatric vs. allopatric pathogens on a given host population. Regardless of which approach is used, the finding of local adaptation of a pathogen deme to its sympatric host population is a clear indication of evolutionary change, and is central to many theoretical models (e.g. the Red Queen hypothesis: Hamilton 1980; Hamilton *et al.* 1990), where there is an expectation that hosts and pathogens will coevolve tightly within local populations through frequency-dependent cycling. In an exhaustive assessment of the reciprocal susceptibility of six host populations in the *Linum–Melampsora* metapopulation to their sympatric and allopatric pathogen populations, P. H. Thrall and J. J. Burdon (unpublished) have shown all possible patterns of interaction ranging from evidence for strong local adaptation through to that for strong local maladaptation. Such results are not particularly surprising, with evidence of both adaptation and maladaptation in host–pathogen interactions being reported in the past (Parker 1985; Lively 1989; Ebert 1994; Lively & Jokela 1996; Kaltz *et al.* 1999).

Of particular interest in the current context is evidence that the mean virulence of individual pathogen demes was very strongly related to the mean resistance of host populations. Comparison of the mean resistance of individual host populations to all six pathogen populations with the mean virulence of each pathogen population on all six host populations uncovered a positive curvilinear relationship such that pathogen demes associated with host populations of high mean resistance were the ones with the higher mean virulence. Such situations are likely to lead to non-congruence between different tests for local adaptation, and further emphasize the need for studies of coevolution to explicitly incorporate multiple populations across a range of distances.

That highly resistant plant populations support pathogen populations with high virulence is perhaps not surprising. However, given the wind-dispersed nature of *M. lini*, its large spore production, and the close physical proximity of many populations to one another, it is highly unlikely that more susceptible host populations would support more avirulent pathogen populations purely by chance. Rather, this provides strong circumstantial evidence for local selection favouring more avirulent pathogens in more susceptible host populations. Just how this is expressed is currently unknown, but the possibility of a trade-off between virulence (ability to

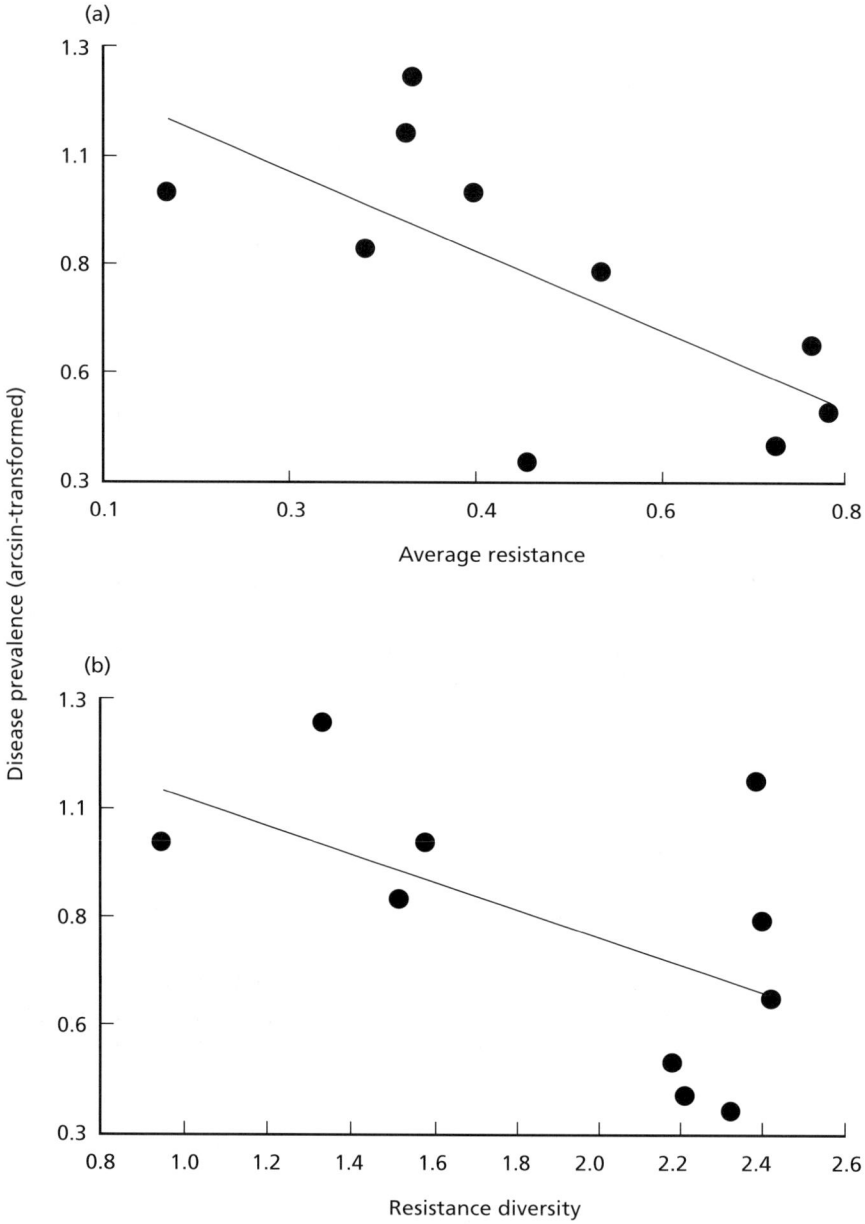

Figure 10.6 Regression analyses showing: (a) the relationship between the average resistance of populations of *L. marginale* and the prevalence of disease caused by *M. lini*, and (b) the relationship between the diversity of resistance phenotypes and disease prevalence in the same populations at the peak of the 1998–1999 epidemic.

attack a particular resistance gene) and aggressiveness (spore production etc.) cannot be discounted. In host populations with low mean resistance, the advantage gained by individual pathotypes with the capacity to attack a wide range of host lines would be more than counter-balanced by increased aggressiveness leading to greater propagule production among isolates carrying sufficient rather than excess virulence. While this possibility has yet to be tested in this metapopulation association, a detailed analysis of patterns of virulence and aggressiveness in *Erysiphe graminis* populations parasitizing monoculture and mixed lines of various barley varieties has clearly demonstrated its occurrence in an agricultural context (Chin & Wolfe 1984).

A final note: from populations to metapopulations and beyond?

Theoretical and empirical studies of single populations of hosts and pathogens have provided major insights into many of the factors (e.g. transmission mode, fitness effects) that influence disease dynamics, persistence and evolution, and form an integral part of any metapopulation study. However, empirical data from multipopulation studies of natural plant–pathogen interactions demonstrates the occurrence of substantial numerical and genetic stochasticity that cannot be explained at the level of individual demes. The degree to which among-population processes must be invoked to explain the coevolutionary dynamics of such associations will depend heavily on the life histories of both host and pathogen. Variation in life history may even lead to qualitatively different coevolutionary trajectories within single host–pathogen interactions. An example of this possibility is to be found in the interaction occurring between *Populus* spp. and the rust *Melampsora* across North America and Canada. In the dry interior of western Canada, *Populus* populations contain major resistance genes, whereas on the wetter Pacific west coast, resistance appears to be due to the collective effect of many minor genes. These differences co-vary with differences in dynamics—boom and bust cycles occur in the dry interior, while on the Pacific coast disease levels are more stable, and pathogen extinction is much less likely (Burdon *et al.* 1996). Such marked evolutionary shifts may be largely a function of the spatial scale and predictability of the interaction (Thrall & Burdon 1997). We have recently shown (Thrall & Burdon 1999) that the relative scales at which hosts and pathogens disperse are a major determinant, not only of pathogen incidence and prevalence, but also of the nature of the dynamics (e.g. endemic vs. epidemic)—factors that clearly underpin the development of coevolutionary patterns.

Overall, as colonization/extinction processes become more important, spatial structure will have ever greater potential to influence local population dynamics. With the incorporation of genetic considerations, the percentage of unexplained variation at the local population scale becomes even larger. In fact, the expectations derived from single population studies may simply not apply to metapopulations (e.g. stochastic colonization and extinction are likely to preclude the tightly coupled frequency-dependent dynamics that underlie many models of host–pathogen coevolution). A more likely scenario may be one in which local coevolutionary processes occur in short bursts that are continually being interrupted and reset by extinction and recolonization. While at the larger scales of the metapopulation, it may be very difficult to empirically demonstrate coevolutionary dynamics, there is substantial scope for theoretical and computer simulation approaches to produce testable hypotheses, and lead towards the development of a conceptual framework for coevolution in spatially realistic settings. Using this approach we should be able to determine what are the crucial life-history features (e.g. transmission mode, dispersal, host longevity) that determine the spatial scale at which coevolution occurs, and ultimately in what ways are patterns of coevolution and local adaptation likely to depend on the underlying genetics of resistance and virulence (i.e. gene-for-gene vs. quantitative systems)?

Summary

Understanding the long-term ecological and evolutionary dynamics of host–pathogen associations is dependent on integration of the apparently stochastic patterns occurring within individual populations across the multiple demes of a metapopulation. Studies focusing on single populations clearly show the potential for pathogen selection pressure to affect host fitness and for the host to affect the structure of the pathogen populations. However, individual local associations are inevitably ephemeral with pathogen and/or host extinctions leading to local collapse of the interaction. At the metapopulation level such local extinctions are part of a broader process in which local unpredictable changes resulting from drift, migration, extinction and local selection contribute to the long-term evolutionary trajectory of the host–pathogen association as a whole.

Acknowledgements

Some of the unpublished work reported here was carried out through the assistance of a research grant from the Swedish government to Professor Lars Ericson. P.H.T. is supported by a QE II Fellowship from the Australian government.

References

Alexander, H.M. & Antonovics, J. (1988). Disease spread and population dynamics of anther-smut infection of *Silene alba* caused by the fungus *Ustilago violacea*. *Journal of Ecology*, **75**, 91–104.

Alexander, H.M., Thrall, P.H., Antonovics, J., Jarosz, A.M. & Oudemans, P.V. (1996). Population dynamics and genetics of plant disease: a case study of anther-smut disease. *Ecology*, **77**, 990–996.

Anderson, R.M. & May, R.M. (1981). The population dynamics of microparasites and their invertebrate hosts. *Philosophical Transactions of the Royal Society London B*, **291**, 451–524.

Anagnostakis, S.L. & Kranz, J. (1987). Population dynamics of *Cryphonectria parasitica* in a mixed-hardwood forest in Connecticut. *Phytopathology*, **77**, 751–754.

Antonovics, J. (1994). The interplay of numerical and gene-frequency dynamics in host–pathogen systems. In: *Ecological Genetics* (ed. L. Real), pp. 129–145. Princeton University Press, Princeton, NJ.

Antonovics, J., Thrall, P.H., Jarosz, A.M. & Stratton, D. (1994). Ecological genetics of metapopulations: the *Silene–Ustilago* host-pathogen system. In: *Ecological Genetics* (ed. L. Real), pp. 146–170. Princeton University Press, Princeton, NJ.

Antonovics, J., Thrall, P.H. & Jarosz, A.M. (1997). Genetics and the spatial ecology of species interactions: the *Silene–Ustilago* system. In: *The Role of Space in Population Dynamics and Interspecific Interactions* (eds D. Tilman & P. Kareiva), pp. 158–180. Princeton University Press, Princeton, NJ.

Augspurger, C.K. (1983). Seed dispersal of the tropical tree, *Platypodium elegans*, and the escape of its seedlings from fungal pathogens. *Journal of Ecology*, **71**, 759–771.

Augspurger, C.K. & Kelly, C.K. (1984). Pathogen mortality of tropical tree seedlings: experimental studies of the effects of dispersal distance, seedling density, and light conditions. *Oecologia*, **61**, 211–217.

Bevan, J.R., Clarke, D.D. & Crute, I.R. (1993). Resistance to *Erysiphe fischeri* in two populations of *Senecio vulgaris*. *Plant Pathology*, **42**, 636–646.

Browning, J.A. (1974). Relevance of knowledge about natural ecosystems to development of pest management programs for agro-ecosystems. *Proceedings of the American Phytopathological Society*, **1**, 191–199.

Burdon, J.J. (1980). Variation in disease resistance within a population of *Trifolium repens*. *Journal of Ecology*, **68**, 737–744.

Burdon, J.J. (1987). Phenotypic and genetic patterns of resistance to the pathogen *Phakopsora pachyrhizi* in populations of *Glycine canescens*. *Oecologia*, **73**, 257–267.

Burdon, J.J. (1994). The distribution and origin of genes for race specific resistance to *Melampsora lini* in *Linum marginale*. *Evolution*, **48**, 1564–1575.

Burdon, J.J. (1997). The evolution of gene-for-gene interactions in natural pathosystems. In: *The Gene-for-Gene Relationship in Plant–Parasite Interactions* (eds I.R. Crute, E.B. Holub & J.J. Burdon), pp. 245–262. CAB International, Oxford.

Burdon, J.J. & Chilvers, G.A. (1982). Host density as a factor in plant disease ecology. *Annual Review of Phytopathology*, **20**, 143–166.

Burdon, J.J. & Jarosz, A.M. (1991). Host–pathogen interactions in natural populations of *Linum marginale* and *Melampsora lini*: I. Patterns of resistance and racial variation in a large host population. *Evolution*, **45**, 205–217.

Burdon, J.J. & Thompson, J.N. (1995). Changed patterns of resistance in a population of *Linum marginale* attacked by the rust pathogen *Melampsora lini*. *Journal of Ecology*, **83**, 199–206.

Burdon, J.J. & Thrall, P.H. (1999). Spatial and temporal patterns in coevolving plant and pathogen associations. *American Naturalist*, **153**, S15–S33.

Burdon, J.J. & Silk, J. (1997). Sources and patterns of diversity in plant pathogenic fungi. *Phytopathology*, **87**, 664–669.

Burdon, J.J., Ericson, L. & Müller, W.J. (1995). Temporal and spatial relationships in a metapopulation of the rust pathogen *Triphragmium ulmariae* and its host, *Filipendula ulmaria*. *Journal of Ecology*, **82**, 979–989.

Burdon, J.J., Groves, R.H. & Cullen, J.M. (1981). The impact of biological control on the distribution and abundance of *Chondrilla juncea* in southeastern Australia. *Journal of Applied Ecology*, **18**, 957–966.

Burdon, J.J., Thrall, P.H. & Brown, A.H.D. (1999). Resistance and virulence structure in two *Linum marginale–Melampsora lini* host–pathogen metapopulations with different mating systems. *Evolution*, **53**, 704–716.

Burdon, J.J., Wennström, A., Elmqvist, T. & Kirby, G.C. (1996). The role of race-specific resistance in natural plant populations. *Oikos*, **76**, 411–416.

Carlsson, U. & Elmqvist, T. (1992). Epidemiology of anther-smut disease (*Microbotryum violaceum*) and numeric regulation of populations of *Silene dioica*. *Oecologia* **90**, 509–517.

Chaboudez, P. & Burdon, J.J. (1995). Frequency-dependent selection in a wild plant–pathogen system. *Oecologia*, **102**, 490–493.

Chin, K.M. & Wolfe, M.S. (1984). Selection on *Erysiphe graminis hordei* in pure and mixed stands of barley. *Plant Pathology*, **33**, 89–100.

Cook, S.A., Copsey, A.D. & Dickman, A.W. (1989). Response of *Abies* to fire and *Phellinus*. In: *The Evolutionary Ecology of Plants* (eds J. Bock & Y.B. Linhart), pp. 363–392. Westview, Boulder, CO.

Cullen, J.M., Kable, P.F. & Catt, M. (1973). Epidemic

spread of a rust imported for biological control. *Nature*, **244**, 462–464.

de Nooji, M.P. & van Damme, J.M.M. (1988). Variation in host susceptibility among and within populations of *Plantago lanceolata* L. infected by the fungus *Phomopsis subordinaria* (Desm.) Trav. *Oecologia*, **75**, 535–538.

Ebert, D. (1994). Virulence and local adaptation of a horizontally transmitted parasite. *Science*, **265**, 1084–1086.

Ericson, L., Burdon, J.J. & Müller, W.J. (1999). Spatial and temporal dynamics of epidemics of the rust fungus *Uromyces valerianae* on populations of its host, *Valeriana salina*. *Journal of Ecology*, **87**, 649–658.

Flor, H.H. (1955). Host–parasite interaction in flax rust — its genetics and other implications. *Phytopathology*, **45**, 680–685.

Frank, S. (1993). Coevolutionary genetics of plants and pathogens. *Evolutionary Ecology*, **7**, 45–75.

Getz, W.M. & Pickering, J. (1983). Epidemic models: thresholds and population regulation. *American Naturalist*, **121**, 892–898.

Hamilton, W.D. (1980). Sex versus non-sex versus parasite. *Oikos*, **35**, 282–290.

Hamilton, W.D., Axelrod, R. & Tanese, R. (1990). Sexual reproduction as an adaptation to resist parasites (A Review). *Proceedings of the National Academy of Sciences of the USA*, **87**, 3566–3573.

Harper, J.L. (1990). Pests, pathogens and plant communities: an introduction. In: *Pests, Pathogens and Plant Communities* (eds J.J. Burdon & S.R. Leather), pp. 3–14. Blackwell Scientific Publications, Oxford.

Holah, J.C., Wilson, M.V. & Hansen, E.M. (1993). Effects of a native forest pathogen, *Phellinus weirii*, on Douglas-fir forest composition in western Oregon. *Canadian Journal of Forest Research*, **23**, 2473–2480.

Holah, J.C., Wilson, M.V. & Hansen, E.M. (1997). Impacts of a native root-rotting pathogen on successional development of old-growth Douglas-fir forests. *Oecologia*, **111**, 429–433.

Janzen, D.H. (1970). Herbivores and the number of tree species in tropical forests. *American Naturalist*, **104**, 501–528.

Jarosz, A.M. & Burdon, J.J. (1991). Host–pathogen interactions in natural populations of *Linum marginale* and *Melampsora lini*: II. Local and regional variation in patterns of resistance and racial structure. *Evolution*, **45**, 1618–1627.

Jarosz, A.M. & Burdon, J.J. (1992). Host–pathogen interactions in natural populations of *Linum marginale* and *Melampsora lini*: III. Influence of pathogen epidemics on host survivorship and flower production. *Oecologia*, **89**, 53–61.

Kaltz, O., Gandon, S., Michalakis, Y. & Shykoff, J.A. (1999). Local maladaptation in the anther-smut fungus *Microbotryum violaceum* to its host plant *Silene latifolia*: evidence from a cross-inoculation experiment. *Evolution*, **53**, 395–407.

Kinloch, B.B. Jr. & Walkinshaw, C.H. (1991). Resistance to fusiform rust in southern pines: how is it inherited? In: *Rusts of Pine* (eds Y. Hiratsuka, J.K. Samoil, P.V. Blenis, P.E. Crane & B.L. Laishley), pp. 219–228. *Proceedings of the 3rd IUFRO Rusts of Pine Working Party Conference*. Forestry Canada, Northwest Region Information Report NOR-X-317.

Lively, C.M. (1989). Adaptation by a parasitic trematode to local populations of its snail host. *Evolution*, **43**, 1663–1671.

Lively, C.M. & Jokela, J. (1996). Clinal variation for local adaptation in a host–parasite interaction. *Proceedings of the Royal Society London B*, **263**, 891–897.

Lukens, R.J. & Mullany, R. (1972). The influence of shade and wet soil on southern corn leaf blight. *Plant Disease Reporter*, **56**, 203–206.

May, R.M. & Anderson, R.M. (1983). Epidemiology and genetics in the coevolution of parasites and hosts. *Proceedings of the Royal Society of London B*, **219**, 281–313.

McDonald, B.A., Bellamy, B.K., Zhan, J. & Appel, D.N. (1998). The effect of an oak wilt epidemic on the genetic structure of a Texas live oak population. *Canadian Journal of Botany*, **76**, 1900–1907.

Morrison, J.A. (1996). Infection of *Juncus dichotomus* by the smut fungus *Cintractia junci*: an experimental field test of the effects of neighbouring plants, environment, and host plant genotype. *Journal of Ecology*, **84**, 691–702.

Miller, P. (1966). The effect of weather on prevalence of disease. *The American Biology Teacher*, **28**, 469–472.

Palti, J. (1981). *Cultural Practices and Infectious Crop Diseases*. Springer-Verlag, Berlin.

Parker, M.A. (1985). Local population differentiation for compatibility in an annual legume and its host-specific legume pathogen. *Evolution*, **39**, 713–723.

Pei, M.H., Royle, D.J. & Hunter, T. (1996). Pathogenic specialization in *Melampsora epitea* var. *epitea* on *Salix*. *Plant Pathology*, **45**, 679–690.

Pinon, J. & Frey, P. (1997). Structure of *Melampsora larici-populini* populations on wild and cultivated poplar. *European Journal of Plant Pathology*, **103**, 159–173.

Schmidt, B. (1994). Effects of genetic diversity in experimental stands of *Solidago altissima*—evidence for the potential role of pathogens as selective agents in plant populations. *Journal of Ecology*, **82**, 165–175.

Snaydon, R.W. & Davies, M.S. (1972). Rapid population differentiation in a mosaic environment. II. Morphological variation in *Anthoxanthum odoratum*. *Evolution*, **26**, 390–405.

Thrall, P.H. & Antonovics, J. (1995). Theoretical and empirical studies of metapopulations: population and genetic dynamics of the *Silene–Ustilago* system. *Canadian Journal of Botany*, **73**, S1249–S1258.

Thrall, P.H. & Burdon, J.J. (1997). Host–pathogen dynamics in a metapopulation context: the ecological and evolutionary consequences of being spatial. *Journal of Ecology*, **85**, 743–753.

Thrall, P.H. & Burdon, J.J. (1999). The spatial scale of pathogen dispersal: consequences for disease dynamics and persistence. *Evolutionary Ecology Research*, **1**, 681–701.

Thrall, P.M. & Burdon, J.J. (2000). Effect of resistance variation in a natural plant host–pathogen metapopulation on disease dynamics. *Plant Pathology*, **49**, 767–773.

Thrall, P.H. & Jarosz, A.M. (1994). Host–pathogen dynamics in experimental populations of *Silene alba* and *Ustilago violacea*. II. Experimental tests of theoretical models. *Journal of Ecology*, **82**, 561–570.

Thrall, P.H., Antonovics, J. & Hall, D.W. (1993). Host and pathogen coexistence in sexually transmitted and vector-borne diseases characterized by frequency-dependent transmission. *American Naturalist*, **142**, 543–552.

Thrall, P.H., Biere, A. & Uyenoyama, M.K. (1995). Frequency-dependent disease transmission and the dynamics of the *Silene–Ustilago* host–pathogen system. *American Naturalist*, **145**, 43–62.

Thrall, P.H., Burdon, J.J. & Bock, C.H. (2001a). Short-term epidemic dynamics in the *Cakile maritima–Alternaria brassicicola* host–pathogen metapopulation association. *Journal of Ecology*, in press.

Thrall, P.H., Burdon, J.J. & Young, A.G. (2001b). Variation in resistance and virulence among demes of a single host–pathogen metapopulation. *Journal of Ecology*, in press.

Watson, I.A. (1981). Wheat and its rust parasites in Australia. In: *Wheat Sciences—Today and Tomorrow* (eds L.T. Evans & W.J. Peacock), pp. 129–147. Cambridge University Press, Cambridge, UK.

Wills, R.T. & Keighery, G.J. (1994). Ecological impact of plant disease on plant communities. *Journal of the Royal Society of Western Australia*, **77**, 127–131.

Wolfe, M.S. (1985). The current status and prospects of multiline cultivars and variety mixtures for disease resistance. *Annual Review of Phytopathology*, **23**, 251–273.

Chapter 11
Spatial dynamics of cytoplasmic male sterility

S. A. Frank* and C. M. Barr*

Introduction

Conflict often leads to nonequilibrium fluctuations as attackers spread, host defences increase, and counter-attack evolves. Spatial processes play a crucial role when attack types arrive from other populations and import of matching defence follows.

We focus on cytoplasmic male sterility (CMS), an ideal system in which to study the spatial dynamics of conflict. Cytoplasmically inherited genes in the mitochondria sometimes cause male sterility by interfering with pollen development. Reallocation from pollen to ovules increases the number of seeds. This reallocation to seeds benefits the mitochondrial CMS genes, which are transmitted through seeds but not through pollen.

Reproductive reallocation causes a conflict with nuclear genes, which are transmitted through both pollen and seeds. Consistent with this idea of conflict, nuclear restorers occur that counteract cytoplasmic effects and restore pollen fertility. A plant appears as a normal hermaphrodite when it has a male-sterile cytoplasm and matching nuclear restorers.

Wild populations of CMS plants maintain distinct cytoplasmic genotypes (cytotypes). Each cytotype causes male sterility by an apparently different mechanism because each responds to a particular subset of nuclear restorer alleles. Nuclear restorer alleles are typically polymorphic at several loci, with each allele specialized for restoring pollen fertility when associated with a particular cytotype. The frequencies of cytotypes, restorer alleles, and male-sterile (female) plants often vary over space.

We focus on the processes that influence spatial variation in gene frequencies. We start by summarizing the key observations and theories. With the theory as our guide, we analyse the best studies of natural populations currently available. Finally, we consider prospects for the future. The arrival of molecular tools brings great opportunity to measure the spatial distributions of genotypes and to test theories about the spatial dynamics of conflict.

In the course of our chapter, we develop a new model of CMS dynamics. We argue that the relative allocation of resources to pollen and ovules by hermaphrodites interacts with the spatial dynamics of gene frequency fluctuations driven by conflict.

* Department of Ecology and Evolutionary Biology, University of California, Irvine, CA 92697–2525, USA.

This interaction leads to an association across species between the physiological patterns of resource allocation and the population-wide frequencies of females.

Observations

Correns (1906) discovered CMS. As of 1972, CMS had been reported in 140 species of flowering plants from 47 genera and 20 families (Laser & Lersten 1972; see also Edwardson 1970; Grun 1976).

Four attributes characterize wild populations with CMS: cytotype polymorphism, nuclear restorer polymorphism, spatial variation in cytotype and restorer frequencies, and spatial variation in the frequency of male-sterile plants. Frank (1989) provides a review of these four attributes, with further data summarized in Couvet *et al.* (1990), Koelewijn and van Damme (1995a,b), Manicacci *et al.* (1996, 1997, 1998), de Haan *et al.* (1997a,b,c,d), Frank (1997, 2000), McCauley (1998), McCauley and Brock (1998), and Taylor *et al.* (1999). Here we give a brief account of the key points. We provide detailed summaries of studies on *Plantago lanceolata* and *Thymus vulgaris* in later sections.

Cytotype polymorphism

Different cytotypes appear to cause male sterility by different mechanisms because each is susceptible only to a particular subset of nuclear restorer alleles. Frank (1997) summarizes data through 1996 on the number of cytotypes per species. In most cases, only two different cytotypes had been clearly established in each wild species, with suggestive data that there may be more. Recently, de Haan *et al.* (1997a) used molecular tools to find a minimum of four different cytotypes in *P. lanceolata*. Mitochondrial genes cause the male-sterile effects of cytotypes in the cases that have been analysed (Brennicke & Kück 1993; Levings & Vasil 1995).

Restorer polymorphism

Restorer alleles typically have a dominant effect in intraspecific crosses and often appear to be specific for a particular cytotype (Edwardson 1970; Charlesworth & Laporte 1998). For some cytotypes, restorer alleles must be present at two or more nuclear loci to restore full pollen fertility (e.g. in maize; Laughnan & Gabay-Laughnan 1983). Incomplete restoration leads to partial male sterility (e.g. in *P. lanceolata*; van Damme & van Delden 1982). No male-sterile plants would be observed if restorer alleles went to fixation. Male sterility is widespread in some species, indicating polymorphism of restorers.

Spatial variation of genotypes

van Damme (1986) found high levels of spatial variation in cytotype and restorer frequencies within a single field of *P. lanceolata*. Three studies of *T. vulgaris* demonstrate spatial variation of genotypes among populations (Couvet *et al.* 1985; Manicacci *et al.* 1996, 1997). We discuss some of these studies later.

Spatial variation in phenotypes

The frequency of male-sterile (female) plants varies widely among wild populations of the same species. For example, 100 populations of *Origanum vulgare* contained 1–62% females (Kheyr-Pour 1980; similar data in Ietswaart *et al.* 1984); 110 populations of *T. vulgaris* contained 5–95% females, with the median greater than 60% (Gouyon & Couvet 1985); and 27 populations of *P. lanceolata* contained 0.4–29% females or partial male-steriles (van Damme & van Delden 1982). Later in this chapter we provide detailed summaries of spatial variation in the frequency of females in *P. lanceolata* and three species of *Thymus*.

Review of previous theories

Equilibrium models for nuclear or cytoplasmic control

Many interesting aspects of CMS follow from the conflict between nuclear and cytoplasmic genes. Matrilineally inherited cytoplasmic genes favour male sterility because females reallocate resources from pollen to ovules (Ashman 1992; Atlan *et al.* 1992; Eckhart 1992). Biparentally inherited nuclear genes favour hermaphroditism, with mixed allocation of resources to pollen and ovules. Comparison of the equilibrium frequency of females favoured by cytoplasmic and nuclear genes provides a simple way to gauge the intensity of the conflict. These equilibria also illustrate the role of traditional breeding system parameters such as selfing rate and inbreeding depression. The derivations follow Frank (1989), based on earlier work cited below.

In most seed plants, mitochondrial genes are transmitted only through ovules (Mogensen 1996). There are two fitness components to consider (see Table 11.1 for notation).

First, the fitness of ovules in a female is proportional to $(1 + f)Cm^x$, where f measures the extra ovule production of females relative to hermaphrodites, m is the frequency of hermaphrodites in the population, and C and x are parameters that describe the availability of pollen. The term Cm^x is the proportion of ovules that successfully achieve outcrossed fertilization.

Secondly, the fitness of ovules in a hermaphrodite is proportional to $s(1 - d) + (1 - s)Cm^x$, where s is the proportion of ovules that are self-fertilized and d measures inbreeding depression. Among the ovules not self-fertilized, a proportion Cm^x successfully achieve outcrossed fertilization.

Equilibrium occurs when the fitness of ovules in a female equals the fitness of ovules in a hermaphrodite

$$(1 + f)Cm^x = s(1 - d) + (1 - s)Cm^x \tag{1}$$

Let $z = 1 - m$ be the frequency of females. The equilibrium frequency of females when controlled by unrestored cytoplasmic genes is

Table 11.1 Some factors influencing the dynamics of cytoplasmic male sterility (CMS).

Selfing rate, s	The probability that a hermaphrodite produces a seed by selfing when there is maximal availability of pollen from other plants
Inbreeding depression, d	One minus the fitness of a seed produced by selfing divided by a seed produced by outcrossing
Female fitness advantage, $1 + f$	The total fitness of all seeds produced by a female divided by the total fitness of all seeds produced by a hermaphrodite under the assumptions that all seeds are outcrossed and pollen is not limited
Pollen limitation, $C(p/P)^x$	The fraction of non-selfed ovules than fail to receive outcrossed pollen, where C is a constant; p is the density of the pollen shadow relative to maximum density, P; and the exponent x defines the shape of the pollen limitation curve; some models set $m = p/P$, where m is the frequency of hermaphrodites
Restorer pleiotropy	The negative effect of a restorer on pollen fertility when not matched to its specific cytotype
Pollen compensation	In hermaphrodites, the enhancement of pollen fertility at the expense of seed fertility
Number of cytotypes	Alternative cytoplasmic genotypes that cause male sterility, each cytotype repressed only by a specific set of matching restorers
Restorer genetics	Number of restorers and their effects on each cytotype
Genetic drift	Loss of alleles from established populations
Demographic extinctions and colonizations	Loss of all plants from a breeding neighbourhood and subsequent recolonization
Pollen and seed shadows	Spatial scale over which pollen normally moves during outcrossing and seeds move during dispersal
Long-distance dispersal	Rare long-distance movement of pollen or seeds can have powerful consequences by introducing locally novel alleles into a breeding neighbourhood

$$z_{cyt}^\star = 1 - \left(\frac{s(1-d)}{C(f+s)} \right)^{1/x} \tag{2a}$$

which is similar to a model first developed by Lloyd (1974, 1975). For no pollen limitation, $C = 1$ and $x \to 0$, $z_{cyt}^\star \to 1$, as first shown by Lewis (1941). For linear pollen limitation, $C = x = 1$, the equilibrium is

$$z_{cyt}^\star = \frac{f + sd}{f + s} \tag{2b}$$

To study the equilibrium favoured by nuclear control, we must also consider the pollen success of a hermaphrodite. Pollen fitness can be divided into two parts.

Pollen success in fertilizing hermaphrodites is the same as the fitness of ovules in hermaphrodites, $s(1-d)+(1-s)Cm^x$, because each successfully fertilized ovule of a hermaphrodite has obtained pollen from a hermaphrodite. Success in fertilizing females is proportional to $[(1-m)/m](1+f)Cm^x$, where $(1-m)/m$ is the number of female plants for each hermaphroditic plant, and $(1+f)Cm^x$ is proportional to the fitness of ovules per female plant.

Nuclear equilibrium occurs when the fitness of ovules in females equals the sum of ovule and pollen fitnesses in a hermaphrodite

$$(1+f)Cm^x = 2\left[s(1-d)+(1-s)Cm^x\right]+\frac{1-m}{m}(1+f)Cm^x \tag{3}$$

For no pollen limitation, $C=1$ and $x=0$, the equilibrium is

$$z^\star_{\text{nuc}} = \frac{f-1+2sd}{2(f+sd)} \tag{4a}$$

as in a model presented by Charlesworth and Charlesworth (1978). For linear pollen limitation, $C=x=1$,

$$z^\star_{\text{nuc}} = \frac{f-1+2sd}{2(f+s)} \tag{4b}$$

where $z^\star_{\text{nuc}} = 0$ when $f < 1 - 2sd$.

When collecting data, one often does not have separate estimates for f, s, d, and the pollen limitation parameters. Instead, one obtains a measure of seed fitness in females relative to hermaphrodites, subsuming aspects of inbreeding and pollen limitation. In our notation, we can define the seed productivity of females relative to hermaphrodites as $F = (1+f)Cm^x/[s(1-d)+(1-s)Cm^x]$. Using F in Eq. 3, the nuclear equilibrium is

$$z^\star_{\text{nuc}} = \frac{F-2}{2(F-1)}, \tag{5}$$

where F is measured at equilibrium. When $F > 2$, the female frequency at the nuclear equilibrium is greater than zero.

Genetic model of restorer polymorphism under nuclear control

We derived the models in the previous section by equating the fitnesses of female and hermaphrodite phenotypes. Phenotypic models highlight the key processes in a simple way, but for CMS one must often understand something of the underlying genetics.

Later we will emphasize that as the nuclear equilibrium rises above zero, restorer alleles decline in frequency. The phenotypic models do not make this point clearly because they hide the important genetic details. In this section, we present a simple genetic model of nuclear control based on Ross and Weir (1975). The genetic model shows the relation between the equilibrium under nuclear control and the frequency of restorer alleles at nuclear loci.

For the purposes of this model, it is best to think of the population as fixed for a single cytoplasmic genotype. This cytoplasmic genotype causes male sterility in the absence of a matching nuclear allele that restores pollen fertility and hermaphroditism. A single nuclear locus controls the frequency of females as follows: homozygotes with two copies of the dominant restorer allele are hermaphrodites, heterozygotes with one copy of the dominant restorer allele are also hermaphrodites, and homozygotes with two copies of the recessive non-restorer allele are females.

The frequencies in the population are D for the dominant homozygote, H for the heterozygote and R for the recessive homozygote. The frequency of the restorer allele is $D + H/2$, because the frequency of the restorer allele in heterozygotes is one-half. As in the previous section, we are interested in the equilibrium frequency of females. In this genetic model with nuclear control by dominant restorer alleles, the equilibrium frequency of females is $z^\star_{nuc} = R^\star$, the equilibrium frequency of recessive homozygotes.

To keep the model simple, we assume no selfing, $s = 0$, and no pollen limitation, $C = 1$ and $x = 0$. With these assumptions, the frequency of the restorer allele in pollen is $r = (D + H/2)/(D + H)$, where the denominator is $D + H$ because the R genotype does not produce pollen. The frequency of the restorer allele in ovules is $p = (D + H/2)/(1 + Rf)$, where the denominator corrects for the fact that the R genotype produces an extra Rf ovules.

With these gametic frequencies, we can write the three genotypic frequencies in the following generation as $D' = rp$, $H' = r(1 - p) + p(1 - r)$, and $R' = (1 - r)(1 - p)$. The equilibrium for this system can be calculated easily (Ross & Weir 1975), yielding $z^\star_{nuc} = R^\star = (f - 1)/2f$, which matches Eq. 4a with $s = 0$. The other genotypes have equilibrium frequencies $H^\star = (1 - R^\star)(1 - x)$ and $D^\star = (1 - R^\star)x$, where $x = f - \sqrt{f^2 - 1}$.

The genetic model produces exactly the same ratio of females to hermaphrodites as the phenotypic model, but we now also have an explicit statement about the frequencies of the restorer allele and the different genotypes. For example, $f \le 1$ yields $R^\star = 0$ and a restorer allele frequency of one, $f = 1.5$ yields $R^\star = 0.17$ and a restorer allele frequency of 0.58, and $f = 2$ yields $R^\star = 0.25$ and a restorer allele frequency of 0.48.

Selfing, inbreeding depression and pollen limitation change the calculations of allele frequency. But for our purposes, we only wish to emphasize the general trend mentioned above: as the nuclear equilibrium rises above zero, restorer alleles decline in frequency.

Definitions of nuclear and cytoplasmic control

We use the phrases 'nuclear control' and 'cytoplasmic control' throughout. Now that we have introduced some genetics, we can be more precise about the meaning of these phrases.

The full genetic system of CMS can be described roughly as follows. There are n different cytoplasmic genotypes (cytotypes) in the population; each individual has a haploid cytotype with one of the n different types. If an individual lacks the particular restorer alleles for its cytotype, then that individual is a female.

A cytotype can interact in a complex way with several nuclear loci. In the simplest case, each cytotype interacts with a unique, diploid nuclear locus. At the nuclear locus, the restorer allele is usually dominant to the non-restorer allele (Edwardson 1970; Charlesworth & Laporte 1998). In an individual with a particular cytotype, if the matching nuclear restorer locus has the restorer phenotype, then the individual is a hermaphrodite.

Genetic control defines the direction of evolutionary change in a local mating population (patch). If, for any of the cytotypes present in that patch, the matching restorers are absent in all individuals, then that cytotype will always cause male sterility. The unmatched cytotype will increase in frequency until the local population reaches the cytoplasmic equilibrium. Thus, cytoplasmic control drives the local population toward the cytoplasmic equilibrium.

If, for each of the local cytotypes, the matching nuclear restorer alleles are present in some individuals in the patch, then the restorers change in frequency until the population reaches the nuclear equilibrium. Thus, nuclear control drives the local population toward the nuclear equilibrium.

The CMS genetic system is sometimes referred to as joint nuclear and cytoplasmic (nucleocytoplasmic) control. This simply means that the outcome depends on the interaction between these two potentially polymorphic components of the genome. In any local population, the particular distribution of polymorphisms determines whether nuclear or cytoplasmic control reigns.

Metapopulation effects on nuclear or cytoplasmic control

This section describes the effects of variable female frequencies among patches of a metapopulation. The models show how the amount of variation among patches raises or lowers the global average frequency of females at equilibrium under either nuclear or cytoplasmic control. The following section takes up theories that analyse non-equilibrium fluctuations caused by conflict between nuclear and cytoplasmic genes.

Local mate competition and group selection

Couvet *et al.* (1998) modelled extinction and colonization of patches in a metapopulation. The number of colonizing seeds contributed by an established patch increases in proportion to the patch's frequency of females because females produce more seeds than do hermaphrodites. This colonizing advantage for female-biased patches favours an increase in the frequency of females controlled by nuclear genes. They interpreted this as a group selection process because it depends on the differential seed productivity of patches.

The model of Couvet *et al.* (1998) is an example of the well-known process of local mate competition from sex-ratio theory (Hamilton 1967, 1979; Charnov 1982;

Frank 1998). In local mate competition, a rise in the genetic relatedness among competing pollen causes an increase in the female bias of the sex ratio. The model requires that seeds disperse and compete over a distance longer than pollen flow. In the model of Couvet *et al.* (1998), empty patches cannot receive pollen but can be colonized by seeds, increasing the effective distance of seed flow relative to pollen flow. Frequent colonizations and extinctions at the patch level increase relatedness within patches, promoting local mate competition.

Pollen limitation

The greater the variation in female frequency among populations, the more often a female occurs within a relatively female-biased population—variation implies females are clumped. A female has difficulty obtaining pollen when in a population with mostly other females. Thus, when females are clumped, female fitness is reduced relative to hermaphrodites (McCauley & Taylor 1997).

McCauley and Taylor (1997) analysed a model of cytoplasmic control with two alternative cytotypes. One causes male sterility and the other produces hermaphrodites. Their model is similar to Eq. 1, with linear pollen limitation, $C = x = 1$, and no selfing, $s = 0$. They also accounted for variation among populations in the frequency of the two cytotypes. Such variation arises by sampling when new populations are established.

If one defines R as the variance among populations in female frequency divided by the total variance in females, then McCauley and Taylor (1997) showed that Eq. 2b with $s = 0$ becomes

$$z^*_{\text{cyt}} = \frac{f - R(1 + f)}{(1 - R)f} \tag{6}$$

If $R = 0$, there is no variation among populations, the frequency of females approaches 1 as in Eq. 2b, and the metapopulation is pushed toward extinction by pollen limitation. An increase in R causes a decline in the equilibrium frequency of females averaged over all populations.

Equation 6 can be understood more easily if one expresses the equilibrium as the number of females to the number of hermaphrodites, $f - R(1 + f) : R$. We note that R is the coefficient of relatedness from kin selection theory (Hamilton 1970; Frank 1998). Here, R measures relatedness of cytotypes within populations. The equilibrium ratio matches the gain to an individual of becoming a female relative to the gain of becoming a hermaphrodite. Becoming a female provides an additional f ovules but incurs the loss of not being able to pollinate neighbouring females, related by R, that have $1 + f$ ovules available to receive pollen. Becoming a hermaphrodite provides pollen to neighbouring hermaphrodites, related by R, that have proportionately one ovule available to receive pollen.

McCauley and Taylor (1997) developed a similar model of pollen limitation under nuclear control. By analogy with the cytoplasmic model, under nuclear control an increase in the variation among populations in female frequency causes a decline in the global frequency of females.

The models of local mate competition and pollen limitation appear to come to opposite conclusions. Spatial variation increases the frequency of females under local mate competition but decreases the frequency of females under pollen limitation. Couvet *et al.* (1998) assumed no pollen limitation in their model, allowing the total seed productivity of groups to rise with the local frequency of females. By contrast, pollen limitation prevents an increase in seed productivity with rising frequency of females, reversing the direction of selection on females. Both models identify important forces. The balance will fall differently in each species depending on the details of pollination ecology and demography.

Pannell (1997) focussed on an extreme form of pollen limitation, in which single females cannot colonize an empty patch but self-compatible hermaphrodites can. If single-seed colonization occurs sufficiently often, this process can bias the sex ratio away from females and toward hermaphrodites.

Nuclear–cytoplasmic conflict: three theories of non-equilibrium dynamics

The equilibrium and metapopulation models above establish the nature of nuclear-cytoplasmic conflict and provide important upper and lower bounds on female frequency. But evolutionary dynamics may often be driven by non-equilibrium fluctuations in which phenotypic control shifts back and forth between cytoplasmic and nuclear genes. The following models emphasize non-equilibrium dynamics driven by conflict.

Demographic extinctions and colonizations

Gouyon and Couvet (1985) noted two striking attributes of *T. vulgaris*. First, the frequency of females per patch varied widely over space. Female frequencies ranged from 5% to 95%, with a median greater than 60%. Secondly, *T. vulgaris* has an ephemeral, patch-structured demography. Fire or other disturbance sometimes clears a patch, followed by subsequent recolonization.

Gouyon and Couvet suggested that patch-level extinctions and recolonizations play a crucial role in CMS dynamics. During colonization of an empty patch, a cytotype may arrive without its associated restorers. An unrestored cytotype drives up the frequency of females toward the cytoplasmic equilibrium. Abundant females favour the introduction and rapid spread of restorers because restored hermaphrodites will donate pollen to the many nearby females.

In this model, patch-level extinctions and colonizations cause local bursts of females followed by return toward the nuclear optimum. Non-equilibrium demography drives spatiotemporal fluctuations in the frequency of females and in the frequency of male-sterility genotypes.

Genetic extinctions and colonizations

Frequent patch-level extinctions and recolonizations occur in some plant species.

However, spatial variation in CMS may be more widespread than such extreme demography. For example, van Damme (1986) observed spatial variation in females and in male-sterility cytotypes over a few hundred metres within a single contiguous patch of *P. lanceolata*.

Frank (1989) developed a model in which genetic extinctions and colonizations occur within established patches. Suppose, for example, that a population lacks a cytotype and its matching restorers. Immigration of that cytotype leads to its rapid increase because it will cause male sterility and increased seed fertility. A high frequency of male-sterile plants favours the introduction and increase of the matching nuclear restorer alleles.

The spread of one cytotype drives down the frequency of other cytotypes, possibly causing local loss of genotypes. Nuclear restorers that match locally extinct cytotypes no longer provide any benefit. They will be driven from the local population if they carry any negative fitness costs because such costs are no longer offset by the benefits of restoration. The local extinction of a cytotype and matching restorers leads eventually to another round of colonization. This process of genetic extinctions and colonizations maintains spatial variation among populations.

The greater the number of alternative cytotypes, the more opportunity for dynamics to be driven by local extinction and colonization processes (Frank 1989, 1997, 2000). Drift can also play an important role — the loss of rare cytotypes and restorers from local populations sets the stage for the next rounds of reintroductions and local genetic turnover.

The model of Gouyon and Couvet (1985) depends on an extreme form of drift, in which severe demographic fluctuations cause local loss of cytotypes and restorers. The model of Frank (1989) combines drift and selection by emphasizing that the spread of a cytotype in a local population deterministically drives down the frequency of alternative cytotypes. Such deterministic selection combined with drift can maintain spatial variation in CMS without frequent demographic extinctions, although such extinctions certainly enhance spatial variation.

Deterministic fluctuations within patches

The previous models depend on stochastic perturbations. Gouyon and Couvet (1985) emphasize local demographic extinctions and recolonizations; Frank (1989) emphasizes genetic extinctions in extant populations followed by subsequent colonizations. Spatial variation in both models increases as the number of alternative cytotypes rises — more cytotypes increase the chance that a particular cytotype can shake free of its matching restorers (Frank 1989).

Studies of *P. lanceolata* in the 1980s found only two alternative male-sterile cytotypes (van Damme & van Delden 1982). In addition, many *P. lanceolata* populations are large and probably not subject to frequent demographic extinctions. In spite of the apparently small number of cytotypes and relative demographic stability, van Damme and van Delden (1982) did observe some spatial variation in the frequency of females.

Gouyon *et al.* (1991) formulated a deterministic model to explain these observations of *P. lanceolata* (see Charlesworth 1981 for a similar model). Gouyon and colleagues assumed two alternative male-sterile cytotypes, each with its own matching, specific nuclear restorer locus. For their parameters, the restorers go to fixation and there are no females unless some process opposes the increase in the restorer allele frequencies.

To oppose fixation of restorers, Gouyon and colleagues assumed that restorers not matched to the resident cytotype reduce pollen fertility when in hermaphrodites. They found that the severity of the fluctuations in gene frequencies and female frequencies depends mainly on the pleiotropic cost of the restorer alleles. When the cost is high, restorer frequency drops as its matching cytotype frequency declines, setting up a strong rise in that cytotype and recovery of the restorers. Thus, high pleiotropic costs lead to a steady cycle of rising and falling frequencies—the classical limit cycle.

Fluctuations within each local population would probably be out of phase with fluctuations in other populations. Asynchronous dynamics lead to spatial variation in females and in gene frequencies. This model requires only two cytotypes and does not depend on stochastic processes or colonizations over space.

This model's simplicity makes it attractive. But we will not discuss it further for three reasons. First, restorer costs needed to drive the fluctuations seem too high to be a widespread explanation for the observed spatial variations. With the most common assumptions about genetic interactions, the model requires restorer costs of about 30%, that is, unmatched restorers in a hermaphrodite lower pollen fertility by about 30%. It has generally been difficult to detect any costs, and when detected such costs tend to be small (de Haan *et al.* 1997d). Because detecting small fitness effects is difficult, costs might be widespread but probably are not very large.

Secondly, Gouyon *et al.* (1991) were compelled to develop their model because the evidence available at that time suggested only two alternative cytotypes in *P. lanceolata*. Recent studies have found additional cytotypes (de Haan *et al.* 1997a), making more plausible the models that work best with higher numbers of cytotypes.

Finally, some level of deterministic fluctuations may occur, but the case studies below on natural populations call attention to spatial processes and to stochastic events.

Runaway allocation: a new theory

We complete our discussion of models by proposing a new theory. We developed this theory as a novel explanation for comparative patterns among species based on the data we will discuss in the second half of this paper. In particular, Manicacci *et al.* (1998) recently studied three species of *Thymus*. Across species, they found that the frequency of females rose with *F*, the seed productivity of females relative to hermaphrodites. Our theory of runaway allocation explains how this positive association may arise.

Our runaway theory follows a cycle. We briefly list each phase and then expand our explanation.

1 A rise in *F* causes a decline in the frequency of restorer alleles and an increase in the frequency of females.

2 A decline in the frequency of restorers increases the probability in a local population that at least one cytotype will exist for which the matching restorers are absent. An unmatched cytotype establishes cytoplasmic control and causes a rapid rise in the frequency of females.

3 When the frequency of females rises above the nuclear equilibrium, hermaphrodites have a higher fitness through pollen than through seeds. This asymmetry favours hermaphrodites to reallocate resources from ovules to pollen, a process we call pollen compensation.

4 Pollen compensation lowers the seed productivity of hermaphrodites, raising *F*, the ratio of seed productivity of females relative to hermaphrodites.

5 A rise in *F* feeds back into the first phase of the cycle, continuing the process and causing a runaway increase in both *F* and the frequency of females. Across species, the theory predicts a positive association between *F* and the frequency of females.

We now provide additional explanation for each phase of the cycle.

1 A rise in *F* causes a decline in the equilibrium frequency of restorers when *F* > 2. We established this in an earlier section in which we presented a genetic model of restorer polymorphism under nuclear control. Note that restorer polymorphism does not require any costs of restoration when *F* > 2. If *F* < 2, a rise in *F* reduces the selective pressure to increase restorer frequency toward fixation. Thus, rising *F* may reduce the frequency of restorers under non-equilibrium fluctuations when *F* < 2. In general, a lower frequency of restorers raises the frequency of females.

2 When restorer frequencies decline, the probability rises that a particular restorer allele will be locally extinct in some patches of a metapopulation. This enhances the probability of cytoplasmic control in a local population. Under cytoplasmic control, the frequency of females rises to a high level.

3 Under cytoplasmic control, a locally high frequency of females favours hermaphrodites to increase pollen productivity at the expense of seed productivity (Charlesworth & Charlesworth 1978; Charlesworth 1989; Maurice *et al.* 1993). Pollen compensation is favoured because the excess females in the local population provide additional ovules for the hermaphrodites to fertilize via pollen, which enhances the value of pollen relative to ovules.

4 Pollen compensation lowers the seed productivity of hermaphrodites, raising *F*, the ratio of seed productivity of females relative to hermaphrodites. Pollen compensation cannot easily be measured. Suppose, for example, that hermaphrodites reduced their seed production by one-half and doubled their pollen production. The outcome would be a doubling of *F*, without any indication that the doubling was caused by pollen compensation rather than inbreeding depression or some other process.

5 A higher value of *F* reduces the selective pressure to raise the frequency of restorers. The lower the frequency of restorers, the more often cytoplasmic control occurs because of an increased probability of local extinction of restorers. Cytoplasmic control favours pollen compensation, which in turn raises F. This causes a further decline in the frequency of the restorers and a rise in the frequency of females, and another turn of the cycle.

Self-compatible species may be particularly prone to this runaway cycle. Selfing and inbreeding depression raise F, and may do so sufficiently such that the initial value of F is high enough to get the cycle started.

Various processes such as pollen limitation may oppose the continued increase of F and the frequency of females. Such processes will stop the runaway increase at different points for different species. Thus, the model predicts a positive association between F and the frequency of females across species.

The first step in our cycle establishes a positive association between F and the frequency of females. We developed our runaway model to explain the wide variations in F observed among *Thymus* species, which we suggest have been driven by pollen compensation.

Case studies

Only a few CMS species have been studied intensively in natural populations. We briefly summarize the key observations. Because these studies guided the development of our runaway allocation theory, we cannot test our theory from available data. Rather, we use our theory along with the other models described above to organize what has been observed and to highlight the kinds of problems that can be studied in the future.

Plantago lanceolata

van Damme and van Delden (1984) measured the seed productivity of female and hermaphroditic plants. In two different plots, females produced 38% and 20% more seeds, respectively. Seeds of females were 20% heavier than those of hermaphrodites. Overall, it appeared that the total seed fitness of females was less than twice that of hermaphrodites. In our notation, $f < 1$, and because this species is self-incompatible, $s = 0$. According to simple models of sex expression in Eq. 4, the nuclear genes would favour a complete absence of females in this species.

Studies by van Damme and van Delden (1982) demonstrated nuclear–cytoplasmic inheritance with two distinct cytotypes, each with its own set of nuclear restorers. The cytotype R causes the male-sterile phenotype MS1 when unrestored and IN1 when partially restored. The cytotype P causes MS2 when unrestored and IN2 when partially restored. All four types are morphologically distinct and can be scored by direct examination. Restored cytoplasms of either type are hermaphroditic, H. The cytoplasmic type of a hermaphrodite can be determined only by crossing until the cytoplasm is exposed in an unrestored nuclear background.

van Damme and van Delden (1982) studied spatial variation of phenotypes. Table 11.2 shows phenotypic frequencies in 12 populations in two habitat groups; the original paper lists data for 27 populations in five categories. The labels for each population are abbreviations for locations.

Table 11.2 Phenotype percentages in natural populations of *Plantago lanceolata.*
(From van Damme & van Delden 1982.)

Population	MS1	IN1	MS2	IN2	H	Sample size
Hayfield						
Dr	0	0	0.2	0.2	99.6	811
Ze	0	0	5.0	0.8	94.1	742
An	0	0	8.2	1.3	90.5	754
Re	0	0	5.0	3.6	91.4	695
Me1	0	0	3.9	5.5	90.6	688
Ve	12.2	2.2	0	0.6	85.0	623
Br	23.0	7.0	0.3	0.2	69.5	601
Pasture						
Wd	4.6	0.6	0.5	0.9	93.4	6902
Bm2	7.3	3.9	0	1.3	87.5	386
Pa	7.6	7.8	0.5	0.9	83.2	437
Ac2	11.8	10.8	0	1.0	76.4	305
Ju	21.5	7.0	0	0.5	71.0	414

Table 11.3 Percentage of phenotypes of *Plantago lanceolate* at a Westduinen field.*
(Data from van Damme 1986.)

Description	MS1	IN1	MS2	IN2	MS3	H	Sample size
Total field	4.6	0.6	0.5	0.9	0.5	92.9	6902
p1	28.6	5.4	0	0	0	66.1	112
p2	25.6	1.6	0	0	0	72.8	188
p3	21.3	3.0	0.3	1.2	0	74.3	695
p4	22.7	1.6	0	4.7	0	71.1	688
Remainder	1.9	0.4	0.6	0.9	0.5	95.7	6140

* MS3 is a rare phenotype controlled by variation at nuclear loci. The locations of populations p1–p4 are shown in Figure 11.1.

The two population groups shown in Table 11.2 are the most differentiated of the five groups listed in the original paper. Five of the hayfield populations either lacked the *R* cytoplasm or were fixed for the *R* restorers. In the pasture populations, either the *P* cytoplasm was very rare or the *P*-specific restorers were common. The other three population groups were relatively more mixed for MS1 and MS2 phenotypes.

van Damme (1986) made an intensive study of spatial variation within the Westduinen (*Wd*) population listed in Table 11.2. A picture of the field at Westduinen is shown in Figure 11.1, with some of the data listed in Table 11.3. Females were rare over the whole population, with MS1 more common than MS2. However, in a few locations the frequency of MS1 was high (Figure 11.1). Within the larger clusters of MS1, p1–p4, the frequency of MS1 phenotypes was close to zero at the borders and rose to 60% near the centre.

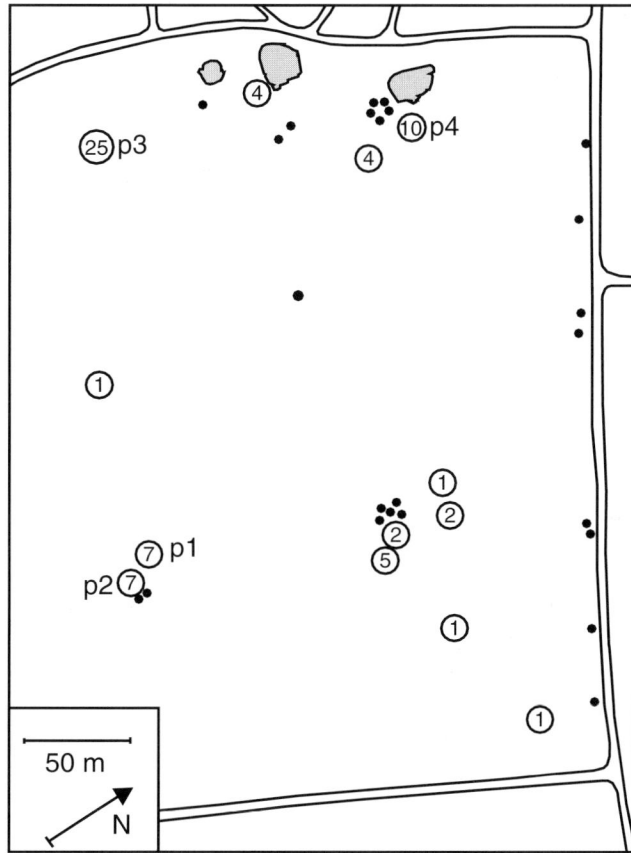

Figure 11.1 Distribution in a pasture of areas with MS1 and IN1 plants of *Plantago lanceolata*. Single plants are represented by dots and groups of plants by circles. The number within each circle is the area in square metres covered by the local group of plants. The four largest groups are labelled p1–p4. The shaded areas are pools that cattle use for water. (From van Damme 1986.)

The field as a whole was dominated by the *P* (MS2) cytoplasm, with an overall frequency of 0.94. The frequencies of the *P*-specific restorer alleles were also high. Thus, most plants were hermaphrodites with a *P* cytoplasm and *P* restorers. The overall frequency of the *R* cytoplasm was 0.06, and the *R*-specific restorers at the two restorer loci had frequencies of 0.02 and 0.08.

Genotypic composition was very different in those few areas that had high frequencies of the MS1 phenotype (Figure 11.1 and Table 11.3). The *R* (MS1) cytoplasm, rare in the population as a whole, had frequencies ranging between 26% and 39% in populations p1–p4. The *R*-specific restorers, also rare in the whole field, were more frequent in the MS1 clusters, although the exact frequencies were difficult to estimate.

van Damme's interpretation suggests colonization by a locally rare cytotype into an established patch. Initially, most of the field was dominated by P cytoplasms and P-specific restorers. R-bearing colonists founded the MS1 spots and, since the R-specific restorers were initially rare, the MS1 females spread from colonizing foci. MS1 plants produce more seeds that are larger and survive better than seeds from hermaphrodites (van Damme & van Delden 1984), so the females have a competitive advantage locally. Seeds disperse at a slow rate (about 0.1 m per generation; Bos *et al.* 1986), thus well-defined patches can form. As the frequency of unrestored R cytoplasms rises in an area, selection favours an increase in R-specific restorers. In an area with a high concentration of R cytoplasms, the main pollen donors will be R-restored hermaphrodites.

The low frequency of the R-specific restorers in the overall population suggests that these alleles are at a selective disadvantage when the R cytoplasm is absent. If so, then a population dominated by the P cytoplasm is likely to have a low frequency of the R restorers, as at Westduinen. That genotypic composition is susceptible to invasion by R cytoplasms, followed by a subsequent change in genotypic composition.

van Damme's (1986) study of a single field calls attention to differing spatial scales. Spatially contiguous populations define physical patches of habitat. Studies often focus on those spatial patches as the unit of study. But key processes may occur on different length scales from the structure of the physical patches.

The field in Figure 11.1 has spatial dimensions on the order of hundreds of metres. By contrast, typical seed flow occurs on the order of 0.1 m per generation and pollen flow at less than 1 m per generation (Bos *et al.* 1986). Thus, the spatial variation that drives the dynamics can occur within a single field. Measures of variation among large patches may hide much of the interesting spatial dynamics that occur within patches.

de Haan (1996) measured the spatial distribution of females in several populations. She found that blocks of length 10–20 m maximized the variation in the frequency of females among spatial units, suggesting that differentiation occurred on a relatively short spatial scale within large aggregations of plants.

The number of different cytotypes can influence CMS dynamics. van Damme and van Delden (1982; van Damme 1983) conducted a series of extensive crossing experiments over many populations and several years. They established the identity of two cytotypes, for each of which they found matching nuclear restorer genotypes.

de Haan *et al.* (1997a) used molecular tools to study the diversity of *P. lanceolata* mitochondria. They sampled 528 plants from 12 populations in the Netherlands and 13 plants from seven European and North American populations. Their tools did not directly identify genes involved in CMS. Instead, they established characteristic restriction fragment length polymorphism (RFLP) patterns for over 20 mitochondrial types, of which nine were relatively common.

de Haan *et al.* (1997a) used the nine common RFLP types as candidates for new CMS specificities, tested by segregation analysis. They clearly established two new mitochondrial CMS specificities and matching nuclear restorer sets—a total of four types have now been identified. Other candidates within their sample may be new

CMS types, but the segregation analyses were not sufficient to identify them unambiguously. This study demonstrates the specificity that had gone undetected in previous, extensive analyses. Given the limited sampling in this first major molecular study of *P. lanceolata*, perhaps more diversity remains to be discovered.

Thymus vulgaris

We describe the biology of *T. vulgaris* by developing contrasts with *P. lanceolata* and other *Thymus* species.

The net ovule fitness advantage of females compared to hermaphrodites is greater in T. vulgaris than in P. lanceolata

Figure 11.2(a) shows the relative seed fitness of females compared with hermaphrodites for three *Thymus* species compared with data for *P. lanceolata*. The plot shows a trend of increasing relative seed fitness for females with a rise in the frequency of females.

Thymus vulgaris is self-compatible whereas *P. lanceolata* is self-incompatible. Thus, measures of the relative ovule fitness advantage of females compared with hermaphrodites in natural populations of *T. vulgaris* confound inbreeding depression, *d*, and the outcrossed ovule fitness advantage of females, *f*. We can instead use the combined measure, *F*, for the seed fitness in females relative to hermaphrodites, which led to the nuclear equilibrium in Eq. 5 as $z_{nuc}^{\star} = (F - 2)/2(F - 1)$.

The nuclear equilibrium predicts that increases in *F* raise the lower bound on the frequency of females. Using the values of *F* in Figure 11.2(a), the nuclear equilibria of female frequency are: 0 for *P. lanceolata*, 0 for *T. zygis*, 0.14 for *T. vulgaris*, and 0.28 for *T. mastichina*. The value of *F* for *P. lanceolata* is less than for *T. zygis*, thus the intensity of selection on nuclear genes to push down the frequency of females toward zero is greatest in *P. lanceolata*.

Figure 11.3 shows the distribution of female frequencies among patches in each of the four species. The locations of the lower bounds and the medians for female frequency follow the trend predicted by the values of *F*.

Pollen compensation appears to increase with female frequency among three species of Thymus

Figure 11.2(b) shows that across three *Thymus* species, as female frequency increases, the relative pollen investment rises. Manicacci *et al.* (1998) calculated the relative male investment in Figure 11.2(b) as full pollen grains divided by germinating seeds per flower. It could be that higher frequencies of females raise this ratio by reducing the seeds per flower because higher female frequency increases pollen limitation. However, Figure 11.2(a) shows that an increase in female frequency correlates with a rise in the relative seed productivity of females compared with hermaphrodites. This argues against severe pollen limitation at high female frequency, because pollen limitation would reduce the seed productivity of females relative to hermaphrodites.

Our runaway model predicts a positive association of *F*, relative pollen invest-

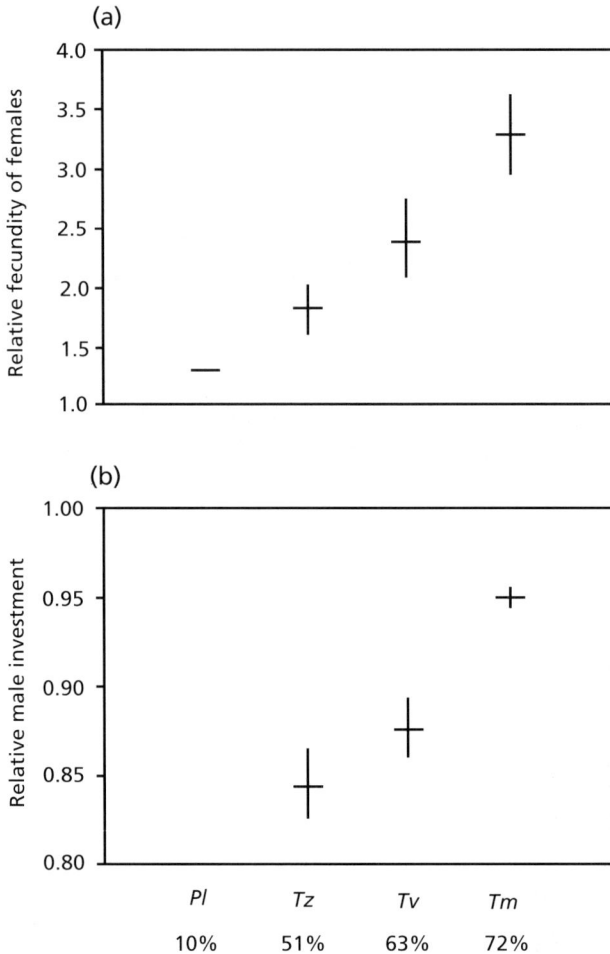

Figure 11.2 Relative female and male investment of sex types. Species abbreviations are: *Pl* for *Plantago lanceolata*, *Tz* for *Thymus zygis*, *Tv* for *T. vulgaris* and *Tm* for *T. mastichina*. The percentages below each species label give the average frequency of females observed in that species. Horizontal lines mark the mean and vertical lines mark ± 1 SE of the mean. (a) Relative seed fecundity of females to hermaphrodites. For the three *Thymus* species, Manicacci *et al.* (1998) measured the number of germinating seeds per fruit. No measures were taken of the number of fruits, differential survival of females and hermaphrodites, or differential survival of seedlings beyond germination. For *Plantago*, van Damme and van Delden (1984) measured total seed production per plant over 2–3 years. Thus, their results include components of adult survival but no measures of seedling fitness. Female frequency taken from van Damme and van Delden (1982). (b) Relative male investment measured as the number of full pollen grains per flower (with stainable cytoplasm) relative to the germinating seeds per flower. (From Manicacci *et al.* 1998.)

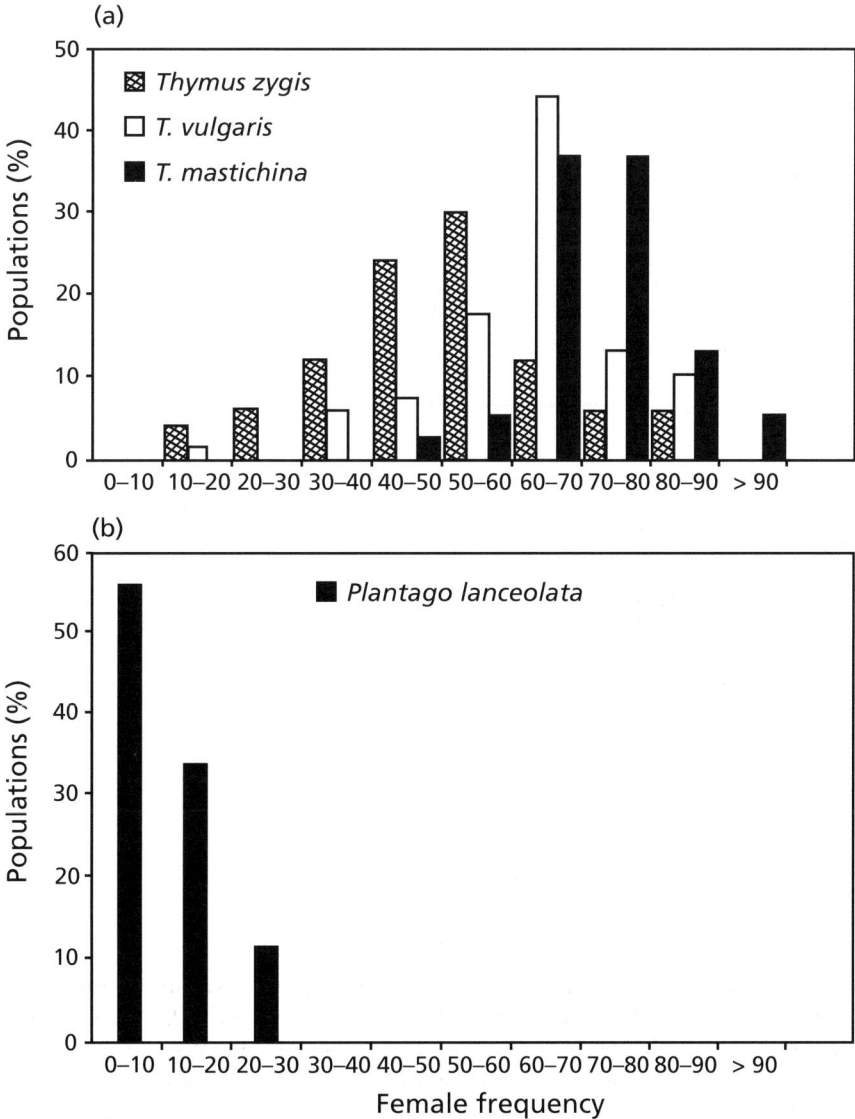

Figure 11.3 Frequency distribution of females among populations in four species. (a) The sex type of 100 individuals in each of 50 *Thymus zygis* populations, 68 *T. vulgaris* populations, and 38 *T. mastichina* populations. (From Manicacci *et al.* 1998.) (b) van Damme and van Delden (1982) measured the sex type in 27 populations of *Plantago lanceolata*, with sample sizes per population ranging from 111 to 6902.

ment of hermaphrodites, and female frequency. The three *Thymus* species show these trends.

Demographic extinctions and colonizations of patches may be more common in T. vulgaris *than in* P. lanceolata

Studies of *T. vulgaris* emphasize that this species has a patch-structured metapopulation in which patches proceed through cycles of colonization and extinction. For *T. vulgaris*, Belhassen *et al.* (1989) note that fire often destroys patches in southern France. *Thymus vulgaris* rapidly colonizes disturbed patches and is often characterized as an early successional species. By contrast, no studies of *P. lanceolata* discuss patch extinctions or colonizations.

Belhassen *et al.* (1989) report data for 15 sites for which the date of a fire had been recorded. The sites varied in age since burn from 1 to 23 years. The data clustered into three groups. The three sites less than 5 years since burn had a median frequency of females of 59%, the six sites between 5 and 11 years had a median frequency of females of 76%, and the six sites between 14 and 23 years had a median frequency of 58% females.

Belhassen and colleagues interpret these data in support of the Gouyon and Couvet (1985) model. Unrestored cytotypes may be relatively common upon colonization of empty patches (founder events). Cytoplasmic control pushes up the frequency of females to high levels until matching restorers arrive. Thus, the frequency of females tends to rise and then fall with the age since colonization. The data match the predicted trend. Given the small sample size and lack of information about the genetics, this study encourages further work.

Manicacci *et al.* (1996) analysed the role of founder events with a molecular study of cytotype diversity and spatial patch structure in *T. vulgaris*. They used RFLP to characterize cytotype in four distantly separated populations. They divided each population into patches with spatially circumscribed groups of plants and separated by regions that lacked *T. vulgaris*.

Almost all of the cytotype diversity was among patches, demonstrating a very strong effect of founder events. None of the 13 patches among the four populations shared a cytotype. Diversity within patches was low. In four patches that contained only female plants, samples of three, five, five and seven plants for each patch revealed only one cytotype per patch.

In two patches with very rare hermaphrodites, all females tested within a patch had one cytotype and a single hermaphrodite from each patch had a different cytotype. This pattern suggests an unrestored cytotype and a restored cytotype, with cytoplasmic control dominating within those patches. Finally, a patch with an intermediate frequency of females had one cytotype in two females and two hermaphrodites, and a second cytotype in two other hermaphrodites, consistent with a joint nuclear–cytoplasmic polymorphism in that patch.

The study by Manicacci *et al.* (1996) has small sample sizes and lacks segregation analyses to correlate RFLP type to genetic control of male sterility. Nevertheless, this study suggests that founder events play an important role in the CMS dynamics of

T. vulgaris. Perhaps more importantly, this work demonstrates the great potential of molecular tools to test hypotheses about spatial process.

Conclusions

We have argued that differing nuclear equilibria strongly influence the broad contrasts between *P. lanceolata* and the three *Thymus* species. The value of the seed productivity of females versus hermaphrodites, *F*, predicts the equilibrium frequency of females under nuclear control, $z^*_{nuc} = (F-2)/2(F-1)$. Using the values of *F* in Figure 11.2(a), the predicted nuclear equilibria of female frequency follows the trend *P. lanceolata* < *T. zygis* < *T. vulgaris* < *T. mastichina*. The lower bounds for female frequency in Figure 11.3 match the trend predicted by the nuclear equilibria.

The value of *F* is confounded with pollen compensation by hermaphrodites. Suppose, for example, that hermaphrodites reduced their seed production by one-half and doubled their pollen production. The outcome would be an apparent doubling of seed productivity of females relative to hermaphrodites. This would increase the apparent female fitness advantage, *F*, which would raise the nuclear equilibrium.

Self-compatible species such as *Thymus* may be particularly prone to pollen compensation and thus to large values of *F*. Selfing may initially cause a nuclear equilibrium frequency of females greater than zero. The higher the nuclear equilibrium, the lower the frequencies of restorers, and the more often control shifts to the cytoplasm. Cytoplasmic control raises the frequency of females and favours additional pollen compensation and an increase in *F*, which in turn further raises the nuclear equilibrium for the frequency of females.

We mentioned the contrast between *P. lanceolata*, which is self-incompatible and has a relatively low frequency of females, and the *Thymus* species, which are self-compatible and have relatively high frequencies of females. Self-compatibility may facilitate high frequencies of females by raising the nuclear equilibrium. However, selfing is certainly not the whole story. *Plantago coronopus*, a congener of *P. lanceolata*, is self-compatible, yet has a relatively low frequency of females when compared with the *Thymus* species (Koelewijn 1993). Clearly, self-compatibility by itself does not explain differences among species, although it may contribute in some way. Broader comparative studies would greatly help in identifying important patterns.

Other differences between *P. lanceolata* and *T. vulgaris* include demography and spatial scaling. *Thymus vulgaris* appears to have more frequent extinctions and colonizations of patches than *P. lanceolata*, probably contributing to relatively greater spatial variation in CMS genetics and frequency of females. Within patches, the spatial scale of pollen and seed dispersal is very short for *P. lanceolata*, allowing significant spatial variation within populations (Figure 11.1).

Manicacci *et al.*'s (1996) molecular study of *T. vulgaris* suggests that most seed dispersal occurs over short distances in that species. They did not mention pollen movement, but isolated females may sometimes set seed, suggesting that pollen can move over relatively longer distances. The relative movement of seeds and pollen plays a crucial role in CMS dynamics—these processes deserve further attention (McCauley 1998; Taylor *et al.* 1999).

The analyses of *P. lanceolata* and the *Thymus* species show the potential for comparative work; almost all CMS species remain unstudied in the wild. The preliminary molecular analyses also hint at the widespread polymorphisms and the powerful interaction between spatial processes and natural selection. Further molecular work tracking the movement of genes will be the key to unraveling this complex and fascinating problem.

Summary

Mitochondria sometimes cause male sterility in hermaphroditic plants by interfering with pollen development. Male-sterile plants usually produce more seeds than do hermaphrodites, probably because male sterility allows resources to be reallocated from pollen to seeds. Enhanced seed production benefits cytoplasmically inherited mitochondrial genes, which are transmitted through seeds but not through pollen. However, reduced pollen success lowers the fitness of nuclear genes, which are transmitted through both pollen and seeds. The different fitness consequences of male sterility for cytoplasmic and nuclear genes create a conflict of interest between these different subsets of the genome. Consistent with this idea of conflict, nuclear restorers occur that counteract cytoplasmic effects and restore pollen fertility.

Wild populations of cytoplasmically male-sterile plants typically have widespread polymorphisms of male-sterile mitochondria and nuclear restorer genes. These polymorphic genes appear to fluctuate over time and space, driven by the genomic conflict between the mitochondrial advantage of male sterility and the nuclear advantage of hermaphroditism.

We review various theories that explain the dynamics of cytoplasmic male sterility. We also propose a new theory, the runaway allocation model, which predicts a positive association across species between the frequency of male-sterile plants and the seed productivity of male-sterile plants relative to hermaphrodites.

Finally, we review observations from wild populations of *Plantago* and *Thymus*. The data suggest that the movement of mitochondrial and nuclear genes in spatially subdivided metapopulations controls the spatiotemporal dynamics of male sterility. The data also show a positive association across species between the frequency of male sterility and the relative seed productivity of male steriles compared with hermaphrodites, supporting the main prediction of our runaway allocation model. Recent studies with molecular tools show great promise for tracking the movement of genes over space and unravelling the processes that drive cytoplasmic male sterility.

Acknowledgements

National Science Foundation grant DEB-9627259 supports S.A.F.'s research.

References

Ashman, T.-L. (1992). The relative importance of inbreeding and maternal sex in determining progeny fitness in *Sidalcea oregana* spp. *spicata*, a gynodioecious plant. *Evolution*, **44**, 1862–1874.

Atlan, A., Gouyon, P.-H., Fournial, T., Pomente, D. & Couvet, D. (1992). Sex allocation in an hermaphroditic plant: the case of gynodioecy in *Thymus vulgaris* L. *Journal of Evolutionary Biology*, **5**, 189–203.

Belhassen, E., Trabaud, L., Couvet, D. & Gouyon, P.-H. (1989). An example of nonequilibrium processes: gynodioecy of *Thymus vulgaris* L. in burned habitats. *Evolution*, **43**, 662–667.

Bos, M., Harmens, H. & Vrieling, K. (1986). Gene flow in *Plantago* I. Gene flow and neighbourhood size in *P. lanceolata*. *Heredity*, **56**, 43–54.

Brennicke, A. & Kück, U. (1993). *Plant Mitochondria: with Emphasis on RNA Editing and Cytoplasmic Male Sterility*. VCH, New York.

Charlesworth, B. & Charlesworth, D. (1978). A model for the evolution of dioecy and gynodioecy. *American Naturalist*, **112**, 975–997.

Charlesworth, D. (1981). A further study of the problem of the maintenance of females in gynodioecious species. *Heredity*, **46**, 27–39.

Charlesworth, D. (1989). Allocation to male and female function in hermaphrodites in sexually polymorphic populations. *Journal of Theoretical Biology*, **139**, 327–339.

Charlesworth, D. & Laporte, V. (1998). The male-sterility polymorphism of *Silene vulgaris*: analysis of genetic data from two populations and comparison with *Thymus vulgaris*. *Genetics*, **150**, 1267–1282.

Charnov, E.L. (1982). *The Theory of Sex Allocation*. Princeton University Press, Princeton, NJ.

Correns, C. (1906). Die Verenbung der Geschlectsformen bei den gynodiócischen Pflanzer. *Berichte der Deutschen Botanischen Gesellschaft*, **24**, 459–474.

Couvet, D., Gouyon, P.-H., Kjellberg, F. & Valdeyron, G. (1985). La différénciation nucléocytoplasmique entre populations: une cause de l'existence de mâle-stériles dans le populations. *Comptes Rendus des Seances de l'Academie des Sciences. Serie III, Sciences de la Vie*, **300**, 665–668.

Couvet, D., Atlan, A., Belhassen, E., Gliddon, C., Gouyon, P.-H. & Kjellberg, F. (1990). Co-evolution between two symbionts: the case of cytoplasmic male-sterility in higher plants. *Oxford Surveys in Evolutionary Biology*, **7**, 225–249.

Couvet, D., Ronce, O. & Gliddon, C. (1998). The maintenance of nucleocytoplasmic polymorphism in a metapopulation: the case of gynodioecy. *American Naturalist*, **152**, 59–70.

de Haan, A.A. (1996). *The maintenance of male sterility in* Plantago lanceolata L. PhD thesis, University of Utrecht.

de Haan, A.A., Mateman, A.C., van Dijk, P.K. & van Damme, J.M.M. (1997a). New CMS types in *Plantago lanceolata* and their relatedness. *Theoretical and Applied Genetics*, **94**, 539–548.

de Haan, A.A., Luyten, R.M.J.M., Bakx-Schotman, T.J.M.T. & van Damme, J.M.M. (1997b). The dynamics of gynodioecy in *Plantago lanceolata* L. I. Frequencies of male-steriles and their cytoplasmic male sterility types. *Heredity*, **79**, 453–462.

de Haan, A.A., Koelewijn, H.P., Hundscheid, M.P.J. & van Damme, J.M.M. (1997c). The dynamics of gynodioecy in *Plantago lanceolata* L. II. Mode of action and frequencies of restorer alleles. *Genetics*, **147**, 1317–1328.

de Haan, A.A., Hundscheid, M.P.J. & van Hinsberg, A. (1997d). Effects of CMS types and restorer alleles on plant performance in *Plantago lanceolata* L.: an indication for cost of restoration. *Journal of Evolutionary Biology*, **10**, 803–820.

Eckhart, V.M. (1992). Resource compensation and the evolution of gynodioecy in *Phacelia linearis* (Hydrophyllaceae). *Evolution*, **46**, 1313–1328.

Edwardson, J.R. (1970). Cytoplasmic male sterility. *Botanical Review*, **36**, 341–420.

Frank, S.A. (1989). The evolutionary dynamics of cytoplasmic male sterility. *American Naturalist*, **133**, 345–376.

Frank, S.A. (1997). Spatial processes in host–parasite genetics. In: *Metapopulation Biology: Ecology, Genetics, and Evolution* (eds I. Hanski & M. Gilpin), pp. 325–352. Academic Press, New York.

Frank, S.A. (1998). *Foundations of Social Evolution*. Princeton University Press, Princeton, NJ.

Frank, S.A. (2000). Polymorphism of attack and defense. *Trends in Ecology and Evolution*, **15**, 167–171.

Gouyon, P.-H. & Couvet, D. (1985). Selfish cytoplasm and adaptation: variations in the reproductive system of thyme. In: *Structure and*

Functioning of Plant Populations, Vol. 2 (eds J. Haeck & J.W. Woldendorp), pp. 299–319. North-Holland Publishing Company, New York.

Gouyon, P.-H., Vichot, F. & van Damme, J.M.M. (1991). Nuclear–cytoplasmic male sterility: single-point equilibria versus limit cycles. *American Naturalist,* **137,** 498–514.

Grun, P. (1976). *Cytoplasmic Genetics and Evolution.* Columbia University Press, New York.

Hamilton, W.D. (1967). Extraordinary sex ratios. *Science,* **156,** 477–488.

Hamilton, W.D. (1970). Selfish and spiteful behaviour in an evolutionary model. *Nature,* **228,** 1218–1220.

Hamilton, W.D. (1979). Wingless and fighting males in fig wasps and other insects. In: *Reproductive Competition and Sexual Selection in Insects* (eds M.S. Blum & N.A. Blum), pp. 167–220. Academic Press, New York.

Ietswaart, J.H., Barel, R.A. & Ikelaar, M.E. (1984). Male-sterility in *Origanum vulgare* populations. *Acta Botanica Neerlandica,* **33,** 335–345.

Kheyr-Pour, A. (1980). Nucleo-cytoplasmic polymorphism for male sterility in *Origanum vulgare* L. *Journal of Heredity,* **71,** 253–260.

Koelewijn, H.P. (1993). *On the genetics and ecology of sexual reproduction in* Plantago coronopus. PhD thesis, University of Utrecht.

Koelewijn, H.P. & van Damme, J.M.M. (1995a). Genetics of male sterility in gynodioecious *Plantago coronopus.* I. Cytoplasmic variation. *Genetics,* **139,** 1749–1758.

Koelewijn, H.P. & van Damme, J.M.M. (1995b). Genetics of male sterility in gynodioecious *Plantago coronopus.* II. Nuclear genetic variation. *Genetics,* **139,** 1759–1775.

Laser, K.D. & Lersten, N.R. (1972). Anatomy and cytology of microsporogenesis in cytoplasmic male sterile angiosperms. *Botanical Review,* **38,** 425–454.

Laughnan, J.R. & Gabay-Laughnan, S. (1983). Cytoplasmic male sterility in maize. *Annual Review of Genetics,* **17,** 27–48.

Levings, C.S., III & Vasil, I.K. (1995). *The Molecular Biology of Plant Mitochondria.* Kluwer Academic Publishers, Dordrecht.

Lewis, D. (1941). Male sterility in natural populations of hermaphrodite plants: the equilibrium between females and hermaphrodites to be expected with different types of inheritance. *New Phytologist,* **40,** 56–63.

Lloyd, D.G. (1974). Theoretical sex ratios of dioecious and gynodioecious angiosperms. *Heredity,* **32,** 11–31.

Lloyd, D.G. (1975). The maintenance of gynodioecy and androdioecy in angiosperms. *Genetica,* **45,** 325–339.

Manicacci, D., Couvet, D., Belhassen, E., Gouyon, P.-H. & Atlan, A. (1996). Founder effects and sex ratio in the gynodioecious *Thymus vulgaris* L. *Molecular Ecology,* **5,** 63–72.

Manicacci, D., Atlan, A. & Couvet, D. (1997). Spatial structure of nuclear factors involved in sex determination in the gynodioecious *Thymus vulgaris* L. *Journal of Evolutionary Biology,* **10,** 889–907.

Manicacci, D., Atlan, A., Rossello, A. & Couvet, D. (1998). Gynodioecy and reproductive trait variation in three *Thymus* species (Lamiaceae). *International Journal of Plant Sciences,* **159,** 948–957.

Maurice, S., Charlesworth, D., Desfeux, C., Couvet, D. & Gouyon, P.-H. (1993). The evolution of gender in hermaphrodites of gynodioecious populations with nucleo-cytoplasmic male-sterility. *Proceedings of the Royal Society of London B,* **251,** 253–261.

McCauley, D.E. (1998). The genetic structure of a gynodioecious plant: nuclear and cytoplasmic genes. *Evolution,* **52,** 255–260.

McCauley, D.E. & Brock, M.T. (1998). Frequency-dependent fitness in *Silene vulgaris,* a gynodioecious plant. *Evolution,* **52,** 30–36.

McCauley, D.E. & Taylor, D.R. (1997). Local population structure and sex ratio: evolution in gynodioecious plants. *American Naturalist,* **150,** 406–419.

Mogensen, H.L. (1996). The hows and whys of cytoplasmic inheritance in seed plants. *American Journal of Botany,* **83,** 383–404.

Pannell, J. (1997). The maintenance of gynodioecy and androdioecy in a metapopulation. *Evolution,* **51,** 10–20.

Ross, M.D. & Weir, B.S. (1975). Maintenance of male sterility in plant populations. III. Mixed selfing and random mating. *Heredity,* **35,** 21–29.

Taylor, D.R., Trimble, S. & McCauley, D.E. (1999). Ecological genetics of gynodioecy in *Silene vulgaris:* relative fitness of females and hermaphrodites during the colonization process. *Evolution,* **53,** 745–751.

van Damme, J.M.M. (1983). Gynodioecy in *Planta-go lanceolata* L. II. Inheritance of three male sterility types. *Heredity*, **50**, 253–273.

van Damme, J.M.M. (1986). Gynodioecy in *Planta-go lanceolata* L. V. Frequencies and spatial distribution of nuclear and cytoplasmic genes. *Heredity*, **56**, 355–364.

van Damme, J.M.M. & van Delden, W. (1982). Gynodioecy in *Plantago lanceolata* L. I. Polymorphism for plasmon type. *Heredity*, **49**, 303–318.

van Damme, J.M.M. & van Delden, W. (1984). Gynodioecy in *Plantago lanceolata* L. IV. Fitness components of sex types in different life cycle stages. *Evolution*, **38**, 1326–1336.

Chapter 12
The evolution of seed heteromorphism in a metapopulation: interactions between dispersal and dormancy

I. Olivieri*

Introduction

Several species, especially in Asteraceae, exhibit seed heteromorphism, such that each individual produces two types of seeds (Venable *et al.* 1987; Venable & Levin 1983; Olivieri *et al.* 1983; Imbert 1999; see Olivieri & Berger 1985 for a review). Venable (1985) addressed the question of the evolution of seed heteromorphism using a graphical (fitness set) approach. He showed that seed specialization would occur more easily if there were trade-offs between performance of seed types in different environments (e.g. one seed type adapted to dry years and performing poorly in wet years; while the other seed type performing well in wet years and poorly in dry years). He also suggested that such seed heteromorphism was more likely to occur if flower polymorphism exists to start with, such as in the Asteraceae (with ray and disc florets). In some Asteraceae, achenes located at the centre of the capitulum bear some dispersal structures while peripheral achenes lack such structures. In many of these species, there are also differences in the germination rate of the dispersed and non-dispersed seeds. When this occurs, it is almost always the case that dormant seeds are not dispersed whereas dispersed seeds are not dormant (Venable & Lawlor 1980; Olivieri & Berger 1985).

Dispersal and dormancy share several potential functions: risk reduction, escape from crowding, and escape from sib-competition (Venable & Brown 1988, 1993; Rees 1996; Levin & Muller-Landau 2000a; Ferrière *et al.* 2000). Using theoretical models, several authors have found that there are selective trade-offs between dispersal and dormancy, such that selection for increased dispersal rate results in less dormancy (e.g. Venable & Lawlor 1980; Klinkhamer *et al.* 1987; Venable & Brown 1988; Wiener & Tuljapurkar 1994; Rees 1993, 1996; McPeek & Kalisz 1998). Similarly, greater dormancy rates select for less dispersal (Levin *et al.* 1984; Wiener & Tuljapurkar 1994). Nevertheless, it is unclear how individuals should allocate resources among the four possible types of seed (dormant and non-dispersed, non-dormant and dispersed, dormant and dispersed, non-dormant and non-dispersed).

* *Institut des Sciences de l'Evolution, UMR 5554, Université de Montpellier 2, Place Eugène Bataillon, 34095 Montpellier Cedex 05, France.*

None of the earlier studies has attempted to answer this question, which amounts to a question regarding the evolution of seed heteromorphism *per se*. To answer this question, it is necessary to compare the outcome of competition between homo-morphic and heteromorphic strategies.

There are at least two reasons why dispersed seeds might not be dormant. First, producing dispersed seeds that enter the seed bank of the new sites might simply be a bad strategy, because the function of dispersal is to colonize, and in order to colonize one must germinate (Venable & Lawlor 1980). In this chapter, I will suggest that, indeed, producing seeds that are both dispersed and dormant is rarely evolu-tionarily stable. The second mechanism is more physiological. It has been suggested that because seed dispersal is more effective when seed weight is low (e.g. Sheldon & Burrows 1973; Greene & Johnson 1993; Peroni 1994; Westoby *et al.* 1996), dispersed seeds should be packed with lighter energy sources such as fat, and thus presumably be viable for a shorter period of time than larger seeds (Rees 1996). In this case, pro-ducing dormant dispersed seeds would be selected against because the viability of efficiently dispersed seeds would be too low for them to persist in the seed bank. Conversely, larger non-dispersed seeds might have a better chance of surviving in the seed bank, as well as better resistance to crowding at the seedling stage when they germinate (Cheplick 1999). It is indeed usually the case that dispersed and non-dispersed seeds also differ by size, although not always in the same direction (Olivieri & Berger 1985; Imbert 1999; see Venable & Brown 1988, for various predictions).

Brief review of published models on the evolution of dormancy

In this section I summarize the literature on the evolution of dormancy, and briefly mention the models dealing only with dispersal when a comparison between the evolution of dispersal and dormancy is useful. Main assumptions and results of the most relevant papers are summarized in Table 12.1.

Since Cohen (1966), various authors have studied the theoretical evolution of dormancy. Most of them have considered annual species. Cohen (1966, 1967), Venable and Lawlor (1980), Klinkhamer *et al.* (1987), Silvertown (1987), Venable and Brown (1988), Wiener and Tuljapurkar (1994), McPeek & Kalisz (1998) con-sider density-independent growth in local populations of infinite size, so that the sole function of dormancy in these models is bet-hedging (escape from local extinc-tions or more generally from bad conditions for reproduction, see Philippi 1993a,b). Conversely, Bulmer (1984), Ellner (1985a,b, 1987), Klinkhamer *et al.* (1987), Rees (1994), and Mathias and Kisdi (2001) considered local density dependence. In these models, population size is infinite (i.e. there is no drift), so that dormancy has two functions: bet-hedging as in the density-independent case, and escape from local competition. Most models suggest that there is a single evolutionarily stable dor-mancy rate (e.g. Ellner 1985a,b; Rees 1994), which decreases as the mortality in the seed bank increases, just as there is a single evolutionarily stable strategy (ESS) for dispersal which decreases as mortality during dispersal increases (van Valen 1971; Olivieri *et al.* 1995).

Table 12.1 Review of main models published on the evolution of dormancy.

Author	Type of local regulation	Local dynamics	Life cycle	Number of sites	Joint evolution	Traits and trade-offs	Type of environmental variance	Condition-dependent dispersal	Analytical predictions	Main result
Cohen 1966	Density independent	—	Annual	1	—	No dispersal, dormancy only	Both local extinctions and decreased productivity	No	Yes	Dormancy is selected for when variance in seed yield exceeds mean yield; ES dormancy rate close to local extinction rate
Cohen 1967	Density independent	—	Annual	1	—	No dispersal, dormancy only	Fecundity and seed viability are environment-dependent random variables	Yes	Yes	Optimal germination fraction depends on temporal correlations
Venable & Lawlor 1980	Density independent	—	Annual	<50	No	Dispersed seeds can be dormant No secondary dispersal	Good years and bad years affect seed viability	Yes	Yes	Increased dispersal selects for less dormancy
Bulmer 1984	Density dependent	Saturated patches	Annual	1 and <50	No	Dispersed seeds can be dormant No secondary dispersal	Both local extinctions and decreased productivity	No	Yes + numerical analyses	Single ES dormancy rate. Analytical predictions under local extinctions and when survival in the bank tends towards 0 or 1.

Continued p. 248

Table 12.1 *Continued*

Author	Type of local regulation	Local dynamics	Life cycle	Number of sites	Joint evolution	Traits and trade-offs	Type of environmental variance	Condition-dependent dispersal	Analytical predictions	Main result
Klinkhamer et al. 1987	Both density dependent and density independent	Saturated patches	Annual	<50	Yes	Dispersed seeds can be dormant. No secondary dispersal	Decreased productivity	No	No	Optimal dispersal rate maximized for an intermediate number of patches. Increased dispersal selects for less dormancy
Ellner 1985 a & b	Density dependent	Saturated and non-saturated	Annual	1	No	No dispersal, dormancy only	Both local extinctions and decreased productivity	No	Yes	Fitness equilibration criteria. ESS germination as a function of bad years frequency and cost of dormancy
Ellner 1987	Density dependent	Intrinsically fluctuating	Annual	1	No	No dispersal, dormancy only	No environmental variation	No	Yes	Competition may favour seed dormancy (sib-competition is studied in Ellner 1986)
Venable & Brown 1988	Density independent	—	Annual	3–50	Yes	Dispersed seeds can be dormant. Secondary dispersal possible (not clearly stated but see Eq. 1 of this paper)	Productivity depends on environmental conditions (simulations with good and bad years)	No	No	Optimum dormancy rate decreases and ES dispersal increases with number of patches. Increased dispersal coevolves with less dormancy
Wiener & Tuljapurkar 1994	Density independent	—	Annual	2–20	Yes	Dispersed seeds can be dormant. No secondary dispersal	Spatial and temporal variance in seed yield	No	Yes + simulations	Dormancy and positive spatial autocorrelation reduce the advantage of dispersal. Predict a broad range of optimum levels of dispersal (flat fitness profiles)

Rees 1994	Density dependent	—	Perennial	1	No	No dispersal, only dormancy	Temporal variance in reproduction and adult survival	Yes in some simulations (ability to detect the presence of an adult)	Mostly simulations	Increased adult survival selects against dormancy. Exceptions occur when adult survival and seedling establishment probability both vary
McPeek & Kalisz 1998	Density independent	—	Annual	2 and 4	Yes	Dispersed seeds germinate. Dormant seeds can be secondarily dispersed and then germinate	Both local extinctions and decreased productivity	No	Numerical analyses	Optimum dormancy rate decreases and optimum dispersal increases with increasing number of patches. Dispersal seems a better bet-hedging strategy than dormancy
Mathias & Kisdi, in press	Density dependent	Saturated	Annual	2	No	Dispersed seeds can be dormant. No secondary dispersal	Spatial and temporal variation of productivity	No	No	Evolutionary branching
This study	Density dependent	Saturated and non-saturated	Annual	1 and 1000	Yes	Cases where dispersed seeds can or cannot be dormant. No secondary dispersal	Local extinctions	No	No	Local extinctions do not always select for increased dormancy. A strategy with non-dormant dispersed seeds beats a strategy with dormant dispersed seeds. Joint evolution might lead to polymorphisms

ES, evolutionarily stable.

One model has considered the evolution of dormancy in a spatially and temporally variable environment (Mathias & Kisdi, in review). In this model, the constant cost of dormancy varies between two patches, which can experience (simultaneously) years with either good or bad recruitment. Under these assumptions, there is first convergence towards a singular strategy with intermediate dormancy, but this strategy is not stable and disruptive selection then produces branching, leading to an evolutionarily stable polymorphism. When applied to the evolution of dispersal, a similar model with many patches and spatial heterogeneity in the distribution of environmental fluctuations, leads to the same result (Mathias *et al.* 2001), which was anticipated by Cohen and Levin (1991) and Ludwig and Levin (1991).

Large dispersal and dormancy rates allow the frequent recolonization of recently disturbed sites in metapopulations with a high local turnover. Therefore, high dispersal rates and large dormancy rates are both selected for when the frequency of local extinction is high (van Valen 1971; Levin *et al.* 1984; Olivieri *et al.* 1995; Cohen 1966; Bulmer 1984). However, it was recently shown that under some conditions the dispersal rate might actually decrease with increasing local extinction rates (Ronce *et al.* 2000). In this density-dependent model, we assumed local extinctions but an infinite number of patches, so the only function of dispersal was escape from crowding. When local extinction rates increase, there is a decrease in competition locally, so that escape from crowding is no longer selected for. Then the advantage of exploiting empty patches is offset by that of filling patches to exclude competitors. These two strategies have been discussed by Bolker and Pacala (1999) in the context of short-distance dispersal and stochastic local individual deaths. The same effect of increased local extinction rates on the evolution of dormancy is expected but only at low fecundity, such that local growth can occur before the patch is saturated. Ellner (1985b) is the only author who considered the general case where there can be growth following a local extinction, rather than immediate saturation. However, the consequence of such growth for the evolutionarily stable dormancy rate as a function of local disturbances was not studied.

Ellner (1987) reanalysed a model by León (1985) and showed that dormancy might be favoured as a strategy to escape crowding even in a constant environment, either because of sib-competition, or because of intrinsic (deterministic) fluctuations in population density (see also Westoby 1981; Ellner 1986). More recently, several authors have also considered the sib-competition function of seed dormancy (Cheplick 1992; Lundberg *et al.* 1996; Hyatt & Evans 1998; Nilsson *et al.* 1994; Koyabashi & Yamamura 2000). Dispersal in the context of sib-competition has been studied by Hamilton and May (1977), Frank (1986), Gandon and Michalakis (1999) and Gandon (1999). Dispersal, like dormancy, allows escape from sib-competition.

Rees (1994) studied the influence of iteroparity on dormancy and showed that increased adult survival would in general select for less dormancy. Conversely, in a metapopulation model with no sib-competition, Ronce & Olivieri (1997) found that increasing reproductive effort (and thus decreased adult survival) selects for less dispersal. This is because in the latter model dispersal evolves to escape local crowding, which is more severe when adult survival is large. In the model by Rees (1994), adult survival buffers against bad conditions for reproduction or establishment, so that seed dormancy and adult survival play similar roles.

Apart from Venable and Lawlor (1980) and Cohen (1967), no model has really formalized the evolution of condition-dependent or age-dependent germination. Age-specific dispersal has been recently studied by Ronce *et al.* (2001a). They showed that iteroparity induces opposing forces on the evolution of dispersal as an escape from sib-competition because offspring of older individuals experience in their natal patch less competition with the adults of that patch, but more competition with related juveniles.

I am aware of only four studies which have considered the joint evolution of dispersal and dormancy (Klinkhamer *et al.* 1987; Venable & Lawlor 1988; Wiener & Tuljapurkar 1994; McPeek & Kalisz 1998). Tsuji and Yamamura (1992) also considered joint evolution but in a very specific, two-patch model. Lavorel and Chesson (1995) and Lavorel *et al.* (1994) considered the coexistence of different strategies but did not look for an evolutionary equilibrium. The four main models differ in their basic assumptions (see Table 12.1). Both Venable and Brown (1988) and McPeek and Kalisz (1998) assumed that dormant seeds could be dispersed at any time, even after they entered the seed bank (secondary dispersal). Once in the seed bank, seeds are very unlikely to be dispersed over long distances, either because they have lost their dispersal structures, or because they never had any. However, such a model would be applicable to diapausing insects such as those studied by Menu (1993). Venable and Lawlor (1980), Klinkhamer *et al.* (1987), and Wiener and Tuljapurkar (1994) conversely, assumed that only newly produced seeds could be dispersed. They also assumed that dispersed seeds could enter the seed bank once they had landed somewhere. All these models found selective interactions between dormancy and dispersal, such that increased dispersal would usually select for less dormancy and vice versa. Venable and Brown (1988), in a density-independent model, studied the influence of the number of patches, of the probability of favourable conditions, and of spatial or temporal autocorrelations on the joint evolution of dispersal, dormancy and seed size. They showed that dispersal is favoured but dormancy is disfavoured by an increasing number of patches. This is because as the global growth rate becomes less dependent upon any particular patches, so the bet-hedging function of dormancy and of dispersal is reduced. However, the efficacy of dispersal is increased at the same time, with a resulting overall advantage to increased dispersal. McPeek and Kalisz (1998) found similar results. In the density-dependent version of their model, however, Klinkhamer *et al.* (1987) found that dispersal rate was maximized for an intermediate number of patches.

Venable and Brown (1988) also found that when the probability of favourable conditions increases, the optimal dormancy decreases while optimal dispersal first increases and then decreases. The same result was obtained by Karlson and Taylor (1992, 1995), also in a non-competitive environment. The reason why dispersal decreases with large extinction rates in Venable and Brown's density-independent model is that in this model the main function of dispersal is to bring individuals from unfavourable to more favourable environments. When there are either very few or very many bad environments, this function of dispersal is less strongly selected. As Venable and Brown (1988) explain, this bet-hedging function of dispersal occurs only in their density-independent model, when there are a finite, but large enough number of patches. If the number of patches is infinite, dispersal does not result in a decrease in the among-generation variance in fitness, so that under density independence the optimum is no dispersal. Conversely if the number of sites is small, dispersal is not a good strategy either, at least compared to dormancy.

A non-saturated, density-dependent metapopulation model for the joint evolution of dispersal and dormancy

I use a metapopulation model (Olivieri *et al.* 1995) of an annual species, that allows the explicit consideration of demographic dynamics in the local populations. As in Ronce *et al.* (2000), the bet-hedging function of dispersal will be reduced as much as possible by assuming a very large number of patches, and the escape from sib-competition function will be cancelled by assuming infinite local population sizes. Because I assume density-dependent mortality, escape from crowding is the main force selecting for increased dispersal. Dormancy is selected both for temporal risk spreading and for escape from crowding.

The deterministic Markovian model of metapopulation dynamics that I use has been extensively described in previous papers (Olivieri *et al.* 1995; Olivieri & Gouyon 1997; Ronce & Olivieri 1997; Brachet *et al.* 1999; Ronce *et al.* 2000). The metapopulation is made up of a very large number of sites, which are favourable for the establishment of the species but can be either occupied or empty with respect to the study species. Spatially and temporally uncorrelated local extinctions occur at a given site, with a probability *e* at each time unit, independently of the size of the local-population. I assume that local disturbances do not affect the seed bank. Seed bank survival occurs at a rate *s*. Dispersal between sites occurs according to an island model. Dispersed seeds join a migrant pool, a fraction *a* of them survive and these are redistributed equally among all sites of the metapopulation. Only newly produced seeds disperse. Dispersal takes place before local population regulation. I assume a simple, haploid asexual model with an infinite number of alleles at a locus determining both germination and dispersal rates. The dormancy rate is the probability that a seed will not germinate any given year (including the year it was produced), and the dispersal rate is the probability that a newly produced seed is dispersed. I consider first the case when the dormancy affects all seeds, regardless of whether they are dispersed or not. I then consider the case when non-dispersed seeds can be dormant, whereas dispersed seeds have no dormancy and germinate immediately. The total fraction of seeds that are dormant is then equal to the dormancy rate times the probability of not being dispersed.

Some form of density dependence is necessary to prevent demographic explosion of the metapopulation (Olivieri & Gouyon 1997). I assume local density-dependent regulation of seedling survival, and a patch carrying capacity, *K*. Contest competition is assumed (i.e. the number of adults is set to K if the number of potential survivors exceeds K), which prevents chaotic dynamics. Following founding, populations grow exponentially until they reach the carrying capacity (unless they go extinct before this). Local densities, although regulated, are effectively considered infinite (real numbers). Thus, there are no effects of genetic drift or sib-competition. In order to keep the model as deterministic as possible, I consider a large number of patches (usually 1000), and use a random number only to determine the state (extinct or not extinct) of each patch each generation.

Although the density-independent case is analytically tractable for both the evolution of dormancy (see the seminal paper by Cohen 1966) and the joint evolution of dispersal and dormancy (Klinkhamer *et al.* 1987; Venable & Brown 1988; Wiener & Tuljapurkar 1994), according to Ellner (1985a,b) it does not seem analytically possible to find the evolutionarily stable germination rate under density-dependent regulation. Klinkhamer *et al.* (1987) reached the same conclusion for the joint evolution of dispersal and dormancy. I thus made no attempt to obtain an analytical solution for the problem in this chapter.

ESSs were determined by pairwise comparisons between two alleles determining dispersal or dormancy rates separated by a discrete step of 0.05. Starting with, for example, dispersal or dormancy rate $d = 0$, I tested resistance to invasion for each strategy when a rare mutant at the next 0.05 interval was introduced. I tested resident strategies with an increment of 0.05 until a strategy resisting invasion was isolated. Then more detailed pairwise comparisons were run in the neighbourhood of this resistant strategy, so as to estimate a locally stable dormancy rate with a precision of 0.01. To test for global stability, such locally stable strategies were then confronted by mutants drawn at random from the whole strategy set. I considered as ESSs those strategies which, once fixed in the metapopulation, resisted invasion from any mutant tested. I also varied the initial frequency of the mutant and the resident, but the outcome was independent of initial frequency. In order to find the joint ESS of dispersal and dormancy, I started with particular dispersal and dormancy rates, and then looked for invasibility by small mutations in, alternatively, dispersal and dormancy rates.

Comparison with analytical results

When patches become saturated immediately after recolonization and when there is no dormancy, the ES dispersal rate is $e/(1 - a(1 - e))$, where e is the patch extinction rate and a is seed survival during migration (Levin *et al.* 1984; Ronce *et al.* 2000). I first verified (results not shown) that with no dormancy and appropriate demographic conditions, my results for the evolution of dispersal were consistent with these analytical predictions, including the numerical predictions in the case of unsaturated patches (Ronce *et al.* 2000). I also checked (results not shown) that in a single saturated patch the ES dormancy rate was always larger than or equal to the local extinction rate, as predicted by Venable and Lawlor (1980), Bulmer (1984) and Ellner (1985b).

I now compare my simulation results with the analytical predictions of Bulmer

Table 12.2 Comparison of observed evolutionarily stable (ES) dormancy rates with analytical predictions from Bulmer (1984) and Ellner (1985b) in the limiting case of no mortality in the seed bank and saturated patches. Simulations were run for 1000 independent patches. Bold values indicate those cases reasonably close to the predictions.

Local extinction rate	Mortality rate of seeds in the bank	Theoretical prediction	ES dormancy from simulations
0.01	0.001	0.55	0.68
0.1	**0.001**	**0.87**	**0.88**
0.3	**0.001**	**0.93**	**0.94**
0.6	**0.001**	**0.96**	**0.97**
0.01	0.003	0.23	0.54
0.1	0.003	0.77	0.81
0.3	**0.003**	**0.88**	**0.9**
0.6	**0.003**	**0.94**	**0.94**
0.01	0.01	0	0.36
0.1	0.01	0.57	0.7
0.3	**0.01**	**0.78**	**0.83**
0.6	**0.01**	**0.88**	**0.9**
0.01	0.03	0	0.21
0.1	0.03	0.27	0.56
0.3	0.03	0.63	0.74
0.6	**0.03**	**0.8**	**0.86**

(1984) and Ellner (1985b) in the limit of a saturated patch with no mortality in the seed bank. When patches are saturated and the survival rate, s, in the seed bank is close to 1, the ES germination rate should approach $[2(1 - s)(1 - e)/e]$ (Bulmer 1984; Ellner 1985b). Note that when $1 - s = 0$ (no mortality at all in the seed bank) this predicts an optimal germination rate of 0, i.e. all seeds should be dormant. This obviously cannot be an ESS. Table 12.2 shows a comparison of the ES dormancy rate with the analytical predictions in the limit of no mortality in the bank. The observed dormancy rates agree reasonably well with this analytical predictions, especially for large extinction rates (Table 12.2). However, the observed ES dormancy rates are invariably larger than expected from the theory (except when mortality $1 - s = 0$); this difference could come from the approximations necessary to derive the analytical expression. When mortality rate $1 - s$ is larger than $0.5 \, e/(1 - e)$, the analytical expression predicts an optimal germination rate larger than 1 (note that in these cases, we set the ES dormancy rate to zero in Table 12.2). It could be that, except when $1 - s = 0$ (no mortality in the bank), the analytical expression systematically underestimates the ES dormancy rate.

Evolution of dormancy under fixed dispersal rates in a saturated metapopulation

As found in all earlier studies, the ES dormancy rate decreases with increasing dispersal rate (Figure 12.1), regardless of whether dispersed seeds germinate readily or whether they join the dormant seed bank. The ES rate of dormancy of non-dispersed seeds is larger when dispersed seeds are not dormant.

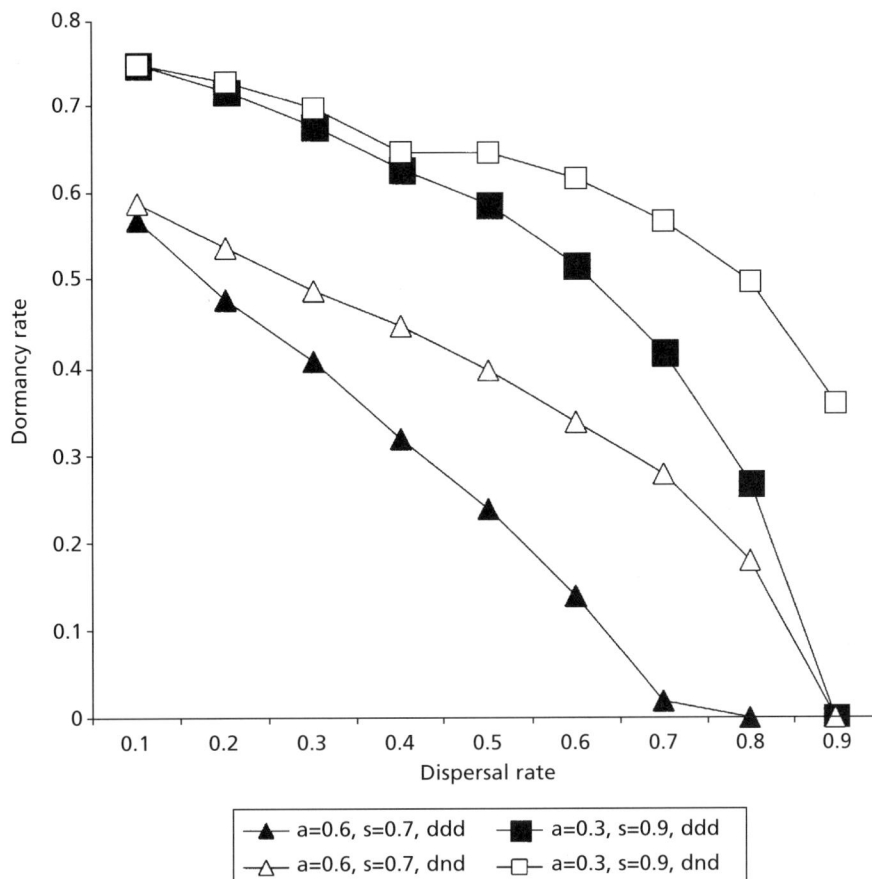

Figure 12.1 Evolutionarily stable (ES) dormancy rate as a function of fixed dispersal rate for different parameter sets. A saturated metapopulation was considered. Local extinction rate $e = 0.6$. Solid symbols indicate that dispersed seeds are possibly dormant (ddd), whereas open symbols indicate that dispersed seeds are never dormant (dnd). Survival during dispersal = a, survival in the bank = s.

As expected, ES dormancy rates increase with local extinction rates, decrease with increasing cost of dormancy, and increases with the cost of dispersal (Figure 12.2). This is because the effective dispersal rate is lowered by mortality during dispersal, which selects for more dormancy.

ES dormancy rates with increasing local extinction rates in an unsaturated metapopulation

As expected, and differently from Venable and Brown (1988), both the ES dispersal rate and the ES dormancy rate show a non-monotonic relationship with increasing

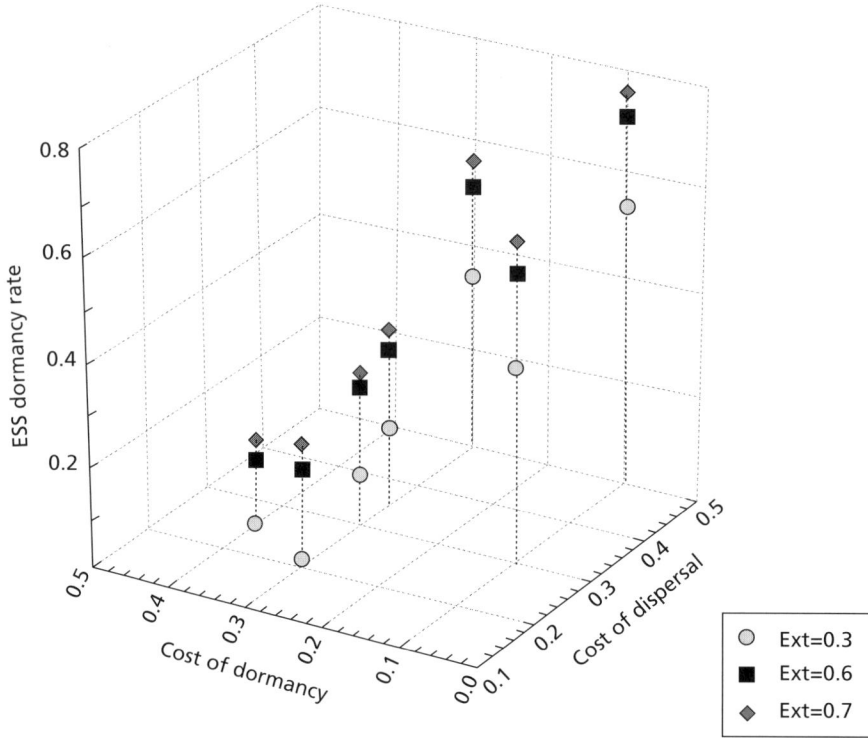

Figure 12.2 Evolutionarily stable (ES) dormancy rate as a function of local extinction rate, mortality in the seed bank, and mortality during dispersal. A fixed dispersal rate of 0.41 was considered (same data as first part of Table 12.2, with dispersed seeds possibly dormant). Circles: $e = 0.3$; squares: $e = 0.6$; diamonds: $e = 0.7$.

local extinction rate when a large number of non-saturated patches are considered (Figure 12.3). Note, however, that the trend is quite weak, probably because the other function of dormancy, bet-hedging (i.e. escape from local extinctions rather than from competition), is insensitive to demographic conditions.

I also studied metapopulations of isolated patches (i.e. no dispersal), where the bet-hedging function of dormancy is expected to be stronger (Venable & Brown 1988; McPeek & Kalisz 1998). Unfortunately, metapopulations of 1000 or even 10 000 independent patches would usually go extinct before an ESS could be found when fecundity was low. In those few cases where I could maintain a viable metapopulation (e.g. up to $e = 0.68$ for a fecundity of 20 and a mortality of 0.4 in the seed bank), the ES dormancy rate would first increase with increasing local disturbance rates, and then reach an asymptotic value (0.69 in the present example) with no apparent tendency to decrease as is observed when patches are connected by dispersal.

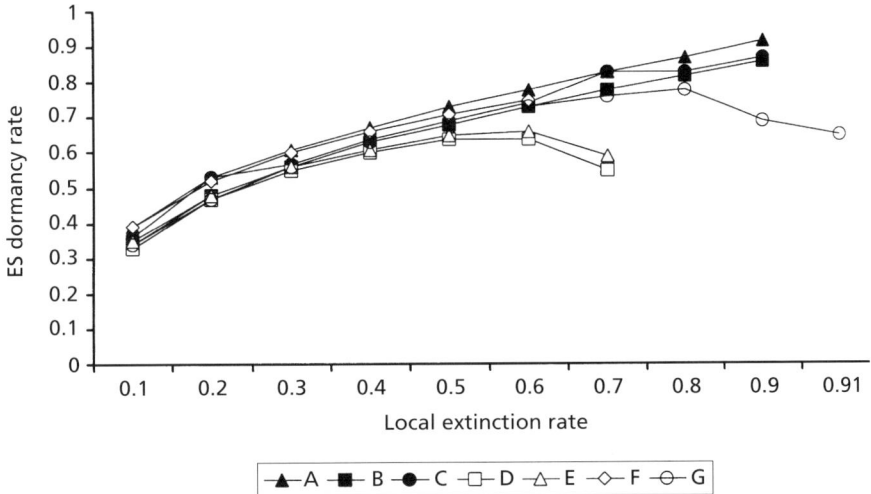

Figure 12.3 Evolutionarily stable (ES) dormancy rate as a function of local extinction rate under various scenarios. Survival in the seed bank is $a = 0.9$. (A) Saturated metapopulation of 1000 independent patches. (B) Saturated metapopulation of 1000 patches connected by 10% dispersal, with dispersed seeds possibly dormant and survival during dispersal, $s = 0.5$. (C) Same as (B), with dispersed seeds never dormant (the dormancy rate indicated in this case is that of resident seeds). (D) Same as (B), with fecundity = 5 only. (E) Same as (C), with fecundity = 5 only. (F) Same as (A), with fecundity = 5 only. (G) Same as (B) and (D), with fecundity = 20.

Joint evolution of dispersal and dormancy

In this section I assume that dispersed seeds can be dormant. Figure 12.4 gives an example of the invasion process when both dispersal and dormancy evolve. In this particular example, the initial values of dormancy and dispersal rates are too low compared to the optimal ones, given the large local extinction rate. Therefore, both start increasing through time. At some point, however, there is a 'branching', such that increased dispersal is favoured, which in turn favours decreased dormancy, until an equilibrium is reached.

With other parameter values, combinations of dispersal and dormancy other than the ESS could coexist in a stable polymorphism with the ESS. For instance, when $e = 0.7$, $a = 0.5$ and $s = 0.9$, the joint ESS is 46% dispersal and 58% dormancy (Figure 12.5). However, once such an ESS has been reached, it is invadable, although not replaceable, by several other combinations of dispersal and dormancy rates. For instance, a genotype with 82% dispersal and 12% dormancy would be maintained at an equilibrium frequency of about 0.4, with the ESS of 46% dispersal, 58% dormancy at a frequency of 0.6. Such an equilibrium did not seem to be invadable subsequently with, for example, a genotype with 81% dispersal and 13% dormancy.

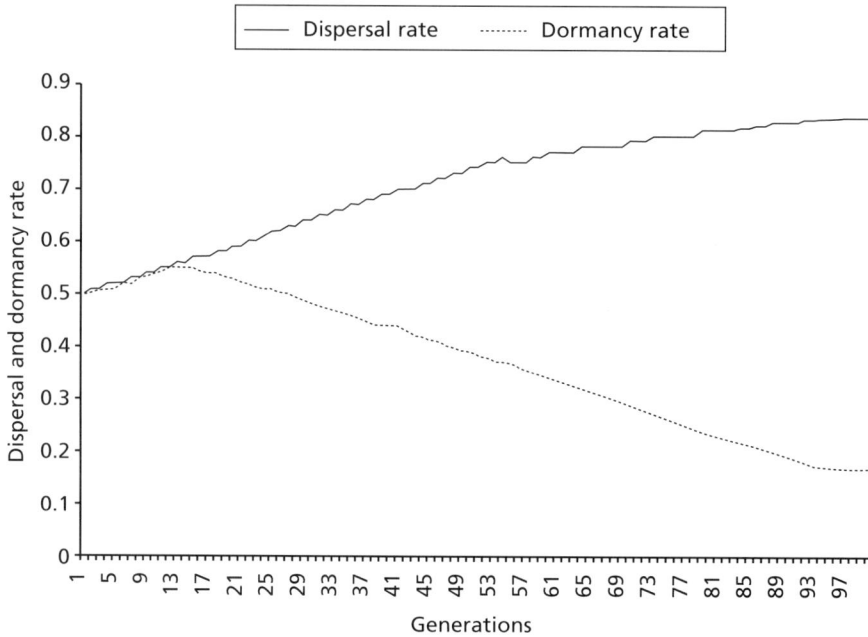

Figure 12.4 Coevolution between dispersal and dormancy. Evolution through time of selected phenotypes. Parameters are $e = 0.8$, $a = 0.5$, $s = 0.9$. Initial condition is 50% dispersal, 50% dormancy. Dispersed seeds can be dormant. Convergent stable strategy is 83% dispersal, 17% dormancy.

Moreover, once disturbed, the frequencies would return to their original values of 0.4 and 0.6, suggesting a protected polymorphism. Similarly, a strategy with 100% dispersal and no dormancy could be stably maintained with the 'ESS' at a frequency of about 30%.

I have not been able yet to describe the whole range of possible dynamics. But it seems that, even though there is a single, convergent, stable, joint ESS, a whole range of polymorphisms may persist, at least for several thousands of generations. For example, starting a simulation with 100×100 genotypes and 50 sites, with dormancy rate ranging from 0 to 0.99 and dispersal rate ranging from 0.01 to 1, each at 0.01 intervals, I found that only genotypes with no dormancy and dispersal rates of 0.89, 0.90 and 0.91, respectively, would occur at a frequency above 5% after 40 000 generations (13%, 36% and 6%, respectively). After 55 000 generations, genotypes with no dormancy and dispersal rates of 0.89 and 0.90 would occur at 13% and 26%, respectively. For each dispersal rate above 3%, a few genotypes, with dormancy rates specific to each dispersal rate, would occur at very low frequencies for several thousands of generations. Figure 12.6(a) and (b) show the situation at generation 60 000. Genotypes closer to but lower than the ESS have increased in frequency, but so has the genotype with 90% dispersal and no dormancy. This polymorphism was stable for several more hundred thousands of generations. This is reminiscent of

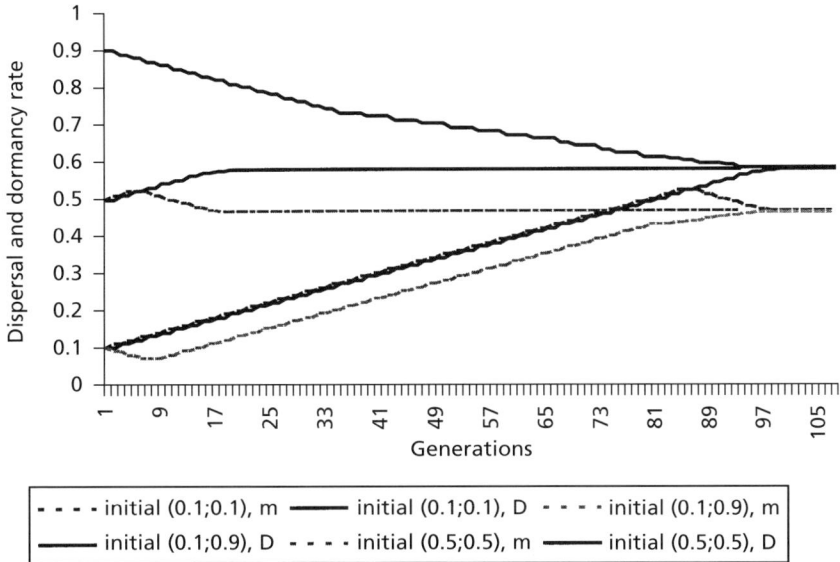

Figure 12.5 Coevolution between dispersal and dormancy. Evolution through time of selected phenotypes. A saturated metapopulation of 1000 patches was considered. Parameters are $e = 0.7$, $a = 0.5$, $s = 0.9$. Several initial conditions with two genotypes are shown. Dispersed seeds can be dormant. Convergent stable strategy is 46% dispersal, 58% dormancy.

Wiener and Tuljapurkar's (1994) density-independent model, in which several strategies share the same geometric growth rate.

Evolutionarily instability of producing dormant dispersed seeds

In this section I compare the two following strategies: either dispersed seeds can be dormant as in the previous section, or only non-dispersed seeds can be dormant. In the former cases, there are in theory four types of seeds (resident non-dormant, dispersed non-dormant, resident dormant, dispersed dormant), whereas in the latter case only the first three types of seeds are produced (dispersed non-dormant, resident dormant and resident non-dormant). Usually, species with individuals of the former case are homomorphic, in the sense that each seed has the same probability of being dispersed and of being dormant. Conversely, species of the latter case are often heteromorphic, that is some seeds are dispersed and not dormant whereas others are not dispersed and have some probability of being dormant. There are thus two types of competing genotypes (homomorphic—seeds are uniform for both dispersal and dormancy probability; and heteromorphic—dispersed non-dormant/non-dispersed possibly dormant).

I first studied the joint ESS in each case, and then the outcome of competition between the best strategy with dormant dispersed seeds, and the best strategy with

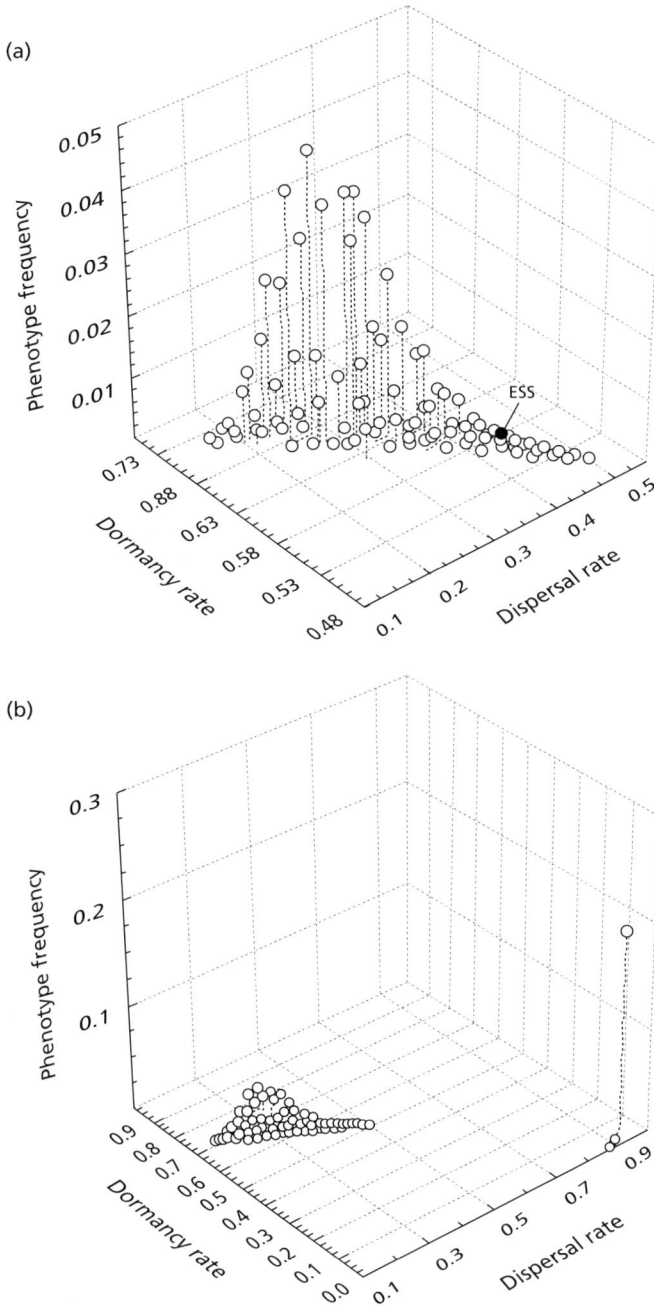

Figure 12.6 Evolution of dispersal and dormancy rates: phenotypic frequencies at generation 60 000. Same as in Figure 12.5, except that initial conditions were 10 000 genotypes in equal frequencies of 0.0001, with dispersal ranging from 0.01 to 1 and dormancy from 0 to 0.99. Convergent stable strategy under mutation of small effect is 46% dispersal, 58% dormancy. (a) Frequencies of genotypes close to the evolutionarily stable strategy (ESS). (b) Frequencies of all phenotypes with frequency larger than 0.00001.

Table 12.3 Competition between strategies producing possibly dormant dispersed seeds (a and b) and strategies whose dispersed seeds are never dormant (c and d), for various sets of parameters. Each pair of values indicate the fixed dispersal rate and the evolutionarily stable (ES) dormancy rate (a and c) or the coevolved dispersal and dormancy rates (b and d). The ES dormancy rate indicated is that of non-dispersed seeds in cases (c) and (d). Bold characters indicate winners of competition between (a) and (c) (fixed dispersal rate of 0.41), and between (b) and (d) (coevolved strategies for dispersal and dormancy, within each type of strategy). Note that the best strategy with non-dormant dispersed seeds always beats the best strategy with possibly dormant seeds, unless ES dormancy rate is close to zero (selective neutrality). Italic values indicate the best strategy among (a), (b), (c) and (d). The best strategy is almost always the coevolved strategy with dispersed seeds non-dormant (column d), at least when some positive level of dormancy is ES. Dispersal values of 0.01 indicate values strictly positive and less than 0.01. Values of 0.001 indicate that dispersal rates of 0 can be maintained as well in a metapopulation of 1000 patches.

Local extinction rate	Cost of dispersal	Mortality of seeds in the bank	Dispersed seeds can be dormant		Dispersed seeds have no dormancy	
			(a) Fixed dispersal (0.41) Only dormancy evolves	(b) Joint evolution of dispersal and dormancy rates for each seed	(c) Fixed dispersal (0.41) Only dormancy of non-dispersed seeds	(d) Joint evolution of dispersal and dormancy of non-dispersed seeds
0.3	0.3	0.3	0.41, 0.01	*0.59, 0*	**0.41, 0.15**	*0.59, 0*
0.6	0.3	0.3	0.41, 0.19	0.83, 0	**0.41, 0.37**	***0.83, 0.01***
0.7	0.3	0.3	0.41, 0.24	0.88, 0	**0.41, 0.45**	***0.88, 0.05***
0.3	0.4	0.4	0.41, 0	*0.52, 0*	**0.41, 0.08**	*0.52, 0*
0.6	0.4	0.4	0.41, 0.13	*0.8, 0*	**0.41, 0.31**	*0.8, 0*
0.7	0.4	0.4	0.41, 0.17	*0.85, 0*	**0.41, 0.38**	*0.85, 0*
0.3	0.6	0.6	0.41, 0	*0.42, 0*	0.41, 0	*0.42, 0*
0.6	0.6	0.6	0.41, 0.05	*0.71, 0*	**0.41, 0.23**	*0.71, 0*
0.7	0.6	0.6	0.41, 0.08	*0.8, 0.01*	**0.41, 0.29**	*0.8, 0*
0.3	0.6	0.3	0.41, 0.15	0.08, 0.39	**0.41, 0.24**	***0.15, 0.36***
0.6	0.6	0.3	0.41, 0.31	0.71, 0.01	**0.41, 0.44**	***0.51, 0.40***
0.7	0.6	0.3	0.41, 0.35	0.79, 0.01	**0.41, 0.50**	***0.65, 0.38***
0.3	0.5	0.1	0.41, 0.38	0.001, 0.61	**0.41, 0.45**	***0.001, 0.60***
0.6	0.5	0.1	0.41, 0.56	0.17, 0.7	**0.41, 0.64**	***0.31, 0.67***
0.7	0.5	0.1	0.41, 0.62	0.48, 0.57	**0.41, 0.70**	***0.47, 0.67***
0.3	0.9	0.1	0.41, 0.55	0.001, 0.61	**0.41, 0.56**	***0.001, 0.61***
0.6	0.9	0.1	0.41, 0.72	*0.001, 0.78*	**0.41, 0.73**	*0.001, 0.78*
0.7	0.9	0.1	0.41, 0.77	*0.001, 0.83*	**0.41, 0.78**	*0.001, 0.83*
0.3	0.5	0.3	0.41, 0.10	0.28, 0.21	**0.41, 0.20**	***0.28, 0.28***
0.6	0.5	0.3	0.41, 0.27	0.75, 0	**0.41, 0.42**	***0.65, 0.28***
0.7	0.5	0.3	0.41, 0.30	0.82, 0	**0.41, 0.48**	***0.75, 0.28***
0.3	0.9	0.3	0.41, 0.34	0.001, 0.47	**0.41, 0.37**	***0.001, 0.47***
0.6	0.9	0.3	0.41, 0.52	0.03, 0.67	**0.41, 0.56**	***0.08, 0.65***
0.7	0.9	0.3	0.41, 0.57	0.13, 0.68	**0.41, 0.62**	***0.20, 0.67***

non-dormant dispersed seeds. As Table 12.3 shows, the best strategy when dormant seeds cannot be dispersed always beats the best strategy when dispersed seeds can be dormant. I tested the robustness of this result by varying the former strategy away from its optimum values (not shown). Only when the strategy with non-dormant dispersed seeds would be really far from the optimum would the ESS with dormant dispersed seeds beat it.

Discussion

The examples studied in this paper suggest that indeed, as envisioned by Venable and Lawlor (1980), it is always better to produce non-dormant dispersed seeds, unless the dispersal and dormancy fractions are really far from the optimum. This prediction holds for both competitive and non-competitive environments, that is whether the functions of dispersal and dormancy are escape to crowding plus bet-hedging (this study) or only bet-hedging. As dispersal and dormancy play similar roles under both competitive and non-competitive environments, this result makes sense.

It would be interesting to determine whether species with no obvious seed heteromorphism actually trade dispersal with dormancy. In those species with no special design for dispersal, seeds that are at the top of the plant are more likely to be dispersed farther than seeds that are close to the ground. Our prediction would be that those seeds at the bottom of the plants, presumably less dispersed, should germinate less easily than those seeds at the top of the plant. Venable (1985), using a fitness set graphical approach, studied the evolution of heteromorphism, but not in the context of dispersal and dormancy and in a model with no density dependence. He showed under which conditions, in a temporally variable environment, a genotype producing different types of seeds, each specialized to a particular environment or year-type, would beat a genotype producing a single generalist seed. Essentially, just as in the model by Levins (1968), specialization will occur if the fitness set between (assuming two types of environments or years) survival of a seed type in one environment vs. in the other environment is convex (second derivative negative). Alternatively, specialization might also occur if fitness sets are concave but differ among seed types. This suggests that seed heteromorphism is more likely to evolve in those species or families with heteromorphic flowers.

Our results confirm analytical predictions from density-dependent models similar to ours. For instance, when survival in the bank tends towards zero, Bulmer (1984) showed that, in a single patch experiencing local extinctions, the ES dormancy rate would be close to e, the local extinction rate. Interestingly, this is also the ES dispersal rate obtained in a competitive (saturated) environment when both the cost of dispersal and the number of patches are very large (van Valen 1971), so that the main function of dispersal is escape from crowding.

Inspection of columns (b) and (d) of Table 12.3 also reveals that dispersal seems to evolve more easily than dormancy: while strategies with no dormancy evolve even for low mortality rates in the bank, strategies with little dispersal evolve only when the cost of dispersal is very large. This is because seeds that do not germinate suffer successive yearly mortality, whereas those that are dispersed in space only suffer mortality once, during dispersal. The fact that seed dispersal in time seems more ubiquitous than dispersal in space argues for the existence of very large cost of dispersal in nature (Venable & Brown 1988).

My study of the consequences of increasing local extinctions confirms the prediction made in the introduction. As expected, when the number of patches was large, the dormancy rate decreased with increasing local extinction rates (for very large extinction rates in an unsaturated metapopulation). When local extinction rates increase from low values, it becomes increasingly valuable to either disperse or remain dormant, as there are progressively more opportunities to escape local crowding. However, when local extinction rates become very large, there are progressively fewer recolonizers, and thus less local competition for resources and space. It then is no longer of benefit to pay the cost of dispersal or of dormancy and delayed germination, as the chance of establishing locally is getting larger with increasing local extinction rates. Note that this effect is likely to be weaker if one assumes instead finite population sizes, and thus sib-competition: as local population growth is slower, the local relatedness is larger, which would select for larger dispersal and dormancy rates (F. Rousset, unpublished). In a density-independent model, the effect of crowding cannot be affected by local extinctions, so that optimal dormancy rates should keep increasing with local extinction rates, as indeed was observed, for example, by Venable and Brown (1988).

The results presented in this chapter are very exploratory and I now present a few ways to expand them. Throughout I assumed constant dispersal and germination fractions. However, germination for instance has been shown to depend on the age of the seed (Philippi 1993a). It is well known that dispersal and dormancy rates can vary with the environment. For instance, Imbert and Ronce (2001) have shown that dispersal rate of *Crepis sancta* was larger under stress. In *Fraxinus ornus* (Brachet *et al.* in prep.), we found that wing–load ratio, a quantity related to dispersal ability of samaras, was a function of population age. Only phenotypic plasticity for dispersal could explain the results. If plants have a way of assessing individual and population age (e.g. through density, see Mandak and Pysek (1999) for an example), plastic dispersal as a function of these quantities are expected to evolve (Levin *et al.* 1984; McPeek & Holt 1992; Olivieri & Gouyon 1997; Ezoe & Iwasa 1997; Ronce *et al.* 1998; Ferrière *et al.* 2000; Ronce *et al.* 2001b), and so is condition-dependent dormancy (e.g. Cohen 1967). The joint evolution of phenotypic plasticity for both dispersal and dormancy rates remains to be studied.

When the only source of environmental variation is local extinction, there is a single ESS for both dispersal and dormancy rates, as found in single trait values (e.g. see Olivieri *et al.* (1995) for dispersal; Ellner (1985a,b) for dormancy). In all simulations, I found convergence towards a single joint ESS. However, I also found that at equilibrium other strategies could coexist at high frequencies: there would be convergence towards a single strategy, but such a strategy, although it might not be displaced, would not be protected from the increase of other strategies. As most models usually study pairwise competition, it is hard to say whether this result is peculiar to joint evolution. Because dispersal and dormancy play similar role, it is probably easier for different phenotypes to have the same function (Wiener & Tuljapurkar 1994). I ran simulations for either dormancy or dispersal fixed starting with 100 genotypes, and always found convergence towards the ESS. At most, five genotypes very close to the ESS (with dispersal and dormancy rates at most 5% above or below the ESS values) could be maintained during several hundreds of generation, and such polymorphism was not protected. The evolutionary stability and evolutionary dynamics of what appears to be protected polymorphisms in the case of joint evolution remains to be studied.

When there is some degree of spatial variation, such that local disturbance probabilities or the cost of dormancy may vary among patches, it was found that two types could coexist for dormancy (Mathias & Kisdi 2001) and dispersal (Mathias *et al.* 2001). We still have to explore the joint evolution between dispersal and dormancy (and possibly seed size) in a spatially and temporally variable environment. Further, as suggested by Ronce *et al.* (2001b), in a spatially structured environment, dispersal distance matters more than dispersal rate.

Finally, recent studies have shown that genetic variation for dormancy and dispersal occur in natural plant populations (Cody & Overtown 1996; Venable & Burquez 1989; Van der Schaar *et al.* 1997; Meyer & Allen 1999). Clearly it will be very interesting to consider how the precise genetic determination of seed dormancy and dispersal might interact with their evolution. In this model, I have assumed an infinite-allele model in an asexual species, in which all possible combinations of dispersal and dormancy could evolve. However, it is likely that dispersal and dormancy rates are determined by several, partly independent loci. Linkage, recombination, and epistatic interactions between these sets of loci are likely to affect the evolutionary dynamics of these two traits.

Summary

The models that have considered the evolution of dormancy are reviewed, in particular those also considering dispersal, with emphasis on their implicit and explicit hypotheses and main results. A model of the joint evolution of dormancy and dispersal in a metapopulation of an annual species is then presented. There is a specific focus on species with seed heteromorphism in Asteraceae, where dispersed seeds germinate immediately whereas non-dispersed seeds often show some dormancy. I ask under which conditions such a dimorphic strategy beats homomorphic genotypes, in which each seed has some probability of germinating and some probability of being dispersed. As dispersal and dormancy are often viewed as adaptations to a variable environment, I study a metapopulation experiencing local disturbances which kill all adults but leave the seed bank intact. There is not the usual assumption that local patches reach saturation immediately after disturbance; taking into account periods of population growth after recolonization leads to new predictions. Although both dispersal and dormancy evolve as a response to variable environments, when fecundity is low enough that sites are not saturated immediately after recolonization the evolutionarily stable dormancy rate and dispersal rate can both decrease with increasing local extinction rates. This is consistent with expectations when the main function of dispersal and dormancy is escape from local crowding.

Finally, I study the dynamics of the joint evolution of dispersal and dormancy, and suggest that there might be no single ESS.

Acknowledgements

Janis Antonovics as well as two anonymous reviewers made very useful comments on the submitted version. Janis Antonovics also extensively edited the last version. Ophélie Ronce made useful comments on an earlier draft of this paper. Earlier discussions with Pierre-Henri Gouyon on the evolution of seed heteromorphism has stimulated much of my work over the last 10 years. Véronique Perrot and Arnaud Martin modified a computer simulation program aimed at studying the evolution of dispersal to incorporate the evolution of dormancy. Renaud Vitalis, apart from sharing my daily simulation results, also helped transferring this Turbo Pascal program into the Delphi language, thereby increasing the potential number of patches by orders of magnitude. This work is supported by EC TMR ('Fragland project') allocated to I. Hanski, EC 'Plant dispersal' allocated to B. Vosman, as well as the French Ministère de l'Aménagement du Territoire et de l'Environnement, through the National Program Diversitas (contract no 98/153), and the Bureau des Ressources Génétiques. This is publication ISEM 2001-050 of the Institut des Sciences de l'Evolution de Montpellier.

References

Bolker, B.M. & Pacala, S.W. (1999). Spatial moment equations for plant competition: understanding spatial strategies and the advantages of short dispersal. *American Naturalist*, **153**, 575–602.

Brachet, S., Olivieri, I., Godelle, B., Klein, E., Frascaria-Lacoste, N. & Gouyon, P.-H. (1999). Dispersal and metapopulation viability in a heterogeneous landscape. *Journal of Theoretical Biology*, **198**, 479–495.

Brachet, S., Ronce, O., Olivieri, I., Clobert, J. & Gouyon, P.-H. (2001). The evolution of age-related dispersal ability in a metapopulation: theoretical predictions and results from an empirical study of *Fraxinus ornus* (L.). (submitted to *Journal of Ecology*)

Bulmer, M.G. (1984). Delayed germination of seeds: Cohen's model revisited. *Theoretical Population Biology*, **26**, 367–377.

Cheplick, G.P. (1992). Sibling competition in plants. *Journal of Ecology*, **80**, 567–575.

Cheplick, G.P. (1999). Assessing the potential for competition on a coastal beach and the significance of variable seed mass in *Triplasis purpurea*. *Journal of the Torrey Botanical Society*, **126**, 296–306.

Cody, M.L. & Overton, J.M. (1996). Short-term evolution of reduced dispersal in island plant populations. *Journal of Ecology*, **84**, 53–61.

Cohen, D. (1966). Optimizing reproduction in a randomly varying environment. *Journal of Theoretical Biology*, **12**, 119–129.

Cohen, D. (1967). Optimizing reproduction in a randomly varying environment when a correlation may exist between the conditions at the time of a choice has to be made and the subsequent outcome. *Journal of Theoretical Biology*, **16**, 1–14.

Cohen, D. & Levin, S.A. (1991). Dispersal in patchy environments: the effects of temporal and spatial structure. *Theoretical Population Biology*, **33**, 63–99.

Ellner, S. (1985a). ESS germination strategies in randomly varying environments. I. Logistic-type models. *Theoretical Population Biology*, **28**, 50–79.

Ellner, S. (1985b). ESS germination strategies in

randomly varying environments. II. Reciprocal yield-law models. *Theoretical Population Biology*, **28**, 80–116.

Ellner, S. (1986). Germination dimorphisms and parent-offspring conflict in seed germination. *Journal of Theoretical Biology*, **123**, 173–185.

Ellner, S. (1987). Competition and dormancy: a re-analysis and review. *American Naturalist*, **130**, 798–803.

Ezoe, H. & Iwasa, Y. (1997). Evolution of condition-dependent dispersal: a genetic algorithm search for the ESS reaction norm. *Researches on Population Ecology*, **39**, 127–137.

Ferrière, R., Belthoff, J.R., Olivieri, I. & Krackow, S. (2000). Evolving dispersal: where to go next? *Trends in Ecology and Evolution*, **15**, 5–7.

Frank, S.A. (1986). Dispersal polymorphisms in subdivided populations. *Journal of Theoretical Biology*, **122**, 303–309.

Gandon, S. (1999). Kin competition, the cost of inbreeding and the evolution of dispersal. *Proceedings of the Royal Society of London B*, **266**, 2507–2513.

Gandon, S. & Michalakis, Y. (1999). The evolution of dispersal in a metapopulation with extinctions and kin competition. *Journal of Theoretical Biology*, **199**, 275–290.

Greene, D.F. & Johnson, E.A. (1993). Seed mass and dispersal capacity in wind-dispersed diaspores. *Oikos*, **67**, 69–74.

Hamilton, W.D. & May, R.M. (1977). Dispersal in stable habitats. *Nature*, **269**, 578–581.

Hyatt, L.A. & Evans, A.S. (1998). Is decreased germination fraction associated with risk of sibling competition? *Oikos*, **83**, 29–35.

Imbert, E. (1999). The effects of achene dimorphism on the dispersal in time and space in *Crepis sancta* (Asteraceae). *Canadian Journal of Botany*, **77**, 508–513.

Imbert, E. & Ronce, O. (2001). Phenotypic plasticity for dispersal ability in the seed heteromorphic *Crepis sancta* (Asteraceae). *Oikos*, **93**, 126–134.

Karlson, R.H. & Taylor, H.M. (1992). Mixed dispersal strategies and clonal spreading of risk: predictions from a branching process model. *Theoretical Population Biology*, **42**, 218–233.

Karlson, R.H. & Taylor, H.M. (1995). Alternative predictions for optimal dispersal in response to local catastrophic mortality. *Theoretical Population Biology*, **47**, 321–330.

Klinkhamer, P.G.L., de Jong, T.J., Metz, J.A. & Val, J. (1987). Life history tactics of annual organisms: the joint effects of dispersal and delayed germination. *Theoretical Population Biology*, **32**, 127–156.

Koyabashi, Y. & Yamamura, N. (2000). Evolution of seed dormancy due to sib competition: effect of dispersal and inbreeding. *Journal of Theoretical Biology*, **202**, 11–24.

Lavorel S. & Chesson, P. (1995). How species with different regeneration niches coexist in patchy habitats with local disturbances. *Oikos*, **74**, 103–114.

Lavorel, S., O'Neill, R.V. & Gardner, R.H. (1994). Spatio-temporal dispersal strategies and annual plant species coexistence in a structured landscape. *Oikos*, **71**, 75–88.

León, J.A. (1985). Germination strategies. In: *Essays in the Honour of John Maynard Smith* (eds P.J. Greenwood, P.H. Harvey & M. Slatkin), pp. 129–142. Cambridge University Press, Cambridge, UK.

Levin, S.A. & Muller-Landau, H. (2000a). The evolution of dispersal and seed size in plant communities. *Evolutionary Ecology Research*, **2**, 409–435.

Levin, S.A., Cohen, D. & Hastings, A. (1984). Dispersal strategies in patchy environments. *Theoretical Population Biology*, **26**, 165–191.

Levins, R. (1968). *Evolution in Changing Environments*. Princeton University Press, Princeton, NJ.

Lundberg, S., Nilsson, P. & Fagerström, T. (1996). Seed dormancy and frequency dependent selection due to sib competition: the effect of age specific gene expression. *Journal of Theoretical Biology*, **183**, 9–17.

Ludwig, D. & Levin, S.A. (1991). Evolutionary stability of plant communities and the maintenance of multiple dispersal types. *Theoretical Population Biology*, **40**, 285–307.

Mandak, B. & Pysek, P. (1999). Effects of plant density and nutrient levels on fruit polymorphism in *Atriplex sagittata*. *Oecologia*, **119**, 63–72.

Mathias, A. & Kisdi, É. (In review). Adaptive diversification of germination strategies. Submitted to the Proceedings of the Royal Society of London, Series B.

Mathias, A., Kisdi, É. & Olivieri, I. (2001). The divergent evolution of dispersal in a heterogeneous landscape. *Evolution*, **55**, 246–259.

McPeek, M.A. & Holt, R.D. (1992). The evolution of dispersal in spatially and temporally varying environments. *American Naturalist*, **140**, 1010–1027.

McPeek, M. & Kalisz, S. (1998). On the joint evolution of dispersal and dormancy in metapopulations. *Ergebnisse der Limnologie*, **0**(**52**), 33–51.

Menu, F. (1993). Strategies of emergence in the chestnut weevil *Curculio elephas* (Coleoptera: Curculionida). *Oecologia*, **96**, 383–390.

Meyer, S.E. & Allen, P.S. (1999). Ecological genetics of seed germination regulation in *Bromus tectorum* L.: I. Phenotypic variance among and within populations. *Oecologia*, **120**, 27–34.

Nilsson, P., Fagerstrom, T., Tuomi, J. & Astrom, M. (1994). Does seed dormancy benefit the mother plant by reducing sib-competition? *Evolutionary Ecology*, **8**, 422–430.

Olivieri, I. & Berger, A. (1985). Seed dimorphism for dispersal: physiological, genetic and demographical aspects. In: *Genetic Differentiation and Dispersal in Plants* (eds P. Jacquard, G. Heim & J. Antonovics), pp. 413–429. Springer-Verlag, Berlin.

Olivieri, I. & Gouyon, P.H. (1985). Seed dimorphism for dispersal: theory and implications. In: *Structure and Functioning of Plant Populations*, Vol. 2 (eds J. Haeck & J.W. Woldendorp), pp. 77–90. North-Holland Publishers, Amsterdam.

Olivieri, I. & Gouyon, P.H. (1997). Evolution of migration rate and other traits: the metapopulation effect. In: *Metapopulation Biology: Ecology, Genetics and Evolution* (eds I. Hanski & M.E. Gilpin), pp. 293–323. Academic Press, New York.

Olivieri, I., Michalakis, Y. & Gouyon, P.-H. (1995). Metapopulation genetics and the evolution of dispersal. *American Naturalist*, **146**, 202–228.

Olivieri, I., Swan, M. & Gouyon, P.-H. (1983). Reproductive system and colonizing strategy of two species of *Carduus* (Compositae). *Oecologia*, **60**, 114–117.

Peroni, P.A. (1994). Seed size and dispersal potential of *Acer rubrum* (Aceraceae) samaras produced by populations in early and late successional envirronments. *American Journal of Botany*, **81**, 1428–1434.

Philippi, T. (1993a). Bet-hedging germination of desert annuals: variation among populations and maternal effects in *Lepidium lasiocarpum*. *American Naturalist*, **142**, 488–507.

Philippi, T. (1993b). Bet-hedging of desert annuals: beyond the first year. *American Naturalist*, **142**, 474–487.

Rees, M. (1993). Trade-offs among dispersal strategies in British plants. *Nature (London)*, **366**, 150–152.

Rees, M. (1994). Delayed germination of seeds: a look at the effects of adult longevity, the timing of reproduction, and population age/stage structure. *American Naturalist*, **144**, 43–64.

Rees, M. (1996). Evolutionary ecology of seed dormancy and seed size. *Philosophical Transactions of the Royal Society of London B*, **351**, 1299–1308.

Ronce, O. & Olivieri, I. (1997). Evolution of reproductive effort in a metapopulation with local extinctions and ecological succession. *American Naturalist*, **150**, 220–249.

Ronce, O., Clobert, J. & Massot, M. (1998). Natal dispersal and senescence. *Proceedings of the National Academy of Sciences of the USA*, **95**, 600–605.

Ronce, O., Gandon, S. & Rousset, F. (2001a). Kin selection and natal dispersal un age-structured populations. *Theoretical Population Biology*, **58**, 143–159.

Ronce, O., Olivieri, I., Clobert, J. & Danchin, E. (2001b). Perspectives for the study of dispersal evolution. In: *Dispersal: Mechanisms and Consequences* (eds J. Clobert, E. Danchin, A. Dhondt & J. Nichols), pp. 341–357. Oxford University Press, Oxford, UK.

Ronce, O., Perret, F. & Olivieri, I. (2000). Evolutionarily stable dispersal rates do not always increase with local extinction rates. *American Naturalist*, **155**, 485–496.

Sheldon, J.C. & Burrows, F.M. (1973). The dispersal effectiveness in the achene-pappus units of selected Compositae in steady winds with convection. *New Phytologist*, **72**, 665–675.

Silvertown, J. (1987). The demographic and evolutionary consequences of seed dormancy. In: *Plant Population Ecology* (eds H. Davy & A.R. Watkinson), pp. 205–219. Blackwell Scientific Publications, Oxford.

Tsuji, N. & Yamamura, N. (1992). A simple evolutionary model of dormancy and dispersal in heterogeneous patches with special difference to phytophagous lady beetles. I. Stable environments. *Researches on Population Ecology*, **34**, 77–90.

Van der Schaar, W., Alonso-Blanco, C., Leéon-

Kloosterziel, K.M., Jansen, R.C., Van Ooijen, J.W. & Koornneef, M. (1997). QTL analysis of seed dormancy in Arabidopsis using recombinant inbred lines and MQM mapping. *Heredity*, **79**, 190–200.

van Valen, L. (1971). Group selection and the evolution of dispersal. *Evolution*, **25**, 591–598.

Venable, D.L. (1985). The evolutionary ecology of seed heteromorphism. *American Naturalist*, **126**, 577–595.

Venable, D.L. & Brown, J.S. (1988). The selective interactions of dispersal, dormancy, and seed size as adaptations for reducing risk in variable environments. *American Naturalist*, **131**, 360–384.

Venable, D.L. & Brown, J.S. (1993). The population-dynamic functions of seed dispersal. *Vegetatio*, **108**, 31–55.

Venable, D.L. & Burquez, A. (1989). Quantitative genetics of size, shape, life-history, and fruit characteristics of the seed-heteromorphic composite *Heterosperma pinnatum*. I. Variation within and among populations. *Evolution*, **43**, 113–124.

Venable, D.L. & Lawlor, L. (1980). Delayed germination and dispersal in desert annuals: escape in space and time. *Oecologia*, **46**, 272–282.

Venable, D.L. & Levin, D.A. (1983). Morphological dispersal structures in relation to growth habit in the *Compositae*. *Plant Systems Evolution*, **143**, 1–16.

Venable, D.L., Burquez, A., Corral, G., Morales, E. & Espinosa, F. (1987). The ecology of seed heteromorphism in *Heterosperma pinatum* in central Mexico. *Ecology*, **68**, 65–76.

Westoby, M. (1981). How diversified seed germination behavior is selected. *American Naturalist*, **118**, 882–885.

Westoby, M., Leishman, M. & Lord, J. (1996). Comparative ecology of seed size and dispersal. *Philosophical Transactions of the Royal Society of London B*, **351**, 1309–1318.

Wiener, P. & Tuljapurkar, S. (1994). Migration in variable environments: exploring life-history evolution using structured population models. *Journal of Theoretical Biology*, **166**, 75–90.

Part 3

Geography

Chapter 13

Inferring glacial refugia and historical migrations with molecular phylogenies

*G. M. Hewitt and K. M. Ibrahim**

Introduction

Ecology and genetics have in many respects gone their own ways, despite repeated attempts to combine them (e.g. Berry *et al.* 1991). Ecology is versed in climatic effects and spatial distribution, while genetics is fundamentally involved in gene history and evolution. Recent advances in climatology are restructuring our thinking on the environment over the last few million years, and coupled with technological innovations in molecular genetics they promise real common ground for the integration of these orthogonal disciplines. In this article contemporary DNA markers are used to describe the present genetic structure of species across their ranges, and in combination with recent palaeoclimatic information to explore and analyse how this has developed over the recent ice ages. This involves range contractions and refugial expansions, and has implications for current biodiversity, community structure and the processes of speciation.

Climatic changes

The earth's climate has been cooling from the Tertiary period some 60 Ma with increasing oscillations to produce ice ages in the Quaternary period of the last 2.4 Ma. As the polar ice sheets grew, they advanced and retreated with roughly a 41-ka cycle until about 0.9 Ma, from when a 100-ka cycle has dominated to the present. Such periodicity implies controlling factors, and the likely drivers of these ice-age cycles are regular variations in the earth's orbit around the sun; this is known as the Croll–Milankovitch theory (Hays *et al.* 1976; Bennett 1997). The main ellipse varies with a 100-ka cycle, the axial tilt of the earth swings over 41-ka, and the wobble of the axis changes precession with a roughly 23-ka cycle. Thus, the earth's insolation energy varies as a composite of these cycles, and it seems probable that these variations are transmitted through the ocean circulation systems, changes in which effect major climatic switches (Duplessy 1999).

Over the last 25 years palaeoclimatic research has produced a vast body of data from many sources, including levels of isotopes of carbon and oxygen, of dissolved

* *School of Biological Sciences, University of East Anglia, Norwich NR4 7TJ, UK.*

gases, mineral and magnetic variation, and various plant and animal remains. The analysis of these past signatures in continuous cores or series from the sea bed, lake bottoms, ice sheets and land exposures is providing satisfyingly coherent explanations, and some exciting revelations (Williams *et al.* 1998).

Within the main 100-ka ice age cycle of the last 1 Ma there is now clear evidence of large millennial scale oscillations, and much shorter nested ones. This has been shown most clearly by the ice cores from Greenland and Antarctica, which have recently been extracted some 2 km in length, going back some 400 ka and covering four ice ages (Stauffer 1999). The annually layered snow is analysed to show variation in the entrapped gases, isotopes, acidity, pollen and dust, providing a rich set of signatures with both temporal continuity and definition. Most cores analysed in detail to date go back some 120 ka through the last ice age to the interglacial before the present one, and within this period the Greenland Ice Core Project (GRIP) revealed some 24 major warmer interstadia with shorter fluctuations (Dansgaard *et al.* 1993).

The details of these oscillations are startling and significant. They are now considered to be caused by the switching off, and then on, of the North Atlantic Deep Water Conveyor due to great ice surges particularly from the Laurentide ice sheet—the so-called Heinrich events (Alley 1998). Estimates of the temperature changes that ensued indicate very rapid warming of some 8°C in decades and a somewhat slower ramped decline. The warm and cold spells lasted from a few hundred to a few thousand years and at times flickered between hot and cold levels (Alley 2000). Furthermore, these estimates from the oxygen isotope record (δ^{18}O) may not capture the sharp extreme fluctuations as well as deviations in the nitrogen–argon isotopic signals. So that, for example the last cold spell, the Younger Dryas 12.5–11 ka, was perhaps some 15°C colder than present, and not 8°C from δ^{18}O. Similar calculations of lower temperature apply to other cold periods (Jouzel 1999).

Whilst these discoveries have emerged from, and apply to, the North Atlantic and its neighbouring lands, they can be related to other parts of the globe. Sediment and ice cores, animal and plant remains have demonstrated the effects of these major climatic oscillations around the world (e.g. Behl & Kennett 1996; Hughen *et al.* 1996; Adkins *et al.* 1997; Schulz *et al.* 1998). As more data become available, differences in the nature and effect of climatic change in tropical, Pacific and southern regions can be assessed in detail.

Fossil record

Naturally, these ice ages and such major nested oscillations in climate greatly affected plant and animal life both on land and in water. The sea bottom cores do not provide the fine resolution of ice cores due to sedimentation turbulence, and lake and land cores also suffer from some mixing of sediments. Nevertheless, the species composition in them reflects major climatic changes; and in favourable circumstances pollen and insects can demonstrate fairly rapid changes on a scale of decades (Coope 1977; Levesque *et al.* 1997; Guiot *et al.* 1989). Indeed, the fast switches clearly demonstrated in the ice cores were presaged in the earlier beetle and pollen data from England and France. Long pollen cores are now available, several going back 100 ka over the last ice age, and even over three or four ice ages in Europe (Beaulieu & Reille 1992; Tzedakis 1994; Reille *et al.* 1998). These provide a fine record of species composition at each site, and when combined into networks, as are available for much of Europe and North America, they allow the reconstruction of vegetational changes through time across the continent (Huntley & Birks 1983; Huntley 1988). While nowhere near so geographically comprehensive, animal fossil remains, particularly beetles (Ashworth *et al.* 1997), can complement this plant series to provide an increasingly clear picture of changes in the biota through the last ice age (Bennett 1997; Williams *et al.* 1998).

Range changes

At the height of the last glaciation 18–24 ka (Figure 13.1), large areas of North America and Europe were covered by ice sheets, while south of these and across northern Asia there was tundra and permafrost. The species now inhabiting these regions mostly survived further south, although fossil evidence shows that some arctic species survived in refugia that were clear of ice. Warmer temperature zones, and the species adapted to them, were condensed toward the equator. Mountain ranges

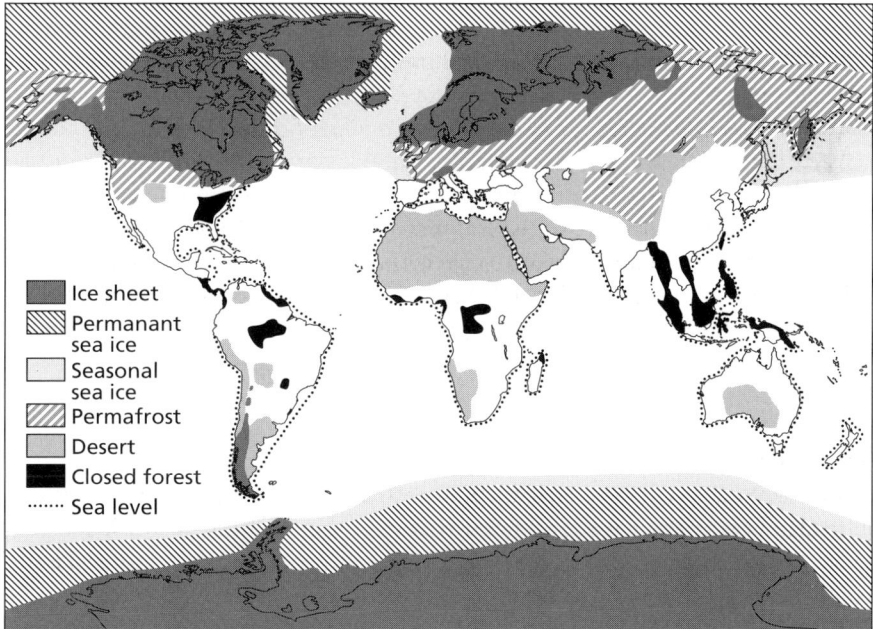

Figure 13.1 A map of the world showing the extent of ice, land, forest and desert during the last glacial maximum 20–18 ka BP (based on several sources including Frenzel *et al.* 1992; Williams *et al.* 1998, and Jonathan Adams *http://www.esd.ornl.gov/projects/qen/nerc.html*).

in Europe, North America and North Asia were also glaciated, and their present species were at lower altitudes or farther south. Tropical regions were generally drier, with reduced and fragmented wet forest and increased savannah and desert. Because of the lowering of sea level by the build-up of ice, shallower seas became land, notably in South-East Asia and the Bering Straits (Williams *et al.* 1998).

Thus, at higher latitudes species underwent considerable changes in range, or else they went extinct. In intermediate latitudes and equatorial regions, events were more complex, and there is unfortunately less detailed information from pollen cores and fossils. There are some good pollen cores from southern Europe (Tzedakis 1994; Bennett 1997), Amazonia (Colinvaux 1997), South-East Asia and other tropical parts (Flenley 1998), which show that many plant species survived through climatic reversals in these regions, possibly by changes in altitude and aspect in suitably environmentally diverse places. For example, in South-East Asia in the last glacial maximum (LGM, 20 ka) many montane tree species descended over 2000 m from their present altitude, while lowland forests were reduced and localized.

The ice core data tell us that these major climatic changes were very rapid; the fossil beetle and pollen data show that many organisms responded by quite rapid changes in their ranges. Information from the last glacial cycle, from the Eemian interglacial (120 ka) to the present interglacial, is now quite detailed in places, and particularly from the LGM through the current warm Holocene period. This recent time has seen some of these abrupt warmings and coolings, which are of particular interest due to the current concern over the instability of modern climate. From about 16 ka the climate improved, flickering considerably, until around 13 ka when there was a major shift, the Bolling warming. Pollen cores record rapid northward advances of trees in Europe and North America; present-day Mediterranean beetle species were found in England (Coope 1990). A major cold period occurred around 11–10 ka (^{14}C years = 13–11.6 ka calendar years) known as the Younger Dryas after the arctic–alpine plant, *Dryas octopetala*, that characterized the first discoveries. In Europe the glaciers readvanced, tundra expanded again and birch and other trees retreated. The fossil data also record its effects in North America and elsewhere. The Holocene warming following the Younger Dryas was very rapid indeed, with some cold oscillations around 7.5 ka as it approached present temperature levels. Recent studies with insects and pollen in the Alps, Britain, Scandinavia and North America demonstrate just how drastic were these changes and how fast organisms responded (Coope *et al.* 1998; Birks & Ammann 2000; Peteet 2000). The colonization response to warming of insects like scavenging beetles was virtually immediate, while trees took variably longer times, presumably due to their life histories. As has been emphasized before, the responses of many species appear individualistic (Huntley 1990), unless of course closely dependent on another species such as host or prey.

Population genetic impact

These major, rapid and repeated changes in climate, with their striking effects on species distributions, would be expected to modify the species genome in a number of ways (Hewitt 1993). Thus, with a sharp reduction of say 10°C average temperature over a few decades, northern populations of most species in Europe would not be able to reproduce and would become extinct. At the southern warm edge of their range, small isolated populations would be able to expand as conditions cooled. When conditions reversed and climate warmed rapidly, small populations on the northern edge of refugial areas would then colonize the new territory, while the southern edge retracted. Such leading edge colonization would be dominated by long-distance dispersants that established populations and expanded rapidly before others arrived. Such colonization would be repeated many times over large expansion distances, and because it involves several founder events would involve progressive loss of allele diversity and ultimately a tendency to homogeneity.

Computer simulation of such events shows that in time leptokurtic dispersal produces large homozygous areas that grow in size, in contrast to stepping stone and normal dispersal models (Ibrahim *et al.* 1996; some further simulation is found in Chapter 14). Furthermore, the repeated reversals seen in the climatic record would accumulate this effect. Evidence for such genetic consequences is now available in many species that have colonized regions that were glaciated or tundra in the last ice age (Hewitt 1996). Particularly good recent demonstrations are found in fishes (Bernatchez & Wilson 1998) and plants from North-West America (Soltis *et al.* 1997; see Chapter 15 for new work in the Pacific North-West).

This rapid postglacial advance northward, and its repeated bottlenecks would not only tend to reduce genome diversity, but rearrange it. It has been proposed from laboratory and theoretical work that such severe bottlenecks should reassort the epistatic relations in the genome, releasing additive genetic variation (Carson & Wisotzkey 1989; Meffert & Bryant 1992; Wade & Goodnight 1998). Recent experiments in the pitcher plant mosquito *Wyeomyia smithii*, show reduced allozyme diversity and heterozygosity in the northern expansion part of its range, which extends from Florida to Labrador, and also an increase in additive genetic variation in development time and photoperiod response (Armbruster *et al.* 1998). Such adaptive changes between populations from the glacial refugia in the south and colonized regions in the north are seen in many plants that evolved their hardiness, flowering and reproductive biology as they advanced (Gray 1997).

Not all species can be expected to show this genetic pattern of southern richness and northern purity; their different dispersal and reproductive abilities and the different geographies of their ranges should affect this. The dispersal and reproduction of weevils is very different from oaks, and the peninsulas of southern Europe are more mountainous than the broad plains of the north. In southern Europe species could have survived climatic fluctuations by ascending and descending mountains. These range changes would cover less distance and probably involve more individuals than rapid northward colonizations, thereby preserving more genetic diversity (Hewitt 1996). The presence of valleys and mountain blocks may produce an island effect, so that several distinct populations may survive climatic expansions and contractions with little gene flow among them. This would preserve genetic variation. They may accumulate genetic differences and diverge significantly, possibly forming species (Hewitt 1996). These arguments may also be applied to other mountainous regions in lower latitudes of America, Africa, Australia or Asia (Hewitt 2000).

Two other dynamic effects of rapid range change and colonization are interesting; namely high-density blocking and low-density hybridization. When a leading edge expansion has filled the territory just occupied, it is then difficult for populations behind to contribute genetically, because their dispersants' growth is logistic and not exponential like the pioneers (Hewitt 1993). This means that those populations and their particular genomes that make this first colonization can block the advance of interior genomes, and that effect may persist to the present. This high-density blocking effect is the converse of the introgression that is possible when two genomes meet and hybridize at low density. Due to long-distance colonists, the first contact between rapidly expanding genomes is broad and sparse, leaving a signal of wide introgression when full density is achieved. This form of contact may be contrasted with that between two slowly advancing genomes, where population density is high and in which diffusion allows very slow introgression over the generations. These two extremes are called pioneer and phalanx forms (Nichols & Hewitt 1994). Interestingly, if there is some genetic unfitness in the hybrid progeny, then a broad contact may sharpen and crystallize into a narrow hybrid zone for the selected parts of the genome. These various outcomes of population genome expansion and contraction will depend on individual species dispersal, reproduction and niche, guided and driven by topography and climate.

Using DNA sequences

Advances in DNA technology in the last decade mean that sequence variation can now be determined to the single base level for many individuals and populations. This rich type of data allows the genetic relationships among individuals and the divergence of lineages to be assessed, and has led to concomitant advances in data analysis. In the present context it can show how populations across the present geographic range of a species are genetically related, and hence allow inferences of ancestry, past refugia and postglacial colonization. This is part of the burgeoning new discipline of phylogeography that uses the geographic distribution of genealogical lineages in species to understand evolutionary processes in space and time (Avise *et al.* 1987; Avise 2000; Hewitt 2001). A variety of DNA markers are being employed for this task. For historical and technical reasons, mitochondrial (mt) DNA is most used in animals, while chloroplast (cp) DNA has been used more in plants. Recently, more nuclear sequences are being tried, such as gene introns, transposons and other noncoding regions. While there are still few direct comparisons of the rates of divergence of these different sequences, in general mtDNA is faster (2% per Ma) than intron (0.7% per Ma) than cpDNA (0.02–0.1% per Ma) (e.g. Hewitt 2000). This means that over the Pleistocene period (2 Ma) of the ice ages, these sequences will have diverged proportionately. Therefore, particularly for the slower evolving molecules, few sequence variants will be recent mutations and most population differences will be the result of the sorting of ancient mutations. Some parts of these molecules diverge at rather different rates, with the mtDNA D-loop region being notable. In humans it is very variable and provides a significant level of sequence variants for population studies.

Other polymerase chain reaction (PCR)-based hypervariable markers are now available, including microsatellites, which are simple sequence repeats (SSR), and amplified fragment length polymorphisms (AFLPs) (Goldstein & Schloetterer 1999; Mueller & Wolfenbarger 1999). Microsatellites have high mutation rates (over 100-fold mtDNA) and provide many alleles of different length. However, because they are repeats, the variants do not show a clear genealogy, and there is homoplasy (Orti *et al.* 1997; van Oppen *et al.* 2000). Nevertheless, their variability makes them very useful for estimating genetic distance among populations and producing within-species phylogeny when analysed carefully (Angers & Bernatchez 1998). AFLP loci are usually scored as the presence or absence of an unsequenced band, and thus do not have genealogical information. However, many bands can be produced in previously uncharacterized species, and can provide genetic distance measures among populations, neighbour-joining trees and spanning networks (Palacios *et al.* 1999). They are being applied to study divergence among populations of plants at all levels. To study fully the evolutionary history of a species through the last few million years ideally requires a combination of more and less variable molecular markers, which is costly (Hillis *et al.* 1996).

Analysing spatial genetic data

There are many ways in which data on genetic variation collected across a species range may be analysed. Allelic data will show geographic genomic structure in the present, but sequence data allows haplotypes to be genealogically related and hence their phylogenetic history can be deduced. Intraspecific phylogenies for individual DNA sequences can be used to make inferences about the history of a species, particularly when placed in the spatial context of past and present ranges of the species.

By far the commonest approaches currently in use for the purpose of phylogeographic inference rely on the three traditional methods of reconstructing gene trees (genealogies) combined with graphical representation of the geographical distribution of the lineages in the tree. Maximum parsimony and maximum likelihood phylogenies as well as those using various distance approaches are now standard methods covered in many textbooks and will not be dealt with in detail. Instead, we present an overview of the methods that were developed or extensively used specifically for the purpose of phylogeographic inference and the more recent network-based representations of the evolutionary history of sequences. These include early techniques such as spatial autocorrelation (Cliff & Ord 1973; Sokal & Oden 1978a,b) and Mantel tests (Manly 1985), methods based on DNA distance measures between sampling locations, recent approaches of constructing haplotype networks, and more recent attempts of hypothesis testing using spatially explicit stochastic simulations of evolutionary and demographic history (Table 13.1).

Table 13.1 A summary of the main analytical approaches discussed, with comments on their attributes and properties.

	Phylogenies: MP, ML and distance methods	Distance and haplotype frequency combined	Mismatch distribution	Nested clades	Haplotype networks			
					Min-spanning	Median	Reduced median	Median-joining
Gene trees (genealogies)	✓				✓	✓	✓	✓
Haplotype networks contain MP tree(s)						✓	✓	✓
Homoplasy (recombination) tolerated or handled		✓	✓	✓	✓	✓	✓	✓
Large amounts of data	✓	✓	✓	✓	✓			✓
Inferred haplotypes in networks				✓		✓	✓	✓
Phylogeographic inference based on: Statistical tests of associations		✓		✓				
Graphical representation	✓	✓			✓	✓	✓	✓
Demographic inference			✓	✓				

DNA distance measures between populations

The genetic differentiation between sample populations can be measured from sequence data by computing statistics analogous to Wright's F indices including Nei's (1982) γ_{st}, N_{st} (Lynch & Crease 1990) and K_{st} (Hudson *et al.* 1992). These statistics make use of the phylogenetic information content in sequence variation as well as the variation between the different sampling sites in the frequencies of the sequence types (haplotypes). When the spatial scale and arrangement of the sampling scheme is representative of a species range, the patterns of genetic differentiation revealed by these measures are good phylogeographic inference tools.

In contrast to Wright's original indices, these statistics do not necessarily measure inbreeding coefficients but are simply estimators of the proportion of the overall molecular variation in a species range ascribable to the differentiation between populations from different localities. The variances associated with these estimators incorporate variance arising from the sampling of populations, the sampling of individuals from within populations, and the sampling of the sequenced DNA fragment from the species' genome. Analytical formulae for estimating these components of variance from sample data exist (see Nei 1982; Lynch & Crease 1990) but require data sets much larger than usually obtained in empirical studies. Even where obtainable, because the distributional properties of these statistics are not well studied, the final tests of significance require the adoption of approximate distributions, most often the χ^2 distribution. In practice, statistical significance of the differentiation estimates is tested using bootstrap techniques (Manly 1997). All the sequences in a study are pooled and randomly subdivided into the N number of populations sampled each of size n as in the original sample sizes. The differentiation estimates between these artificial subdivisions are then computed and the process is repeated usually a thousand or more times. The proportion of randomization-based differentiation estimates that are equal to or greater than the real statistics is used to test for statistical significance. This method was used to investigate the population genetic structure of the European meadow grasshopper *Chorthippus parallelus* and to deduce its postglacial expansion routes into northern Europe (Cooper *et al.* 1995).

A 286-bp region of nuclear non-coding DNA was sequenced in populations of *C. parallelus* from much of Europe. An analysis of genetic distance as K_{st} among these revealed major divergence between Iberian, Italian, Greek, Balkan and Russian samples (Figure 13.2). The rest of Europe to the North was similar to the Balkan populations, and this is best explained by postglacial colonization of these regions from a Balkan refugium. The DNA sequences showed that Iberian and Italian refugial genomes did not expand out past the Pyrenees and Alps, and narrow hybrid zones exist between abutting genomes. The extent of the sequence divergence among these refugial genomes indicates that they have been separate for several ice ages (Hewitt 1999).

It is clear that the above approach, used in the *Chorthippus parallelus* example, concentrates on extracting maximum information from the sequence data followed by inferences about range expansion based on additional knowledge about the sampling sites such as relief, topography, glacial history and various other data. No explicit tests of association between geographical locations and genetic distances are carried out. Furthermore, the analysis represents the combined effects of two evolutionary forces that put in place the observed spatial population genetic structure — current or recent-past gene flow, which determines the frequency of the different haplotypes at different localities, and older historical events, including divergence times that have greater impact on the genealogical relationships between the different haplotypes.

Nested clade analysis

Templeton *et al.* (1987) developed a test of association that is based on hierarchical nesting of clades, which overcomes the above restriction. Initially, the method was developed to test for associations between phenotypic variation and genetic variation as represented by haplotype networks. Subsequently, Templeton and colleagues extended the method to a variety of applications including statistical tests for geographical and genealogical associations as well as discriminating between the effects of recurrent gene flow and historical events.

The first step in the nested clade analysis (NCA) is to construct a haplotype network. To do this, the number of character differences between all pairs of aligned haplotypes is used as a distance measure. Assume there are k distinct distance values:

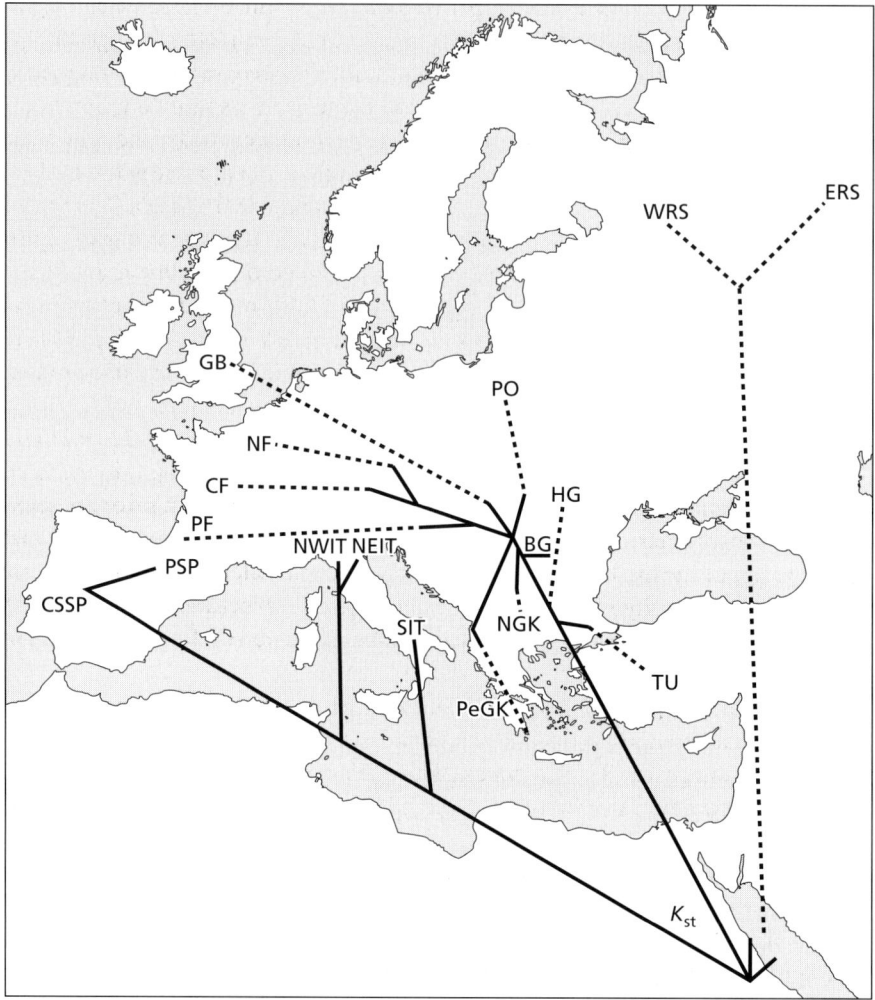

Figure 13.2 A Fitch tree calculated from K_{st} genetic distance s among populations of the grasshopper *Chorthippus parallelus* from different areas of Europe. Note the similarity among Balkan and Northern European regions, indicative of postglacial range expansion. Much larger genetic distances exist among Spanish, Italian, Balkan and Russian samples (see Cooper *et al.* 1995 for detail).

$\delta_1, \delta_2, \ldots, \delta_k$ between the sequences under consideration. Starting at the lowest value, $\delta_1 = 1$, we connect all haplotypes that differ at only one nucleotide position. This may produce a connected one-step network of all the haplotypes but much more often the δ_1 connections divide the data set into several single-step clades. Templeton *et al.* (1987) provide an algorithm for nesting these clades successively into $\delta_2, \delta_3, \ldots, \delta_k$-step clades such that the union of δ_i-step clades produces a δ_{i+1}-step clade; this is repeated recursively until the entire haplotype network is united into a single category. The nesting algorithm has been refined to handle complications arising from limited homoplasy (Templeton 1993; Templeton & Singh 1993).

The second phase of the NCA involves partitioning the geographical data embedded in the distribution of the different haplotypes among the sampling sites using the same nesting design as the clades. Two distance measures are defined. The clade distance, D_c, measures the average distance of a particular haplotype in the clade of interest from the geographical centre of all the haplotypes in that clade. The nested clade distance, D_n, measures the average distance of a haplotype from the geographical centre of all the haplotypes in the next higher-level nesting clade containing the particular haplotype. The statistical significance of both measures is tested using random permutations as in the case of the analogues of Wright's F indices. Where statistical significance is detected, many phylogeographic inferences can be drawn from the relative magnitudes and trends of the two distance measures.

Templeton (1998) describes the expectations in the relative magnitudes of D_c and D_n for spatial genetic structure put in place by: (i) current demography in the form of restricted gene flow; (ii) historical events such as range fragmentation or range expansion. In particular, contrasts between the two measures in the case of clades that form the tips of the haplotype network and those immediately interior to them are informative in identifying the causes of spatial genetic structure. Templeton *et al.* (1995) provide an inference key, which makes the evaluation of the patterns and the inferences from them explicit and consistent.

For example, in Figure 13.3 we show a subset of the *C. parallelus* sequence data discussed above nested into six one-step, three two-step, two three-step and finally a single four-step categories. It is clear that most of the haplotypes are $\delta = 1$ distance apart from the two commonest haplotypes 1 and 2. In addition, most form tip-clades relative to these two haplotypes. Figure 13.3 also lists the locations from which the haplotypes were sampled (for the complete data set refer to Cooper *et al.* 1995). Estimates of D_c and D_n were obtained using an approximate distance matrix between the localities derived from a grid overlay. The patterns observed indicated range expansion in that significantly large values for the two measures were obtained.

Using 383-bp sequence of *cyt-b* gene in mtDNA of hedgehogs *Erinaceus europaeus/concolor* across Europe has revealed a very different pattern of postglacial colonization from southern refugia (Santucci *et al.* 1998). The extent of the divergence between the parapatric western *E. europaeus* and eastern *E. concolor* suggests separation in the early Pliocene, and within each there are two divergent clades that probably date back to the start of the Pleistocene. Interestingly, each of these distinct clades is found in a southern peninsula — Iberia, Italy, Balkans or Turkey. Representatives of these genomes appear to have colonized northward broadly as phalanxes and filled northern Europe as genomic stripes (Hewitt 1999). More recent collections and sequencing provide detail of finer genomic subdivision within each of these major clades (Seddon *et al.* 2001). NCA of the two western clade expansions from Iberia and Italy provide evidence of much past fragmentation and occasional range expansion, a rather different pattern from *C. parallelus* (Figure 13.4). In a number of cases more samples in particular regions are indicated to distinguish

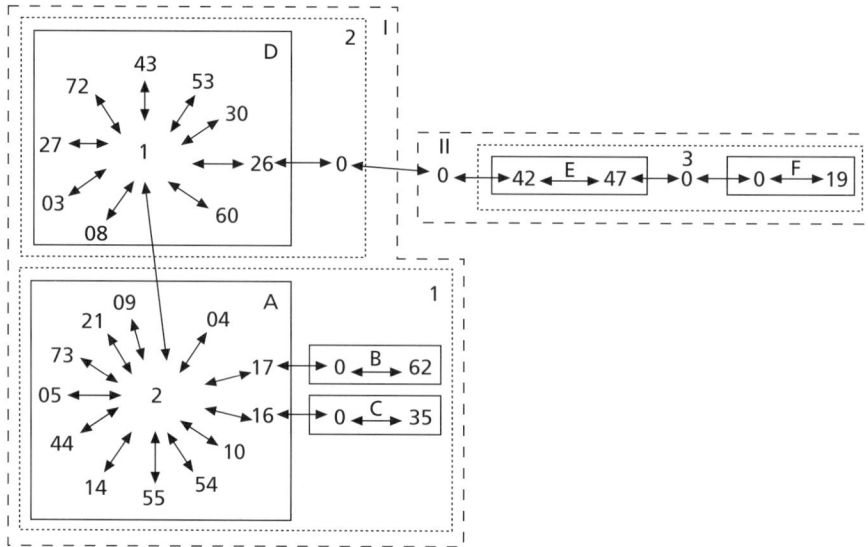

Region	cpnl-1 haplotype number
Central France	1, 2, 3, 4, 10, 16, 30
Alpine France	1, 2, 4, 10, 14,16, 17, 22
Pyrenean France	1, 2, 3, 4, 5, 16, 17, 26
Northern France	3, 4, 17
Germany / Western Austria	1, 2, 3, 10, 14, 30, 35
Eastern Austria	1, 2, 3, 5, 27, 30, 73
Great Britain	1, 2, 44, 72
Holland	1, 2, 4, 8, 9
Rumania	1, 2, 53, 54
Bulgaria	1, 4, 5, 8, 16, 17, 21
Northern Greece	2, 4, 57, 60
Peleponnese Greece	2, 19, 21, 61, 62

Figure 13.3 A haplotype network nested in one-step (A to F), two-step (1 to 3) and three-step (I and II) clades following the nesting algorithms in Templeton *et al.* (1987) and Templeton *et al.* (1987, 1995). Below: geographic distribution of the *Chorthippus parallelus* haplotypes in Europe.

causes other than isolation by distance. A value of this approach is the identification of regions critical to the analysis from which more samples are needed. It has as yet been little performed in plants, but a combination of restriction fragment length polymorphism (RFLP) and heteroduplex analysis of cpDNA provides suitable haplotype variation for the useful application of NCA in *Periqueta caroliniana* (Maskas & Cruzan 2000).

Sequence mismatch comparison

Mismatch distribution (Harpending *et al.* 1993) is a name given to a type of histogram where the frequency of pairs of sequences in a sample is plotted against their

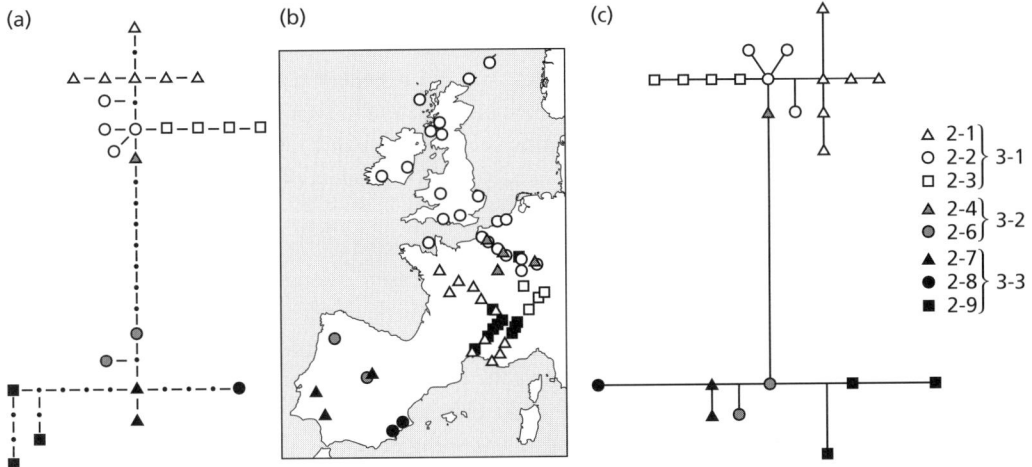

Figure 13.4 The distribution of *cyt-b* mtDNA haplotypes in the western clade of the European hedgehog *Erinaceus europaeus*. (a) A nested clade network (Templeton 1998); (b) the geographic location of the different haplotypes sampled; (c) a median-joining network of these same haplotypes (Bandelt *et al.* 1999). The haplotype clades are designated by symbols for visual simplicity.

genealogical distance represented by a simple count of the nucleotide difference between them. Rogers (1995) summarizes three properties of mismatch distributions that enable inferring whether a population has undergone sudden expansion. First, populations that have undergone reduction in size quickly converge to a new equilibrium mismatch distribution. Secondly, after a large growth, convergence to equilibrium distribution is very slow. Thirdly, an initial expansion obscures the effect of later ones for a very long time. The three combined imply that population expansions leave a lasting signature on mismatch distributions. They produce a wave-shaped distribution compared to the very rugged (multipeaked) distribution of populations at steady state. This inference can be phylogeographically informative when interpreted in a spatial context. For example, in the western-most clade of the hedgehog *E. europaeus*, recent northern expansions are indicated (Seddon *et al.* 2001). These approaches have been used particularly to investigate ancient human population demography (Harpending *et al.* 1998).

Spanning haplotype networks

There are several analytical approaches based on haplotype networks, all of which represent an alternative to the three traditional tree-building methods: distance, maximum parsimony and maximum likelihood. In the latter, gene genealogies are constructed and phylogeographic inferences are drawn from the topologies of trees in comparison to the site distribution of the haplotypes. This approach has been extensively used, and the hedgehog paradigm pattern discussed above utilized some of these methods. Similarly, but in contrast to NCA, the network-based approaches do not explicitly test for associations between gene genealogy and geography but address some significant problems in the reconstruction of intraspecific phylogenies when using the traditional methods, namely, reticulations due to homoplasy. The network-based methods include the minimum spanning network (Excoffier & Smouse 1994), the median and reduced median networks (Bandelt *et al.* 1995), and the median-joining network (Bandelt *et al.* 1999).

A minimum spanning network connects haplotypes sequentially in increasing distance, $\delta_1, \delta_2, \ldots, \delta_k$, measured in the character-state difference between pairs of haplotypes. If this produces a fully connected one-step network, the maximum parsimony evolutionary tree (or trees) is contained in the minimum spanning network. If the network constructed at δ_1 is not connected, the next recursive step adds links between all the haplotypes that are δ_2 distance apart and so forth with δ_3 to δ_k until a single connected network is obtained. Minimum spanning networks are simple to compute and are amenable to phylogeographic inference when haplotype frequency and geographic data are mapped on them (Excoffier & Smouse 1994). However, they may not contain the most parsimonious pathway for the evolutionary relationship between the sample haplotypes unless one assumes that ancestral and intermediate haplotypes are present in the sample. The aim of the other three network-based methods is to ensure this by generating additional inferred haplotypes that reduce tree length.

The construction of median and reduced median networks requires sequence variation to be coded in binary; fortunately, most variable sites in intraspecific sequences exhibit only two character states which facilitates this. Again, consider the case of aligned haplotypes with k, two-state variable sites. In total, there are 2^k possible haplotypes (binary vectors) of length k and these can be connected in a single-step network to form a k-dimensional hypercube. In a sample study, however, only n of these distinct haplotypes are present. The median network obtains a single network of these haplotypes using the consensus intermediate haplotypes. For a limited number of haplotypes, the method is straightforward. It is a representation of the probable evolutionary paths (mutation events) that led to the observed variation among the sample haplotypes. It invariably contains all the most parsimonious trees which a standard parsimony tree would identify.

However, representation of the evolutionary relationships between haplotypes using median networks is only practical if a few haplotypes are involved. Even for haplotypes as few as six, extensive homoplasy makes representation using median networks impractical (Bandelt *et al.* 1995). Reticulation can be resolved by exploiting additional information in the sequence data, such as the frequency distribution of the haplotypes and the base composition of the sequence. Bandelt *et al.* (1995) used both as weighting factors to produce the reduced median networks.

Bandelt *et al.* (1999) proposed yet another network based representation of the evolutionary pathways between haplotypes; the median-joining network. This is a derivative of the previous methods but overcomes the limitations of the median and reduced median networks in that it can handle multistate variation and large data sets. As in the case of the minimum spanning network, haplotypes are linked sequentially according to their distance, δ, into a single network. Where the minimum spanning network contains connections where δ_i is greater than 1, the resulting network generally does not include the most parsimonious tree. The median-joining procedure generates additional inferred haplotypes in order to reduce tree length. The algorithm is described in Bandelt *et al.* (1999) and differs from their previous methods primarily in that it can handle multistate character variation and large data sets. An example of such a median-joining network is presented for the western clade of the European hedgehog (Figure 13.4c); it is quite similar to the NCA network using Templeton's (1998) analysis (Figure 13.4a) (Seddon *et al.* 2001).

The approaches using haplotype networks, particularly those which ensure that the maximum parsimony tree is represented, provide several advantages over conventional phylogenetic trees. Bandelt *et al.* (1999) argue that such networks can predict haplotypes not in the sample, pinpoint the location of homoplasy, frequent mutations and recombination. Phylogeographic inference, however, not only requires an optimal representation of haplotype genealogy but also benefits from the systematic use of the spatial and frequency distribution of the sampled sequences. The network-based methods do not yet address these.

Simulation — genetic and demographic

Powerful desktop computers have opened up the possibility of testing phylogeographic hypotheses using stochastic simulations. Simulating the evolution of DNA sequences under a specified model of nucleotide substitution (e.g. Rambaut & Grassly 1997) coupled with spatially explicit representation of demographic history (e.g. Ibrahim *et al.* 1996, 2000; Ibrahim 2000) is proving to be a useful exploratory tool. We have used a similar approach to gain insight into the stock structure and demographic history of Northern Atlantic fisheries.

Patterns of postglacial colonization

The two species used to illuminate phylogeographic analysis, the grasshopper and the hedgehog, show very different patterns of genomic variation and subdivision across Europe. This means that their ice-age refugia and colonization routes were different. Along with other present-day species in temperate regions, they were reduced to southern refugia in the peninsulas of Iberia, Italy and the Balkans, and around the Black Sea. The genetic differences among the populations from these places indicate separation and divergence over several ice ages, in *C. parallelus* for approximately 400 ka and for *E. europeus* for approximately 2 Ma. This is an indication of when the peninsulas were last colonized by these species. Since then they have survived there through many climatic oscillations, of which major ones have exterminated the species to the north, the most recent being the last glacial maximum (Hewitt 1999). A third pattern has been found in the brown bear *Ursus arctos* (Taberlet & Bouvet 1994; Taberlet *et al.* 1998), which colonized the west of Europe from Iberia and the east from the Balkans or further east. These expansion routes met in

Grasshopper   Hedgehog   Bear

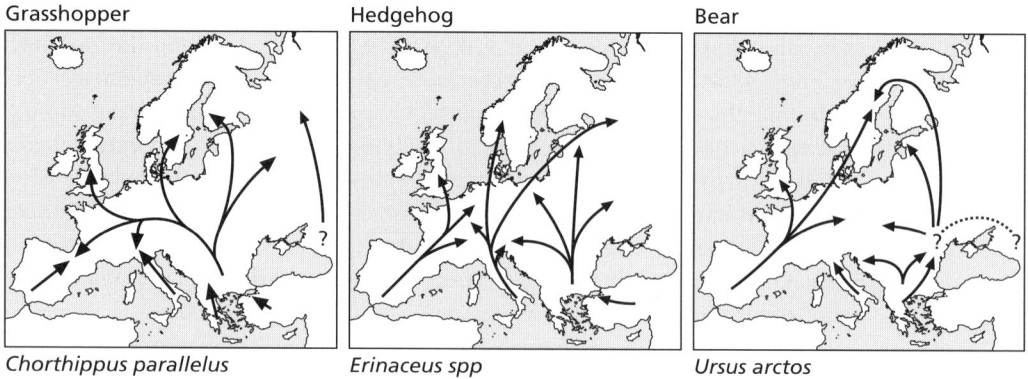

Chorthippus parallelus   *Erinaceus spp*   *Ursus arctos*

Figure 13.5 Paradigm postglacial colonization patterns in the grasshopper, hedgehog and bear. Arrows indicate the proposed spread of distinct refugial genomes with warming climate after the last glacial maximum, with contacts producing hybrid zones (Hewitt 1999)

the centre of Europe and finally in central Scandinavia, where the last of the ice sheet melted some 9 ka (Figure 13.5).

Phylogeographies for several other European species are now available and most resemble one of these three paradigm refugial-colonization patterns (Hewitt 1999). Thus, a number of species including the alder, crested newt and beech follow the grasshopper pattern, and from subspecific taxonomy this seems to be the most common one. This is probably because the Alps and Pyrenees acted as barriers and slowed expansion, and the eastern parts also warmed more quickly allowing rapid Balkan expansion. The second most common pattern is that of the bear, and a number of other mammalian species similarly have eastern and western genomes meeting in central Scandinavia (Jaarola *et al.* 1999). The hedgehog pattern, with divergent genomes colonizing northward in strips from Iberia, Italy and the Balkans, is similar to oaks and firs and is the least common so far (see Chapter 14 for detailed colonization by oaks). It would seem that the Alps were a greater hindrance to colonization than the Pyrenees, and when a species finally crossed them it found the northern side already occupied by a Balkan or Iberian genome expansion, which blocked its progress. There are many hybrid zones in the Alps and central Europe, which were put in place by such postglacial colonization and contact of diverged genomes (Hewitt 1999).

New molecular phylogeographies are emerging all the time, and variant geographic patterns may well be discovered. Thus, for European freshwater fish, such as the chubb and perch, major river systems like the Danube would seem to dominate the colonization pattern (Durand *et al.* 1999a; Nesbo *et al.* 1999).

While the major features of the postglacial colonization of Europe can be deduced from a continuation of palaeontological and genetical analyses, in temperate regions the genetic signal of earlier times has been largely extinguished in the north by the ice ages. It has become fainter in the south, but topography and climate have allowed several lineages to survive in these regions. NCA allows us to look for significant major fragmentation and colonization events from such data, and this has been applied in southern Europe to Greek chubb (Durand *et al.* 1999b) and Spanish leaf beetles (Gomez-Zurita *et al.* 2000). As well as recent colonizations, it identifies older fragmentations and allows the deduction of previous Pleistocene range changes. A number of species phylogeographies for North America have been analysed using NCA, particularly those emanating from the south-east refugial areas. Such analysis discerns known northward postglacial expansions clearly from the genetic data in fish, grasshoppers, mice and salamanders, and indicates earlier range fragmentation and colonization (Templeton 1998).

Phylogeography around the world

Phylogeography is a modern discipline and most studies have been conducted in North American and European species (Avise 2000). This is advantageous in that the patterns of postglacial colonization in these northern regions are simpler than those nearer the equator. Furthermore, the refugial and postglacial colonization patterns would seem to differ among major regions of North America (Hewitt 2000). Thus, the northern part of the continent was largely colonized by species surviving south of the ice sheets, and these commonly show the southern richness to northern purity in genetic diversity that such rapid expansion produces (Hewitt 1996; Bernatchez & Wilson 1998). Considerable phylogenetic data is now accumulating for true arctic species, whose ranges were particularly affected by the ice sheets and extensive tundra through the ice ages (Hewitt 2000). Of particular note is the genetic evidence for a Beringian ice age refugium for a number of species that have since colonized across boreal North America. For example these include fishes (Bernatchez & Wilson 1998), beetles (Reiss *et al.* 1999), collared lemming (Ehrich *et al.* 2000), brown bears (Leonard *et al.* 2000) and *Dryas integrifolia* (Tremblay & Schoen 1999), that classic Arctic genus! Distinct refugia colonized different areas, as is clearly demonstrated by the plants and animals expanding from southerly refugia up the Pacific North West of the continent (Soltis *et al.* 1997; Conroy & Cook 2000) (see also Chapter 15 for phylogeography of the Pacific North-West).

The first phylogeographies, and more since, were produced for the south-east USA, particularly marine, coastal and freshwater species (Avise 1994). These refugial areas have relatively complex genomic subdivision produced over several ice ages, with northward postglacial expansions leaving a genetic signal detectable by NCA (Templeton 1998). Many of the species from this region show phylogeographic concordance, which argues for shared colonization patterns (Walker & Avise 1998; Weisrock & Janzen 2000). Such commonality would be the product of common refugia and rapid climatic amelioration promoting a stampede into new territory. The south-west USA with its mountains and deserts is dissected and diverse, and was so through climatic oscillations. This would produce complex shifts of habitat, and this is reflected in the extent of genome subdivision and divergence in a number of species (Zink 1996; Orange *et al.* 1999).

However, the tropics contain most species biodiversity, and the few studies we have suggest that their subspecific genetic richness is enormous. Intraspecific phylogenies have been produced for the tropics of Africa, Amazonia, Australia, South-East Asia and Central America (Hewitt 2000). While each species phylogeny is individual, most show deeply divergent DNA lineages that indicate the survival of many populations from before the Pleistocene. These phylogeographies are often complex, suggesting repeated range changes accumulating divergent population genomes over time. It is difficult with present data to determine particular refugia and colonization routes in the tropics, but with convenient geography and a combination of palaeobotany and phylogenetics it is possible. This has been demonstrated in the wet forests of north-east Australia. Here, phylogeographies of birds, frogs and reptiles show concordant deep divergences and bottleneck signatures of low diversity, and from them possible colonization routes have been postulated (Schneider *et al.* 1998).

Conclusions

The combination of palaeontology, particularly the pollen networks of Europe and North America, and modern genetics means that it is possible now to deduce the broad pattern of postglacial colonization from refugia in many species in these higher latitudes. The genetic data that comes from the application of PCR-based techniques is providing fine intraspecific detail of allelic distribution, and suitable analyses of their spatial and phylogenetic content are becoming available. With the deduction of ice-age refugia for the component genomes of a number of species, several colonization patterns are emerging, with main refugia contributing differently to expansion.

In Europe and North America there is much genetic diversity in the southern refugial areas, which from DNA divergence measures has apparently accumulated over several ice-age cycles, and suggests a process of speciation (Hewitt 1989). In contrast to this 'southern richness', populations of many species in the north frequently show lower genetic diversity—'northern purity', probably as a result of rapid colonization (Hewitt 1996, 1999). This distribution has important implications for conservation theory and practice.

Interestingly, northern places have been colonized by species emanating from different refugia, hence they would seem to have had little time to become closely coadapted, and they may well have had different colonization patterns, producing different mixtures in previous interstadia. One task for the immediate future is to better understand the effects of earlier climatic oscillations, and for this more long pollen cores and deep species phylogeographies are needed, extending palaeogenetic analysis back into previous ice ages. Whilst phylogenetics and NCA probe previous ice ages, more recent events in the Holocene and Neolithic times are also naturally fascinating. Disentangling the genetic contributions of ancient and modern events is a difficult, but exciting challenge.

As more phylogeographies are produced, it may be possible to discern particular temperospatial patterns correlated with certain attributes of species, like dispersal, reproduction or survival capabilities. For example, are herbs different from trees in some aspects of their phylogeography? Are annuals different from perennials? Are flightless beetles different from flighted species? And so forth. It will be necessary to make such comparisons within a biogeographic region, e.g. Europe, south-east USA, north-west North America, because current evidence suggests congruence of response at such a scale. Furthermore, different patterns of genetic spatial structure and inferred colonizations are suggested in emerging data from the arctic, desert and tropical regions (Hewitt 2000). The tropics are of course particularly important, as they contain so much biodiversity. This needs to be measured at the intraspecific level; the understanding of its genetic basis and structure is a priority.

Summary

Recent advances in climatology are restructuring our thinking on the environment over the last few million years, coupled with technological innovations in molecular genetics, promise real common ground for the integration of the orthogonal disciplines of ecology and genetics.

The severe climatic oscillations of the Quaternary produced great changes in species distributions, as seen in the fossil record, and these occurred repeatedly. Such events had genetic consequences, particularly those produced by colonization, shrinkage and fragmentation, and altitudinal shifts in range, which would tend to homogenize, reduce, subdivide or retain genetic diversity.

Intraspecific phylogenies for particular DNA sequences can be used to make inferences about the history of a species, particularly when placed in the spatial context of past and present ranges of the species. New methods such as DNA distance phenograms, sequence mismatch comparisons, nested clade analysis and spanning haplotype networks are available, which assist this inference. The interpretation of these phylogenies becomes much stronger when combined with knowledge of present species substructure and hybrid zones, and relevant palaeoclimatic, fossil and geographic information.

These approaches have been applied to a number of European species with adequate DNA data sets to deduce from which ice age refugia particular genomes emerged to cover their present distribution. These provide novel insights into species colonization, and unexpected genetic subdivision and mixture of species. Three paradigm patterns are evident and these may be related to other European species distributions to assess their generality.

Comparable data sets and analyses are becoming available in other parts of the world, and several similarities in genome diversity and structure are apparent. These studies have implications for current biodiversity and community structure, and also contribute to understanding the processes and rates of speciation over the Pleistocene.

References

Adkins, J.F., Boyle, E.A., Keigwin, L. & Cortijo, E. (1997). Variability of the North Atlantic thermohaline circulation during the last interglacial period. *Nature*, **390**, 154–156.

Alley, R.B. (1998). Icing the North Atlantic. *Nature*, **392**, 335–337.

Alley, R.B. (2000). Ice core evidence of abrupt climatic changes. *Proceedings of the National Academy of Sciences of the USA*, **97**, 1331–1334.

Angers, B. & Bernatchez, L. (1998). Combined use of SMM and non-SMM methods to infer fine structure and evolutionary history of closely related brook charr (*Salvelinus fontinalis*, Salmonidae) populations from microsatellites. *Molecular Biology and Evolution*, **15**, 143–159.

Armbruster, P., Bradshaw, W. & Holzapfel, C. (1998). Effects of postglacial range expansion on allozyme and quantitative genetic variation of the pitcher-plant mosquito *Wyeomyia smithii*. *Evolution*, **52**, 1697–1704.

Ashworth, A.C., Buckland, P.C. & Sadler, J.P., eds (1997). *Studies in Quaternary Entomology*. John Wiley & Sons, Chichester.

Avise, J.C. (1994). *Molecular Markers, Natural History and Evolution*. Chapman & Hall, New York.

Avise, J.C. (2000). *Phylogeography: the History and Formation of Species*. Harvard University Press, Cambridge, MA.

Avise, J.C., Arnold, J., Ball, R.M., Bermingham, E., Lamb, T., Neigel, J.E., Reeb, C.A. & Saunders, N.C. (1987). Intraspecific phylogeography: The mitochondrial DNA bridge between population genetics and systematics. *Annual Review of Ecology and Systematics*, **18**, 489–522.

Bandelt, H.-J., Forster, P., Sykes, B.C. & Richards, M.B. (1995). Mitochondrial portraits of human populations using median networks. *Genetics*, **141**, 743–753.

Bandelt, H.-J., Forster, P. & Rohl, A. (1999). Median-joining networks for inferring intraspecific phylogenies. *Molecular Biology and Evolution*, **16**, 37–48.

Beaulieu, J.D. & Reille, M. (1992). The last climatic cycle at La Grande Pile (Vosges, France): A new pollen profile. *Quaternary Science Reviews*, **11**, 431–438.

Behl, R. & Kennett, J. (1996). Brief interstadial events in the Santa Barbara basin, NE Pacific, during the past 60 kyr. *Nature*, **379**, 243–246.

Bennett, K. (1997). *Evolution and Ecology: The Pace of Life*. Cambridge University Press, Cambridge, UK.

Bernatchez, L. & Wilson, C. (1998). Comparative phylogeography of nearctic and palearctic fishes. *Molecular Ecology*, **7**, 431–452.

Berry R., Crawford T. & Hewitt, G. (eds) (1991) *Genes in Ecology*. Blackwell Scientific Publications, Oxford, UK.

Birks, H.H. & Ammann, B. (2000). Two terrestrial records of rapid climatic change during the glacial-Holocene transition (14 000–9000 calendar years B.P.) from Europe. *Proceedings of the National Academy of Sciences of the USA*, **97**, 1390–1394.

Carson, H.L. & Wisotzkey, R.G. (1989). Increase in genetic variance following a population bottleneck. *American Naturalist*, **134**, 668–673.

Cliff, A.D. & Ord, J.K. (1973). *Spatial Autocorrelations*. Pion Press, London.

Colinvaux, P. (1997). An arid Amazon? *Trends in Ecology and Evolution* **12**, 318–319.

Conroy, C.J. & Cook, J.A. (2000). Phylogeography of a post-glacial colonizer: *Microtus longicaudus* (Rodentia: Muridae). *Molecular Ecology*, **9**, 165–175.

Coope, G.R. (1977). Fossil coleopteran assemblages as sentitive indicators of climate change during the Devension (last) cold stage. *Philosophical Transactions of the Royal Society, London B*, **280**, 313–340.

Coope, G.R. (1990). The invasion of Northern Europe during the Pleistocene by Mediterranean species of Coleoptera. In: *Biological Invasions in Europe and the Mediterranean Basin* (eds F. di Castri, A. Hansen & M. De Bussche), pp. 203–215. Kluwer, Dordrecht.

Coope, G.R., Lemdahl, G., Lowe, J.J. & Walkling, A. (1998). Temperature gradients in northern Europe during the last glacial-Holocene transition (14-9 C^{14} kyr BP) interpreted from coleopteran assemblages. *Journal of Quaternary Science*, **13**, 419–433.

Cooper, S.J.B., Ibrahim, K.M. & Hewitt, G.M. (1995). Postglacial expansion and genome subdivision in the European grasshopper *Chorthippus parallelus*. *Molecular Ecology*, **4**, 49–60.

Dansgaard, W., Johnsen, S., Clausen, H., Dahl-Jensen, D., Gundestrup, N., Hammer, G.,

Hvidberg, C., Steffensen, J., Sveinbjornsdottir, A., Jouzel, J. & Bond, G. (1993). Evidence for general instability of past climate from a 250-kyr ice-core record. *Nature*, **364**, 218–220.

Duplessy, J.-C. (1999). Climate and the Gulf Stream. *Nature*, **402**, 593–594.

Durand, J.D., Persat, H. & Bouvet, Y. (1999a). Phylogeography and postglacial dispersion of the chub (*Leuciscus cephalus*) in Europe. *Molecular Ecology*, **8**, 989–997.

Durand, J.D., Templeton, A.R., Guinand, B., Imsiridou, A. & Bouvet, Y. (1999b). Nested Clade and phylogeographic analyses of the chub, *Leuciscus cephalus* (Teleostei, Cyprinidae), in Greece: Implications for Balkan Peninsula Biogeography. *Molecular Phylogenetics and Evolution*, **13**, 566–580.

Ehrich, D., Federov, V.B., Stenseth, N.C., Krebs, C.J. & Kenney, A. (2000). Phylogeography and mitochondrial DNA (mtDNA) diversity in North American collared lemmings (*Dicrostonyx groenlandicus*). *Molecular Ecology*, **9**, 329–337.

Excoffier, L. & Smouse, P.E. (1994). Using allele frequency and geographic subdivision to reconstruct gene trees within a species: molecular variance parsimony. *Genetics*, **136**, 343–359.

Flenley, J.R. (1998). Tropical forests under the climates of the last 30 000 years. *Climatic Change*, **39**, 177–197.

Frenzel, B., Pecsi, M. & Velichko, A. (1992). *Atlas of Paleoclimates and Paleoenvironments of the Northern Hemisphere. Late Pleistocene–Holocene.* Hungarian Academy of Sciences, Gustav Fischer Verlag, Budapest. Stuttgard.

Goldstein, D.B. & Schlotterer, C., eds (1999). *Microsatellites: Evolution and Applications.* Oxford University Press, Oxford.

Gomez-Zurita, J., Petitpierre, E. & Juan, C. (2000). Nested cladistic analysis, phylogeography and speciation in the *Timarcha goettingensis* complex (Coleoptera, Chrysomelidae). *Molecular Ecology*, **9**, 557–570.

Gray, A. (1997). Climate change and the reproductive biology of higher plants. In: *Past and Future Rapid Environmental Changes* (ed. B. Huntley), pp. 371–380. Springer-Verlag, Berlin.

Guiot, J., Pons, A., Beaulieu, J.D. & Reille, M. (1989). A 140 000 year continental climate reconstruction from two European pollen records. *Nature*, **338**, 309–313.

Harpending, H.C., Sherry, S.T., Rogers, A.R. & Stoneking, M. (1993). The genetic structure of ancient human populations. *Current Anthropology*, **34**, 483–496.

Harpending, H.C., Batzer, M.A., Gurven, M., Jorde, L.B., Rogers, A.R. & Sherry, S.T. (1998). Genetic traces of ancient demography. *Proceedings of the National Academy of Sciences of the USA*, **95**, 1961–1967.

Hays, J., Imbrie, J. & Shackleton, N. (1976). Variations in the Earth's orbit: pacemaker of the ice ages. *Science*, **194**, 1121–1132.

Hewitt, G.M. (1989). The subdivision of species by hybrid zones. In: *Speciation and its Consequences* (eds D. Otte & J. Endler), pp. 85–110. Sinauer Associates, Sunderland, MA.

Hewitt, G.M. (1993). Postglacial distribution and species substructure: lessons from pollen, insects and hybrid zones. In: *Evolutionary Patterns and Processes* (eds D.R. Lees & D. Edwards), pp. 97–123. Academic Press, London.

Hewitt, G.M. (1996). Some genetic consequences of ice ages, and their role in divergence and speciation. *Biological Journal of the Linnean Society*, **58**, 247–276.

Hewitt, G.M. (1999). Post-glacial recolonization of European Biota. *Biological Journal of the Linnean Society*, **68**, 87–112.

Hewitt, G.M. (2000). The genetic legacy of the Quaternary ice ages. *Nature*, **405**, 907–913.

Hewitt, G.M. (2001). Speciation, hybrid zones and phylogeography — or seeing genes in space and time. *Molecular Ecology*, **10**, 537–549.

Hillis, D., Moritz, C. & Mable, B., eds (1996). *Molecular Systematics*. Sinauer Associates, Sunderland, MA.

Hudson, R.R., Boos, D.D. & Kaplan, N.L. (1992). A statistical test for detecting geographic subdivision. *Molecular Biology and Evolution*, **9**, 138–151.

Hughen, K., Overpeck, J., Peterson, L. & Trumbore, S. (1996). Rapid climate changes in the tropical Atlantic region during the last deglaciation. *Nature*, **380**, 51–54.

Huntley, B. (1988). Glacial and Holocene vegetation history: Europe. In: *Vegetation History* (eds B. Huntley & T. Webb), pp. 341–383. Kluwer, Dordrecht.

Huntley, B. (1990). European vegetation history: palaeovegetation maps from pollen data —

1300 yr BP to present. *Journal of Quaternary Science*, **5**, 103–122.

Huntley, B. & Birks, H.J.B. (1983). *An Atlas of Past and Present Pollen Maps for Europe.* Cambridge University Press, Cambridge, UK.

Ibrahim, K.M. (2000). Plague dynamics and population genetics of the desert locust: can turnover during recession maintain population genetic structure? *Molecular Ecology*, **10**, 581–591.

Ibrahim, K.M., Nichols, R.A. & Hewitt, G.M. (1996). Spatial patterns of genetic variation generated by different forms of dispersal during range expansion. *Heredity*, **77**, 282–291.

Ibrahim, K.M., Sourrouille, P. & Hewitt, G.M. (2000). Are recession populations of the desert locust (*Schistocerca gregaria*) remnants of past swarms? *Molecular Ecology*, **9**, 783–792.

Jaarola, M., Tegelstrom, H. & Fredga, K. (1999). Colonization history in Fenno scandian rodents. *Biological Journal of the Linnean Society*, **68**, 113–127.

Jouzel, J. (1999). Calibrating the Isotopic Paleothermometer. *Science*, **286**, 910–911.

Leonard, J.A., Wayne, R.K. & Cooper, A. (2000). Population genetics of Ice Age brown bears. *Proceedings of the National Academy of Sciences of the USA*, **97**, 1651–1654.

Levesque, A.J., Cwynar, L.C. & Walker, I.R. (1997). Exceptionally steep north-south gradients in lake temperatures during the last deglaciation. *Nature*, **385**, 423–426.

Lynch, M. & Crease, T.J. (1990). The analysis of population survey data on DNA sequence variation. *Molecular Biology and Evolution*, **7**, 377–394.

Manly, B.F.J. (1985). *The Statistics of Natural Selection.* Chapman & Hall, London.

Manly, B.F.J. (1997). *Randomization, Bootstrap and Monte Carlo Methods in Biology.* Chapman & Hall, London.

Maskas, S.D. & Cruzan, M.B. (2000). Patterns of intraspecific diversification in the *Piriqueta caroliniana* complex in southeastern North America and the Bahamas. *Evolution*, **54**, 815–827.

Meffert, L.M. & Bryant, E.H. (1992). Divergent ambulatory and grooming behaviour in serially bottlenecked lines of the housefly. *Evolution*, **46**, 1399–1407.

Mueller, U.G. & Wolfenbarger, L.L. (1999). AFLP genotyping and fingerprinting. *Trends in Ecology and Evolution*, **14**, 389–394.

Nei, M. (1982). The evolution of human races at the gene level. In: *Human Genetics, part A: The unfolding genome* (eds B. Bonne-Tamir, T. Cohen & R.M. Goodman), pp. 167–181. Alan R. Liss, New York.

Nesbo, C.L., Fossheim, T., Vollestad, L.A. & Jakobsen, K.S. (1999). Genetic divergence and phylogeographic relationships among European perch (*Perca fluviatilis*) populations reflect glacial refugia and postglacial colonization. *Molecular Ecology*, **8**, 1387–1404.

Nichols, R.A. & Hewitt, G.M. (1994). The genetic consequences of long distance dispersal during colonization. *Heredity*, **72**, 312–317.

Orange, D.I., Riddle, B.R. & Nickle, D.C. (1999). Phylogeography of a wide ranging desert lizard, *Gambelia wislizenii* (Crotaphytidae). *Copeia*, **1999**, 267–273.

Orti, G., Hare, M.P. & Avise, J.C. (1997). Detection and isolation of nuclear haplotypes by PCR-SSCP. *Molecular Ecology*, **6**, 575–580.

Palacios, C., Kresovich, S. & Gonzalez-Candelas, F. (1999). A population genetic study of the endangered plant species *Limonium dufourii* (Plumbaginaceae) based on amplified fragment length polymorphism (AFLP). *Molecular Ecology*, **8**, 645–657.

Peteet, D. (2000). Sensitivity and rapidity of vegetational response to abrupt climate change. *Proceedings of the National Academy of Sciences of the USA*, **97**, 1359–1361.

Rambaut, A. & Grassly, N.C. (1997). Seq-Gen: an application for the Monte Carlo simulation of DNA sequence evolution along phylogenetic tress. *Computer and Applied Biosciences*, **13**, 235–238.

Reille, M., Andrieu, V., De Beaulieu, J.-L., Guenet, P. & Goery, C. (1998). A long pollen record from Lac du Bouchet, Massif Central, France: for the period ca.325 to 100 ka BP (OIS 9c to OIS 5e). *Quaternary Science Reviews*, **17**, 1107–1123.

Reiss, R., Ashworth, A. & Schwert, D. (1999). Molecular genetic evidence for the post-Pleistocene divergence of populations of the arctic-alpine ground beetle *Amara alpina* (Paykull) (Coleoptera:Carabidae). *Journal of Biogeography*, **26**, 785–794.

Rogers, A.R. (1995). Genetic evidence for a Pleistocene population explosion. *Evolution*, **49**, 608–615.

Santucci, F., Emerson, B.C. & Hewitt, G.M. (1998). Mitochondrial DNA phylogeography of European hedgehogs. *Molecular Ecology*, **7**, 1163–1172.

Schneider, C., Cunningham, M. & Moritz, C. (1998). Comparative phylogeography and the history of endemic vertebrates in the Wet Tropics rainforests of Australia. *Molecular Ecology*, **7**, 487–498.

Schulz, A., von Rad, V. & Erlenkeuser, H. (1998). Correlation between Arabian Sea and Greenland climatic oscillations of the past 110 000 years. *Nature*, **393**, 54–57.

Seddon, J.M., Reeve, N.J., Santucci, F. & Hewitt, G.M. (2001). Phylogeography and colonization routes of European hedgehogs, *Erinaceus europaeus* and *E. concolor*. *Molecular Ecology*. In press.

Sokal, R.R. & Oden, N.L. (1978a). Spatial autocorrelation in biology: 1. Methodology. *Biological Journal of the Linnean Society*, **10**, 199–228.

Sokal, R.R. & Oden, N.L. (1978b). Spatial autocorrelation in biology: 2. Some biological implications and four applications of evolutionary and ecological interest. *Biological Journal of the Linnean Society*, **10**, 229–249.

Soltis, D., Gitzendanner, M., Strenge, D. & Soltis, P. (1997). Chloroplast DNA intraspecific phylogeography of plants from the Pacific Northwest of North America. *Plant Systematics and Evolution*, **206**, 353–373.

Stauffer, B. (1999). Cornucopia of ice core results. *Nature*, **399**, 412–413.

Taberlet, P. & Bouvet, J. (1994). Mitochondrial DNA polymorphism, phylogeography, and conservation genetics of the brown bear (*Ursus arctos*) in Europe. *Proceedings of the Royal Society of London B*, **255**, 195–200.

Taberlet, P., Fumagalli, L., Wust-Saucy, A.-G. & Cossons, J.-F. (1998). Comparative phylogeography and postglacial colonization routes in Europe. *Molecular Ecology*, **7**, 453–464.

Templeton, A.R. (1993). The "Eve" hypothesis: a genetic critique and reanalysis. *American Anthropology*, **95**, 51–72.

Templeton, A. (1998). Nested clade analyses of phylogeographic data and testing hypotheses about gene flow and population history. *Molecular Ecology*, **7**, 381–397.

Templeton, A.R. & Singh, C.F. (1993). A Cladistic analysis of phenotypic associations with haplotypes inferred from restriction endonuclease mapping. IV. Nested analysis with cladogram uncertainty and recombination. *Genetics*, **134**, 659–669.

Templeton, A.R., Boerwinkle, E. & Sing, C.F. (1987). A cladistic analysis of phenotypic associations with haplotypes inferred from restriction endonuclease mapping. I. Basic theory and an analysis of alcohol dehydrogenase activity in *Drosophila*. *Genetics*, **117**, 343–351.

Templeton, A.R., Routman, E. & Phillips, C.A. (1995). Separating population structure from population history: A cladistic analysis of the geographical distribution of mitochondrial DNA haplotypes in the tiger salamander, *Ambystoma tigrinum*. *Genetics*, **140**, 767–782.

Tremblay, N.O. & Schoen, J. (1999). Molecular phylogeography of *Dryas integrifolia*: glacial refugia and postglacial recolonization. *Molecular Ecology*, **8**, 1187–1198.

Tzedakis, P. (1994). Vegetation change through glacial-interglacial cycles: a long pollen perspective. *Philosophical Transactions of the Royal Society of London B*, **345**, 403–432.

van Oppen, M.J.H., Rico, C., Turner, G.F. & Hewitt, G.M. (2000). Extensive homoplasy, nonstepwise mutations, and shared ancestral polymorphism in a complex microsatellite locus in Lake Malawi cichlids. *Molecular Biology and Evolution*, **17**, 489–498.

Wade, M. & Goodnight, C. (1998). The theories of Fisher and Wright in the context of metapopulations: when nature does many small experiments. *Evolution*, **52**, 1537–1553.

Walker, D. & Avise, J.C. (1998). Principles of phylogeography as illustrated by freshwater and terrestrial turtles in the southeastern United States. *Annual Review of Ecology and Systematics*, **29**, 23–58.

Weisrock, D.W. & Janzen, F.J. (2000). Comparative molecular phylogeography of North American softshell turtles (*Apalone*): implications for regional and wide-scale historical evolutionary forces. *Molecular Phylogenetics and Evolution*, **14**, 152–164.

Williams, D., Dunkerley, D., DeDecker, P., Kershaw,

P. & Chappell, M. (1998). *Quaternary Environments*. Arnold, London.

Wright, S. (1978). *Evolution and the Genetics of Populations, Vol 4: Variability within and among natural populations*. University of Chicago Press, Chicago, IL.

Zink, R.M. (1996). Comparative phylogeography in North American birds. *Evolution*, **50**, 308–317.

Chapter 14

From spatial patterns of genetic diversity to postglacial migration processes in forest trees

R. J. Petit,* R. Bialozyt,† S. Brewer,‡,§ R. Cheddadi,‡,§ and B. Comps¶

Introduction

Much of population genetics in the past has been developed without an appropriate historical perspective. This may seem surprising, as the emergence of Darwinism in the 19th century marked a transition to a view of organisms as ultimately accidental and historically contingent. But, in the biological sciences, the search for 'ahistorical' laws remains strong (e.g. Kauffman 1993). According to Gould (1994), the 'pure extrapolationism of Darwin's uniformitarian perspective' (his emphasis on small causes producing unlimitedly large effects because of the immensity of time) has relegated historically bound approaches to the mere role of documenting the phenomenology of evolution, without any possibility to contribute to the development of evolutionary theory. In population genetics, for instance, 'equilibrium' models were designed to be independent of history (Fisher 1930; Wright 1931). The same could be said of the geographical context in which organisms are evolving; although generally acknowledged, it was not given any theoretical importance. Population genetics models therefore lacked a geographical perspective, as in the unstructured 'island model' (Wright 1931). If spatial relationships were to be introduced, as in the isolation by distance or stepping stone models (Wright 1943; Kimura & Weiss 1964), space remained highly uniform and isotropic and was not linked with the history of the populations.

Well into the 1980s, experimental population genetics was dominated by fundamental debates on the mechanisms of evolution that largely kept geneticists away from more pragmatic and ecologically more realistic approaches (Avise 1994). In particular, historical explanations for spatial genetic patterns were dismissed as 'story-telling', and the major question of interest was whether this genetic structure was the result of (geographically variable) selection or of random genetic drift. As a consequence, population genetics has developed largely independently from the more traditional discipline of historical biogeography, whereas many ecologists

* Institut National de la Recherche Agronomique, Station de Recherches Forestières, BP 45, F-33611 Gazinet cedex, France, † Institute of Forest Genetics, Sieker Landstrasse 2, D-22927 Grosshansdorf, Germany, ‡ IMEP, CNRS UPRES A6116, Faculté de St Jérôme, case 451, 13397 Marseille cedex 20, France, § European Pollen Database, Centre universitaire d'Arles, 13200 Arles, France and ¶ Laboratory of Ecological Genetics, University of Bordeaux I, F-33405 Talence, France.

have essentially ignored genetics. Fortunately, a better integration of geography and history in population genetics thinking is currently under way. There is a clear shift in thinking, as it is becoming clear that technological breakthroughs in the analysis of genetic variation have revolutionized our ability to examine the past (Cavalli-Sforza 1998). Furthermore, population genetics theory is being restated using an explicit historical frame (the coalescent approach, Kingman 1982), and spatial simulation models are being developed, while geostatistical methods can now be applied to analyse patterns obtained in empirical surveys. Hence, both space and time are increasingly taken into account in modern population genetic studies.

Typically, recent empirical population genetic surveys simply refer to the history of the species or the ecological setting of the fauna and flora in the region to assist the interpretation of results. We will provide an example that illustrates how available historical information can be better integrated to understand the processes that have produced observed spatial genetic patterns. The orbitally induced migrations of forest tree species will be used as paradigm (see Chapter 13 for a description of the causes of cyclic climatic changes). Our intention in this chapter is to illustrate the importance of the (longer) temporal perspective for the understanding of the spatial genetic structure of plant species and for the maintenance of genetic diversity. Simultaneously, we hope to demonstrate the usefulness of interdisciplinary approaches (specifically the combination of population genetics and palaeoecology) in ecology. The presentation relies on a few case studies, rather than on an exhaustive review of the published evidence, and is organized according to the method of investigation (chromosome, isozyme and DNA markers).

Spatial genetic patterns and history: an early example based on chromosomes

Although frequently ignored by population geneticists (at least until recently), the Quaternary epoch has long been considered important by other biologists interested in evolution, as providing a relevant spatial and temporal framework for the study of speciation: for instance, Darwin devotes 18 pages to this subject in the *Origin of Species*. In plants, one of the best-documented early example is provided in the study by Anderson (1936) of the distribution of *Iris* species in North America. In this model, the direction of evolution is known from chromosome and hybridization studies: the allopolyploid *Iris versicolor* ($2n = 108$ chromosomes), derives from the hybridization of the two progenitor species *I. virginica* ($2n = 72$) and *I. setosa* ($2n = 36$). The hybrid now occupies territories that were covered by ice during the last glacial maximum (Figure 14.1). Although the present range of *I. virginica* partly overlaps with that of the hybrid, this is not the case for *I. setosa*, which is restricted to Alaska. This led Anderson to infer that the former range of *I. setosa* must have extended further towards the south-east, in sympatry with *I. virginica*, providing the prerequisite for the formation of *I. versicolor* through hybridization. As Stebbins (1950) states, 'with some conception of the geological history and fossil flora of the

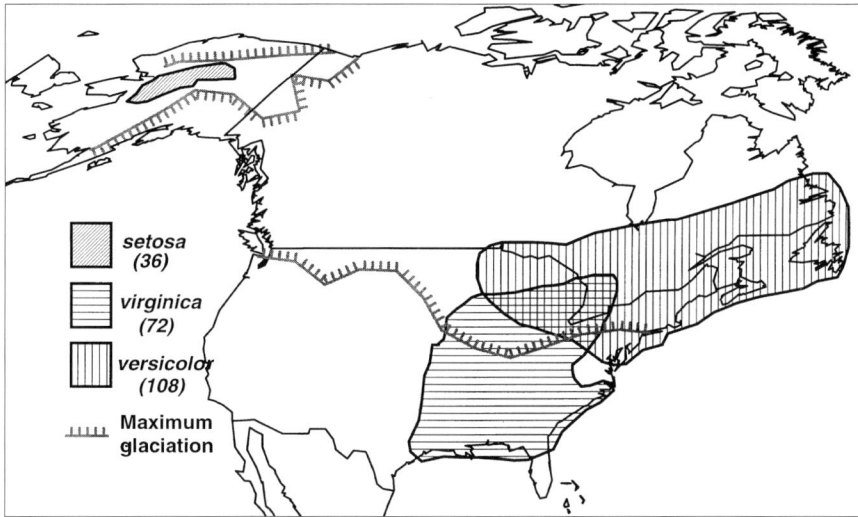

Figure 14.1 Distribution of three iris species in North America: the allopolyploid *Iris versicolor* ($2n = 108$) and its putative progenitors *I. setosa* ($2n = 36$) and *I. virginica* ($2n = 72$). The hybrid species is found mostly north of the limit of the Pleistocene glaciation. (From Stebbins 1950, after Anderson 1936.)

regions in which the species occur, significant inferences can often be made as to the time and place when these hybridizations took place, and therefore of the distribution of certain elements of the flora during past epochs of the earth's history'. For Stebbins, the chief external factor favouring the establishment of polyploidy is the availability of new ecological niches. This classical example appears now as a brilliant demonstration of the potential of 'molecular markers' (*sensu lato*: here, the simple arithmetic of chromosome counts) for the study of 'natural history'.

More recent analyses confirm that polyploidization can be a source of taxonomic and hence of ecological diversification of genera (Petit & Thompson 1999). For instance, Ellstrand and Schierenbeck (2000) have shown that invasiveness can be catalysed by hybridization events, including allopolyploidization. Despite the commonly held view that invasives should be genetically depauperate, as a consequence of the bottlenecks typically associated with colonization, their hybrid origin may actually produce the opposite pattern. First, as already shown for a number of plant species, these allopolyploidization events are often recurrent (Soltis & Soltis 2000), and hence initial diversity levels can be quite high. Second, increased ploidy will result in a mechanical increase of heterozygosity (due to polysomic inheritance).

In the next sections, we show that intraspecific genetic studies can also benefit from a detailed historical background. We focus on forest trees and discuss other mechanisms leading to the maintenance of genetic diversity during colonization.

Spatial genetic patterns and history: allozymes and changes in levels of diversity

In forest trees, several examples exist where geographic differences in levels of allozyme diversity have been attributed to postglacial history. Refugia, i.e. regions where the species has persisted throughout the last glacial maximum (Bennett *et al.* 1991), are expected to act as 'hotspots' for genetic diversity, in contrast to the lower diversity of more recently founded populations (Hewitt 1996). In principle, temperate wind-pollinated trees should constitute outstanding models for such studies. In these long-lived organisms, relatively few generations have elapsed since the outset of postglacial colonization, facilitating the reconstitution of their past dynamics. Furthermore, anemophilous trees produce abundant pollen which is well conserved in sediments, and there is now a sufficient number and coverage of palynological studies in some regions to allow the past distributions of the major tree taxa to be reconstructed (e.g. Huntley & Birks 1983). The palynological studies are, however, often limited in their taxonomic resolution, as most tree pollen can only be identified to the generic level.

Short literature overview for forest trees

Along the Pacific coast of western North America, both allelic richness (the mean number of alleles per locus in standardized sample sizes) and heterozygosity have been shown to decrease during colonization in several tree species, such as *Pinus monticola* (Steinhoff *et al.* 1983), *Pinus jeffreyi* (Furnier & Adams 1986), the coastal variety of *Pseudotsuga menziesii* (Li & Adams 1989) or *Pinus coulteri* (Ledig 2000). A model of cumulative founding events is particularly likely to apply there, due to the narrow size of the ranges of these trees in this region (see also Chapter 15). Other studies report significant decrease of allelic richness associated with little or no decrease of heterozygosity, as in *Pinus contorta* ssp. *latifolia* in western America (Cwynar & MacDonald 1987). Some authors have also reported differences in levels of diversity across the range that could be related to the size of the refugia from which the populations originated, rather than from their proximity to these refugia: this is the case for *Picea abies* and probably also for *Quercus petraea* in Europe (Lagercrantz & Ryman 1990; Zanetto & Kremer 1995). Finally, regions where colonization routes meet may be characterized by high levels of diversity due to this admixture, and care should be taken to distinguish these 'melting pots' from the primary 'hotspots' of diversity, as shown for silver fir or for the oaks in Europe (Konnert & Bergmann 1995; Petit *et al.* 2001a).

The study of Cwynar and MacDonald (1987) is noteworthy, because these authors have adopted a direct quantitative approach to the study of the genetic consequences of range expansion on genetic diversity, which illustrates the advantages of combining palaeobotanical with population genetic data. Their study relies on a previous rangewide survey using 42 isozyme loci in the lodgepole pine *Pinus contorta* (Wheeler & Guries 1982). This wind-pollinated species grows in western North America, from Baja California in the south to Yukon in the north. Palynological studies have demonstrated the northward spread of this tree, following climatic change during the Holocene, and Cwynar and MacDonald obtained direct estimates of the age of the first appearance of the species in each of 15 populations, by identifying and analysing a suitable palynological site near to each of them. The comparison showed that expected heterozygosity was not related to time of establishment, whereas allelic richness was significantly reduced during colonization, most likely as a consequence of the successive founding events that took place. Furthermore, the dispersal abilities of the trees had increased during the 12 000 years needed to cover the 2200 km up to Yukon, as demonstrated by measurements of wing loading of the seeds.

Relationship between genetic diversity and postglacial history in the European beech

The evidence

The approach of Cwynar and MacDonald (1987) cannot easily be repeated, as it requires that palynological investigations be made in the vicinity of every population studied with genetic markers. However, population ages may be estimated using data sets based on palynological records, compiled in order to map the changing distributions of the trees species over time (see, for example, Brewer *et al.* 2001, for the oaks). A geostatistical model is built using estimates of the time of arrival of the species at each palynological site; these times are inferred from the empirical limit corresponding to the start of continuous appearance of the taxon in the pollen record (Smith & Pilcher 1973). This model is then used to predict the age of each population, by a form of interpolation, called kriging, onto the coordinates of the population (Goovaerts 1997). We present here preliminary results based on this novel (and more generally applicable) approach for the European beech *Fagus sylvatica*. In this species, variation at 12 polymorphic isozyme loci has been studied, on the basis of a large sample of 389 populations distributed throughout the range (Comps *et al.* 2001). This allowed the distribution of both allelic richness and heterozygosity to be mapped with great resolution.

Maximum allelic richness is found in the south-eastern part of the range (southern Italy and the Balkans), where beech was confined during the last ice age, but heterozygosity is significantly lower in refugia than in recently colonized regions, resulting in a negative correlation between the two diversity measures (Comps *et al.* 2001) (Figure 14.2).

To simplify the analysis, populations were combined into 55 groups. An estimate of the time elapsed since colonization took place in each region was obtained as described above. The distance covered by the ancestors of the population was obtained by measuring the most likely path linking putative beech refugia with the sampled populations, on the basis of chloroplast (cp) DNA data which help to identify colonization routes (Demesure *et al.* 1996). Multiple regressions were performed between diversity indices and age, distance from refugia, latitude, longitude and altitude of each population. The strongest relationship was found between allelic richness and migration distance ($R^2 = 0.70$) (Figure 14.3). This was expected, because the number of founding events (which must be proportional to the distance

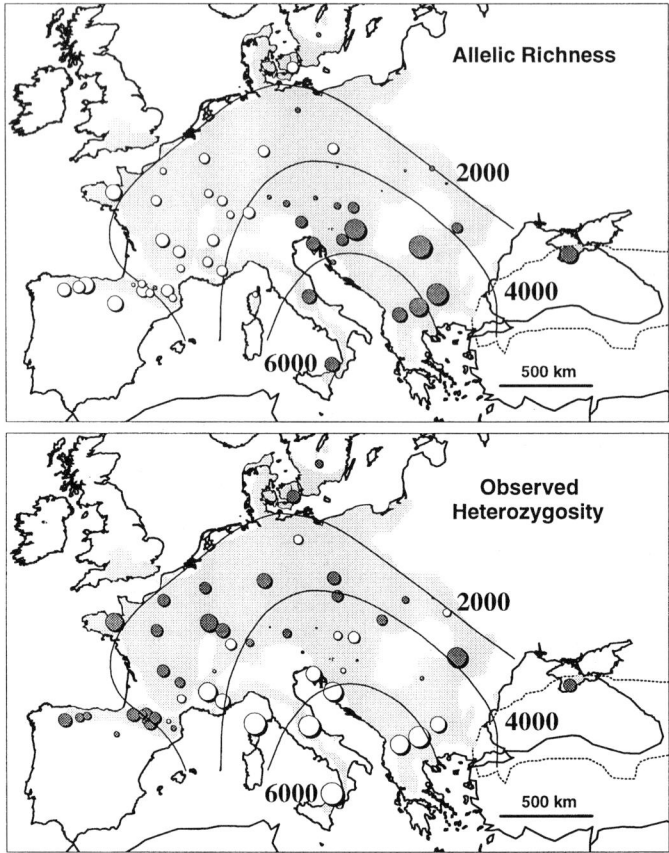

Figure 14.2 Evolution of genetic diversity in the beech *Fagus sylvatica*, in relation to the timing of its postglacial colonization. Genetic diversity was evaluated on the basis of 12 isozyme loci, using two measures: total allelic richness, based on standardized samples of 200 trees, and observed heterozygosity. Each of the 55 points corresponds to the mean of 5–9 nearby populations. Black circles correspond to values above the mean diversity, white circles to values below the mean, and the diameter of the circles are proportional to the deviation from the mean. The two maps are overlaid upon the distribution of the beech at 10 000, 6000, and 4000 years BP (contour lines) and at present (grey shading). (Modified from Comps *et al.* 2001.)

covered during migration), rather than the population age, should determine the intensity of allelic loss. On the other hand, estimated age of the population proved to be the best correlate of heterozygosity (Figure 14.4); together with altitude, population age accounts for 60% of the variation in observed heterozygosity (52% for age alone). Heterozygosity decreased when both parameters (age and altitude) increased. Finally, genetic differentiation (F_{st}) decreased with age and increased with altitude ($R^2 = 0.22$). Latitude and longitude did not further improve the predictions.

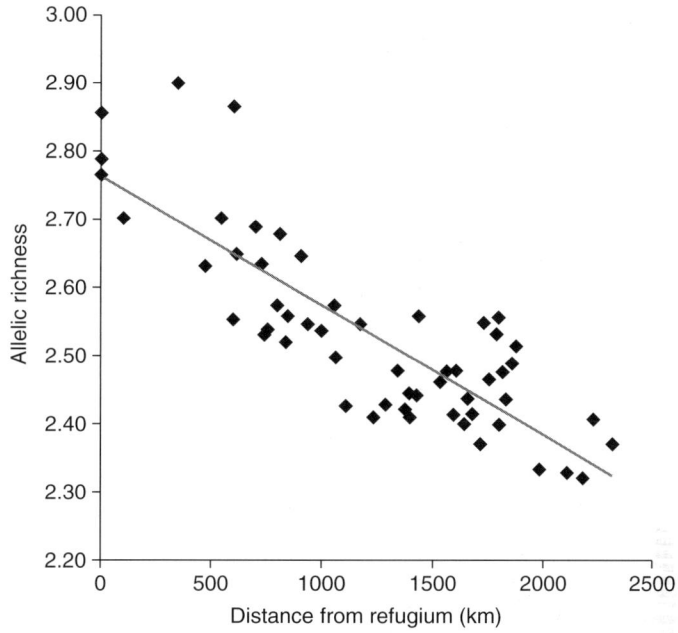

Figure 14.3 Regression curve of total allelic richness vs. the distance from nearest putative full glacial refugium for the European beech ($R^2 = 0.70$).

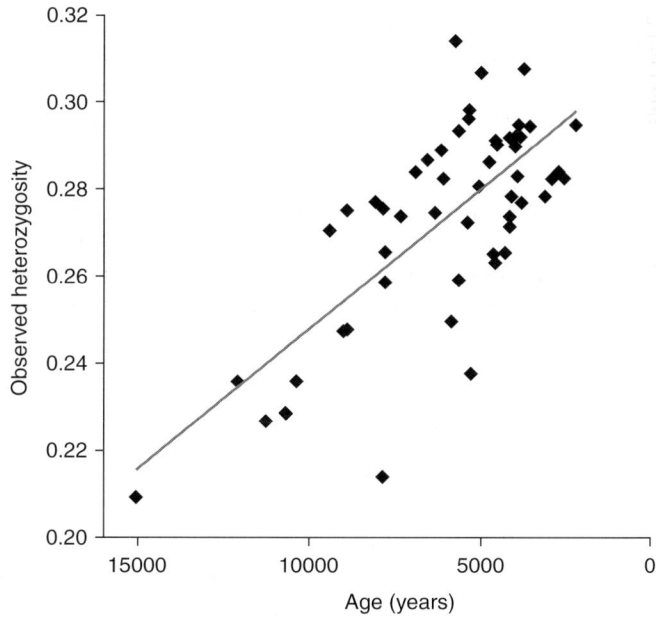

Figure 14.4 Regression curve of observed heterozygosity vs. the estimated time of beech establishment in the region ($R^2 = 0.60$).

Possible mechanisms

Some (but not all) of these results are predicted by neutral models of colonization (e.g. Austerlitz *et al.* 1997; Le Corre & Kremer 1998). Founding events will lead to increased differentiation among populations, whereas in mountains the topography will restrict gene flow and will maintain low levels of diversity at neutral loci following establishment. Nei *et al.* (1975) have shown that the loss of heterozygosity should be less pronounced than the loss of allelic richness during a founding event, especially when it is followed by rapid population growth. Comps *et al.* (2001) suggested that increased pollen flow in the open conditions prevailing during colonization should further help restore heterozygosity close to the initial value before the bottleneck (see also Haase 1993; Young *et al.* 1996). Indeed, despite their isolation, the low size and density typical of newly founded populations implies that they will operate as pollen sinks (Ellstrand & Elam 1993; Ingvarsson 1997). Brown and Marshall (1981) had pointed out that shifts in the mating system often accompanied plant colonization, not always in the 'orthodox' direction of increased selfing. The factors listed above cannot, however, account for an increase in heterozygosity beyond the values observed in the refugia. Carson (1990) has stressed that heterozygosity maintained by balancing selection is especially likely to pass through a bottleneck. Cases of positive association between heterozygosity and fitness have often been reported (e.g. Bush & Smouse 1992; David 1998). Forest trees in particular can produce massive numbers of offspring, so that the potential for differential selection during the early ontogenetic stages is particularly high. Environmental stresses seem to enhance this relationship between heterozygosity and fitness (Parsons 1996; David 1998). In the case of the European beech, Thiébaut *et al.* (1992) have described a pronounced trend of increase of observed heterozygosity with age when beech seedlings are growing under high daylight intensity, which could explain why newly established beech stands maintain more diversity than expected at some loci compared to more mature stands.

One locus (*Mdh*-3) accounted for 44% of the overall increase in heterozygosity during colonization of Europe by the beech; this locus had been shown previously to display strong overdominance in large-scale viability experiments where pollution stresses were applied to several beech seedlots (Müller-Starck 1993; see also Starke *et al.* 1996 for evidence of selection at this locus). The increase in heterozygosity during colonization seems therefore to be driven in part by differential selection at a few of the studied loci (notably through overdominance), and in part by other mechanisms such as a temporary increase in gene flow during colonization and the admixture of genetically differentiated populations; all this will limit the overall erosion of genetic diversity (especially heterozygosity) during range expansion.

Spatial genetic patterns and history: maternally inherited markers in oaks

Useful attributes of maternally inherited markers

In plants, maternally inherited markers are moved either by seeds or by vegetative means, but not by pollen. This means that they may be used to track colonization routes, as the setting in new territories necessarily involves a diploid organism. Furthermore, at least in late successional wind-pollinated trees, gene flow by seeds is likely to be much smaller than that by pollen (Petit *et al.* 1993a; Ennos 1994), and, given the high population sizes, the initial maternal genetic structure should persist thousands of years after the end of colonization (Le Corre *et al.* 1997; Le Corre & Kremer 1998). Given the high level of fixation, a few individuals will generally be sufficient to characterize a population, so that most of the sampling effort can be allocated to the recovery of the spatial structure rather than to the characterization of each population (Pons & Petit 1995). By contrast, in surveys using nuclear markers, larger sample sizes per population will be generally required. The uniparental inheritance of the organelle genomes also implies clonal evolution, a feature that considerably facilitates phylogenetic reconstruction, especially at the intraspecific level. This can ease the integration of an historical frame into population genetics (Avise 1994; Hewitt 1999; Soltis *et al.* 1991; Taberlet *et al.* 1998).

Inferences of refugia and colonization routes in oaks

In the European white oaks, a complex of partly interfertile species, cpDNA variation has been studied in great detail over more than 10 years (Kremer *et al.* 1991; Petit *et al.* 1993b, 1997; Ferris *et al.* 1993, 1998; Dumolin-Lapègue *et al.* 1997, 1998, 1999a). Recently, a consortium of 16 laboratories has joined efforts to produce detailed maps based on over 2600 populations from throughout the range (Petit *et al.* 2001a,b). Out of a total of 32 detected haplotypes, only three were restricted to the northern part of the range (above the 45°N parallel), whereas 12 were found south of this limit, despite a three times higher sampling effort in the north. The majority of the haplotypes (17) were present across this limit. Hence, except for the initial loss of some rarer types, many variants migrated without getting lost on the way.

The rapidity of range expansions in the oaks (up to 500 m yr^{-1}, Huntley & Birks 1983) and the low cpDNA mutation rates imply that no direct 'phylogenetic study' of range expansion (as outlined in Thorpe 1984) can be carried out. This does not imply an absence of phylogeographic structure: during the longer glacial episodes, new variants have appeared, which then followed colonization routes similar to that of the haplotypes from which they derived (Dumolin-Lapègue *et al.* 1997; Petit *et al.* 2001b) (Figure 14.5). However, phylogenetically *unrelated* variants located in the same refugia will also follow similar migration routes, limiting somewhat the level of phylogeographic structure (Petit *et al.* 2001b). Communications between the European peninsulas seem to have occurred during the present interglacial and probably also during previous ones, which could explain the presence of unrelated haplotypes in the same refugial areas (Dumolin-Lapègue *et al.* 1997; Petit *et al.* 2001b). Once in closer contact, further exchanges by pollen flow may have occurred between oak populations having different maternal lineages. Bennett (1997) stressed that 'the representativity of the spreading part of the species (and its subsequent genetic

Figure 14.5 Geographic distribution of some cpDNA variants in European white oaks. The distribution of six closely related haplotypes belonging to one of the major cpDNA lineages is shown. They originate from the western part of the Iberian refugium. Note the very similar distribution and the persistence of the three common types (black, grey and white) up to the northern border of the range. Small dots indicate the distribution of sampled populations characterized by haplotypes of other lineages. (From Petit *et al.* 2001b.)

history) is irrelevant for the long-term genetic history of the species, because it is all lost'. Our results question the generality of this assertion.

As shown by Huntley and Birks (1983) and confirmed by Brewer *et al.* (2001) on the basis of fossil pollen evidence, deciduous oaks were restricted to the extreme southern part of the European continent, in the three southern peninsulas (Iberian, Italian and Balkan), during the last glacial maximum, due to reductions in temperature and in the available precipitation. However, small populations are hard to detect using pollen analysis, and the extent of the identified refugia is not known. Surveys using appropriate genetic markers could be useful to confirm the existence of the refugia or to identify new ones. The pollen studies also indicate the timing of the spread from these refugia, and may therefore give insights into the controlling factors of the spread. However, the rapidity of the colonization and problems of spatial resolution in the pollen studies make it impossible to discern the routes of colonization at finer spatial scales with this technique; furthermore, once the migration routes meet, it becomes difficult to track subsequent movements with pollen data. These problems can be largely circumvented with the genetic approach. The comparison of the two data sets (fossil pollen and cpDNA) has allowed the proposal of spatiotemporal scenarios for oak colonization which could not have been deduced with each data separately (Petit *et al.* 2001b).

Inferences of long-distance dispersal events and maintenance of diversity during colonization

Like spatial ecological patterns (such as the distribution of individuals in space), spatial genetic patterns may present a hierarchy of structure, i.e. they may be scale dependent. Different processes may have given rise to these scale-specific patterns (Lavorel *et al.* 1993). This does not mean that they can be studied separately, as several processes could operate at different scales or influence the processes situated immediately below or above in the hierarchy. In oaks, postglacial recolonization has yielded spatial genetic patterns at more than one scale: at the rangewide scale, as shown above, but also at a more local one (Petit *et al.* 1997); this latter pattern had been attributed to the particular mode of dispersal during colonization (Le Corre *et al.* 1997). We show here, using simulations, how the understanding of postglacial recolonization processes at a finer scale eventually accounts for patterns observed at the broader scale, i.e. the persistence of relatively high levels of cpDNA genetic diversity during colonization.

Long-dispersal events

The convergent interest by modellers, palaeoecologists, and plant ecologists in the modalities of postglacial plant migration (Clark 1998; Clark *et al.* 1998; Pitelka *et al.* 1997; Shigesada *et al.* 1995), has led to the demonstration of the importance of rare long-distance colonization events in plants. Widespread and wind-pollinated tree species, such as oaks (Dyer 1995; Skellam 1951) or beech (Bennett 1988; Davis *et al.* 1986), have been used as model species for such investigations. It was Reid (1899) who pointed out for the first time that pure diffusion could not account for the rapidity of colonization observed during the Holocene for species such as the oak, and this prediction was confirmed analytically by Skellam's (1951) modelling of the dispersal of this species. To account for this paradox (Clark *et al.* 1998), it proved necessary to infer the existence of rare events of dispersal far away from the main colonization front, as these could significantly speed up colonization. Timofeeff-Ressovsky (1940, in Stebbins 1950) went one step futher and pointed out that during the advance of a species in a new territory, isolated 'advance guards' may at first establish small populations, which will then spread and merge with each other. He thought that the spatial structure generated this way was caused by the irregular environment: the hardiest of the seedlings would form the first plant populations in small pockets of favourable terrain. Later treatments emphasized rather the random character of the long-distance dispersal events, and the strong drift resulting from these founding events (Hewitt 1993; Ibrahim *et al.* 1996). Patterns of plant establishment seem from this perspective to be dominated by truly historical, idiosyncratic events, probably subsequently shaped by selection.

Hewitt (1993), Nichols and Hewitt (1944) and Ibrahim *et al.* (1996) predicted that such jumps will leave distinct signatures in the genetic structure of plant or animal populations. In oaks, cpDNA patches were indeed identified at the regional (200 × 270 km) scale, with areas of about 50 km virtually fixed for a single haplotype (Figure 14.6) (Petit *et al.* 1997). This led us to suggest that rare long-distance seed

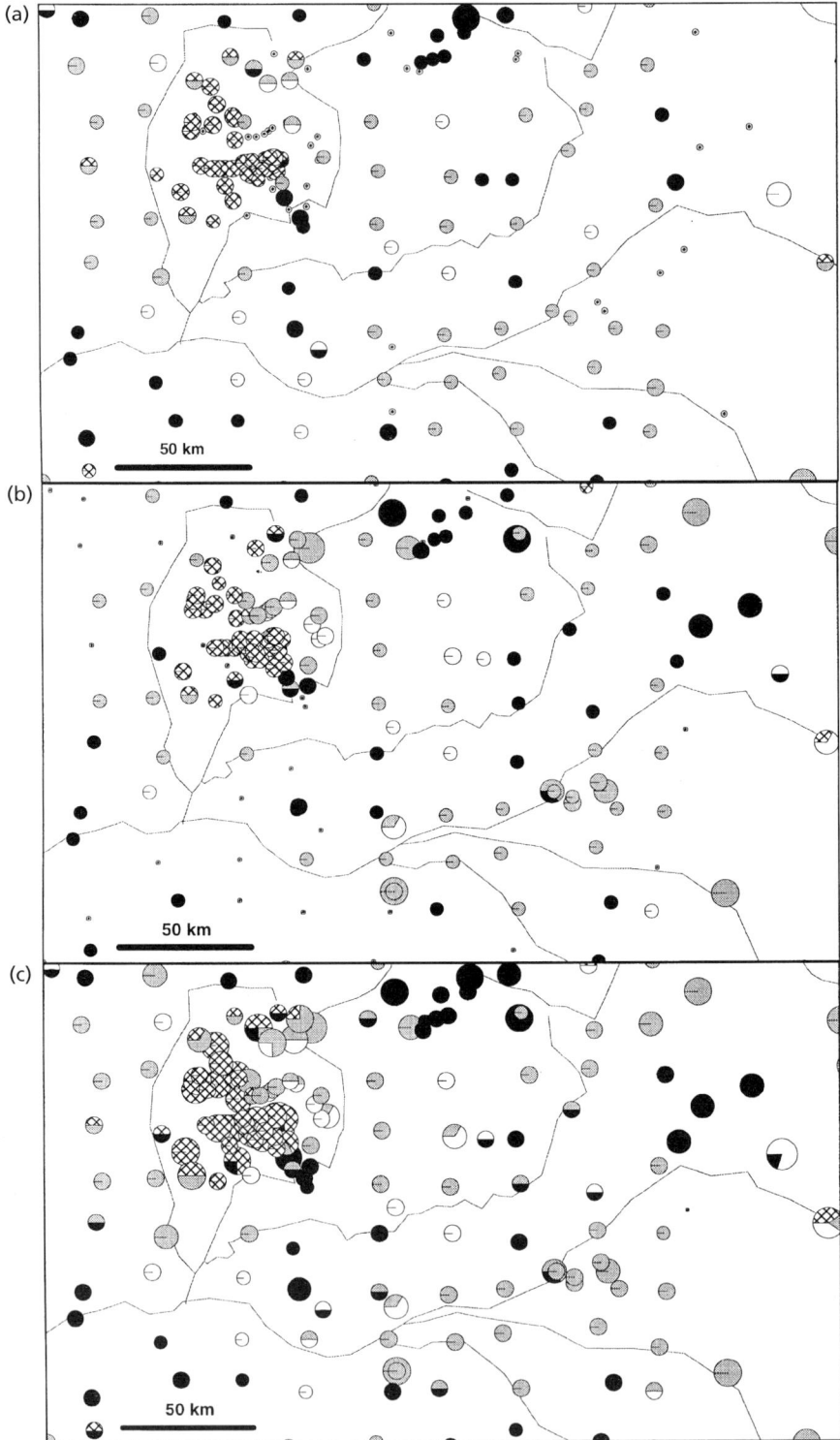

dispersal events of the same magnitude (around 50 km) were involved during colonization, and had generated maternal cpDNA clones extending over kilometres. Simulations confirmed that this scenario could indeed have generated the observed pattern (Le Corre *et al.* 1997). Although very large, this estimate of dispersal distance is in agreement with observations showing that tree species have readily crossed large potential barriers formed by seas, lakes or mountains (Clark *et al.* 1998). Dispersal distances such as 70 km and from 25 to 120 km are cited by palaeobotanists for the lodgepole pine (Cwynar & MacDonald 1987) or the American beech (Webb 1987).

Maintenance of cpDNA diversity

As discussed above, cpDNA diversity has been preserved relatively well in the European oaks, for instance along the Atlantic coast (see Figure 14.5). This seems at first sight incompatible with these scenarios of colonization through long-distance maternal founding events, as these jumps, involving virtually a single seed, should result locally in a complete loss of cpDNA diversity (Petit *et al.* 1997). We show here by simulations using cellular automata that stratified dispersal (diffusion plus long-distance migration) in two dimensions can preserve quite well the overall diversity (R. Bialozyt, unpublished). What happens is that these long-distance jumps maintain a mosaic of cpDNA patches, each nearly fixed for a single variant (see also Nichols & Hewitt (1994) and Le Corre *et al.* (1997)). In our simulations, low-frequency jumps result in the fixation of a single cpDNA variant ahead of the colonization front; however, as soon as the frequency of long-distance dispersal events becomes higher than 5×10^{-5}, stratified dispersal maintains cpDNA diversity better than pure diffusion (Figures 14.7 and 14.8). This means that, at the regional scale, strong founding events do not necessarily imply increased diversity losses.

Hybridization and colonization

Considering the stratified mechanism of dispersal in oaks, and the presence of mountain barriers, many expanding maternal lineages must have involved a single oak species at the outset of recolonization (Petit *et al.* 2001b). Because the oak species can have contrasting ecological behaviours, the direction and speed of colonization may have been affected. Nevertheless, the present day picture is that of systematic cpDNA exchanges between species and hence nearly species independence of cpDNA variation, when the species are sympatric (Dumolin-Lapègue *et al.* 1999a; Petit *et al.* 2001c). A striking example is provided in Figure 14.6 for part of western France (Petit *et al.* 1997). These results led to the hypothesis that oak species are able to colonize a site already occupied by other related species by pollen rather than by seeds (i.e. through pollen swamping) (Bacilieri *et al.* 1996; Petit *et al.* 1997). Potts

---

Figure 14.6 Geographic distribution of cpDNA haplotypes in two species of oaks in central western France. (a) *Quercus robur*; (b) *Q. petraea*; (c): both species. The systematic local sharing of haplotypes across the two species is striking. (Modified from Petit *et al.* 1997.)

Pure diffusion

Simulation 9 (a = 5 × 10E-7, sd2 = 50 km)

Simulation 8 (a = 1 × 10E-6, sd2 = 50 km)

Simulation 2 (a = 5 × 10E-6, sd2 = 50 km)

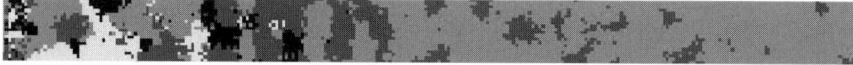

Simulation 6 (a = 1 × 10E-5, sd2 = 50 km)

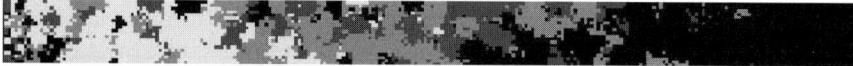

Simulation 5 (a = 5 × 10E-5, sd2 = 50 km)

Simulation 7 (a = 1 × 10E-5, sd2 = 50 km)

0   100   200   300 km

Figure 14.7 Examples of simulations of postglacial recolonization of cpDNA in oaks. The program is based on cellular automata, with 5-km cells, and 1000 trees at carrying capacity (R. Bialozyt, unpublished), and was tested against the individual-based model of Le Corre *et al.* (1997). The simulation plot measures 100×1320 km, and the initial condition was an equal mixture of four cpDNA variants in the first 20 km (diversity of 0.75), whereas the remaining cells were empty. The simulations were carried out using the stratified dispersal approach of Nichols and Hewit (1994), where the probability of the seed density in a given distance is given by: $F = (1 - a)N[0, sd1] + aN[0, sd2]$. The first normal distribution represents the short distance dispersal ($sd1 = 250$ m) and the second represents the long distance dispersal ($sd2 = 50$ km). The parameter a accounts for the proportion between these two distributions. In the pure diffusion model, $a = 0$. In the examples shown, fixation had occurred at 1200 km in the two pure diffusion cases as well as in the simulations characterized by low values of a ($<5 \times 10^{-6}$).

and Reid (1988) had suggested a similar scenario in the case of *Eucalyptus* species in Tasmania. Figure 14.9 details how this might have occurred: the first species to settle (often the more pioneer and cold tolerant, but this will depend on their distribution in the different refugia) necessarily established by long-distance seed movement, generating the characteristic patchy structure shown in Figure 14.6. Once these

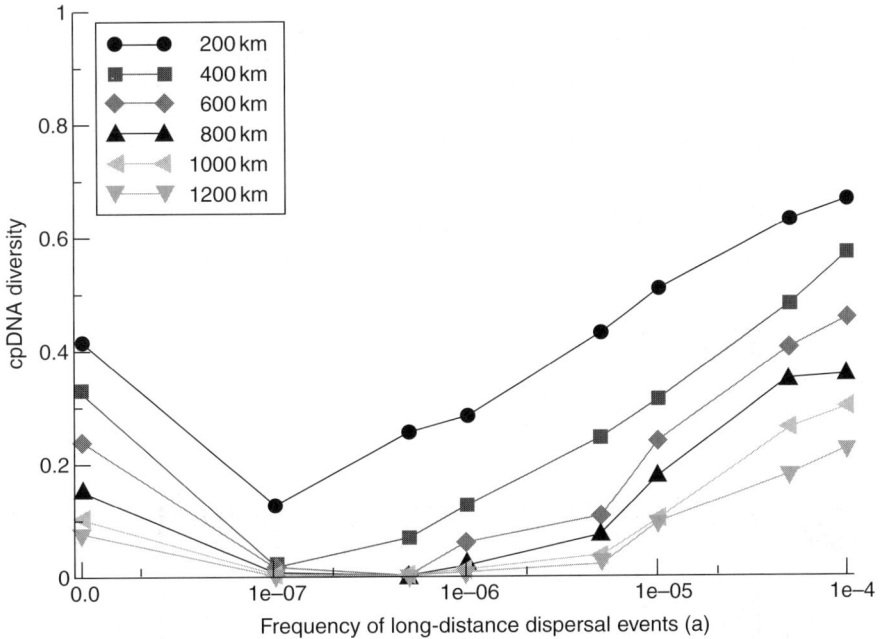

Figure 14.8 Chloroplast DNA diversity maintained during colonization as a function of the distance from refugia and rate of long-distance dispersal events. Total genetic diversity was measured in six 100×100-km regions, at 200-km intervals (see legend). The values are means over 20 replicated simulations. A progressive decrease of diversity during colonization is apparent in all cases, but it is attenuated (compared to the situation of pure diffusion) when sufficiently frequent ($>5 \times 10^{-5}$) long-distance dispersal events are included in the simulations.

pioneer populations mature, a large number of female flowers are produced, which are partly receptive to the pollen of the other oak species brought from very long distances by wind. This would result in hybrids, and eventually in backcrosses and other hybrid derivatives characterized by the original cpDNA structure but an increasing proportion of the nuclear genome of the second species. This provides a very efficient system of dispersal, especially for the later-successional species that cannot invest so much of their resources in the development of efficient acorn dispersal strategies, but are likely to be a good competitor in already established forests (Petit *et al.* 1997). Indeed, in the species pair investigated in more details, the results suggest that interspecific gene flow reinforces the natural succession process (Bacilieri *et al.* 1996; Petit *et al.* 1997). It remains to be investigated whether the asymmetric direction of cross-compatibility observed between the early and late-successional oak species has actually evolved in response to selection pressures for dispersal into new regions. The consequences of these intense interspecific gene flow on the maintenance of diversity in each species should also be investigated further.

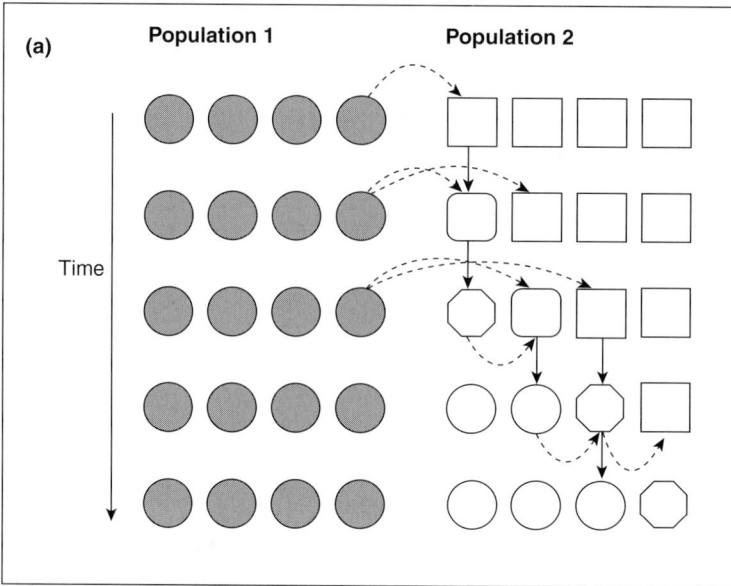

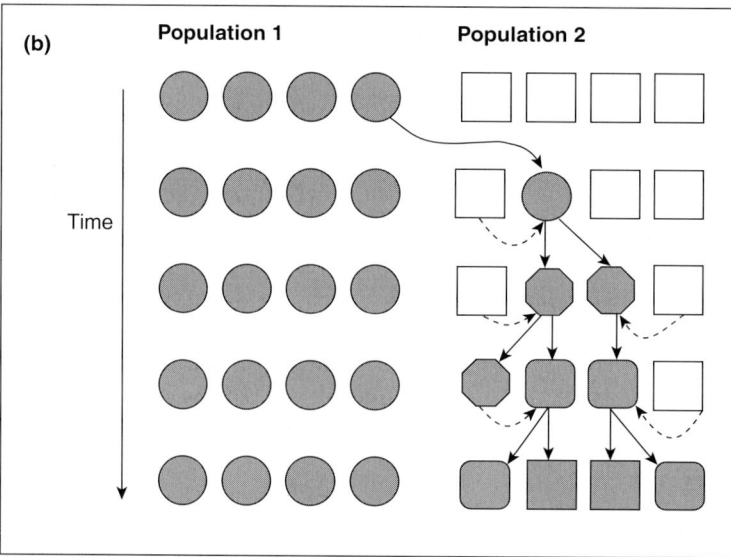

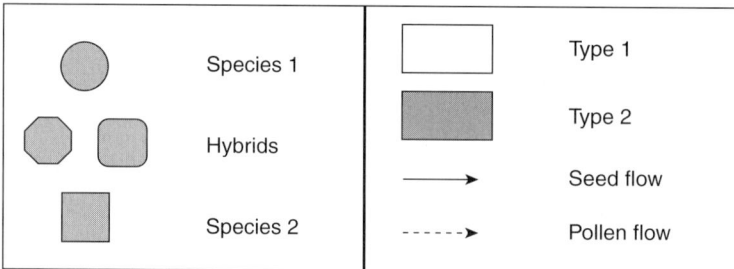

Prospects and conclusion

Working with longer time scales or at broader geographic scales than is generally the case in population genetics may elucidate rare events or slow processes that cannot be captured otherwise, and could bridge the gap with ecologically orientated biogeographic studies. That studies of speciation should be tackled at these broader scales is widely recognized (Stebbins 1950; Hewitt 1996). But historically, population genetics has defined the population as the unit of microevolution. Metapopulation theory, where each population is in disequilibrium but the whole is in equilibrium (see Chapters 7 and 12), goes one step further than conventional models by taking into account extinction of populations and colonization, but this may not suffice when dealing with range shifts driven by ice ages. Gould (1985) has distinguished three biologically significant time scales, corresponding to ecological time (1 ka), geological time (1–10 Ma) and mass extinctions ($\approx$26 Ma). In order to fill the gap between microevolutionary and macroevolutionary studies, models at scales intermediate between ecological and geological times are necessary. This need has been previously expressed by paleoecologists (Bennett 1990, 1997; Webb & Bartlein 1992). For these authors, the antiquity of climate forcing implies that all modern boreal and temperate species must have coping mechanisms that have allowed them to persist until now. They argue that the role of chance should be downplayed at the continental scale, in order to unite explanations of continental migrations with gap-phase succession using a hierarchical scheme. Modified speciation rates, and increased generalism and dispersability have been suggested as possible evolutionary consequences of orbitally induced climate changes (Huntley & Webb 1989; Dynesius & Jansson 2000). As argued here, the ability to maintain sufficient genetic diversity during colonization could constitute another important evolutionary consequence of these cyclic environmental changes. For those species that cannot cope with these changes, the only alternative is to become extinct (Figure 14.10) or to subsist as narrow endemics, providing the opportunity for selection among species. According to Lloyd and Gould (1993) and Gould and Lloyd (1999), selection at supraorganismic levels is expected to lead to emergent fitness, not necessarily to emergent features; indeed, 'benefit may also accrue

Figure 14.9 Two simple models accounting for the sharing of cpDNA variants across species. (a) Nuclear genome displacement through long-distance pollen swamping. No seed flow between populations is required. (b) Cytoplasmic genome displacement through seed dispersal and invasion by the allochthonous cytoplasmic genome. No pollen flow between populations is required. Model (a) appears more parsimonious than model (b), as long-distance pollen flow is often more efficient than long-distance seed flow between established plant populations. Model (b) is hard to conceive without a selective superiority of the type 2 cytoplasm, and does not take into account the dynamic nature of plant populations, especially during postglacial colonization. The popular term of 'cytoplasmic capture', coined by Rieseberg and Soltis (1991) in a more phylogenetic than biological context, could falsely suggest that model (b) is more frequent in nature.

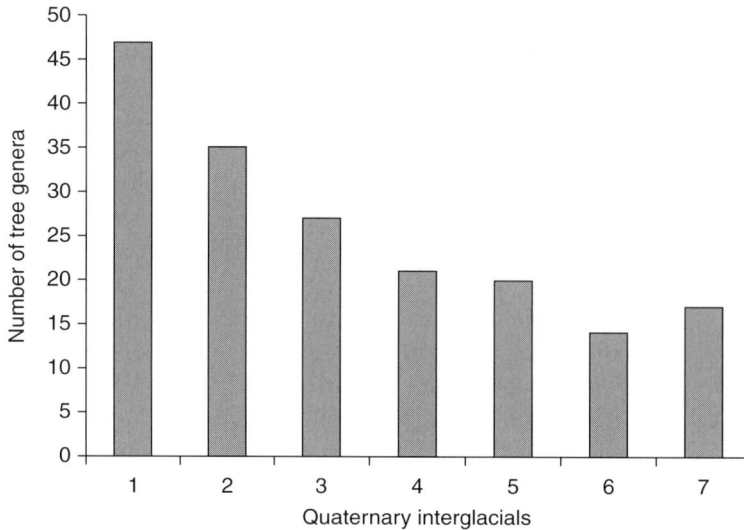

Figure 14.10 Extinctions of tree genera during the Quaternary. (From Bradshaw 1999.)

passively at one level . . . as structural side consequences of causes acting at other levels'.

As in the case of the maintenance of sex, where a seemingly confusing variety of proximal causes have been described (Maynard-Smith 1978), species able to cope with a succession of ice ages must be characterized by a variety of attributes allowing them to maintain sufficient genetic diversity in the face of frequent changes in their ranges. Brown and Marshall (1981) concluded their review on evolutionary changes in colonizing plants by emphasizing that these species are of interest 'not so much because they form a homogeneous group, but because they display a wide range of evolutionary pathways'.

Reviews of the plant isozyme literature have shown that geographic distribution is the best correlate of levels and distribution of genetic diversity (Hamrick *et al.* 1992). In particular, widespread tree species from the boreal–temperate region have significantly higher heterozygosity than those with more restricted ranges and from lower latitudes, despite the fact that they must have gone through periods when they were much more restricted, during the ice ages, providing indirect support for the hypothesis that they constitute a particular class of selected organisms able to cope with large-scale climatic oscillations.

We have described several mechanisms that allow plant species to limit losses of genetic diversity during colonization and hence to survive in the long term, and we expect that others could be found, if more attention was given to the surprising maintenance — rather than to the expected loss — of diversity during ice ages. Hetero-zygote advantage, especially during stress, could constitute one such mechanism, as discussed above for the beech. Self-incompatibility systems will also maintain more diversity than in purely neutral systems due to frequency-dependent balancing selection (Wright 1939). In other biological systems, dispersal may be so efficient that there may be few or no bottlenecks at all during recolonization (e.g. Oddou *et al.* 2000); in particular, the long juvenile phase of trees may allow multiple colonization events before saturation by growth of the newly founded populations (Austerlitz *et al.* 2000); alternatively, there may be locally strong founding events but an overall maintenance of diversity at the regional scale, demonstrating a complete decoupling of the consequences of colonization on diversity at two spatial scales. Interspecific hybridization may also explain the success of some groups in colonizing new territories while maintaining enough diversity, as in the case of the oaks or the irises. The requirements for efficient systems that can maintain diversity in the face of frequent and rapid recolonization may be greater for those species that do not maintain permanent populations in southern regions, near refugia, but rather track environmental changes by migration (Bennett *et al.* 1991).

Although we have chosen here to emphasize studies based on genetic markers, quantitative traits could provide complementary insights; for instance, Carson (1990) has described an increase in genetic variance for quantitative traits following bottlenecks. In addition, the exposure to new environments, both abiotic and biotic (due to the individualistic postglacial colonization behaviour of forest trees), could promote rapid diversification, through the establishment of a geographic mosaic of coevolution, as shown by Benkman (1999) in the case of the lodgepole pine.

The new insights provided by the direct cooperation between palaeoecologists and geneticists show the necessity of extending this interdisciplinary approach. Similar efforts are made in the field of evolutionary developmental genetics, thanks to the association of paleontologists and molecular biologists interested in the evolution of body plans in animals and plants (Carroll 2000). In studies of orbitally induced changes in species' ranges, the genetic and palaeoecological approaches nicely supplement each other (see also Chapters 13 and 15). For instance, genetic surveys can provide a greater spatial and taxonomic resolution than palynological surveys, but palaeobotanical investigations provide the necessary temporal resolution. In the future, it will be necessary to integrate also climatic and ecological data, so that the processes that have led to the observed patterns of recolonization can be better identified. This includes the competitive or facilitating interactions with other forest tree species (MacDonald 1993) and with soil development. Finally, molecular analysis of plant macrofossils may provide an even more direct multidisciplinary approach, if significant amounts of usable DNA could be retrieved in key sites from ancient material. The potential for such studies has already been demonstrated in animals, using archaeological material such as bones (e.g. Hardy *et al.* 1995). Preliminary attempts to amplify DNA from recent and more ancient wood fragments uncovered during archaeological investigations have already given promising results (Dumolin-Lapègue *et al.* 1999b).

Summary

Rangewide studies of the phylogeographic structure and genetic diversity of plants, and especially of forest trees, have produced new insights into their Quaternary history, in particular the location of their ice-age refugia and of their postglacial colonization routes. Although considerable evidence exists for the diminution of genetic diversity during postglacial colonization, this is not a universal feature, as shown by results recently obtained on isozyme variation in the European beech. In this example, a new approach was used to obtain quantitative estimates of the age of each population since founding, using pollen data and geostatistical methods, thus improving estimates of rates of changes in diversity levels. This study, as well as simulations of postglacial colonization in oaks, point to a variety of mechanisms that may limit diversity losses during colonization, perhaps as a consequence of selection at supraorganismic levels. In the future, it is recommended that population genetics explicitly includes approaches dealing with larger temporal and geographical scales, to bridge the gap with macroevolutionary studies.

Acknowledgements

The oak and the beech studies described here were partly supported by the European Union (contracts FAIR PL95-0297, FAIR5-CT97-3795 and FAIR3-CT97-1464). R.J.P. thanks the Institut für Forst Genetik (BFH), for its hospitality during the preparation of the manuscript.

References

Anderson, E. (1936). The species problem in *Iris*. *Annals of the Missouri Botanical Garden*, **23**, 457–509.

Austerlitz, F., Jung-Müller, B., Godelle, B. & Gouyon, P.H. (1997). Evolution of coalescence times, genetic diversity and structure during colonization. *Theoretical Population Biology*, **141**, 148–164.

Austerlitz, F., Mariette, S., Machon, N., Gouyon, P.H. & Godelle, B. (2000). Effects of colonization processes on genetic diversity: differences between annual plants and tree species. *Genetics*, **154**, 1309–1321.

Avise, J.C. (1994). *Molecular Markers, Natural History and Evolution*. Chapman & Hall, New York.

Bacilieri, R., Ducousso, A., Petit, R.J. & Kremer, A. (1996). Mating system and asymmetric hybridization in a mixed stand of European oaks. *Evolution*, **50**, 900–908.

Benkman, C.W. (1999). The selection mosaic and diversifying coevolution between crossbills and lodgepole pine. *American Naturalist*, **153**, S75–S91.

Bennett, K.D. (1988). Holocene geographic spread and population expansion of *Fagus grandifola* in Ontario, Canada. *Journal of Ecology*, **76**, 547–557.

Bennett, K.D. (1990). Milankovitch cycles and their effects on species in ecological and evolutionary time. *Paleobiology*, **16**, 11–21.

Bennett, K.D. (1997). *Evolution and Ecology. The Pace of Life*. Cambridge University Press, Cambridge, UK.

Bennett, K.D., Tzedakis, P.C. & Willis, K.J. (1991). Quaternary refugia of north European trees. *Journal of Biogeography*, **18**, 103–115.

Bradshaw, R.H.W. (1999). Spatial responses of animals to climate change during the Quaternary. *Ecological Bulletins*, **47**, 16–21.

Brewer, S., Cheddadi, R., de Beaulieu, J.-L., Reille, M. & data contributors (2001). The migration of deciduous *Quercus* throughout Europe since the last glacial period. *Forest Ecology and Management*, in press.

Brown, A.H.D. & Marshall, D.R. (1981). Evolutionary changes accompanying colonization in plants. In: *Evolution today, Proceedings of the Second International Congress of Systematic and Evolutionary Biology* (eds G.G.E. Scudder & J.L. Reveal), pp. 351–363. Vancover, British Columbia, Canada.

Bush, R.M. & Smouse, P.E. (1992). Evidence for the adaptive significance of allozymes in forest trees. *New Forests*, **6**, 179–196.

Carroll, R.L. (2000). Towards a new evolutionary synthesis. *Trends in Ecology and Evolution*, **15**, 27–32.

Carson, H.L. (1990). Increased genetic variance after a population bottleneck. *Trends in Ecology and Evolution*, **7**, 228–230.

Cavalli-Sforza, L.L. (1998). The DNA revolution in population genetics. *Trends in Genetics*, **14**, 60–65.

Clark, J.S. (1998). Why trees migrate so fast: confronting theory with dispersal biology and the paleorecord. *American Naturalist*, **152**, 204–224.

Clark, J.S., Fastie, C., Hurtt, G., Jackson, S.T., Johnson, C., King, G.A., Lewis, M., Lynch, J., Pacala, S., Prentice, C., Schupp, E.W., Webb III, T. & Wyckoff, P. (1998). Reid's paradox of rapid plant migration. *BioScience*, **48**, 13–24.

Comps, B., Gömöry, D., Letouzey, J., Thiébaut, B. & Petit R.J. (2001). Diverging trends between heterozygosity and allelic richness during postglacial colonization in the European beech. *Genetics*, **157**, 389–397.

Cwynar, L.C. & MacDonald, G.M. (1987). Geographical variation of lodgpole pine in relation to population history. *American Naturalist*, **129**, 463–469.

David, P. (1998). Heterozygosity–fitness correlations: new perspectives on old problems. *Heredity*, **80**, 531–537.

Davis, M.B., Woods, K.D., Webb, S.L. & Futyma, R.P. (1986). Dispersal versus climate: Expansion of *Fagus* and *Tsuga* into the Upper Great Lakes region. *Vegetatio*, **67**, 93–103.

Demesure, B., Comps, B. & Petit, R.J. (1996). Chloroplast DNA phylogeography of the common beech (*Fagus sylvatica* L.) in Europe. *Evolution*, **50**, 2515–2520.

Dumolin-Lapègue, S., Demesure, B., Le Corre, V., Fineschi, S. & Petit, R.J. (1997). Phylogeographic structure of white oaks throughout the European continent. *Genetics*, **146**, 1475–1487.

Dumolin-Lapègue, S., Pemonge, M.-H. & Petit, R.J. (1998). Association between chloroplast and mitochondrial lineages in oaks. *Molecular Biology and Evolution*, **15**, 1321–1331.

Dumolin-Lapègue, S., Kremer, A. & Petit, R.J. (1999a). Are chloroplast and mitochondrial DNA variation species-independent in oaks? *Evolution*, **53**, 1406–1413.

Dumolin-Lapègue, S., Pemonge, M.-H., Gielly, L., Taberlet, P. & Petit, R.J. (1999b). Amplification of DNA from ancient and modern oak wood. *Molecular Ecology*, **8**, 2137–2140.

Dyer, J.M. (1995). Assessment of climatic warming using a model of forest species migration. *Ecological Modelling*, **79**, 199–219.

Dynesius, M. & Jansson, R. (2000). Evolutionary consequences of changes in species' geographical distributions driven by Milankovitch climate oscillations. *Proceedings of the National Academy of Sciences of the USA*, **97**, 9115–9120.

Ellstrand, N.C. & Elam, D.R. (1993). Population genetic consequences of small population size: implications for plant conservation. *Annual Review of Ecology and Systematics*, **24**, 217–242.

Ellstrand, N.C. & Schierenbeck, K.A. (2000). Hybridization as a stimulus for the evolution of invasiveness in plants? *Proceedings of the National Academy of Sciences of the USA*, **97**, 7043–7050.

Ennos, R.A. (1994). Estimating the relative rates of pollen and seed migration among plant populations. *Heredity*, **72**, 250–259.

Ferris, C., Oliver, R.P., Davy, A.J. & Hewitt, G.M. (1993). Native oak chloroplasts reveal an ancient divide across Europe. *Molecular Ecology*, **2**, 337–344.

Ferris, C., King, R.A., Väinölä, R. & Hewitt, G.M. (1998). Chloroplast DNA recognizes three refugial sources of European oaks and suggests independent eastern and western immigrations to Finland. *Heredity*, **80**, 584–593.

Fisher, R.A. (1930). *The Genetical Theory of Natural Selection*. Clarendon Press, Oxford.

Furnier, G.R. & Adams, W.T. (1986). Geographic patterns of allozyme variation in Jeffrey pine. *American Journal of Botany*, **73**, 1009–1015.

Goovaerts, P. (1997). *Geostatistics for Natural Resources Evaluation*. Oxford University Press, Oxford.

Gould, S.J. (1985). The paradox of the first tier: an agenda for paleobiology. *Paleobiology*, **11**, 2–12.

Gould, S.J. (1994). Tempo and mode in the macroevolutionary reconstruction of Darwinism. *Proceedings of the National Academy of Sciences of the USA*, **91**, 6764–6771.

Gould, S.J. & Lloyd, E.A. (1999). Individuality and adaptation across levels of selection: How shall we name and generalize the unit of Darwinism? *Proceedings of the National Academy of Sciences of the USA*, **96**, 11904–11909.

Haase, P. (1993). Genetic variation, gene flow, and the 'founder effect' in pioneer populations of *Nothofagus menziesii* (Fagaceae), South Island, New Zealand. *Journal of Biogeography*, **20**, 79–85.

Hamrick, J.L., Godt, M.J.W. & Sherman-Broyles, S.L. (1992). Factors influencing levels of genetic diversity in woody plant species. *New Forests*, **6**, 95–124.

Hardy, C., Callou, C., Vigne, J.-D., Casane, D., Dennebouy, N., Mounolou, J.-C. & Monnerot, M. (1995). Rabbit mitochondrial DNA diversity from prehistoric to modern times. *Journal of Molecular Evolution*, **40**, 227–237.

Hewitt, G.M. (1993). Post-glacial distribution and species substructure: lessons from pollen, insects and hybrid zones. In: *Evolutionary Patterns and Processes* (eds D.R. Lees & D. Edwards), pp. 97–123. Linnean Society Symposium Series 14, Academic Press, London.

Hewitt, G.M. (1996). Some genetic consequences of ice ages, and their role in divergence and speciation. *Biological Journal of the Linnean Society*, **58**, 247–276.

Hewitt, G.M. (1999). Post-glacial re-colonization of European biota. *Biological Journal of the Linnean Society*, **68**, 97–112.

Huntley, B. & Birks, H.J.B. (1983). *An Atlas of Past and Present Pollen Maps for Europe, 0-13000 Years Ago*. Cambridge University Press, Cambridge, UK.

Huntley, B. & Webb III, T. (1989). Migration: species' response to climatic variations caused by changes in the earth's orbit. *Journal of Biogeography*, **16**, 5–19.

Ibrahim, K.M., Nichols, R.A. & Hewitt, G.M. (1996). Spatial patterns of genetic variation generated by different forms of dispersal during range expansion. *Heredity*, **77**, 282–291.

Ingvarsson, P.K. (1997). The effect of delayed population growth on the genetic differentiation of local populations subject to frequent extinctions and recolonizations. *Evolution*, **51**, 29–35.

Kauffman, S.A. (1993). *The Origins of Order. Self-organization and Selection in Evolution*. Oxford University Press, Oxford.

Kimura, M. & Weiss, G.H. (1964). The stepping-stone model of population structure and the decrease of genetic correlation with distance. *Genetics*, **49**, 561–576.

Kingman, J.F.C. (1982). The coalescent. *Stochastic Processes and their Applications*, **13**, 235–248.

Konnert, M. & Bergmann, F. (1995). The geographical distribution of genetic variation of silver fir (*Abies alba*, Pinaceae) in relation to its migration history. *Plant Systematics and Evolution*, **196**, 19–30.

Kremer, A., Petit, R.J., Zanetto, A., Fougère, V., Ducousso, A., Wagner, D. & Chauvin, C. (1991). Nuclear and organelle diversity in *Quercus robur* and *Q. petraea*. In: *Genetic Variation in European Populations of Forest Trees* (eds G. Müller-Starck & M. Ziehe), pp. 141–166. Sauerländer's Verlag, Frankfurt am Main.

Lagercrantz, U. & Ryman, N. (1990). Genetic structure of Norway spruce (*Picea abies*): concordance of morphological and allozymic variation. *Evolution*, **44**, 38–53.

Lavorel, S., Gardner, R.H. & O'Neill, R.V. (1993). Analysis of patterns in hierarchically structured landscapes. *Oikos*, **67**, 521–528.

Le Corre, V. & Kremer, A. (1998). Cumulative effects of founding events during colonization on genetic diversity and differentiation in an island and stepping-stone model. *Journal of Evolutionary Biology*, **11**, 495–512.

Le Corre, V., Machon, N., Petit, R.J. & Kremer, A. (1997). Colonization with long-distance seed dispersal and distribution of maternally inherited diversity in forest trees: a simulation study. *Genetical Research, Cambridge*, **69**, 117–125.

Ledig, F.T. (2000). Founder effects and the genetic structure of Coulter pine. *Journal of Heredity*, **91**, 307–315.

Li, P. & Adams, W.T. (1989). Range-wide patterns of allozyme variation in Douglas-fir (*Pseudotsuga menziesii*). *Canadian Journal of Forest Research*, **19**, 149–161.

Lloyd, E.A. & Gould, S.J. (1993). Species selection

on variability. *Proceedings of the National Academy of Sciences of the USA*, **90**, 595–599.

MacDonald, G.M. (1993). Fossil pollen analysis and the reconstruction of plant invasions. *Advances in Ecological Research*, **24**, 67–110.

Maynard-Smith, J. (1978). *The Evolution of Sex*. Cambridge University Press, Cambridge, UK.

Müller-Starck, G. (1993). *Auswirkungen von Umweltbelastungen auf genetische Strukturen von Waldbeständen am Beispiel der Buche (Fagus sylvatica L.)*. Schriften aus der Forstl. Fak. d. Univ. Göttingen u. d. Niedersächs. Forstl. Versuch-sanst., Bd. 112. Sauerländer's Verlag, Frankfurt.

Nei, M., Maruyama, T. & Chakraborty, R. (1975). The bottleneck effect and genetic variability in populations. *Evolution*, **29**, 1–10.

Nichols, R.A. & Hewitt, G.M. (1994). The genetic consequences of long distance dispersal during colonization. *Heredity*, **72**, 312–317.

Oddou, S., Petit, R.J., Le Guerroué, B., Guesnet, D. & Demesure, B. (2001). Pollen- versus seed-mediated gene flow in a scattered forest tree species. *Evolution*, **55**, 1123–1135.

Parsons, P.A. (1996). Conservation strategies: adaptation to stress and the preservation of genetic diversity. *Biological Journal of the Linnean Society*, **58**, 471–482.

Petit, C. & Thompson, J.D. (1999). Species diversity and ecological range in relation to ploidy level in the flora of the Pyrenees. *Evolutionary Ecology*, **13**, 45–66.

Petit, R.J., Kremer, A. & Wagner, D.B. (1993a). Finite island model for organelle and nuclear genes in plants. *Heredity*, **71**, 630–641.

Petit, R.J., Kremer, A. & Wagner, D.B. (1993b). Geographic structure of chloroplast DNA polymorphisms in European oaks. *Theoretical and Applied Genetics*, **87**, 122–128.

Petit, R.J., Pineau, E., Demesure, B., Bacilieri, R., Ducousso, A. & Kremer, A. (1997). Chloroplast DNA footprints of postglacial recolonization by oaks. *Proceedings of the National Academy of Sciences of the USA*, **94**, 9996–10001.

Petit, R.J., Csaikl, U., Bordacs, S., Burg, K., Coart, E., Cottrell, J., van Dam, B., Deans, J.D., Dumolin-Lapègue, S., Fineschi, S., Finkelday, R., Gillies, A., Glaz, I., Goicoechea, P.G., Jensen, J.S., König, A., Lowe, A.J., Madsen, S.F., Mátyás, G., Munro, R.C., Olalde, M., Pemonge, M.-H., Popescu, F., Slade, D., Tabbener, H., Taurchini, D., Ziegenhagen, B. &

Kremer, A. (2001a). Chloroplast DNA variation in European white oaks: synthesis based on data from over 2600 populations. *Forest Ecology and Management*, in press.

Petit, R.J., Brewer, S., Bordács, S., Burg, K., Cheddadi, R., Coart, E., Cottrell, J., Csaikl, U.M., van Dam, B., Deans, J.D., Espiñel, S., Fineschi, S., Finkeldey, R., Glaz, I., Goicoechea, P.G., Jensen, J.S., König, A.O., Lowe, A.J., Madsen, S.F., Mátyás, G., Munro, R.C., Popescu, F., Slade, D., Tabbener, H., de Vries, S.M.G., Ziegenhagen, B., de Beaulieu, J.-L. & Kremer, A. (2001b). Identification of refugia and postglacial colonization routes of European white oaks based on chloroplast DNA and fossil pollen evidence. *Forest Ecology and Management*, in press.

Petit, R.J., Latouche-Hallé, C., Pemonge, M.-H. & Kremer, A. (2001c). Chloroplast DNA variation of oaks in France and the influence of forest fragmentation on genetic diversity. *Forest Ecology and Management*, in press.

Pitelka, L.F. and the plant migration workshop group (1997). Plant migration and climate change. *American Scientist*, **85**, 464–473.

Pons, O. & Petit, R.J. (1995). Estimation, variance and optimal sampling of gene diversity. I. Haploid locus. *Theoretical and Applied Genetics*, **90**, 462–470.

Potts, B.M. & Reid, J.B. (1988). Hybridization as a dispersal mechanism. *Evolution*, **42**, 1245–1255.

Reid, C. (1899). *The Origin of the British Flora*. Dulau, London.

Rieseberg, L.H. & Soltis, D.E. (1991). Phylogenetic consequences of cytoplasmic gene flow in plants. *Evolutionary Trends in Plants*, **5**, 65–84.

Shigesada, N., Kawasaki, K. & Takeda, Y. (1995). Modeling stratified diffusion in biological invasions. *American Naturalist*, **146**, 229–251.

Skellam, J.G. (1951). Random dispersal in theoretical populations. *Biometrika*, **38**, 196–218.

Smith, A.G. & Pilcher, J.R. (1973). Radiocarbon dates and vegetational history of the British Isles. *New Phytologist*, **72**, 903–914.

Soltis, D.E., Mayer, M.S., Soltis, P.S. & Edgerton, M. (1991). Chloroplast-DNA variation in *Tellima grandiflora* (Saxifragaceae). *American Journal of Botany*, **78**, 1379–1390.

Soltis, P.S. & Soltis, D.E. (2000). The role of genetic and genomic attributes in the success of polyploids. *Proceedings of the National Academy of Sciences of the USA*, **97**, 7051–7057.

Starke, R., Ziehe, M. & Müller-Starck, G. (1996). Viability selection in juvenile populations of European beech (*Fagus sylvatica* L.). *Forest Genetics*, **3**, 217–225.

Stebbins, G.L. Jr. (1950). *Variation and Evolution in Plants*. Columbia University Press, New York.

Steinhoff, R.J., Joyce, D.G. & Fins, L. (1983). Isozyme variation in *Pinus monticola*. *Canadian Journal of Forest Research*, **13**, 1122–1132.

Taberlet, P., Fumagalli, L., Wust-Saucy, A.-G. & Cosson, J.-F. (1998). Comparative phylogeography and postglacial colonization routes in Europe. *Molecular Ecology*, **7**, 453–464.

Thiébaut, B., Comps, B. & Leroux, A. (1992). Relation hauteur-génotype dans une régénération naturelle de hêtre (*Fagus sylvatica* L.), équienne et âgée de 18 ans. *Annales des Sciences Forestières*, **49**, 321–335.

Thorpe, R.S. (1984). Primary and secondary transition zones in speciation and population differentiation: a phylogenetic analysis of range expansion. *Evolution*, **38**, 233–243.

Webb, S.L. (1987). Beech range extension and vegetation history: pollen stratigraphy of two Wisconsin lakes. *Ecology*, **68**, 1993–2005.

Webb III, S.L. & Bartlein, P.J. (1992). Global changes during the last 3 million years: climatic controls and biotic responses. *Annual Review of Ecology and Systematics*, **23**, 141–173.

Wheeler, N.C. & Guries, R.P. (1982). Population structure, genic diversity, and morphological variation in *Pinus contorta* Dougl. *Canadian Journal of Forest Research*, **12**, 595–606.

Wright, S. (1931). Evolution in Mendelian populations. *Genetics*, **16**, 97–159.

Wright, S. (1939). The distribution of self-sterility alleles in populations. *Genetics*, **137**, 1157–1165.

Wright, S. (1943). Isolation by distance. *Genetics*, **28**, 114–138.

Young, A., Boyle, T. & Brown, T. (1996). The population genetic consequences of habitat fragmentation for plants. *Trends in Ecology and Evolution*, **11**, 413–418.

Zanetto, A. & Kremer, A. (1995). Geographic structure of gene diversity in *Quercus petraea* (Matt.) Liebl. 1. Monolocus patterns of variation. *Heredity*, **75**, 506–517.

Chapter 15

Comparative phylogeography of north-western North America: a synthesis

S. J. Brunsfeld,* J. Sullivan,† D. E. Soltis‡ and P. S. Soltis§

Introduction

Phylogeography is concerned with the principles and processes that determine the geographic distributions of genealogical lineages, within and among closely related species (Avise *et al.* 1987; Avise 2000). Although this field of study is very new (only a little more than a decade has passed since the term 'phylogeography' was first coined; see Avise *et al.* 1987), the scientific literature in this research area is now voluminous.

To date, most phylogeographic investigations of natural populations have focused on muticellular animals (Hewitt 1993; Patton *et al.* 1994; daSilva & Patton 1998; Eizirik *et al.* 1998; Avise 2000; Hewitt 2000; Schaal & Olsen 2000; Sullivan *et al.* 2000). This bias is due in large part to the ready availability of population-level genetic markers afforded by the animal mitochondrial genome. The more slowly evolving chloroplast genome, in contrast, often does not provide sufficient variation to reconstruct phylogeny at the populational level (Soltis *et al.* 1997; Schaal *et al.* 1998; Schaal & Olsen 2000). Phylogeographic data have accumulated so rapidly for animal taxa that it has been possible to compare phylogeographic structure among codistributed species. In fact, one of the most profound recent contributions of molecular phylogeography is the construction of *regional phylogeographic* perspectives that permit comparisons of phylogeographic structure among codistributed species, and subsequent integration of genealogical data with independent biogeographic and systematic data.

Probably the best-known regional phylogeographic analysis for North America involves animals from the southeastern USA (reviewed in Avise 2000). Avise and colleagues demonstrated that similar phylogeographic patterns are present in a diverse array of animals, including freshwater and marine fish, turtles, birds and invertebrates. A high degree of phylogeographic concordance was observed across taxa, with a pronounced distinction in mitochondrial (mt) DNA haplotypes between populations from the Atlantic coast and those from the Gulf coast. This concordance implicates shared historical factors in shaping the genetic architecture of

* College of Natural Resources, University of Idaho, Moscow, ID 83844, USA, † Department of Biological Sciences, University of Idaho, Moscow, ID 83844, USA, ‡ Department of Botany and the Genetics Institute, University of Florida, Gainesville, FL 32611, USA and § Florida Museum of Natural History and the Genetics Institute, University of Florida, Gainesville, FL 32611, USA.

these diverse taxa. Despite this wealth of data for animals, only one such study has been completed for a plant species from this region (*Liriodendron tulipifera*; Sewell *et al.* 1996). Nevertheless, as recently noted by Avise (2000), one of the earliest regional phylogeographic comparisons of codistributed organisms actually involved plants from the Pacific Northwest of North America (reviewed in Soltis *et al.* 1997). Similarly, a substantial body of phylogeographic data has now accumulated on European trees (see Chapter 14), and the combination of these data with analyses of multiple animal species has allowed a multi-kingdom approach to European phylogeography (see Chapter 13, and references therein; see Willis & Whittaker (2000) on the importance of refugia).

Here we attempt to begin to reconstruct a comprehensive regional phylogeography for north-western North America that encompasses examples from both the plant and animal literature. Our general goals are to: (i) demonstrate the complexity and caveats of such an undertaking for an area that is both geologically and ecologically highly complex; (ii) explore the roles of vicariance, dispersal and refugia in structuring genetic diversity in the region; and (iii) highlight the need for additional data from this region and stimulate similar efforts for other geographic areas.

The geographic scope of this chapter encompasses the western coast of North America from southern Alaska to northern California, east to the Rocky Mountains of British Columbia, western Montana and central Idaho (Figure 15.1). This region contains the world's greatest extent of mesic, temperate coniferous forests, whose unique biota is our principal focus. The area can be divided longitudinally into three parts; the western coastal mountains (the Cascades and Coast Ranges), the northern Rocky Mountains of the eastern interior, and the low-lying intervening Columbia River Basin or Plateau. Moist westerly winds bring a maritime climate (wet, mild winters and cool, relatively dry summers) to the coastal mountains, and this climatic influence penetrates eastward to the northern Rocky Mountains. The rainshadow of the Cascade Range, however, produces a broad extent of steppe and shrub–steppe ecosystems that largely isolate the mesic forests of the coastal mountains from those of the interior. The ecological isolation of the two mountain ranges is partially circumvented in the north by the Okanogan Highlands and in the south by the Central Oregon Highlands (Figure 15.1).

Mesic, temperate coniferous forests are characterized by the late successional dominance of western hemlock, *Tsuga heterophylla*, and often western redcedar, *Thuja plicata*; they have been referred to as the *Tsuga heterophylla* Province or Zone (Franklin & Dyrness 1973; Daubenmire 1978), or simply 'cedar–hemlock' ecosystems (Daubenmire & Daubenmire 1968). Subalpine and boreal forests replace mesic temperate forests at higher elevations and latitudes, respectively, and are generally dominated by mountain hemlock, *Tsuga mertensiana*, spruce, *Picea* spp. and fir, *Abies* spp. West of the summits of the Cascade Range, mesic forests extend from sea level to the subalpine, but on the east slope of the Cascades and in the Rocky Mountains cedar–hemlock forests are sandwiched between xerophytic forest ecosystems at low elevations and a well-developed subalpine zone. Xerophytic

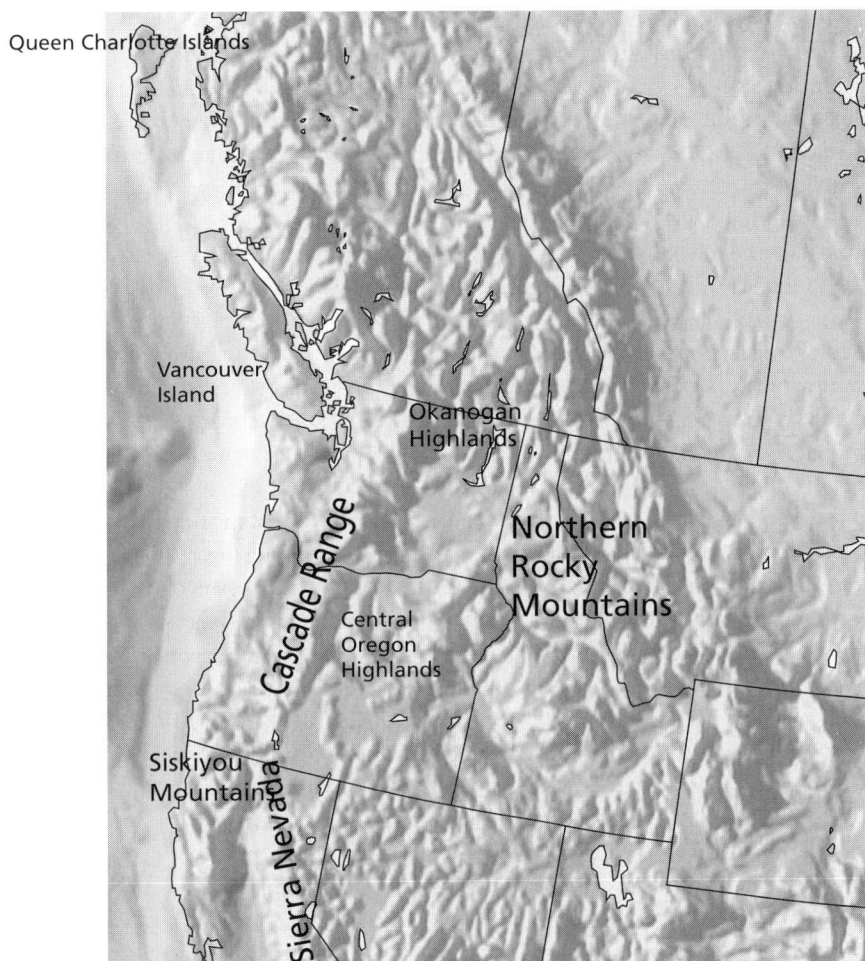

Figure 15.1 The Pacific Northwest of North America, showing relevant geological features.

forests include those dominated by Douglas-fir, *Pseudotsuga menziesii*, ponderosa pine, *Pinus ponderosa*, and in some places juniper *Juniperus* spp. In the Rocky Mountains, the Clearwater River drainage in Idaho is the southern extent of cedar–hemlock ecosystems. This drainage, thought to be a refugium during the Pleistocene or earlier (Daubenmire 1952; Detling 1968), plays a pivotal role in some of the phylogeographic hypotheses proposed below. The southern limit of cedar–hemlock forests in coastal mountains lies in a zone from southwestern Oregon to coastal northern California, i.e. the ecosystem boundary is largely congruent with the southern limit of the Cascade Range. South of the Cascades, the Sierra Nevada Range differs in geology, and a warmer, more Mediterranean climate fosters a substantial change in biota.

Current distributional patterns

A region as complex as north-western North America is, of course, home to species with a wide array of distributional patterns. Although patterns involving species occurring in alpine, boreal, Columbia Plateau, Great Basin and other habitats exist, these will not be discussed here; we will focus on the three major patterns outlined below.

Mesic forest disjunct pattern

One of the most compelling distributional patterns associated with the mesic, temperate forests of the region is the disjunction of conspecific populations between Pacific coastal and interior Rocky Mountain habitats (Figure 15.2). Ecosystem dominants, western hemlock and western redcedar are the most obvious disjuncts, but populations of at least 60 other plants and numerous animal and fungal species (Johnson 1987) are currently separated by 300 km of arid habitats of the Columbia Basin.

Cascade/Sierran pattern

Many coastal species reach their current northern or southern limits at the Cascade/Sierran transition (see Figure 15.1), resulting in the ready distinction

Generalized Mesic Forest
Disjunct Distribution

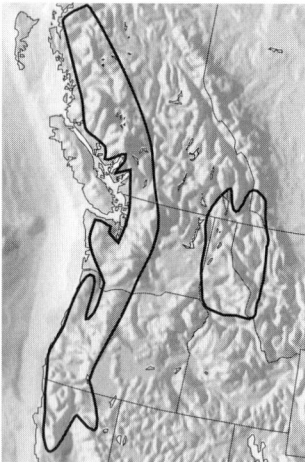

Ancient Vicariance Hypothesis

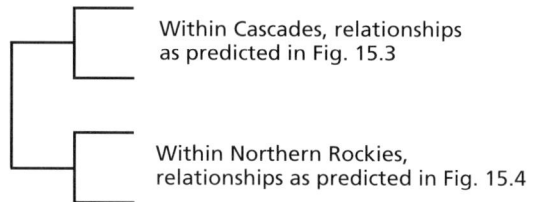

Within Cascades, relationships as predicted in Fig. 15.3

Within Northern Rockies, relationships as predicted in Fig. 15.4

Inland Dispersal Hypotheses
1: Northern Route   2: Southern Route

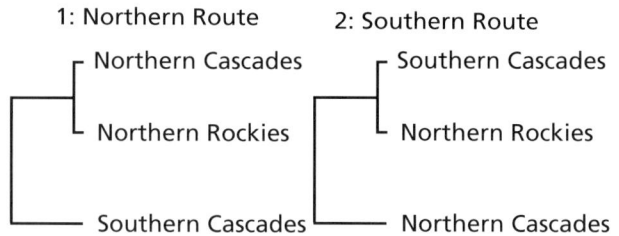

Northern Cascades   Southern Cascades

Northern Rockies   Northern Rockies

Southern Cascades   Northern Cascades

Figure 15.2 Mesic forest disjunct distribution and phylogeographic hypotheses. Over 100 species demonstrate this disjunct distribution, with populations in the Cascade/Sierran region and isolated populations in the northern Rock Mountains. Three hypotheses, involving either vicariance or dispersal, have been proposed for the genesis of the interior populations, and the phylogeographic predictions of each are shown.

Generalized Cascade/ Sierran Distribution

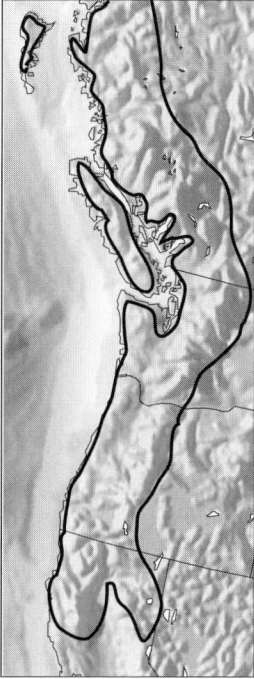

Clinal Environment Hypothesis

Isolation by distance

Single Pacific Coast Refugium Hypothesis

Star phylogeny with very recent coalescence times

Multiple Refugia Hypotheses

1: North-South Recolonization   2: Multiple Coastal Refugia

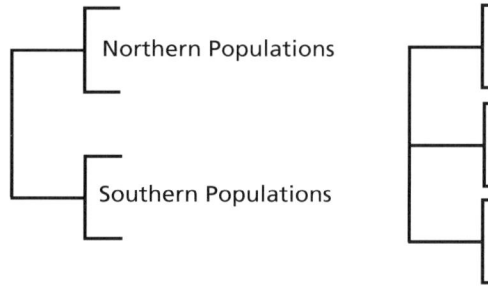

Northern Populations

Southern Populations

Figure 15.3 Cascade/Sierran distribution and phylogeographic hypotheses. Several hypotheses have been erected regarding the role of past events in structuring genetic variation in coastal species. All but one of these involve at least one Pleistocene refugium.

between Cascadian and Sierran ecosystems. Many other species, however, span the boundary, suggesting an ecological and historical connection between the now-contiguous major ecosystems (Figure 15.3).

Northern Rocky Mountain pattern

The mesic, temperate (cedar–hemlock) forests of the Rocky Mountains occur only at middle elevations and only in the northern portion of the range (Figures 15.1 and 15.4). Within this area, however, species with strong affinities to coastal forests are not uniformly distributed. Much of the diversity in inland mesic-adapted species occurs south of the limits of the last Cordilleran glacial advance, with diversity highest in the Clearwater River drainage. In contrast, a few coastal-disjunct species occur only in similar forests north of glaciation. A few plant species (including mountain hemlock) from the subalpine zone of the Cascade/Sierras occur in the subalpine zone of the northern Rocky Mountains. Thus, the biogeographic discontinuity in the Rocky Mountains spans two distinct elevational ecosystems. Species of low-elevation xerophytic forests of the Rocky Mountains, on the other hand, exhibit more complex distributional patterns, including abundant widespread species and more localized low-elevation endemics.

Historical overview

The modern distributional patterns outlined above are best understood in light of the geological history of the region, coupled with evidence of past biotic distributions inferred from palaeobotanical data. The Rocky Mountains are the oldest mountains in western North America, having attained significant relief during the Eocene (45–36 mya). The oldest record of co-occurring coniferous forest elements (including *Thuja* and *Tsuga*) comes from the middle Eocene Republic flora from the west slope of the Rockies in north-eastern Washington (Graham 1999). From that time on, many fossil localities indicate the existence of montane coniferous forests throughout the Rocky Mountains (Graham 1993, 1999). In contrast, major uplift of the Cascade/Sierra chain did not occur until the Pliocene (5–2 mya), and fossil sites with coniferous forests do not predate this time. The rise of the Cascade/Sierras produced a rain shadow that led to the development of essentially modern steppe vegetation on the Columbia Plateau by the end of the epoch (Graham 1999). Thus, by the end of the Tertiary: (i) coniferous forests probably dominated substantial portions of the Cascade/Sierra and Rocky Mountains; (ii) the two ranges were probably largely ecologically isolated; and (iii) mesic temperate (cedar–hemlock) forests were apparently present in the Rocky Mountains, and are predicted to have been supported by the maritime climate in the coastal mountains.

Pleistocene glaciation had enormous impact on the geographic distribution of organisms of the region. During this epoch, 100 000-year cycles created by variation in the earth's orbit (Milanovitch cycles) repeatedly buried at least half of the region under cordilleran and alpine ice for 90 000 years each cycle (Delcourt & Delcourt 1993). For example, during the last glacial maximum ($\approx$20 000 BP), treelines were lowered as much as 1000 m, but forest zones were not necessarily shifted down into low-elevation basins (Barnosky *et al.* 1987). In the Columbia Basin and adjacent lowlands, cold, dry steppe (sagebrush/grass) and, later, pine woodland/steppe occupied most areas until late Holocene (Mack *et al.* 1978a,b). On the coast, relatively wet conditions prevailed during full glacial times, with western hemlock generally present in forests or parklands, often with subalpine (e.g. mountain hemlock or spruce) and tundra elements in the vicinity (Heusser 1985). Thus, a large refugium for mesic temperate forest elements existed along the coast south of glaciation, and additional refugia probably existed in other unglaciated coastal areas (e.g. the western Olympic Peninsula, Vancouver Island and the Queen Charlotte Islands). Pollen records document the northward spread of western redcedar along the Pacific coast during early and middle Holocene, suggesting postglacial dispersal from a southern refugium (Barnosky *et al.* 1987). However, no mesic forest refugium from the Sierras or southern Cascades has yet been identified from fossil data.

The arrival of mesic forests to glaciated portions of the northern Rocky

Mountains appears to have been recent. Based on several sites studied by Mack *et al.* (e.g. 1978a,b), western hemlock did not become established in these areas until 2500–1500 years ago. However, no Quaternary pollen sites have been studied from mesic forest habitats south of glaciation in the northern Rocky Mountains. Thus, the full-glacial fate and Holocene history of cedar–hemlock forests of the inland region '. . . remain a puzzle' (Mehringer 1985).

Hypotheses

The geological and climatic history outlined above suggests a number of hypotheses about the patterns of genetic architecture that might be expected in species exhibiting each of the three major distributional patterns. For each distributional pattern, we propose alternative hypotheses that take into account currently observable aspects of the physical environment (e.g. populations separated by unsuitable habitat) and conditions (e.g. glacial refugia, dispersal avenues) that others have hypothesized to have affected the genetic architecture of multiple species. The historical information in molecular data provides a means of testing and refining biogeographic hypotheses, which until recently have been based on a fragmentary fossil record.

Mesic forest disjunct distributions
'Ancient vicariance'
Our first hypothesis for disjunct distributions requires the continuous occurrence of mesic forests in the Cascades and the northern Rocky Mountains in the past (perhaps dating back to the Eocene), with subsequent attenuation of east–west gene flow by the Cascadian rain shadow of the late Pliocene. Considerable genetic divergence at both cytoplasmic and nuclear loci would be predicted to exist between coastal and inland populations (see Figure 15.2). Recolonization of deglaciated lands would involve differentiated coastal and inland genotypes, which in some cases might come into contact in central British Columbia. Taxa that are not confined to strictly mesic temperate habitats might exhibit even higher levels of east–west differentiation, or even be represented by Cascadian/Rocky Mountain sister species. Members of these lineages might represent early Tertiary colonists of various primordial Cascadian and Rocky Mountain habitats. Within both the coastal and the inland populations, genetic variation would be structured following hypotheses restricted to each of these regions (Figures 15.3 and 15.4).

'Inland dispersal'
A contrasting hypothesis is founded on the presumed absence of mesic forests in the Rocky Mountains until postglacial times and relatively recent colonization coming eastward from the Cascade/Sierra. Assuming north–south differentiation in Cascade/Sierran populations (see below), one subhypothesis ('inland dispersal–north') involves eastward dispersal of northern genotypes across the Okanogan Highlands. This results in an intraspecific phylogeny with a sister relationship between northern Cascadian and Rocky Mountain populations (see Figure 15.2). Alternatively, popu-

Northern Rocky Mountain Distribution

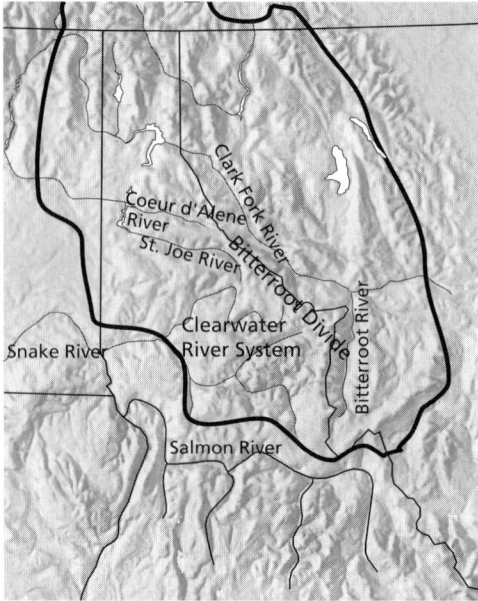

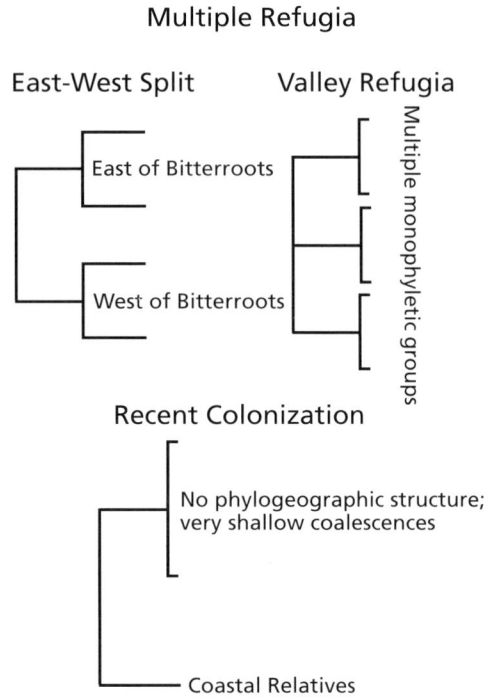

Figure 15.4 Northern Rocky Mountain distribution and phylogeographic hypotheses. The timing of population origin and the isolation associated with geographic features (rivers and mountain ranges) are hypothesized as major factors underlying the structure of genetic variation in inland mesic forest denizens. Phylogeographic predictions are shown for these three hypotheses.

lations from the northern Rockies might be nested within populations from the northern Cascades. Also, because dispersal is hypothesized to be post-Pleistocene, coalescence times should be quite short within the northern Cascades/northern Rockies clade. A second subhypothesis is similar, except eastward dispersal occurs across the central Oregon highlands ('inland dispersal–south'), resulting in a sister relationship between northern Rocky Mountain and southern Cascade/Sierran populations (see Figure 15.2). Because both alternative subhypotheses are based on recent dispersal, predicted genetic patterns include: (i) little or no differentiation between the coast and inland populations, except perhaps in organisms with very short generation times (e.g. insects); and (ii) levels of polymorphism that attenuate with distance from source populations on the coast.

Because dispersal from the coast to the northern Rockies has been hypothesized because of a lack of palaeobotanical records of mesic forest plants in the inland region during the Pleistocene, we restrict our attention to an inland dispersal rather than colonization of the coast ranges from an inland refugium.

Cascade/Sierran distributions

Figure 15.3 illustrates an example of a species with a Cascade/Sierran distribution. Because mountain glaciers covered substantial portions of the region during Pleistocene glacial maxima, all but the first hypothesis below involve refugia in shaping the genetic structure on the landscape.

'Clinal environment hypothesis'

This hypothesis is founded on the fact that the Cascade/Sierran chain is of relatively uniform age, but throughout the Cenozoic a clinal environmental gradient probably existed, from relatively cool and moist in northern latitudes to warm and dry in the south. As is seen today, some species occupy only a portion of this climatic gradient, whereas others have a broad latitudinal distribution. Under this hypothesis, the latter species should exhibit gradual shifts (at most) in the frequencies of neutral nuclear markers, and variation in cytoplasmic genomes, if present, would not show congruent patterns across multiple species.

'Single Pacific Coast refugium'

If a single Pacific Coast refugium existed, and there was apparently at least one (Barnosky *et al.* 1987), relative genetic uniformity would be predicted if the refugium was small. That is, very shallow coalescence times should be seen in all species; neither north–south patterns nor congruent patterns of divergence among species would be predicted.

'Multiple refugia'

Many authors have posited the presence of more than a single coastal refugium (e.g. MacDonald & Cook 1996; Soltis *et al.* 1997). Thus, we can subdivide this hypothesis into: (i) the 'north–south recolonization' subhypothesis in which there are two refugia, one coastal, perhaps in the vicinity of Vancouver Island or the Queen Charlotte Islands, and a second in the mountains south of glaciation, perhaps the Siskiyous; and (ii) the 'multiple coastal' subhypothesis, in which there are more than two refugia scattered along the coast and in other lowlands west of the Cascades. Under the 'north–south' subhypothesis, we would predict a pattern of divergence into northern and southern clades (especially in haploid, uniparentially inherited cytoplasmic genomes), and there should be congruent patterns across multiple species (see Figure 15.3). Within each of these clades coalescence times would likely be short. Under the 'multiple coastal' refugia subhypothesis, we would predict multiple reciprocally monophyletic clades, within which coalescence times would be short. Relationship among these clades might be star-like (i.e. represented by very short internodes that are difficult to resolve), and this pattern should recur across multiple species (Figure 15.3).

Northern Rocky Mountain distributions

'Multiple refugia'

Our first hypothesis associated with the northern Rocky Mountains is based on small-scale isolation of populations across the heterogeneous mountain environ-

327

ment. The Bitterroot crest separates mesic forest habitats on the east and west slopes of the range, and major river canyons (Figure 15.4) result in a series of relatively isolated mid-elevation, mesic, riverside forest ecosystems. This isolation probably increased during glaciation, as mesic habitats contracted at the expense of both expanding subalpine forests and tundra above and cold steppe below (Barnosky *et al.* 1987). This hypothesis thus posits a series of refugia, across the dissected mountain topography. The expected intraspecific phylogeny could contain an 'east–west split', or multiple monophyletic groups associated with multiple 'valley refugia' (Figure 15.4), with differing population sizes and histories potentially fostering differing branch lengths. Refugial areas are expected to be supported by multiple congruent phylogenies. An additional prediction of this model is that northern, glaciated portions of the region would have been colonized by genotypes found in adjacent unglaciated habitats, or by Cascadian genotypes that dispersed eastward across the Okanogan Highlands after glaciation.

'Recent colonization'
This alternative hypothesis for genetic patterns within the northern Rocky Mountains is founded on the assumption of a recent, postglacial colonization of the region. Genetic markers would be unlikely to vary between the east and west slopes of the range, among river canyons, or between glaciated and unglaciated habitats (Figure 15.4). Whether the species dispersed into the area via a northern or southern route might be inferred from its lack of differentiation from one Cascadian genotype in an intraspecific phylogeny, but the place of origin and direction of migration would be equivocal unless a unidirectional attenuation in the frequency of markers existed.

Case studies

Mesic forest disjunct taxa
The genetic structures of several plant species with disjunct distributions in the mesic forests of the Cascades/Coast Ranges and northern Rockies have been examined using cytoplasmic (cp) DNA and/or nuclear markers (Table 15.1). Four of these, *Tellima grandiflora*, *Tiarella trifoliata*, *Alnus rubra* and *Polystichum munitum*, have nearly identical distributions from southeastern Alaska to central California, mostly west of the Cascade crest, with disjunct populations in the Rocky Mountains. All four of these species exhibit the north–south pattern of cpDNA differentiation (reviewed in Soltis *et al.* 1997; see below) in the coastal portions of their ranges. *Tellima grandiflora*, *Tiarella trifoliata* and *Polystichum munitum* show a congruent pattern in which the cpDNA of populations from the northern Rockies is identical to the northern coastal genotype. Isozyme data for western white pine, *Pinus monticola*, show a similar pattern of close relationship between northern Rocky and northern Cascade populations and more distant relationships to populations in the southern Cascades and Sierras (Steinhoff *et al.* 1983). These patterns are consistent

Table 15.1 A compilation of plant and animal taxa that exhibit a disjunct distribution in the mesic forests of the Pacific Northwest and for which genetic data have been examined.

	Major group: family	Life history	Genetic data	Reference
Plant species				
Tellima grandiflora	Magnoliophyta: Saxifragaceae	Herbaceous perennial	cpDNA	Soltis *et al.* (1991)
Tiarella trifoliata	Magnoliophyta: Saxifragaceae	Herbaceous perennial	cpDNA	Soltis *et al.* (1992)
Alnus rubra	Magnoliophyta: Betulaceae	Tree	cpDNA	Strenge (1994)
Polystichum muntium	Pteridophyta: Dryopteridaceae	Herbaceous perennial	cpDNA	Strenge (1994)
Pseudotsuga menziesii	Coniferophyta: Pinaceae	Tree	Allozymes	Li and Adams (1989)
Animal species				
Dicamptodon ensatus/ aterimus/tenebrosi/copei complex	Caudata: Dicamptodontidae	Metamorphic and paedomorphic salamanders	Allozymes	Daugherty *et al.* (1983) Good (1989)
Ascaphus truei/montanus complex	Anura: Ascaphidae	Metamorphic frogs	Allozymes MtDNA RAPDs	C. H. Dougherty unpubl. Nielson *et al.* (2001) Ritland *et al.* (2000)
Microtus richardsoni	Rodentia; Muridae	Semiaquatic vole	mtDNA sequences (cyt b)	Demboski and Sullivan (unpublished)
Rana pretiosa complex	Anura: Ranidae	Metamorphic frog	Allozymes	Green *et al.* (1996)
Plethodon vandykei/ idahoensis complex	Anura: Plethodontidae	Metamorphic salamanders	Allozymes	Howard *et al.* (1993)

cpDNA, chloroplast DNA; mtDNA, mitochondrial DNA; RAPDs, randomly amplified polymorphic DNA.

with the 'inland dispersal–north' hypothesis of recent colonization of the northern Rockies, perhaps via the Okanogan Highlands. In contrast, in *Alnus rubra*, the cpDNA of populations from the northern Rockies is identical to the southern coastal genotype, consistent with recent colonization via a southern route ('inland dispersal–south'), such as the highlands of central Oregon. Contrasting isozyme data were reported for Douglas fir (Li & Adams 1989), a species that extends beyond mesic habitats. In this case, coastal and inland populations are well differentiated, suggesting relatively ancient vicariance.

Studies suggesting both ancient vicariance and inland dispersal also exist in the animal literature. Relatively few animal examples exist for the disjunct mesic forest communities, and most of those are amphibians (Table 15.1). Good (1989) examined allozyme variation in the genus *Dicamptodon* (giant salamanders); Howard *et al.* (1993) examined allozyme variation in the *Plethodon vandykei/ P. idahoensis* complex; Nielson *et al.* (2001) examined mtDNA sequence variation (cyt b and ND2 genes) in *Ascaphus* (tailed frogs). In spite of the differences in methodologies, these studies have a common conclusion; the divergence of the inland forms from the coastal forms is the deepest split. Thus, each of these examples suggests an ancient vicariance and persistence of inland populations throughout the Pleistocene (see Figure 15.2). Unfortunately, the fact that the first two examples involve allozyme data prevents us from applying the statistical phylogenetic hypothesis tests described below (e.g. parametric bootstrap tests) as these are primarily devised for DNA sequence data.

A contrasting case study involves water voles, *Microtus richardsoni*, which occur in moist meadows within conifer forests along the coast, and exhibit a disjunct distribution in the Rocky Mountains. Preliminary cyt b sequence data (J. Demboski & J. Sullivan, unpublished) deviate from the common patterns seen in the amphibians. First, only a single species appears to be present. Secondly, inland populations are nested with populations from the northern Cascades, supporting the hypothesis of recent inland dispersal across the Okanogan Highlands ('inland dispersal–north' hypothesis; see pp. 325–6). A statistical test of this data set is described below.

Thus, the current distributions of the flora and fauna of the northern Rocky Mountains are probably the result of numerous vicariance and dispersal events of varying age, and similarities in the composition of *mesic* forests in the Cascades and northern Rockies apparently arose, at least in part, through a complex series of relatively recent migrations into the northern Rockies. These colonization events appear to have come from multiple refugia, across different inland migration routes.

Cascade/Sierran taxa

Molecular studies of both plants and animals centred primarily on the Cascade/ Sierran region suggest a recurrent pattern of genetic differentiation. In a diverse array of plants, including the angiosperms *Tolmiea menziesii*, *Tellima grandiflora*, *Tiarella trifoliata*, *Alnus rubra* and *Ribes bracteosum* and the fern *Polystichum munitum*, cpDNA data indicate two clades of populations that are geographically structured (Soltis *et al.* 1989a, 1991, 1992, 1997; Table 15.2). A northern group consists of populations from Alaska to central or southern Oregon; populations from central Oregon southward to northern California form a southern clade (reviewed in Soltis *et al.* 1997).

Similar patterns of north–south genetic differentiation are apparent in several animals from north-western North America (Table 15.2). Analysis of mtDNA markers in the moth *Greya politella* revealed the presence of northern and southern clades comprising populations from Washington, Oregon; and Idaho and California, respectively (Brown *et al.* 1997). Allozyme and cytological data suggest a north–south pattern of differentiation in rainbow trout, *Onchorynchus mykiss* (Thorgaard 1983; Hatch 1990; Reisenbichler *et al.* 1992; Ostberg & Thorgaard 1999). For example, Hatch (1990) reported that 'the area south of the Coos River (central Oregon) was marked by sharp transition in four enzymes . . . '. Allozyme data for the urodele

Table 15.2 A compilation of plants and animals that exhibit a Cascade/Sierran pattern of genetic differentiation in northwestern North America.

	Major group: family	Life history	Genetic data	Reference
Plant species				
Tolmiea menziesii	Magnoliophyta: Saxifragaceae	Herbaceous perennial	cpDNA	Soltis et al. (1989a)
Tellima grandiflora	Magnoliophyta: Saxifragaceae	Herbaceous perennial	cpDNA	Soltis et al. (1991)
Tiarella trifoliata	Magnoliophyta: Saxifragaceae	Herbaceous perennial	cpDNA	Soltis et al. (1992)
Alnus rubra	Magnoliophyta: Betulaceae	Tree	cpDNA	Strenge (1994)
Ribes bracteosum	Magnoliophyta: Grossulariaceae	Shrub	cpDNA	Soule et al. (1995)
Polystichum munitum	Pteridophyta: Dryopteridaceae	Herbaceous perennial	cpDNA	Strenge (1994)
Erythronium montanum	Magnoliophyta: Liliaceae	Herbaceous perennial	Allozymes	Allen et al. (1996)
Pinus jeffreyi	Coniferophyta: Pinaceae	Tree	Allozymes	Furnier and Adams (1986)
Pinus contorta subsp. latifolia	Coniferophyta: Pinaceae	Tree	Allozymes	Wheeler and Guries (1982)
Pinus monticola	Coniferophyta: Pinaceae	Tree	Allozymes	Steinhoff et al. (1983)
Animal species				
Greya politella	Lepidoptera: Prodoxidae	Holometabolous insect	mtDNA	Brown et al. (1997)
Onchorynchus mykiss	Actinopterygii: Salmonidae	Anadromous fish	cytogenetic; mtDNA (control region)	Thorgaard (1983) Ostberg and Thorgaard (1999)
Dicamptodon ensatus/ tenebrosi/copei complex	Caudata: Dicamptodontidae	Metamorphic and paedomorphic salamander	Allozymes	Daugherty et al. (1983) Good (1989)
Plethodon vandykei	Caudata: Plethodontidae	Metamorphic salamander	Allozymes	Howard et al. (1993)
Rhyacotriton cascadae/ olympicus/keezeri/ variegatus complex	Caudata: Rhyacotritonidae	Metamorphic salamander	Allozymes	Good and Wake (1992)
Ascaphus truei	Anura: Ascaphidae	Metamorphic frog	Allozymes mtDNA sequences (cyt b and ND2)	Dougherty (1979) Nielson et al. (2001)
Sorex monticolus/ sonomae coastal complex	Insectivora: Soricidae	Insectivorous shrew	mtDNA sequences (cyt b)	Demboski and Cook (2001)

Abbreviations as in Table 15.1.

amphibians *Dicamptodon* and *Plethodon vandykei* complex show an initial deep split between the Cascades/Sierras and the Rocky Mountains (see above), but within the former region a distinct north–south structuring of genotypes (and taxonomy in *Dicamptodon*) is also observed (Good 1989; Howard *et al.* 1993). Demboski and Cook (2001) examined cyt b variation among coastal endemic shrews in the *Sorex monticolus* complex. *Sorex monticolus* has classically been considered to be widespread in western North America, with *S. bendiri* and *S. pacificus* restricted to small areas in coastal Oregon. All of the samples from the coast (coastal *S. monticolus* samples plus *S. bendiri* and *S. pacificus*) form a coastal clade, and within that clade, haplotypes partition in a north–south pattern (Demboski & Cook 2001).

Allozyme and cpDNA data also reveal that some species have lower levels of genetic variation in the northern portion of their ranges than in the southern portion. In *Tolmiea, Tellima* and *Polystichum* the northern clade consists of a single haplotype, whereas multiple cpDNA genotypes occur in the southern clade (Soltis *et al.* 1989a, 1991, 1997). Reduced allozyme variation was detected in northern populations of *Erythonium montanum* and *Pinus monticola* (Steinhoff *et al.* 1983; Allen *et al.* 1996). Such patterns of diversity are observed in multiple European taxa, and are thought to be associated with dispersal from southern refugia (e.g. Hewitt 1999; Chapters 13 and 14 this volume).

Of the hypotheses proposed above for the Cascade/Sierran region (see above), much of the data are in very close agreement with in scenario proposed as part of the 'multiple refugia — north–south recolonization' hypothesis (Table 15.2, Figure 15.3). However, the considerable support for a northern and southern refugium does not preclude the possibility that other of our proposed hypotheses explain the pattern of genetic variation in other species. For example, in *Heuchera micrantha*, another member of Saxifragaceae displaying the Cascade/Sierran distributional pattern, no pattern of north–south genetic differentiation was detected with either cpDNA restriction sites (Soltis *et al.* 1989b) or allozymes (Ness *et al.* 1989), as predicted by the 'clinal environment hypothesis'. Significantly, considerable genetic variation was present among populations of *H. micrantha*, but the phylogeny obtained was essentially a starburst.

Although there is agreement in both the plant and animal literature that refugia have played a major role in the recolonization of areas of the Pacific North-West, there is less agreement as to the possible locations of these refugia. In several of the plant species analysed for cpDNA variation, a few populations having southern genotypes appear to have survived in northern glacial refugia on the Olympic Peninsula of Washington and Prince of Wales Island, Alaska (reviewed in Soltis *et al.* 1997). Studies on three-spine sticklebacks, *Gasterosteus aculeatus* (O'Reilly *et al.* 1993), song sparrows, *Melospiza melodia* (Zink & Ditmann 1993), and black bears, *Ursus americanus* (Byun *et al.* 1997) have suggested that the Queen Charlotte Islands represent an important refugium for animal taxa. However, other interpretations of refugia for these animal species are equally plausible (Orti *et al.* 1994; Demboski *et al.* 1998). Furthermore, there are no genetic data for plants that clearly support the Queen Charlotte Islands as a refugium. Other mtDNA studies have identified the

Columbia River as a possible refugium for populations of white sturgeon, *Acipenser transmontanus* (Brown *et al.* 1992), and bull trout, *Salvelinus confluentus* (Taylor *et al.* 1999).

Northern Rocky Mountain taxa

There are only a limited number of genetic studies of plant species distributed in the northern Rocky Mountains (Table 15.3), and these present a complex picture of phylogeographic history. Sequence data from the cpDNA of *Cardamine constancei*, an endemic species of mesic forests of the northern Rocky Mountains, provide strong support for the 'multiple refugia' hypothesis (see Figure 15.4). Three major haplotype lineages are geographically structured, suggesting long isolation of populations in separate refugia (Brunsfeld & Sullivan, unpublished). Isozyme data from Douglas-fir revealed substantial differentiation between northern and southern Rocky Mountain populations (Li & Adams 1989), leading the authors to suggest that Douglas fir existed in a refugium in the northern Rockies during the Pleistocene. These data, however, do not reveal any differentiation among populations that might suggest multiple refugia. This might be attributable to high gene flow known to occur in conifers, or the species may not have been confined to isolated mesic forest refugia because of its extremely wide ecological amplitude. Similarly, isozyme data from 19 populations of western larch (*Larix occidentalis*) from the northern Rockies (Fins & Seeb 1986) show little interpopulational differentiation, providing possible support for the 'recent colonization' hypothesis (see Figure 15.4).

Examples of genetic studies of animal species restricted to the northern Rockies are also limited. However, Good and Sullivan (unpublished) have examined cyt b

Table 15.3 Plant and animal taxa from mesic forests of the northern Rocky Mountains for which genetic data are available.

	Major group: family	Life history	Genetic data	Reference
Plant species				
Cardamine constancei	Magnoliophyta: Brassicaceae	Herbaceous perennial	cpDNA	Brunsfeld and Sullivan (in prep)
Larix occidentalis	Coniferophyta: Pinaceae	Tree	Allozymes	Fins and Seeb (1986)
Pinus monticola	Coniferophyta: Pinaceae	Tree	Allozymes	Steinhoff *et al.* (1983)
Animal species				
Spermophilus columbianus	Rodentia: Sciuridae	Granivorous rodent	mtDNA restriction sites	MacNeil and Strobeck (1987)
Tamias ruficaudus	Rodentia: Sciuridae	Granivorous rodent	mtDNA sequences (cyt b)	Good and Sullivan In prep
Ascaphus montanus	Anura: Ascaphidae	Metamorphic frog	mtDNA sequences (cyt b)	Nielson *et al.* (2001)

variation in a sample of Columbian ground squirrels collected from across the southern end of their range (Oregon, Idaho and Montana); differentiation ranges up to 4.5% uncorrected divergence among the easternmost and westernmost samples. This is consistent with an east–west pattern of differentiation (see Figure 15.4), although additional sampling is certainly required. Good and Sullivan (unpublished) also examined cyt b variation in 175 red-tailed chipmunks *Tamias ruficaudus*, collected from across the range of this species, and found two well-differentiated eastern and western haplotype clades in this species as well, separated by 4.5% uncorrected sequence divergence (similar to the differentiation seen in Columbian ground squirrels). This example also supports an east–west split, and haplotype diversity appears to be highest among the samples from the Clearwater drainage. Nielson *et al.* (2001) examined cyt b and ND2 variation within the Rocky Mountain tailed frog, *Ascaphus montanus*, and found a deep divergence in populations from the Salmon River Mountains, suggesting a north–south split in this species within the northern Rocky Mountains. Thus, the limited data currently available suggest the existence of multiple refugia impacting the genetic structure of multiple taxa in the northern Rockies. This is not congruent with data (reviewed above) that suggest a recent colonization of the region from the coast. Reconciling these conflicting data will require additional studies employing more comparable genetic data and focusing on taxa that are more ecologically similar (i.e. confined to mesic forests).

Advances in methods of comparison

Because many phylogeographic studies are focused at or near species limits, analyses of phylogeographic data often involve both population genetics analyses and phylogenetic analyses. The suite of population genetics tools available is reviewed by Hewitt and Ibrahim (Chapter 13); here we focus on advances in phylogenetic analyses that elevate comparative phylogeography from a science in which patterns of similarity are described to a more powerful hypothesis-testing perspective. Page (e.g. 1994) has developed methods that allow a more rigorous assessment of the degree to which different potentially coevolved lineages (such as codistributed taxa) experienced shared history. Such methods as TreeMapping (Page 1994) provide inferences of the number of codivergence events (either codispersal or coviciariance) and also allow for randomization tests to estimate the significance of shared history (e.g. Bermingham & Martin 1998; Sullivan *et al.* 2000).

TreeMapping certainly represents an improvement over visual comparisons of topologies; however, the approach ignores phylogenetic uncertainty. Phylogeographies are reconciled with each other as if each were estimated with certainty. If relationships among areas are only weakly supported, spurious conclusions might result. A novel method is a Bayesian approach similar to that developed by Huelsenbeck *et al.* (2000) for the assessment of cospeciation between hosts and parasites. Although this approach is very promising, it will require the development of a biogeographic model similar to the model of cospeciation developed by Huelsenbeck *et al.* (2000). A second approach is use of the parametric bootstrap (e.g. Huelsenbeck *et al.* 1996). One may test for congruence by forcing the data for each species to fit the phylogeographic patterns inferred from the other species of interest, or alternatively, one may test *a priori* hypotheses such as those outlined above.

Hypothesis testing via the parametric bootstrap was performed using data for water voles, *Microtus richardsoni* (Demboski & Sullivan, unpublished). Water voles occur in moist meadows, usually within 3–5 m of streams, and exhibit the disjunct distribution described above. Maximum-likelihood (ML) analysis of the preliminary data (750 bp cyt b for 28 voles) supports the hypothesis of inland dispersal across the Okanogan Highlands during glacial retreat (Figure 15.5). In the ML tree, haplotypes found in the northern Rockies are nested within haplotypes found in the northern Cascades, and haplotypes found in the southern Cascades are sister to these. If the data are constrained to fit the ancient vicariance hypothesis that appears to have generated the disjunct distribution of the three amphibians discussed above (reciprocal monophyly of haplotypes found in the Cascades and northern Rockies; see Figure 15.2), the best-likelihood score is 19.270 lnL units worse than the best unconstrained tree. If the disjunct distribution of *Microtus richardsoni* were the result of an ancient vicariance event (see Figure 15.2), we would expect to see data of the nature we observed less than 1% of the time (see Figure 15.2; *P* < 0.01). Thus, by adopting a rigorous statistical framework, we can go beyond visual inspection of

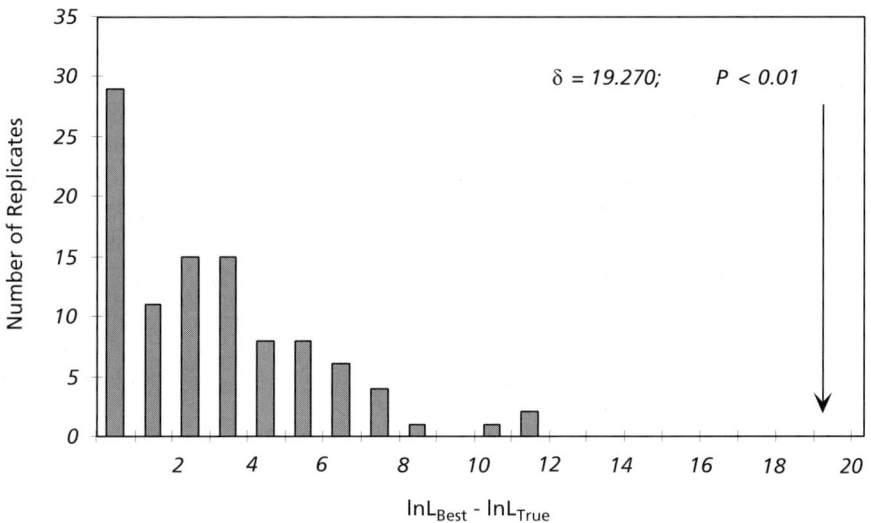

Figure 15.5 Parametric bootstrap test of the ancient vicariance hypothesis in water voles, *Microtus richardsoni*. Phylogenetic analyses of cyt b data for water voles supports the 'inland dispersal—north' hypothesis. Forcing the data to fit the ancient vicariance hypothesis results in a deterioration of the likelihood score by 19.270 lnL units. The null distribution was generated by simulation, and the ancient vicariance hypothesis can be rejected (*P* < 0.01).

patterns and reject the ancient vicariance hypothesis as an explanation of the genesis of the disjunct distribution for water voles.

Conclusion

Phylogeographic studies of plant and animal species from northwestern North America illustrate a complex history for the biota of this region. Current species distributions appear to result largely from the combined effects of orogeny and glaciation. The geological and climatological complexity of this region has created complex patterns of genetic diversity within species. We have laid a foundation for understanding this variation by elaborating alternative hypotheses that are testable using empirical data. The fragmentary data currently available suggest that vicariance, dispersal and the existence of refugia have worked in concert to produce the species distributions and genetic divergence patterns of the region. Inferences to date have been hampered by a lack of consistency in both the types of data gathered and the analytical approaches used. A clear understanding of regional phylogeography requires coordinated analyses, and future studies should seek to use DNA sequence data that are amenable to analyses at multiple hierarchical levels. More robust, statistical analytical methods need to be employed to elevate phylogeography to a level of rigour common in other fields of science.

Summary

Understanding the causative forces underlying the genetic architecture of any species may be difficult, but it is more challenging for species from geographic areas that have experienced complex and dynamic geological and climatological histories, such as northwestern North America. However, as the number of plant and animal species studied phylogeographically in this region increases, patterns are beginning to emerge, providing consistent support for the roles of glacial refugia, vicariance and overland migration routes in shaping the genetic structures of codistributed species. For example, species with coastal distributions typically exhibit a sharp genetic discontinuity between northern populations and southern populations, probably reflecting isolation in multiple glacial refugia and recolonization to form a continuous distribution. The disjunct distributions of many species between the mesic forests of the Cascades/Coast Ranges and the northern Rocky Mountains could have arisen through a number of processes, such as vicariance caused by the rise of the Cascades and the development of the intervening rain shadow of the Columbia Basin, or more recent colonization of the northern Rockies via northern or southern overland routes from Cascade/Sierran communities. Genetic patterns within the northern Rockies reflect the probable variation in colonization times, with some species showing strong divergence patterns suggestive of multiple refugia, and others exhibiting the genetic homogeneity expected in a recent colonist. Studies of additional species are needed to test the alternative hypotheses further. Comparative phylogeographers have a new arsenal of powerful statistical methods with which to make inferences on a regional scale. Statistical phylogenetic methods, such as parametric bootstrap analyses and tree mapping, provide means of expanding the field beyond the simple description of pattern, to one based on the statistical testing of hypotheses of shared history.

References

Allen, G.A., Antos, J.A., Worley, A.C., Stuttill, T.A. & Hebda, R.J. (1996). Morphological and genetic variation in disjunct populations of the avalanche lily *Erythronium montanum*. *Canadian Journal of Botany*, **74**, 403–412.

Avise, J.C. (2000). *Phylogeography: The History and Formation of Species*. Harvard University Press, Cambridge, MA.

Avise, J.C., Arnold, J., Ball, R.M., Berminham, E., Lamb, T., Neigel, J.E., Reeb, C.A. & Saunders, N.C. (1987). Intraspecific phylogeography: the mitochondrial DNA bridge between population genetics and systematics. *Annual Review of Ecology and Systematics*, **18**, 489–522.

Barnosky, C.W., Anderson, P.M. & Bartlein, P.J. (1987). The Northwestern U.S. during deglaciation; Vegetational history and paleoclimatic implications. In: *North America and Adjacent Oceans During the Last Deglaciation* (eds W.F. Ruddiman & H.E. Wright Jr.), pp. 289–321. *The Geology of North America*, Vol. K-3. Geological Society of America, Boulder, CO.

Bermingham, E. & Martin, A.P. (1998). Comparative mtDNA phylogeography of neotropical freshwater fishes: testing shared history to infer the evolutionary landscape of lower Central America. *Molecular Ecology*, **7**, 499–517.

Brown, J.R., Beckenbach, A.T. & Smith, M.J. (1992). Influence of Pleistocene glaciations and human intervention upon mitochondrial DNA diversity in White Sturgeon (*Acipenser transmontanus*) populations. *Canadian Journal of Fisheries and Aquatic Sciences*, **49**, 358–367.

Brown, J.M., Leebens-Mack, J.H., Thompson, J.N., Pellmyr, O. & Harrison, R.G. (1997). Phylogeography and host association in a pollinating seed parasite, *Greya politella* (*Lepidoptera: Prodoxidae*). *Molecular Ecology*, **6**, 215–224.

Byun, S.A., Koop, B.F. & Reimchen, T.E. (1997). North American black bear mtDNA phylogeography: implications for morphology and the Haida Gwaii glacial refugium controversy. *Evolution*, **51**, 1647–1653.

daSilva, M.N.F. & Patton, J.L. (1998). Molecular phylogeography and the evolution and conservation of Amazonian mammals. *Molecular Ecology*, **7**, 475–486.

Daubenmire, R. (1952). Plant geography of Idaho. In: *Flora of Idaho* (ed. R.J. Davis), pp. 1–17. Brigham Young University Press, Provo, Utah.

Daubenmire, R. (1978). *Plant Geography with Special Reference to North America*. Academic Press, New York.

Daubenmire, R. & Daubenmire J.B. (1968). *Forest Vegetation of Eastern Washington and Northern Idaho*. Technical Bulletin 60, Washington Agricultural Experiment Station, Washington State University, Pullman, Washington.

Daugherty, C.H. (1979). *Population ecology and genetics of* Ascaphus truei: *an examination of gene flow and natural selection*. PhD dissertation, University of Montana, IL.

Daugherty, C.H., Allendorf, F.W., Dunlap, W.W. & Knudsen, K.L. (1983). Systematic implications of geographic patterns of genetic variation in the genus *Dicamptodon*. *Copeia*, 1983, 679–691.

Delcourt, P.A. & Delcourt, H.R. (1993). Paleoclimates, paleovegetation, and paleofloras during the late Quaternary. In: *Flora North America*, Vol. 1, pp. 71–94. Oxford University Press, New York.

Demboski, J.R., Stone, K.D. & Cook, J.A. (1998). Further perspectives on the Haida Gwaii glacial refugium. *Evolution*, **56**, 2008–2012.

Demboski, J.R. & Cook, J.A. (2001). Phylogeography of the dusky shrew, *Sorex monticolus* (Insectivora, Soricidae): Insight into deep and shallow history in northwestern North America. *Molecular Ecology*.

Detling, L.E. (1968). *Historical Background of the Flora of the Pacific Northwest*. Bulletin No. 13, Museum of Natural History, University of Oregon, Eugene.

Eizirik, E., Bonatto, S.L., Johnson, W.E., Crawshaw, Jr., P.G., Vie, J.C., Brousset, D.M., O'Brien, S.J. & Salzano, F.M. (1998). Phylogeographic patterns and evolution of the mitochondrial DNA control region in two neotropical cats (Mammalia, Felidae) *Journal of Molecular Evolution*, **47**, 613–624.

Fins, L. & Seeb, L.W. (1986). Genetic variation in allozymes of western larch. *Canadian Journal of Forestry Research*, **16**, 1013–1018.

Franklin, J.F. & Dyrness, C.T. (1973). *Natural Vegetation of Oregon and Washington*. General Technical Report PNW-8, USDA Forest Service, Portland, Oregon.

Furnier, G.R. & Adams, W.T. (1986). Geographic patterns of allozyme variation in Jeffrey pine. *American Journal of Botany*, **73**, 1009–1015.

Graham, A. (1993). History of the vegetation: Cretaceous–Tertiary, In: *Flora North America*, Vol. 1, pp. 57–70. Oxford University Press, New York.

Graham, A. (1999). *Late Cretaceous and Cenozoic History of North American Vegetation*. Oxford University Press, New York.

Green, D.M., Sharbel, T.F., Kearsley, J. & Kaiser, H. (1996). Postglacial range fluctuation, genetic subdivision and speciation in the western North American spotted frog complex, *Rana pretiosa*. *Evolution*, **50**, 374–390.

Good, D.A. (1989). Hybridization and cryptic species in *Dicamptodon*. *Evolution*, **43**, 728–744.

Good, D.A. & Wake, D.B. (1992). Geographic variation and speciation in the torrent salamanders of the genus *Rhyacotriton* (Caudata: Rhyacotritinudae). *University of California Publications in Zoology*, **126**, 1–91.

Hatch, K.M. (1990). *A phenotypic comparison of thirty-eight steelhead* (Oncorhynchus mykiss) *populations from coastal Oregon*. MS Thesis, Oregon State University, Corvallis.

Hewitt, G.M. (1993). Postglacial distribution and species substructures: lessons from pollen, insects and hybrid zones. In: *Evolutionary Patterns and Processes* (eds D.R. Lees & D. Edwards), pp. 97–123. Academic Press, London.

Hewitt, G.M. (1999). Post-glacial recolonization of European biota. *Biological Journal of the Linnean Society*, **68**, 87–112.

Hewitt, G.M. (2000). The genetic legacy of the Quaternary ice ages. *Nature*, **405**, 907–913.

Heusser, C.J. (1985). Quaternary pollen records from the Pacific Northwest coast: Aleutians to the Oregon-California boundary. In: *Pollen Records of Late-Quaternary North American Sediments* (V.M. Bryant, Jr. & R.G. Holloway), pp. 141–165.

American Association of Stratigraphic Palynologists Foundation, Dallas, Texas.

Howard, J.H., Seeb, L.W. & Wallace, R. (1993). Genetic variation and population divergence in the *Plethodon vandykei* species group. *Herpetologica*, **49**, 238–247.

Huelsenbeck, J.P., Hillis, D.M. & Jones, R. (1996). Parametric bootstrapping in molecular phylogenetics: Applications and performance. In: *Molecular Zoology: Advances, Strategies, and Protocols*. (eds J.D. Ferraris & S.R. Palumbi), pp. 19–45. Wiley-Liss, New York.

Huelsenbeck, J.P., Rannala, B. & Larget, B. (2000). A Bayesian framework for the analysis of cospeciation. *Evolution*, **54**, 352–364.

Johnson, P.J. (1987). *Larval taxonomy, biology, and biogeography of the genera of North American Byrridae* (Insecta: Coleoptera). MS Thesis, University of Idaho, Moscow.

Li, P. & Adams, W.T. (1989). Range-wide patterns of allozyme variation in Douglas-fir (*Pseudotsuga menziesii*). *Canadian Journal of Forest Research*, **19**, 149–161.

MacNeil, D. & Strobeck, C. (1987). Evolutionary relationships among colonies of columbian ground squirrels as shown by mitochondrial DNA. *Evolution*, **41**, 873–881.

MacDonald, S.O. & Cook, J.A. (1996). The land mammal fauna of southeast Alaska. *Canadian Field Naturalist*, **110**, 571–598.

Mack, R.N., Rutter, N.W., Bryant, V.M., Jr. & Valastro, S. (1978a). Reexamination of postglacial vegetation history in northern Idaho: Hager Pond, Bonner Co. *Quaternary Research*, **10**, 241–255.

Mack, R.N., Rutter, N.W., Valastro, S. & Bryant, V.M., Jr. (1978b). Late Quaternary vegetation history at Waits Lake, Colville River Valley, Washington. *Botanical Gazette*, **139**, 499–506.

Mehringer, P.J., Jr. (1985). Late-Quaternary pollen records from the interior Pacific Northwest and northern Great Basin of the United States. In: *Pollen Records of Late-Quaternary North American Sediments* (V.M. Bryant, Jr. & R.G. Holloway), pp. 167–189. American Association of Stratigraphic Palynologists Foundation, Dallas, Texas.

Ness, B.D., Soltis, D.E. & Soltis, P.S. (1989). Autopolyploidy in *Heuchera micrantha* (Saxifragaceae). *American Journal of Botany*, **76**, 614–626.

Nielson, M., Lohman, K. & Sullivan, J. (2001). Evolution and phylogeography of the tailed frog

(*Ascaphus truei*): insights on the biogeography of the Pacific Northwest. *Evolution*, in press.

O'Reilly, P., Reimchen, T.E., Beech, R. & Strobeck, C. (1993). Mitochondrial DNA in *Gasterosteus* and Pleistocene glacial refugium on the Queen Charlotte Islands, British Columbia. *Evolution*, **47**, 678–684.

Orti, G., Bell, M.A., Reimchen, T.E. & Meyer, A. (1994). Global survey of mitochondrial DNA sequences in the threespine stickleback: Evidence for recent migrations. *Evolution*, **48**, 608–622.

Ostberg, C.O. & Thorgaard, G.H. (1999). Geographic distribution of chromosome and microsatellite DNA polymorphisms in *Oncorhynchus mykiss* native to western Washington. *Copeia*, **2**, 287–298.

Page, R.D.M. (1994). Maps between trees and cladistic analysis of historical associations among genes, organisms, and areas. *Systematic Biology*, **43**, 58–77.

Patton, J.L., daSilva, M.N.F. & Malcolm, J.R. (1994). Gene genealogy and differentiation among arboreal spiny rats (Rodentia: Echimyidae) of the basin: A test of the riverine barrier hypothesis. *Evolution*, **48**, 1314–1323.

Reisenbichler, R.R., McIntyre J.D., Solazzi M.F. & Landino S.W. (1992). Genetic variation in steelhead of Oregon and northern California. *Transactions American Fisheries Society*, **121**, 158–169.

Ritland, K., Dupuis, L.A., Bunnell, W., Hung, L.Y. & Carlson, J.E. (2000). Phylogeography of the tailed frog (*Ascaphus truei*) in British Columbia. *Canadian Journal of Zoology*, **78**, 1749–1758.

Sewell, M.M., Parks, C.R. & Chase, M.W. (1996). Intraspecific chloroplast DNA variation and biogeography of North American *Liriodendron* L. (*Magnoliaceae*). *Evolution*, **49**, 727–742.

Schaal, B.A. & Olsen, K.M. (2000). Gene genealogies and population variation in plants. *Proceedings of the National Academy of Sciences of the USA*, **97**, 7024–7029.

Schaal, B.A., Hayworth, D.A., Olsen, K.M., Rauscher, J.T. & Smith, W.A. (1998). Phylogeographic studies in plants: problems and prospects. *Molecular Ecology*, **7**, 465–474.

Soltis, D.E., Soltis, P.S., Ranker, T.A. & Ness, B.D. (1989a). Chloroplast DNA variation in a wild plant, *Tolmiea menziesii*. *Genetics*, **121**, 819–826.

Soltis, D.E., Soltis, P.S. & Ness, B.D. (1989b). Chloroplast DNA variation and multiple origins

of autopolyploidy in *Heuchera micrantha* (Saxifragaceae). *Evolution*, **43**, 650–656.

Soltis, D.E., Mayer, M.S., Soltis, P.S. & Edgerton, M. (1991). Chloroplast DNA variation in *Tellima grandiflora* (*Saxifragaceae*). *American Journal of Botany*, **78**, 1379–1390.

Soltis, D.E., Soltis, P.S., Kuzoff, R.K. & Tucker, T.L. (1992). Geographic structuring of chloroplast DNA genotypes in *Tiarella trifoliata* (Saxifragaceae). *Plant Systematics and Evolution*, **181**, 203–216.

Soltis, D.E., Gitzendanner, M.A., Strenge, D.D. & Soltis, P.S. (1997). Chloroplast DNA intraspecific phylogeography of plants from the Pacific Northwest of North America. *Plant Systematics and Evolution*, **206**, 353–373.

Soule, J.A., Soltis, D.E. & Soltis, P.S. (1995). Geographic patterns of chloroplast DNA variation in *Ribes bracteosum* (*Grossulariaceae*). *American Journal of Botany*, **82**, 164.

Steinhoff, R.J., Joyce, D.G. & Fins, L. (1983). Isozyme variation in *Pinus monticola*. *Canadian Journal of Forest Research*, **13**, 1122–1132.

Strenge, D. (1994). *The intraspecific phylogeography of* Polystichum munitum *and* Alnus rubra. MS Thesis, Washington State University, Pullman, Washington.

Sullivan, J., Arellano, E. & Rogers, D.S. (2000). Comparative phylogeography of Mesoamerican highland rodents: Concerted vs. independent response to past climatic fluctuations. *American Naturalist*, **155**, 755–768.

Taylor, E.B., Pollard, S. & Louie, D. (1999). Mitochondrial DNA variation in bull trout (*Salvelinus confluentus*) from northwestern North America: implications for zoogeography and conservation. *Molecular Ecology*, **8**, 1155–1170.

Thorgaard, G.H. (1983). Chromosomal differences among rainbow trout populations. *Copeia*, **3**, 650–662.

Wheeler, N.C. & Guries, R.P. (1982). Populations structure, genetic diversity, and morphological variation in *Pinus contorta* Dougl. *Canadian Journal of Forest Research*, **12**, 595–606.

Willis, K.J. & Whittaker, R.L. (2000). The refugial debate. *Science*, **287**, 1406–1407.

Zink, R.M. & Dittmann, D.L. (1993). Gene flow, refugia, and evolution of geographic variation in the song sparrow (*Melospiza melodia*). *Evolution*, **47**, 717–729.

Chapter 16

A geographical context for the evolution of plant reproductive systems

S. C. H. Barrett,* M. E. Dorken* and A. L. Case*

Introduction

The evolution of reproductive systems in flowering plants necessarily takes place in a geographical context, yet until recently few studies have considered the spatial scale of the ecological mechanisms involved (Olivieri *et al.* 1990; Couvet *et al.* 1998; Barrett & Pannell 1999). Because of the ephemeral nature of the local population, investigations at larger geographical scales are more likely to capture the microevolutionary events signalling changes in reproductive mode. This is especially likely in herbaceous plants of widespread distribution and broad ecological amplitude. Populations in parts of a species' range often confront novel environments resulting in changes to demography and life history. These changes can have important reproductive consequences setting the stage for evolutionary modifications to the reproductive system. Such geographical differentiation can have significant micro- and macroevolutionary consequences leading to reproductive isolation and the diversification of plant lineages (Baker 1959a; Lloyd 1965; Strid 1969; Grant 1971; McNeill & Jain 1983; Wyatt 1988; Olmstead 1990; Barrett 1995).

Evolutionary responses to variation in ecological conditions are invoked to explain many aspects of plant reproduction. These include the diverse mating strategies promoting outcrossing and selfing (Uyenoyama *et al.* 1993; Barrett 1998), the balance between sexual vs. asexual reproduction (Abrahamson 1980; Bierzychudek 1987), and the various forms of gender expression (Lloyd & Bawa 1984; Geber *et al.* 1999). Associations between mating systems and life history (Barrett *et al.* 1996a) and between gender dimorphism and environmental conditions (Sakai & Weller 1999) are just two examples that point to the importance of ecological processes in governing the evolution of reproductive traits. While the role of ecology as a driving force in the evolution of reproductive systems is widely recognized, for most transitions the ecological mechanisms responsible are not well understood. For example, unsatisfactory pollinator service is frequently invoked as a mechanism promoting diverse reproductive outcomes from the transition from outcrossing to selfing (Darwin 1876; Lloyd 1980; Schoen *et al.* 1996), to the evolution of gender dimorphism from monomorphism (Ganders 1978; Bawa 1980; Sakai & Weller 1999). The

* *Department of Botany, University of Toronto, 25 Willcocks Street, Toronto, Ontario, Canada M5S 3B2.*

seeming paradox of a single ecological mechanism favouring the evolution of such contrasting reproductive systems arises because of a failure to appreciate that pollinator service can be unsatisfactory for different reasons. Detailed ecological investigations are required to distinguish *insufficient* from *inferior* pollinator service because of their distinct influences on the quantity and quality of offspring produced by animal-pollinated plants (Harder & Barrett 1996).

Spatial context is of crucial importance for reproduction in plants because of their predominantly sessile habit. Immobility strongly influences the mating process because it requires that plants use vectors (animals, wind, water) to transfer male gametophytes (pollen) between individuals. This reliance has promoted the evolution of diverse floral adaptations associated with the particular agents of pollen dispersal (Proctor *et al.* 1996). The character of gene dispersal by pollen is dependent on the spatial distribution of individuals within populations, their reproductive traits, and the types of pollen vectors involved (Levin & Kerster 1974). At a broader scale, the spatial arrangement of populations across the landscape will determine the extent to which are connected by gene flow or behave as independent evolutionary units. Because most plants are sessile, the reproductive phase is of fundamental significance because it is the only time in the life history when genes have the opportunity to move within and among populations of a species. However, the spatial dynamics of gene movement, and the extent to which gene flow influences evolutionary processes for populations located in different parts of the geographical range, have rarely been investigated.

In angiosperms, the two major evolutionary transitions in reproductive systems are the evolution of separate sexes from combined sexes, and the evolution of uniparental reproduction (predominant selfing or asexual reproduction) from biparental reproduction (Maynard Smith 1978; Charnov 1982; Richards 1997). One approach to analysing these changes is through studies of geographical variation. Indeed, biogeographical information was used by workers in biosystematics and experimental taxonomy to provide evidence for these evolutionary transitions (e.g. Crosby 1949; Hagerup 1951; Baker 1959b, 1967; Carlquist 1966; Rick 1966; Strid 1969; Godley 1979). Unfortunately, during the 1970s and 1980s with the birth of population biology and the requirement for detailed fine-scale studies of local populations, interest in geographical variation declined. However, there is now a resurgence of interest in geographical variation in plants because of the stimulus provided by metapopulation biology (Hanski & Gilpin 1997) and phylogeography (Schaal 1998). With the growing awareness of the importance of spatial processes in genetics and ecology it is now an appropriate time to integrate recent theoretical and conceptual advances with the more traditional biogeographical approaches employed prior to the advent of population biology.

Polymorphic sexual systems, such as heterostyly and the various forms of gender dimorphism, are of particular value for broad-scale spatial analyses of geographical variation in reproductive mode. This is because the small number of mating types that characterize these sexual systems are easily recognized under field conditions, and the large samples required to detect pattern can usually be obtained without difficulty. The genetic control of these polymorphisms is usually governed by a small number of genes enabling the development of theoretical models concerned with their evolutionary dynamics. Moreover, polymorphic sexual systems are often sensitive to variation in ecological conditions and can be vulnerable to genetic and evolutionary modifications in traits influencing mating behaviour and the frequency of sex phenotypes in populations. Hence, polymorphic sexual systems provide valuable model systems for investigating the ecological factors driving evolutionary changes in reproductive mode.

Here we use examples from our own studies of polymorphic sexual systems to illustrate how insights on plant reproductive diversity can be gained by considering ecological and evolutionary processes operating at different spatial scales. These include investigations of local populations, clusters of interconnected populations (metapopulations), and larger assemblages at regional and geographical scales. Our knowledge of each of these case studies largely reflects the duration of our investigations. The examples therefore illustrate a progression in the approaches and tools we have employed to investigate the patterns detected. This progression is of interest because it tends to parallel historical developments in the study of geographical variation. Our studies commence with the search for geographical patterns from large-scale population surveys. Inferences are then made on the likely ecological and genetic mechanisms that are responsible for the variation detected. This is followed by ecological and life-history comparisons of populations differing in reproductive system, the application of genetic markers to measure important reproductive parameters, and studies of the inheritance of variation patterns. Finally, theoretical models that attempt to integrate spatial ecology with genetics to understand the evolutionary dynamics of polymorphic sexual systems are developed and evaluated using field data. A fundamental requirement of these microevolutionary studies is to find plant species that display intraspecific variation in their reproductive systems.

We first examine the ecological conditions associated with the evolution and maintenance of gender monomorphism vs. dimorphism using species that exhibit both cosexual and dioecious populations. We consider how contrasting life-history strategies associated with stress in one case, and competition and disturbance in another, play a role in the evolution of combined vs. separate sexes. We then investigate the forces maintaining outcrossing in several tristylous species, and consider how spatial variation in ecological and genetic factors can destabilize this complex polymorphism resulting in a variety of reproductive outcomes, each of which is preceded by the loss of morphs from populations. Of particular significance for our studies of tristyly are the relative roles that stochastic forces and natural selection play in causing geographical differentiation in reproductive systems.

Gender strategies and the evolution of dioecism

The origin of separate sexes from combined sexes has occurred repeatedly during the evolutionary history of the flowering plants. Dioecious species occur in nearly half of all families but comprise fewer than 10% of angiosperm species (Renner & Ricklefs 1995). Two major evolutionary routes to dioecy are usually recognized; the monoecy–paradioecy and the gynodioecy–subdioecy pathways (reviewed in Webb 1999). These pathways differ in the types of gender variation upon which selection acts and in the genetic architecture of this variation. For transitions involving monoecious populations as the ancestral condition, disruptive selection is thought to gradually increase gender specialization, through effects on the proportion of pistillate and staminate flowers, with female and male morphs as endpoints of selection. In contrast, in the gynodioecious pathway female variants initiate the change by spreading in cosexual populations, with selection then favouring male function in hermaphrodites, through mutations that reduce female fertility. Theoretical models can explain these transitions based on a few key parameters of which selfing rates, inbreeding depression, the genetic control of the sex types, and the reallocation of resources to female and male function, are most important (Charlesworth 1999).

The evolution of dioecy has occurred in taxa possessing a range of life histories, and under diverse environmental and biogeographic conditions, and this has made it difficult to determine whether similar ecological mechanisms are involved (reviewed in Sakai & Weller 1999). The problem is exacerbated because few species maintain variation in sexual systems encompassing the transition from gender monomorphism to dimorphism, restricting opportunities for microevolutionary study. Here we review two recent investigations of taxa in which both gender strategies co-occur, evaluate the mechanisms associated with their maintenance under contrasting ecological conditions, and discuss the implications of these findings for the evolution of dioecy.

Stress and the evolution of dioecy

There is growing evidence implicating harsh or stressful environments in the evolution and maintenance of separate sexes from combined sexes. Species with gender dimorphism are often found in drier habitats than their cosexual relatives (e.g. Weller & Sakai 1990; Costich 1995), and populations of gynodioecious species are often closer to a dioecious state as resources, particularly water, become limiting (Wolfe & Schmida 1997; Ashman 1999). This pattern seems counterintuitive for sessile organisms, because harsh growing conditions might be expected to result in low plant density, insufficient pollination and reduced fertility. However, such allee effects, if indeed they occur (see below), must be outweighed in resource-limited conditions by the benefits that unisexuals gain over cosexuals by not investing in both sex functions. Darwin (1877) first noted that in harsh conditions unisexuals may be favoured over hermaphrodites if they outperform them in the comparable sex function (reproductive compensation). This idea is supported by a recent evolutionarily stable strategy (ESS) model (De Laguérie et al. 1993), and empirical data demonstrating that the seed fitness of females relative to hermaphrodites is greatest in harsh environments (Delph 1990).

These issues have recently been investigated in *Wurmbea* (Colchicaceae), a genus of 41 species of diminutive geophytic herbs almost equally distributed between Africa and Australia (Case 2000). While African species are uniformly monomorphic, gender dimorphism occurs in one-third of those occurring in Australia. The occurrence of gynodioecy and subdioecy in *Wurmbea* indicates that dioecy has evolved via the gynodioecious pathway through invasion of monomorphic populations by females (Barrett 1992).

In Western Australia, monomorphic and dimorphic populations of the widespread and highly variable *W. dioica* occur along an approximately 1000 km latitudinal precipitation gradient running from Geraldton in the north to Albany in the south (Figure 16.1a). Monomorphic populations are more widely distributed, occurring in diverse habitat types including flooded pastures, seeps, forest understory and dry grasslands. In contrast, dimorphic populations are more restricted in distribution, usually occurring in arid sites on shallow, rocky or sandy soils. Investi-

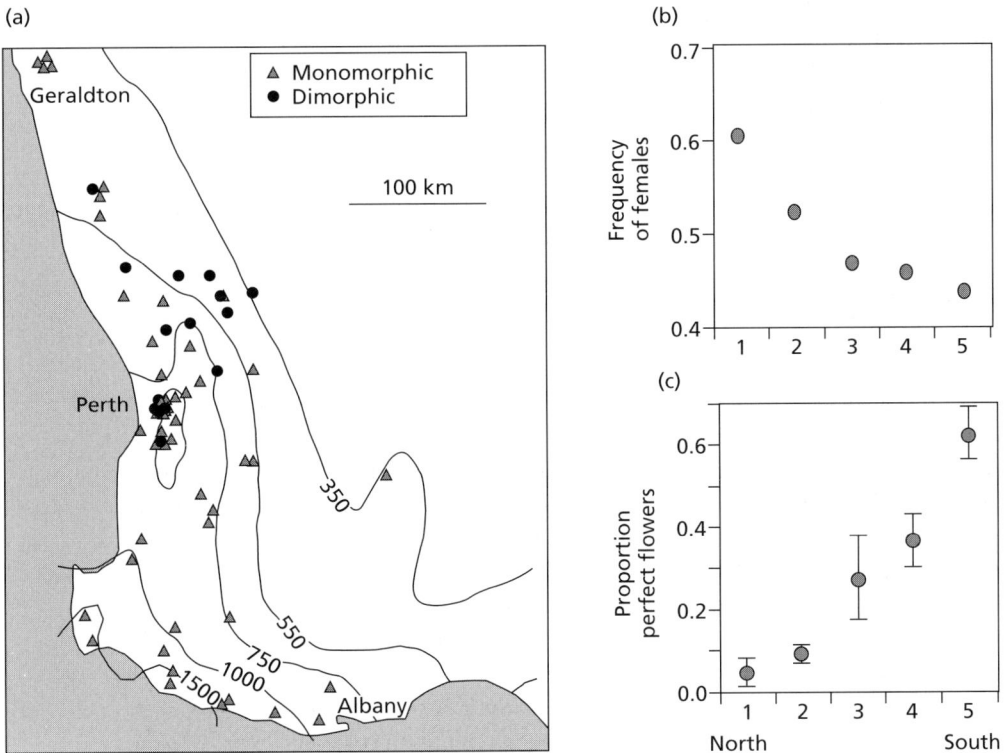

Figure 16.1 The influence of stress on gender expression in *Wurmbea dioica*. (a) The geographical distribution of monomorphic (△) and dimorphic (●) populations in Western Australia in relation to rainfall. Isoheyts indicate mean annual rainfall in millimetres. (b) Changes in female frequency with latitude in five dimorphic populations. (c) Changes in the proportion of perfect flowers produced by hermaphroditic plants in five dimorphic populations. (A.L. Case & S.C.H. Barrett, unpublished.)

gation of gender expression and allocation along this precipitation gradient revealed several latitudinal patterns. In dimorphic populations, lower precipitation was associated with higher frequencies of females (Figure 16.1b) and reduced allocation to female function in hermaphrodites during flowering (Figure 16.1c). This result supports the idea that stressful conditions may influence the transition from gynodioecy to dioecy by enhancing selection for male function in hermaphroditic plants. However, there was no evidence that increasing aridity was associated with the establishment of gynodioecy in *W. dioica*. Female allocation of flowering cosexual plants, which on average gain equal fitness through both sex functions, was unaffected by this same gradient in precipitation. If such changes in allocation reflect female fitness, then stress provides no 'allocation advantage' for female invasion into monomorphic populations. However, aridity could still favour the separation of the sexes if it magnifies the expression of inbreeding depression.

Monomorphic and dimorphic populations of *W. dioica* are spatially isolated throughout most of their geographical range in Western Australia. However, in a remarkable series of sites on the Darling Escarpment near Perth, both monomorphic and dimorphic sexual systems coexist within a few metres of one another (Barrett 1992; Case & Barrett 2001; Figure 16.2a). These sites provide opportunities to examine whether fine-scale differentiation occurs with respect to resource availability. They also raise the question of what ecological and genetic mechanisms maintain the sexual systems in sympatry. Recent investigations of the spatial distribution of the two sexual systems indicate that they are segregated from one another into wet vs. dry microsites and possess contrasting allocation and physiological strategies (Case & Barrett 2001). Gender dimorphism is associated with drier microsites, shallower soil, earlier flowering, lower plant density, and allocation patterns that favour resource acquisition and storage below ground. In contrast, gender monomorphism is associated with wetter microsites, deeper soil, later flowering, higher plant density, and greater investment into leaves and flowers. Strong temporal displacement of flowering time maintains ecological and genetic differentiation between the sexual systems by restricting opportunities for gene exchange (Figure 16.2b). Allopatric populations in other parts of the range tend to flower concurrently, raising the interesting possibility that divergent flowering times in sympatry may have arisen through selection against the inferior products of hybridization.

The lower density of unisexuals of *W. dioica* at sympatric sites on the Darling Escarpment (Figure 16.2a) is most probably associated with the drier soil conditions in which they occur. Low plant density can have important implications for pollination, especially in dioecious species, because the proportion of pollen-dispersing individuals is halved in comparison with cosexes. Differences in allocation, flowering time and plant density between the two sexual systems of *W. dioica* are associated with contrasting patterns of insect visitation (A. L. Case & S. C. H. Barrett, unpublished). Unisexuals are visited exclusively by nectar-foraging flies, whereas pollen-collecting bees are the primary pollinators of cosexuals. Bees present in the community in June ignore unisexual plants, presumably because of their lower density and smaller flowers, signalling lower reward status. Nevertheless, despite the low

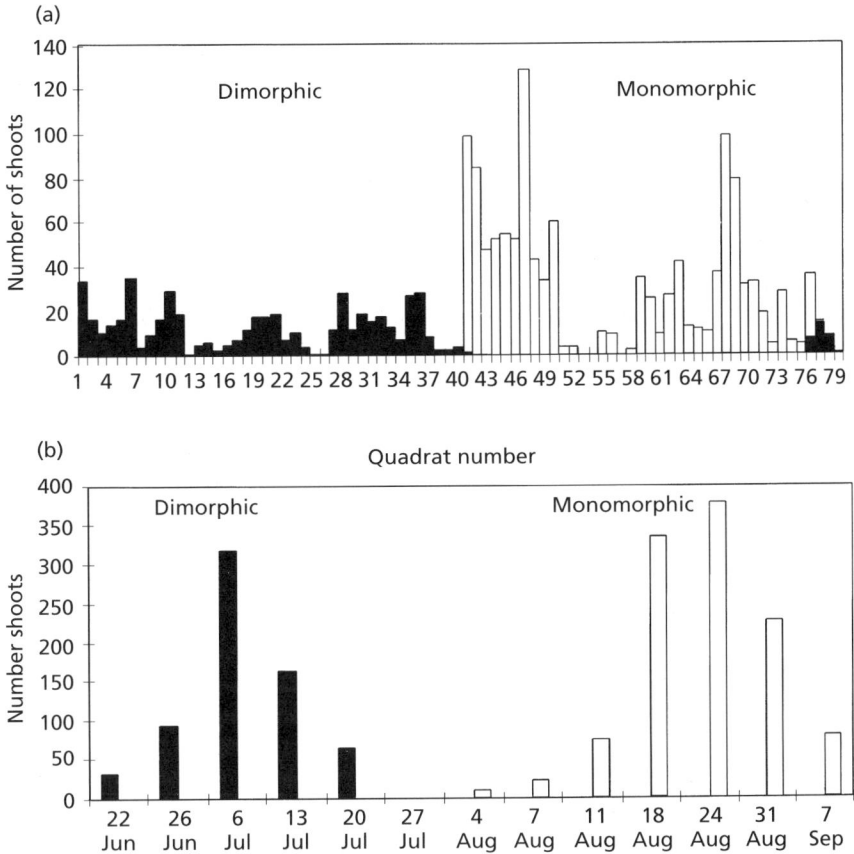

Figure 16.2 Spatial and temporal differentiation of monomorphic and dimorphic sexual systems of *Wurmbea dioica* in sympatry on the Darling Escarpment, Western Australia. (a) Density and distribution of monomorphic (open bars) and dimorphic (solid bars) populations at Lesmurdie in 1995. The number of plants in each 0.25 m^2 quadrat was recorded along a 40-m transect through areas of transition between the sexual systems. (b) Flowering phenology of sympatric monomorphic (open bars) and dimorphic (solid bars) populations at Lesmurdie in 1996. The number of plants in flower in each quadrat was recorded weekly along 10 transects and the data summed to produce the flowering curves for each population. (From Case & Barrett 2001.)

density of plants in dimorphic populations, there is no evidence that female fertility is pollen-limited owing to insufficient pollination, based on experiments using supplemental hand pollination. Flies are abundant in June, visitation rates are high, and floral longevities of up to 3 weeks ensure sufficient pollen is deposited on stigmas. Many sexually dimorphic species are pollinated by either wind, water or generalist insects (Sakai & Weller 1999). This may serve to reduce the incidence of pollinator failure under the harsh conditions that appear to favour the evolution of separate sexes from combined sexes in some plant groups.

Clone size and the evolution of dioecy

Dioecy is commonly associated with large plant size and long-lived perennial life histories. One explanation for this association is that large plants often produce many flowers increasing the likelihood of geitonogamous selfing (de Jong *et al.* 1993; Harder & Barrett 1995), a problem not faced by unisexual plants. On the other hand, dioecy tends to be rather uncommon in short-lived species, presumably because of the risks associated with reproductive failure in the ephemeral habitats that they usually occupy. These contrasting reproductive factors appear to play a role in the ecological differentiation of sexual systems in *Sagittaria latifolia* (Alismataceae), a widespread clonal aquatic native to diverse wetland habitats in North America. Geographical surveys of *S. latifolia* in Ontario indicate that monoecious populations commonly occur in ephemeral aquatic environments such as roadside ditches, farm ponds, and stream and lake edges exposed to frequent disturbance. In contrast, dioecious populations more often inhabit large wetlands associated with the Great Lakes and the major rivers systems that drain into them (Sarkissian *et al.* 2001; M. E. Dorken & S. C. H. Barrett, unpublished). While in Ontario the two sexual systems tend to be ecologically differentiated from one another, they frequently occur in close geographical proximity (Figure 16.3). Establishment and long-term persistence of *S. latifolia* in contrasting aquatic habitats demands different life histories with contrasting reproductive consequences.

Comparisons of monoecious and dioecious populations of *S. latifolia* sampled from southern Ontario indicate that plants belonging to the two sexual systems

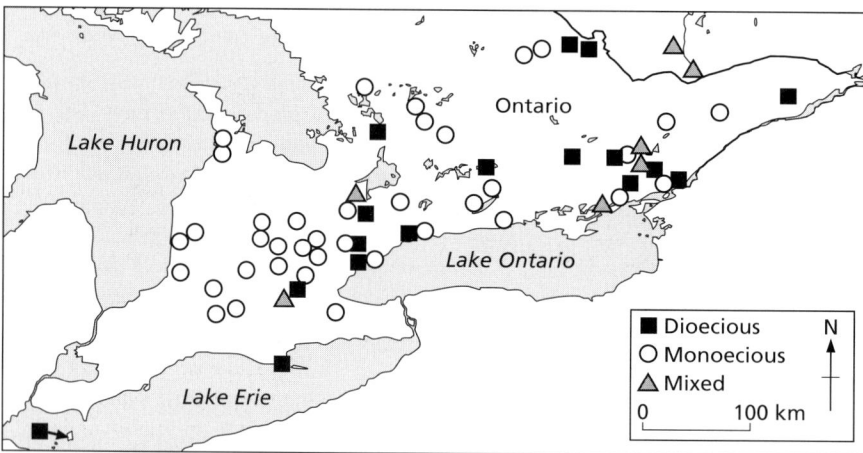

Figure 16.3 The distribution of monoecious and dioecious populations of *Sagittaria latifolia* in Ontario, Canada. Monoecious populations (○) more commonly occur in ephemeral aquatic habitats or those subject to frequent disturbance. Dioecious populations (■) inhabit extensive wetlands associated with the Great Lakes or large river systems. Occasional mixed populations (△) composed of cosexual and unisexual plants also occur. (M.E. Dorken & S.C.H. Barrett unpublished.)

differ in a range of life-history traits. Glasshouse comparisons generally indicate that plants from dioecious populations are taller with larger leaves and produce heavier tubers than plants from monoecious populations (Figure 16.4a,b). These results are consistent with field observations of habitat sorting of the two sexual systems in

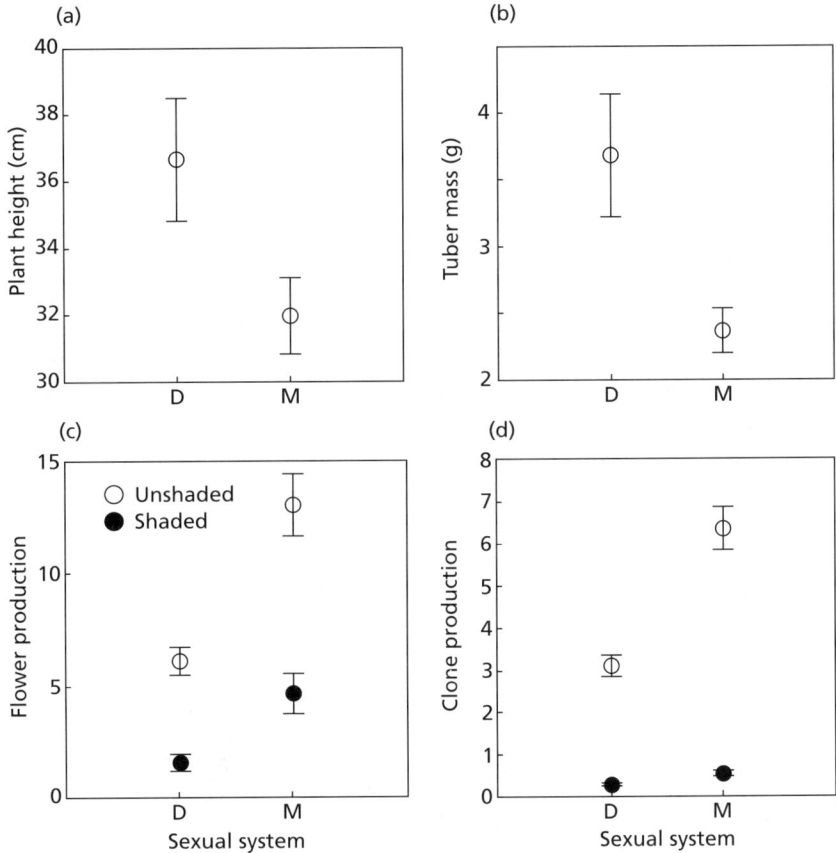

Figure 16.4 Life-history differentiation between monoecious and dioecious populations of *Sagittaria latifolia*. (a) Plant height, measured from the soil surface (cm) and (b) tuber mass, measured as the average tuber mass (g). For both (a) and (b) the data shown are grand population means (±SE) from 18 monoecious (mean = 13 individuals per population) and 13 dioecious (mean = 14 individuals per population) Ontario populations grown under uniform glasshouse conditions for one season. (c) Flower production, measured as the total number of flowers produced by the focal ramet, and (d), clone production, measured as the total number of clonal shoots produced by the focal ramet. For (c) and (d), focal ramets were transplanted into field plots that were shaded by *Typha* (●) vs. those that were unshaded (○) in a wetland in Ontario during 1999 (see text). Data shown are grand population means for 10 monoecious and 10 dioecious populations (24 focal ramets per population) after one seasons growth. (M.E. Dorken & S.C.H. Barrett unpublished.)

Ontario, but it is not known if this ecological differentiation occurs in other areas of the geographical range in North America.

A field experiment provided additional evidence of life-history differences between the two sexual systems of S. latifolia in Ontario. Clones from monoecious and dioecious populations were transplanted into a marsh containing open plots with limited above-ground competition and shaded plots dominated by Typha. The plot conditions were chosen to simulate the contrasting habitats that monoecious (open plots) and dioecious (shaded plots) populations, respectively, commonly inhabit. Size differences observed in the glasshouse were maintained in the field with monoecious populations generally flowering earlier than dioecious populations. Monoecious populations performed relatively poorly in shaded plots compared to open plots with reduced flowering and clonal propagation (Figure 16.4c,d). On the other hand, dioecious populations were less affected by the different growing conditions of the two plot types (and see Costich 1995), with flowering and clonal propagation less influenced by the contrasting levels of competition (Figure 16.4c,d). In open plots, and to a lesser extent in shaded plots, monoecious populations had greater reproductive expenditure than dioecious populations, both in terms of sexual and clonal propagation (Figure 16.4c,d). This finding probably reflects the importance of rapid regeneration for monoecious populations in changing conditions. Adaptation to ephemeral environments is often associated with high reproductive capacities. In contrast, persistence in the competitive conditions that often prevail in large marshes in southern Ontario probably requires large plant size and heavier clonal propagules. Because of the greater stability of these habitats, unisexual plants can be of considerable size. Thus, while annual rates of cloning may be higher in monoecious populations, the spatial extent of clones is often much larger in dioecious populations, presumably because clones live longer.

What are the reproductive consequences of these associations between clone size and sexual systems in S. latifolia and are they relevant for understanding why dioecy has evolved in this group? Whether clone size leads to inferior pollination and the resulting mating costs associated with extensive geitonogamy depends on features of floral biology. Monoecious plants of S. latifolia are self-compatible but exhibit inflorescence-level protogyny with little overlap between female and male function. Inferior pollination from insect-mediated geitonogamy is most likely to occur when inflorescences in staminate and pistillate phases are in flower at the same time. Clearly, this is more likely to occur when clone size increases. Data on outcrossing rates estimated using allozyme markers indicates that geitonogamy does indeed occur with some monoecious populations exhibiting up to 63% selfing ($N = 6$ populations; mean $t = 0.59$; range 0.37–0.87; M. E. Dorken & S. C. H. Barrett; unpublished). Hence, one scenario for the evolution of dioecy in S. latifolia is that ecological radiation into habitats requiring selection for large clone size resulted in the destabilization of outcrossing in monoecious populations through increased geitonogamy. Inbreeding depression and pollen discounting would then provide the necessary conditions favouring the evolution of unisexuality. However, an alternative scenario that cannot be completely ruled out is that large clone size *followed* rather than preceded the evolution of dioecy, because the constraints imposed by geitonogamy were relieved in unisexuals. In either case, interactions between clone size, inferior pollination, and mating can be invoked to explain the associations between sexual systems and life history in *S. latifolia*.

Evolution in tristylous populations

Tristyly is a genetic polymorphism in which populations are usually composed of three mating types (hereafter L-, M- and S-morphs) differing reciprocally in style length and anther height. The polymorphism has evolved independently in at least five flowering plant families, and functions to increase the proficiency of cross-pollination through animal-mediated pollen dispersal (reviewed in Barrett 1993). Like other sexual polymorphisms, tristyly is maintained in populations by frequency-dependent selection. This arises as a consequence of strong intermorph (disassortative) mating enforced by heteromorphic incompatibility and/or reciprocal sex-organ positioning. Theoretical studies indicate that if there are no fitness differences among the floral morphs, an isoplethic equilibrium (1 : 1 : 1) is the only possible condition in large populations with disassortative mating, regardless of inheritance (Heuch 1979). However, a variety of ecological and genetic factors can lead to deviations from isoplethy, and more significantly from an evolutionary standpoint, the loss of floral morphs from populations. Below we review several examples that illustrate how landscape-level approaches can aid in the detection of patterns linked to the causal mechanisms that destabilize tristyly.

Stochastic forces and morph loss

Theoretical work on the influence of stochastic forces on the maintenance of tristyly indicate that bottlenecks and genetic drift lead to different probabilities of morph loss from populations depending on their size (reviewed in Barrett 1993). Small population size results in the S-morph being lost most often, followed by the M-morph, with the L-morph disappearing only rarely. This asymmetry is a form of genetic constraint imposed directly by the particular type of inheritance pattern found in most tristylous groups. Countering stochasticity are the opposing forces of frequency-dependent mating acting to drive morph ratios back to an isoplethic equilibrium, and gene flow from neighbouring populations which can restore missing morphs. Interpreting patterns of morph-frequency variation in a species therefore requires an understanding of the inheritance of tristyly, knowledge of the mating system, the likely ecological and demographic influences on population size, and information on the spatial distribution of populations across the landscape.

Strong evidence for the role of stochasticity in influencing morph-frequency variation in a tristylous species comes from a study of the perennial herb *Lythrum salicaria*. Eckert and Barrett (1992) and Eckert *et al.* (1996) examined the relation between population size and morph loss by surveying populations in the native and introduced ranges of the species, in south-west France and Ontario, Canada, respectively. They predicted a higher level of morph loss in Ontario because *L. salicaria* in this geographical region is an aggressive invader of wetlands, and during range expansion founder effects and periods of small population size frequently occur. As expected, the frequency of populations missing at least one morph differed significantly between the regions (Figure 16.5; France 5% vs. Ontario 23%) with the S-morph lost most often, as predicted by stochastic theory. Although in both regions small populations were more likely to have morphs missing, population sizes were on average smaller in south-west France than Ontario. This seeming paradox can be resolved by considering the spatial distribution and metapopulation structure of populations in the two regions. Populations in south-west France commonly occur in agricultural habitats and their distribution along drainage ditches is probably associated with a high level of connectivity through pollen and seed flow. Modelling studies demonstrated that gene flow on the order of $m \geq 0.05$ would counter the loss of morphs through drift in small populations (Eckert *et al.* 1996). In Ontario, however, the dispersed distribution of dimorphic populations across the landscape indicates the multiple, independent loss of morphs (mostly the S-morph, Figure 16.5), during colonization of new territory. In Ontario, reintroduction of missing morphs is much less likely because of the geographical isolation of *L. salicaria* populations.

High levels of disassortative mating are enforced in *L. salicaria* because the species possesses a conventional heteromorphic self-incompatibility system. This form of incompatibility prevents selfing and intramorph mating, and buffers the mating system against variable pollination environments that could reduce the intensity of frequency-dependent mating. Several tristylous species do not possess heteromorphic incompatibility, and in these, self and/or intramorph matings can occur.

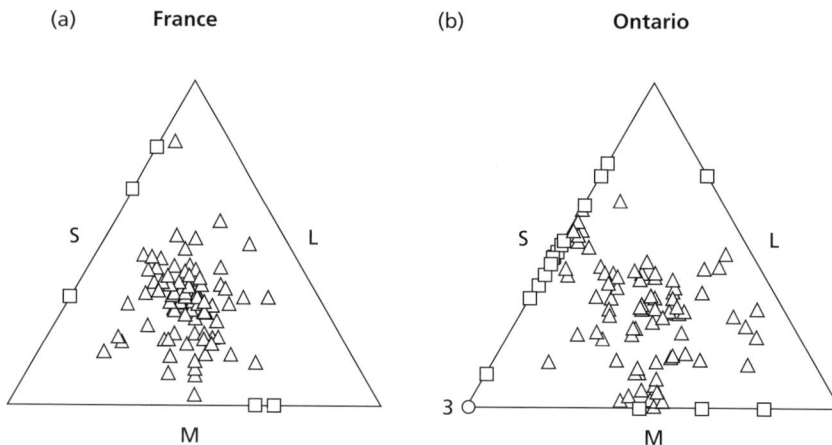

Figure 16.5 The role of stochastic forces influencing style-morph frequencies in populations of *Lythrum salicaria*. Style-morph frequencies from (a) native populations in south-west France and (b) introduced populations in Ontario, Canada. Each side of the triangle represents one of the three floral morphs (L-, M-, S-morph) and each point represents the morph frequencies of a single population. (From Eckert *et al.* 1996.)

If these types of 'illegitimate mating' are common, biased morph ratios and the loss of style morphs from populations will result more often. We next consider several cases in which these effects have resulted in evolutionary changes to reproductive systems.

Pollen dispersal and biased morph ratios

Striking spatial patterns of stylar polymorphism occur in *Narcissus* (Amaryllidaceae), a genus of perennial geophytes native to the Mediterranean (Barrett *et al.* 1996b). In several species (e.g. see Arroyo & Dafni 1995; Baker *et al.* 2000a), populations exhibit strongly biased morph ratios that are geographically structured in a manner that cannot be explained by stochastic forces alone. The key to understanding these patterns is the recognition that *Narcissus* possesses an unusual self-incompatibility system that prevents selfing, but permits outcrossing to any plant regardless of style type (Dulberger 1964; Barrett *et al.* 1997; Sage *et al.* 1999; Baker *et al.* 2000b). Unlike conventional heterostylous taxa, where morphology and mating type are tightly coupled, in *Narcissus* this association is absent, enabling both disassortative and assortative mating to occur. Accordingly, morph ratios are governed by the share of matings that each morph obtains, with mating success largely dependent on how floral morphology affects pollen dispersal and male fertility. As discussed below, geographical variation in the interaction between floral morphology and pollinators visiting populations appears to play a role in influencing mating patterns and hence morph ratios.

Narcissus triandrus is a widespread and highly variable bee-pollinated species native to Spain and Portugal. Most populations contain the three-style morphs but their frequencies are usually strongly skewed in favour of the L-morph, unlike any other tristylous species (Barrett *et al.* 1997). Extensive surveys of this species have revealed clear geographical patterns of morph-frequency variation (S. C. H. Barrett, L. D. Harder & W. W. Cole unpublished). While *N. triandrus* var. *cernuus* displays L-biased morph frequencies throughout its range (southern and central Spain and Portugal), morph frequencies in *N. triandrus* var. *triandrus* show complex clinal patterns in central and northern Portugal and northern Spain. In the northwest of the Iberian Peninsula there is a general reduction in the M-morph, culminating in its loss from populations (Figure 16.6). An important feature of this latitudinal pattern is that the decrease in the M-morph is accompanied by an increase in the L-morph only. The frequency of the S-morph is insensitive to changes in the other two morphs, remaining stable throughout the geographical range. This pattern indicates that the intensity of frequency-dependent selection varies among the floral morphs.

To explain the complex patterns of morph-frequency variation in *N. triandrus*, S. C. H. Barrett, L. D. Harder & W. W. Cole (unpublished) have recently developed a model based on the relation between morph-specific floral morphology, pollen transfer and rates of assortative and disassortative mating. The model predicts morph ratios based on empirical data on the mean and variance of sex-organ position, and assumes that pollen is more likely to be transferred between anthers and

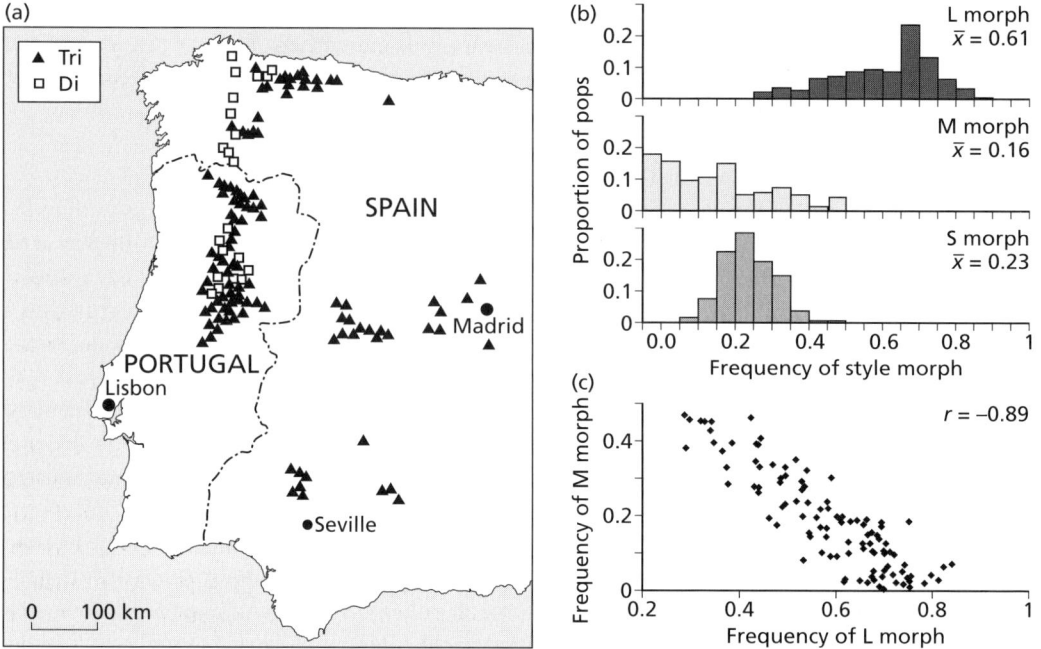

Figure 16.6 Patterns of morph-frequency variation in tristylous *Narcissus triandrus*. (a) Geographical distribution of trimorphic (▲) and dimorphic (□) populations in the Iberian peninsula. (b) The distribution of morph frequencies in 133 populations. (c) The relationship between the frequencies of the L- and M-morphs in 109 tristylous populations. (S.C.H. Barrett, L.D. Harder & W.W. Cole unpublished.)

stigmas of similar height, as demonstrated experimentally for other tristylous species (Barrett & Glover 1985). The results of the model indicate a good fit between predicted and observed morph ratios for most populations. This supports the view that skewed morph ratios are largely governed by differences among morphs in male fitness resulting from variation in the proficiencies of pollen transfer. Fitness comparisons of components of female fertility including seed set and maternal outcrossing rate have failed to reveal any morph-specific effects. This suggests that insufficient or inferior pollination of the floral morphs is unlikely to play a significant role in causing biased morph ratios.

Populations in the north-west part of the range of *N. triandrus* var. *triandrus*, where the M-morph is often missing, produce larger flowers and more flowers per inflorescence than populations in central Spain and Portugal. These size differences in floral traits are likely to be associated with the effects of rainfall on overall plant stature. A precipitation gradient occurs in the Iberian Peninsula from the dry, southern Mediterranean climate to the wetter, northern Atlantic climate. These latitudinal changes in floral biology may be important in pollinator interactions and the mechanics of pollen dispersal. While our pollinator observations are limited, there is some indication that northern populations are visited by bumble bees, whereas to the south solitary anthophorid bees are the primary pollinators. Changes in floral traits and pollinator service with latitude may alter pollen transfer patterns in ways that make it more difficult to maintain the M-morph in northern populations of *N. triandrus* var. *triandrus*.

The loss of sex in clonal populations

Our third example involving tristylous systems concerns the replacement of sexual reproduction by asexual propagation in *Decodon verticillatus* (Lythraceae), a long-lived clonal aquatic that inhabits marshes, swamps and bogs in eastern and central North America. *Decodon verticillatus* is highly self-fertile with most populations exhibiting a mixed mating system with approximately 30% selfing (Eckert & Barrett 1994a,b). However, selfed offspring rarely establish under field conditions owing to strong inbreeding depression (Eckert & Barrett 1994c). Clonal propagation and weak disassortative mating reduce the intensity of frequency-dependent selection resulting in populations with a wide range of morph frequencies. This variation tends to be geographically structured with populations at the southern end of the range (south-east USA) more often trimorphic than northern populations where stylar monomorphism is common (Eckert & Barrett 1992). Recent surveys of populations along a 500-km latitudinal gradient in New England have revealed a particularly striking pattern with a steep transition from trimorphism to monomorphism (Figure 16.7). While monomorphic populations should be capable of reproducing sexually, studies of allozyme variation in *D. verticillatus* suggest otherwise. Patterns of genetic diversity in trimorphic populations indicate regular sexual recruitment, while populations monomorphic for style length are usually composed of single clonal genotypes (Eckert & Barrett 1993; Dorken & Eckert 2001).

A variety of ecological and genetic factors regulate the balance between sexual and asexual reproduction in clonal plants, raising the issue of their relative importance in *D. verticillatus*. Field studies of components of reproduction along the 500-km transect illustrated in Figure 16.7 revealed dramatic differences between trimorphic and monomorphic populations. Monomorphic populations flowered infrequently, exhibited weak pollen-tube growth, and seed production was severely reduced in comparison with trimorphic populations (Figure 16.8; Dorken & Eckert 2001). Moreover, these differences were maintained when clones from these populations were grown in the glasshouse, indicating that low fertility is largely due to genetic factors. Indeed, crossing studies implicate a single recessive mutation that impairs normal pollen-tube growth in causing low fertility (Eckert *et al.* 1999). However, in one monomorphic population with low fertility in the field, seed production in the glasshouse was similar to fertile, trimorphic populations. Therefore, even in the absence of sterility mutations disrupting sexual reproduction, seed production in northern populations can be reduced by one or more environmental factors that covary with latitude. Furthermore, because ecological conditions in some northern populations prevent fertile clones from producing seed, sterile genotypes are unlikely to experience an allocation advantage through increased clonal propagation.

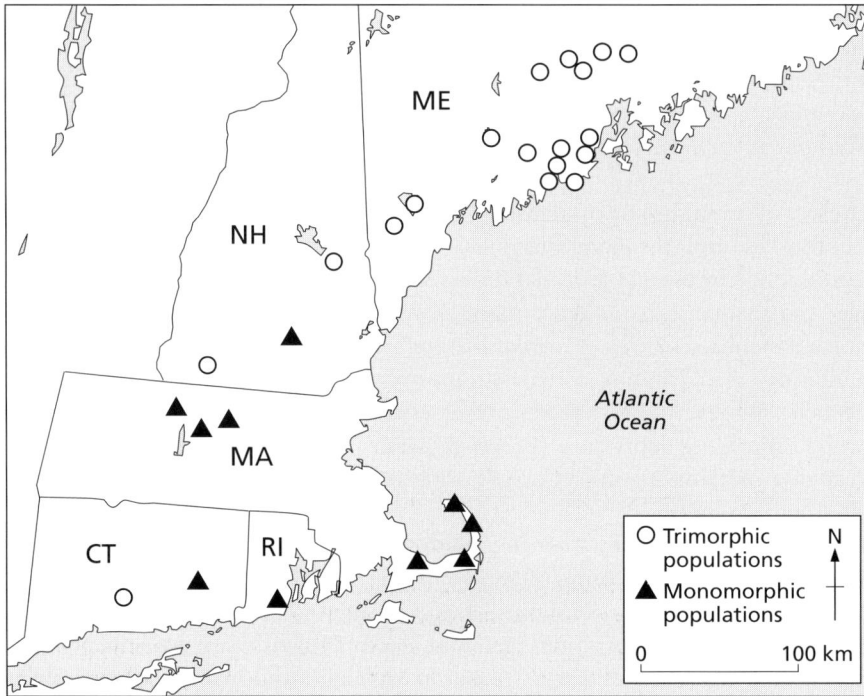

Figure 16.7 Steep transition from sexuality to asexuality at the northern margin of the range of tristylous *Decodon vertcillatus* in New England, USA. Trimorphic populations (▲) have high seed fertility whereas monomorphic populations (○) are largely sterile. The populations mapped were examined for components of fertility under field and glasshouse conditions, see text. (From Dorken & Eckert 2001.)

In fact, sterility in *D. verticillatus* is not generally associated with either increased or decreased vegetative vigour, and mutations impairing sexual reproduction are thus probably selectively neutral in northern populations.

The common occurrence of the loss of sex in *D. verticillatus* raises the question of the origin and spread of sterility mutations in northern populations. It seems most probable that infertile genotypes have become fixed in populations through stochastic influences such as founder effects or drift, rather than through antagonistic pleiotropy, or by direct selection because of advantages associated with reduced investment in sexual reproduction (Eckert *et al.* 1999). However, how often has this process occurred during the northward migration of *D. verticillatus* following glaciation? At least two possibilities exist. All sterile populations may be genetically identical because of the origin and spread of a single sterile genotype. Alternatively, multiple founder events may be involved, as suggested by the geographical distribution of style morphs in northern populations (see Eckert & Barrett 1995). Recent evidence from allozyme variation indicates that sterility is unlikely to have evolved only once in northern populations of *D. verticillatus* (Dorken & Eckert 2001). Most

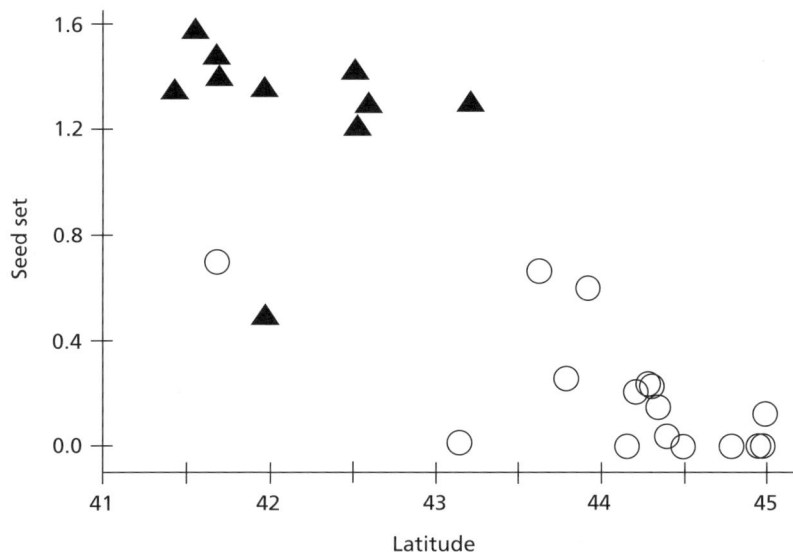

Figure 16.8 Strong decline in seed production with latitude at the northern limit of the range of tristylous *Decodon verticillatus* in New England. Trimorphic populations (▲) have much higher seed set than monomorphic populations (○) further north. The data shown are grand population means of log10 (seeds/fruit + 1) for 10 trimorphic populations and 18 monomorphic populations. (From Dorken & Eckert 2001.)

monomorphic populations are fixed for single multilocus genotypes, as predicted based on the absence of sex, but these genotypes differ among infertile populations, indicating that sterility mutations have probably arisen on numerous occasions.

Variation in the balance between sexual and asexual reproduction is likely to be common whenever clonal propagation occurs over a wider range of environmental conditions than sexual reproduction. In *D. verticillatus*, variation in the relative importance of sexual vs. asexual reproduction was detected through large-scale geographical surveys of the patterns of style-morph distribution and the discovery of monomorphic populations. Sexual polymorphisms are especially useful for investigating this type of problem because they are sensitive indicators of the reproductive systems of populations. Where sex occurs regularly, all mating morphs are likely to be represented, often at similar frequencies. In contrast, where clonal propagation dominates, biased morph ratios and floral monomorphism are common.

Joint action of drift and selection
The most comprehensive study of the evolutionary breakdown of tristyly involves the evolution of selfing from outcrossing in *Eichhornia paniculata* (reviewed in Barrett *et al.* 1993). This represents one of the only known examples of an evolutionary peak shift resulting from the joint action of genetic drift and natural selection (see Coyne *et al.* 1997). This annual, emergent aquatic from north-east Brazil and

the Caribbean is highly self-fertile and therefore vulnerable to ecological and demographic factors influencing mating patterns. Indeed, *E. paniculata* displays among the widest range of selfing rates reported in flowering plants. In large, dense populations high levels of disassortative mating serve to maintain tristyly. However, periodic bottlenecks and dispersal events associated with the ephemeral aquatic habitats that *E. paniculata* occupies often result in small effective population sizes and periods of low density (Husband & Barrett 1992a,b). Under these conditions, genetic drift predominates and selection favours predominant selfing. Selfing variants of the M-morph have arisen on multiple occasions in several parts of the geographical range with floral modifications governed by different recessive modifier genes (Husband & Barrett 1993; Fenster & Barrett 1994).

The shift from outcrossing to selfing in *E. paniculata* occurs in two successive stages (Barrett *et al.* 1989; Figure 16.9). First, the S-morph is lost from small populations through drift resulting in dimorphic (L, M) populations. Secondly, selfing variants of the M-morph spread to fixation in dimorphic populations resulting in the loss of the L-morph. Selfing variants are favoured in dimorphic populations because the transmission bias of selfing genes is not countered by strong inbreeding depression or pollen discounting (Barrett *et al.* 1989; Kohn & Barrett 1994). Selfing variants also benefit from reproductive assurance when pollinator service is insufficient and episodes of colonization and extinction of populations are frequent. Indeed, selfing variants predominate on the island of Jamaica, where the normal long-tongued pollinators of the species that service populations in Brazil are absent, and the species occupies ephemeral aquatic habitats such as rice fields and roadside ditches. The benefits of reproductive assurance in the context of metapopulation dynamics have been explored theoretically by Pannell and Barrett (1998). Their

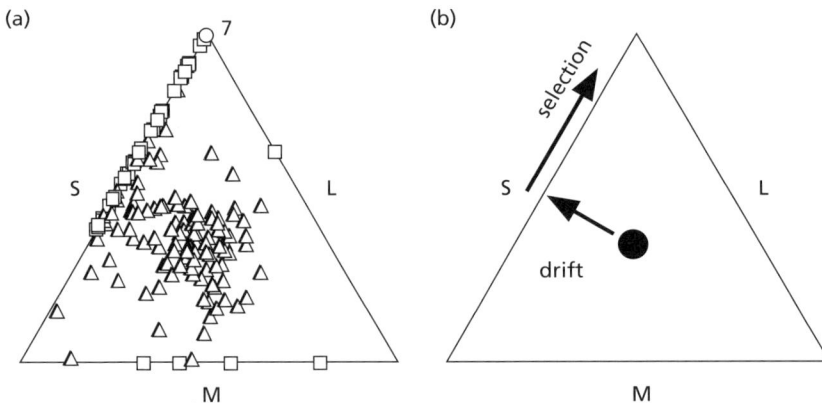

Figure 16.9 Patterns of variation in style-morph frequencies implicate the joint action of genetic drift and natural selection in the evolutionary breakdown of tristyly in *Eichhornia paniculata*. (a) Style-morph frequencies in 167 populations sampled from north-east Brazil. (b) Model of the evolutionary forces transforming outcrossing tristylous populations to populations composed of selfing variants. (From Barrett 1995.)

results indicate that selection for reproductive assurance will be strongest where a species is uncommon across the landscape, such as at range margins, and this agrees with empirical observations on the geographical distribution of selfing in *E. paniculata*, and other species where selfing has evolved at the geographical limits of the range (Lloyd 1980).

These inferences on evolutionary processes in *E. paniculata* have been based on extensive geographical surveys of a large number of populations during 10 years of field studies in north-east Brazil and Jamaica (Husband & Barrett 1995, 1999; Barrett & Husband 1997). Census data on population-size fluctuations, the spatial and temporal dynamics of floral-morph frequencies, and measurements of mating patterns and gene flow jointly implicate metapopulation dynamics as playing a critical role in the population biology of the species and in the evolutionary breakdown of tristyly. A recent metapopulation model, simulating conditions in dimorphic populations of *E. paniculata*, confirms that mixed populations containing selfing and outcrossing morphs are difficult to maintain and that selfing can often evolve (Pannell & Barrett 2001). An important feature of this model is that mating in populations is context dependent, varying with population size and the frequency of selfing and outcrossing morphs. As a result, recently founded populations have higher selfing rates than larger, older populations. Studies of mating patterns in *E. paniculata* indicate these forms of context dependence (Barrett & Husband 1990; Kohn & Barrett 1994) which may be common in self-compatible species with population-size fluctuations and frequent cycles of colonization and extinction.

Conclusions

While experiments on the mechanisms of selection at the population level are necessary to understand how evolutionary modifications to plant reproductive systems occur, studies of geographical variation of the type described here can be informative in identifying the ecological and genetic factors involved. For each of the groups we have discussed, there is good evidence of spatial genetic variation governing reproductive systems related to ecological conditions. The scale at which this variation is manifested differs among the groups considered. In *Wurmbea*, contrasting sexual systems coexist on the same hillside ecologically differentiated into wet vs. dry sites, although regional patterns of segregation associated with precipitation were also evident. Ecological sorting at a local scale also occurs in *Sagittaria*, where monoecious and dioecious populations can be found in aquatic habitats in the same general area that differ in stability and competition. In contrast, large-scale geographical surveys at regional (*Narcissus, Decodon*), continental (*Eichhornia*) and intercontinental (*Lythrum*) scales were required to detect variation in tristylous systems. The common theme in each of these studies was the value in examining large numbers of populations over a wide geographical area. Large samples are required to detect the stochastic signature of genetic drift and they also increase the likelihood of observing reproductive differentiation related to spatial variation in ecological conditions. Research that integrates traditional biogeographical perspectives with modern theoretical and experimental approaches is most likely to provide novel insights into the ecological mechanisms that govern the evolution of plant reproductive systems.

Summary

There is a strong theoretical foundation to explain the evolution of plant reproductive systems. However, for most transitions the ecological mechanisms and spatial scale in which they operate are poorly understood. Studies of geographical variation can provide insights into the role of ecology as the principal driver of shifts in reproductive mode because variable demographic and environmental conditions are commonplace in wide-ranging species. The two major transitions in reproductive systems of flowering plants are the evolution of separate sexes from combined sexes, and the evolution of uniparental reproduction (asexual reproduction or predominant selfing) from biparental reproduction. Here we investigate these changes using experimental and theoretical approaches to intraspecific variation in species with polymorphic sexual systems. We examine microevolutionary processes operating in a variety of spatial contexts including local populations, metapopulations, and larger assemblages at regional, geographical and continental scales. We first investigate the maintenance of gender monomorphism vs. dimorphism in species with both cosexual and dioecious populations. We analyse how contrasting life histories associated with aridity in one case, and competition and disturbance in another, influence the evolution of unisexuality from hermaphroditism. We then consider the evolutionary forces modifying the sexual systems of several tristylous species. This analysis reveals how spatial variation in ecological and genetic factors can destabilize this complex genetic polymorphism resulting in a variety of reproductive outcomes, including clonal reproduction and autogamy. Our studies illustrate the benefits of looking beyond the scale of local populations and incorporating the broader geographical perspective that was central to early evolutionary research.

Acknowledgements

We thank Bill Cole, Chris Eckert, Lawrence Harder and Brian Husband for advice and permission to cite unpublished work and Janis Antonovics and Richard Abbott for useful comments on the manuscript. Our research was funded by grants from the Natural Sciences and Engineering Research Council of Canada and graduate student scholarships from NSERC, the Ontario Government, and the Connaught Foundation of the University of Toronto. We thank the many colleagues who have helped us on our travels.

References

Abrahamson, W.G. (1980). Demography and vegetative reproduction. In: *Demography and Evolution in Plant Populations* (ed. O.T. Solbrig), pp. 89–106. Blackwell, Scientific Publications, Oxford.

Arroyo, J. & Dafni, A. (1995). Variations in habitat,

season, flower traits and pollinators in dimorphic *Narcissus tazetta* L. (Amaryllidaceae) in Israel. *New Phytologist*, **129**, 135–145.

Ashman, T.-L. (1999). Determinants of sex allocation in a gynodioecious wild strawberry: implications for the evolution of dioecy and sexual dimorphism. *Journal of Evolutionary Biology*, **12**, 648–661.

Baker, A.M., Thompson, J.D. & Barrett, S.C.H. (2000a). Evolution and maintenance of stigma-height dimorphism in *Narcissus*. I. Floral variation and style-morph ratios. *Heredity*, **84**, 501–515.

Baker, A.M., Thompson, J.D. & Barrett, S.C.H. (2000b). Evolution and maintenance of stigma-height dimorphism in *Narcissus*. II. Fitness comparisons between style morphs. *Heredity*, **84**, 516–526.

Baker, H.G. (1959a). Reproductive methods as factors in speciation in flowering plants. *Cold Spring Harbor Symposium of Quantitative Biolology*, **24**, 177–191.

Baker, H.G. (1959b). The contribution of autecological and genecological studies to our knowledge of the past migration of plants. *American Naturalist*, **93**, 255–272.

Baker, H.G. (1967). Support for Baker's Law — as a rule. *Evolution*, **21**, 853–856.

Barrett, S.C.H. (1992). Gender variation and the evolution of dioecy in *Wurmbea dioica* (Liliaceae). *Journal of Evolutionary Biology*, **5**, 423–444.

Barrett, S.C.H. (1993). The evolutionary biology of tristyly. In: *Oxford Surveys in Evolutionary Biology* (eds D. Futuyma & J. Antonovics), pp. 283–326. Oxford University Press, Oxford.

Barrett, S.C.H. (1995). Mating-system evolution in flowering plants: micro- and macroevolutionary approaches. *Acta Botanica Neerlandica*, **44**, 385–402.

Barrett, S.C.H. (1998). The evolution of mating strategies in flowering plants. *Trends in Plant Science*, **3**, 335–341.

Barrett, S.C.H. & Glover, D.E. (1985). On the Darwinian hypothesis of the adaptive significance of tristly. *Evolution*, **39**, 766–777.

Barrett, S.C.H. & Husband, B.C. (1990). Variation in outcrossing rates in *Eichhornia paniculata*: the role of demographic and reproductive factors. *Plant Species Biology*, **5**, 41–55.

Barrett, S.C.H. & Husband, B.C. (1997). Ecology and genetics of ephemeral plant populations: *Eichhornia paniculata* (Pontederiaceae) in northeast Brazil. *Journal of Heredity*, **88**, 277–284.

Barrett, S.C.H. & Pannell, J.R. (1999). Metapopulation dynamics and mating-system evolution in plants. In: *Molecular Systematics and Plant Evolution* (eds P. Hollingsworth, R. Bateman & R. Gornall), pp. 74–100. Taylor & Francis, London.

Barrett, S.C.H., Morgan, M.T. & Husband, B.C. (1989). The dissolution of a complex genetic polymorphism: the evolution of self-fertilization in tristylous *Eichhornia paniculata* (Pontederiaceae). *Evolution*, **43**, 1398–1416.

Barrett, S.C.H., Kohn, J.R. & Cruzan, M.B. (1993). Experimental studies of mating-system evolution: the marriage of marker genes and floral biology. In: *Ecology and Evolution of Plant Reproduction: New Approaches* (ed. R. Wyatt), pp. 193–230. Chapman & Hall, New York.

Barrett, S.C.H., Harder, L.D. & Worley, A.C. (1996a). The comparative biology of pollination and mating in flowering plants. *Philosophical Transactions of the Royal Society, London, B*, **351**, 1271–1280.

Barrett, S.C.H., Lloyd D.G. & Arroyo, J. (1996b). Stylar polymorphisms and the evolution of heterostyly in *Narcissus*. In: *Floral Biology: Studies on Floral Evolution in Animal-Pollinated Plants* (eds D.G. Lloyd & S.C.H. Barrett), pp. 339–376. Chapman & Hall, New York.

Barrett, S.C.H., Cole, W.W., Arroyo, J., Cruzan, M.B. & Lloyd, D.G. (1997). Sexual polymorphisms in *Narcissus triandrus* (Amaryllidaceae). Is this species tristylous? *Heredity*, **78**, 135–145.

Bawa, K.S. (1980). Evolution of dioecy in flowering plants. *Annual Reviews of Ecology & Systematics*, **11**, 15–40.

Bierzychudek, P. (1987). Resolving the paradox of sexual reproduction: A review of experimental tests. In: *The Evolution of Sex and its Consequences* (ed. S.C. Stearns), pp. 163–174. Birkhäuser Verlag, Basel.

Carlquist, S. (1966). The biota of long-distance dispersal. IV. Genetic systems in the floras of oceanic islands. *Evolution*, **20**, 433–455.

Case, A.L. (2000). *The evolution of combined versus separate sexes in* Wurmbea (*Colchicaceae*). PhD Thesis, University of Toronto, Canada.

Case, A.L. & Barrett, S.C.H. (2001). Ecological

differentiation of combined versus separates sexes of *Wurmbea dioica* (Colchicaceae). *Ecology*, (in press).

Charlesworth, D. (1999). Theories of the evolution of dioecy. In: *Gender and Sexual Dimorphism in Flowering Plants* (eds M.A. Gender, T.E. Dawson & L.F. Delph), pp. 33–60. Springer-Verlag, Berlin.

Charnov, E.L. (1982). *The Theory of Sex Allocation.* Monographs in population biology 18. Princeton University Press, Princeton, NJ.

Costich, D.E. (1995). Gender specialization across a climatic gradient: experimental comparison of monoecious and dioecious *Ecballium. Ecology*, **76**, 1036–1050.

Couvet, D., Ronce, O. & Gliddon, C. (1998). The maintenance of nucleocytoplasmic polymorphism in a metapopulation: The case of gynodioecy. *American Naturalist*, **152**, 59–70.

Coyne, J.A., Barton, N.H. & Turelli, M. (1997). Perspective: A critique of Sewall Wright's shifting balance theory of evolution. *Evolution*, **51**, 643–671.

Crosby, J. (1949). Selection of an unfavourable gene-complex. *Evolution*, **3**, 212–230.

Darwin, C. (1876). *The Effects of Cross- and Self-fertilization in the Vegetable Kingdom.* John Murray, London.

Darwin, C. (1877). *The Different Forms of Flowers on Plants of the Same Species.* John Murray, London.

De Laguérie, P., Olivieri, I. & Gouyon, P.-H. (1993). Environment effects on fitness-sets shape and evolutionarily stable strategies. *Journal of Theoretical Biology*, **163**, 113–125.

de Jong, T.J., Waser, N.M. & Klinkhamer, P.G.L. (1993). Geitonogamy: the neglected side of selfing. *Trends in Ecology & Evolution*, **8**, 321–325.

Delph, L.F. (1990). Sex-differential resource allocation patterns in the subdioecious shrub *Hebe subalpina. Ecology*, **71**, 1342–1351.

Dorken, M.E. & Eckert, C.G. (2001). Severely reduced sexual reproduction in northern populations of a clonal plant, *Decodon verticillatus* (Lythraceae). *Journal of Ecology*, **89**, 339–350.

Dulberger, R. (1964). Flower dimorphism and self-incompatibility in *Narcissus tazetta* L. *Evolution*, **18**, 361–363.

Eckert, C.G. & Barrett, S.C.H. (1992). Stochastic loss of style morphs from populations of tristylous *Lythrum salicaria* and *Decodon verticillatus* (Lythraceae). *Evolution*, **46**, 1014–1029.

Eckert, C.G. & Barrett, S.C.H. (1993). Patterns of genotypic diversity and clonal reproduction in *Decodon verticillatus* (Lythraceae). *American Journal of Botany*, **80**, 1175–1182.

Eckert, C.G. & Barrett, S.C.H. (1994a). Self-compatibility, tristyly and floral variation in *Decodon verticillatus* (Lythraceae). *Biological Journal of the Linnean Society*, **53**, 1–30.

Eckert, C.G. & Barrett, S.C.H. (1994b). Post-pollination mechanisms and the maintenance of outcrossing in self-compatible *Decodon verticillatus* (Lythraceae). *Heredity*, **72**, 396–411.

Eckert, C.G. & Barrett, S.C.H. (1994c). Inbreeding depression in partially self-fertilizing *Decodon verticillatus* (Lythraceae): population genetic and experimental analyses. *Evolution*, **48**, 952–964.

Eckert, C.G. & Barrett, S.C.H. (1995). Style morph ratios in tristylous *Decodon verticillatus* (Lythraceae): selection versus historical contingency. *Ecology*, **76**, 1051–1066.

Eckert, C.G., Manicacci, D. & Barrett, S.C.H. (1996). Genetic drift and founder effect in native versus introduced populations of an invading plant, *Lythrum salicaria* (Lythraceae). *Evolution*, **50**, 1512–1519.

Eckert, C.G., Dorken, M.E. & Mitchell, S.A. (1999). Loss of sex in clonal populations of a flowering plant, *Decodon verticillatus* (Lythraceae). *Evolution*, **53**, 1079–1092.

Fenster, C.B. & Barrett, S.C.H. (1994). The inheritance of mating system modifier genes in *Eichhornia paniculata* (Pontederiaceae). *Heredity*, **72**, 433–445.

Ganders, F.R. (1978). The genetics and evolution of gynodioecy in *Nemophila menziesii* (Hydrophyllaceae). *Canadian Journal of Botany*, **56**, 1400–1408.

Geber, M.A., Dawson, T.E. & Delph, L.F., eds (1999). *Gender and Sexual Dimorphism in Flowering Plants.* Springer-Verlag, Berlin.

Godley, E.J. (1979). Flower biology in New Zealand. *New Zealand Journal of Botany*, **17**, 441–466.

Grant, V. (1971). *Plant Speciation.* Columbia University Press, New York.

Hagerup, O. (1951). Pollination in the Faroes—in spite of rain and poverty in insects. *Kongelige Danske Videnskabernes Selskab-Biologiske Meddelelser*, **18**, 1–47.

Hanski, I.A. & Gilpin, M.E. (1997). *Metapopulation*

Biology; Ecology, Genetics, and Evolution. Academic Press, San Diego.

Harder, L.D. & Barrett, S.C.H. (1995). Mating cost of large floral displays in hermaphrodite plants. *Nature*, **373**, 512–515.

Harder, L.D. & Barrett, S.C.H. (1996). Pollen dispersal and mating patterns in animal-pollinated plants. In: *Floral Biology: Studies on Floral Evolution in Animal-Pollinated Plants* (eds D.G. Lloyd & S.C.H. Barrett), pp. 140–190. Chapman & Hall, New York.

Heuch, I. (1979). Equilibrium populations of heterostylous plants. *Theoretical Population Biology*, **15**, 43–57.

Husband, B.C. & Barrett, S.C.H. (1992a). Effective population size and genetic drift in tristylous *Eichhornia paniculata* (Pontederiaceae). *Evolution*, **46**, 1875–1890.

Husband, B.C. & Barrett, S.C.H. (1992b). Genetic drift and the maintenance of style length polymorphism in tristylous populations of *Eichhornia paniculata* (Pontederiaceae). *Heredity*, **69**, 440–449.

Husband, B.C. & Barrett, S.C.H. (1993). Multiple origins of self-fertilization in tristylous *Eichhornia paniculata* (Pontederiaceae): inferences from style morph and isozyme variation. *Journal of Evolutionary Biology*, **6**, 591–608.

Husband, B.C. & Barrett, S.C.H. (1995). Estimates of gene flow in *Eichhornia paniculata* (Pontederiaceae): effects of range substructure. *Heredity*, **75**, 549–560.

Husband, B.C. & Barrett, S.C.H. (1999). Spatial and temporal variation in population size of *Eichhornia paniculata* in ephemeral habitats: implication for metapopulation dynamics. *Journal of Ecology*, **86**, 1021–1031.

Kohn, J.R. & Barrett, S.C.H. (1994). Pollen discounting and the spread of a selfing variant in tristylous *Eichhornia paniculata*: evidence from experimental populations. *Evolution*, **48**, 1576–1594.

Levin, D.A. & Kerster, H.W. (1974). Gene flow in seed plants. *Evolutionary Biology*, **7**, 139–220.

Lloyd, D.G. (1965). Evolution of self-compatibility and racial differentiation in *Leavenworthia* (Cruciferae). *Contributions from the Gray Herbarium of Harvard University*, **195**, 3–134.

Lloyd, D.G. (1980). Demographic factors and mating patterns in angiosperms. In: *Demography and Evolution in Plant Populations* (ed. O.T. Solbrig), pp. 67–88. Blackwell Scientific Publications, Oxford.

Lloyd, D.G. & Bawa, K.S. (1984). Modification of the gender of seed plants in varying conditions. *Evolutionary Biology*, **17**, 255–338.

Maynard Smith, J. (1978). *The Evolution of Sex.* Cambridge University Press, Cambridge, UK.

McNeill, C.L. & Jain, S.K. (1983). Genetic differentiation studies and phylogenetic inference in the plant genus *Limnanthes* (section Inflexae). *Theoretical and Applied Genetics*, **66**, 257–269.

Olivieri, I., Couvet, D. & Gouyon, P.H. (1990). The genetics of transient populations: research at the metapopulation level. TREE, **5**, 207–210.

Olmstead, R.G. (1990). Biological and historical factors influencing genetic diversity in the *Scutellaria angustifolia* complex (Labiatae). *Evolution*, **44**, 54–70.

Pannell, J.R. & Barrett, S.C.H. (1998). Baker's Law revisited: reproductive assurance in a metapopulation. *Evolution*, **52**, 657–668.

Pannel, J.R. & Barrett, S.C.H. (2001). Effects of drift, selection and population turnover on a mating-system polymorphism. *Theoretical Population Biology* **59**, 145–155.

Proctor, M., Yeo, P. & Lack, A. (1996). *The Natural History of Pollination.* Timber Press, Portland, OR.

Renner, S.S. & Ricklefs, R.E. (1995). Dioecy and its correlates in the flowering plants. *American Journal of Botany*, **82**, 596–606.

Rick, C.M. (1966). Some-plant animal relations on the Galápagos islands. In: *The Galápagos* (ed. R.I. Bowman), pp. 215–224. University of California Press, Berkeley, CA.

Richards, A.J. (1997). *Plant Breeding Systems.* Allen & Unwin, London.

Sage, T.L., Strumas, F., Cole, W.W. & Barrett, S.C.H. (1999). Differential ovule development following self- and cross-pollination: the basis of self-sterility in *Narcissus triandrus* (Amaryllidaceae). *American Journal of Botany*, **86**, 855–870.

Sakai, A.K. & Weller, S.G. (1999). Gender and sexual dimorphism in flowering plants: a review of terminology, biogeographic patterns, ecological correlates, and phylogenetic approaches. In: *Gender and Sexual Dimorphism in Flowering Plants* (eds M.A. Geber, T.E. Dawson & L.F. Delph), pp. 1–31. Springer-Verlag, Berlin.

Sarkissian, T.S., Barrett, S.C.H. & Harder, L.D. (2001). Gender variation in *Sagittaria latifolia* (Alismataceae): is size all that matters? *Ecology*, **82**, 360–373.

Schaal, B. (1998). Phylogeographic studies in plants: problems and prospects. *Molecular Ecology*, **7**, 465–474.

Schoen, D.J., Morgan, M.T. & Bataillon, T. (1996). How does self-pollination evolve? Inferences from floral ecology and molecular genetic variation. *Philosophical Transactions of the Royal Society, London, B*, **351**, 1281–1290.

Strid, A. (1969). Evolutionary trends in the breeding system of *Nigella* (Ranunculaceae). *Botaniska Notiser*, **122**, 380–397.

Uyenoyama, M.K. Holsinger, K.E. & Waller, D.M. (1993). Ecological and genetic factors directing the evolution of self-fertilization. In: *Oxford Surveys in Evolutionary Biology* (eds D. Futuyma & J. Antonovics), pp. 327–381. Oxford University Press, Oxford.

Webb, C.J. (1999). Empirical studies: evolution and maintenance of dimorphic breeding systems. In: *Gender and Sexual Dimorphism in Flowering Plants* (eds M.A. Geber, T.E. Dawson & L.F. Delph), pp. 61–95. Springer-Verlag, Berlin.

Weller, S.G. & Sakai, A.K. (1990). The evolution of dicliny in *Schiedea* (Caryophyllaceae), an endemic Hawaiian genus. *Plant Species Biology*, **5**, 83–96.

Wolfe, L.M. & Schmida, A. (1997). The ecology of sex expression in a gynodioecious Israeli desert shrub (*Ochradenus baccatus*). *Ecology*, **78**, 101–110.

Wyatt, R. (1988). Phylogenetic aspects of the evolution of self-pollination. In: *Plant Evolutionary Biology* (eds L.D. Gottlieb & S.K. Jain), pp. 109–128. Chapman & Hall, London.

Chapter 17

Adaptation at the edge of a species' range

*N. H. Barton**

Introduction

A species' range often ends more or less abruptly, even when physical conditions change gradually. Almost by definition, the range corresponds to the limits of the species' niche—that is, to the set of conditions in which individuals can reproduce rapidly enough to sustain a population. Thus, sharp edges to a species' range imply a failure to adapt to conditions beyond the current niche. From an evolutionary point of view, such limits to adaptation are puzzling (Antonovics 1976; Barton & Partridge 2000). There may be absolute physical constraints, such that it is impossible for organisms to survive and reproduce in more extreme environments. More often, it may be impossible to produce such genotypes by gradual evolution of the present population. However, it is more usual for populations to be able to adapt to moderate changes in conditions: the ready response of almost all quantitative traits to artificial selection is strong evidence of this.

Natural selection may fail to establish fitter genotypes at the edge of the range because selection is opposed by the flow of genes from the centre of the distribution. Moreover, because gene flow tends to be from dense regions into those that are less dense, and because poorly adapted populations tend to be less dense, there is a feedback between fitness and population size which may cause a catastrophic failure to adapt, and set a sharp limit to the species' range. (There is an analogy here with the conflict between selection and random drift. Here, there is also a positive feedback in which poorly adapted and hence less numerous populations suffer more drift, which may cause catastrophic accumulation of deleterious mutations; Lynch *et al.* 1995.) A species' range may also be limited by competition with other species. Competition can sustain a sharp, stable boundary at an arbitrary position even within a uniform habitat (Bazykin 1998); along an environmental gradient, the fitness of new genotypes which are better adapted to more extreme conditions may be reduced by the presence of another species which is already well adapted to those conditions.

Haldane (1956) first explicitly identified the feedback between maladaptive gene flow and population size as a factor limiting geographic distribution. However, until recently there has been no quantitative analysis of the effects of gene flow on range

Institute of Cell, Animal and Population Biology, University of Edinburgh, West Mains Road, Edinburgh, EH9 3 JT, Scotland.

limits, or of its interaction with other limiting factors such as competition. Pease *et al.* (1989) follow the adaptation and spread of a species across a continuous habitat with a linear change in optimum; they obtain conditions for initial increase, in which case density regulation is negligible. Holt and Gomulkiewicz (1997) considered the simplest case of adaptation of a quantitative trait in a single population experiencing immigration. Kirkpatrick and Barton (1997) considered a quantitative trait under stabilizing selection towards an optimum which changes linearly across a one-dimensional habitat. They found that if the optimum changes slowly in space, the population can remain perfectly adapted everywhere. However, above a critical spatial gradient, the population becomes restricted to a narrow region to which it is well adapted. Peck *et al.* (1998) argued that the adaptation of asexuals would not be impeded in this way, and so could gain an advantage at the edge of the range; this might explain the tendency for parthenogens to occur at range margins. Case and Taper (2000) have extended Kirkpatrick and Barton's (1997) model to include several species, and find that the interaction between competition and gene flow can greatly sharpen species' ranges.

Here, I extend this theoretical work by asking whether an increase in genetic variance in extreme environments can facilitate adaptation, and hence allow indefinite expansion of the species' range. In evolutionary ecology, it is usual to assume a fixed genetic variance. This is a reasonable approach, because we observe consistently high additive genetic variance, and because the causes of this variance are not well understood. However, there are many plausible models for the genetic basis of quantitative traits that do permit the genetic variance to change, and examining a variety of such models may lead to robust conclusions about the likely effects of an evolving genetic variance. I consider the effects of both changing allele frequencies (which will dominate measures of variance when few loci are involved, and linkage is loose), and of linkage disequilibrium (which is significant when selection is strong relative to recombination, and large numbers of loci affect the trait). At each locus, I assume either very many alleles, or just two alleles. The causes of genetic variance are unclear: in particular, it is not known whether it is maintained primarily by mutation or by balancing selection. However, because gene flow generates substantial genetic variance, no restrictive assumptions need be made about the causes of the standing genetic variability. I begin by summarizing Kirkpatrick and Barton's (1997) model and approximations.

The basic model

Population size as a direct function of mean fitness
As in Kirkpatrick and Barton (1997), Peck *et al.* (1998) and Case and Taper (2000), I consider a quantitative trait under stabilizing selection towards an optimum that changes along a one-dimensional habitat. Suppose that the density of the population at position x and time t is $n(x, t)$, and the mean of the quantitative trait is $\bar{z}(x, t)$. The trait mean changes as:

$$\frac{\partial \bar{z}}{\partial t} = \frac{\sigma^2}{2} \frac{\partial^2 \bar{z}}{\partial x^2} + \sigma^2 \frac{\partial \log(n)}{\partial x} \frac{\partial \bar{z}}{\partial x} + v_g \frac{\partial \bar{r}}{\partial \bar{z}} \tag{1}$$

(Pease *et al.* 1989; Eq. 1 of Kirkpatrick and Barton 1997). The first term represents the diffusion of genes from place to place; σ^2 is the variance of distance between parent and offspring. The second term represents asymmetric gene flow, which tends to carry genes from dense into less dense regions. The final term represents natural selection; v_g is the additive genetic variance, and $\bar{r}$ is the mean Malthusian fitness of the population. (If fitness is frequency dependent, as with some types of competition, then the partial differential in the last term must include only the direct effect of changes in genotype frequencies on fitness, and not the indirect changes in genotypic fitness due to those changing frequencies). Equation 1 can be derived either from a continuous model, or as the limit of a model with discrete generations and discrete demes as selection becomes weak. The selection term requires the assumption that the distribution of breeding values is Gaussian. For the moment, we take the genetic variance v_g to be fixed and the same everywhere.

Stabilizing selection towards an optimum at z_{opt} is defined by setting the fitness of an individual with phenotype z as:

$$r = r_e(n) + r_g(z) \quad \text{where} \quad r_g = -\frac{(z - z_{opt})^2}{2V_s} \tag{2}$$

Here, individual fitness is the sum of two terms: an ecological component, $r_e(n)$, and a genetic component $r_g(z)$, which is a function of the trait, z. V_s is the inverse of the strength of selection. The mean fitness is:

$$\bar{r} = r_e(n) - \bar{r}_g \quad \text{where} \quad \bar{r}_g = -\frac{v_p}{2V_s} - \frac{(\bar{z} - z_{opt})^2}{2V_s} \tag{3}$$

where v_p is the phenotypic variance.

If the optimum changes linearly through space, as $z_{opt} = bx$, then there is always an equilibrium in which the population is everywhere perfectly adapted ($\bar{z} = z_{opt}$), so that mean fitness and population density are constant. Gene flow has no effect because the influx from populations on one side, with higher $\bar{z}$, is precisely balanced by the influx from the opposite side, with lower $\bar{z}$ (Felsenstein 1977). To find whether this equilibrium is stable, and whether other equilibria exist, we must make some assumption about the relation between n and $\bar{z}$. The simplest is to assume that population size is a definite function of the genetic component of mean fitness; I refer to this as the simple one-variable model. Assume $n \sim \exp[\bar{r}_g \gamma]$, so that numbers increase exponentially with mean fitness; γ is a measure of the weakness of density-dependent regulation. If the gradient in the optimum exceeds a certain value, b_{crit}, the perfectly adapted equilibrium becomes unstable, and the population collapses to become adapted to only a limited region:

$$\bar{z} = \beta x \quad \text{where} \quad \beta = \frac{b}{2}\left(1 - \sqrt{1 - \left(\frac{b_{crit}}{b}\right)^2}\right) \quad \text{and} \quad b > b_{crit} = \sqrt{\frac{4v_g}{\sigma^2 \gamma}} \tag{4}$$

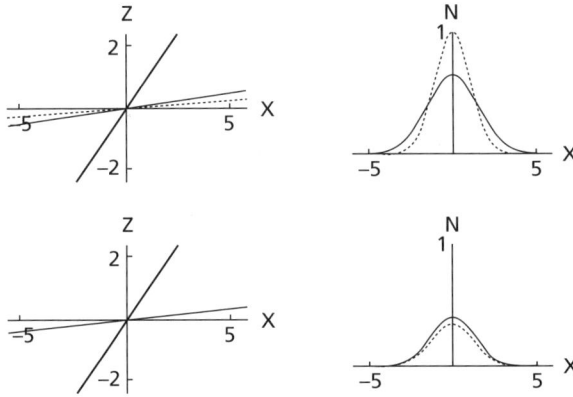

Figure 17.1 Example of the collapse of adaptation when the optimum changes too steeply. The upper panel is for the logarithmic model of density dependence, $r_e = -\log(n/K)/\gamma$, with $A = \gamma v_g/V_s = 0.1$; $B_{crit} = 0.467$. On the left, the solid lines show the optimum ($Z_{opt} = BX$, with $B = 1$; steep line), and the trait mean (Z; shallow line), plotted against scaled distance, X. The right panel shows the density, N, against X. The dashed line shows the one-variable approximation, $n \sim \exp(\gamma \bar{r}_g)$. The lower row shows the logistic model of density dependence, $r_e = 1 - n/K$, with $A = v_g/r^*V_s = 0.1$; $B_{crit} = 0.071$. The dashed line shows the Gaussian approximation (Kirkpatrick & Barton 1997, Eqs 12–14), and the solid line the exact solution of Eqs 8 and 9; these are indistinguishable for Z, on the lower left. All values are scaled as in Eq. 7.

The dashed lines in the upper row of Figure 17.1 show an example of such an equilibrium. The trait mean changes linearly, but at a slower rate than the changing optimum (upper left of Figure 17.1). The population density has a Gaussian form, with 95% of the population confined within a region of width

$$\sigma \sqrt{\frac{2}{L} \frac{b_{crit}}{b - \beta}}, \quad \text{where} \quad L = \frac{v_g}{2V_s}$$

is the standing load due to genetic variation around the optimum. The critical gradient is such that the change in optimum over one dispersal distance, relative to the genetic standard deviation ($b\sigma/\sqrt{V_g}$) is related to the strength of density-dependent regulation, $2/\sqrt{\gamma}$. Note that this critical gradient is independent of the strength of selection, V_s.

Joint evolution of the trait mean and population density

It is more realistic to consider the joint evolution of the trait mean with population density. The density changes as a result of dispersal and reproduction:

$$\frac{\partial n}{\partial t} = \frac{\sigma^2}{2} \frac{\partial^2 n}{\partial x^2} + n\bar{r} \tag{5}$$

In this chapter, I will consider two specific forms of density dependence: a logarithmic form which is consistent with the simple one-variable model, and logistic regulation. First, suppose that fitness, r_e, depends on density, n as $r_e(n) = -\frac{1}{\gamma}\log\left(\frac{n}{K}\right)$; this implies an indefinitely high fitness at low density ($-\log(n) \to \infty$ as $n \to 0$). At a spatially homogeneous equilibrium, $\bar{r} = r_e + \bar{r}_g = 0$, and we recover the one-variable model $n = K\exp(\gamma\bar{r}_g)$. With spatial heterogeneity, the diffusion of individuals from place to place alters n, and so the coupled equations for density and trait mean, Eqs 1 and 5, have a different solution from the one-variable model (Eq. 1 with $n = K\exp(\gamma\bar{r}_g)$). However, the solution has the same form, with a linear change in $\bar{z}$ and a Gaussian decline in density around the point at which the population is best adapted (see Appendix 1). The one-variable model $n \sim \exp(\gamma\bar{r}_g)$ can be seen as a limiting case of this model, in which selection is so weak that the population reaches a quasi-equilibrium density at each point. The exact solution of Eqs 1 and 5 is compared with the simple one-variable model in the upper panels of Figure 17.1 (solid and dashed lines, respectively). In this example, selection is strong ($A \equiv \gamma v_g/V_s = 0.1$), and so dispersal causes a substantial reduction in density at the centre below that predicted by the local mean fitness. Because the gradients in density are broadened by dispersal, adaptation is impeded less by gene flow, and so the exact solution (assuming v_g constant) predicts a higher mean fitness than does the simple approximation of Kirkpatrick and Barton (1997). However, with weaker selection ($A = \gamma v_g/V_s < 0.01$, say) the approximation becomes accurate.

Kirkpatrick and Barton (1997) used a linear density dependence, $r_e = r_{max}\left(1 - \frac{n}{K}\right)$, as in the logistic equation. The qualitative conclusion is the same: above a critical spatial gradient in the optimum, perfect adaptation becomes unstable, and the population collapses to survive within a limited niche. Linear density dependence makes relatively little difference to the shape of the equilibrium solution (lower panels of Figure 17.1): the trait mean changes approximately linearly, and the numbers are approximately Gaussian. For equivalent parameters, equilibrium density is lower (compare right-hand panels of Figure 17.1). This is because in the logistic model, fitness is bounded at low density. However, with logistic regulation the critical gradient now has a qualitatively different form from the logarithmic case (Eq. 4):

$$b_{crit} = \frac{v_g}{\sigma\sqrt{V_s}} = \frac{\sqrt{2Lv_g}}{\sigma} \tag{6}$$

where $L = v_g/(2V_s)$ is the standing genetic load due to genetic variation around the optimum (from Kirkpatrick and Barton 1997, Eq. 18). Because we expect the standing load $L = v_g/(2V_s)$ to be small, the critical change in optimum over one dispersal range, measured in genetic standard deviations, is also small ($\sigma b_{crit}/\sqrt{v_g} = \sqrt{2L}$). However, note that Eq. 6 is a criterion for an equilibrium with imperfect adaptation

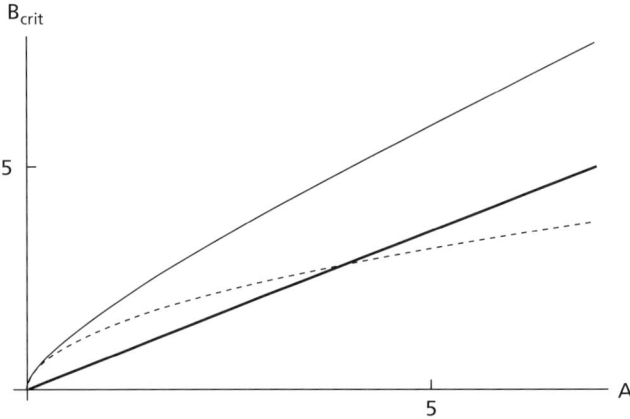

Figure 17.2 The critical gradient, B_{crit}, plotted against the scaled strength of selection, $A = v_g/r^* V_s$. The curves show the critical gradient for the three models compared in Figure 17.1: one-variable model (dashed line), logarithmic density dependence (thin line); and logistic density dependence (thick line).

to exist in the margins. Kirkpatrick and Barton (1997) found that Eq. 6 can be a substantial underestimate of the critical gradient: for steeper gradients, the equilibrium with imperfect adaptation (and hence a limited range) exists but is unstable, so that the mean moves towards the optimum everywhere.

These different forms for the critical gradient are compared in Figure 17.2 and summarized in Table 17.1. Note that the critical gradient for the logistic model is shallower than for the logarithmic model, especially for weak selection (left of Figure 17.2). This is because under the logarithmic model, the high fitness of sparse populations buffers the species against extinction.

These two models of density dependence are only two arbitrary examples: other relations between density and fitness in the limit of small n can be treated in the same way. The logarithmic model was introduced as a bridge between the one-variable model and the two-variable logistic model of Kirkpatrick and Barton (1997). Because it has an exact solution, and includes the one-variable model as a special case, it will be useful in the extensions of the theory set out below. Moreover, we will see that the qualitative outcome depends on evolution at the margins: thus, it is the form of $r_e(n)$ as $n \to 0$ that matters.

In the following, it is convenient to rescale distance, trait and time so as to work with dimensionless variables. Let:

$$T = r^* t \quad X = \frac{\sqrt{2r^*}}{\sigma} x \quad N = \frac{n}{K^*} \quad Z = \frac{\bar{z}}{\sqrt{r^* V_s}}$$

$$B = \frac{b\sigma}{r^* \sqrt{2V_s}} \quad A = \frac{v_g}{r^* V_s} \quad \bar{R} = \frac{1}{r^*} \left(r_e(n) - \frac{V_P}{2V_s} - \frac{(\bar{z} - z_{opt})^2}{2V_s} \right)$$

(7)

Table 17.1 Summary of critical gradients for the various models of density dependence (columns) and of the genetic variance (rows). Above this value, an equilibrium exists in which the species is maintained in a limited range. The gradient is scaled such that

$$B_{crit} = \frac{b_{crit}\sigma}{r^* \sqrt{2V_s}},$$

B_{crit} is a function of

$$A = \frac{v_g}{r^* V_s},$$

where v_g is the standing variance in a spatially homogeneous population, apart from the two-allele model, in which case it is the maximum possible variance. The symbol on the right of each cell indicates the stability of the alternative equilibria.

Genetic variance	One-variable $n \sim \exp(\bar{r}_g\, \gamma)$	Logarithmic $r_e = -\frac{1}{\gamma}\log\left(\frac{n}{K}\right)$	Logistic $r_e = r_{max}\left(1 - \frac{n}{K}\right)$
Fixed	$\sqrt{2A}$ **PU**	$\sqrt{2A}$ **IS** for $A \ll 1$	$\sqrt{2} + \frac{A}{\sqrt{2}}$ **IS**
Gaussian	$\frac{1}{\sqrt{2}}$ **BS** for $A \ll 1$	∞	∞
Two alleles	∞	∞	∞
Linkage equilibrium (infinitesimal)	$2.45\ \sqrt{A}$ **BS** for $A \ll 1$	$2.45\ \sqrt{A}$ **BS** for $A \ll 1$	$\frac{A}{\sqrt{2}}$ **BS**

PU, perfect adaptation unstable when imperfect adaptation is possible; BS, both equilibria stable; IS, imperfect adaptation stable only for a steeper gradient $B > B_{crit}$. Where the only possible equilibrium is one with perfect adaptation, $B_{crit} = \infty$.

where K^* is some measure of the carrying capacity, and r^* some measure of the growth rate (the choice of these measures is defined below). The dimensionless parameter A is twice the ratio between the standing load due to genetic variation and the reproductive rate: $A = 2L/r^*$.

Assuming a linear change in optimum, $Z_{opt} = BX$, the scaled equations for trait mean and density are:

$$\frac{\partial Z}{\partial T} = \frac{\partial^2 Z}{\partial X^2} + 2\frac{\partial \log(N)}{\partial X}\frac{\partial Z}{\partial X} + A(BX - Z) \tag{8}$$

$$\frac{\partial N}{\partial T} = \frac{\partial^2 N}{\partial X^2} + N\bar{R} \tag{9}$$

For the logistic model used by Kirkpatrick and Barton (1997), setting

$$r^{\star} = r_{max} - \frac{v_p}{2V_s} \quad \text{and} \quad K^{\star} = \frac{Kr^{\star}}{r_{max}}$$

gives $\bar{R} = 1 - N - \frac{1}{2}(BX - Z)^2$. For the logarithmic model, setting

$$r^{\star} = \frac{1}{\gamma} \quad \text{and} \quad K^{\star} = K\exp\left(-\frac{\gamma v_p}{2V_s}\right)$$

gives $\bar{R} = -\log(N) - \frac{1}{2}(BX - Z)^2$. This rescaling allows a direct comparison of the logarithmic and logistic models, as in Figure 17.1: for both models, $r^{\star}$ equals the local strength of density dependence (defined as $n\partial_n(\partial_t n)$) at a spatially homogeneous equilibrium.

Evolution of the variance

Although a key aim of population genetics has been to explain the genetic variability that is the basis of evolution, and although there is an extensive empirical and theoretical literature on spatial variability, there has been surprisingly little study of how quantitative genetic variation changes through space (for exceptions, see Felsenstein 1977; Slatkin 1978; Lande 1982; Goldstein & Holsinger 1992; Barton 1999). This is largely because the evolution of the genetic variance depends on its detailed genetic basis, which is poorly understood. I will consider three cases: a continuum of allelic effects; two alleles per locus; and changes due to linkage disequilibrium (the 'infinitesimal model'). First, however, it is helpful to consider what the optimal genetic variance would be in the absence of any genetic constraints.

The genetic variance that maximizes the total fitness summed over all individuals, $\int nr dx$, is set by the trade-off between the reduction in mean fitness due to variation around the optimum, and the ability to adapt over the whole range of conditions. Naively, one might imagine that the optimum variance would be just large enough to allow the trait mean to follow the optimal mean everywhere, but no larger (i.e. v_g such that $b = b_{crit}$). However, a smaller genetic variance can suffice. Kirkpatrick and Barton (1997) showed that with a linear gradient in optimum and an infinite range, a state of perfect adaptation is locally stable, even if an alternative state of collapse *also* exists and is stable. This perfect state is only unstable at the boundaries of the range, or where the gradient changes. Thus, a higher genetic variance in such boundary regions, and zero variance where the gradient in optimum is constant could permit a stable and highly adapted equilibrium. Of course, there is no reason why populations should in fact evolve to such an optimal outcome: the genetic variance is strongly constrained by the underlying genetics, and this constraint may limit the mean fitness and the range of the species.

Changes in allele frequency: a continuum of alleles

Suppose that at each genetic locus there are alleles with an infinite variety of effects on a quantitative trait. A general model for such a 'continuum of alleles' is set out in Appendix 2. It can be solved numerically, or can be approximated by assuming that the distribution of allelic effects is approximately Gaussian at each locus. This may seem a dangerous assumption, because in nature mutation rates are unlikely to be high enough to maintain such a distribution (Turelli 1984). However, if most genetic variation is maintained by migration rather than by mutation, the Gaussian approximation is accurate (Barton 1999). We will see that the contribution of a low rate of mutation does not affect the ultimate outcome, because at the edge of the range most variability is maintained by gene flow.

It is convenient to rescale the genetic variance relative to the variance that would be maintained in the absence of gene flow, v_∞; thus, $V \equiv v_g/v_\infty$. Other scalings are made as in Eq. 7, with the strength of density-dependent regulation being $\gamma = 1/r^*$. Assuming that the optimum changes linearly, as $z_{opt} = bx$, Eq. 8 extends to:

$$\frac{\partial Z}{\partial T} = \frac{\partial^2 Z}{\partial X^2} - \left[2(BX - Z)\left(B - \frac{\partial Z}{\partial X}\right) + A\frac{\partial V}{\partial X}\right]\frac{\partial Z}{\partial X} + A(BX - Z)V \qquad (10a)$$

$$\frac{\partial V}{\partial T} = \frac{\partial^2 V}{\partial X^2} - \left[2(BX - Z)\left(B - \frac{\partial Z}{\partial X}\right) + A\frac{\partial V}{\partial X}\right]\frac{\partial V}{\partial X}$$

$$+ \frac{A}{2n_L}(1 - V^2) + \frac{1}{n_L A}\left(\frac{\partial Z}{\partial X}\right)^2 \qquad (10b)$$

I assume that all n_L loci have the same mean and variance; if there is heterogeneity over loci, the n are replaced by $n_{L,e}$, $n_{L,e}^*$, which are effective numbers weighted by genetic variance or by squared gradients. These $n_{L,e}$ may themselves evolve, and so the equations are no longer closed. The scaled equation for the mean is the same as Eq. 8, with $\partial_X \log(N)$ replaced by $\gamma \partial_X \bar{r}$, which leads to the middle term: asymmetric gene flow is caused by spatial variation in mean fitness, which in turn is caused by variation in the deviation of the mean from the optimum, and in the variance. The variance changes as a result of gene flow, in the same way as does the mean (first two terms). It also changes as a result of mutation and selection, which force it towards the mutation–selection balance $V = 1$ (third term), and as a result of the mixing of populations with different means (last term).

There are (at least) two kinds of equilibrium. First, the population may be everywhere perfectly adapted ($Z = BX$); the variance is then uniformly inflated by gene flow:

$$V = \sqrt{1 + \frac{2B^2}{A^2}}$$

Second, the population may fail to adapt: $Z = \beta(X - X_0)$. The variance is still inflated everywhere, although to a lesser extent because the gradient is now shallower ($0 < \beta < B$; see Appendix 2). The increase in variance due to gene flow necessarily increases the gradient β at equilibrium: adaptation is facilitated by the evolution of the variance. When stabilizing selection is weak (A small), the variance is less tightly constrained (third term in Eq. 10b), and so can increase much more as a result of gene flow. Thus, the critical gradient can become much greater than if the variance were

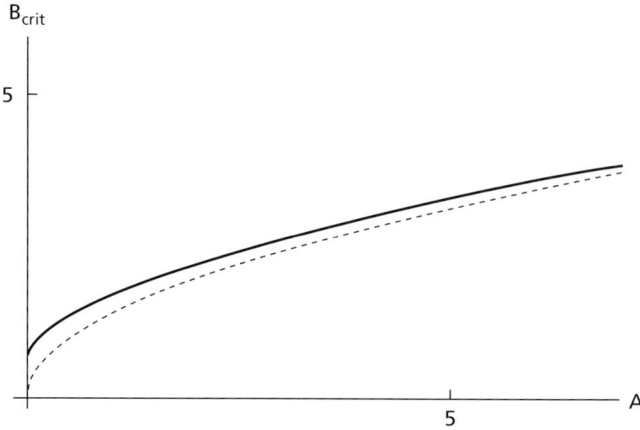

Figure 17.3 The critical gradient, B_{crit}, above which an equilibrium with imperfect adaptation is stable, plotted against the scaled strength of selection, $A = v_g/r^* V_s$. The heavy curve shows B_{crit} when the variance evolves under the Gaussian continuum-of-alleles model, under the one-variable approximation, $n \sim \exp(\gamma \bar{r}_g)$ (from Eq. 10). The light curve shows the corresponding values when the variance is fixed.

fixed at $V = 1$: as A becomes small, $B_{crit} \to 1/\sqrt{2}$ rather than $\sqrt{2A}$ (Figure 17.3). This implies that a population can always adapt to a scaled gradient $B < 1/\sqrt{2}$, even if the standing genetic variance generated by mutation is negligible.

Iteration of Eq. 10 for small A shows that the stability of the equilibria is qualitatively different when the genetic variance is free to evolve. Recall that with a fixed genetic variance, a local stability analysis shows that equilibria with both perfect and imperfect adaptation are locally stable whenever they exist (Kirkpatrick & Barton 1997). When the variance is allowed to evolve under the Gaussian approximation, a similar analysis of Eq. 10 yields the same conclusion. However, with a fixed genetic variance, numerical calculations showed that whenever an equilibrium with imperfect adaptation exists, the alternative equilibrium is unstable towards the substantial perturbations that occur at the edges, or at points where the gradient in optimum changes. In practice, therefore, a population with fixed variance will collapse to a state of imperfect adaptation whenever such an equilibrium exists. In contrast, when the variance can evolve, both equilibria can be stable. Figure 17.4 shows an example with $A = 0.1$, $B = 1.2$; $B_{crit} = 0.93$ for $A = 0.1$, and so if the population begins in a badly adapted state $(Z = 0)$, it remains poorly adapted, and with low variance $(V = 1.24$; thin lines in Figure 17.4). However, if the population begins well adapted $(Z = BX)$, then it remains well adapted, because gene flow generates a high genetic variance

$$\left(V = 16.61 \approx \sqrt{1 + \frac{2B^2}{A^2}} \text{; thick lines in Fig. 4} \right)$$

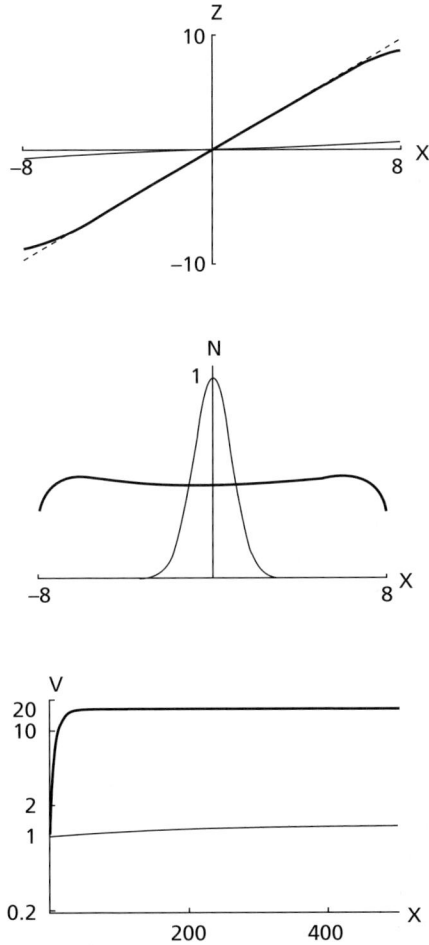

Figure 17.4 An example of the joint evolution of trait and variance under the Gaussian approximation, and with the simple one-variable model of density regulation; $A = 0.1$, $B = 1.2$. The top panel shows the scaled trait mean at equilibrium, Z, and the optimum, BX (dashed line), plotted against distance, X. If the population is started at $Z = 0$, $V = 1$, it evolves to an imperfectly adapted equilibrium (thin line). If it starts perfectly adapted, and with variance either at zero, or in a balance between mutation and stabilizing selection ($V = 1$), it evolves to a well-adapted equilibrium (thick line, following $Z = BX$ except near the edges). The middle panel shows the population density at these alternative equilibria. The bottom panel shows change in genetic variance at the centre ($X = 0$) over time, on a log scale. Numerical values were calculated using a stepping-stone model with spacing between demes $\delta X = \frac{1}{2}$, and time interval $\delta T = \frac{1}{16}$; the recursions were iterated until $T = 200$, when equilibrium had been reached. Ten loci are assumed.

In this example, a well-adapted equilibrium is reached regardless of whether the population starts with no genetic variance ($V = 0$), or with a genetic variance set by a balance between mutation and stabilizing selection ($V = 1$). Note that the mean fitness, and hence population density, is greatly reduced by this inflation of variance: density is reduced by $\exp[-AV/2] \rightarrow \exp[-B\sqrt{2}]$ as B becomes large, and is much lower than when the population occupies a limited range ($N = 0.44$ vs. 0.94; middle panel of Figure 17.4). However, the increased variance allows the species to occupy an indefinitely wide range, rather than being confined to a limited region, and so reach a higher density.

This simple one-variable model for the evolution of the variance depends on the assumption that the population size can be taken as a direct function of mean fitness, $n \sim e^{\gamma \bar{r}}$. We now relax this assumption by following the joint evolution of trait mean, variance and population density. The scaled equations are given in Appendix 2. Now, the only solution in which the gradient in trait mean is linear is one of perfect adaptation ($Z = BX$).

The inevitability of evolution towards perfect adaptation is confirmed by numerical examples, for a variety of starting conditions and parameter values. Figure 17.5 shows one such example, with $A = 0.1$, $B = 1.2$ and logarithmic density dependence. Initially, there is no genetic variance, and the trait mean is zero everywhere. The variance increases slowly, primarily by mutation. As it does so, the gradient in the trait mean increases in proportion. At $T \sim 270$, the variance and gradient reach a threshold, and increase rapidly as a result of gene flow; this increase occurs first at the margins, and slightly later at the centre. The population mean thus becomes perfectly adapted throughout its range. This sudden increase in variance and hence in mean fitness allows the population to rapidly spread across the whole range. The scaled density at equilibrium is still substantially less than 1, because the high genetic variance imposes a large genetic load (Figure 17.5).

This conclusion does not depend critically on the form of density dependence. Following Kirkpatrick and Barton (1997), consider the solution to Eq. 16 for large X, where the population is very poorly adapted. The change in population density is then dominated by the high mortality due to deviations of the trait mean from the optimum, $-\frac{1}{2}(BX - Z)^2$. Provided that fitness does not increase as fast as logarithmically as density decreases, the density-dependent term $r_e(n)$ is negligible, and the high mortality is balanced by diffusion of individuals from more abundant regions, $\partial^2 N / \partial X^2$. For given V, Eqs 16(a,c) rapidly tend towards a Gaussian solution for N, and a linear change in trait mean, of the form

$$Z \sim \beta X, \quad N \sim \exp\left[-\frac{(B-\beta)X^2}{2\sqrt{2}}\right]$$

The gradient β equilibrates at the solution of Eq. 16(a), which is either $\beta = B$ (perfect adaptation), or

$$\beta = \frac{AV}{\sqrt{2}} \quad \text{if} \quad V < \frac{B\sqrt{2}}{A}$$

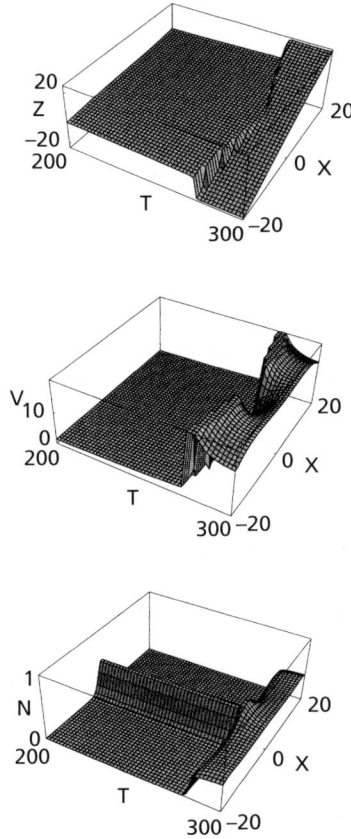

Figure 17.5 An example of the joint evolution of trait and variance under the Gaussian approximation, and with logarithmic density dependence; $A = 0.1$, $B = 1.2$. The top panel shows the scaled trait mean, Z, plotted against time, T, and distance, X. The middle panel shows the scaled genetic variance, and the bottom panel the scaled density, N. Numerical values were calculated as in Figure 17.4. The final values are

$$V = 16.4 \sim \sqrt{1 + \frac{2B^2}{A^2}}; \quad \overline{R} \sim -\frac{AV}{2} = -0.82; \quad N = 0.446 \sim \exp[-\overline{R}].$$

Now, consider the change in variance (Eq. 16b). With a large number of loci, $n_L \gg 1$, the first two terms dominate, and the variance rapidly moves to an arbitrary but spatially uniform value. It then evolves more slowly, at a rate $\sim 1/n_L$ (last two terms). Crucially, if

$$\partial_X Z = \beta = \frac{AV}{\sqrt{2}}$$

the variance generated by gene flow precisely cancels that eliminated by stabilizing selection, leaving a gradual increase as a result of mutation, until

$$V = \frac{B\sqrt{2}}{A}, \beta = B$$

and the population is perfectly adapted. This account matches the behaviour seen in simulations, in that the variance initially increases by mutation at a rate $A/2n$, and the gradient $\partial_X Z$ increases in proportion (Figure 17.5). However, the solution

$$\beta = \frac{AV}{\sqrt{2}}$$

becomes unstable at a critical variance much smaller than

$$\frac{B\sqrt{2}}{A}$$

at which point the population moves rapidly to perfect adaptation of the mean.

Changes in allele frequency: two alleles

Thus far, we have assumed that there is a continuum of alleles at each locus, and that this continuous distribution is approximately Gaussian. At the opposite extreme, we can suppose that there are just two alleles at each locus, of effect $\pm\alpha/2$ and at frequencies p_i, q_i. The trait mean is then $\bar{z} = \Sigma_i \alpha(p_i - q_i)$, and the genetic variance is $v = 2\Sigma_i \alpha^2 p_i q_i$. Mutation occurs at an equal rate μ in either direction. We now scale the genetic variance relative to the maximum possible, $v_{max} = \frac{1}{2}\Sigma_i \alpha_i^2$. The scaled equations for this model are set out in Appendix 3.

The key parameter is $\tilde{A}$, which is the product of the maximum possible genetic variance, and the strength of selection, relative to the population growth rate ($\tilde{A} = v_{max}/(r^* V_s)$). The reduction in fitness arising from the maximum polymorphism at one locus is

$$\frac{\alpha^2}{2V_s} = \frac{\tilde{A}r^*}{n_L}$$

This is expected to be small compared with the growth rate of the population, so that $\tilde{A} < n_L$; from Eq. 19 (Appendix 3), $\tilde{A}/n_L$ is a measure of the selection on each locus, and should be small. On the other hand, the reduction in fitness if the trait takes on its maximum possible variance may be large ($1 < \tilde{A}$). The maximum scaled mean is $Z_{max} = \sqrt{2\tilde{A}n_L}$, which is large for large $\tilde{A}$ and n_L. Note that we are now scaling the variance relative to its maximum value, so that $V \ll 1$; for comparison with the previous section, the scaled standing variance in mutation–selection balance is $4n_L\mu V_s/v_{max} = 8\mu V_s/\alpha^2 = 2\gamma/\tilde{A} \ll 1$.

We can first ask whether it is possible for gene flow to maintain genetic variance, and hence a perfectly adapted mean, in the absence of mutation ($\mu, \gamma = 0$). If the mean matches the optimum everywhere ($\delta = 0$), then stabilizing selection acts to reduce genetic variance, and tends to fix one or other allele at each locus; this is represented by the term $p_i q_i(p_i - q_i)$ in Eq. 19. Such selection, combined with gene flow, maintains a cline $p_i = 1/(1 + \exp[-4x/w])$, where the cline width is $W = 4\sqrt{n_L/\tilde{A}}$ (or

$w = 4\sqrt{\sigma^2 V_s / \alpha^2}$ in the original units). A steadily changing mean must correspond to a series of staggered clines, each shifting from $p_i = 0$ to 1, and contributing a shift in the mean of 2α, and a total genetic variance $\int 2\alpha^2 p_i q_i \, dx = 2\alpha\sqrt{\sigma^2 V_s}$. A scaled gradient in optimum, b, requires $b/2\alpha$ such clines per unit distance, and hence maintains genetic variance $b\sqrt{\sigma^2 V_s}$, or in scaled units,

$$V = \frac{B\sqrt{2}}{\tilde{A}}$$

Note that this is independent of allelic effect, α, and numbers of loci, n_L. More remarkable is that this result is the same as for the Gaussian approximation, even though derived by an entirely different argument (see Barton & Turelli 1989; Barton 1999, p. 235). (The scaling relative to mutation–selection balance, v_∞, or maximum possible variance, v_{max}, is immaterial, because it appears in both V and A, $\tilde{A}$ in the same way, and cancels.)

For comparison, a low mutation rate maintains genetic variance $4n\mu V_s$; this is negligible if the genomic mutation rate $U = 2n_L \mu$ is much smaller than $\sqrt{2L}$, where $L = \dfrac{\sigma^2 b^2}{2V_s} = (r^* B)^2$ is the loss of fitness due to the change in optimum over one dispersal range. In order for the trait mean to change smoothly, these clines must overlap; this requires that $w \gg \dfrac{2\alpha}{b}$, or

$$\sqrt{2L} \gg \frac{\alpha^2}{2V_s}, \quad B\sqrt{2} \gg \frac{\tilde{A}}{n}$$

the latter being the selection on an individual allele. The two conditions

$$\sqrt{2L} \gg U, \quad \sqrt{2L} \gg \frac{\alpha^2}{2V_s}$$

can both be satisfied for moderate spatial gradients in optimum. (Barton 1999, Eqs 12 and 13, gives a somewhat more sophisticated argument, which takes account of deviations from the optimum, δ, and of the variance contributed by mutation.)

Figure 17.6 shows an example in which a population that is initially poorly adapted, and restricted to a limited region, adapts and spreads over the whole habitat. The scaled gradient in optimum is $B = 1$, similar to that in the examples of Figures 17.4 and 17.5; there are $n_L = 40$ loci, and density dependence is logarithmic. We now scale the genetic variance, and strength of selection, relative to the maximum possible variance, $v_{max} = n_L \alpha^2 / 2$. Therefore, $\tilde{A} = 10$ is an appropriate choice, because it implies weak selection on individual loci, but substantial selection on the total trait variance. Initially, allele frequencies are spatially uniform, and take a random value in $\{0, 0.01\}$ at half the loci, and in $\{0.99, 1\}$ at the other half. Thus, the mean is initially near zero, and the variance is low ($V \sim 0.02$). The population density rapidly collapses outside the region near $X = 0$ where the mean coincides with the optimum (Figure 17.6, bottom panel). The genetic variance increases near the edges, where

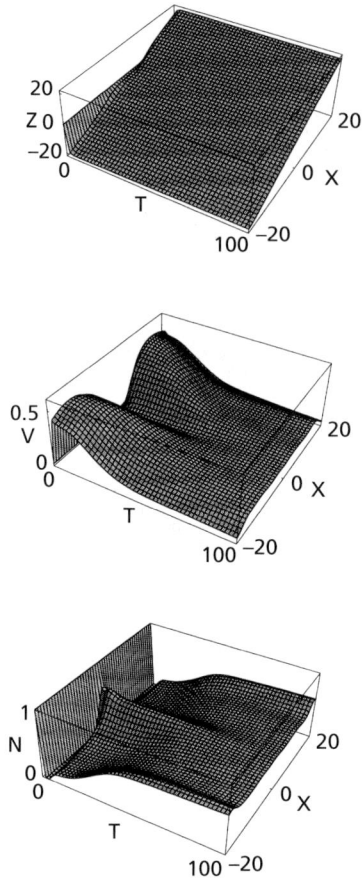

Figure 17.6 An example of the joint evolution of trait and variance with two alleles at each of $n = 40$ loci, with logarithmic density dependence; $A = 10$, $B = 1$. The top panel shows the scaled trait mean, Z, plotted against time, T, and distance, X. The middle panel shows the scaled genetic variance, and the bottom panel the scaled density, N. Initially, allele frequencies were set to a random value, constant in space; this value was uniformly distributed in $\{0, 0.01\}$ at half the loci, and in $\{0.99, 1\}$ at the other half. Numerical values were calculated as in Figure 17.4. At equilibrium, $V \sim 0.14$, as predicted by $B\sqrt{2}/\tilde{A}$; density is then reduced by

$$0.5 \sim \exp\left[-\frac{\tilde{A}V}{2}\right] \sim \exp\left[-\frac{B}{\sqrt{2}}\right].$$

there is strong directional selection on allele frequencies; this allows the trait mean to rapidly approach the optimum (Figure 17.6, top panel). Density remains low, however, because the high genetic variance at the edges imposes a substantial load on the population. The genetic variance slowly decreases, allowing the density to increase to a uniform value across the whole habitat. Note that although the trait mean

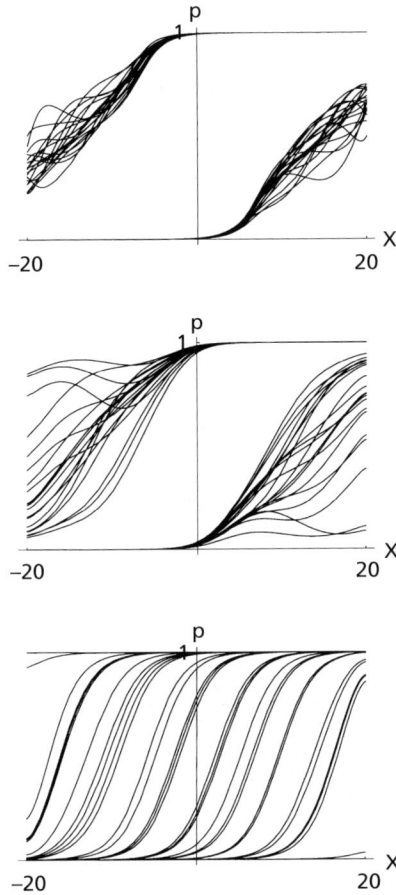

Figure 17.7 Allele frequencies for the example of Figure 17.6, at $T = 2, 20, 100$ (top to bottom).

matches the optimum almost perfectly, the genetic variance imposes a substantial load on the population. Moreover, the reduction in density depends only on the scaled parameter B.

Figure 17.7 shows how the underlying allele frequencies change. At first, all '+' alleles decrease on the left, where the mean lies far above the optimum, and increase on the right. Directional selection quickly brings the mean close to the optimum (via the term $-2p_i q_i \delta$ in Eqs 17–19); allele frequencies then change linearly, matching the linear change in optimum (top panel of Figure 17.7). Stabilizing selection now acts to fix one or other allele at each locus, amplifying slight random differences between the clines. A series of staggered clines emerges (Figure 17.7, bottom panel). These have width close to $W = 4\sqrt{n_L/\tilde{A}} = 8$, as predicted.

In the example of Figures 17.6 and 17.7, density dependence is logarithmic: sparse populations have high fitness, which facilitates their adaptation. Simulations of the simple model of density regulation lead to the same outcome, as do those with logistic density dependence. In the latter case, however, it takes much longer for the initially high genetic variance to dissipate, and so allow the species to spread over the whole range.

Simulations for steeper gradients show a similar pattern, in which genetic variance increases as the trait mean evolves towards the optimum, and then declines to an equilibrium of

$$V = \frac{B\sqrt{2}}{\tilde{A}}$$

Examination of the allele frequency equations for large X suggest that perfect adaptation to a linear optimum is always possible in this model. In the margins, the density must follow a Gaussian of the form

$$N \sim \exp\left[-\frac{(B-\beta)X^2}{2\sqrt{2}} \right]$$

The allele frequency equation (Eq. 19) is then dominated by the terms $2\partial_X \log[N]\partial_X p_i - 2\frac{\tilde{A}}{n}p_i q_i \delta$. The solution for small p_i is for an exponential increase in allele frequency with distance ($p_i \sim \exp[-\tilde{A}X/n]$), which takes the mean towards the optimum. Unlike the Gaussian case, there is no equilibrium with imperfect adaptation in the absence of mutation.

Linkage disequilibrium: the infinitesimal model

Thus far, we have only followed allele frequencies, and have neglected the linkage disequilibria that must be generated by gene flow and by stabilizing selection. This is valid when selection is weak relative to recombination, and when the number of loci involved is small. At the opposite extreme of strong selection on very many loci, we obtain the infinitesimal model (Bulmer 1985), in which selection on each locus is so weak that the effect of changes in allele frequency on the variance can be neglected. We now consider whether the linkage disequilibria generated by gene flow can inflate the genetic variance sufficiently to allow the population to expand its range into extreme environments (see Appendix 4 for details).

Barton (1999, Eqs 14–16) derived the change in the density and the genetic variance, on the assumption that the distribution of breeding values is Gaussian. This is a remarkably good approximation even when selection is strong (Barton 1999, Fig. 10; Turelli & Barton 1994). We can find solutions (Eqs 16 and 20, Appendices 2, and 4) that are valid at the margins ($|X| \gg 1$). As under the Gaussian approximation, there is always an equilibrium with perfect adaptation, and above a critical value of the gradient there is an alternative equilibrium in which the population is adapted to only a limited region. Figure 17.8 shows this critical value for three alternative models of density dependence. Comparison with Figure 17.2 shows that

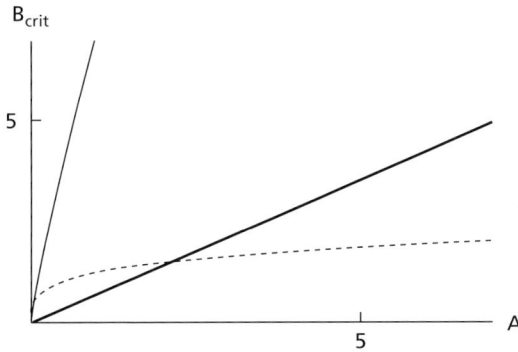

Figure 17.8 The critical gradient, B_{crit}, plotted against the scaled strength of selection, $A = V_g/r^* V_s$ (Eq. 7). Genetic variance changes due to linkage disequilibria, under the infinitesimal model. The curves show the critical gradient for the three models compared in Figures 17.1 and 17.2: one-variable model (dashed line), logarithmic density dependence (thin line); and logistic density dependence (thick line).

under both logistic and logarithmic density dependence, the inflation of variance due to linkage disequilibrium makes it possible for populations to adapt to steeper spatial gradients in the optimum (solid lines in Figures 17.2 and 17.8). However, for the simple one-variable model $n \sim \bar{r}^\gamma$ (dashed lines in Figures 17.2 and 17.8), and for large A, stabilizing selection can reduce the variance below its linkage equilibrium value, and thus make it harder for the species to adapt.

Numerical calculations suggest that where alternative equilibria exist, both are stable. This contrasts with the cases considered previously. When the variance is fixed, perfect adaptation of the mean is unstable (Kirkpatrick & Barton 1997). When the variance evolves because of changes in allele frequency, perfect adaptation is inevitable. To understand why a state of imperfect adaptation is stable, consider the case of logistic density dependence (or indeed, of any model in which fitness tends to a finite positive value at low density). In the margins, density follows a Gaussian curve, and the mean changes linearly

$$N \sim \exp\left[-\frac{(B-\beta)X}{2}\right], \quad Z \sim \beta X$$

where $\beta = AV/\sqrt{2}$. The genetic variance then changes according to Eq. 20 (Appendix 4), and (as we saw in the previous section) the increase in variance due to gene flow precisely cancels with the decrease due to local stabilizing selection. In the Gaussian continuum-of-alleles model, the variance increased slowly as a result of mutation, and so the population eventually became perfectly adapted. In contrast, linkage disequilibria decrease as a result of segregation $(-\frac{1}{2}(V-1))$, and so the population remains poorly adapted in the margins.

Conclusions

The effects of an evolving genetic variance, and of the various models of density dependence are summarized in Table 17.1. Regardless of its genetic basis, the variance is inflated by gene flow at a rate proportional to the square of the gradient in mean. The variance is reduced by stabilizing selection, at a rate that is sensitive to the underlying genetics. If there are very many alleles at each locus, and if there is an extra source of variation such as mutation, then the genetic variance gradually increases until a threshold is reached, at which point the population rapidly becomes well adapted, and spreads over the whole range (see Figure 17.5). This outcome depends on the diffusion of individuals away from the well-adapted centre: if density is taken as a direct function of mean fitness ($n \sim \exp(\bar{r}\gamma)$), then the species may remain restricted to a limited region if the gradient in optimum is steeper than $1/\sqrt{2}$ (see Figure 17.4). With two alleles per locus, adaptation is more effective: the only equilibrium is one where the trait matches the optimum everywhere. In contrast, if genetic variance varies as a result of changes in linkage disequilibrium among large numbers of unlinked loci, the effects are less marked: a stable state of imperfect adaptation exists below a critical gradient, albeit one that is usually somewhat larger than for a fixed variance. Note that although an inflation of the genetic variance allows the mean to come close to the optimum, it imposes a substantial load on the species: density is reduced by $\sim\exp(-B/\sqrt{2})$ at equilibrium, where B is the scaled gradient in optimum.

The conclusions from different forms of density dependence are similar. This is because adaptation first occurs at the margins, where population growth depends only on the limiting fitness at low density. The model for the genetic variance also has rather little consequence; this may be because in all models the mean changes in proportion to the variance, and the variance is inflated at a rate proportional to the square of the gradient in mean. However, the neglect of random drift may be more restrictive—particularly because we are most concerned with the evolution of marginal populations. Random drift will reduce genetic variance at a rate inversely proportional to population density. Demographic and environmental stochasticity will also cause absolute extinction at low average densities, and lead to a fragmentation of the population. It is not obvious whether this will impede adaptation: on the one hand, genetic variability is reduced by random extinction and recolonization, but on the other, local isolates may be shielded from gene flow and hence be better able to adapt. Such effects are suggested by simulations in which the variance evolves as a result of linkage disequilibria. When these are simulated on a fine grid, populations can remain trapped in limited regions. However, well-separated local populations can adapt and spread. It would be fruitful to investigate the effects of different kinds of stochasticity and population structure.

The assumption of a linear gradient may also be restrictive. Because the genetic variance at each locus increases slowly, at a rate inversely proportional to the number of loci, n_L, it is expected to change over large spatial scales ($\sim\sigma\sqrt{n_L}$; Barton 1999). Therefore, a low variance in regions with a shallow gradient may prevent the evolution of a high variance in restricted regions where the gradient is steep. However, this argument is not supported by (limited) simulations of accelerating gradients. For example, Figures 17.9 and 17.10 show that a species can adapt to an abrupt change in the optimum, suggesting that it can spread beyond it into regions where it was originally absent. The final outcome exhibits localized increases in genetic variation near the steps, associated with localized reductions in density (Figure 17.9).

Adaptation to abrupt changes can be understood as follows. Suppose that initially the population is adapted to (say) $z_{opt} = 0$, and that there is a sharp shift in optimum to $z_{opt} = z^*$ over some region. The population essentially becomes extinct where it is

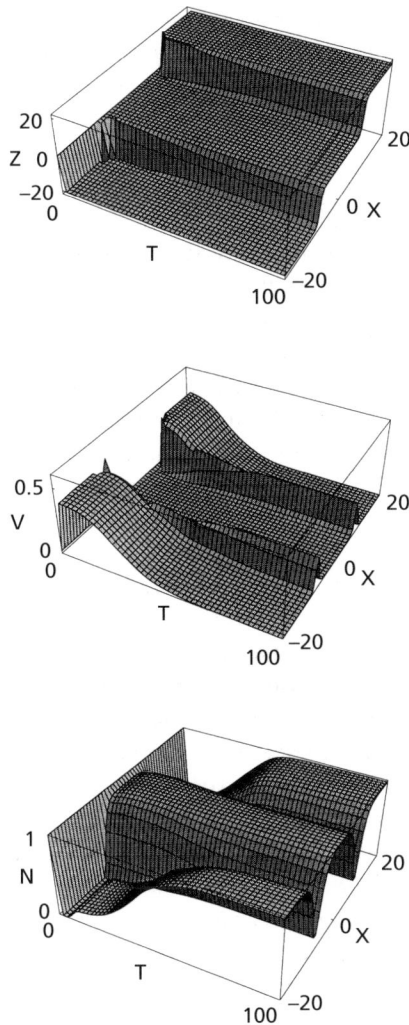

Figure 17.9 Adaptation to a sharp change in the optimum. There are two alleles at each of $n = 40$ loci, with logarithmic density dependence; $A = 10$. The optimum is -20 for $X < -8, 0$ for $-8 < X < 8$, and $+20$ for $8 < X$. Otherwise, as for Figure 17.6.

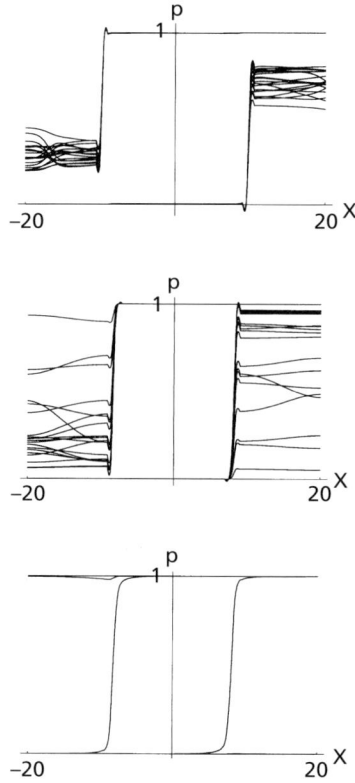

Figure 17.10 Allele frequencies for the example of Figure 17.9, at $T = 2, 20, 100$ (top to bottom).

poorly adapted, and density decreases exponentially into the sink region. Within that region, there is a steady gradient in log(density), which displaces any clines generated by selection. However, such a gradient does not prevent an increase in the mean and in the genetic variance far from the step, and so populations at the margins can recover, allowing indefinite spread. A more detailed examination is needed, however: the outcome will depend on random variation in density and allele frequency in sparse regions, and on just how the optimum changes with distance. Moreover, if other species are already well adapted to conditions at the margins, competition between species that are both evolving may prevent either from spreading (Case & Taper 2000).

Spatially varying selection can maintain substantial variability, making adaptation to those varying conditions possible. A strong argument against the general importance of this source of variability, however, is that high heritabilities are observed in domesticated and laboratory populations (Barton & Turelli 1989). In the present context, however, the key point is that even if gene flow usually maintains little genetic variation, it may still have a transient importance in generating variation while populations adapt to new conditions.

Case and Taper (2000, Fig. 13) review evidence on dispersal rates and geographic gradients, and suggest that these are unlikely to be large enough to limit the ranges of single species, in the absence of competition. However, if many traits, n_{traits}, were adapting to changing optima, maladaptation of each would depress fitness and hence population size: the threshold gradient would therefore be reduced by a factor $\sqrt{n_{trait}}$. Also, Case and Taper (2000) estimated gradients in optima from broad clines in morphological traits. These may be much shallower than the selective optima if the populations are failing to adapt, and the local gradients at the edge of the range may be considerably steeper.

Direct tests of the importance of gene flow in maintaining variation, and in limiting species' ranges, would be both valuable and difficult. There are several related questions: Do species adapt to local conditions? Does local adaptation allow them to extend their range? Does gene flow interfere with local adaptation? Does genetic variance increase in regions of steep spatial variation, and does this increase facilitate adaptation? The best empirical evidence comes from heavy-metal tolerance in grasses, which answers all but the last of these questions in the affirmative (see Antonovics 1976). However, while there is abundant evidence of local adaptation (especially in plant species: see Chapter 6), there is still little evidence on how this affects abundance and range. The theory presented here and in Barton (1999) makes the robust prediction that the genetic variance should increase in regions where the mean changes rapidly, and that the genic component of this decrease should be spread over a broader spatial range than the change in mean. However, it is hard to use measures of means and variances to test whether gene flow limits adaptation and hence the species' range: if the range is limited in this way, there will be little change in mean and little inflation of variance at the margin. The ideal experimental manipulation would be to prevent gene flow into a set of marginal populations, and ask whether traits that adapt them to marginal conditions change in mean; whether the genetic variance decreases; and whether fitness increases as a consequence. Such a test would be demanding, but well worthwhile.

Summary

A species' range is necessarily limited by its failure to adapt to conditions elsewhere. One limitation on adaptation is imposed by gene flow: alleles or traits favoured only within a limited region may be swamped by an influx of differently adapted genes from more abundant populations elsewhere. Because sparse populations are more sensitive to gene flow, and because a failure to adapt reduces population density, there is a positive feedback which can restrict a population to a limited region. A model of stabilizing selection on a quantitative trait shows that if the genetic variance is fixed, there is a critical spatial gradient above which the population collapses outside a restricted region. This chapter investigates the consequences of evolution of the genetic variance on a species' range. The genetic mixing caused by gene flow inflates the genetic variance and facilitates further divergence. This feedback allows species to adapt to an indefinitely wide range and can maintain substantial genetic variance. This outcome can be achieved for arbitrarily steep but constant gradients, and with either two alleles, or a continuum of alleles at each locus.

Appendix 1: Exact solution with logarithmic density dependence

For the logarithmic model of density dependence, substituting $\bar{R} = -\log(N) - \frac{1}{2}(BX - Z)^2$ into Eqs 8 and 9 gives the solution:

$$z = \beta X \quad N = \exp\left[-\frac{A(B-\beta)}{2\beta}\left(1+\frac{X^2}{2}\right)\right]$$

where $\beta = \frac{1}{3}\left(B + \sqrt{a}\cos\left[\frac{\theta+\pi}{3}\right]\right)$,

$$a = 2(2B^2 + 3A^2 - 3A), \theta = \arccos\left[\frac{2B(9A + 18A^2 - 4B^2)}{a^{3/2}}\right] \tag{11}$$

The critical gradient is:

$$B_{\text{crit}} = \frac{1}{4}\sqrt{(8A^2 + 20A - 1) + (1 + 8A)^{3/2}} \tag{12}$$

For small A, this tends to $\sqrt{2A}$, as for the simple model of density regulation.

Appendix 2: A continuum of alleles

Suppose that at locus i there is some distribution, $\psi_i(z_i)$, of allelic effects on an additive trait, z. For a diploid, the value of the trait is the sum of the contributions of each of k loci, with contributions z_i, z_i^* of the two copies of each gene: $z = \Sigma_{i=1}^k(z_i + z_i^*)$. Suppose that density is regulated to $n \sim \exp[\bar{r}\gamma]$. Then, from Eq. 1 of Barton (1999), the distribution of allelic effects is:

$$\frac{\partial \psi_i}{\partial t} = \frac{\sigma^2}{2}\frac{\partial^2 \psi_i}{\partial x^2} + \sigma^2\gamma\frac{\partial \psi_i}{\partial x}\frac{\partial \bar{r}_g}{\partial x} - \frac{1}{2V_s}(z_i - z_{\text{opt}})^2 \psi_i$$

$$-\bar{r}_g\psi_i + \mu_i\left(\int_{-\infty}^{\infty} m_i[y]\psi_i(z_i - y, x)dy - \psi_i(z_i, x)\right) \tag{13}$$

The first term on the right represents diffusive gene flow; the second, asymmetric gene flow out of fitter and hence denser regions; the third and fourth terms, stabilizing selection; and the last term, mutation at a rate μ_i to new alleles that differ by y in their effect on the trait. I can find no analytic solution to Eq. 13. However, its Fourier transform can readily be solved numerically (Barton 1999).

Equation 13 has a Gaussian equilibrium solution in which the trait mean changes linearly through space, as is the case in all the solutions we consider below. The dynamics of genetic variability may involve deviations from a Gaussian, however. Assuming a Gaussian with mean z_i and variance v_i at locus i:

$$\frac{\partial \bar{z}_i}{\partial t} = \frac{\sigma^2}{2} \frac{\partial^2 \bar{z}_i}{\partial x^2} - \frac{\sigma^2 \gamma}{V_s} \left[\left(b - \frac{\partial \bar{z}}{\partial x} \right)(bx - \bar{z}) + \frac{1}{2} \frac{\partial v}{\partial x} \right] \frac{\partial \bar{z}_i}{\partial x} + \frac{V_i}{V_s}(bx - \bar{z})$$

$$\frac{\partial v_i}{\partial t} = \frac{\sigma^2}{2} \frac{\partial^2 v_i}{\partial x^2} - \frac{\sigma^2 \gamma}{V_s} \left[\left(b - \frac{\partial \bar{z}}{\partial x} \right)(bx - \bar{z}) + \frac{1}{2} \frac{\partial v}{\partial x} \right] \frac{\partial v_i}{\partial x}$$

$$+ \sigma^2 \left(\frac{\partial \bar{z}_i}{\partial x} \right)^2 - \frac{v_i^2}{V_s} + v_{m,i} \tag{14}$$

With no gene flow, and assuming a Gaussian distribution, the variance at each locus is $v_i = \sqrt{v_{m,i} V_s} \equiv v_{\infty,i}$, where $v_{m,i} = \mu_i \int_{-\infty}^{\infty} m_i[y] y^2 dy$ is the variance introduced into a gene at locus i per generation. The total variance with no gene flow is $v_\infty = \Sigma_{i=1}^{n} 2 v_{\infty,i}$.

Equation 14 can be rescaled in terms of dimensionless parameters, giving Eq. 10, above. We seek an equilibrium solution which has a linear gradient in the mean ($Z = \beta X, 0 < \beta < B$). Substituting into Eq. 10 gives simultaneous equations for β, V:

$$AV = 2(B - \beta)\beta \quad V^2 = 1 + \frac{2\beta^2}{A^2} \tag{15}$$

This is a family of neutrally stable equilibria, centred on X_0. Equation 15 has an explicit (but ugly) solution as the solution to a cubic. Graphically, one can see that either there is no solution (in which case the population must be perfectly adapted, $\beta = B$), or there are two solutions (in which case the lower solution should be stable, by analogy with the case of constant V).

If both the trait mean and population density can evolve separately, Eqs 8 and 9 extend to give scaled equations:

$$\frac{\partial Z}{\partial T} = \frac{\partial^2 Z}{\partial X^2} + 2 \frac{\partial \log(N)}{\partial X} \frac{\partial Z}{\partial X} + AV(BX - Z) \tag{16a}$$

$$\frac{\partial V}{\partial T} = \frac{\partial^2 V}{\partial X^2} + 2 \frac{\partial \log(N)}{\partial X} \frac{\partial V}{\partial X} + \frac{A}{2n}(1 - V^2) + \frac{1}{nA} \left(\frac{\partial Z}{\partial X} \right)^2 \tag{16b}$$

$$\frac{\partial N}{\partial T} = \frac{\partial^2 N}{\partial X^2} + N\bar{R} \tag{16c}$$

With logarithmic density dependence, $\bar{R} = -\log(N) - \frac{1}{2}(BX - Z)^2 - (AV/2)$, and with logistic density dependence, $\bar{R} = 1 - N - \frac{1}{2}(BX - Z)^2 - (AV/2)$. As before, we can seek exact equilibrium solutions to the logarithmic model, in which the population density has a Gaussian form, the trait mean has constant slope β, and the trait variance is uniform.

Now, the only equilibrium solution in which the trait mean changes linearly is one of perfect adaptation. We can understand why this is by noting that at equilibrium the only difference between the explicit model of logarithmic density dependence, and the simple one-variable model where $n \sim e^{\gamma \bar{r}}$, is the term $\partial^2 N / \partial X^2$ in Eq. 16. Examination of Eq. 16, for population density of Gaussian form, shows that this term, which represents diffusion of individuals out of well-adapted regions of high density, makes gradients in density shallower, and therefore weakens the maladaptive effects of gene flow on the trait mean. This makes imperfectly adapted equilibria (at least, of the form considered above) impossible for all parameter values.

Appendix 3: Two alleles

With two alleles per locus, allele frequencies then change as:

$$\frac{\partial p_i}{\partial t} = \frac{\sigma^2}{2} \frac{\partial^2 p_i}{\partial x^2} + \sigma^2 \frac{\partial \log(N)}{\partial x} \frac{\partial p_i}{\partial x}$$

$$+ \frac{\alpha_i^2}{2V_s} p_i q_i (p_i - q_i - 2\delta) - \mu(p_i - q_i) \quad \text{where} \quad \delta = \frac{(\bar{z} - z_{\text{opt}})}{\alpha} \tag{17}$$

To reduce the number of parameters and to make the comparison with the previous results, we scale time, distance and trait mean as before (Eq. 7), and scale the genetic variance relative to the maximum possible variance, $v_{\text{max}} = \frac{1}{2}\Sigma_i \alpha_i^2$:

$$\tilde{A} = \frac{v_{\text{max}}}{r^* V_s} \quad V = \frac{v}{v_{\text{max}}} \quad \gamma = \frac{U}{r^*} \tag{18}$$

where $U = 2 n_L \mu$ is the total genomic mutation rate. Then:

$$\frac{\partial p_i}{\partial T} = \frac{\partial^2 p_i}{\partial X^2} + 2 \frac{\partial \log(N)}{\partial X} \frac{\partial p_i}{\partial X} + \frac{\tilde{A}}{n_L} p_i q_i (p_i - q_i - 2\delta) - \frac{\gamma}{2 n_L}(p_i - q_i)$$

$$\text{where} \quad \delta = (Z - BX)\sqrt{\frac{n_L}{2\tilde{A}}} \quad Z = \sqrt{\frac{2\tilde{A}}{n_L}} \Sigma_j (p_j - q_j) \quad V = \frac{4}{n_L} \Sigma_i p_j q_j \tag{19}$$

The same scaled equation for the population density, Eq. 16(c), applies.

Appendix 4: The infinitesimal model

In the present notation, the equations for the mean and the density are as in Eq. 16 (Appendix 2, above), while the scaled equation for the variance is:

$$\frac{\partial V}{\partial T} = \frac{\partial^2 V}{\partial X^2} + 2 \frac{\partial \log(N)}{\partial X} \frac{\partial V}{\partial X} - \hat{A} V^2$$

$$- \frac{1}{2}(V - 1) + \frac{2}{\tilde{A}}\left(\frac{\partial Z}{\partial X}\right)^2 \quad \text{where} \quad V \equiv \frac{V}{v_{LE}}, \quad \hat{A} \equiv \frac{v_{LE}}{r^* V_s} \tag{20}$$

and v_{LE} is the additive genetic variance in the absence of linkage disequilibria. Equation 20 is the same as for the Gaussian approximation (Eq. 16b), except that the effects of selection $(-\hat{A}V^2)$ and gene flow $((2/\hat{A})(\partial_x Z)^2)$ are greater by a factor of twice the number of loci, $2n_L$, and the variance is strongly regulated towards its linkage equilibrium value, v_{LE}, by the segregation of unlinked loci $(-\frac{1}{2}(V-1))$. With perfect adaptation of the mean, $\partial_x Z = B$, and a genetic variance of approximately $1 + 4B^2/\hat{A}$ is maintained when selection is weak and the gradient shallow $(4B^2 \ll \hat{A} \ll 1)$.

Acknowledgements

This work was supported by the Darwin Trust of Edinburgh, and by grants from the BBSRC and NERC. I am grateful for thoughtful comments on the manuscript from Janis Antonovics, Sarah Otto and Michael Whitlock.

References

Antonovics, J. (1976). The nature of limits to natural selection. *Annals of the Missouri Botanical Garden*, **63**, 224–247.

Barton, N.H. (1999). Clines in polygenic traits. *Genetical Research (Cambridge)*, **74**, 223–236.

Barton, N.H. & Partridge, L. (2000). The limits to selection. *BioEssays*, **22**, 1075–1084.

Barton, N.H. & Turelli, M. (1989). Evolutionary quantitative genetics: how little do we know? *Annual Review of Genetics*, **23**, 337–370.

Bazykin, A.D. (1998). *Nonlinear Dynamics of Interacting Populations*. World Scientific, New York.

Bulmer, M.G. (1985). *The Mathematical Theory of Quantitative Genetics*. Oxford University Press, Oxford.

Case, T.J. & Taper, M.L. (2000). Interspecific competition, environmental gradients, gene flow, and the coevolution of species borders, *American Naturalist*, **155**, 583–605.

Felsenstein, J. (1977). Multivariate normal genetic models with a finite number of loci. In: *Proceedings of the International Conference on Quantitative Genetics* (eds E. Pollak, O. Kempthorne & T.B. Bailey), pp. 227–246. Iowa State University Press, Ames, Iowa.

Goldstein, D.B. & Holsinger, K.E. (1992). Maintenance of polygenic variation in spatially structured populations: roles for local mating and genetic redundancy. *Evolution*, **46**, 412–429.

Haldane, J.B.S. (1956). The relation between density regulation and natural selection. *Proceedings of the Royal Society, London, B*, **145**, 306–308.

Holmes, E.E., Lewis, M.A., Banks, J.E. & Veit, R.R. (1994). Partial differential equations in ecology: spatial interactions and population dynamics. *Ecology*, **75**, 17–29.

Holt, R. & Gomulkiewicz, R. (1997). How does immigration affect local adaptation? A re-examination of a familiar paradigm. *American Naturalist*, **149**, 563–572.

Kimura, M. (1965). A stochastic model concerning the maintenance of genetic variability in quantitative characters. *Proceedings of the National Academy of Sciences of the USA*, **54**, 731–736.

Kirkpatrick, M. & Barton, N.H. (1997). Evolution of a species' range. *American Naturalist*, **150**, 1–23.

Lande, R. (1982). Rapid origin of sexual isolation and character divergence in a cline. *Evolution*, **36**, 213–223.

Lynch, M., Conery, J. & Burger, R. (1995). Mutational meltdowns in sexual populations. *Evolution*, **49**, 1067–1080.

Pease, C.M., Lande, R. & Bull, J.J. (1989). A model of population growth, dispersal and evolution in a changing environment. *Ecology*, **70**, 1657–1664.

Peck, J.R., Yearsley, J.M. & Waxman, D. (1998). Explaining the geographic distributions of sexual and asexual populations. *Nature*, **391**, 889–892.

Slatkin, M. (1978). Spatial patterns in the distribution of polygenic characters. *Journal of Theoretical Biology*, **70**, 213–228.

Turelli, M. (1984). Heritable genetic variation via mutation-selection balance: Lerch's zeta meets the abdominal bristle. *Theoretical Population Biology*, **25**, 138–193.

Turelli, M. & Barton, N.H. (1994). Genetic and statistical analyses of strong selection on polygenic traits: what, me normal? *Genetics*, **138**, 913–941.

Chapter 18

The unified neutral theory of biodiversity and biogeography: a synopsis of the theory and some challenges ahead

S. P. Hubbell[*]

Introduction

Theoretical community ecology is due for a major overhaul. One indication that an overhaul is needed is the conspicuously large number of well-established and pervasive patterns in community ecology—including basic patterns of species richness, relative species abundance, species–area relationships and phylogeny—that remain largely or totally unexplained by contemporary theoretical ecology. There are many reasons for this state of affairs, but in my view one of the most important hindrances has been ecology's half-century preoccupation with the issue of species coexistence in equilibrium models of ecological communities, which has led us away from asking the right questions. New perspectives are needed to resolve the long-standing dispute in ecology over the principal rules governing the assembly of ecological communities. The mainstream paradigm is the *niche-assembly perspective*, which holds that ecological communities are limited membership assemblages of species that coexist at demographic and adaptive equilibrium under strict niche partitioning of limiting resources (e.g. Levin 1970; MacArthur 1970; Diamond 1975; Tilman 1982; Weiher & Keddy 1999). In contrast, the *dispersal-assembly perspective* asserts that ecological communities are open, continuously changing, non-equilibrium assemblages of weakly or non coadapted species whose presence, absence and relative abundance are dictated by random speciation and dispersal, ecological drift and extinction (MacArthur & Wilson 1963, 1967; Hubbell 2001). This argument is long standing because both perspectives have strong elements of truth and because reconciling them is non-trivial. Actual communities are undoubtedly governed by both niche-assembly and dispersal-assembly rules, so the challenge is to find appropriate theoretical and empirical approaches that permit a synthesis.

In a recent book, I argue that the theory of island biogeography can serve as the intellectual foundation for such a synthesis, provided certain changes are made in the original theory (Hubbell 2001). I constructed a formal, neutral, dispersal-assembly theory on this foundation in the expectation that the next generation of

[*] *Department of Botany, University of Georgia, Athens, GA 30602 and Smithsonian Tropical Research Institute, Box 2072, Balboa, Panama.*

theory could build upon it, incorporating both niche-assembly rules as well as ecological drift. In the process of developing the neutral theory, however, I was surprised by, and unprepared for, how well it performed across disparate spatial and temporal scales. The neutral theory was also unexpectedly rich in new, testable predictions, many of which proved to be qualitatively and quantitatively quite accurate. Although consistency of the neutral theory with data of course does not prove that the communities in question are neutral, nevertheless the precision of the fit in many cases led me to question just how much of or how often our contemporary niche-assembly theory is correct and/or necessary. Even in cases in which the neutral theory could be rejected under very stringent fitting requirements, the overall fit is often still quite close, suggesting that random dispersal and ecological drift play a significant if not exclusive role in assembling ecological communities. Therefore, I believe that the theoretical frontier in community ecology is now to develop mixed models that incorporate both the dispersal-assembly and the niche-assembly perspectives, and that do so in an explicitly spatial context. Some promising initial theoretical efforts in this direction suggest that it is likely to be filled with surprises (Tilman 1994; Hurtt & Pacala 1995; Durrett & Levin 1996; Hubbell 2001; Chave *et al.* 2001). It is hard to know exactly what form this new theory will take, but I predict it will resemble the synthesis that has occurred in theoretical population genetics.

In order to build a successful neutral theory on the foundations of the theory of island biogeography, it was necessary to make some fundamental changes in the original theory, which are: (i) to include a process of speciation; (ii) to change the level of the neutrality assumption from the species level to the individual level; and (iii) to treat space explicitly, not implicitly, as was done in the original theory. These changes permit the development of a formal neutral theory for much more than simply the equilibrium number of species on islands (Hubbell 2001). The neutral theory merits serious attention because, for the present, it does a better qualitative and quantitative job of explaining patterns of relative species abundance, species–area relationships and phylogeny than current niche-assembly theory does.

Before outlining the main results of the neutral theory, it is important to define some terms. A *community* in the theory is a group of trophically similar, sympatric species whose individuals actually or potentially compete for the same or similar limiting resources. A *metacommunity* is a large regional collection of communities that share a common biogeographic and evolutionary history. *Neutrality* in the present context means the ecological equivalence of individuals at least in terms of their probabilities of giving birth, dying, dispersing, and even of speciating. This is not the same thing as the qualitative notion of 'nothing going on', because this definition allows complex ecological interactions among individuals so long as all individuals obey the same rules of ecological engagement. Demographic equivalence is not as unreasonable an assumption as it might at first seem. All persistent species in ecological communities have essentially identical long-term per capita relative fitnesses, by an almost self-evident proof. Species may win a little here, and lose a little there, but on large landscapes and over long time periods, all permanent members of the community must have net population growth rates of essentially zero. If this were not true, such that one or another species had a persistently higher fitness, then this species would eventually displace all of its competitors in the community. *Speciation* in the theory has been studied in two generic modes, dubbed the point mutation and the random fission modes. Under *point-mutation* speciation, new species always arise as very small populations, in analogy to a rare mutant. Under *random fission* speciation, a randomly chosen species (selected by choosing an individual in the metacommunity at random and then determining its species) divides randomly into two daughter species. In the latter mode, species may be quite abundant at origination. Putting speciation into the theory of island biogeography has the remarkable effect of unifying the theories of relative species abundance and island biogeography, two bodies of theory that until now have had completely independent intellectual histories.

The basic theory has just four parameters:

1 v, the per capita speciation rate in the metacommunity;

2 J_M the size of the regional metacommunity, equal to the sum of the population sizes of all species in the metacommunity;

3 J, the size of the local community, the sum of the population sizes of all species in the local community; and

4 m, the probability that a death in the local community is replaced by an immigrant from the metacommunity.

Synopsis of major results

Relative species abundance

Adding speciation to the theory of island biogeography enables it to predict relative species abundance for the first time. In the original theory, no new species were permitted to arise on the island or on the mainland metacommunity. Mainland species were treated as a permanent pool of species to be sampled for island immigrants. In reality, of course, all species become extinct. One can in fact solve for the equilibrium relative abundance distribution among these transient species that arises at steady state in the metacommunity between speciation and extinction. The nature of this distribution depends upon the mode of speciation. Under *point-mutation* speciation, the metacommunity relative abundance distribution is completely controlled by a single composite parameter, θ, which is mathematically equal to

$$\theta = 2J_M v \tag{1}$$

Under the random fission speciation, v and J_M also uniquely determine the relative abundance distribution in the metacommunity, but they must be specified separately because they have different quantitative effects in this case.

The parameter θ is the critical parameter under point-mutation speciation in the sense that it crops up in the theory at all spatial and temporal scales. Therefore, it is deservedly named the *fundamental biodiversity number*. One of the truly remarkable results is that in the limit of no dispersal limitation ($m = 1$) and in the infinite metacommunity limit ($J_M \rightarrow \infty$), the distribution of relative species abundance in the metacommunity is asymptotically identical to Fisher's logseries (Fisher *et al.* 1943), and θ is asymptotically identical to Fisher's α. Finding a theoretical explanation of Fisher's α is most important because of its ubiquity, universality and the theoretical invariance of Fisher's α as sample size varies (Magurran 1988). Fisher and colleagues did not have an underlying dynamical theory of ecological communities to explain why Fisher's α and the logseries worked so well, an explanation that the unified neutral theory now provides.

Although the distribution of relative species abundance in the metacommunity is asymptotically the logseries, at least under point-mutation speciation, the relative abundance distribution on islands or in local communities is not (or only rarely), a difference that is also explained for the first time by the neutral theory. Preston (1948, 1960), in a critique of the logseries, noted that it always predicts that the rarest abundance category (i.e. singletons) will have the most species. In contrast, Preston empirically found that distributions of relative abundance were more nearly lognormal, with the largest frequency of species at intermediate abundances. In the decades since Preston's papers were published, a greater number of local distributions of relative species abundance have been found to fit the lognormal better than the logseries. Although Preston had no theoretical explanation for the interior mode of the relative abundance distribution, the unified neutral theory does. Under the neutral model of relative species abundance, the interior mode arises as a result of the dynamic immigration–extinction equilibrium in relative abundance in the local community. Under this dynamic equilibrium, rare species are more extinction prone and will be less abundant and less frequent in local or island communities than a random sample of the metacommunity would predict. Herein lies an explanation and resolution of the half-century-old conflict between Preston and Fisher. In hindsight, it becomes clear that Fisher was describing the limiting relative abundance distribution for the metacommunity, whereas Preston was describing the corresponding distribution expected for a local community at immigration–extinction equilibrium with the metacommunity.

If the unified neutral theory is true, it turns out that Preston's distribution is only approximately correct. As larger data sets on relative species abundance in local communities have become available, it has become clear that observed distributions are seldom symmetrical as predicted by the lognormal, but instead are strongly and negatively skewed with a long tail of very rare species. The unified neutral theory predicts this negative skewing, and, moreover, that the extent of this skewing—as well as the overall shape of the local relative abundance distribution—will functionally depend on the immigration rate m. The predicted relative abundance distribution is a new statistical distribution that I have named the *zero-sum multinomial*. The shape of this distribution is controlled by three parameters, the fundamental biodiversity number θ for the metacommunity, the per capita immigration rate, m, and the size of the local community, J. The zero-sum multinomial looks like a perfectly good lognormal on the right tail, but it departs strongly from the lognormal in the left tail, rare-species end of the distribution. Thus, for the first time, we have a theory of relative species abundance that factors in the effects of dispersal and dispersal limitation. Explorations of this new statistical distribution of relative species abundance can be found in Bell (2000) and in Hubbell (2001).

The theory predicts that steeper dominance–diversity relative abundance curves will be found in local communities that are derivative of a species-poor metacommunity, or in communities that are very isolated (low immigration rate) from a species-rich metacommunity. Figure 18.1 compares the dominance–diversity curves for four 50-ha plots of tropical forest in South-East Asia. The data were kindly provided by my colleagues at the Center for Tropical Forest Science of the Smithsonian Tropical Research Institute. The most diverse forest, with nearly 1200 species having stem diameters >1 cm d.b.h., is found in Lambir Hills National Park, Sarawak. The maximum-likelihood estimate of θ for Lambir is 310. The second most diverse forest illustrated in Figure 18.1 is the Pasoh Research Forest in peninsular Malaysia, several hundred kilometres north of Lambir. Pasoh has slightly more than 800 species, and a fitted value of θ of 190 for stems >1 cm d.b.h. Both Lambir and Pasoh are closed-canopy, evergreen, mixed dipterocarp forests. Moving farther north, to the northern limit of dipterocarp forest, into a seasonal semideciduous forest at Huai Kha Khaeng, in western Thailand, we have a much poorer forest in

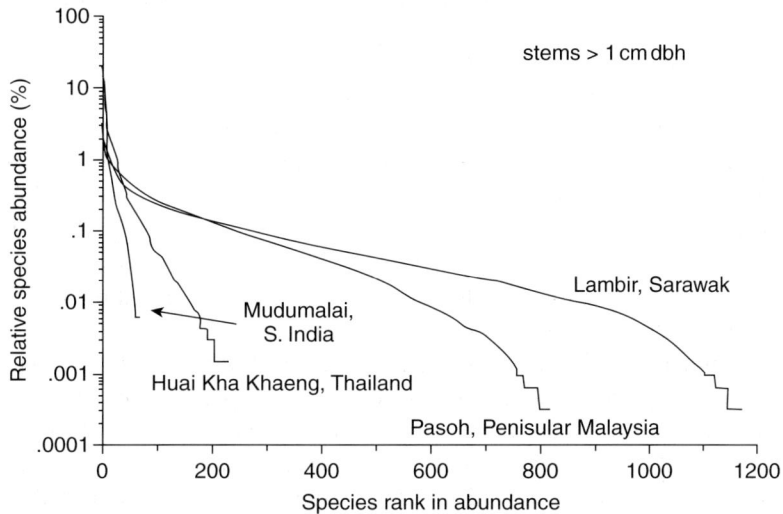

Figure 18.1 Comparison of the dominance–diversity curves for four South-East Asian tropical forests, each of which is represented by a 50-ha permanent plot. Each curve represents all free-standing woody stems > 1 cm diameter at breast height. The most diverse plot of the four is Lambir Hills National Park, which had a toal of 1197 species. The second most diverse plot is located in Pasoh Research Forest in central peninsular, Malaysia; the Pasoh plot had 817 species. The next most diverse plot (200 species) is further north in Huai Kha Khaeng Wildlife Sanctuary, western Thailand. Finally, the least diverse plot (71 species) is located in Mudumalai Game Reserve in the foothills of the Western Ghats of southern India. See text for further explanation.

species richness, with a fitted θ of 30. The forest is mostly closed canopy, but there are some large, herb-dominated openings, and portions of the forest have been disturbed by fire. Finally, the most species-poor site in this set is from the 50-ha plot in Mudumalai Game Reserve. This is an open-canopy, seasonal, semideciduous woodland with a grass understory and regular fire and elephant disturbance. The fitted value of θ for Mudumalai is approximately 10.

The fitting of dominance–diversity curves by the unified neutral theory is often excellent, but sometimes not. I first illustrate two extremely good fits in the cases of the two most species-rich, evergreen tropical forests (Figure 18.1), Lambir (Figure 18.2), and Pasoh (Figure 18.3). Two lines have been fitted in each case, one line for the metacommunity limiting distribution, in which only θ is fitted, and a second line, fitting θ and also the parameter m, the per capita probability of immigration from the metacommunity. Parameter J, local community size, is also needed but it does not need to be fitted because it is already known. The metacommunity line is the diagonal dotted line in each figure extending off the graph at the rare end of the dominance–diversity curve. The actual dominance–diversity curves depart most from the expected metacommunity curve at the rare end of the distribution. This differentiation of local relative abundance is due to the immigration–extinction equilibrium of the local community with the metacommunity, according to the

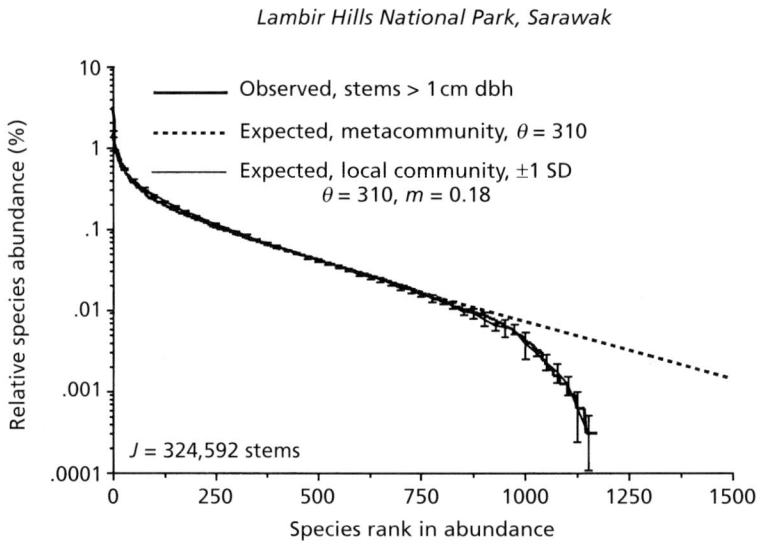

Figure 18.2 The excellent fit of the unified neutral theory to the Lambir dominance–diversity curve. The dotted line extending diagonally down to the right is the best-fit metacommunity curve for $\theta = 310$, assuming no dispersal limitation ($m = 1$). The relative abundance for the 50-ha plot was best fit with $\theta = 310$ and $m = 0.18$. The error bars are ± 1 SD. The heavier solid line is the observed dominance–diversity curve. Note the excellent fit even for very rare species. This fit to 1197 species is achieved with just three parameters, θ, m and local community size, J, the latter of which is known from the plot census data ($J = 324\,592$).

Pasoh, Peninsular Malaysia

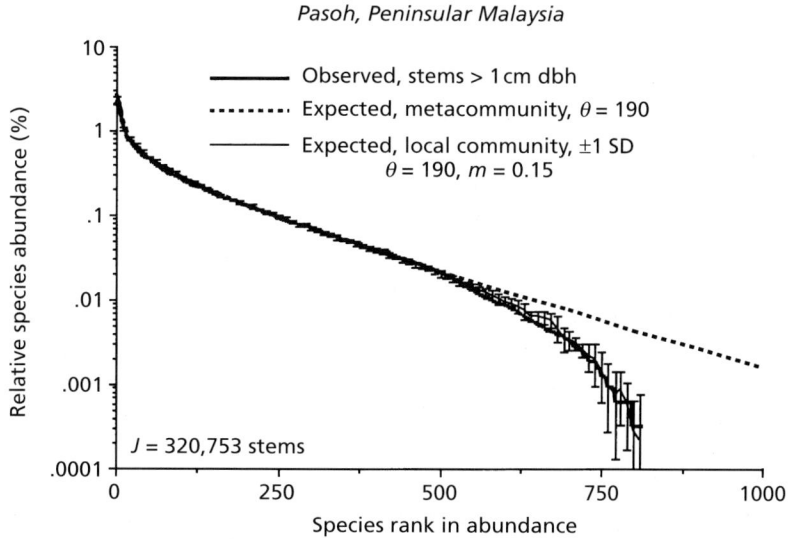

Figure 18.3 The equally excellent fit of the unified neutral theory to the Pasoh dominance–diversity curve. The dotted line extending diagonally down to the right is the best-fit metacommunity curve for $\theta = 190$, assuming no dispersal limitation ($m = 1$). The relative abundance for the 50-ha plot was best fit with $\theta = 190$ and $m = 0.15$. The error bars are ± 1 SD. The heavier solid line is the observed dominance–diversity curve. Again, note the excellent fit even for very rare species. And once again, this fit to 817 species is achieved with just three parameters, θ, m, and local community size, J, the latter of which is known from the plot census data ($J = 320\,753$).

theory. When dispersal is not infinite ($m < 1$), then rare species are expected to be less abundant in the local community than expected from a random sample of the metacommunity. Note the excellent fit, even for the very rare species, well within the predicted standard deviation of each rank abundance. Parameter m has a fitted value of 0.18 for Lambir and 0.15 for Pasoh. This means that an estimated 18% of the stems in the Lambir 50-ha plot originated from immigrant propagules, whereas an estimated 15% of the stems at Pasoh did so.

By contrast, the case of the Mudumalai forest illustrates a poor fit (Figure 18.4). The best fit θ has a value of about 10 (not shown), but it is quite clear that the dominance–diversity curve is diphasic. The most abundant 15 species are best fit by a curve having a θ of about 5, whereas the remaining rarer species are parallel to but depressed below the curve for $\theta = 16$. This diphasic curve is significantly non-random. One can fit the most common 15 species, but then the rare species depart significantly from expectation. Alternatively, if the rare species are fit, then the common species are too common. The implication is that the assembly rules organizing the common species in the Mudumalai forest are different from those organizing the rare species. Thus, the neutral theory is useful in detecting either positive or negative *ecological dominance deviations* that cannot be ascribed to pure ecological drift and

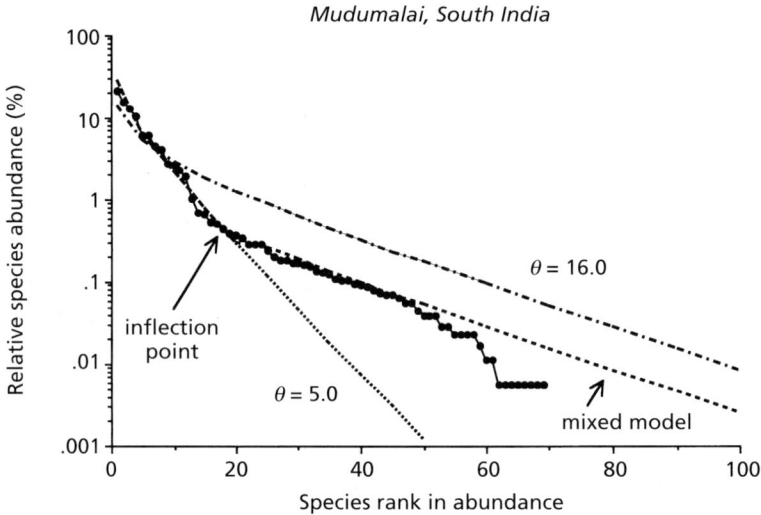

Figure 18.4 The poor fit of the neutral theory to the dominance–diversity curve for the Mudumalai forest. The curve is clearly diphasic, one phase consisting of the 15 most abundant species, and a second phase of all remaining rarer species. The best fit metacommunity θ is 10, but this does not fit well (not shown). The 15 most common species exhibit a steep dominance–diversity curve that is fit well by a θ of 5, but this does not fit the rarer species. Conversely, a θ of 16 yields a curve parallel to the rare-species portion of the curve, but not coincident with it. However, a mixed model can be made to fit, in which the 15 most common species have a survival advantage over the rare species. See text for more explanation.

random dispersal. Assuming that two different domains of assembly rules exist in this forest, one can estimate the fitness differentials for the common species necessary to produce excess dominance in the commonest 15 species by simulation and maximum likelihood. If each of the common species enjoys a slight advantage over the rare species in its per capita probability dying or reproducing, then each of these species will increase in steady-state abundance. When estimates of the competitive advantage of the common species are put into the equations, a mixed model fits the data very well and yields a diphasic curve. In this case each of the common species has a slight survival advantage, estimated by maximum likelihood. The mean advantage of the 15 most common species was small, only averaging 3.2%. One should then ask, why do these common species not dominate completely? In the spatially explicit model, competitive exclusion is indefinitely delayed by dispersal limitation. In classical models of competition that do not treat space explicitly, relatively rapid competitive exclusion is expected (Zhang & Lin 1997). However, in spatially explicit models with dispersal limitation, slight competitive advantages do not have this result (Tilman 1994; Hurtt & Pacala 1995; Hubbell 2001).

How does the Mudumalai forest differ from Lambir and Pasoh? One of the principal differences as mentioned is that the Mudumalai is really a woodland with a very open canopy of about 15% cover. The understory is grass dominated and it burns most years, and this disturbance, along with elephant predation, causes heavy mortality in the sapling layer. In contrast, the Lambir and Pasoh forests have very low disturbance rates, and the canopy is nearly completely continuous and closed. It is possible to prove mathematically that in communities in which all space or limiting resources are taken, such that the dynamics of the community are a zero-sum game, and if the rules of this game are neutral on a per capita basis, then local relative abundance will be given by the zero-sum multinomial distribution under dispersal limitation (Hubbell 2001). The neutral theory says that Mudumalai fails to fit precisely because it has a very open canopy, so that the dynamics of the Mudumalai tree community are not, in fact, a zero-sum game. I hypothesize that this is because the population dynamics of individual tree species are largely decoupled from one another. However, even if true, this hypothesis does not explain the diphasic nature of the curve observed in Figure 18.4. One possibility is that the commonest 15 species are the principal members of the community, perhaps because they are fire tolerant and therefore dominate the resource space, whereas the remaining rare species are sink populations that are maintained at low frequency solely by repeated immigration. We currently lack the data to test this and other alternative hypotheses.

As it happens, among the four data sets discussed here, the worst fit is also the plot with the fewest species. This may be coincidence because I have analysed data from species-poor temperate and boreal forests much poorer in species than Mudumalai that have very good fits (Hubbell 2001). However, in general we might expect that niche assembly would be more important in species-poor communities because of the potential for more frequent and stronger pairwise interactions among the smaller set of species. The potential for pairwise rather than diffuse coevolution among competing species is clearly greater if species encounter each other more often (Connell 1980; Hubbell & Foster 1986). Brown *et al.* (2001) have recently argued that the strength of pairwise interactions in communities should decrease approximately as the square of the number of species in the community. Thus, a plausible explanation for the very good fits for Lambir and Pasoh to the unified neutral theory is that their megadiversity reduces the importance of niche assembly relative to dispersal assembly and neutral forces.

Species–area relationships and metacommunity biodiversity

The neutral theory under explicit space also predicts species–area relationships. According to the theory, species–area relationships are best understood as a spatially distributed biodiversity steady state at dynamic equilibrium among speciation, dispersal and extinction across large landscapes. One of the qualitative predictions of the neutral theory that no other theory makes is that the functional form of the curve is triphasic as a function of spatial scale, which agrees with all species–area relationships I am aware of that cross all spatial scales, from individual organism scales to global scales. The qualitative shape of the predicted curve on a log–log plot of

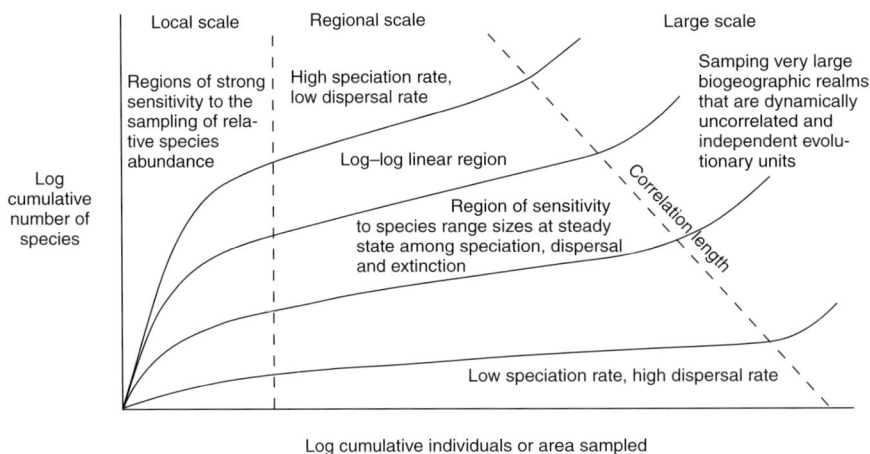

Figure 18.5 The qualitative shape of the triphasic species–area curve, as predicted by the unified neutral theory. On local spatial scales, the species accumulation curve is most sensitive to relative abundance of species in the local community. On intermediate spatial scales, the domain of log–log linear species–area curves, the curve is less sensitive to relative species abundance and more to the encounter of the ranges of species at steady state between speciation, dispersal and extinction. The slope z of the log–log curve is a function of the fundamental biodiversity number θ and the dispersal rate m. When θ is large and m small, the z slope is steep. Conversely, when θ is small and m is large, the z slope is shallow. On very large spatial scales, the correlation length of the biogeographic process has been exceeded, and sampling is of biogeographic realms with completely separate evolutionary histories. The correlation length defines the natural length scale of the biogeographic process. The correlation length decreases with increasing θ and decreasing m.

cumulative species number against cumulative area sampled is shown in Figure 18.5. The theory says that the well-known linear log–log species–area power law relationship (Rosenzweig 1995)

$$S = cA^z \tag{2}$$

is predicted to occur only on landscape to regional spatial scales, but not on local or very large (e.g. intercontinental) scales. The reason for the predicted triphasy is that the curve exhibits scale-dependent changes in sensitivity to the effects of dispersal and speciation rate. On very local scales, the species–area curve is curvilinear on a log–log plot because it is primarily responsive to local relative species abundance, as first common and then increasingly rare species are collected. On local scales, the effect of dispersal limitation is negative on the rate of species accumulation, a fact responsible for the drop-off of local dominance–diversity curves from the metacommunity expectation (see Figures 18.2 and 18.3). On regional scales, the sampling is more responsive to the steady-state distribution of species' range sizes under the dynamical speciation–dispersal–extinction equilibrium in the metacommunity. On this spatial scale, the effect of dispersal limitation switches from being negative to positive as newly encountered, increasingly dispersal-limited species are intercepted for the first time.

In the neutral theory, knowing the size of the metacommunity, the speciation rate, and the dispersal function are sufficient to predict the z value of the log–log power law of the species–area curve on intermediate spatial scales. If dispersal is rapid with respect to the speciation rate, species will have time to disperse over the metacommunity landscape before new species arise, and the slope of the species–area curve will be shallow (Figure 18.5). Conversely, if the speciation rate is relatively fast compared to the dispersal rate over large distances, such that new species arise more quickly than they manage to disperse over the metacommunity landscape, then the species–area curve will be steep. These qualitative conclusions are always true, but the quantitative value of the slope of the species–area curve depends on which dispersal function is used.

At very large spatial scales, an upward inflection point in the species–area curve is predicted by the theory (Figure 18.5). This is the *correlation length, L,* the natural biogeographic length scale under the neutral theory. The correlation length in species–area relationships has largely gone unnoticed, but it is important because it describes the natural biogeographic scale on which metacommunity species spend their entire evolutionary lives. Among other applications, L could have important value to large-landscape conservation planning. Above this spatial scale, the slope of the species–area curve approaches unity because biogeographic processes become increasingly uncorrelated and decoupled dynamically. On transregional correlation length scales, sampling is among completely different biogeographical realms, a phenomenon also discovered by Durrett and Levin (1996). Under the neutral theory, the predicted correlation length increases with increasing dispersal rate, and decreases with increasing speciation rate (Figure 18.5). This is intuitive because increasing dispersal will increase the interaction distance of species populations on regional scales, whereas increasing the speciation rate will tend to fragment the biogeographic region into smaller zones of high endemism.

The rate of dispersal over the metacommunity landscape also turns out to have profound effects on the distribution of α- and β-diversity (Hubbell 2001). When dispersal rates are high, equilibrium metacommunity diversity is lower and local diversity higher than when dispersal is slow. This is because high dispersal will transport abundant species throughout the metacommunity. However, because these abundant species are very resistant to global extinction, they have a large mass effect on local communities everywhere they go, tending to overwhelm the reproduction of rare, local endemics. Thus, high dispersal rates distribute common species more widely, but in so doing they reduce the overall species richness of the metacommunity by accelerating the extinction of rare species everywhere (Hubbell 2001). Conversely, when dispersal rates are slow, there is little force of dispersal to displace rare, local endemics, and species richness in the metacommunity remains much higher. Thus, even though this is a neutral model, the fate of common and rare species in general is very different.

Speciation and phylogeny

There are several important conclusions about speciation, phylogeny and the nature of biodiversity itself that come from the unified neutral theory, some of which are very different from current neutral theory in phylogeny and phylogenetic reconstruction. Most current theory assumes that the lineage is the unit and that lineages have the same probability of going extinct and of speciation (e.g. Raup *et al.* 1973; Nee *et al.* 1994). This assumption flies in the face of abundant evidence, both from ecological as well as palaeobiological studies, showing that widespread and abundant lineages on average are much more resistant to extinction and have much longer lifespans. Under the unified neutral theory, lineages do not have assigned probabilities of speciating or going extinct, because they are predicted by the abundance of the lineage. Factoring in lineage abundance gives more realistic patterns of phylogeny that are qualitatively more consistent with observed patterns (Hubbell 2001). Among other things, the theory predicts that most rare and endemic species will be relatively recent in origin, and widespread abundant species are expected to be older and closer to stem ancestors. In fact, one can calculate analytically the relationship between the steady-state metacommunity distribution of relative species abundance and the distribution of lineage lifespans. The rarest species in metacommunities are 10–20 orders of magnitude shorter in lifespan than are the most common metacommunity species. Abundant metacommunity species are expected to persist for millions to tens of millions of years and to be very resistant to extinction, as just mentioned, whereas the rarest species may last for only a very brief time.

The unified neutral theory also predicts that different modes of speciation will leave different signatures in the metacommunity distribution of relative species abundance. This is a very exciting development because for the first time we have a formal theory in which biogeographic patterns of diversity and modes of speciation are explicitly mathematically linked. Under point-mutation speciation, as discussed previously, the limiting distribution of metacommunity relative species abundance is Fisher's logseries, characterized completely by the fundamental biodiversity number θ. However, under random fission speciation, the logseries is not the expected distribution. Instead, it is the zero-sum multinomial distribution, just as in the local community at immigration–extinction equilibrium with the metacommunity. Another difference is that the composite parameter θ no longer uniquely specifies the metacommunity distribution under random fission speciation. One must specify both the metacommunity size J_M and the speciation rate v separately because the steady-state metacommunity distribution is differently affected by the speciation rate and how large the metacommunity is. Under random fission speciation, when the metacommunity is larger, the average population size of incipient species will also be larger for a given speciation rate, which slows down the extinction rate. This increases the number of species maintained in the metacommunity at steady state. The difference in speciation signature should be detectable in many metacommunities if the neutral theory is correct. A mathematically as yet unproven conjecture is that there should also be a complete continuum in the shape of metacommunity relative abundance distributions between the logseries and the zero-sum multinomial, depending upon the fraction of speciation events in the metacommunity that are by one or the other speciation mode (Hubbell 2001). This newly discovered connection between modes of speciation and patterns of metacommunity biodiversity gives a strong theoretical justification for efforts to obtain improved estimates of global species abundances and metacommunity sizes.

A final result to highlight in this brief synopsis of the neutral theory is the prediction that phylogenetic clades will often be fractal and self-similar on all taxonomic scales from individuals upwards to higher taxa. Under point-mutation speciation, the fractals exhibit homogeneity and a single scaling domain at all taxonomic scales of resolution. The fractal dimension of a clade can be found by plotting the log of the number of lineages in a clade against the log of the time depth into the past of the sampling point of the clade (Figure 18.6). The fractal dimension D of a clade under point mutation speciation is functionally related (one-to-one mapping) to the fundamental biodiversity number θ (Figure 18.7). This homogenous scaling domain arises because ecological drift (demographic stochasticity) and speciation are identical processes at the per capita level under point mutation (all new species arise as if rare singleton mutants). Conversely, under random fission speciation, the

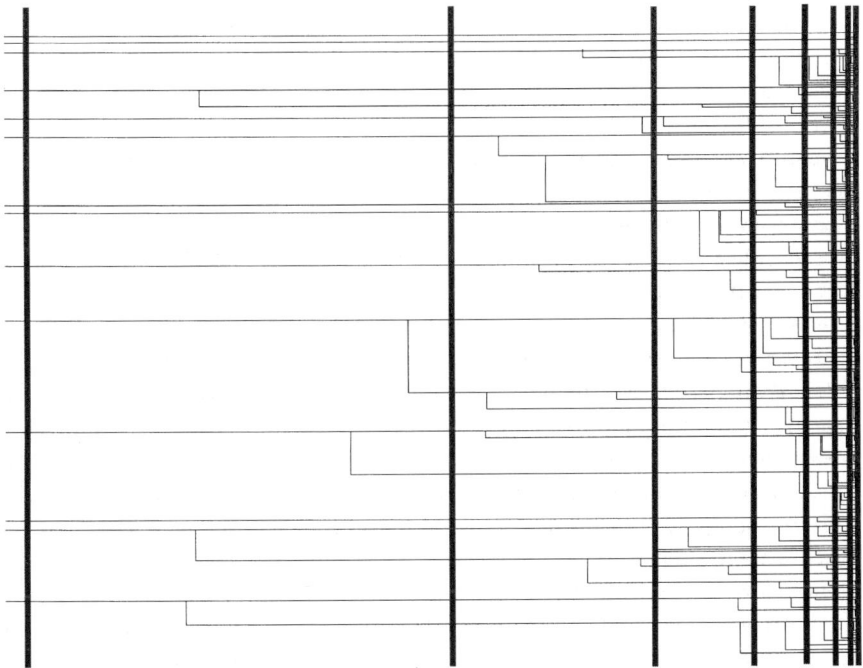

Figure 18.6 Sampling of a phylogeny produced by the unified neutral theory for measuring its fractal dimension. The number of lineages is counted at exponentially deeper sampling points into the past, and then the logarithm of the number of lineages is plotted against the logarithm of the time depth. This phylogeny was produced by a fundamental biodiversity number θ of 100. (From Hubbell 2001.)

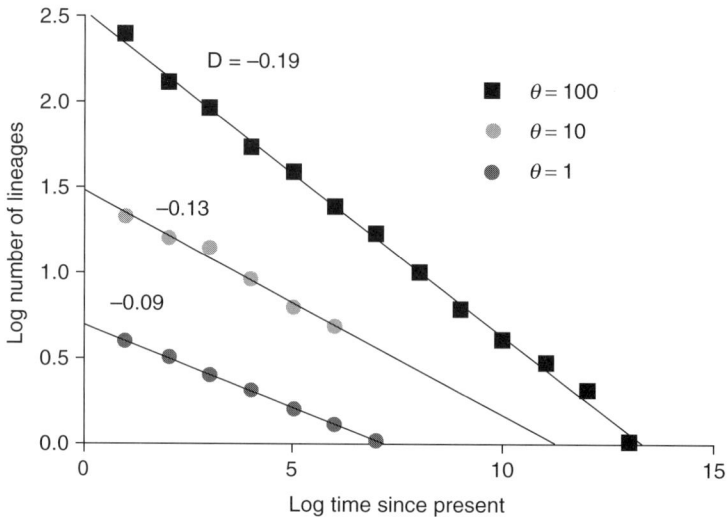

Figure 18.7 The relationship between the log of number of lineages in a clade and the log of the time since the present that the clade is sampled. The fractal dimension of the phylogeny is functionally related to the fundamental biodiversity number θ. Each line is fit to the data from one phylogeny, for θ = 100, 10 or 1. The lines are not ensemble means of many runs. I chose to illustrate single runs to show the precision of the relationship for single phylogenies. The fractal dimension of a phylogeny decreases with decreasing θ. (From Hubbell 2001.)

speciation process (random cleavage of an ancestral species into two daughter species), is a fundamentally different process than ecological drift, and this produces a 'kink' in the fractal plot of log number of lineages against log time. Figure 18.8 illustrates an example of such a kinked fractal, in this case for cactophilic drosophila (data from T. Markow, pers. comm.). Not all relationships are expected to have kinks that are this sharp. The larger the metacommunity, the more variable will be the population sizes of species at their origination, which in turn will produce a more rounded and gradual transition from one fractal scaling domain to the next.

If the neutral theory is correct and phylogenies are fractal and self-similar at all taxonomic scales, then this implies that species, and indeed biodiversity itself, are fractal. This has potentially profound implications for how we think about, categorize and manage biodiversity. Under point-mutation speciation at least, the theory says that we should not expect to find any demographic or metacommunity signature of the special existence of species because the finer and smaller the taxonomic and genetic scale we look, the more diversity we will find. However, this is not true under random fission speciation, where the signature of the origination of species can be found in the change in the slope of the log–log lineage–time graph.

Finally, some colleagues have argued that the speciation rates required to fit the fundamental biodiversity number θ are too large. However, I would argue that we really do not know enough to reach this conclusion. My reasoning is as follows. If many species arise like rare point mutations, or even by random fission but in small

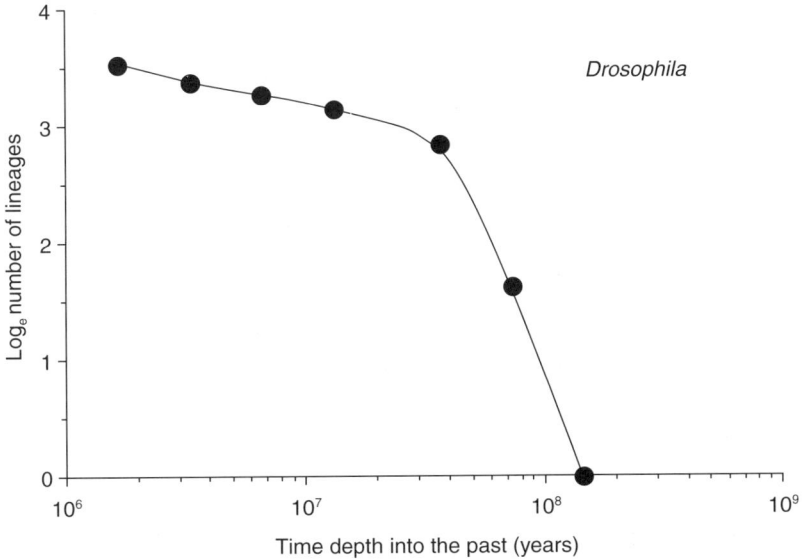

Figure 18.8 The relationship between log number of lineages and log time depth for the molecular phylogeny of cactophilic species of *Drosophila*, showing a 'kinked' curve with two scaling regions. According to the neutral theory, this is indicative of random fission rather than point mutation speciation. (Data from Pitnick *et al.* 1995.)

peripheral isolates, then the vast majority of these new rare species will go extinct rapidly and before they can be detected and classified by taxonomists. An average species will be found only after it is already old and has achieved a significant level of global abundance. So I respond by predicting a positive relationship between the mean age of species and their global abundance. If this is found, then there is a strong reason to suspect that a large sampling bias exists in our current estimates of real speciation rates in nature, which will tend to be underestimates. The neutral theory offers some promise that it will be possible to estimate true speciation rates from the fractal geometry of biodiversity. At least under point-mutation speciation, if we can estimate the fractal dimension D of a particular phylogeny, and if we can further estimate the population sizes of all living members of the phylogeny, then we can estimate what the branching rate must have been at the level of individuals to give rise the lineage diversity observed at higher taxonomic levels. This would be an exciting development because it would allow us to estimate the net rate at which minor variations among individuals survive and become amplified by population growth into new and sufficiently common species to be detectable.

Conclusions and some challenges ahead

An attempt to unify the divergent perspectives of dispersal assembly and niche assembly of ecological communities is made elsewhere (Hubbell 2001), but here it might be useful to outline some challenges that this theoretical unification must confront. One is the fact that the neutral theory does as well as it does. I believe that this is powerful, hard-to-ignore testimony to the fact that ecological communities are probably a lot simpler dynamically than their species richness might lead us to believe. If we always had to specify a set of unique interaction rules between each and every species, as in the Lotka–Volterra equations or in their mechanistic resource-based counterparts, then the neutral theory simply would not work at all.

Another challenge is to better understand the degree to which species are ecologically and evolutionarily opportunistic, facultatively able to exploit varied resources as they become available. A critical element of the current neutral theory, on which much of its success depends, is the assumption of zero-sum dynamics, such that resources collectively limit the total abundance of species in the community. How applicable and general are zero-sum dynamics in actual ecological communities? I suspect that species are far more labile than our current typological and static concept of the niche would suggest. Most species are released ecologically when their closest competitors are absent. Facultative resource use and ecological release may have huge but still largely unexplored implications for community ecology (Mac-Nally 1995). We need to reinvigorate research on niches and the phenomenon of ecological release, subjects that used to be hot topics more than two decades ago. I believe that such research, done from a strong evolutionary perspective, in which individual variation in limiting resource use and its fitness consequences are evaluated, will expose the extent to which our current niche assembly theory and typology is valid or not.

One common misconception about the neutral theory is that it mandates helter-skelter, constantly changing collections of species, randomly chosen from the metacommunity. Nothing could be farther from the truth. Under the dynamic immigration–extinction equilibrium of local communities with the metacommunity, common metacommunity species will be much more frequently present in local communities than rare species, and their relative abundances will be stabilized by their dynamic coupling to the metacommunity. Thus, the neutral theory does not predict a random collection of species on islands, but a distribution weighted by species abundances on the mainland or in the metacommunity. For this reason local community composition will be much more stable and predictable than might be thought. Local communities under the neutral theory will also exhibit resilience because they will return to their predisturbance compositions to the extent that they are coupled through dispersal to the size-stabilized metacommunity.

To the extent that niche-assembly rules are proven to be necessary, one predictable consequence of niches will be to increase the stability of particular species assemblages over that predicted by the neutral theory. But beyond this, niche-assembly rules should also increase the steady-state biodiversity that can be maintained for a given speciation rate, metacommunity size, and dispersal rate. For example, in a recent paper, Chave et al. (2001) carried out simulations of communities that had both ecological drift and predator-mediated density dependence and frequency dependence. Among other things, they modelled the Janzen–Connell mechanism. Janzen

(1970) and Connell (1971) argued that seeds not dispersed sufficiently far from maternal parents would be at greater risk of discovery by these predators and pathogens, and that high mortality near parents would prevent any one species from replacing itself in the forest, thereby opening space for other species to grow. Chave and colleagues put such effects into their model, and discovered that total steady-state metacommunity diversity was increased over that predicted by the purely neutral model. The relative abundance distributions were still zero-sum multinomials. One challenge created by niche assembly rules that increase the steady-state diversity in the metacommunity is that such rules will cause overestimates of the fundamental biodiversity number θ, which describes the predictive metacommunity biodiversity in the absence of niche-assembly rules.

There are few more critical challenges facing humanity in the next century than slowing the rapid loss of biodiversity on earth. Improving our theoretical understanding of the origin, maintenance and loss of biodiversity will help to formulate better science-based biodiversity policies. In developing the unified neutral theory, I hope to have made a useful contribution to improving our theoretical understanding of biodiversity, but much work remains theoretically and empirically. If nothing else, the theory has generated a host of non-obvious, novel and testable predictions that should stimulate ecological and evolutionary research in many new directions. Resolving the old controversy between niche-assembly and dispersal-assembly perspectives is one of the most important unsolved ecological problems of our time. Which perspective is closer to the truth under what circumstances, is important — not just to theoretical ecology, but also to the design and implementation of our efforts to conserve global biodiversity.

Summary

Unlike population genetics, community ecology has lacked a good formal neutral theory. In a recent book, I have attempted to develop such a theory on the premise that it would be highly beneficial to the intellectual growth and maturation of ecology (Hubbell 2001). The theory explores the consequences of assuming that ecological communities are assembled purely by ecological drift (demographic stochasticity), random but limited dispersal, and random speciation. In this chapter I present a non-technical synopsis of some of the more salient concepts and predictions of the theory with particular reference to plant community ecology, highlighting the role of dispersal in organizing large-scale patterns of biodiversity under the theory. The theory is remarkably rich in testable predictions for plant ecology, many of which are novel and surprisingly accurate. These predictions include qualitative and quantitative patterns of relative species abundance in plant communities, species–area relationships, the landscape-level distribution of species diversity, and even phylogeny. Among other things, the theory generates a remarkable dimensionless biodiversity number, θ, that is fundamental in the sense that it crops up throughout the theory at all spatial and temporal scales. I discuss some issues involved in testing the theory. I conclude by discussing some challenges ahead for attempts to unify the neutral, dispersal-assembly and niche-assembly perspectives into a single synthetic theory of biodiversity and biogeography for community ecology.

References

Bell, G. (2000). The distribution of abundance in neutral communities. *American Naturalist*, **155**, 606–617.

Brown, J.H., Bedrick, E.J., Ernest, S.K.M., Cartron, J.-L.E. & Kelly, J.F. (2001). Constraints on negative relationships: mathematical causes and ecological consequences.

Chave, J., Muller-Landau, H. & Levin, S.A. (2001). Comparing classical community models: Theoretical consequences for patterns of diversity.

Connell, J.H. (1971). On the role of natural enemies in preventing competitive exclusion in some marine animals and in rain forest trees. In: *Dynamics of Populations* (eds P.J. den Boer & G.R. Gradwell), pp. 298–312. Centre for Agricultural Publishing and Documentation, Wageningen, The Netherlands.

Connell, J.H. (1980). Diversity and the coevolution of competitors, or the ghost of competition past. *Oikos*, **35**, 131–138.

Diamond, J.M. (1975). Assembly of species communities. In: *Ecology and Evolution of Communities* (eds M.L. Cody & J.M. Diamond), pp. 342–444. Belnap, Harvard University Press, Cambridge, MA.

Durrett, R. & Levin, S.A. (1996). Spatial models for species-area curves. *Journal of Theoretical Biology*, **179**, 119–127.

Fisher, R.A., Corbet, A.S. & Williams, C.B. (1943). The relation between the number of species and the number of individuals in a random sample of an animal population. *Journal of Animal Ecology*, **12**, 42–58.

Hubbell, S.P. (2001). The *Unified Neutral Theory of Biodiversity and Biogeography*. Princeton Monographs in Population Biology, no. 32. Princeton University Press, Princeton, NJ.

Hubbell, S.P. & Foster, R.B. (1986). Biology, chance and history and the structure of tropical rain forest tree communities. In: *Community Ecology* (eds J.M. Diamond & T.J. Case), pp. 314–329. Harper and Row, New York.

Hurtt, G.C. & Pacala, S.W. (1995). The consequences of recruitment limitation: Reconciling chance, history, and competitive differences between plants. *Journal of Theoretical Biology*, **176**, 1–12.

Janzen, D.H. (1970). Herbivores and the number of tree species in tropical forests. *American Naturalist*, **104**, 501–528.

Levin, S.A. (1970). Community equilibria and stability, and an extension of the competitive exclusion principle. *American Naturalist*, **104**, 413–423.

MacArthur, R.H. (1970). Species packing and competitive equilibrium for many species. *Theoretical Population Biology*, **1**, 1–11.

MacArthur, R.H. & Wilson, E.O. (1963). An equilibrium theory of insular zoogeography. *Evolution*, **17**, 373–387.

MacArthur, R.H. & Wilson, E.O. (1967). *The Theory of Island Biogeography*. Princeton Monographs in Population Biology, no 1. Princeton University Press, Princeton, NJ.

MacNally, R.C. (1995). *Ecological Versatility and Community Ecology*. Cambridge University Press, Cambridge, UK.

Magurran, A.E. (1988). *Ecological Diversity and Its Measurement*. Princeton University Press, Princeton, NJ.

Nee, S., May, R.M. & Harvey, P.H. (1994). The reconstructed evolutionary process. *Philosophical Transactions of the Royal Society, London, B*, **344**, 305–311.

Pitnick, S., Markow, T.A. & Spicer, G.S. (1995). Delayed male maturity is a cost of producing large sperm in Drosophila. *Proceedings of the National Academy of Sciences of the USA*, **92**, 10614–10618.

Preston, F.W. (1948). The commonness, and rarity, of species. *Ecology*, **29**, 254–283.

Preston, F.W. (1960). Time and space variation of species. *Ecology*, **41**, 611–627.

Raup, D.M., Gould S.J., Schopf, T.J.M. & Simberloff, D.S. (1973). Stochastic models of phylogeny and the evolution of diversity. *Journal of Geology*, **81**, 525–542.

Rosenzweig, M.L. (1995). *Species Diversity in Space*

and Time. Cambridge University Press, Cambridge, UK.

Tilman, D. (1982). *Resource Competition and Community Structure*. Princeton Monographs in Population Biology, no. 17. Princeton University Press, Princeton NJ.

Tilman, D. (1994). Competition and biodiversity in spatially structured habitats. *Ecology*, **75**, 2–16.

Weiher, E. & Keddy, P. (1999). *Ecological Assembly Rules: Perspectives, Advances, Retreats*. Cambridge University Press, Cambridge, UK.

Zhang, D.-Y. & Lin, D. (1997). The effects of competitive asymmetry on the rate of competitive displacement: How robust is Hubbell's community drift model? *Journal of Theoretical Biology*, **188**, 361–367.

Index

Note: page numbers in *italics* refer to figures; those in **bold** refer to tables.